SOCIAL PSYCHOLOGY AND ITS APPLICATIONS

SOCIAL PSYCHOLOGY AND ITS APPLICATIONS

Michael J. Saks
University of Iowa

Edward Krupat
Massachusetts College of Pharmacy
and Allied Health Sciences

1817
HARPER & ROW, PUBLISHERS, New York
Cambridge, Philadelphia, San Francisco, Washington,
London, Mexico City, São Paulo, Singapore, Sydney

Sponsoring Editor: Leslie Carr
Development Editor: Marian Wassner
Project Editor: Susan Goldfarb
Text Design: Emily Harste
Cover Design: Joan Greenfield
Cover Illustration: Luigi Russolo, *The Revolt* (1911). Collection Haags Gemeentemuseum, The Hague, Netherlands.
Text Art: Fineline Illustrations, Inc.
Photo Research: Mira Schachne
Production Manager: Willie Lane
Compositor: Ruttle, Shaw & Wetherill, Inc.
Printer and Binder: The Murray Printing Company
Cover Printer: NEBC

Photo credits begin on page P-1.

SOCIAL PSYCHOLOGY AND ITS APPLICATIONS

Library of Congress Cataloging-in-Publication Data

Saks, Michael J.
Social psychology and its applications.

Bibliography: p.
Includes indexes.
1. Social psychology. I. Krupat, Edward. II. Title.
HM251.S255 1988 302 87-33456
ISBN 0-06-045698-1

88 89 90 91 9 8 7 6 5 4 3 2 1

To Roselle and Barbara

CONTENTS IN BRIEF

CONTENTS

CHAPTER 2
Social Perception and Cognition 35

CHAPTER 3
The Self and Personality 81

CHAPTER 5
Attitudes 165

CHAPTER 6
Attitude Change 209

APPLICATIONS

Listings in italics refer to the untitled Applications that begin and end each chapter.

TO THE INSTRUCTOR

Writing a text about social psychology has never been easy, but it has become even harder in the past five to ten years. There is a need to cover the sheer breadth and depth of this growing field, thereby giving students a thorough grounding in the theories and research that have shaped social psychology and driven it forward. Yet there is an equal need, many of us feel, to give students a strong sense of the social concerns of the field and to offer them an appreciation of the ways in which its theories and findings have been applied to modern life.

Today social psychologists are being called upon to apply their knowledge and skills in order to solve problems in settings as diverse as hospitals and factories, courtrooms and corporations. Research findings in social psychology have been used to improve productivity on assembly lines, evaluate the reliability of eyewitness testimony, help the victims of child abuse, plan political and advertising campaigns, design apartment complexes and public spaces, and devise strategies to resolve large-scale conflicts. We believe that the true vision of social psychology unites the basic and the applied, the laboratory and the field. We want students not only to gain a healthy respect for each aspect, but also to see that the aspects work together. Therefore, we have chosen not to isolate applied social psychology in separate chapters at the end of the book, or even in boxed inserts, but rather to make the applications an integral part of the discussion.

Each chapter begins with an applied problem from the real world, and then poses a set of basic questions we need to examine in order to deal with the problem. The text then proceeds with a thorough discussion of classic and contemporary theory and research in the field, incorporating two additional case-study applications. At the end of the chapter, one or more solutions to the initial problem are presented. Each solution is based on key concepts and findings presented in the chapter. In this way, students see how research, theory, and practice interact, and how real-world solutions can derive from basic knowledge.

The applied issues brought into focus reflect the diversity and excitement of the field and show students how social psychology can be applied to issues at both a personal level and a broader societal level. In the chapter on aggression, for example, students examine the evidence that television contributes to violence. In the chapter on personality, they consider some specific steps for overcoming Type A behavior. In the chapter on small groups, they study findings on the optimum size for a jury. By viewing applied subjects in context, students can better understand the connections between abstract principles and practical applications. And they do not lose sight of the larger picture that social psychology has always sought to elucidate.

OTHER FEATURES

"From the Field" boxes focus on the work of social psychologists in key areas. These brief profiles offer students insight into the questions that provided the impetus for research.

"In the News" boxes present actual press stories closely related to the text discussion. This feature helps students recognize the many relationships between social psychological findings and the problems that face us all.

SUPPLEMENTS

Social Psychology and Its Applications is supported by a teaching and learning package that includes the following supplements:

Study Guide Written by Ann L. Weber of the University of North Carolina at Asheville, the Study Guide includes annotated chapter outlines, questions for review (including true/false, fill-in, matching, and multiple-choice items), and intriguing application problems that send the student back into the chapter to find solutions.

Test Bank The Test Bank, also written by Ann L. Weber, consists of multiple-choice and essay questions that reflect a balance of applied, interpretive, and factual material.

Harper Test This computerized test-generating system allows instructors to edit items easily, add new items, set up criteria for selection of items, and print tests.

Instructor's Manual Debra McCallum and Richard McCallum of the University of Alabama at Birmingham have written the Instructor's Manual, which includes annotated outlines, lecture ideas, demonstrations and projects, and annotated reading lists for each chapter.

ACKNOWLEDGMENTS

As any social psychologist knows, and as we hope the readers of this book will come to appreciate, people do not live or work in a vacuum. Any given product—this textbook, for instance—is really the result of a group effort, and the credit for it goes to many people, not just the authors.

We would like to acknowledge the many valuable suggestions made by the following reviewers:

Joel Aronoff, Michigan State University
Ellen Berscheid, University of Minnesota of Minneapolis–St. Paul
Leonard Bickman, Peabody College of Vanderbilt University
Kenneth S. Bordens, Indiana University–Purdue University at Fort Wayne
Sharon S. Brehm, University of Kansas
James V. P. Check, York University
James H. Davis, University of Illinois at Urbana–Champaign
Marsha Epstein, Middlesex Community College
Jeffrey D. Fisher, University of Connecticut
Donelson R. Forsyth, Virginia Commonwealth University
James R. Friedrich, Mount St. Mary's College
Russell G. Geen, University of Missouri, Columbia
Martin F. Kaplan, Northern Illinois University
Stuart A. Karabenick, Eastern Michigan University
John P. Keating, University of Washington
Ross J. Loomis, Colorado State University
Debra Moehle McCallum, University of Alabama at Birmingham
Robert Montgomery, University of Missouri, Rolla
Lynn M. Musser, Oregon State University
Gary Nickell, Moorhead State University
Richard Petty, University of Missouri, Columbia
Anthony R. Pratkanis, University of California, Santa Cruz
Leonard Saxe, Boston University
David Simpson, Carroll College
Ralph B. Taylor, Temple University
Shelley E. Taylor, University of California, Los Angeles
Rhoda K. Unger, Montclair State College
Robin R. Vallacher, Florida Atlantic University
Ann L. Weber, University of North Carolina at Asheville
Russell H. Weigel, Amherst College
Gary L. Wells, University of Alberta
David A. Wilder, Rutgers University—New Brunswick Campus

At Harper & Row there are many people we would like to thank. First and foremost is our development editor, Marian Wassner. From the early stages of planning and writing through the final stages of revising and editing, she coordinated our efforts. She knew just when to insist on something and when to compromise, and how to communicate concern and encouragement when they were most needed.

Leslie Carr worked to keep us on target with the marketplace and stayed with us through to publication. Lauren Bahr and Judy Rothman were there throughout to oversee the project and to move us along when things got bogged down. In addition, Susan Goldfarb served as a most able project editor during the production stages of our work.

Other people have contributed in a range of important ways. Bill DeJong produced a first-rate chapter on attraction and worked on and worried about it to the end. Terri Amabile wrote an early draft of the chapter on social cognition and attribution, and it served as a useful resource for the chapter that appears in the book. Ann Weber did a fine job on the Study Guide and Test Bank that accompany the text, and Debra and Richard McCallum deserve equal credit for generating an excellent Instructor's Manual. Roselle Wissler tirelessly searched out books and articles and provided suggestions and references to help get us going; and three librarians at the Massachusetts College of Pharmacy and Allied Health Sciences—Mary Chitty, Nancy Occhialini, and Beth Banov—were of invaluable assistance in tracking down a variety of bibliographic sources. Bob Doty helped by typing fast and accurate drafts, and Donna Boardman was far more than a secretary and typist, providing a sense of humor and a voice of sanity in addition to turning out beautifully typed copy under outrageous deadlines.

Finally, we would like to thank our families. Families are always listed last by some strange custom, even though they are the most important people to acknowledge. Through the many years of this project, when the work was dragging on and kept us from them, our families helped and understood. We did the writing, but it was their love and support that kept us going, and for that we are truly grateful.

Michael J. Saks
Edward Krupat

TO THE STUDENT

Why are we attracted to some people, but "turned off" by others? Why are we likely to act differently as members of a group than we would on our own? Chances are that you already have some of your own ideas about why people behave the way they do toward others and in various social situations. Here is a chance to test those ideas. Read over the 10 statements below and decide which ones seem true and which ones you believe to be false. Then check your answers against those given below.

True/False Test

T	F	1. Women are more cautious than men in entering a relationship and also more likely to end one that is going badly (Chapter 7).
T	F	2. Urban crowding is one of the most direct causes of crime and violence in cities (Chapter 11).
T	F	3. Eyewitness testimony is one of the most reliable and accurate sorts of evidence in the courtroom (Chapter 2).
T	F	4. The more people present at the scene of an accident, the more each onlooker will feel the urge to help (Chapter 9).
T	F	5. People's attitudes are not usually good predictors of their behavior (Chapter 5).
T	F	6. Decisions reached by groups are usually more extreme than those reached by individuals (Chapter 12).
T	F	7. The more money someone offers you to change your opinion, the more likely you are to do so (Chapter 6).
T	F	8. The quality and quantity of social relationships do not vary greatly between people in cities and people in small towns (Chapter 11).
T	F	9. We tend to believe that people do the things they do because of the circumstances they are in (Chapter 2).
T	F	10. Frustration always leads to aggression (Chapter 8).

Answers: 1. T 2. F 3. F 4. F 5. T 6. T 7. F 8. T 9. F 10. F

As you can see, some of the findings of social psychology will challenge the assumptions you may have made about how and why people act the way they do. They may even change some of the ways you think about social interactions—particularly your own. What makes a person offer help in one situation and not in another? Why do we form positive impressions of some people and negative impressions of others? Why do some groups make good decisions while others get mired in "groupthink"? These are just a few of the questions that this book will help you explore.

Probably the most important—and most interesting—issue to you is the way in which the theories and research findings discussed in this book can be put to use. Social psychology has served as a tool for solving problems and improving life in areas ranging from dormitory design and roommate selection to psychotherapy and rape counseling, doctor-patient relations and medical care. You will encounter issues such as these throughout this book.

Two special features in each chapter highlight the work of social psychologists and the implications of their findings. "From the Field" boxes offer a glimpse behind the scenes at some of the people whose work has shaped social psychology. "In the News" boxes feature recent press stories that focus on some of the key issues discussed in the chapter. In them you will see how current events can serve as good illustrations of social psychological concepts.

This first course in social psychology probably won't change your life, but it will certainly enhance it. It is one course in which the answer to the question "What does this have to do with me?" will be self-evident and, we hope, enriching and intriguing.

Michael J. Saks
Edward Krupat

SOCIAL PSYCHOLOGY AND ITS APPLICATIONS

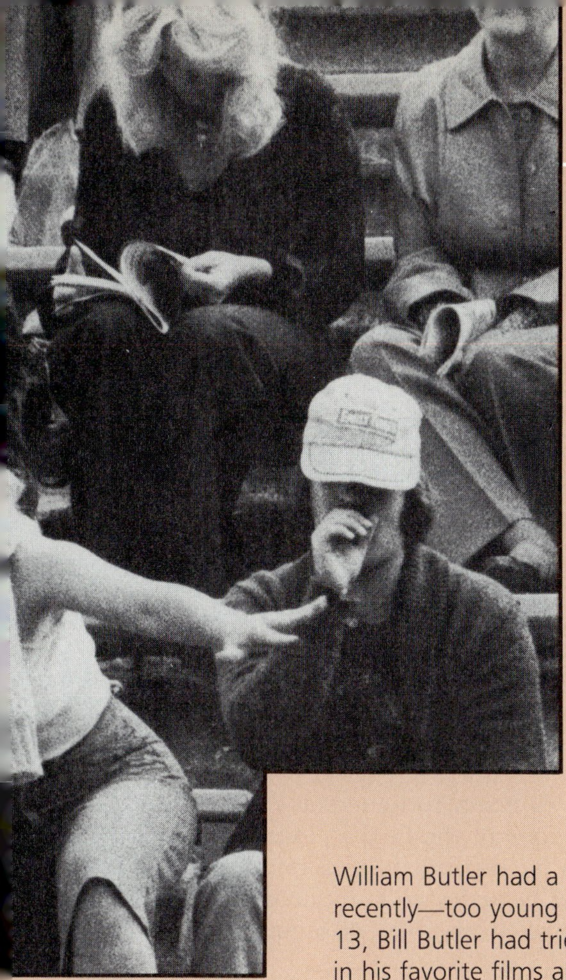

CHAPTER 1
Introduction

William Butler had a lust for life. We must say "had" because he died recently—too young and a victim of lung cancer. When he was only 12 or 13, Bill Butler had tried to emulate the strong and handsome men he saw in his favorite films and in cigarette advertisements by starting to smoke. It was also a way to prove to his friends (and to himself) that he was every bit as much an adult as they were. Years later, with that same objective in mind, he tried without success to quit. He could do anything else he set his mind to, but he could not quit smoking. Once, in desperation, he even went to the local police and asked them to lock him up for a few weeks without cigarettes, no matter how much he might plead. The harder he tried to quit, the greater became his hatred for the cigarette company that had "gotten him hooked."

When he was only in his late forties, what he feared might happen did happen. He developed lung cancer. Less than a year after the diagnosis, he stopped breathing for good. Before he died, Bill Butler asked his lawyer to file a suit against the tobacco company whose advertisements he had been influenced by as a boy and whose cigarettes he smoked for the rest of his life. He was angry at the company for what it had done to him, and he wanted to get even. He wanted a jury to decide whether the product was so dangerous, the warnings so inadequate, and the advertising so deceptive that the tobacco company would have to pay for the costs of his illness and for the support of his wife and children after his death.

Butler's lawsuit lived on after he was gone. His lawyer knew that winning such a case would not be easy. The tobacco company claimed that Butler had "assumed the risk" by choosing to smoke, and that people who choose to smoke know they might be running such a risk. Butler's lawyer argued that a teenager is not equipped to make such choices; by the time Butler was old enough to be legally responsible, he was already addicted to the nicotine. Experts from both sides debated what the scientific evidence did or did not mean.

How are such issues communicated to a jury? Which experts would be believed? Would a jury blame Butler for his own death or hold the tobacco company liable? More generally, can we believe "scientific evidence" about behavior such as Butler's? How is such evidence derived? In this chapter we will introduce you to the perspective, content, and methods of social psychology. Then, with a basic understanding of what the field is all about, we will return to see how a social psychologist's knowledge could be applied to this issue.

SOCIAL PSYCHOLOGY: AN OVERVIEW

What is social psychology? One way to begin to understand the field is through a definition. Gordon Allport, one of the field's pioneers, offered this definition: "Social psychology is an attempt to understand and explain how the thoughts, feelings, and behavior of individuals are influenced by the actual, imagined, or implied presence of others" (Allport, 1968, p. 3).

This definition means, first, that social psychology is focused on the behavior of *individuals,* not groups or institutions, which makes it different from sociology. Second, social psychologists focus on the **social factors** that influence behavior: other people and the institutions, artifacts, situations, and social and physical structures that people have created. Despite differences in their topics of primary concern, the particular theories to which they subscribe, and the roles and settings in which they work, social psychologists share this unique perspective, which differentiates their work from that of other disciplines and from other areas within psychology.

Another way to understand the field of social psychology is to look at the topics it covers. Take a look at the table of contents of this book and you will know what social psychology is about. First we will look at human (and sometimes nonhuman) social behavior at the level of the individual: perception and cognition in Chapter 2, the self and personality in Chapter 3. Next we'll learn about the ways in which people connect with the social world around them: socialization and social roles (Chapter 4), attitudes (Chapter 5), and attitude change (Chapter 6). We then move to small social units that involve behavior ranging from love (Chapter 7) to violence (Chapter 8), and branch out to altruism (Chapter 9) and conformity (Chapter 10). The final three chapters of the book deal with social behavior in the larger environment (Chapter 11) and in groups, both small (Chapter 12) and large (Chapter 13). As you can see, social psychology covers a wide territory, from the phenomena at the level of the individual to the level of large organizations and nations.

We can see some of these social processes at work in William Butler's life, as his attitudes toward cigarettes changed. He adopted a certain image of himself, and others held certain perceptions of him and feelings about him. He sought help from people, including those whose formal role it is to give certain kinds of help—doctors and lawyers. And he wanted to hurt the company he felt had done him harm.

Social Psychology's Perspective

All social psychologists share certain common denominators. They are referred to as social psychology's "perspective" (Brickman, 1980; Krupat, 1982; Saxe, 1983; McGuire, 1973). Perhaps the dominant theme in social psychology's perspective is **situationalism** (Cartwright, 1978); that is, the ideas created and tested by social psychologists nearly always reflect awareness of the importance of the situation in which behavior occurs. The situationalist view is that behavior is a product of an organism's interaction with its environment.

Sensitivity to the context of behavior is especially important to those who want to solve real-world problems, because the most feasible solutions are those that can be brought about by changing variables in people's environment. Theories of behavior that locate causes within people—be they genetic tendencies or personality traits—point to variables that are less easily changed.

An illustration of this is provided by Caplan and Nelson (1973), who found that psychological researchers tend to attribute causes of behavior to the *characteristics of the individual,* rather than looking for explanations in the person's relationship to the social world (Pepitone, 1981). For example, when poor children were found to arrive late for classes and other appointments, many psychologists looked for the cause in the individual child's "makeup": perhaps he or she had failed to inherit or to develop the proper compulsiveness, or lacked the ability to delay gratification, or had some other defect in personality, intelligence, or genes.

Ryan (1971) has argued, however, that this is little more than "blaming the victim." An alternative was to study the *circumstances* of these children, which revealed that their poverty deprived them of having the wristwatches most middle-class children have. The poor children were given watches, and their punctuality improved dramatically.

Another common denominator of social psychologists is that they try to be systematically **empirical.** To be empirical is to acquire knowledge through the senses, through observation, and through experience. Truth, the empiricist believes, is found not in the pronouncements of authorities or from logic alone, but from encounters with reality. But that is not enough.

The empirical approach must be carried out systematically. Every one of us gains knowledge of the world empirically each morning when we venture out from under the covers. But any old foray into reality—worthwhile though it may be—does not mean that the knowledge gained is representative, reliable, or capable of leading to trustworthy inferences about relations among events, especially cause-effect relations.

What we are talking about here is the difference between common sense and science. When we engage in scientific empiricism, we recognize that unsystematic experience can distort reality and mislead us. Thus, the scientific method was invented to guard against possible distortions of observation and inference. The key word in that phrase is *method.* Careful methods provide the systematic empirical evidence on which ideas in social psychology are built and tested. (For those with a deeper interest in social psychological research methods, we have provided an appendix on research methodology at the end of the book.) In short, social psychologists appreciate that a fact is only as good as the methods used to find it.

What makes a person start smoking? What makes a jury reach a certain verdict? To assert possible answers is relatively easy. To test the proposed answers against empirical evidence is quite another matter. Social psychologists do far more than speculate about the answers to complex issues. They go out and collect data in a systematic and careful manner. Walter Stephan (1980) has called social psychology "a discipline with a scientific mind and a humanistic heart" (p. 196), and a student we knew once said the field seemed to be characterized by "soft topics and hard tactics."

The Origins and Evolution of Social Psychology

Social psychology is a field with a dual interest in both understanding and application, and its history is filled with examples of both. One of the field's earliest textbooks, *Psychology and the Social Order* (Brown, 1936), sought, much as our book does, to consider what help social psychology might be to the solution of societal problems. The Society for the Psychological Study of Social Issues (SPSSI), now a division of the American Psychological Association, was founded in 1936 with a similar objective. In World War II the military put social psychologists to work solving a variety of problems, such as developing and testing methods of countering propaganda and studying the way soldiers adapt to and function in military life. The energy put into such problem solving paid dividends in important new knowledge about behavior in organizations, attitude measurement and change, mass communication, international relations, and leadership (Cartwright, 1948; Hilgard, 1978; Hovland, Lumsdaine, & Sheffield, 1949; Stouffer et al., 1949a, 1949b).

Most social psychologists trace their modern lineage to Kurt Lewin (1890–1947), who emigrated from Germany to the United States at the age of 43, in the early years of Hitler's reign. Though Lewin had to begin a new professional life in a new place, and had only 14 years of life remaining to him, he succeeded in starting a number of institutions and projects of central importance to the field. One of the most notable features of Lewin's work is the importance he placed on a marriage of the basic and the applied, the theory-oriented and the problem-centered. He saw the two as serving one another. The problems Lewin researched were motivated by real-world social problems: intergroup relations (especially the reduction of prejudice), attitudes and behavior (to adjust to the needs of the war effort), studies of the effects of authoritarian and democratic social climates, and conflict and its resolution.

Lewin devoted himself to trying to solve these and similar problems while gaining an improved theoretical understanding of the phenomena at issue. One of the methodological inventions he developed was **action research,** whereby people attempt simultaneously to study and to solve their problems. He believed that problems could not be held in abeyance forever, awaiting basic knowledge to accumulate enough to provide perfect answers. Instead, solutions should be tested in real-world settings in a way that would also yield improved understanding of the problems themselves. Knowledge would grow out of problem-solving efforts, and solutions would grow out of knowledge-building efforts. So complete was Lewin's merging of theory and practice that his biography is titled *The Practical Theorist* (Marrow, 1969).

In the years following Lewin's death, social psychologists nurtured the theoretical side of his legacy. The practical side was preserved by his heirs largely as an ideal (Sanford, 1970). Academic social psychologists could—and did—carry out a wealth of theory-testing experiments from the comfort of their university laboratories. That these projects would some day have applied value was rarely doubted, but they represented only one side of the Lewinian bequest.

By the mid-1960s the field's preoccupation with theoretical issues and laboratory research led to what has been called the "crisis" of social psychology. The crisis was felt most acutely when the social movements opposing racial, sexual, and class injustice, the Vietnam War, and the arms race erupted inside as well as outside academe. Social psychology, along with other disciplines, could not ignore the question of whether its accumulated knowledge had anything of value to contribute to the resolution of these social problems (Elms, 1975; Sherif, 1970; McGuire, 1969, 1973; Smith, 1972, 1973).

Let us take a look at the theories that social psychology has developed, and then ask whether they have relevance to real-life problems and solutions.

Theories in Social Psychology

Contrary to popular belief, the growth of knowledge in science (including social science) is measured not by accumulating facts but rather by making changes in the theories that are constructed to explain those facts. The goal of science is not to create an encyclopedia of observations about a topic, such as attitude change, but to provide explanations of those observations. Such explanations are called **theories.** Theories are not guesses that stand in until facts can be found; they are explanations of observed facts.

Coming up with explanations for behavior is something all of us do. Common sense and folk wisdom can always be counted upon to provide "explanations" after the fact. If two people of similar backgrounds like each other, we can say "birds of a feather flock together." If two friends are as different as night and day, we can say "opposites attract." But the real test of a theory—the test to which it is put in science—is its ability to predict. Similarly, its practical value comes from its ability to predict or to prescribe actions to be taken.

Theories are abstractions. They compete with each other to provide the best account of an observed phenomenon (Murphy & Medin, 1985). Good theories, as opposed to bad theories, (1) explain more of the observations and relations among observations; (2) use fewer concepts (this is called *parsimony*); (3) are internally consistent; (4) lead to testable hypotheses; and (5) are therefore capable of being disconfirmed (this is called *falsifiability*). In order for one theory to be found superior to a competing theory, both must lead to testable hypotheses. Ideally a critical test can be constructed in which one theory leads to one set of predictions and the other to different predictions about a given phenomenon.

Not only does falsifiability allow us to choose among competing theories, but it permits knowledge to advance, since it is the displacement of older, poorer theories by newer, better theories that marks the growth of knowledge. A theory that is incapable of disconfirmation cannot contribute to the development of further knowledge. Francis Bacon, the early-seventeenth-century philosopher and a founder of modern science, made the point that a clear and incorrect theory is preferable to an unclear, untestable theory by observing that "truth will sooner come out of error than from confusion."

Cognitive theories are among the most popular theories in social psychology today. They focus on the processes by which human beings perceive, store, and process social information and how they use this information to guide their everyday interactions with others (Fiske & Taylor, 1984). Though an oversimplification, we might say that cognitive theories regard human beings as sophisticated computers. People "output" behavior as a function of the kind of information that has been "input" and the way that the information has been centrally processed. Like all cognitive theorists, students of social cognition are interested in understanding both the hardware (central nervous system) and the software (the learned programs) that determine how people think and behave.

Another major theory in social psychology is **social learning theory,** an outgrowth of the stimulus-response (S-R) school of thought. The two most familiar S-R theories are *classical* conditioning, associated with Ivan Pavlov, and the *operant* conditioning of B. F. Skinner. To the basic learning processes of classical and operant conditioning, social psychologists have added a third kind of learning, **modeling.** In learning by modeling, people do not receive rewards or punishments directly; rather, they observe the responses of others and note the consequences (either positive or negative). Later, they may choose to imitate the observed behavior if they believe it will bring positive results (a reward). Social learning theory has provided some of the major explanations for attitude change, interpersonal attraction, and aggression, as we shall see in Chapters 6, 7, and 8.

Psychoanalytic theory, most prominently associated with Sigmund Freud, is most concerned with biological drives and early development. Freud assumed that current functioning is best understood by looking at the early conflicts of infancy and childhood. He believed that unresolved unconscious conflicts of a person's earliest years are responsible for today's feelings and behavior. Psychoanalytic theory, although it has had a good deal of impact on twentieth-century thought, has had less influence among social psychologists than among other psychologists because many of its major principles are not testable and, therefore, not falsifiable. Some discussions of psychoanalytic theory, however, will be found in our review of the topics of aggression, authoritarianism, and personality.

Where psychoanalytic theory looks to internal conflicts as the source of behavior, **role theory** directs its attention to the impact on behavior of roles that are created by the society of which we are a part. A **role** is a set of behaviors prescribed for certain categories of people such as students, doctors, or fire fighters. We step in and out of roles, but whenever we do so we find that our behavior changes in line with the expectations for the role we are currently in. Concepts from role theory will be discussed when we consider such matters as behavior in organizations, love and friendship relationships, and socialization and social roles (especially sex roles).

Field theory was developed primarily by Lewin (1936, 1951). It conceives of behavior as a joint product of all the forces acting on the person, both internal (psychological and biological) and external (social and physical environment). All the relevant forces exist in a "field," which is the individual's *life space.* Our behavior is thought of as motion within that field, as people are pulled toward positive goals or away from negative situations. These various forces manifest themselves in different behavior.

Let us see how the different theories might view the same social behavior; for instance, Why did William Butler start and continue to smoke?

A cognitive social psychologist would be interested in Butler's perception and interpretation of the world and what it meant to Butler to be a person who smokes. Butler's image of a smoker seemed to be that of an adventurous, competent, attractive man. His behavior was aimed at trying to fit himself to that image.

A social learning theorist would consider the way in which Butler began to smoke, looking at the social reinforcement he sought in smoking and the models (peers and movie stars) who influenced him to take up the habit. Once he was addicted to cigarettes, the thought of quitting was so unpleasant and the need for nicotine was so strong that the behavior of smoking was accompanied by powerful physiological reinforcement. In addition, learned habits and social reinforcement also maintained the behavior.

A psychoanalytically oriented social psychologist might argue that Butler must have been plagued by some unresolved problems in the oral stage of his psychosexual development, and for that reason was likely to fall into some habit that served his unconscious need for oral gratification.

A role theorist would point to the social forces operating on a teenager of Butler's generation, including the expectations of his friends that he would smoke.

Field theory would look to the variety of forces operating on the young Butler: present life goals, survival and comfort needs, parental expectations, perception of the situation, and so on. Unlike those in psychoanalytic theory, these forces would be primarily here-and-now, and their resolution would result in the decision to start or to quit smoking.

The various theories employ different concepts in trying to understand a behavior. And the different theories imply different strategies for trying to achieve a solution.

BASIC AND APPLIED RESEARCH

The process of building knowledge through the development and testing of theories, described in the preceding section, is what is known as pure or **basic research.** It is aimed at testing theories and sorting out the better from the lesser ones. A social psychologist doing basic research might try to determine which of the theories just sketched provides the best explanation of smoking, or might conduct a study designed to test which theory provides the best explanation of the effects of televised violence.

Psychoanalytic theory, for example, predicts that violent entertainment reduces the level of actual violence among viewers by providing an outlet for pent-up aggressive energy (such an outlet is known as "catharsis"). By contrast, social learning theory predicts that much aggressive behavior is learned and that the more we observe people resorting to violence, the more we behave violently. The results of studies of the effects of televised and other observed violence cast light on the validity of these competing theories. (Details of the outcome of this particular debate can be found in Chapter 8, "Aggression and Violence.")

Basic research is the activity to which many social psychologists devote most of their energy and time, but it is not all they do. A second important and growing activity of social psychologists is **applied research.** While pure research is "theory-oriented," applied research is "problem-centered"—it addresses itself to finding or testing the validity of solutions to human problems (Deutsch, 1980).

A social psychologist doing problem-centered research might carry out a study to assess the effectiveness of a number of techniques that promise to reduce the level of violence in our society. Knowing the results of basic research findings helps. The research done by basic and applied researchers might not look very different, but the answers they seek are aimed at different purposes: building knowledge versus solving problems.

Theory-oriented research builds the conceptual bridges, and problem-oriented research uses these bridges to find solutions and expand the theories further. And, although applied researchers sometimes work to turn their conclusions into real-world solutions, others—social psychological technologists—specialize in turning knowledge into action (Reyes & Varela, 1980). The different kinds of orientation held by basic and applied social psychologists are highlighted in Table 1.1. Though they sometimes seem to be at odds, these two kinds of orientation really complement each other (Saxe & Fine, 1980). In fact, Donald Campbell, one of social psychology's most celebrated methodologists, has noted that any social reform can and should be seen as a social experiment that provides us with empirical evidence.

The close relationship that can exist between the basic and applied approaches is exemplified in a "debate" that took place between *New York Times* columnist James Reston and Senator William Proxmire on the value of research on attraction and love (the topic of Chapter 7). As can

FROM THE FIELD
Donald T. Campbell

Donald Campbell, the originator of evaluation research, has developed important ways of thinking about research design and measurement. His work has been especially important to applied research, since it shows, for example, how legal reforms can be studied as if they were independent variables in quasi-experimental designs. In addition to his methodological achievements, Professor Campbell has made contributions to the study of prejudice, public opinion, and attitude change. A past president of the American Psychological Association, he spent much of his career at Northwestern University and is now at Lehigh University.

TABLE 1.1
Comparison of Basic and Applied Approaches

Basic	Applied
1. Cartesian view of research as an individualistic, competitive, intrinsically satisfying activity	1. Baconian view of research as a collaborative social means for contributing to the public welfare
2. Tradition of academic freedom: the individual researcher follows own interests in deciding what is to be studied	2. Tradition of mission orientation: the area of study is determined by collective needs
3. Emphasis on knowledge relating to controlled laboratory conditions	3. Emphasis on knowledge relating to actual conditions "in the field," "in the real world"
4. Emphasis on hypothesis testing	4. Emphasis on the systematic standardized observation and classification of natural phenomena
5. Emphasis on theoretical payoff: the goal is theory-based knowledge	5. Emphasis on pragmatic payoff: the goal is to reduce problems in the most cost-effective and ethical manner
6. Emphasis on publication in highly technical specialized journals	6. Emphasis on communication with lay decision makers concerning programs and policies
7. Emphasis on deriving general statements about human behavior	7. Emphasis on deriving particular evaluations of specific programs

Source: D. B. Fishman & W. D. Neigher (1982). American psychology in the eighties: Who will buy? *American Psychologist, 37,* 540.

be seen in the In the News box (see pp. 14–15), Reston argues that basic knowledge has the capacity to enlighten our approaches to solving significant real-world problems. This is a position we agree with and will attempt to illustrate throughout this book. The value of each approach to the other has been summarized by Lewin in one of the most venerated quotations in social psychology: "There is nothing so practical as a good theory" (1951, p. 169).

Early social psychologists regarded the combination of the scholarly pursuit of theory-oriented knowledge and a concern for solving human problems as both possible and desirable. This attitude was reflected in much of their work. Today, both inside and outside of social psychology, this interest has seen a rebirth, and social psychological knowledge has found its way into the public arena. Ronald Fisher (1980) has suggested several "touchstones" that provide a test of the progress of social psychology's knowledge and its application. They help summarize this discussion of basic and applied research. Social psychological knowledge should reflect

1. A central focus on fundamental social problems.
2. The continuous integration of theory, research, and practice.
3. The development of theories stressing the interaction of the person and the environment.
4. The application of numerous complementary research methods.
5. The expansion of practical expertise through collaboration with other disciplines and professions.
6. The adherence to humanistic values and a professional code of ethics.

Applied social psychology has by no means displaced what is now referred to as "traditional" social psychology. Yet it has extended its basic principles and methods into new spheres. The explosion of applied research in the last decade has taken social psychology into the fields of law, health care, education, energy conservation, international relations, public policy analysis, and communications, among others. In addition to the kinds of settings and issues applied research has touched upon, new courses, new journals, and new books have begun to appear reflecting the "new"—yet not altogether new—social psychology. Table 1.2 provides some sense of the diversity of problem areas addressed by contemporary (applied) social psychologists by presenting some of the journals and book series being published in the field.

The expansion of social psychologists' interests and activities has enlarged the settings where they work and the roles they undertake. For most of its history, social psychology has been based in familiar territory: college and university campuses. Whatever topics they focused on, whatever theoretical orientation they worked from, and however pure or applied their research, most social psychologists could be found at universities. The basic and the applied researcher might well be the same person, doing one kind of work one day and the other the next day. Social psychologists committed to applied work could be at university research centers or professional schools (of law, medicine, business, or education) instead of academic departments. Forays into real-world problem solving, government service, and consulting to public and private agencies could also be done from a university base.

Today, however, social psychologists in growing numbers are taking jobs in nonacademic settings. Table 1.3 shows the distribution of job settings taken by a sampling of social psychologists who recently received their Ph.D.'s. Note that while more than half of the new social psychologists took positions in academic settings, about a third work in government, business, and other such applied settings. In the latter they often provide research and consulting services aimed at trying to solve society's problems—ranging from poverty to defense, justice to transportation, health to communication.

TABLE 1.2
Journals and Book Series About Social Psychology

Basic Research in Social Psychology

Journal of Personality and Social Psychology
Journal of Experimental Social Psychology
Personality and Social Psychology Bulletin
Journal of Social Psychology
Advances in Experimental Social Psychology
Progress in Social Psychology

Applied Research in Social Psychology

In General
Journal of Applied Social Psychology
Journal of Social Issues
International Journal of Applied Social Psychology
Advances in Applied Social Psychology
Applied Social Psychology Annual
Evaluation Studies Review Annual
Basic and Applied Social Psychology

Environmental Psychology
Environment and Behavior
Population and Environment
Advances in Environmental Psychology

Health
Health Psychology
Journal of Health and Social Behavior
Handbook of Psychology and Health

Law and Policy
Law and Human Behavior
Law and Psychology Review
Policy Studies Review Annual
Perspectives in Law and Psychology

In the realm of problem solving, the social psychologist can occupy roles other than researcher or adviser. In giving advice on what policies or courses of action might be adopted, a social scientist can take the role of an *expert witness.* An expert witness is a neutral, honest broker between knowledge and a consumer's need to know. In this role the social psychologist shares information as neutrally as possible with people whose job it is to make policy decisions. A social psychologist in an *advocate* role has a specific outcome or program in mind and seeks to have it adopted; such a social psychologist is often hired by or represents the interests of particular groups. The social psychologist as *evaluator* comes in after a policy or solution has been implemented and collects data to provide feedback to the policymakers on how successful their attempted solution

TABLE 1.3
Where Social Psychologists Work

Setting	Percentage of All Social Psychologists
Academic settings, including psychology departments and schools of medicine, law, and business	62.7
Schools and school systems	3.9
Organized human service setting	5.9
Independent practice	1.0
Business, government, and other	26.5

Source: A. Howard, G. M. Pion, G. D. Gottfredson, P. E. Flattau, S. Oskamp, S. M. Pfattlin, D. W. Bray, & A. G. Burstein (1986). The changing face of American psychology. *American Psychologist, 41(12),* 1323. Copyright 1986. Adapted by permission of the publisher.

has been (APA Task Force on Psychology and Public Policy, 1984; DeLeon, O'Keefe, & VandenBos, 1982; Segall, 1976).

As social psychologists take positions in nonacademic settings, their work and their roles take on increased diversity and specialization which reflect the structure of the world in which they are working. In virtually all of these roles social scientists have the responsibility to create knowledge or to evaluate and put research knowledge to use. For all of them an understanding of research methods is necessary.

EMPIRICAL RESEARCH METHODS

Every discipline defines itself by the questions it seeks to answer and relies on a set of methods that brings its knowledge into being. To answer applied and basic questions, social psychologists need to have methods by which these answers can be developed. And, to understand and to assess their findings, it is helpful for students to have a grasp of the methodology by which the knowledge was created. As we mentioned earlier in the chapter, a fact is only as good as the methods used to find it. And a theory is only as good as the empirical evidence that supports it. Accordingly, research methodology, especially the experiment, has come to be a central feature of the discipline of social psychology (Danziger, 1985).

Theory and Observation

Theories, as we noted earlier, are explanations for sets of observations. Observation comes into play in the life of theories at two major points. First is the **inductive,** or theory development, phase. In this phase facts

IN THE NEWS

PROXMIRE ON LOVE

Senator William Proxmire of Wisconsin has discovered that the National Science Foundation is spending $83,000 a year out of the Federal Treasury to find out why people fall in love, and he wants it stopped. Not the love but the spending. "Biggest boondoggle of the year," he says. "I don't want the answer." . . .

Mr. Proxmire is a modern man who believes that government should help people with their problems . . . but he is against basic research on the alarming divorce rate or break-up of the human family in America. You have to assume he was kidding.

The National Center for Health Statistics of the Department of Health, Education and Welfare has just reported that there were 970,000 divorces in the United States in 1974, compared to 913,000 in 1973, and 479,000 in 1965. The *rate* of population growth in the United States is down over the last decade, but in 1974, the excess of births over deaths was still up over a million and a quarter, while the rate of marriages was down and the rate of divorces up.

All the National Science Foundation was suggesting, and the Federal Government was financing, was a modest inquiry into these statistics. Why this increase in divorce, this decrease in marriage, this disbelief in the family as the basis of American life?

Were the expectations of married life unreasonably high? Were the assumptions of courtship, and of economic security an enduring reality or a trap? What was romantic love anyway—a basis for secure family and national life, or a dangerous illusion?

With these questions in mind, the National Science Foundation was given $83,000 to see whether it could come up with any answers or at least clues, and the burden of research fell on Ellen Berscheid, a professor of psychology at the University of Minnesota. When Senator Proxmire spotted this $83,000 item as chairman of the Senate Appropriations subcommittee in

are established on the basis of observations, and theories are constructed to explain or account for the facts. Thus, observations are important at the origin of a theory.

The second occasion for observation is the **deductive** phase, in which a theory is subjected to empirical verification; that is, hypotheses based on the theory are derived and tested against new empirical observations. The theory will stand or fall in large part on its ability to survive such attempts to test its validity (see Figure 1.1).

Research Settings

The controlled observation that constitutes research is conducted in a variety of settings. **Laboratory research** is the most common kind of social psychological research. In such controlled settings social psychologists construct analogs of the social phenomena they wish to study. For example, a researcher might create mock juries and present different versions of a case to them to see which version is more persuasive. Such

charge of the National Science Foundation's budget, he almost blew his new hairdo. "Get out of the love-racket," he told the foundation.

Obviously, he had a point. The reasons why people fall in love, or think they do, will always be a mystery, and many people, like Mr. Proxmire, probably "don't want the answer." But if the sociologists and psychologists can get even a suggestion of the answer to our pattern of romantic love, marriage, disillusion, divorce—and the children left behind—it could be the best investment of Federal money since Mr. Jefferson made the Louisiana Purchase. . . .

It is the illusion of romantic love among the young that leads to broken marriages, [Professor Berscheid] says, and broken families, which in turn contribute to the disorientation, instability, disunity and even violence of American life. Therefore, she concludes, research on how and why young men and women marry is fundamental, even if the researchers never find the answers. . . .

Mr. Proxmire . . . saw what seemed to be an obvious boondoggle in the budget, and he attacked it as a budgetary swindle. It was good politics but probably bad history, for the world is being transformed now, not by political leaders, but by the fertility of the human mind and body, by the creation of life at the beginning and the prolongation of life at the end.

The politicians don't quite know how to find the jobs, schools, houses, food, fuel and transportation to deal with this torrent of people and problems. Therefore, the social scientists have to think about why new life is created in the first place, where the pill, and the concepts of romantic love, easy sex, marriage and divorce fit into the life of the nation.

Source: "Proxmire on Love," by James Reston from *The New York Times*, Friday, March 14, 1975.

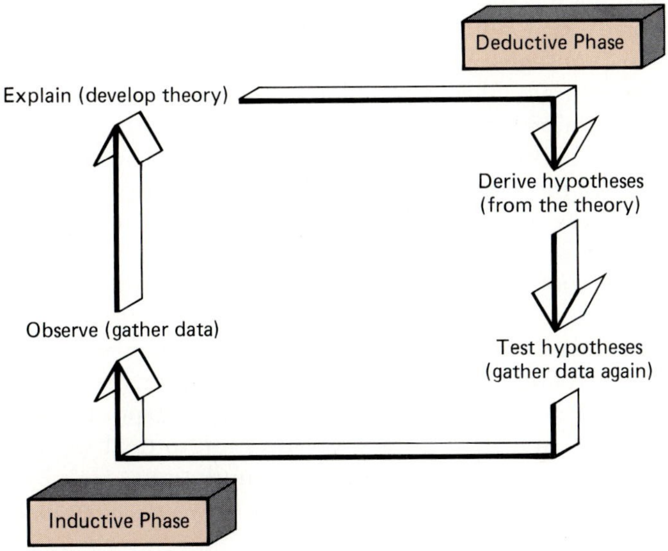

FIGURE 1.1
Phases of Theory Development and Testing Theories are explanations of what is observed, and their validity needs to be tested. In the inductive phase of science, we go from particular observations to general concepts designed to explain those observations. In the deductive phase we go in the other direction, deriving from general theories particular hypotheses which are tested against further observations.

Social psychologists constantly generate data from surveys, experiments, and systematic observation. Once the data are collected, however, they must be interpreted. In this photo, a researcher is trying to determine whether or not his hypothesis has been confirmed.

laboratory studies can vary in their realism. Some studies can be highly artificial; others capture quite realistically the phenomenon of interest.

Because social psychologists have become increasingly concerned that the findings obtained in the laboratory should be generalizable beyond the laboratory, they have turned increasingly to **field research**—research that takes place in the setting they want to generalize to. Field research has the advantage of providing all the complexity and reality of a natural setting. It also has disadvantages. In natural settings variations are more difficult to introduce, data are harder to collect, and the work is more inconvenient, time-consuming, and expensive. But doing such research may be worth the costs if it produces more generalizable findings.

Research can take place in still other "places," such as a computer. The behavioral or social process of interest can be represented as a series of equations in a computer program and the process studied in what is termed a *computer simulation*. Another strategy is to tell people to **role-play** a social phenomenon. This is different from a laboratory analog. In the laboratory, people typically are led to believe that what they are doing is real or a simulation of reality. In role playing, people might be told to make believe they are a head of state, the director of a corporation, a judge, or a married couple, and then be given a situation to deal with or a problem to solve. Role playing and computer simulations are often useful, but their results are treated cautiously because they look at models

This interview might concern anything from the couple's feelings about foreign policy to their preferences in breakfast cereals. Survey methods enable us to learn about people's attitudes, and even their behavior (through self-report), allowing us to answer both basic and applied questions.

of behavior that are distant from behavior in its naturally occurring form. More details on the methodology of research in social psychology can be found in the appendix on research methodology at the end of the book.

APPLICATION
DO MALES MISPERCEIVE FEMALES' FRIENDLINESS?

Sometimes social psychologists get ideas for research from everyday experiences. Such was the case for Antonia Abbey. She reports that she and a few women friends were at a crowded campus bar, sharing a table with two male strangers. It seemed to Abbey that the men misinterpreted the women's friendliness as a show of sexual interest—so much so, apparently, that the women "finally had to excuse themselves from the table to avoid an awkward scene" (Abbey, 1982, p. 830).

This appears to be a casual conversation between a young man and a young woman, but do they attach equal significance to it? Research suggests that, in comparison to females, males tend to read greater interest and potential attraction into encounters such as these.

For a social psychologist, such an experience is often the beginning of theorizing about a phenomenon and applying empirical research methods to cast more light on it. Abbey wanted to find out why men would see a woman's words and actions as more seductive than she intended them. Do males and females perceive behavior differently? Or might it instead be a person's role (sender versus receiver of signal) that makes the difference in perception?

Abbey designed a laboratory experiment to try to answer these questions. She assigned 144 people to 4-person groups, each with two males and two females. Each group was then divided into two randomly paired mixed-sex couples. While one pair engaged in a brief conversation, the other was taken to a room from which they observed the conversation.

The researcher could thus obtain information about perceptions that could not be found in natural settings. The conversing pair would be able to record their perceptions of each other, and the passive observers would be able to record their perceptions also, providing a measure of how outside observers perceived each participant. This would permit a comparison of males' versus females' perceptions as well as a comparison of the perceptions of the people interacting (the "actors") versus the perceptions of those watching from outside the conversation (the "observers") (see Figure 1.2).

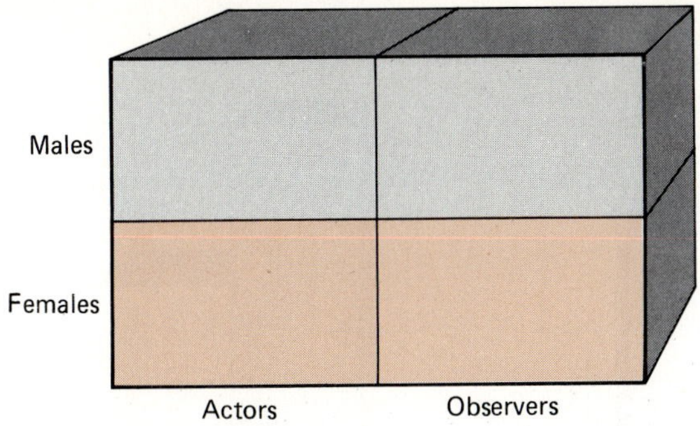

FIGURE 1.2
Basic Design of Abbey's Study Abbey's study consisted of two major independent variables: gender (male or female) and role in the action (whether a person was an actor or an observer). This produces a 2 × 2 design, with four sets of conditions.

After the conversation, all four people filled out questionnaires in which they indicated their perceptions of the actors' personality traits and their perceptions of how each actor was "trying to behave." Among other characteristics, Abbey wanted to find out how flirtatious, seductive, or promiscuous the four people perceived the actors to be.

What did Abbey find? First, males rated females' behavior as significantly more promiscuous and seductive than females rated females' behavior. Also, male observers thought the women actors were more attracted to and interested in their partners than female observers thought they were. As Figure 1.3 illustrates, male actors were significantly more attracted to their partners than their partners were to them. Similarly, male observers were more sexually interested in the female actors than the female observers were in the male actors.

The central research question seems to have been answered: Men perceive women's friendliness as sexually provocative, while women observing the same behavior do not see it as sexual. But this conclusion seems no more than a manifestation of the apparent tendency for men to see the world of male and female interaction as more sexual than women do. In addition, the role a person occupies also plays a part. *Actors* of both sexes gave themselves and their partners higher ratings on evaluations of personality and conversational style than either of the *observers* did.

This study illustrates how social psychologists can test hypotheses against empirical data in an effort to determine which ideas are supported and which are not. Sometimes they uncover additional phenomena worth investigating further, such as the actor/observer differences. In this study, Abbey translated a messy social encounter into a laboratory analog and designed a true experiment (at least with respect to the actor/observer variable; we cannot randomly assign people to be males or females). As in many such studies, the participants were

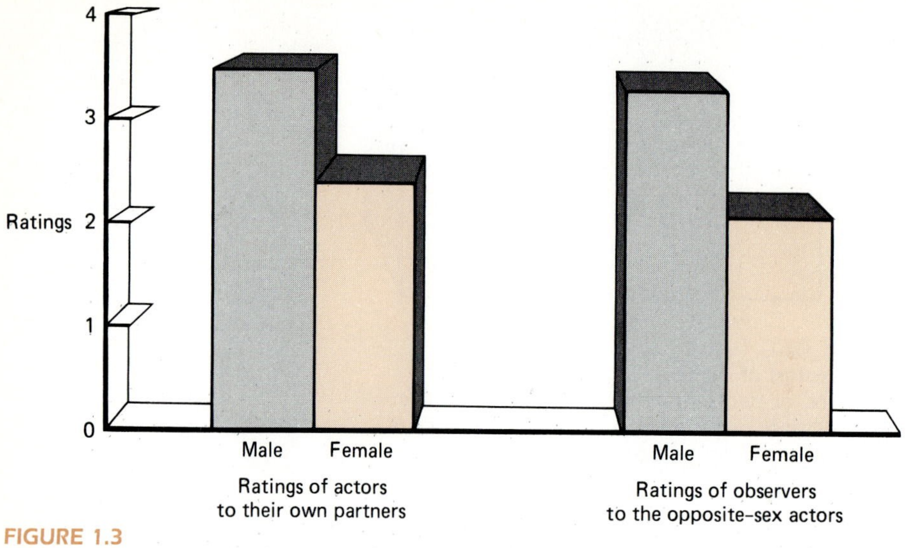

FIGURE 1.3

Sexual Attraction in Abbey's Study This figure summarizes Abbey's findings concerning sexual attraction. In rating their own partners, men were more sexually attracted than women were. When observers were asked to rate their sexual attraction to the opposite-sex actors, again men were more attracted than were women. *Source:* After A. Abbey (1982). Sex differences in attributions for friendly behavior: Do males misperceive females' friendliness? *Journal of Personality and Social Psychology, 42,* 830–838.

college students. Abbey collected her data from written questionnaires that contained both open-ended items and rating scales. The most important data are presented as averages in tables, along with significance test results. Is this an example of basic or applied research? Can you think of other kinds of studies that you could design to get at the questions that Abbey was examining?

THE SOCIAL PSYCHOLOGY OF RESEARCH

Doing research is itself a social process, and the behavior and perceptions of scientists are subject to social psychological processes just as other human behavior is (Barber, 1976; Rosenthal, 1967; Rosenthal & Rosnow, 1969, 1984). This is true of all kinds of research, whether involving people or not, but the consequences can be most serious when the research participants are humans.

Investigator Paradigm Effect

All researchers operate out of a conceptual framework of what the world they are studying is like. Whatever they are trying to study, they inevitably make assumptions about the nature of the world surrounding it. Such assumptions constitute a **paradigm.** The particular paradigm scientists hold affects what they choose to study, how they study it, and what sense they make of their research findings (Kuhn, 1962). Scientists can thus sometimes "fail to 'see' events that are incongruent with the assumptions of a prevailing paradigm" or "'see' nonexistent phenomena" (Barber, 1976, pp. 6, 7). For example, chemists once assumed that noble gases could not combine, so it was not until 1962 that they found they could (Abelson, 1962). And despite the publication of hundreds of scientific papers on "N-rays" early in the century, scientists decided in 1904 that there was no such thing.

In psychology, the substantial theoretical differences between, say, social learning theorists and cognitive theorists may lead them to ask different research questions and look to different evidence for answers. The only real "cure" for such paradigm effects is to encourage a variety of paradigms and to enjoy healthy skepticism and open debate.

Observer Effects

Even when scientists share a common paradigm, they are still subject to error. One source of potential error, the **observer effect,** is due to differences in human perception. For example, in astronomy different observers perceive star movements as occurring at different speeds. Different social psychologists judging whether a given behavior is aggressive may draw the dividing lines in different places and categorize the same behavior differently. The opportunity for such error increases as the level of complexity and room for interpretation of observations rises. Skepticism about the accuracy of one's own observations is necessary. Social scientists have learned to regulate their observations in order to calculate the extent of agreement among raters and to test the reliability of their measuring instruments. Only findings based on high reliabilities (for example, agreement among observers) should be trusted.

Interactional Experimenter Effects

As we have seen, in true experiments people in different conditions should be treated differently only with respect to the independent variables. On all other variables they must be treated equally or randomly. A researcher who is administering a treatment or collecting information, however, might unconsciously treat people differently and thereby affect the data. This is known as an **interactional experimenter effect.**

One kind of interactional experimenter effect is called the *biosocial effect.* That is where the characteristics of the experimenter and the participant interact to produce systematically different treatments of people. For instance, in one investigation it was found that only 12 percent of experimenters smiled at male participants while 70 percent smiled at females (Rosenthal, 1967). Thus any differences between the responses of males and females might be due not to differences between the male and female participants but to differences in the way experimenters *treated* the male and female participants.

The **experimenter expectancy effect** is a second problem of interaction between experimenter and participant. The researcher testing a hypothesis usually has an expectation about how it will turn out and, in fact, may be quite committed to a particular outcome. Medical researchers may be hoping that a new drug will prove effective. Social psychological researchers may be optimistic that a new dispute resolution procedure will support their theory about conflict resolution. The researcher's expectations may unintentionally affect the ways participants are treated in different experimental conditions. If the expectations are communicated to people, they may behave differently. In drug research, for example, it is known that a patient's mere expectation of a drug's action (known as a "placebo effect") produces an effect equal to about one-third the pharmacological effect of the drug.

In research on social variables the impact of the experimenter expectancy effect can be great. Research has shown that experimenters can unintentionally behave in ways that produce the effects they hope to find. In a series of studies on this issue, Rosenthal and his colleagues (Rosenthal, 1963, 1966; Rosenthal & Rosnow, 1969) have shown that experimenters who set out to test a hypothesis they strongly expect to confirm tend to find what they were looking for. Such effects have been found when animals as well as humans were the subjects of the experiments.

Research procedures have been invented to deal with this problem. One is the *double-blind* design, in which both the experimenter and the participant are kept "blind" to (not allowed to know) which condition—experimental or control—a person is in. If this is not possible, the experiment can be carried out by research assistants who are uninformed of the experimental hypotheses. Without clear expectations about what might happen, they are less likely to transmit expectations to participants.

Experimenter expectancy effects are more pronounced when research participants are volunteers. Rosenthal and Rosnow (1975) have found that people who volunteer for experiments differ from the population at large in ways that may affect an experiment's outcome. Volunteers tend to be more sociable and more intelligent, as well as having a higher need for approval. Concerning the external validity of such studies, it is appropriate to wonder whether the behavior of volunteers should be generalized to nonvolunteer populations.

Demand Characteristics

We can rule out the effects of experimenters' expectations when they are blind to treatments, but what about the expectations and perceptions of the research participants? A participant who figures out the expectations of the research may then choose to behave so as to confirm the experimental hypotheses. Martin Orne (1962) has called this the **demand characteristics** of the experimental situation. Orne found, first, that people do things in experimental situations that they would never do in ordinary situations: perform boring tasks for hours, submit to bodily intrusions, and so on. Second, they may view the experimental situation as a problem to be solved. If they can determine what the experimenter "wants" them to do, they usually do it even if it is contrary to their natural behavior. The characteristics of the research situation may thus "demand" certain behaviors of participants which do not represent their behavior in situations beyond the experimental setting.

In sum, the validity of conclusions—in research as in all human efforts to improve our understanding of the world—depends on being aware of the numerous problems that can mislead us and on fashioning methods to resist those problems.

METHODS OF APPLICATION

Because social psychology has, historically, been a research enterprise, its methodology of application is not as advanced as its research methodology. For many years social psychologists assumed that if they produced knowledge, someone else would find ways to put it to use. Now that more social psychologists are actively involved in generating knowledge, they have begun to think more about the means by which this knowledge comes to be used, not used, or even misused.

The Technological Method

The scientific method is a reflection of a philosophy of science that is now widespread in the intellectual life of Western civilization. It is a set of instructions for generating and, especially, for testing the validity of knowledge. Reyes and Varela (1980) have pointed out that if we apply knowledge to solving problems, we must have a "technological method" to guide the process of putting knowledge to work. A former engineer, Varela was experienced in the way physics is put to work to solve physical problems. In some respects, the technological method is the mirror image of the scientific method.

While science breaks problems down into components for analysis, technology puts these components together into a coherent and useful whole. The technological method seeks to create solutions by integrating principles and to get them to act jointly to produce an effect. It must take into account the combination of forces that make something work as it does. For example, the problems of education, poverty, and slum housing are usually treated separately by researchers, those involved in generating knowledge. But neighborhood location will affect what schools children go to and whom they associate with, which will affect what kind of jobs and incomes they will eventually have, which will affect the kind of housing they will be able to afford (Nelson & Caplan, 1983). Changing just one thing may change nothing. Since problems are related as whole "systems," solutions must take a systems approach and integrate the many aspects involved.

Utilization of Research

As we have said, social psychologists had long held the simple hope that if they stuck to producing knowledge through their research, someone would eventually put that knowledge to use (Weiss, 1977a, 1977b). Examples of just such a sequence appear throughout this book, but they mostly represent utilization by accident more than by design. Most social psychologists today feel that more systematic application is needed. If decision makers in both the private and public sectors have no effective or systematic means for locating, digesting, and incorporating available social science knowledge into their decisions, social science knowledge will be underutilized and decisions will not be as informed and effective as they might be.

Although this chemical plant may seem very distant from the university laboratory of the social psychologist, each year more and more research is being done in, and applied to, industrial and organizational settings.

Some studies have examined how high-level federal executives actually find and use social science knowledge (Caplan, Marson, & Stambaugh, 1975; Caplan, 1979). Caplan and his colleagues found that policymakers, unfortunately, do not distinguish between empirical and other types of knowledge. They are also more likely to use social science knowledge to revise preexisting perceptions of a problem rather than to find new answers to it. They think not about individual studies but about a cluster of studies that bears on an issue. Most important, their "information-seeking" systems are relatively closed. Rather than searching widely for all relevant information, they rely on internal studies or work contracted by their agency. In order to improve the utilization of social science knowledge, methods will have to be developed for information needs and available information resources to match each other better and to be more readily brought together (Braskamp & Brown, 1980; Siegel & Tuckel, 1985).

ETHICAL PROBLEMS OF RESEARCH AND APPLICATION

As social science becomes more involved in affecting people's lives, it encounters ever more numerous and profound ethical dilemmas. Ethical principles are sometimes thought of as the etiquette of research or intervention and, like etiquette in other spheres of life, are thought by some to serve little purpose aside from getting in the way of doing real work. On the other side of this coin is an equally simplistic view, which sees researchers and practitioners as the mad scientists of horror films, so obsessed with the pursuit of their own interests that the rights of others are trampled. From this viewpoint, ethical principles are the long, thin leash that holds such fiends in check.

A more sophisticated view of ethics usually sees neither good guys nor bad guys. Instead, the problem is that two positive values sometimes find themselves on a collision course with one another: (1) the search for knowledge and solutions to human problems; and (2) the desire to respect the autonomy and self-determination of the individuals affected. Ethical principles are the tools for guiding these two values into a peaceful coexistence.

Science's search for empirically verified knowledge offers the possibility for solving many human problems and improving the quality of our lives. But along the way the search itself can cause harm. And the consequences of knowledge are not invariably good, as the advent of nuclear weapons has made evident. In the balance of this section we will discuss the nature of the values at stake in the ethical dilemmas of research and application—the impact on the people affected, and social psychologists' responsibilities to the public (Diener & Crandall, 1978; Sieber, 1982a, 1982b; Steininger, Newell, & Garcia, 1984). Because social psychology's focus has been on research, our discussion of ethical issues will also focus on research.

Impact on Participants

The major focus of ethical concern for social psychologists is the people whose minds and bodies provide the data for our research and who are the targets of behavioral change programs. Should these people be subjected to harm or discomfort, have their privacy intruded upon, or even have an hour of their time taken by a researcher, in order to serve the researcher's goals? May their lives and behavior be altered without their consent?

Informed Consent On the one hand, the goals of research are humane ones: to advance knowledge both as an end in itself and in order to solve human problems. If society chose not to develop and advance new knowledge, we would all be condemning ourselves permanently to the status quo. On the other hand, Western values hold that each individual is the owner of himself or herself. Without your consent, no doctor can examine or treat you, no social worker can serve you, no scientist can gather data from you. If you do not want to fill out a questionnaire, submerge your hand in icy water, or give electric shocks to another person, you have the right to refuse before or during an experiment. Furthermore, consent is considered meaningful only when a person has been provided with adequate information on which to base a decision. This adds up to the moral and legal requirement of **informed consent** before a researcher or service provider can do anything to or for a person (see National Research Act PL 93-348; 45 Code of Federal Regulations 46; APA, 1982).

We must strike a balance between two values: the search for knowledge and the integrity of the individual. All people invited to participate in research must decide if the costs to them are outweighed by the contribution they will be making to the growth of knowledge. The American Psychological Association code of ethics directs researchers to weigh the potential benefits of research against the costs to participants in deciding whether and how to carry out research. Most research organizations, including universities, have committees called Institutional Review Boards (IRB's). IRB's are composed of representatives of the population to be studied, philosophers, and other citizens, as well as researchers. They review proposed research to identify ethically troublesome procedures and try to work out improvements. They can prohibit research from being performed.

Some social psychological research presents difficult problems for the requirement of informed consent. Suppose you wanted to examine public records or to study the behavior of crowds. How could you obtain informed consent? Suppose you wanted to see how people responded in an emergency, such as a crime taking place. If you told people in advance that you wanted to study a mock crime, the act of informing them would probably alter their behavior so much that the study would not be worth doing. Sometimes research can be done only when the participants are not fully informed or are misled about the true purpose of the research. This problem of *deception* has been much debated in social psychology (Geller, 1982; Menges, 1973; Ring, 1967). By 1969, 66 percent of studies used deception. Gross and Fleming (1982) found that in spite of the concerns raised about deception in the late 1960s (e. g., Kelman, 1967), its use did not decline in the following decade.

Sometimes it is questionable whether people are in a position to grant truly voluntary consent. Prisoners used to "volunteer" for dangerous medical experiments in the hope that their act would be smiled upon by the parole board and result in early release, assuming they survived the research. The law no longer permits such experiments to be carried out on prison populations. The comparable ethical dilemma for psychologists today is the subject pool. Because students in psychology classes are the people most available to university research psychologists, they (you) are the people most often required/urged/invited/induced to participate in research. Years ago the requirement was simply imposed. Increased ethical sensitivity in recent years has led to an improved balance of interests. Guidelines provided by the American Psychological Association for setting up subject pools urge that students be told about research participation requirements when they enter a course and be given alternative opportunities should they choose not to participate.

Confidentiality Another concern about research participants is that of confidentiality (Turner, 1982). Sometimes social psychological research involves obtaining sensitive information from people, such as data on sexual behavior, drug use, or criminal conduct. In order to protect people who are willing to provide such information—indeed, in order to encourage people to be candid about such matters—researchers offer to preserve the confidentiality of the information. The promise of confidentiality to research participants is among the highest ethical duties a researcher undertakes.

Ethical Problems of Applied Research

Applied research has all the problems of basic research plus some additional wrinkles of its own (Ruback & Greenberg, 1985). Their potential for doing good frequently puts social psychologists in a position to do harm. The most intense clash is in evaluation research on the effectiveness of different programs. We know that the surest road to clear answers is the true experiment. The effectiveness of interventions such as prisons, psychotherapy, and increased control for the elderly can be assessed most clearly when we subject them to study by randomly created experimental and control groups. Such a study requires that some people be given a treatment of unknown effect while others are denied such treatment, and that the participants be deliberately selected to receive or not receive it on a random basis. How can we, for example, send some people to prison while others, convicted of identical crimes, are given some alternative sentence? And yet, if we truly want to know about effectiveness, how can we not? Without such true experimental studies, the effectiveness (or harmfulness) of an intervention cannot be evaluated unambiguously.

Applied research may be in conflict with other values. For example, it is important to the law and to society to understand how juries decide cases. But few judges or lawyers have ever seen a jury operate. Some researchers, with the court's approval, "bugged" actual jury deliberations (Amrine & Sanford, 1956). But this authorized, and in many respects desirable, invasion of the jury's sanctity caused an uproar that reached the halls of Congress and led to new laws protecting juries from researchers.

Even less intrusive (and so far perfectly legal) surveys can upset our political process. Pollsters conduct exit interviews of voters on the East Coast during presidential elections and then project the winner. The exit interviews could be unrepresentative and the computer projections could be inaccurate, but nevertheless, the television networks race to broadcast the projections hours before West Coast polls close. These reports could affect the outcome of a close presidential race. Researchers are not merely in the business of gathering and disseminating data; the work they do is part of the larger society. They must judge themselves and set standards in light of the needs of the world of which they are only one part.

APPLICATION
PEER MONITORING IN SCHOOLS

Try to spot the ethical dilemmas in the following research. Several social psychologists were concerned that schools were too competitive, working to the disadvantage of many students (Fraser et al., 1977). They reasoned that the competitive nature of grading prevented students from working together and helping each other, and wondered whether an alternative might be found to encourage students to work with and help each other. If students tutored each other, learners would receive the benefit of an explanation of the material and tutors would have the benefit of organizing and practicing the material. In going over the material with others, students would better prepare themselves, discover gaps in their grasp of the material, and obtain clarification. Active learning would produce more learning.

The researchers devised a grading system that rewarded students for doing well as a group. Instead of giving grades to individuals, grades would be based on the average performance of a group. The researchers paired students in one section of a course. The final grades of both students in the pair would be the average grade earned by each. Thus, if one got an A and the other a C, both would receive a course grade of B. The goal of the system was to get the students to work together, to help each other, and to monitor each other, since one's own grade would depend on how the other person did. Another group taking the same course served as a control condition. Both classes were taught the same material in the same way, but the control section did not have the pairings.

The results showed that the peer monitor students did substantially better on exams than the control class students. The findings indicated that the paired grading system did promote more peer tutoring and more learning, which was reflected in higher exam grades. Eleven percent of the students in the control class earned a D or an F, but no students in the peer monitor class performed that poorly.

In a second experiment the researchers found that group size (up to four people) had no differential effects. Students in a partnership of any size performed significantly better than students working as individuals. Those in partnerships achieved an average of 81.3 percent of the total possible points in the course; those working alone earned only 77.5 percent. Only six of the students in partnerships received a grade lower than what they would have received under the usual system.

This study and the innovation in grading that it suggests raise some ethical dilemmas. For example, students who did not want to participate in the study had to drop the course. Suppose that peer monitoring were implemented in your classroom. The research findings alert you to the fact that, as a group, you

This is an experiment in peer monitoring. Although research has shown that many benefits can come from this sort of arrangement, others have been critical of it on ethical grounds. What problems do you believe it raises?

will learn more and get higher grades than without peer monitoring. But a given individual might get a lower grade than he or she might receive in a conventional grading system. Can you think of other ethical problems in this research or in its application? Can you think of ways to free either the research or the application from these ethical difficulties?

Responsibilities to the Public

Social scientists also have ethical obligations to the society at large. At the very least, the responsibility of scientists to the public is to do what is in the nature of science to do: research. A scientific enterprise exists within and is supported by the society. Social psychologists who do no knowledge building, or who do worthless research, are not serving the public any more than they are serving themselves. The society has a deep interest in having scientists of all disciplines search, ponder, study, and test in order to continually replace less correct or useful knowledge with more valid knowledge. Scientists thus have an important obligation to do high-quality research.

This obligation carries with it the obligation to report research findings to the public completely and honestly. If scientists were to report false data, the scientific enterprise would crumble. Falsification of findings is therefore the unethical act that is most dangerous to the discipline and to the public. But occasionally it does happen. Known informally as "fudging" or "dry-labbing," examples can be found in physics, biomedical research, and elsewhere (Broad & Wade, 1982; Zinder, 1983). The most dramatic example in psychology was the discovery that Britain's once-eminent psychologist Sir Cyril Burt had fabricated much of his research on the genetic origins of human intelligence (Gillie, 1976).

Sometimes social scientists who have every intention of conducting their work with competence and integrity are subjected to pressures to do otherwise. A private organization or the government may feel threatened by the findings of research they have sponsored and may try to distort or suppress those findings. To try to offset these pressures, the American Anthropological Association ethical code admonishes that "no secret research, no secret reports . . . of any kind should be agreed to . . . no reports should be provided to sponsors that are not also available to the general public." The American Sociological Association code of ethics calls upon researchers to "clarify publicly any distortion by a sponsor or client of the findings of a research project in which [s]he has participated." People who speak the truth against the wishes of their employer or sponsor are sometimes called "whistleblowers." Donald Campbell has spoken of such unauthorized release of data as "Xerox democracy."

Sometimes the duty to reveal and the duty to keep confidential are at odds with each other. Suppose a group of judges is concerned that they may be imposing sentences on defendants inequitably. They want help in determining whether and why this is happening, and they want to correct it. But they do not want the embarrassment of having the data made known to the press, so they invite a social scientist to help them on the condition that the findings will be kept confidential. If the social scientist refuses, the necessary improvements might not get made. But if the social scientist agrees, the principle of public ownership of research is violated.

Some commentators feel that the public responsibilities of social scientists cover not only candid communication of their knowledge but even the choice of research topics. Baumrin (1970) has argued that our world cannot afford the luxury of basic research, and that the only ethical research is applied research. As we saw earlier, most social psychologists disagree. They believe that theory-centered research contributes to the solution of human problems by providing a basic understanding of human behavior; indeed, effective solutions might be more difficult to attain without basic knowledge.

This discussion should serve to illustrate that social psychological research is not only the study of social behavior but is itself a part of society. It affects and is affected by society. The many values and interests we try to serve are often in conflict with each other. At their best, ethical principles help us to think about these dilemmas and to make wiser choices about what we will, and will not, do.

Let us return to the question of what social psychology has to do with the story of William Butler, with which we began this chapter.

We have seen, first of all, that his case raised a number of questions that fall within the domain of social psychology. These include such issues as what influences lead a person to begin and to continue smoking, what perceptions people develop of themselves and others, and what kinds of reactions people will have, such as Bill Butler's anger at those he believed took his life and his money. These are particular instances of the larger topics of social influence, social perception, and aggression. This case can also be analyzed by determining what sort of person Butler was, what roles he was socialized into, and the effects on his behavior of group membership.

Theories to account for such phenomena are tested and refined by basic research, and are in turn useful in understanding and changing such behavior. Applied research in the social psychology of health can use this knowledge to help people stop smoking or prevent them from starting.

The lawsuit that will be brought on behalf of William Butler's survivors illustrates the importance of social psychology to the law. Jurors will be called upon to attribute responsibility for Butler's death, and to make judgments about both Butler and the tobacco company. These processes can be better understood by social psychological research on attribution of responsibility and other aspects of social cognition. The lawyers on both sides will try to convince the jurors of a number of things, and their efforts can be informed by social psychological findings about the determinants of attitude change. The attorneys might also put social psychological research methods to work in conducting surveys to see what kinds of people might serve on the jury, and in determining what kinds of presentations would be most effective in getting the jurors to accept the arguments and evidence they will offer.

In this introductory chapter we have done little more than give a glimpse of the content of social psychological knowledge, how it is developed and tested, and how it might be applied to the wide range of issues that constitute social behavior. You are now ready to begin a more thorough examination of basic social psychology and its applications.

SUMMARY

1. Social psychology attempts to understand and explain "how the thoughts, feelings, and behaviors of individuals are influenced by the actual, imagined, or implied presence of others." Social psychology studies a number of topics, including attitudes and attitude change; the behavior of people in groups; aggression; helping; friendship and love; social influence; the self and personality; socialization and gender roles; and the effects of the physical environment on behavior. The chapters of this book are organized around these topics.
2. All social psychological work has the common denominators of an interest in the effect of situational variables on behavior and in the importance of empirical testing of proposed explanations of behavior.
3. From its inception, social psychology has been interested in using knowledge to try to understand and to solve social problems such as conflict, race relations, organizing people, and persuasion. The simultaneous interest in developing knowledge and in solving problems is reflected in the work of one of the founders of the field, Kurt Lewin, who has been called "the practical theorist."
4. Theories are sets of concepts that seek to explain observations. Different theories compete to provide the best explanation of the phenomenon they address. The advance of knowledge is measured by the evolution of theories, rather than by the accumulation of observations.
5. The major theories in social psychology, as in psychology generally, can be classified as cognitive, social learning, and psychoanalytic. In addition, social psychologists have developed role theory and field theory.

6. Basic research is concerned with testing theories, and is sometimes called "theory-centered" research. Applied research is concerned with using knowledge to solve human problems, and is sometimes called "problem-centered" research. They are really two complementary sides of the same coin, rather than being in opposition to one another. This is captured by the social psychological saying "There is nothing so practical as a good theory."
7. In the past decade there has been a major resurgence of applied social psychology. Applied social psychologists have become involved with problems of law, health, energy, public policy, international relations, communications, and numerous other areas.
8. Carefully designed empirical research is the means by which social psychologists advance knowledge about the phenomena they study and test the theories that evolve to explain them.
9. Since research is itself a kind of social psychological phenomenon, some researchers have studied its properties and the ways in which its social psychology might influence findings, for example, through the investigator paradigm effect, observer effects, interactional experimenter effects (notably, expectancy effects), and demand characteristics.
10. As social psychologists have become more interested in applied problems, they have also become concerned with the ways in which social scientific knowledge comes to be used or not used in the effort to solve social problems or to establish social policy.
11. Similarly, as social scientists have become increasingly involved in solving real-world problems and in doing research in field settings, they have had to become increasingly alert to new and more complicated ethical dilemmas. Ethical concerns center on such issues as the impact of research on the participants (raising such issues as informed consent and confidentiality); controlling, withholding benefits from, or invading the privacy of people; and the possibility that research findings may not be reported accurately.

FORMING IMPRESSIONS OF OTHERS
Implicit Personality Theory
Expectancy Effects
Central Traits
Order Effects
The Effect of Appearance
The Role of Nonverbal Behavior
Putting the Pieces Together

MAKING ATTRIBUTIONS
The Early Work of Fritz Heider
Jones and Davis: From Acts to Dispositions
Kelley and Covariance
Errors and Biases in Attribution
Weiner's Analysis of Attributions About Success
The Attribution of Emotion

APPLICATION:
ATTRIBUTION THERAPY: THE INTERFACE OF CLINICAL AND SOCIAL PSYCHOLOGY

PERSONAL CONTROL
Types of Control
Reactions to the Loss of Control
Reactions to Gaining Control

PROCESSES IN SOCIAL COGNITION
Attention
Memory

APPLICATION:
SOCIAL MEMORY: EYEWITNESS TESTIMONY ON TRIAL

Inference

SOCIAL SCHEMAS
Types of Schemas
Development and Change of Schemas
Schemas and Impression Formation

SUMMARY

CHAPTER 2
Social Perception and Cognition

She could not get the thoughts out of her mind. Everywhere she went, day or night, Sue Collins looked over her shoulder to see if she was being followed. It was just two weeks ago that she had been raped, and since then she had felt extremely vulnerable. She looked for and saw danger in even the most common occurrences.

Why had it happened? she wondered. More important, she wanted to know, "Why did it happen to me?" Her trust in other people, in the predictability of the world, and her basic confidence in herself had been shattered. She could not stop asking herself why this terrible thing had had to happen to her.

Sue's reactions are quite common. In fact victims of many kinds, of rape and other crimes of violence, of serious disease or medical misfortunes, or of natural and technological disasters, all experience similar problems and feelings. They have to make sense of a world in which many of their beliefs, cognitions, and assumptions have gone haywire. They must find a reason for their particular victimization, integrate it into the rest of their beliefs about the world, and then find a way to go on with life.

While the problems of victims may seem special because they deal with particularly vivid and unpleasant experiences, the kind of cognitive work they have to do follows the same basic principles as that which all of us perform every day. This chapter is about the topic of social cognition. It deals with questions of how people make sense of events and other people, and even how we make sense of ourselves and our own actions. How do we form positive and negative impressions? What factors in a social situation do we pay attention to and remember? How do we process information about the world around us? And what is the manner by which we make inferences about the motives of ourselves and others? Once we have discussed the answers to some of these questions, we shall return to ask whether social psychological knowledge in this area can be applied to helping the victims of such events as rape so they can understand and cope with the stressful events of their lives.

The example of Sue Collins is emotionally charged, but it points out that people are constantly doing cognitive work in order to understand, predict, and exert control over the events in their lives. A cognitive approach focuses on the human being as a *thinker* and *reasoner*, although this does not necessarily mean that people always reason well or behave in a "thinking" manner. In fact, we shall be noting throughout this chapter that people often take cognitive shortcuts and jump to the first acceptable set of conclusions rather than work through a problem until they find the best possible explanation or solution. Therefore we shall be describing the way in which people actually seek out and process information rather than the way they might ideally do so.

In discussing the social cognition approach we will introduce four general areas of research and application, in the approximate order that social psychologists have approached them historically. First, we will consider the ways in which general *impressions* of others are formed, looking at the roles of personality traits, physical features, and nonverbal behavior and considering how we put information together to form an overall impression. Next, we will consider the topics of *attribution* and *control*, asking first how we infer the motives behind people's actions, and second how we try to maintain a sense of personal control over events. Finally, we will consider how basic cognitive processes such as *attention*, *inference*, and *memory* help account for social perception, and how *schemas* (the cognitive packages that hold together our ideas about ourselves and others) affect the ways in which we perceive and evaluate other people.

FORMING IMPRESSIONS OF OTHERS

The field of social cognition borrows its basic concepts and methods from broader cognitive theories in psychology. But social cognition is different because the object of perception is another person rather than another object, and therefore the process is both more complicated and more interesting.

Each of these people is trying to generate a quick but accurate impression of the others. Although surface qualities such as physical appearance and dress make a great deal of difference at this point, less obvious characteristics such as personality and values begin to play a greater role as people come to know one another better.

In what ways does the perception of people differ from the perception of objects? First and foremost, social cognition is *mutual* cognition: when you view or judge another person in the course of interaction, that person is doing the same to you. You are as much an object of perception as a perceiver, and as a result social perception constantly has implications for the self (see Chapter 3 for more on this topic). Another important distinction is that people have *intentions,* but objects do not. The book that fell on my foot could not have been "motivated" by any other reason than gravity, but the person who dropped the book could have been clumsy or spiteful, or might have been accidentally pushed by someone else—among many other possible reasons. People are far more complex than objects. They have hidden qualities, they are more likely to change over time, and it is often harder to check the accuracy of people's observations about other people than their observations of objects (Fiske & Taylor, 1984).

Implicit Personality Theory

Let us begin considering the processes of person perception and impression formation by noting that people within the same culture often share certain assumptions about others. We usually think we know what traits belong together. For instance, most of us believe that a person who is open is more likely to be friendly than unfriendly and a person who is

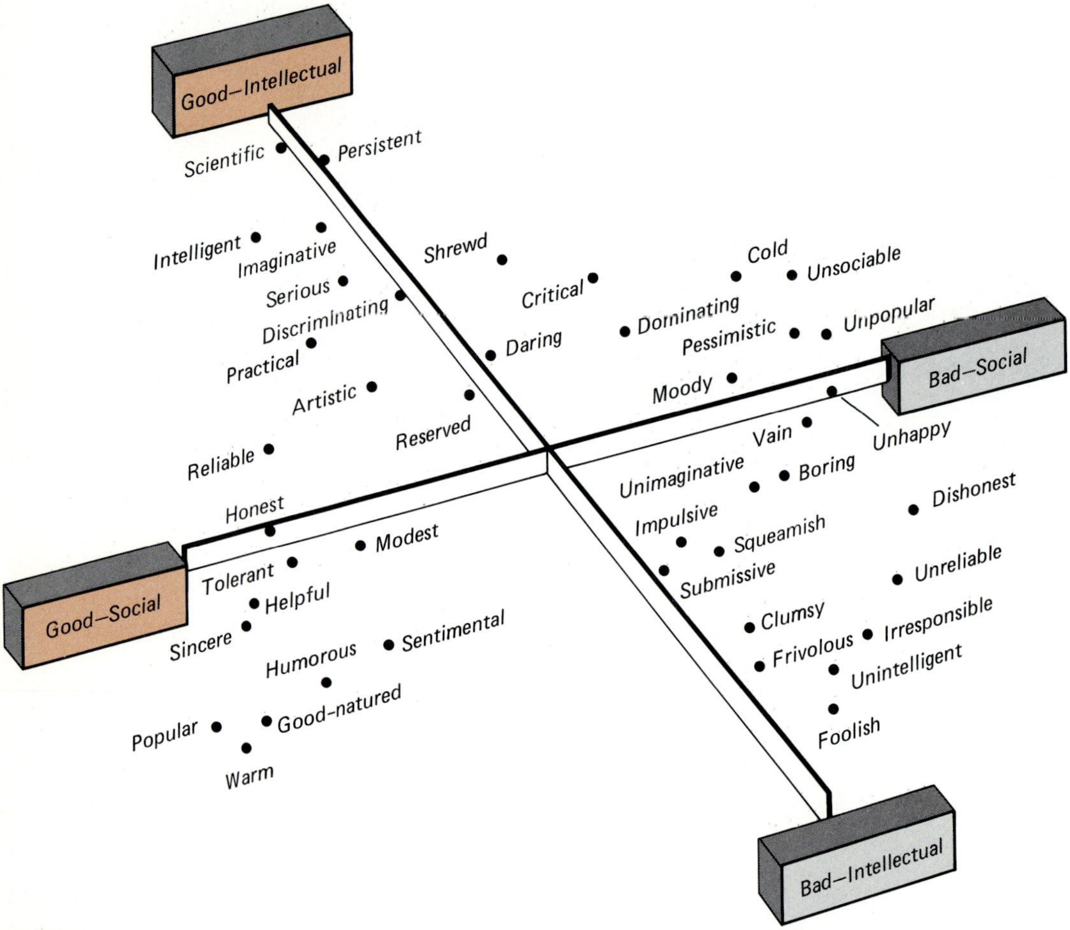

FIGURE 2.1

Two Dimensions of Traits with the Relative Placement of Specific Characteristics

Each of the specific traits shown here falls somewhere in relation to the two key dimensions of general traits (intellectual and social). For instance, "imaginative" (upper left) is positive intellectually, but is not closely related to the social dimension. "Helpful" (far left) is a positive social trait, but is not closely related to the intellectual dimension. *Source:* After S. Rosenberg, C. Nelson, and P. S. Vivekananthian (1968). A multidimensional approach to the structure of personality impressions. *Journal of Personality and Social Psychology, 9,* 283–294.

cruel is more likely to be deceitful than honest. This set of beliefs about the interrelationship among human characteristics has been called an **implicit personality theory.** That is, we each possess a theory of personality, but it is implicit because we are not usually aware of these assumptions.

Rosenberg, Nelson, and Vivekananthian (1968) looked at the shape and form of our "theories" by asking college students to sort 60 traits, each on a separate index card, into piles representing particular people. Using sophisticated statistical techniques, they were able to determine which traits these students as a whole felt belonged together. As you can see in Figure 2.1, these traits fit into two dimensions: an intellectual dimension, from good (scientific, persistent) to bad (foolish, frivolous); and a social dimension, from positive (helpful, sincere) to negative (unpopular, vain). Regardless of where they fell relative to each of the axes, the closer any two characteristics were, the more people generally felt they went together.

Expectancy Effects

In addition to the more general relations that we believe exist among traits, people usually enter into specific situations with certain expectancies. For instance, you may be led to believe in advance of meeting her that your new roommate is arrogant or that your new boss is hard-driving. What effects do such expectancies have on our impressions and our behavior?

In a classic series of studies to test the expectancies of teachers on the evaluation of their students, Robert Rosenthal and his colleagues (Rosenthal & Jacobson, 1968) administered a series of tests to sixth graders. The researchers told the teachers that the tests would allow them to identify "late bloomers," who could be expected to show a marked improvement in their school performance. The tests actually had nothing to do with this trait, but were just an excuse to offer the teachers the expectancy that some of their students (approximately 20 percent of the class) were likely to show improvement soon. The most important feature of this experiment is that the supposed late bloomers were chosen completely *at random*. In reality, they did not differ from the rest of their classmates in any systematic way—except for the expectancy planted in the minds of their teachers.

At the end of the year, the researchers came back to the school, administered additional tests, and recorded the grades of the students and the impressions of the classroom teachers. They found that the "late bloomers" showed significantly greater gains in IQ than the rest of the class, and had been rated by their teachers in a manner consistent with this finding. Using a term coined by Robert Merton (1948), this phenomenon has been labeled a **self-fulfilling prophecy:** the creation or confirmation

Teachers have expectancies about the abilities and interests of their young students. If you were the teacher in this classroom, which of these eager children would you call on? Why?

of an event, experience, or behavior by the mere expectation that it will occur.

Having generated well over 300 studies since its publication (Rosenthal & Rubin, 1978), the self-fulfilling prophecy has been subjected to intense criticism and debate (see Dusek, Hall, & Neger, 1984, for a complete discussion). Still, this effect has been found in the laboratory (Skrypnek & Snyder, 1982) and in field settings from the classroom (Cooper, 1979) to army boot camp (Eden & Shani, 1982). Recently researchers have noted a tendency for a reverse effect, a self-*dis*confirming prophecy, to occur. The direction of the effect of expectancies, whether to confirm or disconfirm, apparently depends on how we respond to our expectancies and how people react to our behavior toward them (Hilton & Darley, 1985; Miller & Turnbull, 1986).

Central Traits

Expectancies can affect the way we see others, but not all the information we receive has the same impact on our evaluations. For instance, traits such as "warm" or "cold" can color the way we see others far more than traits such as "polite" or "blunt." Characteristics such as "warm" and "cold" have been labeled **central traits** because they are closely related to many other traits, and therefore have a strong impact on the way in which we see people (Wishner, 1960).

Asch (1946) initially found support for the idea of central traits using a simple list of personal characteristics, and a follow-up study by Kelley

TABLE 2.1
Ratings of Guest Lecturer According to the Expectation *Warm* vs. *Cold*[a]

Characteristic	Students Believed the Person to Be: Warm	Cold
Considerate of others	6.3	9.6
Informal	6.3	9.6
Modest	9.4	10.6
Sociable	5.6	10.4
Popular	4.0	7.4
Good-natured	9.4	12.0
Humorous	8.3	11.7
Humane	8.6	11.0

[a] The lower the score, the more positive the rating.
Source: Adapted from H. H. Kelley (1950). The warm-cold variable in first impressions of persons. *Journal of Personality, 18,* 431–439. Copyright © 1950 Duke University Press.

(1950) was done more realistically. Kelley told students in psychology classes that they were going to have a guest lecturer, and then briefly described him in advance. For half of the students, the description included the word *cold* along with traits such as industrious, practical, and determined; the other half heard an identical description, except that the word *warm* was substituted for *cold.* Then all the students saw and heard the very same instructor.

Even though all the information was identical with the exception of one word, Kelley found that the students' perceptions of the speaker were quite different (see Table 2.1). What is even more important is that their behavior toward him differed in line with their impressions. Students who believed the speaker to be warm came up in greater numbers after class. They initiated more conversation and asked more questions than those who believed he possessed the central trait "cold." When people are perceived as holding one highly positive central trait, they can sometimes be perceived as doing no wrong. This spread of positive response from one salient aspect of the person to all of his or her characteristics has been called a **halo effect.**

Order Effects

While central traits rely for their impact on their closeness to other traits, other kinds of information generate their impact according to the order in which they are received. Research has shown that information that comes first is usually more powerful than that which follows it. This is known as the **primacy effect.**

Two explanations for this phenomenon have been offered. Anderson (1981) has suggested an *attention decrement* hypothesis. He believes that perceivers are most attentive early in the process but get bored, distracted, or tired as more information comes in. Therefore, they place more weight on what comes at the beginning. Asch (1946), however, has proposed that early information works by providing a context for all future information to be received. It therefore *changes the meaning* of all that follows it.

A potentially important application of this phenomenon is in the courtroom. In simulated criminal trial studies, Pennington (1982) has found that jurors were more likely to vote "guilty" when the strongest incriminating evidence came early in the trial. Pyszczynski and his colleagues (Pyszczynski et al., 1981) studied this question by asking jurors their opinions either midway or at the end of a simulated trial. They found that jurors tended to stay with the first impressions created by the opening statement when deciding on a final verdict.

Can primacy effects ever be undone or reversed? Can people who start off on the wrong foot undo a poor first impression? While it is sometimes difficult to accomplish, research evidence as well as our own experience tells us that primacy can sometimes be undone, and *recency*—a tendency to place greater weight on *final* information—may even take place. Several strategies aimed at counteracting a person's loss of attention have been tested and found effective. They include having people reformulate their impressions after each new bit of information (Stewart, 1965) and telling people not to discount any of the information they are given (Kaplan, 1973). In addition, when people believe that the judgments they will make are especially important, and if they are given enough time to consider all the available information, primacy effects are often reduced (Kruglanski & Freund, 1983).

The Effect of Appearance

Much of the research we have focused upon so far deals with the utilization and integration of trait information provided in written format. There are certain occasions when we do form impressions in this way, such as when letters of recommendation are used for school or job applications, but MacArthur and Baron (1983) point out that this approach de-emphasizes one key aspect of impression formation: the appearance and behavior of the other person.

First impressions based on physical appearance are strong, apparently a part of our implicit personality theories about the relationship between appearance and personality. People in our culture seem to believe that

1. Redheads are tense and excitable; blonds are delicate and weak-willed; and people with brown hair are intelligent, sincere, and dependable (Lawson, 1971).

2. Men with beards are psychologically strong, and men with hairy chests are virile (Roll & Virinis, 1971; Virinis & Roll, 1970).
3. Obese people are lazy, talkative, and unpopular, and muscular people are self-reliant, energetic, and well adjusted (Dibiase & Hjelle, 1968; Sleet, 1969).

As we will note in greater detail in Chapter 7, attractiveness often acts as a central trait, and people seem to believe that physically attractive people are somehow "better" overall. For instance, teachers who were given identical report cards from two children, one attractive and one unattractive, rated the attractive child more intelligent, more popular, and more likely to go to college (Clifford & Walster, 1973). Although physical attractiveness is important in initial impressions, it is important to recognize that it becomes less critical over time as personality and values (characteristics that are more than skin-deep) become increasingly important.

We often feel that we can tell a good deal about people from their style of dress as well as from the nonverbal cues they emit. Try to imagine this couple in standard business clothes. How would their appearance change the way others think of them—and the way they think about themselves?

The Role of Nonverbal Behavior

When we first perceive others, we notice certain obvious physical qualities such as attractiveness. But then we begin to look at and listen to other things such as facial expressions, posture, voice quality, and voice tone. **Nonverbal behavior**, from channels other than spoken content, primarily communicates emotion. Nonverbal cues are transmitted through several channels and are more ambiguous than verbal cues. We make judgments about others using a *visible* channel—for example, facial expressions, posture, and gestures; and a *paralinguistic* channel—the noncontent aspects of speech such as pitch, rate, and voice quality (Barnard, Barr, & Schumacher, 1985).

People's faces capture our attention and are used greatly in our attempts to "read" others. Charles Darwin (1872) believed that facial expressions not only were capable of communicating our emotional condition and relationship to others but that they were universal, the remnants of our biological heritage. Testing Darwin's notion about universality over a century later, a group of researchers from the United States, Brazil, West Germany, and Thailand (Keating et al., 1981) found, in all the cultures they tested, that smiles were always associated with happiness and that nonsmiling faces tended to be associated with dominance. In addition, a good deal of cross-cultural research performed by Ekman and his colleagues (Ekman, Friesen, & Bear, 1984; Ekman & Friesen, 1975) demonstrates that people in cultures that have never even had contact with each other (for example, Americans and isolated natives of New Guinea) closely agree on the meanings of facial expressions for basic emotions such as happiness, sadness, anger, fear, surprise, and disgust. Before going any further, take a look at the set of faces on page 45 to see whether you are good at identifying emotional expressions.

Other visible nonverbal cues include gaze, gestures, body posture and position, touch, and interpersonal spacing. Several different lines of research all point to the importance these cues have in creating an impression. Gestures and touch help define positions of dominance and submission between people. The individual who stands tall, uses broad and expansive gestures, and feels free to touch the other is seen as "in charge" in male-female interaction (males more typically take the dominant role) and business transactions (Henley, 1977; Pearson, 1985). In a medical context, doctors are liked better when they maintain an opened (rather than closed) arm position and nod with their heads to indicate attention or agreement (Harrigan & Rosenthal, 1983).

While some nonverbal behaviors have a constant meaning, others can vary, depending on the context. In the hospital or geriatric setting, a doctor's or nurse's touch may or may not create positive expectations or communicate warmth (Friedman, 1979; Kreps & Thornton, 1984). In geriatric facilities, for example, touch may be used to offer reassurance

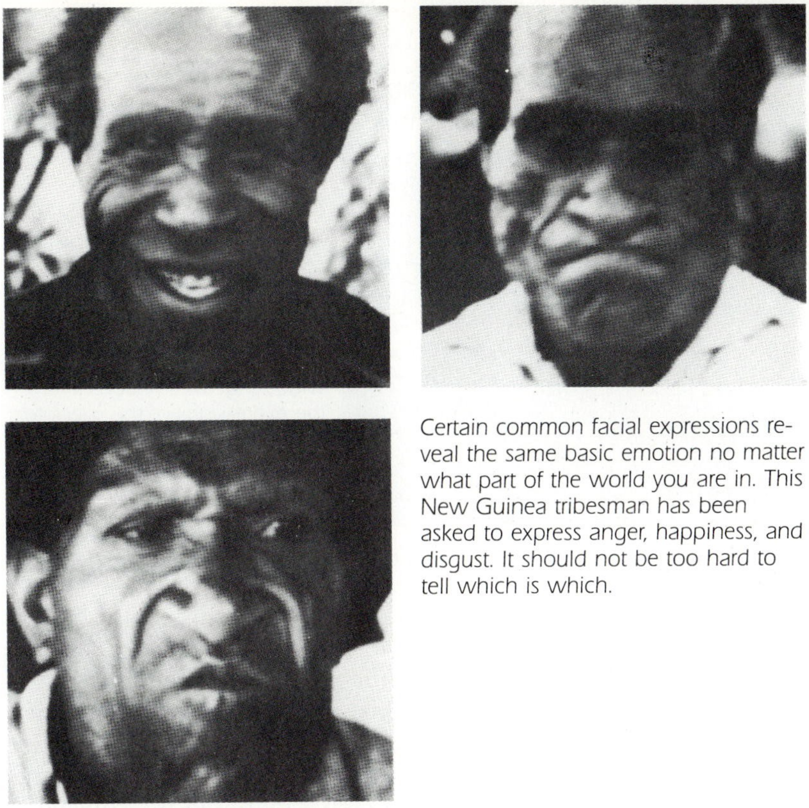

Certain common facial expressions reveal the same basic emotion no matter what part of the world you are in. This New Guinea tribesman has been asked to express anger, happiness, and disgust. It should not be too hard to tell which is which.

and support, but sometimes it is reserved for strictly task-related purposes. Those who are worst off and especially in need of a caring touch may rarely be touched, or may be touched in a way that indicates coldness rather than warmth.

Another way in which we form impressions is by listening to what others say. The same words can mean many different things depending on the emphasis, pitch, tone, and inflection of a person's voice. To demonstrate this, two actors recorded a seven-minute dialogue consisting only of the words *John* and *Martha*. In spite of the limited vocabulary, the varied meanings of their two-word dialogue were crystal-clear from the way in which the words were uttered.

The importance of paralinguistic cues has been studied by comparing regular speech to filtered speech. In filtered speech, the words cannot be understood but the tone of voice remains clear. For instance, Hall, Roter, and Rand (1981) have provided some surprising findings about the verbal and nonverbal styles that patients prefer in their doctors. They found that patients were most satisfied when *reassuring* words were accompanied by

Facial expressions can illustrate a wide range of emotions. From the expressions of the spectators at this hockey game, what do you think has just happened, and which side is each of the spectators rooting for?

an *angry* or *anxious* tone of voice on the part of their doctors. They believe that the message sent by a combination of positive words and negative tone is that the doctor is concerned with the patient's problems.

While nonverbal cues can often reinforce or supplement verbal messages to create an impression, the two do not always coincide. In many instances, they may even directly contradict one another. While sometimes people integrate the two messages, Zuckerman and his colleagues (Zuckerman, Koestner, & Alton, 1984; Zuckerman, DePaolo, & Rosenthal, 1981) suggest that people often discount the words and believe only the nonverbal cues. The "true" message seems to leak out through the nonverbal channels because it is under less conscious control. Most of us are accomplished at deceit by speech content and facial expressions, but gestures, tone, and other nonverbal, nonfacial channels are likely to give us away when our verbal and nonverbal meanings are at odds.

In a realistic demonstration of this, Kraut and Poe (1980) recruited passengers waiting for or departing from Allegheny Airlines flights in Syracuse, New York. Asked to take part in a simulated study on smuggling, each participant was given a camera and small pouches of white powder to conceal. Participants were offered a reward of up to $100 if they could convince customs inspectors (who were all part of the simulation, of course) that they had nothing to hide. While many were successful, others were not. The "smugglers" gave themselves away by avoiding eye contact, shifting posture, hesitating before answering, and giving short answers, all of which signaled their nervousness nonverbally (see Chapter 5 for additional information on the use of nonverbal methods to measure attitudes).

Putting the Pieces Together

Some of the most crucial aspects of forming an overall impression have now been identified. We begin with an implicit personality theory that helps us know what goes with what. In addition, we are influenced by specific expectancies that we bring to each interaction, and we place special importance on those characteristics that are related to many others (central traits). In general, information that reaches us first rather than last has a strong effect on our perceptions, and physical attractiveness plays an especially strong role in generating a first impression. Finally, we pay attention to an array of nonverbal cues such as voice tone, posture, and eye contact that can either reinforce verbal messages or "leak out" to reveal a person's true feelings and sentiments. These are the components of impression formation, but how do we put them all together?

The Cognitive Algebra Approach Two major approaches have dominated social psychologists' work on the ways we form an overall impression. One approach has been referred to as the *elemental* approach by Fiske and Taylor (1984), because it focuses on the way in which each trait, or element, of an impression combines mathematically with other traits or elements (see Kaplan, 1974; Ajzen & Fishbein, 1980).

According to an early version of this approach, the *additive model*, each of us forms an impression by taking the sum total of positive traits minus the sum total of negative traits that we know about another person in much the same way as a banker or an accountant deals with credits and debits. Let's say we know that Bob is cheerful (+3), intelligent (+3), and honest (+2), but that he is also lazy (−2) at times. According to this approach we would come out with an overall positive impression (+6), which could be increased by the addition of positive information or decreased with negative information.

But what happens if we know that Bob is an absolutely splendid person and the rest of the information that comes in about him is positive, yet not as enthusiastic as before. Does our impression continue to build (after all, according to the additive model, the new information does go on the positive side of the ledger), or does it begin to become diluted by faint praise? In other words, are impressions formed from the *sum* of all the things we know about a person, or from the *average* of those traits?

Norman Anderson and his colleagues (Anderson, 1965, 1971; Kaplan, 1975) have shown that the averaging model does a much better job of predicting people's impressions. In addition, he and others (Fiske, 1980; Hamilton & Zanna, 1974) found that even the averaging model needed to be modified to account better for people's impressions. As a result, the *weighted average* model was developed. According to this more refined model, we do not take a simple average but instead place greater emphasis, or weight, on certain traits according to several factors. Among the most important of these are (1) the extremity of the trait (extreme traits are weighted more); (2) the negativity of the trait (negative information is weighted more than positive); (3) the order in which the information is received (early information tends to be weighted more than later information); and (4) the credibility of the source from which we receive the information (Anderson, 1981; Fiske, 1980).

The Holistic Approach Several social psychologists, beginning with Solomon Asch (1946), have been critical of the cognitive algebra approach because they believe it is too mechanical. They argue that it is incorrect to reduce an impression to its smallest possible elements while considering each of these independently. Consistent with the Gestalt school of psychology, they believe we must take a more *holistic* approach by looking at the way each trait *changes in meaning* in relation to other traits. Recalling the research of Asch and Kelley on central traits, we see that being *determined* may mean one thing when paired with *warm,* but it may take on a completely different meaning when paired with *cold.* Theorists of this school assert that no simple (or even complex) formula can capture the final impression because the final impression, the whole, is somehow more than the sum of its parts.

To demonstrate this, Asch and Zukier (1984) gave people two pieces of inconsistent information to see how they would reconcile them. Rather than adding or averaging, they found that people used several different modes of cognitive resolution. For some traits, *segregation* was used; each trait was seen as operating in a different sphere of the person's life. A scientist might be "brilliant" intellectually, but "foolish" when it comes to managing money. A second mode was to see the two traits as representing different *levels of depth,* such as an inner versus outer aspect. For instance, a person could be outwardly "sociable," but inwardly "lonely." Third, opposite traits might be seen as deriving from a *common source;* that is, a person might be both "gloomy" and "cheerful" if considered a generally moody person. In each case, the person presented with two seemingly opposite characteristics did cognitive work that changed the meaning of each trait in relation to the other.

In sum, we must note that social psychologists have been better able to identify the elements of a person's impression than to agree on how these pieces come together to form an overall impression. Those who favor each of the two approaches have been able to explain the ratings people give to others. By varying the scale value and weight of various traits from setting to setting and by applying more complex algebraic integration rules to the combination of traits, the elemental approach has been able to account well for final impressions. Yet those who believe that meaning changes with context have been able to do an equally good job of accounting for the ratings people make. All we can do at this point is to agree with Ostrom (1977) that we should not worry about finding a "winner" or a "loser," but rather explore further the ways in which each kind of cognitive process operates in people's minds and identify the occasions for which or the people for whom one model fits better than the other.

MAKING ATTRIBUTIONS

We have noted so far that in the course of trying to understand, predict, and control our environment, we form generalized impressions of others on the basis of their physical, psychological, and behavioral characteristics. Another critical element of understanding people deals with understanding their *reasons* and *motives,* the general causes of their actions. This process of making attributions—*causal attributions*—occurs every time we ask the question *why:* Why did I do less well on that exam than I expected? Why did my roommate dye his hair blue? Why did the president decide to speak before the UN? **Attribution theory** deals with the process of making attributions. This process can occur at any time, although Hastie (1984) points out that it is most likely to occur in response to a direct question or an unexpected event, when we fail to perform a task properly, or when we depend on others for important outcomes.

Two viewpoints have characterized social psychologists' thinking about the way in which we make attributions. The early view saw all people as commonsense or *naive psychologists* in the way they think about and infer meaning from the world. Given sufficient time, we are capable of gathering all the relevant information and arriving at rational conclusions about causality in much the same manner as scientists do.

More recently, social psychologists have come to recognize that people are not always so careful or thorough. We take shortcuts, simplify complex problems, and accept the first reasonable solution that comes along. Because it emphasizes how stingy we can be at committing ourselves to mental work, this view has been called the *cognitive miser* model. It has led some people to say that humans are sloppy thinkers and biased inference makers, but Fiske and Taylor (1984) point out that our goal in deciding *why* need not always be total accuracy. Rather, if we judge our information processing according to its *efficiency,* cognitive misers do a pretty good job after all.

The Early Work of Fritz Heider

In tracing the history of work on attributions, we come first to the work of Fritz Heider (1958). Heider argued that people make one of two types of attributions for any given behavior: an *internal attribution,* in which the behavior is explained by a cause within the person (a dispositional characteristic, such as personality, ability, or mood); or an *external attribution,* in which the behavior is explained by a cause outside the person (such as the object the person was reacting to, something about the circumstances, or luck). This dichotomy of internal and external causes does not exist only in the minds of social psychologists; it is precisely the sort of decision that people make every day. For instance, when juries and judges decide about guilt versus innocence, or light versus heavy sentence, they have to decide whether a criminal act was caused internally (did this woman intend to shoot her lover?), or externally (was it simply an unfortunate accident with a gun?) (Saks & Hastie, 1978).

Jones and Davis: From Acts to Dispositions

Influenced by the work of Heider, Edward Jones and Keith Davis (1965) have suggested that people are best able to understand and predict other people's behavior when they can attribute it to their stable characteristics. Jones and Davis's model tells us about the ways in which people make *internal* (synonymous with dispositional) attributions about people. As Figure 2.2 illustrates, they propose that we begin by observing an *action* of a person and noticing its *effects*. We then ask whether the person had (1) prior knowledge of the action's effects; (2) a choice in performing the act; and (3) the ability to perform it. If the answer to these questions is yes, we infer that the behavior was performed intentionally and attribute it to specific characteristics (that is, the disposition) of the individual. The personality inference that is made corresponds to the behavior, or, in their terms, a *correspondent inference* has been made.

In choosing among causal attributions, Jones and Davis suggest that we find certain types of information particularly useful. First, we analyze *common* and *noncommon effects*. That is, when people have more than a single course of behavior open to them, we ask what effect the chosen

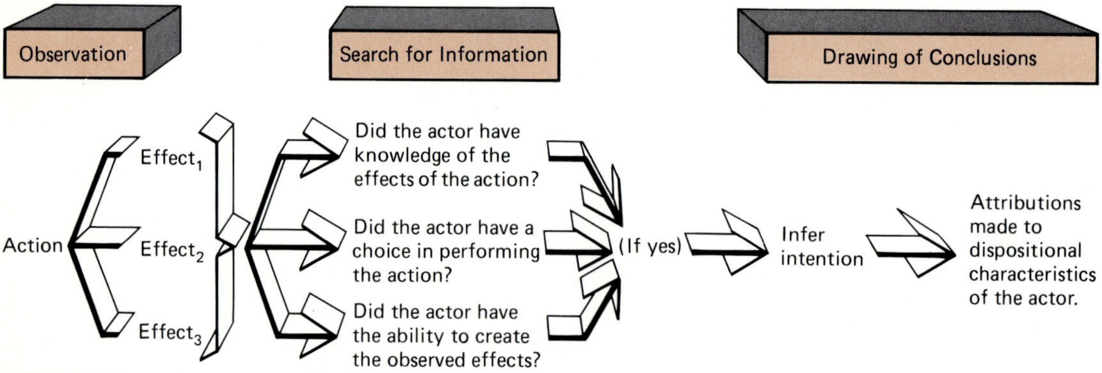

FIGURE 2.2
Making Dispositional Attributions In order to make a dispositional attribution, Jones and Davis suggest that we note the effects of an action and ask a set of questions about the actor's ability, choice, and knowledge of the action's effects.

behavior produced that the nonchosen behavior did not produce. For example, you may be offered two different jobs, both in attractive places, both paying well. But the first requires that you work on your own and the second offers a greater opportunity for a team approach. If you choose the second, it can be inferred that working with other people—the one noncommon effect of your choice—must be important to you.

Two other kinds of information that people use involve the issues of *social desirability* and *in-role/out-of-role behaviors.* Most people prefer to act in a manner that would be approved of by others, one that is socially desirable. When we observe this kind of behavior it is difficult to infer whether the cause has to do with the situation ("she was only doing what was expected of her") or with something about the person ("that's what she's really like"). However, when a person's behavior is not socially desirable—for instance, when someone hits or insults another person for little or no reason—we are more likely to be certain about making an internal attribution. In a similar light, it is equally difficult to know whether behaviors that are in-role really tell us something about the person or merely about the pressures of the situation. When people act in a way that is counter to role expectations, however, we are sure about making a dispositional attribution.

The usefulness of these kinds of information was illustrated in a classic study by Jones, Davis, and Gergen (1961), in which students saw a tape of a young man being interviewed for the position of solo astronaut, a job requiring an ability to work alone and to live without much human contact. When the applicant acted in line with the qualifications for the role, the students were not confident about what he was like as a person. But when the applicant acted just the opposite of what was expected, they made confident dispositional attributions. Therefore, behaviors that are undesirable or that run counter to expectations are thought to be revealing, but "standard" behavior tells us little about what a person is "really" like.

Harold Kelley (1973) has offered a more generalized set of rules about the ways in which information such as social desirability and role relatedness are used. According to the *discounting principle,* any single causal explanation is discounted (given less weight) to the extent that other plausible reasons are available. In the study just referred to, when the astronaut-to-be sounded introverted, his real personality was discounted as the explanation for the behavior. We realize that the applicant knew he was expected to behave in such a way.

Kelley labels the opposite side of the coin the *augmenting principle:* When a given behavior occurs in spite of pressures against it, we feel more certain that it reveals something about the person. So when an applicant for solo astronaut acts extroverted, or a person rushes to save someone in a burning building, or a student tells an instructor that she gave him too many points on an exam, we feel certain in making an attribution about that person's disposition.

Kelley and Covariance

In each of the examples just given, the individual is trying to make an attribution based on a one-shot observation of someone else's behavior. However, Harold Kelley (1967, 1972) has noted that often we have access to more information. Let us take an example. At a restaurant, you notice a friend at the next table who has just finished his meal. Having been out to eat with him before, you are surprised when you notice him paying the bill without leaving a tip. Why? you ask yourself. According to Kelley, we make attributions according to the *covariance principle*: We attribute behavior to causes that are present when the behavior occurs and, conversely, to causes that are absent when the behavior does not occur. In other words, a behavior is attributed to causes that "co-vary" with it over time.

To infer a cause, Kelley believes that we ask three critical questions. The first is about *consensus:* Is the behavior unique to the person, or are many other people doing it? Is my friend the only one not leaving a tip for this waitress, or are many other people failing to do so? Second is the question of *distinctiveness:* Is his behavior unique to this waitress, or does he act in the same manner toward other people (e.g., cab drivers, other waitresses)? Is my friend always tight on tipping in restaurants, or is it just this time? Third is the question of *consistency:* Has this person acted in the same way in this very situation, or is his behavior unique to this instance? Did my friend leave a tip for this waitress the last time he was served by her or did he not?

According to Kelley, the types of attributions we make, whether to external or internal causes, depend on the pattern of answers found to these three questions. As Figure 2.3 demonstrates, when there is a combination of high consensus (nobody is leaving her a tip), high distinctiveness (he is usually generous), and high consistency (he didn't leave her a tip last time either), we lean toward an explanation of the behavior in situational terms. On the other hand, a clear case can be made for a dispositional explanation when there is low consensus (leaving a tip for this waitress is unique to this person), low distinctiveness (he always guards his pennies, no matter who else is involved), and high consistency (he didn't leave a tip for her last time either).

Kelley's model has been generally confirmed by several programs of research using both hypothetical and real-world situations (Ferguson & Wells, 1980; Pruitt & Insko, 1980; MacArthur, 1972), but several modifications have also been necessary. First of all, the Kelley model implies that the search for information is systematic and thorough—as scientists are in their search for explanations—but people are rarely as thorough or systematic as they might be. In addition, consistency information is most often preferred (Kruglanski, 1977), and consensus information is most often underutilized (Major, 1980; Kassin, 1979). Therefore, Kelley's model

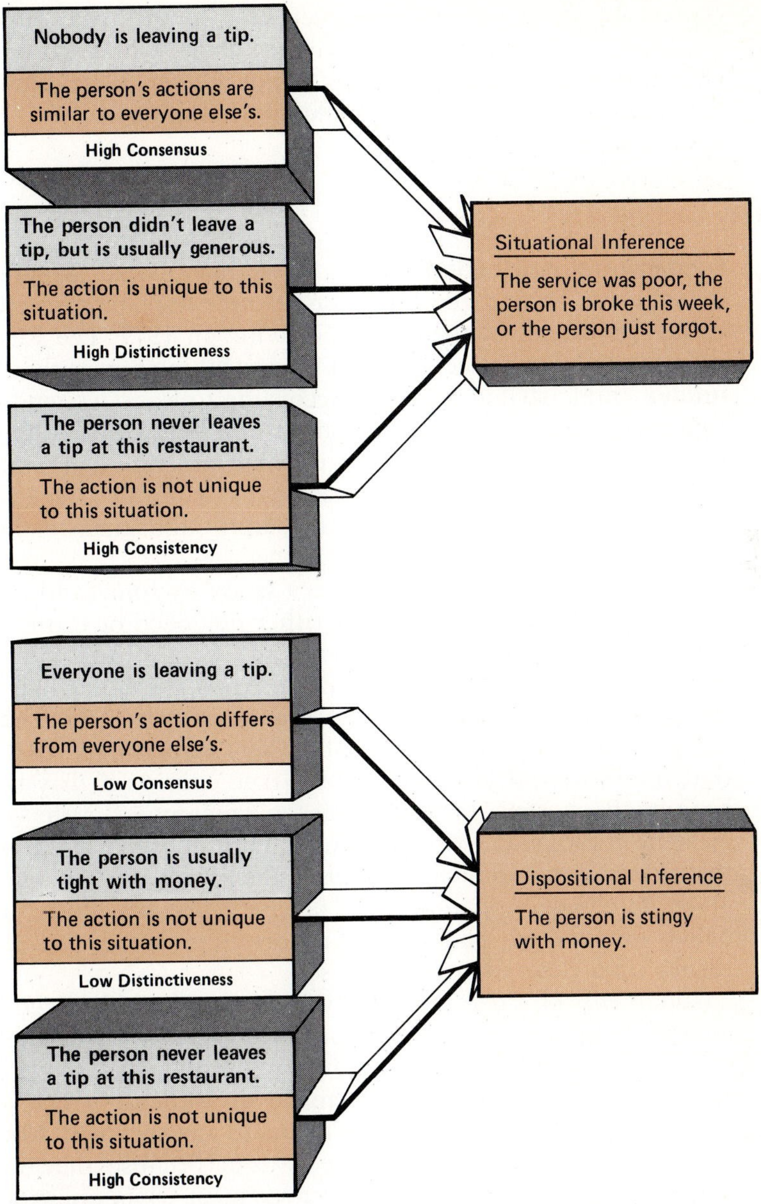

FIGURE 2.3

Making Attributions Based on More Than One Instance of Behavior
According to Kelley, we ask three questions to decide whether a situational or a dispositional inference should be made: (1) Is the person acting like or unlike everyone else? (2) Is the person acting as he or she usually does in the same situation? (3) Are the person's actions in this situation similar to how he or she would react in other situations?

represents the way we draw inferences in the ideal situation but not necessarily how we do it in reality. In short, while there is a naive psychologist in each of us, more often than not we act as cognitive misers as we go through the process of making attributions.

Errors and Biases in Attribution

Fundamental Attribution Error As we have noted, people may confuse the motives behind the behavior of others or may deceive themselves about the causes of their own behavior. In 1977, Lee Ross identified a general tendency in the formation of causal inferences that he labeled the **fundamental attribution error.** According to Ross, we tend to draw hasty conclusions about the *internal* causes of a behavior while overlooking or underestimating the importance of environmental and situational forces. That is, we tend to accept dispositional attributions too easily, especially when a more careful attributional search might uncover important situational causes.

This effect was demonstrated in a study by Jones and Harris (1967) in which students read essays that either defended or criticized the Cuban leader Fidel Castro. Half of the students were told that the writer of the essay had freely chosen the position, while the other half believed that the position had been assigned. Then they were asked to estimate the writer's true opinion about Castro. Not surprisingly, the students said that the essay reflected the writer's true opinion if they believed it had been freely chosen. Yet, in spite of their awareness of the constraints put on some of the essay writers, students also believed that the essay reflected the writer's true opinion even when they knew that the writer had been given no choice. Apparently the behavior was attributed to the writer's beliefs even though a nonbiased or more careful analysis could easily have turned up a clear situational cause.

Judgments of a person's abilities, too, can be influenced by the fundamental attribution error. To demonstrate this, Ross, Amabile, and Steinmetz (1977) conducted a simulated television quiz show. One group of randomly selected participants made up difficult trivia questions, and another group (the "contestants") tried to answer them. Not surprisingly, the contestants had a hard time. Was it because they were stupid (a dispositional reason), or was it because most trivia questions are hard (a situational cause)? Clearly the roles assigned allowed the questioners to show off their knowledge of obscure facts but forced the contestants into a position where they would fare badly. Had the roles been reversed, would the contestants-turned-questioners have looked superior? A reasoned and sophisticated analysis of causes would determine that they would. But what did a set of observers—and even the contestants themselves—say? In both cases the questioners were rated as more knowledgeable than the contestants, showing a bias or preference toward dispositional attributions.

In spite of the many demonstrations of this effect, there are two important points to keep in mind. First, several exceptions to the rule have been demonstrated, such as when a person's behavior is clearly inconsistent with prior expectations about his or her personality, or when attention is focused on situational factors (Kulik, 1983; Quattrone, 1982). Second, we must recognize that in many cases an internal attribution is clearly appropriate. Therefore, as Fiske and Taylor (1984) have noted, we should acknowledge the existence of a fundamental attribution *bias,* but recognize that it does not always result in an attributional *error.*

Actor-Observer Differences People are quick to note that the driver who cut them off must be an "idiot" rather than "in a hurry because of an emergency." This is consistent with the fundamental attribution "bias." But Jones and Nisbett (1972) point out that while we see the behavior of others as dispositionally determined, we are more likely to attribute our own behavior to situational causes: "John handed his paper in late because he is a born procrastinator—but my paper was late because I was busy studying for an exam." This is called the actor-observer bias.

West, Gunn, and Chernicky (1975) demonstrated this effect quite dramatically in a study inspired by the infamous Watergate burglary. In this ethically controversial study (see Chapter 1), some students, not realizing they were part of an experiment, were approached by a "private investigator" and asked to participate in a burglary of a local advertising firm. Various rationales for the burglary were offered, such as the need to help the Internal Revenue Service recover unpaid millions in corporate taxes. Of course, no burglary was in fact committed, but once they agreed, the would-be burglars were asked to make attributions about their behavior, and their responses were compared with those of a second group of people who were merely given a description of the study. Consistent with the **actor-observer effect,** the original student participants (the actors) attributed their own behavior to various factors in the situation. The members of the second group (the observers), however, were more likely to attribute their agreement to assist in the burglary to the potential burglars' personalities.

Two major explanations can be offered for actor-observer differences in attributions. The first concerns available information. As actors, we usually know about the environmental factors influencing our behavior. We know what we are responding to and how our behavior varies over time and across situations (i.e., we have consistency and distinctiveness information). When we observe other people, though, we are less likely to have this sort of information, and therefore we are more likely to assume that the behavior we observe on a single occasion is typical of the person.

The second explanation concerns the focus of attention that each person has. In a given situation, we do not see ourselves. Our eyes focus outward on the elements of the situation itself—other people or the physical environment—and these factors become plausible or salient causes for our behavior. When other people observe someone's behavior, however, the center of attention is that person, and therefore internal explanations become likely. As evidence of this explanation, Storms (1973) had people make attributions of their own behavior and later showed them videotapes of themselves that had been taken during the conversation—in effect making them observers of themselves. In the first case, they tended to make situational attributions, but after focusing on themselves in the videotape, they were more likely to attribute their behavior to their own dispositions.

Self-centered and Self-serving Biases Another kind of self/other bias that exists attributionally is the **self-centered,** or egocentric, **bias,** the tendency to take more responsibility for yourself in a joint task than the other person grants you. For instance, Ross and Sicoly (1979) asked husbands and wives to indicate the extent to which each was responsible for twenty household tasks such as laundry, cleaning, and child care. Not surprisingly, each member of the couple believed that he or she had contributed more than the other member of the couple gave the spouse credit for.

This tendency to see oneself as sharing more of the load than one's partner occurs in a variety of situations from married couples to basketball teams, and can be explained in several ways. Ross and Sicoly (1979) suggest that our own actions may be more noticeable and easily remembered, and therefore we give ourselves more credit than the other person does. However, Thompson and Kelley (1981) suggest a different reason. They believe that people could avoid this bias by asking themselves two questions: (1) Am I the sort of person who does this kind of activity? and (2) Is my partner the sort of person who does it? Consistent with the view that people are cognitive misers, Thompson and Kelley find that people ask only the first question and overestimate their own contributions as a result.

While the self-centered bias describes a situation where a person takes more credit for an activity regardless of its nature or outcome, the **self-serving bias** represents a tendency to take credit for successful endeavors but not for failures. It is captured by the tendency of a husband to tell his wife that he got a promotion because of his ability, or that he did not get promoted because of the stupidity of his boss. As this is being written, for instance, the winners of the World Series are praising themselves for their hard work and discipline, while the losers are blaming bad breaks and awful umpires (see Lau & Russell, 1980, for their analysis of sports teams).

One particular exception to this rule suggests an explanation for the self-serving bias: when people fear that they may seem arrogant or selfish by accepting credit, they may act quite modestly (Tedeschi & Reiss, 1981; Wetzel, 1982). This suggests that the self-serving bias is a *self-presentation* mechanism. It flourishes when it helps a person come out in a positive light, but it disappears if a complementary motive, such as the desire to appear honest or modest, is present.

Weiner's Analysis of Attributions About Success

Research on the self-serving bias deals with attributions about success and failure, but it is not a systematic treatment of this sort of causal inference. Bernard Weiner and his colleagues (Weiner, 1980, 1985) have proposed an attributional model of achievement behavior that not only describes the nature of this process but also points out the importance of a second dimension of causal inference. Consistent with previous analyses of attribution, Weiner believes that the internal-external dimension is important because people experience varying amounts of emotion depending on whether they perceive that they are personally responsible for their success. When people attribute success to their own ability or effort (internal causes), they feel pride; when they fail for lack of effort or ability, they experience guilt or shame. Yet, if the cause of either success or failure is perceived as external (e.g., luck or the difficulty of the task), strong feelings are not as likely to be aroused.

Although an internal attribution leads people to feel pride or shame, it does not help them predict whether they will continue to be successful. To do this, we need to consider the dimension of *stability*. Effort and intelligence are both internal, but effort can vary greatly from one situation to the next while intelligence is generally more stable. By combining the two dimensions, internal versus external, and stable versus variable, Weiner has come up with the pattern of attributions shown in Figure 2.4.

Weiner's model indicates that, depending on the type of attribution made for success, people may work harder and raise their sights or merely hope they will be lucky again. In failing, people may be encouraged to try harder next time, or may give up and feel helpless. For instance, as

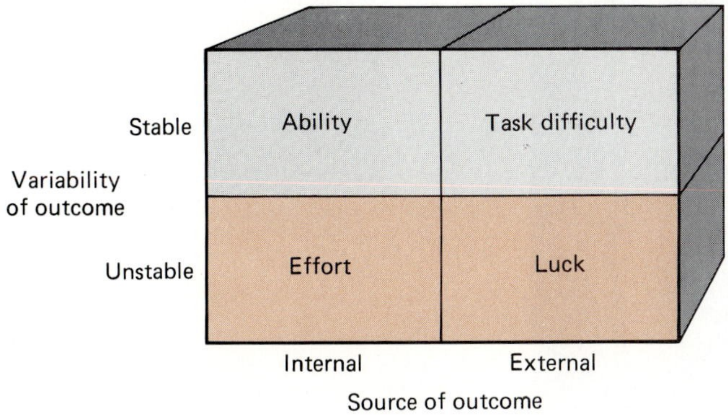

FIGURE 2.4
Attributions About Success or Failure, According to Variability and Source
According to Weiner, different attributions about success are a function of two independent factors: (1) Was the cause of success within or beyond the person's control? (2) Was the outcome caused by something variable or invariable?

we will see in our discussion of male-female success in Chapter 3, acceptance of stereotypes about low ability among females may lead many women toward attributions that rob them of pride and positive expectations even when they do succeed (Ross & Fletcher, 1985; Hansen & O'Leary, 1983).

The great importance of success-related explanations has been demonstrated in an application of the attributional approach to student counseling. Wilson and Linville (1985, 1982) identified a set of freshmen at Duke University who were worried about their grades, and randomly assigned half to an experimental and half to a control group. The experimental group was told that most students' grades improve as they adapt to college, and they heard juniors and seniors report that they found things easier as they went on. This information helped them attribute their problems to temporary (i.e., unstable) factors rather than to permanent factors that were not likely to change. The researchers hoped that this intervention would help the freshmen anticipate improvement and put effort into doing better.

Members of a winning team—such as the New York Mets shown here celebrating their 1986 World Series victory—are more likely to attribute their success to internal causes, both stable (ability) and unstable (effort). You can bet that the Boston Red Sox, who let victory slip away from them in the final game, were more likely to explain the outcome by citing bad breaks (unstable external causes).

The results of this simple experiment were quite dramatic. Test scores and grades of those in the experimental group improved greatly compared with scores of those in the control group, who did not receive any special information. Most notably, 25 percent of the academically troubled control group actually dropped out of school over the next year, whereas only 5 percent of those in the changed-attribution group did.

The Attribution of Emotion

Success and failure can lead us to feel emotions such as pride or shame. But some attribution theorists have asked whether the experience of all emotions can be understood from an attributional point of view. Stanley Schachter (1964, 1971) has pointed out that the physiological component of many different emotions is similar; what differentiates them is the label that people place on their arousal. You may wake up in the morning feeling tense and uneasy, not quite knowing why. According to Schachter, you will engage in a cognitive search for explanations, often focusing on the external environment rather than looking inward as a source of explanation.

Schachter and Singer (1962) tested this two-component (arousal × cognition) theory in an ingenious experiment. Student participants reported to the experiment with an experimental confederate. After being told that the research was concerned with testing a new vitamin, the student was given an injection of epinephrine (an arousal-generating substance), believing that the confederate was receiving the same.

Some students were then told what to expect as a side effect of the drug ("Your heart will start to pound, and your face may get warm and flushed"). These people became aroused and had an appropriate explanation or label for what they felt. Two other groups also received the epinephrine, but they were either told nothing about side effects or were misinformed about what to expect. The researchers reasoned that these people would not know what to attribute their aroused state to, and would be extremely sensitive to information in the environment that might help provide a cognitive label for their arousal. The student and confederate were left alone in the room, and the confederate either began to act euphorically (flying paper airplanes and using a hula hoop) or angrily (ripping up the experimental questionnaire when it began asking intimate and embarrassing questions).

Those who were told what to expect from the injection attributed their arousal to the injection and did not imitate the emotion of the confederate. Subjects in the other two conditions, however, not having an appropriate attribution for their aroused feeling, apparently labeled their own emotional state in line with the confederate's behavior, because they also began to act euphorically or angrily. Considerable debate over the strength and generalizability of these effects has taken place (Maslach, 1979; Marshall & Zimbardo, 1979; Reisenzein, 1983), yet a good deal of evidence exists that people often use environmental cues to infer their own emotions. In effect, this line of research tells us that emotions are not as stable or as internally determined as we might have thought; and that people are capable of attributing—or misattributing—an aroused state to any number of possible causes around them.

APPLICATION
ATTRIBUTION THERAPY: THE INTERFACE OF CLINICAL AND SOCIAL PSYCHOLOGY

Attribution theory was born in the social psychologist's experimental laboratory and has grown and matured there as well. But just as people develop and expand their horizons, so attribution theory has spread its influence farther and wider. One useful expansion of the attributional approach has been to the analysis of behavior problems and the practice of psychotherapy (Henry & Galvin, 1984; Fincham, 1983).

The seeds of a connection between attribution theory and clinical practice grew directly out of Schachter's work on the attribution and misattribution of emotion, and several successes have been reported with problems such as insomnia and phobias. In an early demonstration of this approach, Storms and Nisbett (1970) recruited a group of insomniacs and gave them all placebo pills to take before going to bed. Some were told the pills would arouse them, and others believed the pills would help them relax.

The researchers recognized that these people all felt aroused rather than restful at night, and believed that the insomniacs would be able to fall asleep faster if they could attribute the arousal to the pill rather than to their own problems. And that is what happened. Those in the group who could attribute their uncomfortable feelings to something external (the pill) rather than something internal (their own worries or problems) were able to fall asleep more easily and more quickly (Lowery, Denney, & Storms, 1979). The use of this particular technique has met with mixed success. However, current evidence suggests that it can be effective when the therapist turns the person's attention inward on his or her own feeling states (Bockner & Swap, 1983).

A second area where social cognition approaches have been influential is in the treatment of depression. At any given time, about 15 percent of the U.S. population shows signs of depression (Coleman & Butcher, 1984). This problem, the single most common complaint, has long been addressed by cognitive theories but is now being studied and treated using *social* cognitive approaches (Kuiper & Higgins, 1985; Shaw, 1985). Let us briefly consider several routes of treatment that have been proposed and tried.

Seligman and his colleagues (Seligman, 1975; Peterson & Seligman, 1984) believe that there is an attributional style that makes people depression-prone. Such people attribute their shortcomings and failures to factors that are internal ("It was my fault; I'm just not a very adequate person"); stable ("Things are bad and it doesn't look like they are going to change''); and global (''Everything seems to go wrong, not just some things''). In particular, these people come to believe that they cannot control events around them, a state known as *learned helplessness,* and thus feel depressed (Anderson & Arnoult, 1985).

Can this style of self-blaming be overcome? A first step might be to lower the performance standards of these people to more reasonable levels. If this is accomplished, they are less likely to feel they have failed and will not have the need to blame themselves (Higgins, Klein, & Strauman, 1985). Second, *attributional retraining* may be a practical solution. For example, Dweck (1975) taught a group of children to attribute their failures to a lack of effort rather than a lack of ability. After a period of training, she found that when these children had trouble with a task, their response was to work harder rather than to give up. Similar successes have been reported with college students who have a depression-prone style (Anderson, 1983).

Although the application of attributional and other social cognition approaches to therapy is a relatively recent phenomenon, the number of new developments and reported successes is noteworthy. In addition, the connections made between social and clinical psychologists has helped each group develop and test new ideas. Finally, if we learn enough about the cognitive and attributional patterns that predispose people to depression, perhaps we may even be able to ''inoculate'' them beforehand rather than simply treat them once they are already troubled.

PERSONAL CONTROL

Some psychologists have proposed that people are motivated by a desire for power or by sexual urges or a need to achieve. The cognitive social psychologist believes that people act in order to *understand* and thereby to exert *control* over the events of their lives. In fact, some psychologists believe that the generalized attribution, "I do things because I *want* to," rather than, "I *have* to," is critical to the development of a positive self-image. In this section and throughout this book we will see how people work to maintain control, and also how they react to its loss.

Types of Control

Thompson (1981) has pointed out that there can be many different kinds of control, each helping to reduce the stress of unpleasant events. *Behavior* control is direct and concrete. It involves the feeling or knowledge that you can take specific steps to change the nature of a situation. The belief that you can shut off the VCR if the movie becomes too scary or leave the meeting if it goes on too long is reassuring. Most important, behavior control can apparently reduce anxiety and increase a person's tolerance for pain—even if the control is not real. As long as you believe you have the power, as long as you have the *illusion of control,* stress and discomfort are likely to be reduced (Glass & Singer, 1972; Sherrod & Downs, 1974).

Decision control involves the ability to choose how, when, or where an event will occur, or which of two options to experience. Patients are more satisfied when they are involved in the choice of which form of treatment they will receive (Strull, Lo, & Charles, 1984); and housing residents are most satisfied with their own quarters when they are living there by choice (Michelson, 1977). *Information* control is closely related, involving the feeling that you know everything about an event that is about to occur. If you were going to have an operation, information control would mean knowing what the benefits are, what procedures will be done, and what the short- and long-range effects will be.

Cognitive control is a means of dealing with stress by restructuring the event in your mind. A woman in labor may exercise cognitive control by focusing on pleasant thoughts or reinterpreting the labor pains as indications that her baby is about to be born. Even though there is no real control involved, cognitive control allows a person to see an event differently or to dwell on something else (like the music in the dentist's office) in order to avoid an unpleasant experience.

A different cognitive manipulation to maintain control has been termed *retrospective* control: the belief that an event that has already occurred can be controlled when it happens again. For instance, cancer victims, even though they do not know why they got cancer in the first place, often try to exert retrospective control through the belief that they can reduce their chances of a recurrence through proper diet or stress reduction (Taylor, Lichtman, & Wood, 1984).

Reactions to the Loss of Control

People prefer to believe they have control over their lives. We will encounter this theme in many different forms throughout this book, whether talking about the behavior of hospital patients (see Chapter 4) or the actions of city-dwellers (see Chapter 11). But what happens when people perceive that events are controlled by others or by chance factors? According to Taylor (1979), people often react in either of two opposite and extreme manners: reactance (Brehm & Brehm, 1981) or helplessness (Seligman, 1975). *Reactance* is the unpleasant feeling that people experience when control is taken from them. It motivates them to reassert their control by saying, "Yes, I can," when someone tells them, "You may not."

As opposed to adopting a defiant attitude toward a loss of control, *helplessness* involves an acceptance of it. As a result of specific experiences in which people see that they cannot control events, they may develop a generalized belief that they are powerless. Such a person feels helpless and will give up just when some effort might bring results.

Several factors determine which of these two responses a person will adopt. If the loss of control occurs only occasionally or in relation to unimportant events, people are likely to show reactance and try to reassert control. However, if events in a person's life seem chronically out of control, or if a person's best efforts seem continually to fail, learned helplessness is likely to result (Wortman & Brehm, 1975) and a person will act passive and depressed.

Reactions to Gaining Control

The elderly often have the ability to exercise control taken from them, especially when they are placed in nursing homes. For instance, surveys have reported that less than 10 percent of skilled nursing care facilities allow residents to plan their own entertainment activities; 84 percent offer residents a range of less than one hour to come to dinner; and more than half strictly determine when residents get up, take a bath, and go to bed (Moos, 1980; Lemke & Moos, 1980).

Is it possible to restore control to the residents of nursing homes? And what would be the effects of restored control on their health and well-being? To answer this, Langer and Rodin (1976) compared three groups of nursing home residents who were randomly given varying degrees of control. One group of residents heard a talk from the administrator in which he emphasized the message "*You* have the responsibility of caring for yourselves, of deciding whether to make this a home you can be proud of and happy in." The second group heard the same general content, but with a different message: "*We* feel its our responsibility to make this a home you can be proud of and happy in." People in the first group were also told they could *decide* which of two nights to have a movie shown, and were allowed to *choose* a plant "to keep and take care of as you'd like." Those in the second group were told they would be *informed* later in the week which night the movie would be shown, and were each *given*

FROM THE FIELD
Shelley E. Taylor

Shelley Taylor's approach to social cognition has focused on people's beliefs about events and situations that are important to them. Some of her earlier work dealt with the ways people respond to someone who is distinctive in a social context, such as the lone black person or woman in a group. Now at UCLA, Dr. Taylor has looked at the role of social cognition in health and illness. She has found that the information people have about their condition and its treatment (for example, surgery) affects the course of their recovery. Similarly, she has studied the cognitive strategies people adopt to make sense of their plights and to regain a sense of control when faced with life-threatening diseases or personally shattering events such as rape.

Older people who have a sense that they can exercise control over the events in their lives are more likely to be healthy and happy than those who do not. Unfortunately, many nursing homes fail to reinforce this sense of control, and their residents are worse off as a result.

a plant and told that the nurses would water and care for it. A third control group was given no talk at all.

The results of this intervention were clear. Although the two groups had been equally healthy before the intervention, those given more control generally were more sociable, vigorous, and healthy afterward. Eighteen months later, 30 percent of the people in the we'll-take-care-of-you (i.e., lack of control) group had died, as compared with only 15 percent in the personal control group (Rodin & Langer, 1977).

Why did these people do better? They were given behavior and decision control, and were given it permanently. Rather than being caught up in a vicious cycle where failure to control leads to helplessness followed by fewer and fewer attempts at control, Langer and Rodin's participants fell into a positive cycle. Their newly found sense of control started the sequence of trying, leading to success, followed by further attempts at self-assertion and more success.

In sum, the desire for control and the self-attribution of control are important to maintaining a sense of self-worth. When control is taken away, some people may feel reactance and attempt to assert themselves. Others, especially vulnerable people, are likely to experience a sense of helplessness and to accept their status. When a sense of control, especially behavior control, becomes available, people may feel better both physically and psychologically.

PROCESSES IN SOCIAL COGNITION

Much of the early work on person perception and social cognition that we have discussed has involved *outcomes* of information processing, such as the attributions we make or the impressions we form. In recent years the work in social cognition has grown by leaps and bounds by focusing on the *processes* that determine our perceptions. In particular, social cognition researchers have gotten back to basics by using and extending the principles of experimental psychologists who study such topics as attention and memory. In this section, we will briefly review some of the major issues in attention and memory, and see how they affect the kinds of inferences we make about others.

Attention

Before a piece of information can affect our thoughts or feelings, it goes without saying that it must first be noticed. What factors distinguish between information that is attended to and information that gets overlooked or disregarded?

The most critical factor affecting attention is *salience.* A piece of information is salient when it stands out against its immediate context, when it deviates from the perceiver's expectations, or when it is relevant to the perceiver's needs (MacArthur, 1981; Fiske & Taylor, 1984). For example, by being different from its background, a red rose in a bunch of daisies draws attention. So does a senior citizen in a college classroom. The person stands out as "figure" against "ground," in the terms of Gestalt psychology, and draws attention or even stares from others (MacArthur & Ginsburg, 1981).

People become salient sometimes by choice and sometimes by accident. Salience increases when a person acts differently than usual, acts out of role, or behaves in any extreme manner. A simple means of becoming perceptually salient and attracting attention is to sit opposite someone or to choose the seat at the head of the table in a meeting (Taylor & Fiske, 1975).

Being salient can bring both advantages and disadvantages. It exaggerates our perceptions, both causal and evaluative, in whichever direction they are already leaning. What is good is seen as better if it is salient, and what is bad is perceived as worse. People who are salient get closer scrutiny, especially if they are "one of a kind." Kantor (1977) has noted that female executives attract attention and have their every move scrutinized. As a result, their positive contributions attract attention and have greater impact, but so do their errors.

Berscheid and her colleagues (Berscheid et al., 1976) told students they might have the opportunity to go out with certain others, thereby making the potential dates salient. At that point, the potential partners attracted more attention, received exaggerated attributions, and were evaluated in a highly positive manner. In contrast to Berscheid's study, in which the dates got more positive evaluations by becoming salient, Eisen and MacArthur (1979) had students act as jurors in a videotaped mock trial where the evidence made the defendant appear guilty. In this instance, where the information was largely negative, the more visibly salient the defendant was, the more harshly he was evaluated.

Memory

The contents of our memories of people and events are tremendously rich. Try to remember information about a high school English teacher, your favorite relative, or your best friend. Recall your first date, freshman orientation, or a favorite vacation. Without doubt a range of images, thoughts, and details come to mind.

When people try to remember a specific individual, they usually recall things in a certain order, starting with the most concrete features and moving to more abstract characteristics that need to be inferred. Most likely you will recall first what a person looked like, then his or her traits, and finally the ways in which he or she acts (Fiske & Cox, 1979). In trying to recall, sometimes the reason for remembering can affect the way in which the memory is organized as well as our ability to recall. One surprising finding in this area is that a direct attempt to memorize aspects of a person is less successful than the more general purpose of forming an impression (Hamilton, Katz, & Leirer, 1980; Srull, 1983; Wyer & Gordon, 1982). Apparently people who simply try to memorize facts about others use a variety of organizing strategies, most of which offer only moderate success (Hamilton, 1981a). Forming an impression requires an elaborate processing of information. It encourages people to create meaningful categories in their minds which create links among traits, and it allows memories to be retrieved through several alternate routes (Anderson, 1980; Hamilton, 1981b).

Priming How much we remember and what we remember are affected by priming. **Priming** refers to "the effects of prior context on the interpretation and retrieval of information" (Fiske & Taylor, 1984, p. 231)—that is, thoughts and ideas that have been activated frequently or recently are more easily recalled, and are also recalled in terms of the mental set that the priming has created. For instance, in the context of the word *adventurous*, Higgins, Bargh, and Lombardi (1985) found that a person who liked to sky dive and to sail across the Atlantic was recalled in one way; but the same person described in the context of the prime *reckless* was recalled much differently.

Explanations for the effectiveness of priming vary. Wyer and Srull (1980) have offered a *storage bin* hypothesis, suggesting that memories are stored in layers from the top down. At the top are memories that have been most recently or frequently primed, and therefore they are most likely to be found in the course of a memory search. Higgins and King (1981) suggest an *excitation transfer* model, in which priming increases the level of excitation of a stored memory and therefore its likelihood of recall. This may work like a car's battery, in which those memories that are "charged" more often will be the strongest; or like the synapse between two neurons, where a memory is activated on an all-or-nothing basis depending on whether it reaches some minimum threshold. Higgins, Bargh, and Lombardi (1985) have offered evidence that the last of these models best fits the process.

Accuracy Memories as we recollect them are not carbon copies of people as they were or of events as they occurred. Loftus and Palmer (1974) showed students a movie of an automobile accident and then questioned them about it. Some people were asked how fast the cars were going when they "hit"; others were asked the speed when the cars "smashed into" one another. Not surprisingly, those people asked about the "smash" reported higher speeds than those asked about the "hit." In accord with their biased recollections, twice as many people remembered seeing broken glass at the accident scene when the cars had "smashed"—even though there had been none.

Buckhout (1979) performed an even more dramatic demonstration. He had an actor barge into a classroom, shoot a gun at a professor (which the students did not know was loaded with blanks), and then leave. The students, all eyewitnesses to the "crime," were asked a standard set of questions immediately after the event. On the average, they said the incident took twice as long as it actually did and they added almost 25 pounds to the suspect's weight. Seven weeks later, they were asked to identify the suspect from a set of six photos. Sixty percent chose the wrong person and, of these, 25 percent chose someone else who had just happened to be in the classroom at the time. Based on such research, social psychologists refer to memory for people and events as *reconstructive,* implying that it is an idiosyncratic and dynamic process rather than a matter of static recall.

APPLICATION
SOCIAL MEMORY: EYEWITNESS TESTIMONY ON TRIAL

The judge asked the young woman, "Is there any doubt in your mind as to whether this man you have identified here is the man who had the sexual activity with you on October 3, 1977?" The woman answered, "No doubt." The judge reiterated, "Could you be mistaken?" The woman responded, "No, I am not mistaken." On the basis of a positive identification by the victim, Bernard Jackson was sentenced to jail for rape even though several defense witnesses had testified that he had been at home when the crime was committed. Five years later another man admitted to the crime, and Jackson was released from prison. How could such a tragic mistake have occurred? Is eyewitness testimony not trustworthy?

The answer to this question has three parts. First, eyewitness testimony is not very reliable. Violent incidents seem to be particularly subject to errors in recall (Loftus, 1983). Second, almost no correlation exists between the stated confidence of witnesses and their accuracy. Eyewitnesses who incorrectly identify a suspect from a lineup or set of photos are just as confident as those who are correct (Kassin, 1985; Wells & Murray, 1984). Nevertheless, the Supreme Court has stated that confidence is one of five key factors to use in assessing the admissibility of eyewitness testimony, and ordinary citizens believe that confidence is tied to eyewitness credibility (Yarmey & Jones, 1983; Brigham & Bothwell, 1983). Third, as we saw in Loftus's research, the phrasing of questions by lawyers on both sides can mislead witnesses who are trying to recall accurately an event that may have taken place months ago.

A variety of approaches have been suggested for dealing with this issue. Malpass and Devine (1981) point out that psychologists cannot be present at the moment of a crime to assist witnesses in storing events in their memories, but they can be present at the time of retrieval in the courtroom. At this point they can help generate more accurate eyewitness testimony through priming, by reinstating the cognitive context of the original event using appropriate descriptions and instructions.

To test this assumption, Malpass and Devine had two groups of students witness a crime, and five months later they called upon them to identify the perpetrators. The members of one group were first asked to recall their original feelings and reactions, and also to think about details of the crime scene. The other group received no special memory priming. The students for whom the context was reinstated performed 20 percent better than the control group in correctly identifying the people who had committed the crime.

Other suggestions have been offered as well. Deffenbacher (1984) has argued for the use of psychologists as expert witnesses, for instance, to inform jurors about the uses and problems of eyewitness testimony. Wells, Leippe, and Ostrom (1979) have proposed guidelines for assessing the fairness of a lineup in order to determine the value of an eyewitness identification. And Kassin (1985) has demonstrated that by having eyewitnesses later view *themselves* in the process of choosing photos, the correlation between accuracy and confidence increases significantly.

Each of these many and different approaches derives from basic theory and research in social cognition, and each has the capacity to have a major impact on the way the legal system treats eyewitness testimony. As you can see in the In the News box (see pp. 70–71), newspapers and popular periodicals are finally becoming more aware of these issues and letting their readers know of the potential contribution of social psychological research.

Inference

After information has been stored in memory, the final step involves generating a decision or behavior from it. This process, known as *social inference,* appears straightforward, yet considerable research shows that we are cognitive misers at this point in the process as well. By simplifying complex cognitive tasks, we sometimes end up making errors and falling prey to biased reasoning.

Sampling Biases Even if psychologists were satisfied with how much information people collect and use, the question of how we *sample* from that information would still be a problem. Have you ever noticed that people tend to generalize about what "most people" believe from what they and their friends believe. People on the San Andreas Fault infer that "most people" feel that earthquakes are important matters; and conservatives and liberals both overestimate the degree to which "most people" agree with their respective political philosophies.

This tendency to overgeneralize from a small sample, especially from oneself to others, has been called the *false consensus effect* (Ross, Greene, & House, 1977). This label derives from the fact that people underutilize consensus information—information that tells what others are doing or believing. For instance, students who were willing to walk around campus wearing an "Eat at Joe's" sign thought that over 60 percent of their fellow students would be willing to do the same. But those who refused estimated that two-thirds of their peers would refuse (Ross, Greene, & House, 1977). In the area of attitudes, Judd and Johnson (1981) found that feminist women estimated support for women's rights among adults in the United States to be higher than did a comparison group of nonfeminists.

Underutilization of Base Rates Just as people are often not aware of generalizing from small samples, they also fail to make use of *base rates,* information about broader characteristics of the population. That is, when a person acts in a given manner, is that behavior (1) typical of the person, or (2) typical of the group to which he or she belongs? Is a mother who collects welfare but drives a fancy car and lives in an expensive condo typical of all welfare mothers? According to Hamill, Wilson, and Nisbett (1980), students tend to believe this is so—even after they have been given considerable contradictory information about the population as a whole.

It has been suggested that this problem may result from people's inability to understand broader—base rate—information about people in general. This seems unlikely, however, because people can and do use it when it is the only information they can rely on (Nisbett & Borgida, 1975). More likely, the impact of a specific vivid instance is strong, and people do not see the relevance of considering whether the instance is typical (Ginosar & Trope, 1980).

IN THE NEWS

SOCIAL SCIENCE AND THE CITIZEN

Eyewitness Testimony

Eyewitness testimony that condemns the innocent and lets the guilty go free is not a problem that threatens the collapse of modern jurisprudence—only about 5 percent of the convictions won by American prosecutors are based primarily on eyewitness identification; but recent studies show that eyewitness testimony may be far from the sturdy evidence it is widely thought to be by police, attorneys, jurors, and judges. After his own study in 1972, New York surrogate court judge Nathan Sobel suggested that incorrect eyewitness identifications have led to more miscarriages of justice than all other factors combined.

Only for the past decade or so have researchers such as Dr. John C. Brigham of Florida State University (FSU) seriously investigated the potential for error in eyewitness testimony.

A social psychologist, Brigham first became interested in the accuracy of eyewitness testimony in 1971 when five black men were charged with the murder and robbery of a Tallahassee man. The case against the "Quincy Five" (all the men were from Quincy, Florida) was based solely on the testimony of several white eyewitnesses to the crime. When defense attorneys asked FSU psychologists for help in determining the reliability of "cross-race" identification, Brigham and his colleagues could find only one study on the subject. Even then, the judge refused to let the psychologists tell the jury what they had found.

Following what Brigham calls "a textbook case of how to get flawed testimony from eyewitnesses," the state won two convictions and was well on its way to getting a third when a prisoner in New York's Sing Sing prison confessed to the killing. Fingerprint evidence subsequently confirmed the prisoner's story. Several months later, the state dropped all charges against the Quincy Five.

"Here was a case," Brigham said, "where five innocent men escaped life sentences or the death penalty almost by accident. From the start, the only evidence against them was eyewitness testimony, which turned out to be completely wrong."

Most people have little idea, for example, of just how bad they are at identifying persons of another race. Some people, for instance, think their interracial friendliness and interaction makes them more adept at differentiating among members of other races. This is not so. Regardless of their racial attitudes or their social habits, white people are just as poor at identifying blacks as blacks are at identifying whites, Brigham said. "The old stereotype of one race thinking that people of another race all look alike seems to be true. Social scientists have suspected this for years, but only recently has enough good research borne this out."

Corroborative evidence for such "own-

The Use of Heuristics Some people gather more information than others in making decisions. Some implicitly sample in a biased fashion; others are more attentive to sampling biases and base rates. Yet, in the course of trying to reach conclusions quickly, we all take cognitive shortcuts. Social cognition researchers refer to the criteria that reduce complex decisions to simpler ones as *heuristics* (Tversky & Kahneman, 1973).

race bias'' poses alarming implications for almost every stage of eyewitness identification in which race is a factor. The findings suggest that white law enforcement officials may not be the best qualified to arrange line-ups of black suspects, and vice versa. Fair line-ups, whether of live suspects or of photographs, are only possible when they are composed of individuals who all roughly fit the description of the criminal. This forces eyewitnesses to be careful about who they implicate.

In the Quincy Five case, not only were all the eyewitnesses white and all the suspects black, but the photo and live line-ups were arranged by white law enforcement personnel. The original line-up was of ten photographs, four of which were of the Quincy Five suspects. ''Unless these four guys had been identical twins of each other or something there's no way this could have been a fair line-up,'' Brigham said. ''Beyond that, a fair line-up never includes more than one suspect at a time.''

The role that race plays in determining the quality of eyewitness identification is becoming better understood today by legal authorities, and yet the issue of race was entirely overlooked twelve years ago when the U.S. Supreme Court established five criteria for evaluating eyewitness testimony. That law is still the final word on judging the worth of what an eyewitness says. ''The irony is that compared to the five criteria the court listed, the influence of race is quite powerful. And yet the law doesn't take [race] into account at all,'' Brigham said.

In *Neil v. Biggers* in 1972, the Supreme Court drew upon the meager research evidence available at the time to establish the conditions it declared necessary to evaluate the accuracy of eyewitness testimony. The five criteria are: (1) the witness's opportunity to see the criminal (length of time, lighting conditions, etc.); (2) the length of time between the crime and the identification; (3) the level of certainty demonstrated by the witness; (4) the witness's degree of attention during the crime; and (5) the accuracy of the witness's prior description of the criminal (or to what degree the witness's first description of the criminal matches that of the suspect).

Since 1972, only one of the five criteria—how long and under what conditions the criminal is seen—has been generally supported by scientific evidence, Brigham said. The other four have been shown to be either faulty or fundamentally wrong ideas about what constitutes accurate eyewitness testimony.

Source: Society (1986), *23*, 2–3.

One type of heuristic that is often used in the *representativeness* heuristic, which allows us to save cognitive energy by categorizing an individual and then making a judgment about him or her based on that category. We thus make inferences without having to take the specific characteristics of the person into account. If you believe that Jack is representative of all premed students, then you can begin to make inferences about his intelligence and diligence without closely observing his behavior. When representativeness is assumed, however, it can lead to stereotypical judgments.

The heuristic that has received the greatest attention is the *availability* heuristic, according to which people estimate the likelihood of an event or a given cause according to their ability to summon to mind the event or cause. An explanation or event is highly "available" when we can say, "Oh sure, I can think of lots of cases like that," or "I know many people who are that way."

For example, what do you think is more common, homicide or suicide? Do more people die each year from drowning or from fires? If you guessed that homicides are more common than suicides, and that many more people die in fires than from drowning, you are among the majority. But you are also wrong. There are about 6000 more suicides than homicides per year, and drowning and fires cause about an equal amount of deaths.

Why are so many people in error about these "facts"? First, we tend to over-recall causes of death that are dramatic and sensational, while underestimating undramatic causes (Slovic, Fischhoff, & Lichtenstein, 1982). By virtue of being less spectacular, they are less likely to be accessed in memory or called to mind. Second, because the media more often highlight murders and fires than suicides and drownings, we notice and attend to these more. In short, the availability heuristic works because we notice and call to mind more quickly available than nonavailable information, perhaps causing us to overestimate the probability or frequency of certain events and causes.

SOCIAL SCHEMAS

Given all the information that exists in the form of attributions, appearances, and actions; given the various stages of processing to consider, such as attention, memory, and inference; and given the need to form impressions and make attributions, social psychologists have searched for a central concept to account for the way in which all this information is held together in the human mind. The concept of the **schema** (referred to in the plural as either schemas or schemata) fits the bill. Schemas are "knowledge structures that impose meaning on the blooming, buzzing confusion around us" (MacArthur & Baron, 1983). They simplify and organize an individual's knowledge about a given person, group, or event, and contain information about its attributes and the relationships among these attributes. Schemas allow us to form expectations about people and events, to focus our attention and energies on relevant, important information, and to interpret ambiguous information into preexisting frameworks (Fiske & Linville, 1980; Taylor & Crocker, 1981).

Most of us have a schema for, say, "the politician." That person is outgoing, ambitious, intelligent, a good speaker, and probably not as candid (or even honest) as we might wish. In fact, in thinking about the politician, you can probably come up with a typical or ideal example, known as a *prototype*. It could be Ronald Reagan, Ted Kennedy, or any number of other people who would epitomize your schematic representation of a politician (Cantor & Mischel, 1977).

Types of Schemas

We have several different kinds of schemas, about ourselves, other people and groups, roles, and events. *Person schemas* contain our understanding of the traits, goals, and behaviors of specific individuals or types of individuals, like "extroverts" or "introverts." Often in deciding about another, we think of a prototypical person and compare how the characteristics of the person fit the prototype.

Self-schemas are much like person schemas, except that they deal with the most important "object" in the world: ourselves. Self-schemas are packages of ideas about ourselves that focus on certain traits we may see as central to our personality, although different people are schematic on different traits (Markus, 1977; Markus & Sentis, 1982). For traits on which we are self-schematic, we pay careful attention to what others say about us and even notice them in other people (Fong & Markus, 1982; Cacioppo, Petty, & Sidera, 1982).

Role schemas are the ideas, beliefs, and expectations we hold for people who fit into particular social categories. When we judge people as members of categories (as blacks or whites, Arabs or Jews) rather than as separate persons, we can be guilty of *stereotyping*. From the point of view of social cognition, we can understand stereotypes in a different light. First, we can see that stereotyping is not necessarily an irrational process, but more a natural by-product of the use of role schemas. When we see people as members of categories, we tend to see them as either like or unlike ourselves. As a result we form in-groups, people who are like us, and out-groups, people who are not known or liked.

Our perceptions of out-groups tend to be less variable and less complex than those of in-groups. For instance, young people use fewer dimensions in thinking about older people and are more likely to agree that "they are all alike" (Linville & Jones, 1980). In addition, we tend to place more negative interpretations on the actions of out-group members and recall in memory those instances that reinforce the stereotype (Cohen, 1981; Hastie, 1981). Given these facts, it is not hard to see why stereotypes are so hard to change. This analysis may seem pessimistic concerning the possibility of minimizing stereotypes and the conflict that often comes with them, but we will see in some detail in Chapter 13 that this minimizing can be accomplished by applying a number of approaches from social psychology.

A fourth type of schema, an *event schema,* involves the knowledge structures people hold about certain specific situations, such as a baseball game, a wedding, a final exam, or a high school prom (Abelson, 1981).

They are also called *scripts* because our knowledge about them almost dictates the words to be spoken and the actions to be carried out, like the script for a play. In fact, one highly perceptive social psychologist, Erving Goffman (1967), suggests that behavior is determined by scripts in various social events to such an extent that they are really like rituals.

Take, for instance, the ritual of the used-car sale. As the customer, you see a car that you want badly, but you express only mild interest to the salesman. The salesman points out to you what great condition it is in, how little gas it will use, and what a perceptive person you must be to have picked out the best buy on the lot. You complain that the price is too high, and he says he might be able to do just a bit better. You come up a little, he comes down a little, the two of you shake hands, and the deal is made—all in line with the script you both had in your heads.

Development and Change of Schemas

People develop schemas through experience with objects, events, and people. At first their schemas are specific to the experiences they have, but eventually they get more generalized, abstract, and complex. An example of this is offered by Lurigio and Carroll (1985) in their study of probation officers' schemas of criminal offenders. Although most people have varied ideas of different types of criminals, probation officers have more experience with them and must get to know them in order to make referrals and recommendations. As a result, they have many different and discrete schemas for criminal types (as shown in Table 2.2). Lurigio and Carroll found that the more experienced the probation officers, the more their schemas agreed with each other's, and the richer they were in information.

Although role schemas are particularly hard to affect, all schemas tend to resist change. When specific people or situations do not fit into a broader schema, our perception often yields to the schema rather than vice versa (Crocker, Hannah, & Weber, 1983). Seeing schemas as more sophisticated versions of the *expectancies* we spoke of earlier in the chapter can help us understand the existence of the self-fulfilling prophecy in a broader cognitive context. We should recognize, however, that schemas can gradually change when faced with information where the poor fit is undeniable. In such instances, new subcategories develop and old structures slowly begin to crumble (Weber & Crocker, 1983; Rose, 1981).

Schemas and Impression Formation

By way of bringing the earlier work on impression formation together with the more recent research on social cognition, let us consider what processes occur between the time information comes in and the final impression of a person is formed. According to Burnstein and Schul (1982) there are four stages. First is *initial encoding;* that is, all the information that we take in from a person or situation is analyzed, broken down, and

TABLE 2.2
Probation Officers' Schemas of Various Criminal Types

Schema Type	Brief Description
Burglar	Early 30s, married, any race, intelligent, extensive burglary record, professional—expert. *Prognosis:* very poor (set lifestyle).
Drug addict	Early 20s, black, unintelligent, uneducated, lacking any social skills, parasite—uses people, varied criminal background, crime supports habit. *Prognosis:* some hope in a program.
Gang member	Under 21, Hispanic, cocky at first, gang involvement causes crime, needs lots of supervision. *Prognosis:* good—matures out of gang activities
"Uncle Tom"	40s–60s, black, sporadic history of petty crimes, crime by impulse. *Prognosis:* excellent—fears prison, respectful, cooperative.
Female welfare fraud	20s, black, unmarried but involved with male who controls her life; easily manipulated, feels forced to crime through concern for kids or her man. *Prognosis:* guarded to good depending on getting her away from the man.
Career criminal (con man)	Black, well dressed, street-smart, manipulative, bad person, unreachable, no concern for others; extensive, diverse criminal history. *Prognosis:* very bad.
Violent ("macho man")	20s, Hispanic, short fuse—walking time bomb; assaults and bar fights when manhood challenged; may act out while under supervision.
Suburban kid	Teens, minor first offense; good kid in bad crowd; contrite about crimes; parents heavily involved in case. *Prognosis:* excellent.
"Dumb hillbilly"	Dumb, very easily influenced, impulsive, many petty crimes, cooperative. *Prognosis:* guarded if controlled by probation officer.
White-collar criminal	35–45, white, middle class, employed, family, businessman; looking for a fast buck; irresistible impulse, drug dealing, not a criminal type. *Prognosis:* excellent—cooperative, although insulted by this process.

Source: Adapted from A. J. Lurigi & J. S. Carroll (1985). Probation officer's schemata of offenders: Context development and impact on treatment decisions. *Journal of Personality and Social Psychology, 48,* 1115.

transformed into symbolic codes. Very simply, it is prepared to be stored in our memory. Once in memory, the process of *elaborative encoding* takes place. At this point the information as initially encoded is linked with prior knowledge and ideas. So if I am told that John is a professor at an Ivy League college, I might also infer that he wears tweed jackets and

Self-defense classes not only make people better able to defend themselves physically, but also induce cognitive changes as well. As a result of her training, this woman's sense of vulnerability, and possibly her whole self-image, may be undergoing change.

glasses and is intelligent and married. Once encoded in this way, the third process involves the *integration* of all information. As pointed out earlier, we attempt to place all the information we have (verbal and nonverbal, consistent and inconsistent) into a neat schematic package that fits together as well as possible. This process is of critical importance because subsequent thinking is referred back to the schema without much reference to the fuller, more complex packet of information that was initially received (Wyer & Gordon, 1982). Finally, on the basis of this processing of information, we make an attribution or form an impression of the person, and we *behave* in one way or another.

In summary, schemas are cognitive structures that help people organize their beliefs and perceptions about themselves, other people and groups, roles, and events. They develop through experience, becoming more refined and complex as individuals become more familiar with a given person or situation. They make the processing of information more efficient by substituting our knowledge about general cases for each specific instance we encounter, and often they help people make good predictions about the world they live in. When the schema concept is combined into a process model of impression information, it provides a broad framework for understanding the way we form impressions, make attributions, and handle information in general.

At the beginning of this chapter we read about a rape victim. Having reviewed the basic principles and processes involved in forming impressions, making attributions, and processing information, we now return to ask how they can be applied to understand and assist victims of such crimes as rape. A prerequisite to helping is comprehending the cognitive world of the victim. We begin by recognizing that most people (nonvictims) see themselves as relatively invulnerable. They judge themselves as less likely than the average person to get cancer or heart disease, to become divorced, or to end up in an auto accident (Perloff, 1983).

But the cognitive structure of victims is not like that of most people. Their beliefs about invulnerability have been shattered. The negative outcomes in their lives become more *salient,* the experience of victimization becomes more *available* in their memories, and they come to feel that their sense of control had been nothing more than an illusion. Their self-schemas, which may have included characteristics such as capable and self-sufficient, are likely to undergo change; and their person, role, and event schemas may also have to accommodate the increased fear of victimization (Perloff, 1983).

How can victims be helped? First, Burgess and Holmstrom (1979) have noted that women who consciously adopt some form of coping strategy usually recover more quickly than those who do not. Whether this strategy is behavioral (keeping busy or getting involved in meditation or other stress-reduction techniques) or cognitive (involving rethinking about oneself), some active strategy ought to be encouraged in order to avoid maladaptive patterns like withdrawal from interaction or substance abuse. Taylor and her colleagues (Taylor, Wood, & Lichtman, 1983) have identified five cognitive mechanisms that seem to help minimize negative feelings from victimization: making comparisons with others who are less fortunate; focusing on attributes that make one seem relatively well-off; imagining hypothetical worse cases; finding some benefit from the event; and believing that one is adjusting better than others.

Janoff-Bulman (Janoff-Bulman & Lang-Gunn, in press; Janoff-Bulman, 1979) has proposed that certain forms of internal attributions can be harmful, while others may be helpful. *Characterological blame,* the feeling that some permanent or unchangeable aspect was at fault, can lead to feelings of helplessness and depression. *Behavioral blame,* the feeling that "I didn't act cautiously," helps make the unfortunate incident something that "I could have controlled" and that "I can still control in the future." However, an initial test (Meyer & Taylor, 1986) found that both these forms of blame were associated with poor adjustment, and therefore further work will be needed before we know whether this pattern should be encouraged.

Two other strategies are worth mentioning. The first, which has met with mixed success, involves the fostering of social support. By having friends and relatives around, it is hoped that victims can share their emotional reactions and receive comfort and support from those who know and love them. However, friends and relatives may accompany positive and supportive statements with nonverbal behavior that indicates ambivalence or disappointment (Gotlib & Robinson, 1982). They may also be subject to the fundamental attribution error as they subtly blame the victim for the event itself. The formation of support groups is a more formal version of this strategy, which has been tried with some success to help victims redefine and to find something of value in their experiences (that is, to gain cognitive control) (Coates, Renzaglia, & Embree, 1983).

The final approach we shall discuss, personal defense and assertiveness training, is hardly the invention of social psychologists. But social psychologists have begun to offer explanations for *why* this training works. For instance, victimized women often report feeling fearful and helpless. Self-defense and assertiveness training makes them think, "I can handle myself," or "I can stand up for my rights," thereby offering them a sense of behavior control. When threatened, these women experience the same physiological arousal as before, except now they label it anger instead of fear. In addition, assertiveness and defense training reduces feelings of vulnerability even when characterological blame has occurred. The woman who develops self-defense skills can now say, "My former self was vulnerable, but that could never happen to me again."

SUMMARY

1. The field of social cognition deals with the manner in which people make sense of events, of other people, and of themselves. It focuses on the human being as a thinker and reasoner who desires to understand the environment in order to make it predictable and controllable.
2. Several factors affect impressions. Central traits such as "warm" and "cold" affect the rating of other traits, and also affect behavior toward others. Primacy effects occur when preliminary information exerts a stronger force than information that comes after it. Likewise, expectancies can create a self-fulfilling prophecy, wherein people are perceived in a certain manner merely because we expect to see them that way.
3. Physical appearance exerts a strong effect on first impressions. Attractive people are generally rated more positively than less attractive people, but the impact of attractiveness becomes weaker over time.
4. Nonverbal behavior involves visible characteristics (e.g., facial expression and posture) and paralinguistic characteristics (e.g., voice tone and rate) that can affect our impressions of others. When verbal and nonverbal messages contradict one another, people often rely upon the nonverbal cues to determine the true meaning of a message.
5. There is a debate about how people combine pieces of information to form impressions. Some social psychologists believe that all the trait

information is added or averaged, while others believe that the final impression is something more than the combination of its parts.

6. The topic of attribution theory deals with the process by which people infer the cause of their own and others' behavior. Fritz Heider, one of the pioneers in the field, noted that attributions are to either an internal cause (e.g., one's disposition) or an external cause (circumstances or luck).
7. Harold Kelley has suggested that we ask three questions in making an attribution. Consensus asks whether the behavior is unique to that person; distinctiveness, whether it is unique to the situation; and consistency, whether it is unique to the particular instance.
8. The fundamental attribution error refers to a tendency to attribute behavior to dispositional rather than situational causes. Due to actor-observer differences, however, we are more likely to attribute our own behavior to situational causes.
9. Attributions for success can fall into four categories: internal and stable (ability); internal and variable (effort); external and stable (task difficulty); and external and variable (luck).
10. People attempt to exert control over their lives in several ways. When people have behavior control they can take specific steps to change a situation. Decision and information control involve the ability to choose among events or at least to have full knowledge of the choices. Cognitive control allows people to deal with a situation by restructuring it in their minds.
11. When people are threatened by loss of control, they often react in either of two contrasting ways. They may demonstrate reactance, the desire to regain control in an assertive manner; or they may show helplessness, a generalized acceptance of their powerless state.
12. Attention to a stimulus in the environment is affected by its salience, its tendency to stand out against its context. Individuals who are salient are judged in a more extreme manner.
13. When we recall information about a person, we remember concrete features first and abstract characteristics last. Thoughts and ideas that are primed (i.e., activated frequently or recently) are more easily recalled.
14. Inferences about people and events may be inaccurate, owing to several processes. People often generalize from their own experiences (the false consensus effect) and underutilize information about base rates in the population. Heuristics, or cognitive shortcuts, often help us make quick, efficient inferences, but they can also lead to cognitive biases.
15. Social schemas are knowledge structures that simplify and organize complex packages of information about others, ourselves, roles, and events. They develop through experience with objects, are resistant to change, but can be modified by encounters with information that provides an undeniably poor fit.

CHAPTER 3
The Self and Personality

What type of person is George Rivers? George was pleased with his accomplishments, but not with himself. His hard work had paid off for his company and for his career. At 42 he was a vice president of his company. He was highly regarded, highly paid, and had impressive responsibilities for a large number of people and dollars.

But George's body was letting him down—or more likely the reverse. As a teenager he had been strong, athletic, and unquestionably healthy. Now he was lucky to spend one hour per week doing what could be called "exercise." Many of his business meetings took place over meals. Entertainment was part of his job: rich food and drinking (though George was by no means an alcoholic) were a big part of the social side of business. As a teenager, he had begun smoking to appear more attractive. Now he worked sporadically and unsuccessfully at stopping. He was getting pudgier, weaker, and less attractive each week, and he didn't like it.

But that wasn't the worst of his concerns. George's doctor told him he was headed for serious trouble. His smoking alone made him a good candidate for a heart attack, a stroke, and cancer. His blood pressure and cholesterol level were too high. In fact, his doctor said that he did not hold out much hope for him because George was a "classic Type A."

George Rivers was a workaholic. He felt guilty when he was not working. He moved, walked, talked, and ate rapidly. He was often impatient with the slow pace of other people. To try to speed things up, he would sometimes finish their sentences for them. He tried to schedule more and more activity into less and less time. He had a "chronic sense of time urgency."

The symptom that his doctor thought clinched it was George's "polyphasic" thought and actions. He always tried to do more than one thing at a time. He would try to watch the business news while reading *The Wall Street Journal* and eating dinner. (George was not ignoring family members at the table—he got home too late to eat with them.) And when he did give time to his family—taking them to the beach or to a baseball game—he would be thinking through a business problem or drafting a memo in his mind.

George's doctor explained that research had shown that Type A personalities keep themselves under constant stress and that such people were two to seven times more likely to die of coronary heart disease than their more relaxed Type B counterparts. If George could not be transformed into a Type B, he was not long for this world.

The case of George Rivers confronts us with a number of questions about the nature of differences among individuals. What does it mean to talk about the kind of person someone is? In what meaningful ways can people be classified or measured? Do these characteristics have much to do with one's behavior or one's health? Is the self relatively stable or does it change? Can it—can George—change?

THE MEANING OF SELF AND PERSONALITY

As with other abstract terms that have suffered from centuries of overuse, **personality** has many meanings. In fact, more than 50 years ago, Gordon Allport (1937) was able to identify 50 different definitions of the word. For our purposes (and for most purposes in psychology), *self* or *personality* are terms for dealing with the issues that are raised when a person asks, Who am I? What am I like? What am I *really* like? The two areas of research, into personality and self, differ in several ways. One important difference is that research on the self is typically concerned with how a person conceives of himself or herself, whereas personality research generally takes the perspective of an outside observer.

Most research in social psychology focuses on how social and physical factors affect people in general, assuming that we are all fairly similar in our responses to varying situations. Questions about the self and personality, however, are raised from the opposite point of view: How do people differ in their responses to the same situations? These two approaches—how different situations affect people in general, and how the same situation affects people differently—constitute the two sides of the psychology of social behavior. As Blass (1984) has pointed out, they can be complementary rather than competing approaches, as you can note from the title of social psychology's leading journal: *Journal of Personality and Social Psychology.* Blass's perspective clearly reflects Kurt Lewin's well-respected belief that behavior is a *joint* function of personality and situation.

The Unique Self

By *self,* we mean one unique person who shows a physical and psychological continuity. People who have been badly injured in an accident—who are disfigured, for example, or have had a limb removed—often question whether they are the "same person." In contrast, a person whose *personality* is drastically altered—by joining the Unification Church or the Marines, or perhaps by going to law school—may be regarded by friends and family as no longer his or her former self. In this case, the external physical self is the same, but the individual seems "like a different person." Therefore, *self* does not refer to a physical or psychological entity alone but to the unique combination of the two.

People may not be regarded in a similar way either as they move through places or statuses, or simply begin dressing differently. If someone wins a million dollars, gets a promotion at work, or suddenly becomes a rock star or professional athlete, people who knew the person "back when" tend to feel that the person is different. People who move to another part of the world take on a different identity for those who knew them in a former situation. Thus it appears that external surroundings, or geographic or societal "place," have something to do with who you are (Proshansky, Fabian, & Kaminoff, 1983).

Each individual is constantly changing in small ways, and most changes in personality are slow and gradual, not dramatic and abrupt. But observers do not necessarily see you from such a perspective, especially people with whom you do not interact often. If you see a friend after 30 years, for instance, you may each regard the other as quite changed—in appearance, friends, values, cognitive style, and interests. Yet having been through each day of your own life, you see yourself as not really changed—just the product of a continuous, almost imperceptible progression through life.

Much of this discussion suggests that the perceived self or personality is in some degree a product of the characteristics of the perceiver and not simply the characteristics of the perceived (e.g., Allen & Ebbesen, 1981; Miller, Jones, & Hinkle, 1981). It may seem obvious to most of us that the self is a relatively integrated, constant, and continuous whole, but the most accurate piece of that picture may be the word *seem.* Research findings about the self and personality sometimes clash with commonsense impressions. Our tendency to see consistency and unity in personality may be more a consequence of the casual observer's characteristics than those of the people observed. This issue touches on the topic of social perception we discussed in Chapter 2, and it is one we will return to later in this chapter.

Sources of the Self

We have already hinted at several possible sources of the self. One part of our identity is our biological inheritance. Our genes give us psychological as well as physical traits that differ from those of other people. For example, evidence exists that the general characteristics we call **temperament** are genetically inherited. From infancy, people seem to vary in four aspects of temperament: activity (sheer level of energy output); emotionality (tendency to respond either strongly or sedately); sociability (along a dimension from gregarious to solitary); and impulsivity (from impulsive to deliberate) (Buss & Plomin, 1975).

Another major source of our selves is learning. The family we are born into and other social institutions pass on to us the cultural, ethnic, and other traditions that we come to identify as "us." We belong to various groups and have particular relationships, each of which adds something to our identity and teaches us particular lessons. We "feel" like Americans or Canadians, like members of a particular religion, region, class, and so on. If you or I had been born in the thirteenth century, or in a province of China, or as the fourteenth child of a migrant farm worker, we would not be the same persons that we are here and now. The particular expe-

Just by looking at them, it is hard to tell whether these triplets are more alike now than they were as infants. A social psychologist would be quick to note that their genetic endowments are identical, but the environments in which they were raised were highly similar as well.

riences each of us has, in addition to our genetic uniqueness, leads to the learned uniqueness that distinguishes us from others.

Some people believe in other sources of our selves, such as the position of planets and stars (astrology) or of previous lives (reincarnation). Many efforts to confirm such supernatural forces empirically have been undertaken. H. J. Eysenck and D. K. B. Nias (1982) reviewed about 300 empirical studies testing the relationship between astrological predictions and the actual behavior of people. Almost without exception the studies failed to confirm the astrological predictions. Thus empirical research can be useful in disconfirming hypothesized sources of individual differences, in spite of their appeal.

THE SOCIAL SELF

The sources of personal identity, of the self, with which social psychologists are primarily concerned are those dealing with the social self. By **social self** we mean the parts of a person's identity that have been learned from interaction with other people (Babad, Birnbaum, & Benne, 1983). The social aspects of the self are more interesting and useful than genetic inheritance to an applied social psychologist because social aspects are more subject to conscious change. While genetic engineering or other biological interventions may be possible someday, changes induced through learning and interaction with the external (especially social) environment are and will long continue to be the modes of change most available to us. In this section we will discuss a number of aspects of the social self that psychologists have studied. We will begin with some early formulations and then turn to the construction of images of oneself and the relationship of the self to behavior.

Early Formulations

The role other people might play in the formation of a person's self was first noted by William James (1890), one of the founders of American psychology. He discussed three selves: the material self, that is, one's body, property, friends, and other physical "possessions"; the spiritual self, by which he meant awareness of one's mental processes; and the social self, one's view of one's self as seen through others.

Charles Horton Cooley (1922) developed a more refined notion of the social self, the idea of a "**looking-glass self.**" According to this concept the primary way by which we come to know who we are is through the reflection of ourselves provided by others. To find out about certain aspects of ourselves, such as our looks or hair color, we look in a mirror. But to find out social things, such as our popularity or our lovableness, we have to use others as our mirror or looking glass. Thus we develop a self-image through the reflected appraisal of others. Of course, we do not see clearly what others think of us but have to infer it from their behavior toward us. Thus we see ourselves as we *believe* others see us. The knowledge we gain from the looking glass leaves room for selective attention, distortions, and error. To better understand and perhaps to change ourselves, we might want to be less self-focused (introspective) and more attentive to how others respond to us. This notion is put to practice in some forms of group therapy, as we shall discuss in Chapter 13.

The notion of the looking glass was developed further by George Herbert Mead (1934), who theorized that the self is not a thing but a process. Our understanding of ourselves as social objects comes only after we realize that we exist as objects in the social world of others. Once that awareness has been achieved, we can interact symbolically in the social world by imagining our behavior and how it will be reacted to in a given social context. This process is known as **symbolic interactionism.** Indeed, most people become so good at anticipating reactions that it becomes second nature to adjust their behavior in order to create the image or obtain the response that they desire from others.

Constructing Images of Oneself

To summarize the discussion so far, the social self consists largely of a cognitive construction of who or what we believe we are, based on our social worlds. From these early notions, a number of areas of research and theory have flowed. Each has expanded our knowledge and understanding of who we are and how we see ourselves.

Self-space The **self-space** is defined as "the content that is available to the person when he/she reflects upon the self. Operationally, it is the material that the person records when asked in a nonspecific context, 'Tell us about yourself' " (McGuire & McGuire, 1982, p. 71). Research on self-space has found that children define themselves in terms of the significant people in their lives. Girls' self-concepts are focused on mothers and brothers; boys' self-concepts are in relation to fathers and sisters. As people mature from age 7 through 17, a time during which they become involved in the larger world, they report progressively less about others, but the others they choose are a more varied and sophisticated assortment.

The content of one's awareness of self differs according to whether one is considering the *public* or the *private* self. We have a self that we show the public and a self we keep private, and we are aware of their differences (Buss, 1980; Scheier & Carver, 1983). Erving Goffman, a noted student of the self, has referred to this aspect of "presented" self in terms of the theater, calling the public self "front stage" and the private, or hidden, self "back stage" (Goffman, 1959).

Social Comparison The looking-glass self and symbolic interaction concepts see us as learning about ourselves through the perceptions and reactions (real or anticipated) of others. Other people serve as the standards of measurement, the yardsticks that provide the means for comparison. Are you energetic or lethargic, loving or cold, bright or stupid? The only way to make a judgment—in fact, the only meaning such terms can have—is in comparison with the range of selves, others' selves, that exists in the social world around us.

The theory of **social comparison** (Festinger, 1954) seeks to spell out this process and its implications for our behavior, including our choice of which others we will use for comparison. According to social comparison theory, we evaluate ourselves by comparison with some standard or measure. The fewer objective standards that are available, the more we rely on subjective or social standards. For example, to calculate how fast you are, you might time how long it takes you to run 100 meters or to complete a marathon. But if you wonder how attractive you are, the answer can be found only by comparing yourself with others. Even an objective standard, however, depends for its meaning on other people. Suppose you run 100 meters in 12 seconds. Does that mean you are fast, slow, or average? The answer depends on how other people perform. If you earn $40,000 per year, are you rich or poor? Again, it depends on whom you compare yourself to (Morse & Gergen, 1970).

Social comparison theory also tries to explain which other people we will look to for comparison. We learn little about ourselves by looking to people who are very different from us. Instead, we tend to make our comparisons with people we regard as being similar. In trying to judge whether we are satisfied with, say, our success, our goodness as a human being, or even our independence, we will look to our peers rather than to someone who differs greatly in age, experience, expertise, or other important characteristics. You learn more about your tennis skills from playing a person of about equal age, physique, and experience than you would from playing a child of five or Martina Navratilova.

The Self as Theorist Building on the work of Kelly (1955), Epstein (1973) suggests that our self-concepts are in essence theories we hold about ourselves. Facing much the same problems as a scientist does when trying to construct a coherent theory out of diverse and sometimes contradictory evidence, the self-concept is formed by testing a set of hypotheses about who I am, what kind of person I am. The behavior the person enacts each day and the way the person responds to a variety of situations provide the "data" against which the person may test his or her self-theory. A good self-observer, like a good scientist, will modify the self-concept in line with the data, which will change over time, place, and circumstance. A bad observer, like a bad scientist, will cling to a theory even when it is contradicted by the evidence.

The Self as Historian Will one's theory of oneself, one's emotion-laden conception of one's being, be an accurate mapping of one's motives and preferences? Greenwald (1980) has reviewed a large and diverse body of research that leads to the conclusion that the self (or "ego") makes little more than a pretense of objectivity about itself, and is best characterized as a biased historian.

From the research he reviewed, Greenwald constructed a portrait of how the ego as a historian operates. "The most striking features of the portrait are three cognitive biases, which correspond disturbingly to thought control and propaganda devices that are considered to be defining characteristics of a totalitarian political system" (p. 603). The ego behaves in much the same way as the government did in George Orwell's *1984*, the classic novel on totalitarian control of information.

The first of the biases Greenwald discusses is *egocentricity.* "The past is remembered as if it were a drama in which self was the leading player" (p. 604). When reflecting on an incident, we tend to see it as revolving about us and report it as it affected or was affected by us. Not only is the self the central character but it is seen as the "axis of cause and effect." That is, the self is seen as more influential in causing the events around it and as more often the target of influence attempts by others than is actually the case.

The second bias is *beneffectance.* The ego is a self-aggrandizing historian. It sees itself as the cause of or participant in desirable results but not in undesirable results. For example, people have a remarkable ability to explain the causes of their automobile accidents in ways that absolve them of responsibility. College students at football games are more likely to include themselves in victories ("We won") and to dissociate themselves from defeats ("They lost") (Cialdini et al., 1976). We have seen equivalent biases in our perception of other people and events, as well as of ourselves, in the discussion of the attribution process in Chapter 2.

The third bias is *cognitive conservatism,* the tendency to preserve existing structures rather than to modify one's conception of oneself in the face of conflicting evidence. People selectively search their memories for supporting evidence and distort old memories to move them in line with present needs. Greenwald suggests that the ego's cognitive biases assist us in maintaining relatively positive feelings about ourselves. All of us are likely to say we are thoughtful, intelligent, and wise, and can defend these contentions by retrieving examples that support these claims while overlooking events that contradict them. Just as politicians fare better if they try never to admit error and seek to have their predictions come true, so does the self. And for most of us, the ego has the advantage of an almost completely unwritten history, which can be endlessly revised. Both Epstein's and Greenwald's theories point to the importance of the selection, use, and distortion of self-data as critical to the self-concept.

The Self and Behavior

How we feel about ourselves and how we behave are in part a function of the self that we construct and of how we attend to that self. Among the lines of research that bear on this point are studies of objective self-awareness, self-efficacy, self-monitoring, and self-presentation.

Objective self-awareness A person's attention can be focused on the self to varying degrees, and it can fluctuate according to different features of a situation. If you find yourself sitting opposite a mirror or if you enter a room where a group of people are waiting to hear you, you will be more aware of yourself than usual. This state of heightened attention to the self is known as **objective self-awareness.**

Duval and Wicklund (1972; Wicklund, 1980) have tested this notion by playing tape-recordings of people's voices or seating them before a large mirror. They found that under conditions of heightened self-awareness, people's usual reactions to praise and criticism are exaggerated. Their self-esteem goes up more in response to praise and down more in response to criticism than it would under conditions of less heightened awareness. In the face of negative feedback, heightened self-awareness makes them try to avoid the awareness or to distract themselves from themselves with nervous mannerisms. In one study it was shown that people who were given ways of distracting themselves, such as by squeezing a rubber ball before and during a public speaking appearance, experienced less nervousness than would commonly accompany such a situation.

Wicklund (1982) has suggested that, in order to control its members, society creates situations where people are made more (or less) self-aware. For example, we ask children to tell a class about themselves, their families, or their summer vacation. Merely by focusing attention on themselves, they begin to engage in behavior that is more consistent with societal expectations. Exposing ourselves, our ideas, and our feelings to others provides an occasion for their approval or criticism. Thus children asked to speak about themselves learn what behavior and ideas win approval. Given an apparently safe opportunity to steal, children and adolescents have been shown to be dramatically less likely to do so when a mirror was positioned in such a way that they could see themselves engaging in the theft (Beaman et al., 1979). On the other hand, there are times and circumstances where self-awareness can be decreased. For instance, we shave the heads of soldiers and put them into identical uniforms. By enabling them to lose themselves in a sea of other people, it is

Some people, such as this busy executive, are able to perform well under demanding circumstances. Self-efficacy research suggests that part of what helps us stand up to pressure is the very way in which we perceive our effectiveness.

easier to get them to abandon their individual behavior patterns and to adopt new ones (see the discussion of deindividuation in Chapter 13).

Self-efficacy People differ in their ability to perform various tasks and to cope with various stressors. Albert Bandura (1982) has reviewed a wide range of research evidence showing that perceiving oneself as effective is an important determinant of a person's actual success or failure at various tasks. Bandura notes that knowledge and skills are necessary for performing at a high level, but are insufficient without self-perceptions that connect the capability to the actions themselves. People who perceive themselves as **self-efficacious** (i.e., personally able) show fewer physiological stress reactions, less depression in response to failure experiences, and more striving for achievement.

Self-monitoring Another recent development that is related to the looking-glass self is Mark Snyder's concept of **self-monitoring** (Snyder, 1974, 1979; Snyder & Campbell, 1982). Snyder's findings show that some people more than others are tuned in to—tend more to "monitor"—their social surroundings and people's reactions to them. High self-monitors are more in touch with their surroundings and with what people in various situations expect of them. They would endorse statements such as "When I am uncertain how to act in social situations, I look to the behavior of others for cues"; "I may deceive people by being friendly when I really dislike them"; and "In different situations with different people, I often act very differently." They are flexible, adaptive, and shrewdly pragmatic, and their behavior is more situation-specific. Low self-monitors have a more "principled" self. They are more behaviorally consistent across situations and show a greater similarity between their private and public selves.

Self-presentation: Impression Management Research on self-monitoring also indicates that some people are more able than others to modify the impressions they create (Miell & LeVoi, 1985; Miell & Duck, 1983). This aspect of the presentation of oneself to others is called **impression management.** It involves the manipulation of verbal and nonverbal information with the intent of affecting the impression or image that others come to have of us.

The study of self-presentation began with Goffman's work, discussed earlier. Social psychologists continued his work in a number of areas of interpersonal behavior, usually using laboratory experimental techniques (in contrast to Goffman's participant observation methods). The major area of impression management research has been on *ingratiation,* how we use impression management to get others to like us (Jones, 1964; Jones & Wortman, 1973). Other concerns include *intimidation,* how we get others to perceive us as dangerous or powerful so that they will acquiesce to our wishes; and *self-promotion,* how we get others to see us as competent or skilled (Jones & Pittman, 1982).

An interesting example of such research is Berglas and Jones's (1978) work showing that in order to preserve an image of competence, people may resort to self-handicapping. **Self-handicapping** occurs when a person has favorably impressed others with the appearance of competence, but thinks the performance that won the respect was due more to luck than ability. As a result, the person tends to sabotage or avoid later performances so that a clear test of ability cannot be made and the initial favorable impression is protected. By avoiding occasions for reevaluation of ability, the earlier evaluation cannot be revised. In one experiment, Berglas and Jones set up situations in which people were led to believe that they had achieved success through either luck or ability. Those who thought their success was based on luck were likely to choose a performance-inhibiting rather than a performance-facilitating drug when taking a later test. By handicapping themselves, they could protect the image of competence they had initially created.

THE SEARCH FOR THE "TRUE SELF"

For many of us, adolescence and young adulthood is a time of trying to discover who we are. This seems to be especially true in modern postindustrial society; knowing oneself is less complicated in a "traditional" society, where a person's fate is determined almost from birth. In industrialized societies we have an enormous array of choices, and with them come uncertainties about who we are and where we are going. Since survival is no longer a problem, we have the luxury of indulging in such questions as "Who am I?" In fact, the quest to "find" ourselves has become almost a cultural obsession.

The search for the self seems to be guided by a number of assumptions, among them the very definition of the self. We may feel that somewhere inside us our "true" self waits to be found, like a mystery to be solved. And how do we know when we have found the true self of others? Perhaps they have projected only that image of themselves they wished us to know. In this section we will examine a number of findings and theories that raise doubts about the existence of a single, unvarying self. In addition, we will discuss the factors that affect the self we adopt, the possibility of multiple selves, and the way we present different selves to different people in different situations.

Adopting a Self-concept

When we find ourselves behaving differently with different people or in different settings, our notion of the self can seem very elusive. If we seem to be one kind of person with our parents, another kind of person with friends or lovers, and yet another with our teachers, how can we know which is the one true self?

We may falsely assume that a core self could be found if only we knew where or how to look. Perhaps we have as many different selves as there are other people and situations in which to reflect them. As William James put it nearly one hundred years ago, "A man has as many social selves as there are individuals who recognize him and carry an image of him in their mind. . . . He generally shows a different side of himself to each of these different groups" (1890, vol. 1, p. 294).

That we behave, feel, and think differently with different people in different settings may be an important clue to understanding the nature of the self. Each of us is a mass of potential, capable of displaying a wide array of behavior, although we usually focus on a few attributes from the assortment of possibilities. Which self-concept people adopt varies according to the situation they find themselves in.

William McGuire has introduced the term **spontaneous self-concept** to refer to the habit of some people of defining themselves on the basis of the specific situation in which they find themselves. For example, a white male may not perceive those attributes (being white and male) as central features of himself. But if he finds himself one of the few males among a group of females, or the only white in a group of blacks, he quickly regards those attributes as important to his identity (McGuire & McGuire, 1981; McGuire, McGuire, & Winton, 1979). As long as you are in your own country, being an American or a Canadian or any other nationality is hardly noticed. But if you meet a compatriot in a foreign country, your common nationality becomes important to your identity and is enough to form the basis of a new relationship. In one study, children in first through eleventh grades were asked to "tell us about yourself." Boys who came from homes in which there were more females than males, and girls in male-dominated homes, were more likely to mention their sex as a defining feature of their identity (McGuire, McGuire, & Winton, 1979) (see Figure 3.1).

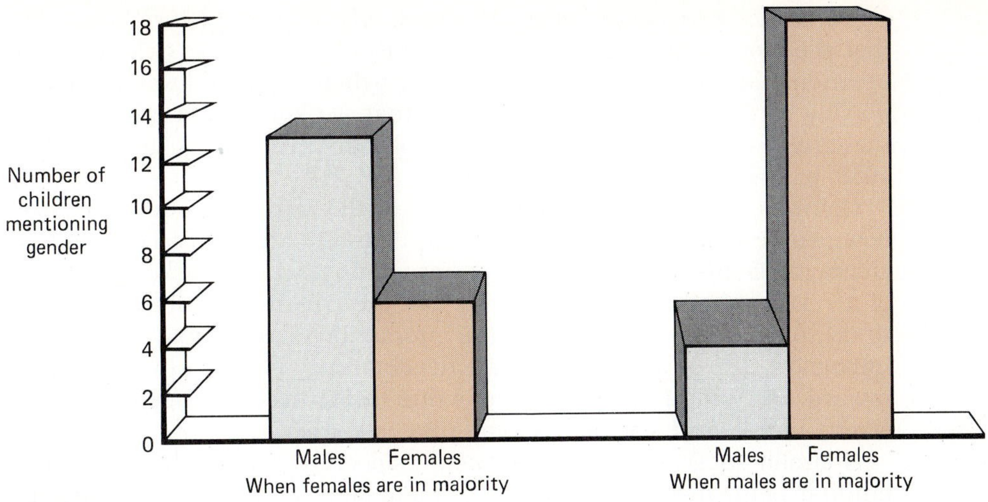

FIGURE 3.1

Children Spontaneously Mentioning Their Gender When asked to describe themselves, male children are more likely to mention their gender when females are in the majority in their households, and female children are more likely to mention their gender when males are in the majority. *Source:* Adapted from W. J. McGuire, C. V. McGuire, & W. Winton (1979). Effects of household sex composition on the salience of one's gender in the spontaneous self-concept. *Journal of Experimental Social Psychology, 15,* 86.

Similarly, the theory of **situated identities** holds that as people move from situation to situation, they bring forth the aspects of themselves that are most appropriate to that setting and most likely to achieve for them what they seek in that situation (Alexander & Knight, 1971; Alexander & Lauderdale, 1977; Alexander & Sagatun, 1973).

Our Multiple Selves

Kenneth Gergen (1972, 1982; see also Greenwald, 1982) has suggested that the notion of "**multiple selves**" is a more accurate characterization of the self than the one true, real self that many people seek. He suggests that we are more flexible, adaptable, and changeable than has usually been supposed. We adopt different styles of responding to different people in various situations; and this adaptation reflects our ability to learn to cope with a multitude of situations. If a person seems to someone else to be a stable and consistent self, it is more likely a reflection of stability in that person's relationships and situations than of stability in the person himself or herself.

Erving Goffman (1959) has discussed our multiple selves as subidentities, "faces" or "masks," using the metaphor of the theater. He believes that people adopt various roles and engage in various techniques to present and sustain their "performances," much as an actor does in presenting a character to an audience: "It is probably no mere historical accident that the word person, in its first meaning, is a mask. It is rather a recognition that everyone is always and everywhere, more or less consciously, playing a role. . . . It is in these roles that we know each other; it is in these roles that we know ourselves" (Goffman, 1959, p. 19, quoting Park, 1950, p. 249).

Goffman emphasizes the importance of the initial encounter between new people in a new situation, since it commits a person to a particular character. Goffman suggests it is easier to adopt a new mask at the outset of a relationship and call forth appropriate treatment from others than to try to create alterations once the interaction is under way. Thus, to an important degree we acquire and develop our selves from the outside inward. Our seeming consistency is due to the need to appear "in character." In different settings, we can play our other roles.

Goffman suggests that many people sincerely believe that their most familiar performances are not performances at all, but "reality." Indeed, he suggests that the more the performers and the audience believe in the enactment, the more successful social life is for all of them. "All the world is not, of course, a stage, but the crucial ways in which it isn't are not easy to specify" (Goffman, 1959, p. 72). A major task we all face is creating the character we wish to project in a given sphere of life. Goffman refers to these as "impression management skills."

The line of reasoning developed by Goffman and others suggests that an exploration of the self is best pursued by experiencing a variety of people and circumstances and seeing how we deal with them. We can try a variety of responses to common situations to discover which "I" feels best. Gergen (1973) has suggested that in choosing a mate, a career, or a circle of friends, we choose one of the selves we could be, giving up in the process many other possible selves. In choosing other companions in different roles and circumstances, we may choose a different self. If true, the theory of multiple selves may disappoint seekers of the true self; but it suggests the potential for change and for adaptability. Instead of trying to find who you "truly" are, you can discover the many selves that you can be.

APPLICATION
OVERCOMING SHYNESS

A remarkable number of people consider themselves shy and regard it as a personal problem. A survey of 2482 American students aged 18–21 revealed that 42 percent of them considered themselves to be shy people (Zimbardo, 1977). Young adults around the world confirmed the widespread problem of shyness, from a high of 60 percent among Japanese to a low of 31 percent among Israelis.

Table 3.1 describes the kinds of situations that young people report make them feel shy. Avoiding these situations is no solution, since many people are

TABLE 3.1
Situations That Make People Feel Shy

What Makes You Shy?	Percentage of Shy Students
Other People	
Strangers	70
Opposite sex	64
Authorities by virtue of their knowledge	55
Authorities by virtue of their role	40
Relatives	21
Elderly people	12
Friends	11
Children	10
Parents	8
Situations	
Where I am focus of attention—large group (as when giving a speech)	73
Large groups	68
Of lower status	56
Social situations in general	55
New situations in general	55
Requiring assertiveness	54
Where I am being evaluated	53
Where I am focus of attention—small group	52
Small social groups	48
One-to-one different-sex interactions	48
Of vulnerability (need help)	48
Small task-oriented groups	28
One-to-one same sex interactions	14

Source: P. G. Zimbardo (1977). *Shyness.* Reading, MA: Addison-Wesley, p. 37. Reprinted with permission.

pained *because* they cannot enjoy the company or attention of other people. Whatever the causes of shyness, much can be done to overcome it (Zimbardo, 1977; Phillips, 1981). Even researchers who have found evidence that shyness is a genetically inherited disposition regard it as a problem that can be remedied (Cheek & Zonderman, 1983).

Philip Zimbardo examines the nature of the problem in his book *Shyness* (1977), in which he devotes a large section to "what to do about it." The following list contains some of his suggestions.

1. Avoid saying bad things about yourself. Especially avoid attributing to yourself irreversible negative traits such as [being] stupid, uncreative, or a failure [p. 159].
2. Do not tolerate people, jobs, or situations that make you feel inadequate. If you cannot improve them or your reactions to them, walk away from them [p. 159].

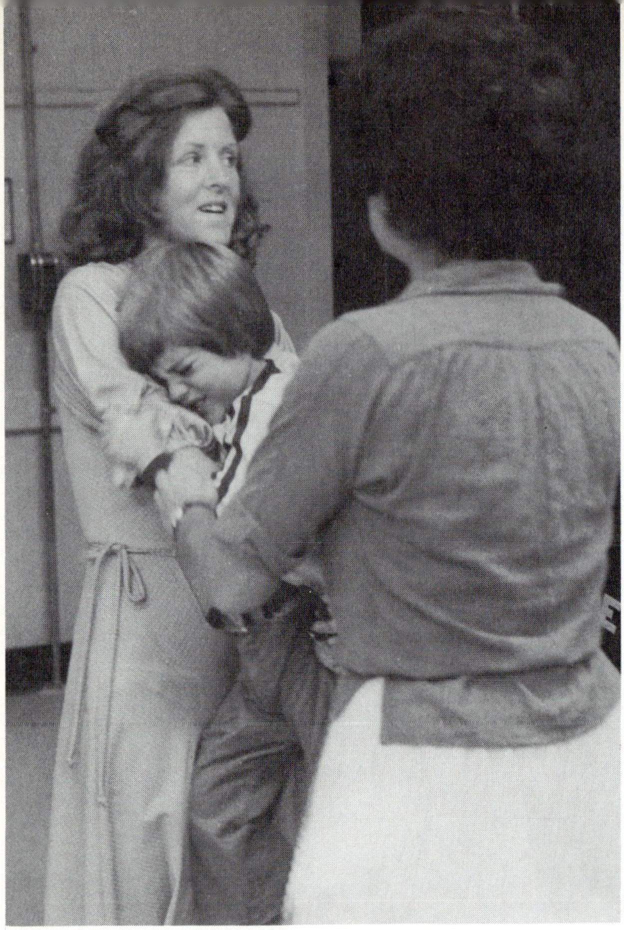

This child appears to be extremely shy, but will the shyness last? While many people do shed their shyness as they mature, according to research 42 percent of college students still regard themselves as shy people.

3. Be specific in your description of yourself. Don't say to yourself, "I am a shy person." Say "I get nervous when I have to talk to groups," or "I am uncomfortable in singles bars" [pp. 161–162].
4. In your mind, go over in detail specific situations that make you feel shy. Imagine what you would do and say in [such] situation[s] if you were not shy. Think about this positive image the next time you start to feel shy in that situation [p. 162].
5. Try "role playing" a part that allows you to enter into social contact, such as an interviewer on a research project. Most students who did this found they were able to be less shy in the "role," and eventually they were able to transcend the role, merging their un-shy interviewer behavior with the other roles of their lives [pp. 170–171].
6. Practice social skills by making phone calls (e.g., to a department store to check on the price of something), or start a brief, "safe" conversation with a stranger in a public place, [as] in a supermarket line, a waiting room, or a library [p. 176].
7. To get into good conversations you need to have something to say. The easiest way to do that is to keep yourself informed. Read the newspaper and/or magazines . . . read movie and book reviews—then go to some movies and read some books [p. 178]. [Reprinted with permission of Addison-Wesley, Reading, MA.]

Note that these suggested techniques focus on changing behavior, not on changing some notion of a real self. If you can change your behavior in a few situations, and gradually in more and more situations, eventually you will not act shy or feel shy or be treated as shy; you will no longer *be* shy. The techniques work on situation-specificity—when, where, and what makes you feel shy—and suggest what to do to prepare for and to act on each situation. They focus on changing the labels we apply to ourselves and the images and feelings we hold about ourselves in various situations, and about ourselves in general. If the labels, images, and feelings can change, then *we* gradually come to change.

SCIENTIFIC MEASURES OF PERSONALITY

When psychologists want to study personality, they encounter problems not unlike those we ourselves encounter in the search to understand the self. But unlike the self studying the self, wherein distortions of data may serve a useful function, when a scientist studies personality, biased selection or distortion of data to fit a theory is not a desirable practice. Thus objective measures have been devised, tests that are subjected to evaluation of their reliability and validity. Such measures avoid some of the problems inherent in the casual and haphazard observation of others we engage in daily.

Casual measures of personality can fool us—a fact put to profitable use by astrologers, fortune-tellers, and, unfortunately, even some mental health professionals. The problem is illustrated by the **Barnum effect,** recalling the nineteenth-century circus entrepreneur who profited from his assessment that "a sucker is born every minute" (Johnson et al., 1985).

FROM THE FIELD
Philip G. Zimbardo

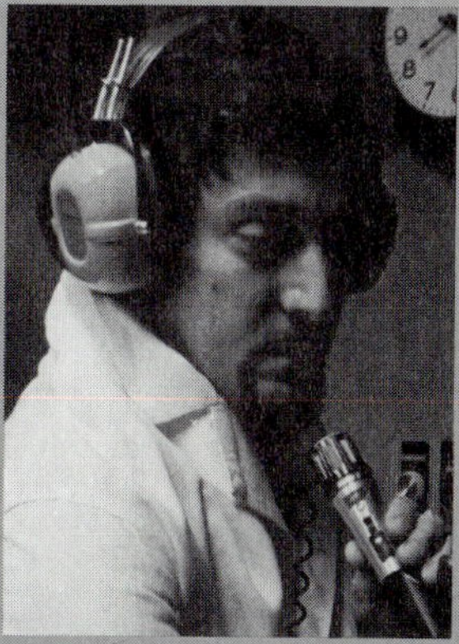

Philip Zimbardo's research has covered a considerable range, and one important theme that unites it is the effect of situations not only on behavior but also on the self and personality. In his earlier work Zimbardo demonstrated the effects of "deindividuation"—how loss of identity can lead to increased deviation from social norms, including violence. In his controversial Stanford prison study, he showed how people assigned at random to the role of prisoner or guard exhibited behavior and emotions consistent with their assigned roles. And, as discussed in this chapter, he has also studied the causes and cures of shyness.

Imagine that a psychologist gave you a test and, after examining you and your responses, presented the following personality profile of you:

> You have a strong need for other people to like you and for them to admire you. You have a tendency to be critical of yourself. You have a great deal of unused capacity which you have not turned to your advantage. While you have some personality weaknesses, you are generally able to compensate for them. Your sexual adjustment has presented some problems for you.
>
> Disciplined and controlled on the outside, you tend to be worrisome and insecure inside. At times you have serious doubts as to whether you have made the right decision or done the right thing. You prefer a certain amount of change and variety and become dissatisfied when hemmed in by restrictions and limitations. You pride yourself on being an independent thinker and do not accept others' opinions without satisfactory proof.
>
> You have found it unwise to be too frank in revealing yourself to others. At times you're extroverted, affable, sociable, while at other times you are introverted, wary, and reserved. Some of your aspirations tend to be pretty unrealistic (Ulrich, Stachnik, & Stainton, 1963, p. 832).

This profile may strike you as a surprisingly insightful description of yourself. Ulrich, Stachnik, and Stainton gave it to a number of people, telling each person that it was an individually tailored description of them. The researchers asked the people to rate the accuracy of the description. As you can see in Table 3.2, about 75 percent believed that the profiles displayed "excellent" or "good" insight into them individually.

The Barnum profile states a number of generalities that fit nearly everybody yet are intimate traits that people do not discuss with each

TABLE 3.2
Students' Ratings of the Accuracy of "Barnum" Personality Interpretations

Rating	Percentage of Students[a]
Excellent	37
Good	38
Average	19
Poor	6
Very poor	0

[a] $n = 79$

Source: From R. E. Ulrich, T. J. Stachnik, & N. R. Stainton (1963). Student acceptance of generalized personality interpretation. *Psychological Reports, 13,* 831–834.

other. Thus each person thinks it describes him or her, when in reality it describes everyone. A measure that gives the same reading for nearly everyone is useless as a research or diagnostic tool. It can, nevertheless, make clients into believers. Reputable scientists and clinicians rely on instruments that have been empirically validated, and even then they exercise reservations about the insights provided by the tests and by their own, even more fallible, clinical judgment (Meehl, 1954, 1965).

Certain tests of personality that have been behaviorally validated are of special interest to social psychologists. We will turn to a description of some of them both to elaborate on the construct and to illustrate some issues in personality measurement and theory.

Sense of Control: The I-E Scale

Table 3.3 contains items from the Internal-External Locus of Control (I-E) Scale. You may want to answer these items before reading about the scale.

Internal-external locus of control involves the notion that people differ in the extent to which they believe they are in command of their lives (Rotter, 1966). At one extreme are those people—*internals*—who believe that all of the good and bad that befalls them is a consequence of their own actions or inactions. By contrast, *externals* see no such relationship.

Some tasks, such as playing the slot machines, offer people no opportunity to exercise control over the outcomes. People high on internal locus of control waste little time on such tasks.

TABLE 3.3
Items from the Internal-External Locus of Control Scale[a]

For each pair of statements, choose the one that you feel is more nearly correct.

1. a. Promotions are earned through hard work and persistence.
   b. Making a lot of money is largely a matter of getting the right breaks.
2. a. Many times the reactions of teachers seem haphazard to me.
   b. In my experience I have noticed that there is usually a direct connection between how hard I study and the grades I get.
3. a. Marriage is largely a gamble.
   b. The number of divorces indicates that more and more people are not trying to make their marriages work.
4. a. It is silly to think that one can really change another person's basic attitudes.
   b. When I am right I can convince others.
5. a. Getting promoted is really a matter of being a little luckier than the next guy.
   b. In our society a man's future earning power is dependent upon his ability.
6. a. If one knows how to deal with people they are really quite easily led.
   b. I have little influence over the way other people behave.
7. a. In my case the grades I make are the results of my own efforts; luck has little or nothing to do with it.
   b. Sometimes I feel that I have little to do with the grades I get.
8. a. It is only wishful thinking to believe that one can really influence what happens in society at large.
   b. People like me can change the course of world affairs if we make ourselves heard.
9. a. A great deal that happens to me is probably a matter of chance.
   b. I am the master of my fate.
10. a. Getting along with people is a skill that must be practiced.
    b. It is almost impossible to figure out how to please some people.

Answers indicating internal locus of control are as follows:

1. *a* 2. *b* 3. *b* 4. *b* 5. *b* 6. *a* 7. *a* 8. *b* 9. *b* 10. *a*

[a] Items are taken from an earlier version of the test and are no longer in use.

Source: J. B. Rotter (1971). External control and internal control. *Psychology Today,* June 1971. Reprinted with permission from *Psychology Today* Magazine. Copyright © 1971, APA.

To them, life is a game of chance. What they do and the consequences that follow are seen as unrelated. Luck has as much to do as anything else with happiness and success. Rotter theorized that differences in locus of control may lead to important differences in how people orient themselves toward others and how they behave in life. It may, for example, explain why some people set high goals for themselves or decide that wearing a seat belt will make a difference if they are involved in a car or plane accident.

Regardless of how theoretically interesting or potentially useful a personality variable sounds, the question to ask is whether it can be measured

A game such as chess affords the player a considerable opportunity to exercise control over the outcome. People who are high on internal locus of control are attracted to these kinds of activities and give them a great deal of time and attention.

reliably and will help predict behavior. The first step is to devise an operational measure of the construct, and typically that is accomplished with the construction of a test, such as the I-E Scale. The first question Rotter answered to his satisfaction was whether the measure was sensitive: Is there a wide range or variety in the scores of different people?

The next question was whether these differences are stable, that is, reliable. **Reliability** is often assessed by administering the test repeatedly to the same people and correlating the sets of scores. For the I-E the test-retest reliability studies yielded coefficients ranging from 0.55 to 0.72 (Rotter, 1966). While this is quite respectable for a personality measure, it falls notably short of perfection.

What has made the I-E construct and Rotter's scale so respectable is their demonstrated ability to predict differences in people's responses to different situations—differences consistent with the theory of locus of control (Lefcourt, 1982; Joe, 1971; Strickland, 1977; Phares, 1976). In other words, the measure has predictive **validity.** Table 3.4 lists some of the diverse types of behavior found to be related to a perception of external locus of control.

TABLE 3.4
A Sampling of Behaviors Related to External Locus of Control

People perceiving external control have been found to

- Attack real-life problems less actively
- Show lower achievement in school
- Participate less in political activity
- Make lower estimates of their own success (even when their actual success is equal to that of internals)
- Smoke more
- Get less exercise
- Be more likely to commit suicide
- Believe more in astrology
- Wear seat belts less often
- Recover more slowly from coronary heart disease

I-E seems to measure a difference among people, a difference that is fairly stable and that has been shown to correlate with a wide array of behaviors predictable by locus of control theory. Particularly with respect to its predictive validity, the I-E construct is an exceptional personality measure.

Recently the locus of control approach has been extended to the medical arena, with the development of the Health Locus of Control Scale (Wallston, Wallston, & DeVellis, 1978; Wallston & Wallston, 1983). People who score at the internal end of the scale believe that their own actions determine whether they get sick, that they can play an active role in their own treatment and recovery, and that chance plays little role in determining their state of health. Internals have been found to seek out health information more than externals, although this particular scale of locus of control apparently does not have the high predictive validity of the original scale (Wallston & Wallston, 1984).

Authoritarianism: The F Scale

Ideas for personality research come from a wide range of sources. The horrors of Nazi Germany prompted a group of social and clinical psychologists at the University of California at Berkeley to carry out a large research program aimed at discovering the psychological basis of facism and prejudice (Adorno et al., 1950).

Beginning with questions about the nature and causes of anti-Semitism, they constructed and administered opinion surveys to approximately 2000 people around the United States. They found that people who were prejudiced against Jews also tended to be prejudiced against other minority groups, such as blacks, Hispanics, foreigners, and Catholics. But the "widening circle of covariation" (Brown, 1965) did not end there. Not only were attitudes toward ethnic groups correlated with each other; they were also correlated with political and economic attitudes. Thus the various attitudes and beliefs did not seem to be isolated from and independent of each other, but to form a coherent syndrome. The next step was to find out why.

Borrowing from psychoanalytic concepts to guide their methods, the Berkeley researchers conducted in-depth interviews and administered projective psychological tests to 80 of the most and the least prejudiced of their survey respondents. The researchers came to believe that the discovered syndrome of attitudes was the product of a pre-fascist (that is, disposed to fascism) personality type, the **authoritarian personality:** prejudiced against minority groups, politically and economically conservative, overconcerned about social status, valuing obedience to authority, and believing in conventional conduct in all spheres of life. This type of person had been raised by parents who were relatively harsh disciplinarians, giving or withdrawing affection in order to control the child's behavior.

This package of findings and ideas about the authoritarian personality was translated into a paper-and-pencil test known as the F Scale. Table 3.5 presents the nine characteristics of which the authoritarian personality was thought to be composed, and lists sample items designed to measure that characteristic. But research has never confirmed that the characteristics are linked or form a structure with any psychological reality. Thus the F scale is best regarded as a complex, undifferentiated measure of authoritarianism (Robinson & Shaver, 1973).

The authoritarian personality research and the fascism personality scale that resulted from it were not carried out as an academic exercise. The researchers' goal was nothing less than to save the world from another Third Reich. If the attitude syndrome exists and is caused by the theorized personality development process, then it ought to be possible both to identify pre-fascists and to try to "treat" them or to prevent their development in the first place. Such efforts may be occurring to some extent through books and programs on how to raise children successfully. The F Scale's primary use today is to help explain more focused behavior patterns, such as the tendency of jurors to react to a case one way rather than another.

Machiavellianism: The Mach IV Scale

Niccolò Machiavelli was a philosopher-adviser to the Prince of Florence in the sixteenth century. Machiavelli's advice, noted for its theme of ruthless manipulation, is recorded in his books *The Prince* and *The Discourses,* in which people are viewed as objects to be manipulated in the pursuit of one's own purposes. Machiavelli's advice on power was unusual in that it did not encourage people to use physical power or force, but rather *psychological* manipulation.

TABLE 3.5
Fascism Scale—Components and Sample Items

1. *Conventionalism.* Rigid adherence to and overemphasis on middle-class values, and overresponsiveness to contemporary external social pressure.
   Sample item: "A person who has bad manners, habits, and breeding can hardly expect to get along with decent people."
2. *Authoritarian Submission.* An exaggerated emotional need to submit to others; an uncritical acceptance of a strong leader who will make decisions.
   Sample item: "Obedience and respect for authority are the most important virtues children should learn."
3. *Authoritarian Aggression.* Favoring condemnation, total rejection, stern discipline, or severe punishment as ways of dealing with people and forms of behavior that deviate from conventional values.
   Sample item: "Sex crimes, such as rape and attacks on children, deserve more than mere imprisonment; such criminals ought to be publicly whipped, or worse."
4. *Anti-Intraception.* Disapproval of a free emotional life, of the intellectual or theoretical, and of the impractical. Anti-intraceptive persons maintain a narrow range of consciousness; realization of their genuine feelings or self-awareness might threaten their adjustment. Hence, they reject feelings, fantasies, and other subjective or "tender-minded" phenomena.
   Sample item: "When a person has a problem or worry, it is best for him or her not to think about it, but to keep busy with more cheerful things."
5. *Superstition and Stereotypy. Superstition* implies a tendency to shift responsibility from within the individual onto outside forces beyond one's control, particularly to mystical determinants. *Stereotypy* is the tendency to think in rigid, oversimplified categories, in unambiguous terms of black and white, particularly in the realm of psychological or social matters.
   Sample item: "Although many people may scoff, it may yet be shown that astrology can explain a lot of things."
6. *Power and Toughness.* The aligning of oneself with power figures, thus gratifying one's need both to have power and to submit to power. There is a denial of personal weakness.
   Sample item: "What this country needs is fewer laws and agencies, and more courageous, tireless, devoted leaders whom the people can put their faith in."
7. *Destructiveness and Cynicism.* Rationalized aggression; for example, cynicism permits the authoritarian person to be aggressive because "everybody is doing it." The generalized hostility and vilification of the human by highly authoritarian persons permits them to justify their own aggressiveness.
   Sample item: "Human nature being what it is, there will always be war and conflict."
8. *Projectivity.* The disposition to believe that wild and dangerous things go on in the world. In the authoritarian personality, the undesirable impulses that cannot be admitted by the conscious ego tend to be projected onto minority groups and other vulnerable objects.
   Sample item: "The sexual orgies of the old Greeks and Romans are kid stuff compared to some of the goings-on in this country today, even in circles where people might least expect it."
9. *Sex.* Exaggerated concern with sexual goings-on, and punitiveness toward violators of sex mores.
   Sample item: "Homosexuality is a particularly rotten form of delinquency and ought to be severely punished."

Source: Adapted from L. S. Wrightsman & K. Deaux (1984). *Social psychology in the '80's* (4th ed.). Monterey, CA: Brooks/Cole. Copyright © 1984, 1981, 1977, 1972 by Wadsworth, Inc. Reprinted by permission of Brooks/Cole Publishing Company, Pacific Grove, CA.

TABLE 3.6
Items from the Mach IV Scale

Each of the following statements represents a commonly held opinion. Indicate the extent to which you agree or disagree.

If you strongly agree, write +3	If you disagree slightly, write −1
If you agree somewhat, write +2	If you disagree somewhat, write −2
If you agree slightly, write +1	If you disagree strongly, write −3

1. Never tell anyone the real reason you did something unless it is useful to do so.
2. The best way to handle people is tell them what they want to hear.
3. One should take action only when sure it is morally right.
4. Most people are basically good and kind.
5. It is safest to assume that all people have a vicious streak and it will come out when they are given a chance.
6. Honesty is the best policy in all cases.
7. There is no excuse for lying to someone else.
8. Generally speaking, men won't work hard unless they're forced to do so.
9. All in all, it is better to be humble and honest than to be important and dishonest.
10. When you ask someone to do something for you, it is best to give the real reasons for wanting it rather than giving reasons which carry more weight.

Items 3, 4, 6, 7, and 9 are worded to indicate low Machiavellianism. Add your score on these, reverse the sign, and combine that with your total score for items 1, 2, 5, 8, and 10. The higher the score the more Machiavellian you are.

Source: R. Christie and F. L. Geis (1970). *Studies in Machiavellianism.* New York: Academic Press.

Richard Christie and his associates (Christie & Geis, 1970) developed a scale called the Mach IV to measure a possible personality trait of **Machiavellianism,** characterized by a willingness to manipulate other people and skill at doing so. As you can see in Table 3.6, which contains some sample items, the scale consists of Machiavellian statements to which people are asked to indicate their agreement or disagreement. People who score high, Christie expected, would be more willing and more able to manipulate other people. While authoritarians tend to react to others in moralistic terms ("people are no damn good but they should be"), Machiavellians react to people in opportunistic terms ("people are no damn good, and let's see how I can use them"). The F Scale and the Mach IV Scale do not correlate with each other.

Like the I-E Scale, the Mach IV is a personality test that has been validated by actual behavior. Christie and others (e. g., Christie & Geis, 1970) have set up experimental situations where high and low "Machs" were asked to perform tasks that involved the manipulation of others or where they were pitted directly against each other in contests where manipulation would lead to victory. The prediction that high Machs would show more interpersonal manipulation (lying, cheating, bluffing, distracting) has not been confirmed in all studies, but, particularly where a premium is placed on face-to-face contact and the opportunity for improvisation, the high Machs typically win more, persuade others more, or otherwise outmaneuver low Machs (Robinson & Shaver, 1973). Consistent with this behavior, high Machs endorse ethical positions that are less idealistic and more realistic (Leary, Knight, & Barnes, 1986).

THEORIES ABOUT PERSONALITY THEORIES

In the preceding section we discussed tests that measure personality, some more formal than others. But such measures are just stabs in the dark without theories to hold them together. This section will deal with personality theory in both its more traditional and its modern approaches.

The goal of traditional personality theory was to discover the person-centered dimensions that underlie behavior. It was believed that once these were identified, people could be described accurately and their behavior could be understood, predicted, and possibly even changed. That effort, however, has met with only mixed success. Because of the inability of personality theory to predict the behavior of all of the people all of the time, the fields of personality and social psychology have moved closer together. And by this merger we have learned more about the ways in which complex social behavior can be truly understood by combining notions of personality *and* situation.

Problems of Classical Personality Theory

The trouble with global notions about personality is that they have not been able to predict behavior with very much success. As noted by Rotter, "the very best techniques we have are of doubtful validity for predicting the specific behavior of any person in a particular situation" (Rotter, 1954, p. 334). Let us first discuss some of the shortcomings of the traditional ideas about personality, and then look at some of the solutions being considered to improve it.

Accounting for the Variance in Behavior Like any single factor in a complex equation, the predictive power of personality measures rarely accounts for more than a fraction of the variance in people's behavior. For instance, Rotter's I-E Scale, by far one of the best-validated personality measures, accounts for no more than about 15 percent of the variance in any area of behavior. Walter Mischel, in a landmark book, *Personality and Assessment* (1968), reviewed a wide array of research on personality and concluded that the correlation between behavior predicted by personality variables and actual behavior usually did not exceed 0.30, or less than 10 percent of the variance (Hunt, 1965).

Consistency Across Situations A central feature of all traditional personality constructs is the assumption that personality variables are stable characteristics that guide a person's behavior in different situations. But the less similar situations across which behavior is measured are, the less likely it is that these personality measures will predict the behavior (Allport, 1966). As Mischel has noted, "Even seemingly trivial situational differences can reduce correlations to zero" (Mischel, 1968, p. 177). The single best predictor of behavior in a situation is not personality but the person's past behavior in the same kind of situation.

Person Versus Situation In studying many of the topics mentioned in this book—altruism, obedience, aggression, conformity, and so on—researchers administered personality tests that had been expected to account for differences in observed behavior. For example, Latané and Darley (1970) administered five different personality tests (among them the F Scale and the Mach IV Scale) to people who participated in their experiments on whether people help in an emergency. None of the scales was able to predict clearly who would and who would not help. By contrast, several situational variables exerted substantial influences on how quickly people helped. Another experiment, by Darley and Batson (1973), exemplified the power of situational variables: whether people stopped to help a sick and moaning person sprawled along a campus sidewalk was most potently determined by how much of a hurry they were in to get to an appointment (see Chapter 9 for more on this research).

Early critics of authoritarian personality research (Hyman & Sheatsley, 1954; Christie, 1954; Christie & Jahoda, 1954) pointed out that an alternative situational explanation existed for the "syndrome" of intercorrelated attitudes held by authoritarians. Instead of being the manifestation of an underlying personality trait, they said, the same pattern of attitudes could be the product of group norms. In research that compared the various combinations of attitudes from sample to sample, they found differences among demographic groups. These differences imply that authoritarian behavior could be accounted for by the influence of situational factors (Prothro, 1952; Hartley, 1957; Christie & Garcia, 1951; Brown, 1965).

Dramatic changes in behavior are not easily accounted for by traditional personality theory. Indeed, since consistency is a fundamental tenet of traditional personality theory, dramatic changes in behavior are seen as aberrations. But when circumstances change dramatically, behavior

IN THE NEWS

FUGITIVE'S OHIO FRIENDS SAY HE WAS RELIABLE, WORKAHOLIC

Sandusky, Ohio—He is only 27 years old, but already he has lived two lives.

He lived one life in the Boston neighborhoods of Hyde Park and Roslindale, where he grew up as Kenneth Ray Wightman and where a legend grew around his criminal skills. He lived the other life in this gray industrial city on the shores of Lake Erie where, for the past three years, he has gone by the alias of Ray Dilly.

In Massachusetts—where he has been one of the most wanted criminals of the decade, according to State and Boston Police—his life was marked by convictions on a variety of crimes from car theft to the attempted murder of two Boston Police detectives. By the age of 21, he had made 38 court appearances, gained a reputation as an expert driver, master of disguise and escape artist.

In Sandusky, he was known as a superb mechanic and auto body man, reliable friend, workaholic.

But nine days ago, after he had spent four years and three months as a fugitive, nearly 50 law enforcement officers, led by the FBI, descended upon Wightman in his Sandusky apartment. Deborah Cole, Wightman's girlfriend of three years, was lying next to him in bed at 11:05 P.M. when they heard the door of his apartment being broken down. Wightman knew instantly what was happening. He quickly rolled over to her, kissed her and said, "Goodbye, babe."

Lloyd Bodi, a Sandusky police officer, is typical of the people who knew Wightman in Ohio.

"We had a good friendship going," Bodi says. "My feelings haven't changed as far as Ray Dilly is concerned. This other guy—this Kenneth Wightman—I have no idea who that guy is. None whatsoever."

One side of the story—the story of Wightman's life before he went to Sandusky—is a story of trouble and crime.

He started out stealing cars, but his crimes escalated and he was convicted of more serious offenses and confined in Department of Youth Services facilities. At various times, he escaped from three different jails.

But the other side of the story has nothing to do with guns or crimes or police or

usually does, too. Consider the man described in the In the News box. What can seem to be stable personalities may be a consequence of stable life situations. And changed personalities may reflect changed life situations.

When all is said and done, it turns out that the proponents of both personality and situational variables have been guilty of making greater claims for their positions than their data justify. On some occasions the situation overwhelms personality factors, and on others the opposite is true. In fact, careful overviews of a range of studies (Sarason, Smith, & Diener, 1975; Funder & Ozer, 1983) lead us to conclude that the amount of variability in social behavior accounted for by situational variables is somewhat greater overall than that accounted for by personality—but the margin of difference is not great.

prisons. It is the story of Kenny Wightman as Ray Dilly—the man Cole and the others here knew so well.

During an interview at her Sandusky home, Cole offers a photograph taken on Easter Sunday 1981, showing Wightman—with her youngest son on his lap—having dinner at her parents' home in Sandusky. She cries and talks about the gifts he gave to her and the children.

Many of Wightman's friends in Sandusky said he often worked seven-day weeks and 14-hour days and that the quality of his work was excellent.

Jack Butts was Wightman's big brother–father figure as well as his closest friend in Sandusky. Butts sat in his apartment, which is on the same floor in the same house as Wightman's, and talked emotionally about his friend one night last week.

He is bewildered by Wightman's past, but more than that, he is anguished by it.

Fran Voltz says she has seen people "sit and cry over this. Men included."

Robert Krueger, 62, Cole's father, says if he was to describe the man he knew as Ray Dilly to a stranger he would say Dilly was "kind-hearted, very enjoyable to be around . . . if you needed help he'd give it to you. He's an ideal guy that you'd want for a son-in-law."

"I'm just numb about the whole thing," says Bodi. "I don't know what happened. All I ever knew him to be was exactly what he was around here. . . . It's too bad what happened in his past—nobody can change that—but he was a great guy around here."

Wightman called Butts from jail late last week.

"He told me the years he spent here," Butts says, "were the happiest years of his life."

And there could be more happy years ahead, says Fran Voltz.

"I didn't know Ken Wightman," she said. "But I did know Ray Dilly, and our door will always be open to him. If he serves 20 years and wants to come back, our door is open."

Source: Charles Kenney, in *Sunday Boston Globe,* August 14, 1983, p. 1.

New Directions in Personality

For the past decade or so, personality and social psychologists have grappled with solutions to the shortcomings of the traditional approaches to personality. The immovable mass of the intuitively obvious—that *something* about people makes their behavior coherent, if not consistent; that they have "personalities"—has come into collision with the irresistible force of data showing that conventional concepts of personality just do not explain or predict as well as they should.

The most interesting approaches to resolving the dilemma brought on by this collision of intuition with evidence have sprung from questioning some of the fundamental assumptions of traditional personality theory. Solutions based on faulty assumptions are not likely to work. Some of the new approaches incorporate social psychological concepts, particularly that of explaining behavior by examining persons-in-situations, as discussed in Chapter 1. This "situational revolution" in personality theory has begun to bring personality and social psychology closer together (Byrne & Kelly, 1981; Magnusson & Endler, 1977; Mischel, 1976). Let us examine some of these new approaches.

The Idiographic Approach Each of the traditional theories of personality reflects a set of **nomothetic** assumptions. A nomothetic approach leads us to believe that the important underlying processes or structures of personality are the same for everyone (just as we all have the same bodily organs and systems); that people vary according to where they fall along particular dimensions of traits; and that these traits or structures co-vary in coherent and predictable ways. These assumptions give researchers marching orders to find universal underlying dimensions—they must be out there somewhere.

A major alternative to nomothetic personality theories is the **idiographic approach.** According to this approach, people do have consistent patterns of responding, but their patterns are highly individualized. Rather than a universal grid of dimensions, each person is capable of learning a unique set of responses to the various situations encountered in the world. Only by knowing a person's unique response patterns to a wide spectrum of situations can accurate predictions be made. This is a far more complicated, time-consuming, and expensive approach to predicting behavior, but it has proved to be more useful than mass personality testing or the psychiatric interview.

The idiographic approach emphasizes learned responses to different situations, responses that may vary from individual to individual and that need not necessarily show any underlying logic or organization. Whatever underlying "themes" might exist are not generalizable across individuals. For example, one person may be highly achievement-oriented in academic endeavors but not in sports. Another person may be highly achievement-oriented in business but not in athletics or academics. Achievement is a characteristic that differentiates one person from another, but there is not an "achievement" trait that is reflected throughout these persons' lives. The psychological learning processes are probably the same for both people, but how they came to have a particular pattern of achievement behavior is a riddle more likely to be answered by tracing their respective histories than by looking to a theory of universal traits or motives.

The best-known idiographic study aimed at improving the prediction of behavior is Bem and Allen's "On Predicting Some of the People Some of the Time" (1974). They reasoned that if people have unique patterns and if stimuli have unique meanings, then any attempt to measure a hypothesized trait will reflect the test maker's or observer's definition of the trait. Thus low trait-behavior correlations in part reflect this highly plastic, largely negotiable meaning of behavior and personality.

For example, you may think one manifestation of friendliness would be to strike up a conversation with a salesperson, but the individual being measured may not agree. Bem and Allen designed a procedure for measuring people's "friendliness" and "conscientiousness" not only by asking people to fill out a personality test of items sampling behavior reflecting these concepts, but also by indicating how consistently they engaged in the various behaviors being sampled. People were divided into those whose traits for friendliness and conscientiousness were either consistent or inconsistent with the measure used, and those who fluctuated. The measured traits were then correlated with ratings of the individuals made by their peers and their parents as well as with direct measurements of certain friendly behaviors via observation.

Using these tests in the traditional way, the prediction of behavior from the measured trait produced the customarily low accuracy. But when consistency with the particular definition of the measured trait was taken into account, the accuracy of prediction became significantly higher for the consistent group and lower for the nonconsistent group. Thus this particular technique informed by idiographic assumptions was able to show improved prediction and more cross-situational consistency.

Several researchers have tried to improve upon Bem and Allen's study. Kenrick and Stringfield (1980) asked people to complete a standardized personality inventory and to indicate which dimensions they thought represented their most consistent characteristics. The correlations between ratings made by the self and by others on consistent dimensions did show higher cross-situational consistencies than was the case for people's less consistent characteristics. They and other researchers suggest that this technique combines the best of both the nomothetic and the idiographic approaches (Tellegen, Kamp, & Watson, 1982).

Taking Situations into Account The idiographic approach implies that the situation in which the behavior will take place is as important to making accurate predictions of the behavior as is knowing the response patterns that make up the personality. Thus another major improvement in personality theories and the measuring instruments that derive from them comes from paying attention to the social environment of the person.

We often talk about behavior and personality as though they exist in a vacuum or could be discussed "in general," but every behavior a person exhibits is within a certain context. You walk into a room in a particular place for a particular purpose, and if other people are present, they bear some particular relationship to you. Your behavior as predicted by personality traits alone could easily be influenced by the context in which the behavior takes place. A visit to the home of the university president will call forth different feelings and behavior from you than would a visit to your best friend's apartment.

Fredericksen (1972) has pointed out that in order to predict individual behavior from one situation to another, it is necessary to develop a taxonomy of situations and to tie the person's characteristics to the situation's characteristics. The same effort that has gone into trying to measure and categorize persons will need to go into describing situations. And the two taxonomies will need to connect (Stagner, 1976; Magnusson, 1974; Argyle, Furnham, & Graham, 1981).

Interactionism In Chapter 1 we discussed the perspective of social psychology as including a sensitivity to the characteristics of both persons and situations in trying to explain behavior. **Interactionism** turns that general perspective into a more detailed approach to understanding personality.

Let us begin to understand the interactionist approach by comparing it to the alternatives we have touched upon already. Figure 3.2 presents a graphic comparison of four different approaches to the study of personality. Approach 1 reflects the traditional assumption that all variation in behavior is due to characteristics of the person, and that different traits (in this case, assertiveness) of different people (P_1, P_2, P_3) will manifest themselves similarly across all kinds of situations.

Just as the first approach ignores situations, Approach 2 ignores individual differences among persons; it focuses purely on situations. A somewhat more sophisticated approach is the third, which sees person characteristics as creating dispositions, or tendencies, which will manifest themselves somewhat differently across situations. But the rank ordering of persons remains consistent: P_3's assertiveness may vary greatly across situations, but P_3 is always the most assertive while P_1 is always the least assertive.

The fourth approach, the interaction approach, sees behavior as the joint product of person characteristics and situational variables. Even saying the terms separately creates a misleading impression, because in this approach they are inseparably connected. As Figure 3.2 shows, any attempt to predict level of assertiveness using situations alone or persons alone will be erroneous. Accuracy requires knowing how different people react to different situations, which the interaction approach takes into account. P_1 is the most assertive person in Situation 1, but the least assertive in Situation 3. Given the complexity of even this simple example, you can understand the appeal of the traditional Approach 1. Psychologists as well as others prefer simple solutions—if they work.

Let us take a careful look at one illustration of the interactionist approach. Recall the concept of locus of control. We might ask how internals and externals differ in handling a decision task. Does one kind of person take more time to make a decision, expect to achieve a higher level of success, or pay more attention to the task at hand? Several studies have shown that the answers depend upon the kind of task being confronted (Rotter & Mulry, 1965; Lefcourt, Lewis, & Silverman, 1968).

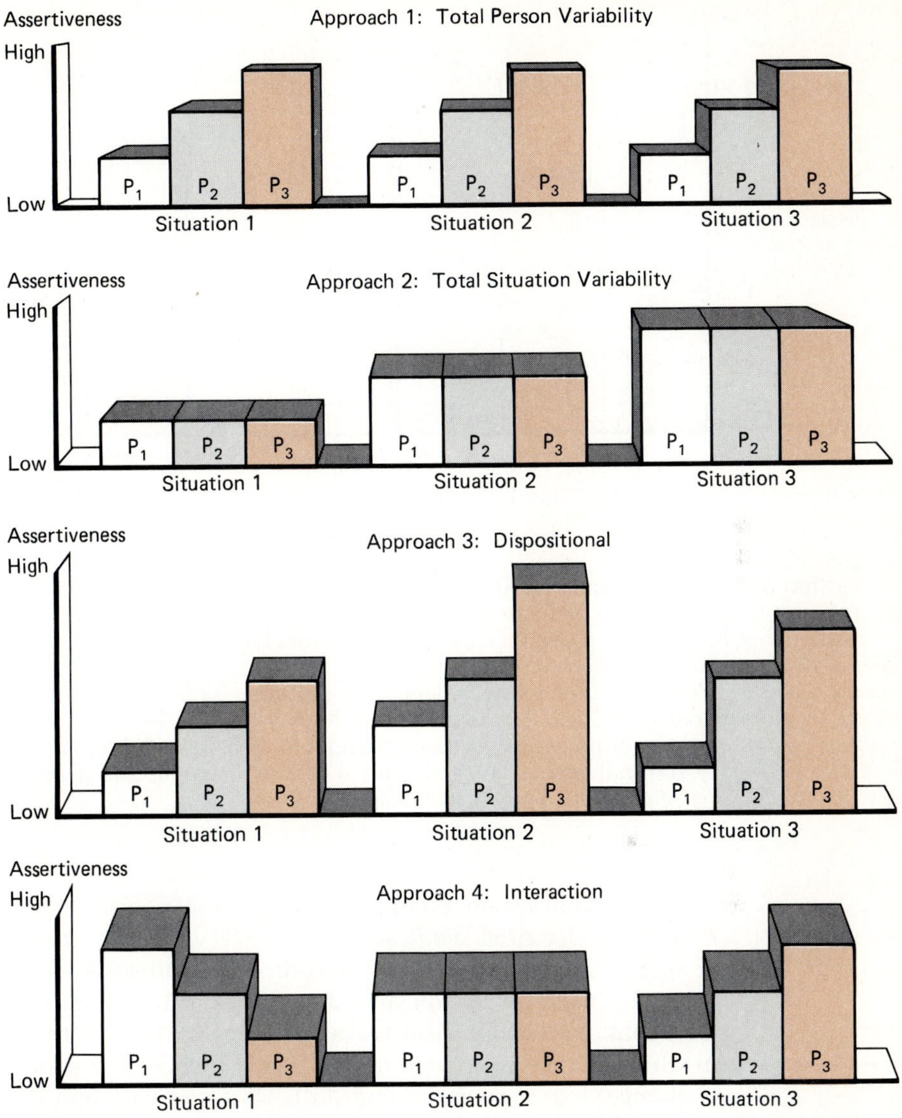

FIGURE 3.2

Approaches to the Study of Personality Approach 1 assumes that personality accounts for all of the differences in behavior and that situations have no effect. Approach 2 assumes that personalities do not matter and that situations account for all of the differences in behavior. Approach 3 assumes that situations moderate the level of behavior but that personality ensures that in any situation people will perform consistently. Approach 4 assumes that situational and personality influences interact in powerful ways, so that a person could be very assertive in one situation and hardly assertive at all in another. *Source:* M. Argyle and B. R. Little (1972). Do personality traits apply to social behavior? *Journal of the Theory of Social Behavior, 2,* 1–35.

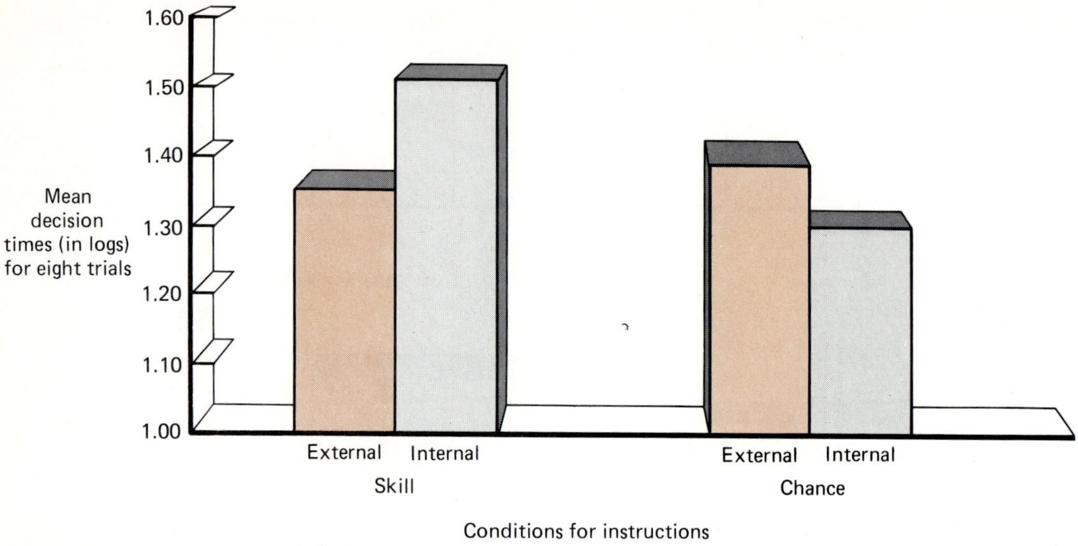

FIGURE 3.3
Interaction of Personality and Situation Who takes longer to make decisions in games, people who are high on locus of control or people who are low? These data show that it depends on whether the task is one of chance or of skill. People who score high on internal locus of control take more time (compared to people who score low) when the game is defined as requiring skill, and less time when the game is one of chance. People who score low on internal locus of control do not adjust as dramatically to the situation. *Source:* J. B. Rotter & R. C. Mulry (1965). Internal versus external control of reinforcement and decision time. *Journal of Personality and Social Psychology, 2,* 598–604.

As you can see in Figure 3.3, for example, internals generally spend more time deciding what actions to take when making a choice on tests of skill. The most interesting and dramatic effect is the interaction—the joint effect of the person and the situation. Internals spend much more time making decisions on tasks involving skill than they spend on tasks in which chance is important. Externals spend more time pondering tasks of chance than tasks requiring skill. Thus accurate predictions about how much time a person would spend making decisions on a task, attending to it, and being distracted from it would require taking both the kind of person and the kind of situation (or task) simultaneously into account.

Ekehammar (1974) has suggested that throughout much of its history, psychology has been aware of and concerned about the person-situation issue and that the recent flowering of interactionism is really due to methodological and statistical advances (especially computers) that have made person-situation research feasible. (See also Alker, 1977; Cronbach, 1975.) Improvements in the conceptual and technical ability to take interaction effects into account have enlarged our ability to explain, predict, and change behavior.

APPLICATION
PERSONALITY AND SOCIAL ENVIRONMENT IN THE CLASSROOM

Who does better in school—students who are independent ("I like to structure tasks for myself") or those who are conformant ("I like to meet requirements set for me by others")? And what kind of class structure results in more student learning and satisfaction—one in which the students' preferences for activities are the order of the day, or one in which the instructor dominates?

The interactionist approach to personalities and situations would lead us to suppose that the answer to each of these questions depends on the answer to the other. That is, students with more independent personalities will do better in classes that allow for more student autonomy, and students with more subordinate and conforming personalities will do better when the instructor controls the class's structure and activities.

To test this assumption, Domino, (1968, 1971) first gave college students the California Personality Inventory, a general purpose personality screening test. Scores on two subscales indicated which students tended toward independence and which toward conformance. Domino assigned half the independent students to a class in which student independence and autonomy would be encouraged, and half to a class in which the instructor would set the tasks. Similarly, half the conforming students were assigned to an independent and half to a conforming class. Domino could then compare student performance and satisfaction in the four different kinds of classes. The results are given in Table 3.7. Notice that when student personalities and the social environment of the class matched (independent student in independent class; conforming student in conforming class), the students' course grades and satisfaction ratings were at their highest.

We can see in this example how the notion of interactive relationships between personality differences and situational variables could be applied to mak-

TABLE 3.7
Performance and Satisfaction in College Classes as a Function of Student Personality and Classroom Social Environment

Student Pattern	Classroom Style	Course Grade[a]	Student Satisfaction
Independent	Independence	100	100
	Conformity	83	88
Conforming	Independence	66	82
	Conformity	89	94

[a] The value of 100 was assigned to the average score of the highest ranking group, and other averages were scaled proportionately. Likewise, two satisfaction measures have been pooled.

Source: G. Domino (1971). Interactive effects of achievement orientation and teaching style on academic achievement. *Journal of Educational Psychology, 62,* 427–431.

ing improvements in education. The concept raises the possibility of improving other areas of human activity as well, such as fitting jobs, cities, and homes to people.

IMPLICATIONS FOR PREDICTING AND CHANGING BEHAVIOR

New understanding leads to new possibilities. Contemporary understanding of the self and personality, and the sometimes counterintuitive evidence on which those views are based, carry implications for our conception of human behavior and for the possibility of changing it.

The Image of Human Nature

The contemporary image implied by the findings we have reviewed is one of human beings as far more flexible and adaptable than had been previously thought. Walter Mischel, one of the leading personality theorists, has stated:

> The image is one of the human being as an active, aware problem solver, capable of profiting from an enormous range of experience and cognitive capacities, possessed of great potential for good or ill, actively constructing his or her psychological world, interpreting and processing information in potentially creative ways, influencing the world but also being influenced by it lawfully—even if the laws are difficult to discover and hard to generalize. . . . It is an image that highlights the shortcomings of all simplistic theories that view behavior as the exclusive result of any narrow set of determinants, whether these are habits, traits, drives, constructs, instincts, genes, or reinforcers. [Mischel, 1976, p. 506]

This perspective is compatible with theories of human beings as constant observers and learners, always changing, adapting to new circumstances and settings. Social learning theory and cognitive theories have thus entered the marketplace of personality theorizing with considerable vigor, with consequences for both the theoretical value and the practical utility of personality theories as well as for the personality measures that were developed based on earlier assumptions.

The Uses of Personality Tests

The initial hope of developing personality tests that would allow quick and powerful predictions of human behavior has evaporated. We cannot use personality to predict who will become a president and who a presidential assassin; who will make an ideal spouse for you; or who will benefit from a particular kind of psychotherapy. And it is unlikely that through the use of conventional personality tests alone we ever will be able to make such predictions. Instead, personality tests should be seen as rough categorizations of people, and predictions based on them should

This person is taking the Minnesota Multiphasic Personality Inventory, usually referred to as the MMPI. Each item is a statement, and the test taker indicates either that it fits or that it does not. The answers can be scored by machine and then summed to create a profile of scores for each person.

be seen as highly tentative. Even tests that predict the behavior of groups of people with reasonable accuracy are not capable of predicting well the behavior of any single individual. The nature of the setting and circumstances in which the behavior occurs can render the prediction wrong. Clinicians using such tests, for example, have to be skeptical of their own predictions and might try to observe the person in the settings in which the predicted behavior will take place. (Intuitive clinical judgments, having less reliability and validity, must be regarded with even greater tentativeness.)

Ironically, while personality tests and theories were designed to provide general readings of broad, underlying traits, what they usually do best is just the opposite. That is, some tests are able to make reasonably accurate predictions for behavior in limited circumstances. For example, Elms and Milgram (1966) tried to predict individual differences in the obedience of people called upon to deliver electric shocks to others (see Chapter 10 for more detail). Some of the most widely used global personality measures were incapable of distinguishing people who were highly obedient from those who were not. Only the F Scale—which, after all, is partly a test of respect for authority—predicted differences in obedience. But for behavior in other kinds of situations, the F Scale does not predict well. Thus, we must take heed of the limits of the range of application of any personality measure.

The Potential for Change

Many people have a concern for the possibilities for change in their own personalities. If much of one's personality is set and fixed at an early age or, indeed, at the time of conception, then change is difficult at best. If, however, change is a realistic possibility, then the question becomes one of how to bring it about.

We have already begun to doubt theories that see human personality as a fixed quality which manifests itself in everything a person does. We have seen considerable possibilities for change across situations and roles. But we have also seen that unique individual patterns (the idiographic approach) do have a consistency, a coherence. The question is whether, over time, people can alter those patterns of behavior, that is, "change their personalities." Studies of personality consistency over many years have found enough stability to give a personality theorist hope, and enough change to give the rest of us some hope (Kagan & Moss, 1962; Block, 1977; Rubin, 1981).

The reason for both change and the failure to change may be found in the pattern of responses people learn in particular settings and roles. Any given behavior style you engage in becomes the "you" that people know. Their image of your personality, of who you are, is more set than your behavior is. Your behavior style fits in with their expectations of you and with the social patterns that you are a part of—you are ensnared in a social web. What happens when you try purposefully to change your behavior? People are likely to object, tease, question, or otherwise nudge you back to your "old self." Merely having your hair cut or coming to school dressed differently can evoke questions. Try changing your behavior in more extreme ways and see how your friends or family react.

Thus the people with whom we interact shape and maintain our behavior in fairly constant ways. And each of us is a part of the "situation" that sets the conditions for the behavior of people we know. We tend to keep each other's behavior stable. Gormley (1983) found that although people's behavior could not be predicted well by personality measures, their choice of settings could be. This may reflect our knowledge that the easiest way to be the kind of person we want to be is to select situations that teach, encourage, or require that kind of behavior.

This suggests, then, that the most effective way to bring about change is not only to practice new behavior but to do so among new friends, in a new city, at a new job. The more a new setting and role permit new patterns to be practiced, the easier it will be to change, and the social situation and the people in it will learn to enforce and reinforce the new behavior. Most people cannot exercise such control over where they live and work, but we can try to exploit opportunities for changed behavior to be tolerated or even supported by those around us. Are there times when "personality" change is more likely to be seen as appropriate by those who form our immediate social world? Major changes in status (such as acquiring a new job), gains (new baby), or losses (death of a loved one) may be such times. New Year's resolutions are a socially acceptable avenue for change. Changes attributable to such occasions might not only be seen as acceptable but may even be reinforced by your network of friends.

In sum, our ability to change our personalities is constrained by our inability to change the external dynamics as much as the internal dynamics in our lives. The more control we can gain over the circumstances in which we live, the more control we gain over ourselves.

Let us return to George Rivers. Can he change from the competitive, time-urgent, hostile Type A personality that he is toward the less driven Type B that he would like to become? A simple personality approach has not been helpful in identifying or explaining the differences between the Type A and Type B patterns (Dembroski & MacDougall, 1982; Mordkoff & Parsons, 1968). Some researchers who recognize the Type A problems as a person-situation interaction, however, have adopted an explicitly interactionist approach to understanding and dealing with it (Chemers et al., 1985; Glass, Contrada, & Snow, 1980; Rosenman & Friedman, 1974).

They have asked, first, How does the Type A pattern work and how does it lead to the heightened likelihood of a coronary? Research indicates that such a pattern emerges in susceptible people (Glass et al., 1980) who are faced with situations they perceive as not being under their control, especially situations involving a competitive challenge (Scherwitz, Burta, & Leventhal, 1978). The resulting stress can apparently lead to coronary heart disease through elevated blood pressure, platelet aggregation (leading to blood clots), cardiac arrhythmia, and other physiological mechanisms. People who respond to these competitive or uncontrollable situations with the Type B pattern apparently do not suffer the consequent cardiac damage.

This research implies that two kinds of psychological-situational changes could reduce the chance of coronary heart disease. One is for susceptible people to stay out of situations that elicit Type A responses from them—that is, one way to "change" George from a Type A is to move him to a job situation that does not bring out the Type A pattern in him. For example, the particular atmosphere and demands of George's position in the corporate world might arouse his Type A responses. A different set of responsibilities in a different department or company, or even a different performance evaluation system, might permit George to respond differently (Strube, Berry, & Moergen, 1985). The jump from Wall Street stockbroker to Vermont furniture maker will not be lost on one's nervous system.

If a person prefers not to move to a safer situation, the second line of attack is to try to change the Type A pattern itself. Many methods currently are being tried (Glass et al., 1980; Dembroski & MacDougall, 1982), such as those in the sampling that follows.

1. Improve work efficiency and time management, thereby giving a person more actual control over the ability to get work done. These are learnable skills which, once adopted, may reduce the need for Type A responses.
2. Change the perception that a situation is uncontrollable. This may be

done through psychotherapy, through greater democratization of the workplace, or by allowing workers to select the time, place, or order of the tasks they face.

3. Reduce stressful responses to the situation and to the Type A responses through development of insight, or anxiety management through behavior modification. Both of these techniques have been found to reduce serum cholesterol, although the insight therapy patients later showed a pronounced return to earlier levels (Roskies, 1979; Roskies et al., 1986).
4. Increase the frequency of Type B responses and decrease the Type A responses. This has been done with simple skills training and with behavior modification, wherein Type A responses are displaced by Type B responses which are reinforced (Roskies & Avard, 1982; Glass et al., 1980). Rosenman and Friedman (1977) suggest that behavior changes can be increased by helping the person gain insight into the widespread effects of Type A—helping George understand just what he is doing, and what that is doing to him.

The diversity of approaches to change reflect the early stage of development of such intervention techniques. Over time, they will be evaluated empirically, and the most effective will become more widely used and refined. But nearly all of the approaches to helping Type A's like George reflect the growing appreciation for the interactive nature of selves and situations, and for how that expands both the options for intervention and the likelihood of success.

SUMMARY

1. Research on the self is concerned with how a person conceives of and reacts to himself or herself. Personality research usually takes the perspective of an outside observer of individual differences among people.
2. Social and personality psychology complement one another. Social psychology is primarily concerned with how all people respond to particular environmental situations. Personality psychology is concerned with how different people respond to the same situations.
3. The self is regarded as unique and continuous, a perception that may be due more to the characteristics of the observer than of the observed.
4. Early formulations of the notion of self included the concept of a social self as the view of oneself seen through the reflected appraisal of others, the "looking-glass self." Modern outgrowths of the earlier ideas about the self include the self-space, that is, what cognitions a person draws on in describing the self. Social comparison is concerned with how we use others as bases for making assessments of ourselves.
5. The self has been compared to a scientific theorist who forms concep-

tions of the self based on observations of behavior. Greenwald likens the self to a historian for a totalitarian government, because of its tendencies to distort and change the "facts" for its own benefit.

6. Manipulating cognitions about the self affects behavior. For example, turning attention to the self (objective self-awareness) produces extreme reactions. Perceptions of self-efficacy affect the ability to transform potential into successful action.
7. People vary in the degree to which they self-monitor their environments and the responses of others to their behavior. High self-monitors vary their behavior more in response to the circumstances in which they find themselves. Self-presentation, or impression management, refers to the ability and tendency of people to manipulate the impressions they make on others in order to create or to preserve certain attributions others make about them.
8. The search for a single "true self" may be based on an erroneous assumption. We behave differently at different times and in different situations, and this may reflect the existence of multiple selves.
9. Personality measurement seeks to construct instruments that are reliable and valid. A reliable test is one that produces consistent measurements. A valid test is one that measures what it claims to measure.
10. The Internal-External Locus of Control Scale distinguishes between people who believe that consequences are contingent upon their own behavior and attributes (internals), and those who see life as a game of chance (externals).
11. The F Scale measures the authoritarian personality, a syndrome of ethnocentric attitudes, political and economic conservatism, and excessive concern with social status, obedience, and conventionality.
12. People who are high in Machiavellianism are more successful in situations involving face-to-face contact and the opportunity to manipulate other people.
13. Empirical research on personality has raised questions about classical personality theory and its assumptions. For instance, personality variables have been found to account for less of the variance in people's behavior than had been accepted. In addition, there is much inconsistency across situations, and situational variables often predict behavior better than personality does.
14. These problems in traditional approaches have led to new directions in personality theory and measurement that make more use of the idiographic approach, take situation into account, and show more concern with interactionism.
15. These new findings and strategies have new implications for successful behavior prediction and change. They create an image of humans as flexible and adaptable. In addition, they suggest that change can be enhanced by changing a person's circumstances, not just trying to change personality.

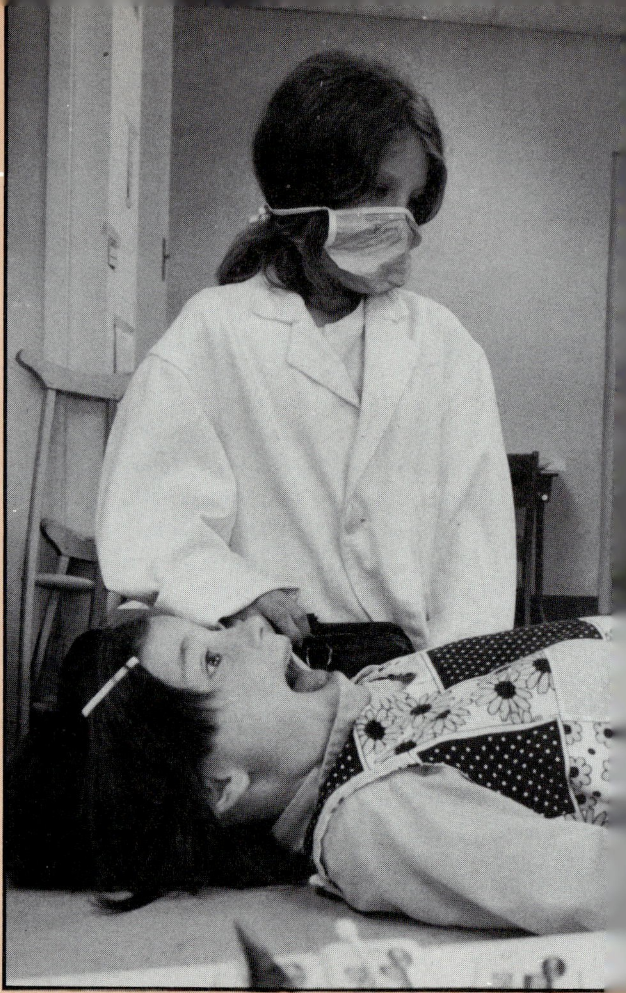

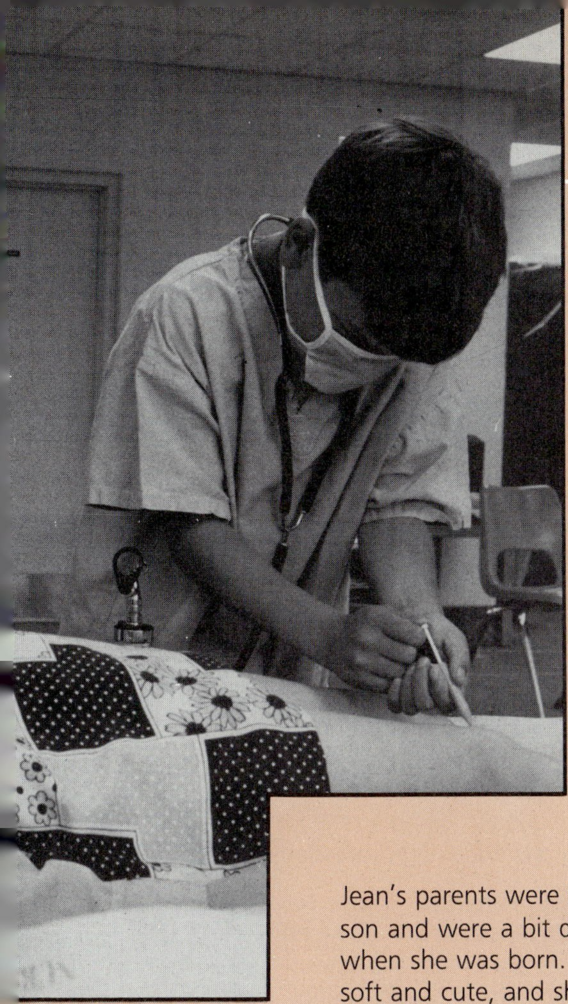

CHAPTER 4
Socialization and Social Roles

Jean's parents were hoping for a son and were a bit disappointed when she was born. She was soft and cute, and she loved it when her mother dressed her up and called her Sugar. As she grew up she got lots of dolls to play with and spent most of her time indoors playing house.

At school Jean was a good reader and speller, and her teacher always praised her for being so neat and polite. In her science books she saw many pictures of famous men who had done important things, so she decided quite early that she could not be like them and wanted to be a teacher when she grew up. By the fourth grade she was as bright as anyone else in the class, but she

Gene's parents were hoping for a son and were quite pleased when he was born. He was strong and sturdy, and he loved it when his father tossed him up and called him Tiger. As he grew up he got lots of blocks to play with and spent most of his time outdoors playing ball.

At school Gene was a good reader and speller, and his teacher always praised him for being so accurate and smart. In his science books he saw many pictures of famous men who had done important things, and he decided quite early that he could be like them and wanted to be an engineer when he grew up. By the fourth grade he was as bright as anyone else in the class, and he was pleased that

was upset that when she did well, especially in math or science, other kids teased her and called her a bookworm.

By the time she was in junior high and high school, she noticed that her interest and her grades in many academic subjects were dropping, and she doubted her ability to make it in college. After four years of college as an education major with a C+ average, Jean met a brilliant young man and they settled down to have a family.

All in all, Jean was pleased with her life. Her husband provided her with the tangible means to live in a style she enjoyed, and she knew that the people around her respected her as a good mother and wife.

when he did well, especially in math or science, other kids respected him and called him a genius.

By the time he was in junior high and high school, he noticed that his interest and his grades in many academic subjects were rising, and he was optimistic about his ability to make it in college. After four years of college as a chemistry major with a B+ average, Gene met a beautiful young woman and they settled down to have a family.

All in all, Gene was pleased with his life. His wife provided him with the love and support to work at the pace he enjoyed, and he knew that the people around him respected him as a hardworking professional.

We have here two people named Jean and Gene. In one sense they are separated by nothing more than a Y chromosome, yet they are worlds apart. By virtue of the fact that one was born male and the other female, their self-images, behavior, and aspirations have been modified to fit different molds, and their lives have taken very different paths. A large part of the difference seems to have taken place in connection with schools—the skills learned there and the careers that grow out of such learning.

Does this important and influential institution help reduce the differences that are presumed to exist between males and females, or does it tend to reinforce and perpetuate them? Are the most important teachings that boys and girls receive in school contained in the official curriculum, or is there a "hidden curriculum" that places them on different tracks and leads them in opposite directions? What can be done to make the school a place in which stereotypes are overcome rather than accepted and internalized?

From infancy on, pressures are applied to people in order to make their behavior conform to the rules of society. This process places each person into a set of *roles* as son or daughter, friend, and student, as well as a host of others, and each role carries with it a set of acceptable or expected behaviors. In this chapter, we will analyze the ways in which the roles we play affect our behavior and our relationships with each other, and also how we deal with conflict and strain within these roles. The major portion of the chapter will be a discussion of gender roles, a consideration of how young boys and girls are socialized into different patterns and modes of interaction as well as the ways in which males and females are thought to differ. We will explore how much of our understanding of gender roles is reality and how much is myth, and, where real differences do seem to exist, we will consider the extent to which they are the result of biological forces versus social and cultural forces. Finally, we will look at changes these roles have undergone in recent times and what these changes have involved.

SOCIALIZATION

Socialization is one of the most basic and important concepts for social psychologists. It is defined as an ongoing process by which people come to adopt the attitudes, behaviors, and ways of seeing the world that are held by the groups to which they belong and relate. Examining the word itself—*social-ization*—makes clear that it involves becoming social. To be *social* means to recognize and be willing to meet the expectations of those around us.

The behavior of *social-ized* people follows the **norms,** or unwritten rules, of society. Norms are prescriptions for behavior; they tell us how to act in a given situation. When people follow the norms, their interaction with others flows smoothly and their behavior is more or less predictable. When a person violates a norm—for instance, facing the rear of an elevator—we all feel uncomfortable and unsure how to act. In fact, we have a word for people who constantly act in violation of accepted normative standards: they are ab-*norm*-al.

Acting socialized and following the norms is not always a simple matter. Sometimes norms are not clear and we are unsure what to do, or we may be faced with conflicting expectations (e.g., from friends versus parents) and not know which to follow. Also, the norms for a given situation may not be shared by all the people in it, especially when the people come from different national or cultural groups. For instance, Bedouins consider it proper to belch as loudly as possible to indicate pleasure after a host's meal. If you had invited a person from this culture to dinner without being aware of Bedouin norms, you would probably not recognize the 40-decibel belch as a compliment, and you might feel insulted rather than gratified. When norms are clear, explicit, and shared, social behavior goes smoothly and comfortably. But when they are not, problems can arise because each person questions whether the other is properly socialized.

Socialization involves several different social psychological processes, and we will encounter it again, particularly when we look at attitudes

(Chapter 5) and groups (Chapters 12 and 13). In this chapter, we will focus on one of the major things we learn from our socialization experiences, namely, a set of social roles.

SOCIAL ROLES

From movies and the theater, we are all familiar with the concept of *role*. It is a part played by an actor in a theatrical production. Assuming that the "production" is the social system, the theatrical concept is much the same as what we mean when we speak of social roles. More formally, the definition of a role contains two elements. First, **role** refers to a category of people: students, doctors, or bus drivers, for example. Second, it refers to a set of expectations of how people in that category should act.

Role Expectations and Performance

An important aspect of the concept of role and one that helps us distinguish it from the concept of *self*, is that we cannot define a role by pointing to one person or even one category of persons. A role is characterized by a *relationship* between two people or two groups of people. You cannot be a parent if you do not have children, nor a wife without a husband, a doctor without patients, or a teacher without students.

Each party in a role relationship, the *role partners* as we shall call them, has a set of rights and obligations (or responsibilities). These rights and obligations are *complementary*, meaning that the rights of person A are the obligations of person B, and the rights of B are the obligations of A. For instance, teachers have the right to expect students to work hard and

The behavior of these people is guided by the norms appropriate for the particular roles they are playing. Who do you think is in charge here, and how does that affect the behavior that is expected and shown?

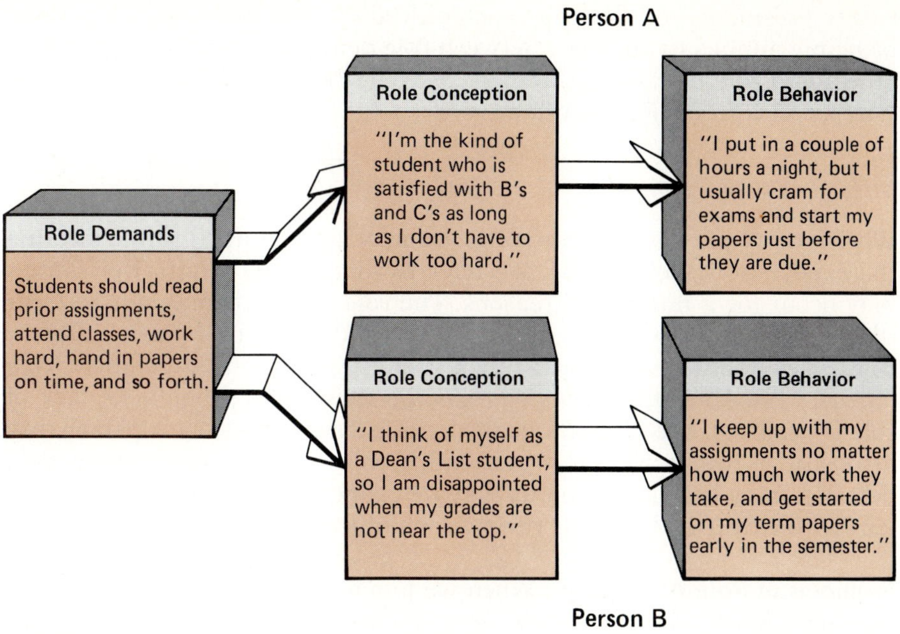

Person A
Role Demands
Students should read prior assignments, attend classes, work hard, hand in papers on time, and so forth.
Role Conception
"I'm the kind of student who is satisfied with B's and C's as long as I don't have to work too hard."
Role Behavior
"I put in a couple of hours a night, but I usually cram for exams and start my papers just before they are due."
Role Conception
"I think of myself as a Dean's List student, so I am disappointed when my grades are not near the top."
Role Behavior
"I keep up with my assignments no matter how much work they take, and get started on my term papers early in the semester."
Person B

FIGURE 4.1
The Effect of Role Conception on Role Behavior Although the same role demands may be communicated to two individuals, they may each interpret their roles in a different manner. As a result, their behavior may be very different.

the obligation to come to class prepared and to communicate effectively. Students have the complementary set of rights and obligations: they have the right to expect their teachers to be prepared and to offer information clearly, and the obligation to study hard.

Roles affect our behavior through a series of links (as indicated in Figure 4.1). First, those in the complementary role positions (our role partners) communicate their role demands. These demands (or role expectations) may be clear and specific or vague and ambiguous. Some role demands are permissive, allowing for greater flexibility of interpretation, whereas others require strict adherence to the norms.

No matter how explicit role demands might be, role performance is likely to vary depending on who occupies the role. Depending upon his or her personality, capabilities, and past experiences, each person will interpret (within the limits of the circumstances) those demands and shape the role according to his or her role conception. Franklin Roosevelt, John Kennedy, and Ronald Reagan are three people who have served as president of the United States during the twentieth century. Each had a somewhat different personality and style and a unique conception of the role of president, and therefore each played the role differently. The same principle applies to all roles. Between role demands as communicated by others and role behavior as actually played, the individual's role conception serves as a critical mediator.

Role Strain and Its Resolution

Whenever we play one or more roles, we may have a difficult time meeting the expectations held for us. We refer to this as **role strain.** Role strain may occur for a number of reasons. The role demands may not be clear (the problem of role ambiguity); the demands of two or more different roles may conflict with each other (the problem of role conflict); role partners may not agree about proper behavior (the problem of lack of role consensus); the obligations of the role may not fit one's personality dispositions (the problem of personality-role conflict); or so many role demands may be made upon us that we cannot fulfill them all (the problem of role overload). Let us review each of these.

Problems of Role Ambiguity When we join a new group, take a new job, or enter a new culture, we often feel stress because we fear that we might make a mistake through a lack of knowledge about proper behavior (Vansell, Brief, & Schuler, 1981). When expectations are unclear, people and the social systems in which they live often make deliberate efforts to spell out a person's obligations and rights. Business organizations, for example, sometimes draw up elaborate corporate plans specifying who reports to whom and which individuals have what decision-making responsibilities.

In less formally defined social relationships, especially those that are new or in transition, a good deal of person-to-person role negotiation may take place. Consider the newly married couple who must decide how to coordinate their schedules and to agree on their responsibilities around the house. Until they can clearly spell out the complementary rights and responsibilities of each, the relationship will experience a good deal of strain.

Problems of Conflict Between Roles We fill many roles simultaneously and have many role partners who make differing demands on us. Often the demands are separate from or are at least compatible with each other. But what happens when our roles call for different or conflicting behaviors at the same time?

Imagine a classic example: You are in a rowboat with your spouse and your mother. The rowboat tips over, you are the only one who can swim, and you have enough time to save only one of them. It is a melodramatic example, but it is a perfect instance of a conflict between the demands of two (or more) roles. You cannot do two things at once or be in two places at once; the demands of each role and each role partner are incompatible.

We usually avoid this type of conflict by playing each of our roles on a different "stage," by separating them in time or space. When this is not possible, however, we are forced to resolve the situation by deciding that one demand is more immediate or more important, thereby forming a *hierarchy of obligations* (Secord, Backman, & Slavitt, 1976). Doctors feel obliged to leave their children's birthday parties to perform emergency operations because one responsibility is more immediate than the other. Yet, to resolve the conflict, the child is likely to be promised a special treat the next day to fulfill the doctor's obligation of being a good parent as well.

We should recognize that the common expression "conflict of interests," often heard in the news, is really a conflict of expectations between two roles. We cannot expect politicians to be unbiased in deciding whether to award a contract to a business in which they have financial interests, or judges to decide a case objectively if it involves a relative. In the latter example, to act properly as a judge might call for a harsh sentence, but to act properly as a cousin might involve going easy on the defendant. The strain could be resolved by temporarily relinquishing one role: removing oneself as judge of the case.

Problems of Consensus People do not need to occupy two roles to experience role conflict. A situation in which a person has more than one role partner—for example, a teacher who has to answer to students, colleagues, and administrators—may bring conflict if the role partners cannot reach a consensus on how the person should behave. The university administration may discourage the giving of final exams at any time other than finals week, but what would happen if a whole class of students were to request that the final be given on the last day of classes? How can the person in that single role satisfy both sets of role partners? Or what happens when you, in the role of student, have to choose between studying hard for two different exams that will be given on the same day?

Some social psychologists have recently become concerned with the role conflict confronted by expert witnesses in trials (Saks & Van Duizend, 1983). An expert witness is expected by the lawyer who hired him or her to help that lawyer's case, by the other side's lawyer to distort the truth, by the judge and jury to share knowledge in a balanced and helpful way, and by the expert's profession to give a complete and accurate account of the field's knowledge. To do all of these at once is impossible, and expert witnesses often feel their role conflict acutely.

Within-role conflicts are difficult to resolve. Gross, Mason, and McEachern (1957) studied a set of school superintendents in Massachusetts who were caught between the school board, which wanted minimal increases in teachers' salaries, and the teachers, who wanted large salary increases. They found that the superintendents generally took one of two orientations toward the demands made on them. Either they had a *moral* orientation and questioned the legitimacy and appropriateness of each group's demands; or they took an *expedient* orientation, weighing the relative number of problems each group could cause if the other group's request were honored. These two considerations, the moral and the expedient, play a large part in determining how people resolve this kind of conflict, and research has shown that the orientation that predominates is likely to depend on the specific issues and the groups involved.

Problems of Personality-Role Fit A fourth form of role strain, traditionally called personality-role conflict, reflects a much broader type of problem. It occurs when an inconsistency exists between any type of personal characteristic (e.g., personality, attitudes, interests, skills) and the demands of a role. People may lack the ability to perform a role successfully, their attitudes or values may be inconsistent with the requirements of the role, or their self-concept may not fit the part. The shy salesperson and the loudmouthed librarian are two extreme examples of personality-role conflict. Among young Catholic priests, Reilly (1978) found a good deal of conflict between their own personal views and the Church's official position on critical matters such as birth control, divorce, and celibacy.

This type of conflict is usually most severe when a person has underlying personal values that conflict with role demands or lacks specific skills necessary for the role. At work, such problems can be avoided through careful selection and screening in the job recruitment process. Many corporations spend large sums of money each year developing tests and screening procedures to try to fit the "right person" to the "right job."

Problems of Role Overload A final type of role strain people experience does not result from a lack of clarity or any inherent contradictions among role demands or role partners. Rather, role overload occurs when a single role (or set of roles) places so many demands on a person that he or she cannot meet them all. It is not that role expectations are incompatible with each other; there are simply too many of them.

People adjust to role overload in much the same way that they resolve conflicts between roles: by setting priorities on the demands made of them according to their general importance or their time immediacy. The demands that cannot be delayed are fulfilled first, and those that are deemed least important are taken care of last or maybe not at all (Gray, 1983; Hall, 1972). People in overloaded occupational roles are often dissatisfied because of the pressures they feel and will attempt to renegotiate and redefine the limits of their obligations; or else they may simply quit.

Role Strain and Health People who have to live or work under circumstances of role conflict or role overload must suffer the consequences (Kasl, 1982; Katz & Kahn, 1978). These problems each have been deemed critical mediators of general life dissatisfaction as well as job dissatisfaction, worker absenteeism, and job turnover. In addition, a range of physical symptoms and diseases such as elevated rates of coronary heart disease, ulcers, high blood pressure, and neurotic behavior have been associated with role strain (see House & Cottington, 1986).

Stress-related problems can occur in a wide variety of occupational roles, both white-collar and blue-collar (House et al., 1986; Cottington et al., 1984), though certain roles have been noted as being particularly stressful. One of the most stressful occupations studied is that of air traffic controller (Cobb & Rose, 1973), which involves monitoring details about the location and progress of several airplanes at once, with the knowledge that the safety of hundreds of airline passengers hinges on making correct decisions. Air traffic controllers have been found to have very high rates of hypertension and peptic ulcers—a result, it is suspected, of the overload of demands in this role.

Doctors and Patients: A Case Study of Roles in Action

The roles of doctor and patient provide some excellent examples of the principles of role theory that we have discussed. Talcott Parsons (1951) has stated that doctors and patients share expectations for one another's behavior that neatly complement each other. Doctors are expected to be highly knowledgeable, to use their skills on the patients' behalf, and to

Physicians are allowed great power over their patients, although sometimes patients exert subtle influence to "manage" their doctors.

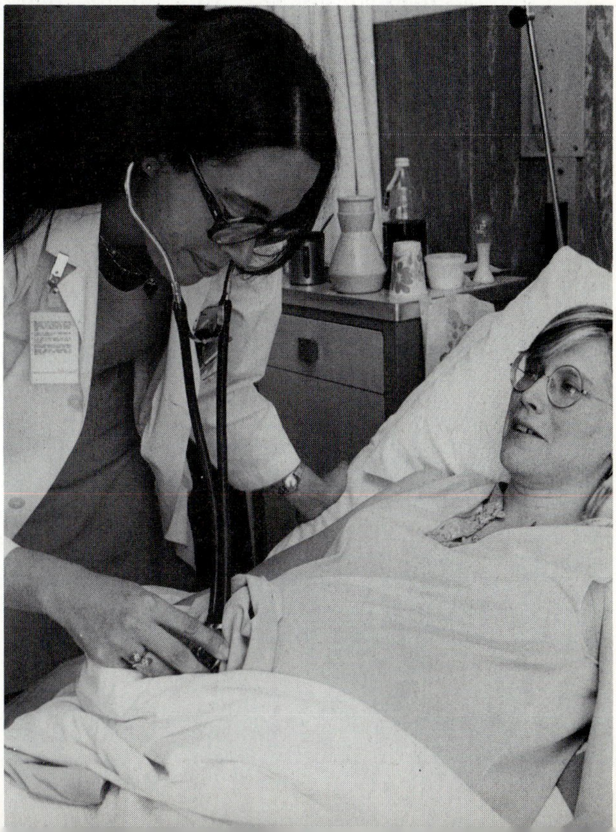

take an attitude toward patients that shows an understanding of their problems. In short they are expected to be competent, dominant, and unemotional.

In return for these role obligations, they are allowed great power over patients. Imagine anyone in any other role granting or denying "permission" to presidents, kings, and popes to get out of bed or to go to the bathroom. "Doctor's orders," of course, have no legal power at all—in fact, legally, the patient is the boss—but normative expectations for this role relationship require that doctors give orders and patients obey them.

Patients in what Parsons has called the **sick role** are not blamed for their current state of illness, are relieved from performing their normal everyday duties, and are allowed to become dependent on others. In return for these rights, they are expected to be motivated to get well, to cooperate with their doctors, and to follow all recommendations. In this role relationship as described by Parsons, the distribution of power is uneven. But both doctor and patient are satisfied because they accept this inequality and recognize the doctor's right to greater power (Krupat, 1983).

Other people who have studied these roles, however, do not believe that the expectations between doctor and patient are always so neatly complementary (Freidson, 1970; Waitzkin & Stoeckle, 1976; Hays-Bautista, 1976). They claim that the relationship between doctor and patient is really characterized by a struggle for power in which doctors attempt to maintain control over patients by using jargon, pulling rank, and controlling the information available to patients. On the other hand, patients use a variety of "doctor management" techniques from subtle strategies of influence to deliberately refusing to take their medications. In the Application that follows we will see that when people play the role of hospital patient, their rights and obligations are often not well defined, and the ways in which they conceive of and play their roles can affect the kinds of reaction and treatment they receive from the staff.

APPLICATION
THE HOSPITAL PATIENT: AN ILL-DEFINED ROLE

When patients check into a hospital, they enter an organizational and social structure unlike any they are used to on the outside. Here they are stripped not only of their clothes and possessions but also of the roles and routines they are accustomed to. The hospital patient role presents them with a problem in role ambiguity. First, they have a variety of new role partners: interns, residents, nurses, and pharmacists, as well as their regular physician. Second, hospital patients are not sure whether and how their sick role obligations have changed once they begin a hospital stay. More important, they have no clear conception of their complementary rights. In fact, when one group of hospital patients were asked what their rights were, 25 percent said they did not know; the majority responded by making vague references to "good care"; and some patients stated that they were not aware of having any rights (Tagliocozzo & Mauksch, 1979).

A critical problem is that hospital patients typically receive little explanation and information about the why, when, and how of their treatment, nor are they asked to do anything but passively cooperate. As a result, they often feel depersonalized and experience a loss of control (Taylor, 1986, 1979). They may react by developing one of two extreme role conceptions: either the role of the "good patient" who never complains and never questions, or the role of the "problem patient" who demands a great deal of time from doctors and nurses and refuses to cooperate.

Shelley Taylor has pointed out that both ways of enacting the role of hospital patient can have harmful consequences. Good patients may become so passive that they fail to provide information relevant to their conditions, or to complain when they are in real distress. Bad patients may demand so much attention that their important problems cannot be distinguished from their unimportant ones, or they may even sabotage themselves (e.g., by not taking their pills) to "show them who is in charge."

A number of approaches have been advocated and tested to overcome some of the problems of the hospital patient role. The expectations for the role can be made clearer. One basis for this approach is the Patient's Bill of Rights, drafted by the American Hospital Association in 1975 (shown in Table 4.1). It spells out what a patient can expect and demand from a hospital staff. These rights are, however, quite general, and each patient is faced with the risk of incurring the wrath of the hospital staff by demanding specific rights.

Recognizing this problem, some hospitals have created new roles in the hospital organization such as patient advocate, or patient relations nurse coordinator. The obligations of such new roles do not involve providing direct medical care. Rather, a person fulfilling this role mediates conflict and represents the interests and concerns of patients to the health professionals who are caring for patients directly (Lorber, 1979; Huttman, 1981). Instead of developing new staff roles, some hospitals have redefined and broadened the role of the patient. For instance, self-help units have been created in which patients who are physically able to move around make their own beds, run many of their own errands, and even help other patients who are more severely disabled (Hoge, 1964; Kornfeld, 1972). In addition, specific attempts have been made to provide patients with better information about the nature of their disease and the course of their treatment. Based on the pioneering work of Irving Janis (1958), a number of highly successful programs have been developed to inform surgical patients about matters such as severity and duration of postoperative pain and to teach them ways of dealing with the pain themselves (Anderson & Masur, 1983; Johnson, 1983).

As patients assume some of their normal role obligations and become more involved in decision making about their own care, the patient role is redefined from passive to active in the curing and healing process. The results of allowing hospital patients to be more active in their own treatment are considerable. For instance, patients who participate actively in their own treatment generally re-

TABLE 4.1
A Patient's Bill of Rights

According to the American Hospital Association, hospital patients have a number of rights, but they are very generally stated. Do you believe that these rights could be stated more concretely? Are there any rights you think are missing?

1. The patient has the right to considerate and respectful care.
2. The patient has the right to obtain from his physician complete current information concerning his diagnosis, treatment, and prognosis in terms the patient can be reasonably expected to understand.
3. The patient has the right to receive from his physician information necessary to give informed consent prior to the start of any procedure and/or treatment. Except in emergencies, such information for informed consent should include but not necessarily be limited to the specific procedure and/or treatment, the medically significant risks involved, and the probable duration of incapacitation.
4. The patient has the right to refuse treatment to the extent permitted by law, and to be informed of the medical consequences of his action.
5. The patient has the right to every consideration of his privacy concerning his own medical care program. Case discussion, consultation, examination, and treatment are confidential and should be conducted discreetly. Those not directly involved in his care must have the permission of the patient to be present.
6. The patient has the right to expect that all communications and records pertaining to his care should be treated as confidential.
7. The patient has the right to expect that within its capacity a hospital must make reasonable response to the request of a patient for service. . . . When medically permissible a patient may be transferred to another facility only after he has received complete information and explanation concerning the needs for and alternative to such a transfer.
8. The patient has the right to obtain information as to any relationship of his hospital to other health care and educational institutions insofar as his care is concerned.
9. The patient has the right to be advised if the hospital proposes to engage in or perform human experimentation affecting his care or treatment. The patient has the right to refuse to participate in such research projects.
10. The patient has the right to expect reasonable continuity of care. He has the right to know in advance what appointment times and physicians are available and when. The patient has the right to expect that the hospital will provide a mechanism whereby he is informed by his physician or a delegate of the physician of the patient's continuing health.

—American Hospital Association

Source: Reprinted with permission of the American Hospital Association, copyright 1972.

quire fewer narcotics and leave the hospital sooner than those who receive little information (Taylor & Clark, 1986). Although the experience of hospitalization is never likely to be pleasant, it can be modified within the framework of the role concepts we have discussed, and as a result can be more successful both medically and interpersonally.

SEX, GENDER, AND ROLES

In moving from situation to situation, we take on and then leave behind a series of roles. An adult can move from being parent and spouse in the morning, to employee at work, to teammate at the gym, and back to parent and spouse in the evening. But one of our roles, involving the expectations placed on us by virtue of being born male or female, is different. It follows us wherever we go.

From the time of birth, males and females are subject to differing personal expectations, and are praised and reinforced for different kinds of activities. In this section of the chapter, we will explore gender roles by considering the traditional expectations and stereotypes held of men and women, by noting the extent to which differences embodied in these stereotypes are actually true, and by discussing the kinds of socialization pressures to which boys and girls are subjected.

Before going any further, however, it is important to distinguish two key terms: sex and gender. We will use the term **sex** to refer to those characteristics of males and females that are attributable exclusively to biology. A male has a penis and produces sperm; a female has a vagina and produces eggs. Men and women also have different hormones which regulate certain physiological and psychological functions. These are *sex differences*. Behaviors and characteristics that are affected by culture and learning are matters of **gender** (Unger, 1979). Sex, then, refers to characteristics that are biologically determined and deals with the dimension of male versus female. Gender refers to characteristics that have a strong environmental determinant and deals with the role-related dimensions of masculine versus feminine (see Stewart & Lykes, 1985). The ability to bear children is a sex-linked trait. The ability to raise children has been traditionally associated with gender.

Stereotypes About Men and Women

When we consider the differences between any two roles, we most often ask in which ways their expectations for behavior vary. For gender roles, however, people not only hold different expectations for behavior, they also ascribe different traits to people who fill masculine and feminine roles. "Sugar and spice and everything nice. That's what little girls are made of," reads the well-known children's rhyme. Contrast this with "Snips and snails and puppy dogs' tails. That's what little boys are made of." The belief that girls are soft and gentle and boys are characteristically tough and aggressive represents one key element of the stereotypes we hold of the two sexes.

Defined as a structured set of beliefs about the personal attributes of a group of people (Ashmore & Del Boca, 1984), **stereotypes** lead us to believe that a given individual possesses certain characteristics because he or she

Little girls are often given dolls to play with, while boys tend to get balls and bats. What do you think this girl will be when she grows up?

is a member of a group. Inge Broverman and her colleagues (Broverman et al., 1972) surveyed a large group of college students to determine how they perceived men and women. Table 4.2 presents a summary of their results, showing 41 traits that 75 percent of the subjects agreed differentiated men from women. The researchers found two distinct clusters of traits, one centering around competency, in which the masculine end was seen as more desirable, and the other centering around warmth and expressiveness, in which the feminine role was seen as preferable. Being male was associated with dominance and controlling others. Being female was associated with submissiveness and being controlled. Although this research has been subject to criticism (see Ashmore & Del Boca, 1984) and results have varied somewhat in more recent studies (Williams & Best, 1982; Ashmore & Del Boca, 1979), the general pattern of results has remained similar over time. In addition, Williams and Best (1982) have found a remarkable similarity in male-female stereotypes among young adults and children in research covering 30 countries on 5 continents.

More recent research has pointed out that gender role stereotypes are not as simple as initially believed. For instance, the stereotype for each sex is hardly absolute. As noted in Table 4.3, if a person is male we feel it highly likely that he is independent and competitive. But we believe that a female also has at least a 50-50 chance of exhibiting these traits (Deaux, 1984). In addition, the use of generalized labels may miss the ways in which people are flexible in judging the behaviors as well as the traits of men and women (Deaux & Lewis, 1984). When given other information, such as one's position of power in a corporation, people are capable of making relatively complex judgments of behavior that go well beyond the simple application of stereotypes (Eagly & Wood, 1982).

TABLE 4.2
Characteristics Attributed to Males and Females as Part of the Sterotype

Competency Cluster: Masculine Pole Is More Desirable	
Feminine	**Masculine**
Not at all aggressive	Very aggressive
Not at all independent	Very independent
Very emotional	Not at all emotional
Does not hide emotions at all	Almost always hides emotions
Very subjective	Very objective
Very easily influenced	Not at all easily influenced
Very submissive	Very dominant
Dislikes math and science very much	Likes math and science very much
Very excitable in a minor crisis	Not at all excitable in a minor crisis
Very passive	Very active
Not at all competitive	Very competitive
Very illogical	Very logical
Very home oriented	Very worldly
Not at all skilled in business	Very skilled in business
Very sneaky	Very direct
Does not know the ways of the world	Knows the ways of the world
Feelings easily hurt	Feelings not easily hurt
Not at all adventurous	Very adventurous
Has difficulty making decisions	Can make decisions easily
Cries very easily	Never cries
Almost never acts as a leader	Almost always acts as a leader
Not at all self-confident	Very self-confident
Very uncomfortable about being aggressive	Not uncomfortable about being aggressive
Not at all ambitious	Very ambitious
Unable to separate feelings from ideas	Easily able to separate feelings from ideas
Very dependent	Not at all dependent
Very conceited about appearance	Never conceited about appearance
Thinks women are always superior to men	Thinks men are always superior to women
Does not talk freely about sex with men	Talks freely about sex with men

Warmth-Expressiveness Clusters: Feminine Pole Is More Desirable	
Feminine	**Masculine**
Doesn't use harsh language at all	Uses very harsh language
Very talkative	Not at all talkative
Very tactful	Very blunt
Very gentle	Very rough
Very aware of feelings of others	Not at all aware of feelings of others
Very religious	Not at all religious
Very interested in own appearance	Not at all interested in own appearance
Very neat in habits	Very sloppy in habits
Very quiet	Very loud
Very strong need for security	Very little need for security
Enjoys art and literature	Does not enjoy art and literature at all
Easily expresses tender feelings	Does not express tender feelings at all easily

Source: I. K. Broverman et al. (1972). Sex-role stereotypes: A current appraisal. *Journal of Social Issues, 28*, 63.

TABLE 4.3
Probability That a Male or Female Would Possess a Given Characteristic

Characteristic	Judgment[a] Men	Women
Trait		
Independent	0.78	0.58
Competitive	0.82	0.64
Warm	0.66	0.77
Emotional	0.56	0.84
Role Behaviors		
Financial provider	0.83	0.47
Takes initiative with opposite sex	0.82	0.54
Takes care of children	0.50	0.85
Cooks meals	0.42	0.83
Physical Characteristics		
Muscular	0.64	0.36
Deep voice	0.73	0.30
Graceful	0.45	0.68
Small-boned	0.39	0.62

[a] Probability that the average person of either sex would possess a characteristic.

Source: K. Deaux (1984). From individual differences to social categories: Analysis of a decade's research on gender. *American Psychologist, 39,* 105–116. Reprinted by permission of the author and the American Psychological Association.

Differences Between Men and Women

One of the many problems with stereotypes is that often they do not reflect reality. A belief about a group may be generated by certain circumstances and then perpetuated even though the belief is no longer—or may never have been—true. In this section we will evaluate popular stereotypes about men and women in light of the evidence. In addition, where we find that such differences do exist, we will discuss the degree to which they are *sex* differences (due to biological causes such as heredity or hormones) versus *gender* differences (due to socialization experiences in a given culture or environment).

Do differences really exist? In 1974, Eleanor Maccoby and Carol Jacklin set out to answer this question by reviewing more than 1400 published studies. Their conclusion, backed by another intensive review of the literature published 10 years later (Nicholson, 1984), was that few sex differences could be substantiated by the evidence, and that even these differences were small.

It is important to realize that such differences are not all-or-none differences. To say that men are more aggressive than women is not to say

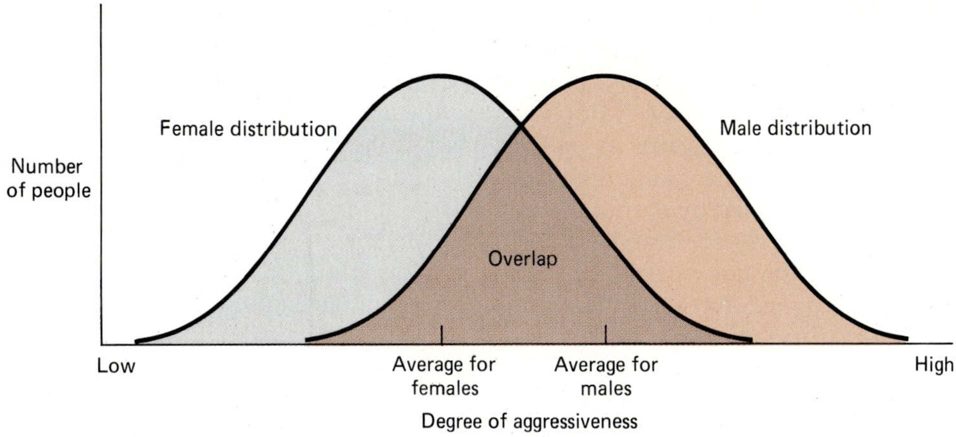

FIGURE 4.2
Overlapping Distributions for Males and Females on a Given Trait Such as Aggressiveness Although males may be more aggressive than females *on the average,* the figure shows clearly that many females are more aggressive than the average male and many males are less aggressive than the average female.

that all men and no women are aggressive, but only that on the average women act less aggressively than men. As shown in Figure 4.2, among men a given trait, let us say aggressiveness, might be distributed widely. Some men are quite docile, some very hostile, and many fall somewhere in between. As noted in the figure, for women this distribution might be similar in shape, but somewhat higher or lower on the scale. Therefore, while the average male might exhibit more aggressiveness (or more of whatever trait), it is important to realize that (1) the distributions overlap to a great degree, and some women are considerably more aggressive than some men, and (2) there are greater differences within each group itself than between males and females.

Aggressiveness Of all the characteristics that are part of the standard gender stereotype, aggressiveness is the one with the greatest evidence for actual male-female differences. In their survey of the literature, Maccoby and Jacklin (1974) concluded not only that males on the average are more aggressive than females, but that this difference may have a biological basis. They base this conclusion on a number of factors. First, in most societies that have been studied, males are stronger and more likely to hunt and to fight. Second, differences in aggression between males and females show up at an early age, before children are likely to have fully developed sex role conceptions. Third, greater male aggressiveness is not limited to humans, but has been found among many different species of animals. Fourth, the presence of male hormones is associated with aggressive behavior in both humans and animals.

A *predisposition* to aggressiveness may be more a part of the male's sex makeup than the female's. The effects of socialization, however, are so strong and interact with biology so early that it is impossible to say the extent to which each is important to the *expression* of aggression (Deaux, 1984). In our culture as well as many others, boys and men are often encouraged to express anger directly and are allowed to experience the rewards gained by their aggressiveness, but girls and women are criticized and made to feel anxiety and guilt for acting aggressively. The same patterns do not exist in all cultures. Among the Luo of Kenya, some boys are assigned household tasks and they grow up to show little aggressiveness (Ember, 1973). And in Pueblo society, aggression is not often displayed by members of either sex.

In our culture, the type of situation and the type of aggression called for most often determines whether males and females differ in aggressiveness. Although women are less likely than men to instigate aggression, when insulted or attacked they are just as likely to respond aggressively as males (Frodi, Macauley, & Thome, 1977). In sum, the direct expression of aggression in our society is condoned more widely for males than for females. When aggression is socially appropriate or clearly justified, however, the crystal-clear differences once thought to exist between men and women become more muddy.

Dominance and Power In general, males are more likely than females to take roles of leadership in task-oriented activities, and their style of exercising power is more direct, both verbally and nonverbally. They tend to maintain eye contact and feel more free to touch another person and to express their desires in an assertive manner. Women, on the other hand, are socialized toward taking a more social-expressive role in groups, helping the group accomplish its goals by maintaining harmony among members (Lockheed & Hall, 1976). Their style is more subtle and indirect. They tend to look away and ask or hint rather than assert (Henley, 1977; Falbo & Peplau, 1980).

Situational factors, once again, are important. For instance, women are especially unlikely to assume a dominant role when paired with males. Golub and Canty (1979) demonstrated this tendency by measuring dominance on the California Personality Inventory and then pairing a dominant woman with either a female or a male partner who was also rated as dominant. With the female peers, 60 percent of the women assumed a dominant role, but when paired with a male, two-thirds of the same women failed to assert themselves.

Intelligence and Ability Another part of the age-old gender stereotype is that men are smarter than women, but the evidence shows that on all available measures of general intellectual ability, reasoning ability, and problem solving, almost no evidence exists to indicate that one sex is any "smarter" than the other (Maccoby & Jacklin, 1974; Block, 1976). Still, on specific abilities such as verbal, quantitative, and spatial skills, we have a good deal of evidence indicating that differences do exist. Generally, females outperform males on verbal tasks, and males do better when spatial or quantitative skills are tested. These differences are hardly dramatic—and, again, there is a good deal of variation within the sexes as well—but the differences are consistent.

When it comes to explaining these differences, a great deal of controversy exists (Basow, 1986; Caplan, MacPherson, & Tobin, 1985). Some researchers believe that they derive from biological factors (i.e., that they are sex differences). They suggest that visual and spatial abilities are genetically sex-linked traits associated with the X chromosome and mediated by differences in hormones and brain functioning (Allioti, 1978; Vandenberg & Kuse, 1979). Levy (1976) has suggested that the left hemisphere is more highly specialized among females; and Davidson et al. (1976) have proposed that males excel at tasks requiring the simultaneous use of both hemispheres, while women are better on those that require a focus on only one. Geschwind and Galaburda (1985) believe that a fetus subjected to an excess amount of the male hormone testosterone—and male fetuses are more likely to be so exposed—is affected in terms of brain organization and development in ways that would predispose it toward mathematical giftedness. Benbow and Stanley (1983) have provided evidence to support this claim.

In addition to evidence for biological determination of differences between the sexes with regard to intelligence and ability, there is equally strong support for an explanation in terms of gender role socialization. For example, as early as the second grade, children in the United States begin to label verbal and artistic skills as feminine, and mechanical, spatial, and athletic skills as masculine (Nash, 1979; Hoferek & Hanick, 1985). Girls are considered odd if they are good at math, boys dull if they are not. Math anxiety is common among young women and may even be reinforced by teachers (Tobias, 1982). As soon as math courses become optional in high school, girls are far more likely than boys to forsake them. In the freshman class at the University of California, Berkeley, Sells (1978) reported that only 8 percent of the females had taken four years of high school math compared with 54 percent of the males. In addition to any biological differences that might account for this difference, is it any surprise, since they receive greater encouragement and training, that men score significantly higher—on the average—than women on the SAT math section?

Achievement The history books are chock-full of "great men"—males who have made major contributions to the progress of Western civilization. But "great women" are far less apparent. Although this may be due in part to the biased perceptions of historians, even in current times the occupational representation of men and women in positions of importance and areas of high recognition and achievement shows a clear margin in favor of men.

Why? As we have noted, males are no brighter than females on the average, nor can we find evidence to suggest any biological causes for differences in the achievement levels of men and women. Therefore, it would seem that the results of socialization and differential expectations for proper role behavior must play a large part.

One such explanation is the concept of **fear of success** proposed by Matina Horner (1970, 1972). Fear of success involves a concern that achievement in competitive situations might lead to negative consequences. Horner suggested that while men desire success and fear only failure, women are made to feel ambivalent about achieving, fearing that success is likely to bring social rejection and questions about their femininity. Male subjects, when asked to write stories about John, "at the top of his medical school class," most often imagined him happy and successful. Women who wrote about Ann in the same situation often characterized her as isolated, rejected, and uncertain about herself.

Further research in this area suggests that the women who wrote stories expressing a fear of success were not expressing conflicts about achievement and success *in general,* but conflicts about achievement and success in situations that deviated from sex-role expectations and behavior (Darley, 1976; Tresemer, 1974). In fact, males express just as much fear-of-success imagery when asked to write about Tom doing well in nursing school (O'Connell & Perez, 1982). Success in this domain is just not "masculine," and is therefore threatening to men.

Males have traditionally received awards for academic achievement, athletic achievement, and a variety of professional and occupational pursuits. They feel it is acceptable to compete for more office space and bigger paychecks. Traditionally, women have been rewarded for different kinds of activities, those centering around physical attractiveness, home, and family. They have found it acceptable to compete in those arenas, but until recently not in the office. We can conclude therefore that some of the major factors keeping women from seeking success are not inborn or permanent parts of their personalities, but rather situation-specific sets of perceptions about the appropriateness of success and the perceived likelihood that their efforts will lead to disapproval.

In summary, our review of the findings reiterates the conclusions of Maccoby and Jacklin (1974) that differences between the sexes on indications of ability and behavior are relatively few, and even then are small. Differences in the predisposition toward aggressiveness appear to have a biological basis, and there is some evidence that differences in verbal and spatial ability may have also. Even on these characteristics, however, biological predispositions interact strongly with socialization practices and cultural norms from the time of early infancy. Other differences, such as styles of dominance and achievement, appear to be attributable mostly to socialization pressures and role expectations. We will now survey a set of theories of socialization that attempt to explain these results. Each offers a different perspective on the process by which males and females develop a gender-role identity and learn appropriate behaviors for their roles.

Perspectives on Gender-Role Socialization

As suggested by the research on male-female differences, the socialization process plays a critical role in the development of behavior patterns of males and females. How and when do young girls and boys learn what behavior is appropriate for them? How do they develop a self-conception as masculine or feminine? Three major theoretical positions are widely cited to explain how children come to understand and enact their gender roles.

Freudian Theory The Freudian, or psychoanalytic, position revolves around the Oedipal period (approximately ages 5 to 7), in which boys and girls become aware of the anatomical differences between the sexes. According to Freud, at this stage boys and girls each desire the parent of the opposite sex, but they experience guilt and anxiety concerning their rival, the same-sex parent. To resolve this conflict, they each identify with that rival and thereby adopt the values and behaviors of the same-sex parent. Boys reject anything feminine and want to be "just like Daddy." Girls renounce masculine activities and want to be "just like Mommy." Each adopts an identity as male or female and tries to act in ways that are gender-role appropriate. According to this view, such developments are automatic, evolving as part of a child's biological heritage. This position is not easily testable, however, and there is little evidence to support

Children tend to identify with the parent of the same sex. This little boy can't wait to be old enough to shave—just like Daddy.

it (Tavris & Wade, 1984). And if a resolution of the Oedipal conflict is the way sex-role identity develops, how is it that the many children brought up today in single-parent families ever develop a clear sex-role identity?

Social Learning Theory Social learning theory proposes that gender roles are neither inborn nor the result of a psychosexual conflict, but that they are the result of direct and observational learning—just as *all* behaviors are. Children are reinforced or punished for various behaviors (direct learning) and also imitate the behavior of others at home, at school, and in the media (social learning). The people who are imitated serve as *role models.* Merely by acting in one way or another, they provide clear messages about what males and females are capable of and good at doing. When young children see and read about daring male adventurers and charming female winners of sewing contests, they learn what kind of pursuits they will be rewarded and praised for.

Cognitive Theory Cognitive theorists are critical of the social learning model. Rather than rely on the process of imitation, they place a greater emphasis on what goes on inside a child's head. They believe that children form an image of who they are or what they would like to be, and then choose from among the many influences available to them (Bem, 1981).

On the basis of Piaget's stage theory of cognitive development, Lawrence Kohlberg (1966, 1969) has proposed that children under the age of 5 have a basic sense of sex differences but that their conception is still very concrete. They think that to be a girl is to have long hair, and they aren't quite sure whether a girl changes her sex if she gets a short haircut. By about 6 to 7 years of age, a child is complex enough cognitively to understand the basic characteristics of people, to learn sex-role stereotypes and norms, and to begin to show a full repertoire of sex-appropriate behaviors.

While varying degrees of evidence exist for each of these positions, social learning and cognitive theories are generally more accepted than Freudian theory. Moreover, it is likely that both cognitive images and reinforcement contribute to gender-role acquisition. Acting in a manner appropriate to one's sex is undoubtedly the result of a cognitive construction of oneself as masculine or feminine as well as a long and complex series of social learning experiences.

The Agents of Socialization

The process of socializing girls and boys into masculine and feminine roles begins early, and the family is the first and most vital agent of socialization. From the moment of their child's birth, parents are likely to have different perceptions and expectations of the little bundle of joy, depending on its sex. Infant girls are seen by their parents—especially their fathers—as smaller, softer, and more fine-featured. Infant boys are seen as firmer, stronger, and more alert, even though hospital personnel who examine children find no overall differences by sex in children's health, size, or dispositions (Rubin, Provenzane, & Luria, 1974).

By the time children can express their knowledge, at about age $2\frac{1}{2}$, it is clear that they know which sex they are and have a good idea about sex-role stereotypes. Seventy-five percent of the children interviewed at this age knew which sex "smokes a pipe," "wears lipstick," and so on. Such knowledge becomes more complete and more refined as children grow older (Reis & Wright, 1982). In general, parents—even those who do not consciously maintain traditional sex roles—give their sons and daughters different chores to do around the house, provide them with different toys, and see them as having different characteristics.

Will, Self, and Datan (1974) demonstrated this by telling one group of mothers that they were playing with 6-month-old Beth and another group of mothers that they were playing with Adam. Each mother actually played separately with the same child. The mothers then had the choice of giving Adam/Beth a doll (traditionally feminine), a train (traditionally masculine), or a fish (neutral) to play with. As we might expect, Beth more often got the doll and Adam the train. Yet, when they were interviewed later, the vast majority of mothers were not only unaware of their biased actions but believed that they were treating their own boys and girls equally in terms of the toys they provided at home.

As children expand their horizons beyond the home, they come under the influence of teachers and school. Beginning in nursery school, teachers are more accepting of girls who cling than of boys who do so; of boys who fight than of girls who do. As they grow older, boys get praised more for academic performance, while they are criticized more for causing trouble in the classroom. For girls the pattern is much the opposite: their schoolwork draws less attention, praise usually being reserved for being good, quiet, and passive. What messages are conveyed when boys receive verbal and nonverbal signals that they are valued for their active contributions, and girls learn that neatness and passivity are traits for which they are valued (LaFrance, 1985)? What is especially surprising and disturbing about these findings is that they come from schools where teachers are making a conscious effort to treat boys and girls equally (Guttentag & Bray, 1976; Serbin & O'Leary, 1975).

Textbooks in schools further compound this situation by rarely mentioning the accomplishments of notable women. Marie Curie, the winner of two Nobel prizes, is referred to in one text as her husband's "helpmate" (Weitzman & Rizzo, 1974). The very organizational structure of the school tends to reinforce sex-role learning in indirect ways. A majority of the teachers are female, but the principal and the school superintendent are more often males. The male teachers are usually in the science and math departments, and the music and reading teachers are women. Thus patterns of dominance and achievement tend to be perpetuated because they are reflected in the organization of the school and the school system.

Beyond the influence of parents and teachers is the ever-present television in addition to popular books, movies, and magazines. Here the research shows a clear consensus: regardless of the medium in question, extreme sex-role stereotypes are portrayed. On TV, in particular, there are three times as many male characters as females. Males are far more likely to be associated with the world of work and are depicted as rational, capable, powerful, stable, and tolerant. Females are attractive, happy, sociable, peaceful, and fair (Weigel & Loomis, 1981).

While we might like to dismiss much standard television fare as "junk," the evidence suggests that these stereotypes persist even in the best children's books and most respected TV programming. The Muppets on the award-winning "Sesame Street" series are all male, and though all the live adult characters, male and female, are warm and nonaggressive, the males are more tied to occupations than are their female counterparts. Kolbe and LaVoie (1981), in reviewing the children's books that won the esteemed Caldecott Medal from 1972 to 1979, found that portrayals of male and female characters were stereotyped here as well. Regardless of the source—the family, the school, or the media—traditional gender-role learning continues throughout childhood. Although the content may be more subtle now than it was years ago, the message remains the same.

SEX ROLES IN THE 1980s AND BEYOND

Attitudes and behavior associated with gender roles are in a period of transition. As late as 1920 women in this country were not even allowed to vote, and in 1930 there were still no women in the Senate. Yet in the 99th Congress elected in 1984 there were 24 women serving in the Senate and House of Representatives, and at last a woman was serving on the Supreme Court. Today, more women go to college and enter the professions than ever before. Women run important governmental agencies and serve on corporate boards. They feel free to speak out, to express anger, and to compete with men. Yet, for all this change, there is also great resistance, both overt and subtle. In this section of the chapter we will explore the extent to which changes have occurred and discuss the forces that act against change. We will see that the unfreezing of sex-role attitudes and behavior has caused greater freedom for men and women, but in some cases it has created greater uncertainty and conflict for members of both sexes.

Changes in Attitudes Toward Women

In recent years the attitudes of both sexes toward women and their role-related rights and obligations have changed significantly. Mirra Komarovsky (1946, 1982), a pioneer in this field, surveyed the future orientations of female freshmen at Barnard College in 1943 and again in 1979, and found tremendous changes. In 1943, 61 percent of the women she surveyed indicated that they preferred not to work after marriage, but in 1979 this figure had decreased to 5 percent. In 1979, Komarovsky identified almost half of her sample as "career salient," women who were at least as achievement-oriented as they were domestic-oriented. In 1943, only 2 percent of the sample fit this description.

Janet Spence, Robert Helmreich, and their colleagues at the University of Texas at Austin developed an Attitudes Toward Women Scale and administered it to nearly 2000 undergraduates and their parents at four-year intervals between 1972 and 1980 (Helmreich, Spence, & Gibson, 1982). In this eight-year period, significant shifts in attitudes toward educational and occupational roles as well as in beliefs about dating, marriage, and family occurred for men as well as women. These changes were sharper between 1972 and 1976, however, and a leveling-off seems to have occurred between 1976 and 1980. In fact, women have shown a slight overall shift in the direction of conservatism in that four-year period, especially in the area of social behavior. As a result, the attitudes of male and female college students about motherhood and achievement are not only more liberal than they were in 1972 but also tend to resemble each other more (see Figure 4.3).

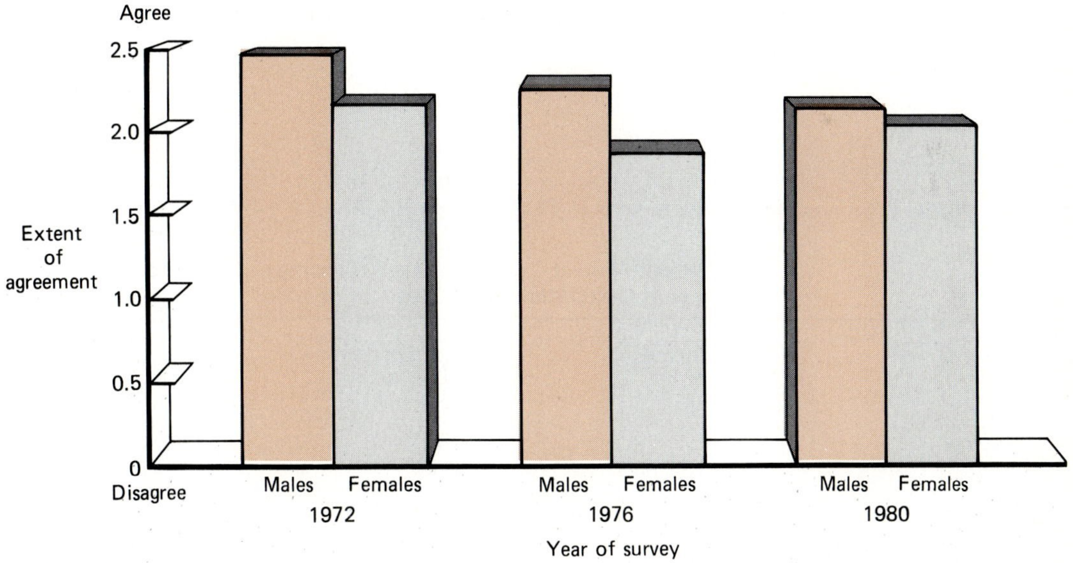

FIGURE 4.3

Changes in Both Sexes' Attitudes About Sex Roles, 1972–1980 From 1972 to 1980, male attitudes became consistently more liberal, while female attitudes became more liberal and then more conservative. As a result, by 1980 the attitudes of the two sexes about motherhood became quite similar. *Source:* Adapted from R. L. Helmreich, J. T. Spence, & R. H. Gibson (1982). Sex-role attitudes: 1972–1980. *Personality and Social Psychology Bulletin, 8,* 656–666.

Sources of Resistance

If women have become more involved in pursuing careers and men have become more accepting of women in positions of responsibility, are these changes reflected in the success women are achieving and in the rewards they get in the workplace? As Table 4.4 shows, equality in this area is still quite distant. In many cases, women are paid only three-quarters of what a man makes in an equivalent occupation; and this difference is large even after variables such as skill, education, and time on the job are controlled for (Mellor, 1985). Why is this so? Lott (1985) points out that such discrimination can be either official or unofficial, overt or subtle, conscious or unconscious. In this section we will explore some of the social psychological forces that act against rewards and recognition for women.

Unconscious Ideologies Sandra and Daryl Bem (1975) suggest that behavior toward women reflects two kinds or levels of underlying value systems. The first involves the attitudes, beliefs, and values that we consciously espouse. For instance, many people consciously tell themselves—and others—that they believe in equality and fairness. Yet the Bems suggest that in addition an **unconscious ideology** exists, a set of beliefs and values in the form of assumptions about what men and women can and should be doing.

Consider the following riddle: A man and his son are out for a drive and they are in a terrible automobile accident. The father is killed in-

TABLE 4.4
Median Weekly Earnings of Workers in Selected Fields According to Sex, 1983

Occupation	Percent Female Workers in Occupation	Earnings of Males	Earnings of Females	Percent Female-to-Male Earnings
Engineers	5.9	$604	$500	82.8
Lawyers	20.2	656	576	87.8
Doctors	22.8	508	421	82.9
College teachers	28.5	508	403	79.3
Bus drivers	29.2	365	260	71.2
Financial managers	38.7	573	359	62.7
Editors and reporters	47.0	524	388	74.0
Real estate sales	52.4	458	307	67.0
Social workers	62.8	398	308	77.4
Elementary-school teachers	82.4	404	351	86.9
Registered nurses	94.4	403	402	99.8
Secretaries	98.5	340	250	73.5

Source: E. F. Mellor (1985). Weekly earnings in 1983: A look at more than 200 occupations. *Monthly Labor Review,* January, pp. 55–59.

stantly, and the son is rushed to the hospital and taken into emergency surgery. About to operate, the surgeon takes one look at the patient and says, "Oh my God, I can't operate on that child. He's my son." How can this be? Some of you may be puzzled, while to others the answer may be obvious: the surgeon is the boy's mother.

When one of us first posed this riddle to a class in 1970, it was followed by a long silence. Eventually students came up with answers such as "It's his grandfather," or "His parents were divorced and this is his real father." What makes the riddle potentially difficult is the unconscious ideology we carry around with us that surgeons are male. These biases are rarely challenged because we do not even realize we have them, and they can creep into seemingly egalitarian marriages in which the husband does half of the housework, glad to "help" the wife with "her" chores. The In the News box presents the problems of Sarah Danca in her construction job. Whether or not she is a victim of conscious discrimination, there seems little doubt that she also suffers from the unconscious ideology held by others.

Evaluation Biases When a woman generates a product, is it judged the same as an identical product generated by a man, or is it subject to a bias in evaluation? To find the answer to this question, Philip Goldberg (1968) performed a simple yet telling study. He asked 40 college women to read and evaluate six journal articles, some in traditionally male-dominated fields (e.g., law and city planning) and others in female-oriented fields (e.g., elementary-school teaching and dietetics). Half the students were told that the author of the article was John T. McKay, while the other half believed the author was Joan T. McKay. Although the essays were identical and the evaluators were themselves female, Goldberg found that the essays attributed to John were rated consistently higher than those written by Joan, regardless of the field.

Since that classic study, numerous replications and variations have been performed to see whether such biases would disappear with changing times, and the evidence is mixed (Basow, 1980; Nieva & Gutek, 1981). On the one hand, 15 years after the publication of Goldberg's study, Paludi and Bauer (1983) reported that the students they tested showed a pro-male bias regardless of the topic of the essay or the sex of the evaluator. On the other hand, others have reported no differences or, in a few cases, a bias in favor of women. For instance, Montgomery and Haemerlie (1986) found that male and female engineering students were biased in favor of female authors when the topic involved their major. This suggests that exposure to competent females may weaken or even overcome anti-female evaluation biases.

Anti-female biases have been demonstrated on other fronts as well. Male applicants for scholarships were judged as more intelligent and likable than their female counterparts (Lao et al., 1975); males were preferred over females for a study-abroad program (Deaux & Taynor,

IN THE NEWS

C'MON, LADY, WE KNOW YOUR HUSBAND'S IN CHARGE: WOMEN FIND BIAS IN SET-ASIDE RULES FOR CONSTRUCTION JOBS

Boston—Sarah E. Danca says she runs her own construction firm. The state of Massachusetts says she doesn't.

Unquestionably, her title is president and she owns 55 percent of Danca Co. She does the hiring, the banking, the bookkeeping, the purchasing of supplies and equipment, final job estimates and some manual labor, sanding, painting and finishing cabinet work in her garage.

But John J. Danca, Sarah's husband, owns 45 percent of the company. A journeyman carpenter, he long worked for other companies while Sarah Danca raised their three children. Since the couple began the company 10 years ago, John Danca has made the on-site estimates, supervised on-site operations and done carpentry along with 10 employees.

In this age of affirmative action, should Danca Co. get preference for state and federal contracts as a business owned by a woman?

Massachusetts says no, and last year it turned down 84 percent of the firms—63 out of 75—that applied for state certification as "women-owned businesses." The rejections in effect labeled them fronts for male-owned firms.

"We're not saying every woman is fraudulent," says David Harris Jr., head of the state Office of Minority Business Enterprise. "But many companies blatantly don't meet the requirements. . . . Women have not traditionally been involved in construction." . . .

"There are tremendous obstacles and frustrations for women-owned businesses trying to get certified in Pennsylvania, Ohio, Michigan, Washington state and all across the country," says Mary A. Johnson, chairman of the Women-Owned Business Committee of the National Association of Women in Construction.

"If you have any male partner, you have to be prepared for an inquisition you wouldn't believe. There's a prejudice that you aren't really running the business."

On the federal level, various agencies, including the Department of Transporta-

1973); and males were more likely than females to be favored for a job (Firth, 1982). Even presumably enlightened heads of psychology departments were shown to rate men higher and were willing to offer them higher-level positions when sent equivalent resumes that they were told came from either a male or female (Fidell, 1976).

Attributions for Success Another factor that works against the perceived value of women's work has to do with attributions people make about success and failure. As we discussed in Chapter 2, whenever people do a task well, their performance can be attributed to (1) ability, (2) hard work, (3) having an easy task, or (4) plain luck. People tend to see men's success as an indicator of their skill, but when women succeed, people more often believe that they were lucky or that the task was not difficult (Frieze et al., 1982; Deaux & Emswiller, 1974). When men and women fail, the pattern is reversed. This attributional pattern holds for success in school

tion, the Environmental Protection Agency and the Housing and Urban Development Department, reserve business for women contractors. But many federal programs rely on the Small Business Administration (SBA) definition of "socially and economically disadvantaged" companies.

Only a dozen of more than 2000 SBA-certified companies last year were owned by nonminority women, according to the National Association of Women Government Contractors.

"I agree that just because momma goes to work in daddy's business, that doesn't make her qualify," says the group's president, Karen Olson. "But the SBA consistently attacks every single application by a married woman as a front."

In Massachusetts, a group of irate women contractors, including Danca and other members of the National Association of Women in Construction, complained to Gov. Michael S. Dukakis and is threatening a class-action suit.

"The woman construction company owner has been treated as a front from the outset," says Donna Hardiman, who led the protest. "We were guilty until proven innocent." . . .

The state's regulations for certifying women and minority firms are 44 pages long. But their bottom line in cases like that of Sarah Danca is this: If the man has the resume and the experience—as John Danca did—it creates "an irrebuttable presumption that the woman owner [does] not have dominant control of the company."

That presumption is sexist, female contractors say, because many of them took time out of the job market to raise children and, once they were ready to step back in, it was natural to enlist the aid of male relatives to penetrate an industry notorious for its exclusivity.

Source: Margot Hornblower, *Washington Post,* November 5, 1984, p. 33.

(Feather & Simon, 1973), in sports (Croxton & Klonsky, 1982), and on the job (Deaux, 1979); and it is shown by women evaluating their own performance as well as by men evaluating women. Even among women who serve on the boards of directors of major American corporations, luck is the one reason they themselves cite most often for their success (Klemesrud, 1979).

This pattern of attributions has its origin in the expectations for performance that both sexes hold for women (Deaux, 1984). As Figure 4.4 shows, by accepting the stereotypes about the lesser ability of women, women as well as men come to have low expectations for the performance of females. Success is therefore inconsistent with expectations for women, but consistent with expectations for men. As a result, men's success is attributed to ability, while women's failure is attributed to lack of ability; men's failures are thought to be the result of bad luck, but women's successes come from good luck.

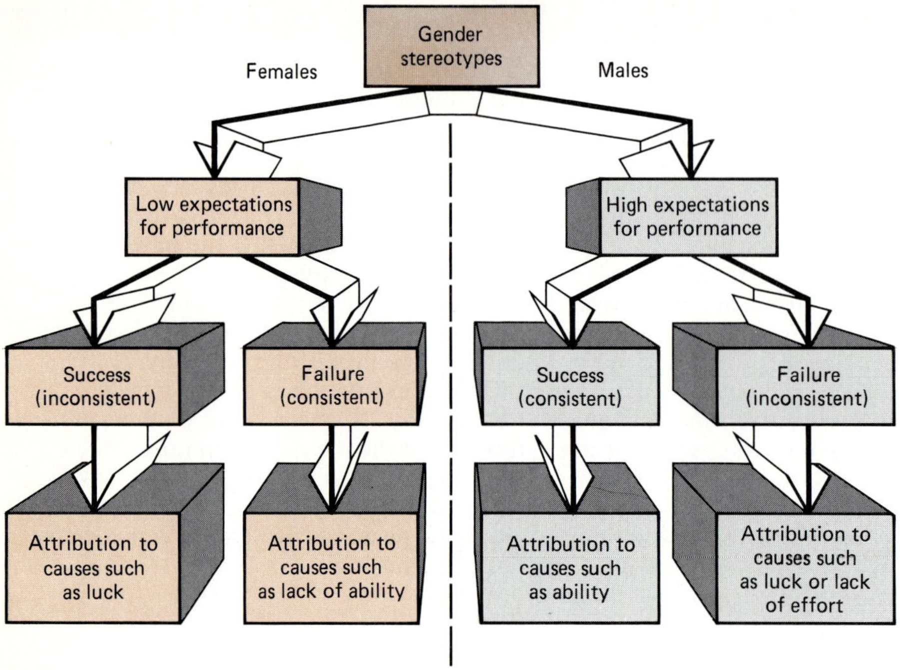

FIGURE 4.4

The Effect of Gender Stereotypes on Attributions for Success According to Deaux, the low performance expectations held for women make it likely that their successes will be attributed to luck and their failures to a lack of ability. The high performance expectations held for men cause their successes to be attributed to ability and their failures to bad luck or insufficient effort. *Source:* Adapted from K. Deaux (1984). From individual differences to social categories: Analysis of a decade's research on gender. *American Psychologist, 39,* 101. Reprinted by permission of the author and the American Psychological Association.

FROM THE FIELD
Kay Deaux

Kay Deaux, who is on the faculty of Purdue University, is best known for her work applying social psychology to problems of sex discrimination. In her most-cited research, she discovered that even when males and females performed equally well at a task, the explanations people offered for their success depended upon the person's sex: "What is skill for the male is luck for the female." Professor Deaux's research has extended to the study of women in traditionally male workplaces—for example, female blue-collar workers in the steel industry. Her work spans the range of gender-related behaviors.

Together, attributional differences, evaluation biases, and unconscious ideologies all lead us to perceive the contributions of women as not as good as those of men. Unlike overt discrimination practices, such psychological barriers are difficult to attack directly. Yet until these subtle biases are recognized and dealt with, real changes in gender roles and gender-role stereotypes will be difficult to attain.

Working Mothers and Role Strain

One result of our changing gender-role expectations is that more and more women are finding their way into the work force. While the primary motivation for working was once economic necessity, greater numbers of women are now taking jobs by choice. According to the Department of Labor almost half of all married women, and 55 percent of all mothers, work outside the home (Nieva, 1985). What is the effect on women of combining the roles of motherhood and paid work?

Two contrasting positions have been offered, each with a good deal of supporting evidence (Warr & Parry, 1982). The first argues that in modern society the role of housewife has been devalued and, without the presence of an extended family, work in the house isolates a woman from others. Work on the outside offers a woman a sense of participation as well as satisfaction and accomplishment. It allows her to develop higher self-esteem, to have greater access to social contacts and a support network, and to gain greater power in family decision making. According to this viewpoint, outside work is a buffer against stress and provides an outlet for the married woman to express herself while being reinforced by others outside the home. Those who believe in this position point out that the employment of married women and of women with children has been associated with greater marital happiness (Birnbaum, 1975) and more positive mental (Kessler & McRae, 1982) and physical health (Nathanson, 1980).

On the other side is the position that work outside the home is a source of stress for women rather than a buffer against it. This position points out that not all mothers take jobs by choice and not all work is pleasant and satisfying. In most cases, the married woman who works still does the majority of the cooking, shopping, and cleaning and is still primarily responsible for child care. In short, the working woman has one job, the working wife and working mother have two, and this creates guilt, strain, and a host of negative consequences. In support of this, research finds that working wives have high rates of alcohol consumption (Johnson 1982), emotional problems, and a higher rate of suicide attempts (Newman, Whitmore & Newman, 1973) than women who do not work.

We can begin to understand the conflicting evidence by analyzing these roles in the same terms in which we discussed other roles earlier in the chapter (see Darley, 1976, for an extended role theory analysis). One major difference between the roles of housewife/mother and employee that may account for the problem of low self-esteem among working women has to do with role ambiguity. There are no clear standards for how to be a parent (should you be permissive or strict, a pal or authority figure?), and it is difficult to know whether one is doing the job well. Workers, on the other hand, usually have specific role descriptions and receive more immediate and clear feedback on performance. As a result, the housewife may be unsure how well she is playing her role and is more likely to be critical of herself.

Between-role conflict is another concept that can apply to the problems of the working mother. Typically, working mothers still maintain the vast majority of domestic duties. If the children are sick or school is closed, it usually falls upon her to make arrangements or to personally take care of the children at the expense of her work. In this way, we might say that working women experience role conflict because two of their roles (mother and worker) are *simultaneous* and therefore often conflicting, whereas a working man's roles are more typically *sequential* and therefore do not conflict.

Another important type of problem that was discussed earlier is role *overload*. That is, regardless of whether a working woman's roles actually conflict, the absolute number of commitments she assumes makes it almost impossible for her to fulfill all of them well—or even at all. Most of us experience some sort of overload, for instance at the end of the semester when all sorts of papers and exams are due, but it is usually of brief duration and can be endured without major alterations in behavior patterns. Working mothers, however, can be subject to constant role overload and must devise long-term strategies to deal with it.

In sum, it is not surprising to find that some women who work outside the home are better off, while others suffer problems. If a woman is working by choice, holds a job that is interesting and rewarding, and has the moral and material support of her husband and family, then work can be a fulfilling experience and serve as a buffer against stress. If these conditions are not met, however, the working mother is likely to experience role strain and find that maintaining a job and a home is stressful. In the following Application we will consider possible role conflicts involved in work at home and at the office and consider ways in which they might be handled in light of our knowledge of the resolution of role strain.

APPLICATION
DEALING WITH THE DEMANDS OF WORK AND FAMILY

Mothers with jobs, even when the work is interesting and is performed by choice rather than economic necessity, face daily problems of role strain. More often than not, the chores of housecleaning, laundry, and meal preparation fall more to them than to their spouses. As opposed to the male, whose occupational role is allowed to intrude into the family role—"I'm sorry, dear, but I'll have to work late at the office all this week"—the working mother's family role most often takes precedence over her occupational role when the two conflict—"I'm sorry, I can't come to work today. My child is sick and I have to stay home with her." The most direct solution, of course, is for a husband and wife to agree on a truly equitable division of home responsibilities so that the woman is not overburdened. Barring that, a number of arrangements and suggestions have been offered to avoid or to resolve the ensuing role strain. In light of our knowledge of role theory, let us review these suggestions and determine which ones are associated with successful resolutions (Nieva & Gutek, 1981).

One route that some women have taken to avoid the conflicts involved in marriage and child rearing is to remain single or childless. Women faculty members, administrators, and clerical workers are all less likely to be married than are males in similar roles (Herman & Gyllstrom, 1977). Yet, assuming that a woman wants to have a family, many accommodations are possible, both bureaucratic and personal.

On the bureaucratic side, new role configurations are evolving to make it easier for both husbands and wives to work. Employers have begun to offer shortened work weeks, flexible time schedules, and permanent part-time employment to workers, enabling them to arrange their occupational role responsibilities to mesh with their other obligations (Polit, 1979; Nieva & Gutek, 1981). One imaginative role redefinition is the job-sharing couple, both members working part-time—in some cases sharing the very same job—while splitting domestic and child-care responsibilities. Members of job-sharing couples feel liberated from role overload, and report high levels of satisfaction that are matched by their employers' evaluations of them (Arkin & Dobrofsky, 1979).

For women whose jobs cannot be arranged in innovative ways, a number of personal accommodations have been proposed to reduce role strain. Two suggestions, although widely proposed, appear to produce more, not less, dissatisfaction among working mothers (Gray, 1983). The first involves separating one's roles completely, and the second involves learning to be more organized and efficient in order to accomplish both roles better (known as the "superwoman" strategy). Total separation is very difficult to accomplish, and women report that when they attempt to isolate the two roles completely they cannot do justice to either of them (Hennig & Jardim, 1977). The superwoman strategy places the whole burden for the resolution of role strain on the woman's shoulders and makes her feel like a failure if she cannot meet her very high standards for both roles.

A recent study by Janet Dreyfuss Gray (1983) helps identify some of the coping strategies that professional women use successfully. She interviewed more than 200 married women doctors, lawyers, and professors in Philadelphia and found that more than 80 percent of her sample subscribed to the resolutions generally proposed for between-role conflict and role overload—that is, these women formed a hierarchy of role obligations, rotating their attentions among them depending on which was most pressing.

Two other strategies used by more than 80 percent of the women that were particularly effective involved getting family members to share household tasks, thereby reducing overload; and reducing their standards for performance in their various roles. For instance, as mothers they might not plan such elaborate meals, or as professors they might not get their papers graded as quickly.

We can see, therefore, that assumptions about women's traditional roles and obligations are still alive and functioning even in the families of highly educated professional women. Yet, by applying some of the basic principles of role strain resolution, these women are able to lead satisfying and challenging lives, as evidenced by the finding that only 16 percent of them were dissatisfied with the way in which they had balanced their multiple roles.

The Concept of Androgyny

The working woman is often expected to be assertive and independent on the job (i.e., to act in ways that are traditionally masculine) and to be warm and supportive with her family at home (to act in a traditionally feminine manner). Is it possible for a person to blend masculine and feminine traits? For many years, the ways in which we thought about these concepts led us to say no. People made the assumption that the concepts of masculine and feminine represented endpoints on a single continuum (see Figure 4.5), and that each person fell at one point somewhere along this dimension. The more masculine you were, the less feminine you could be; and the more feminine you were, the less masculine. The two concepts were therefore not only opposite, but mutually exclusive.

More recently, researchers in this area have suggested that such an assumption is incorrect (Bem, 1981; Spence, Helmreich, & Stapp, 1974). They believe and have demonstrated that masculinity and femininity are two independent dimensions, and that a person—either male or female—is capable of acting in ways that reflect both. The person who combines the orientations, traits, and behaviors thought to be characteristic of both sexes is known as *androgynous.*

The term **androgyny** is derived from the Greek *andro,* meaning male, and *gyn,* meaning female. In order to determine if someone is androgynous, several measures have been developed, although the most commonly used instrument is the Bem Sex-Role Inventory (Bem, 1981). This scale contains sixty adjectives. Twenty of these terms—for example, *ambitious, self-reliant,* and *forceful*—have been traditionally associated with masculinity; another twenty—for example, *affectionate, helpful,* and *friendly*—have been more commonly associated with femininity; and the remaining twenty terms are neutral and serve as filler items. For each of

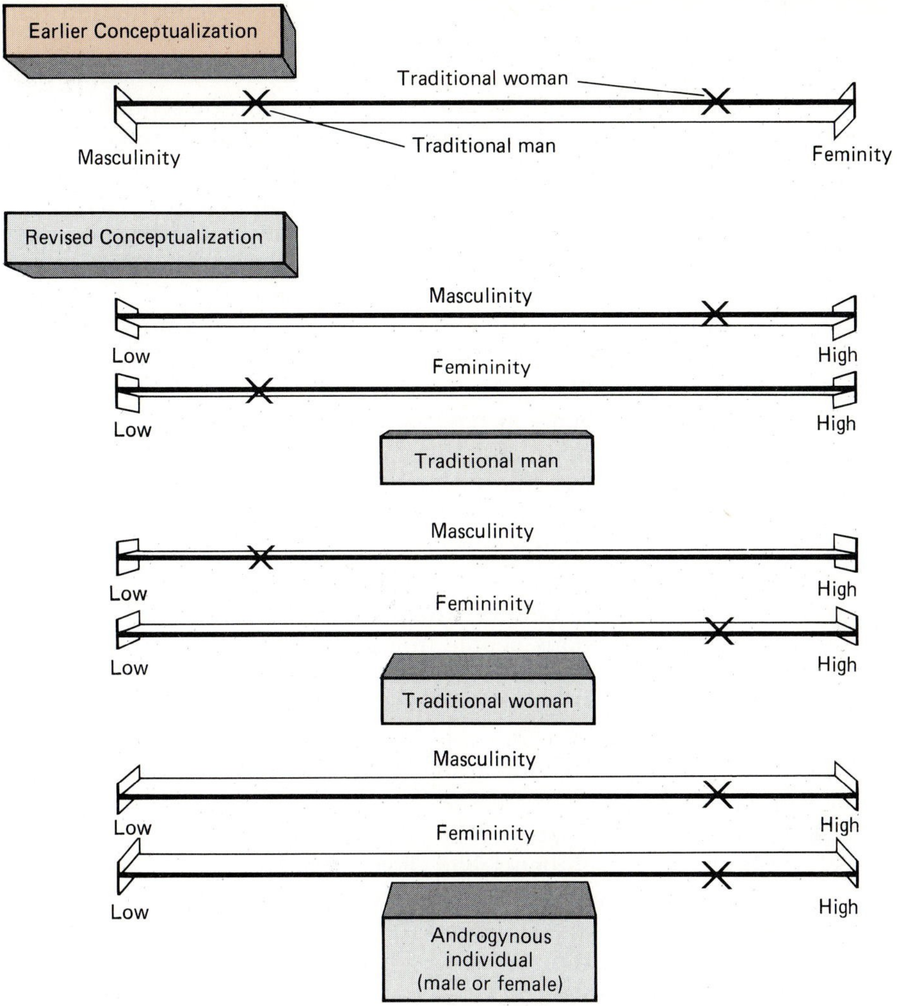

FIGURE 4.5
Earlier and Revised Conceptualizations of Masculinity and Femininity Earlier ways of thinking about masculinity and femininity pictured them as opposite ends of a single dimension. When we think of masculinity and femininity as two separate dimensions, however, it is possible not only to account for people who are masculine or feminine in the traditional sense but also to see that androgynous people may possess both kinds of traits.

the terms the test taker indicates how well that characteristic describes him or her.

Males who score high on masculinity and low on femininity, and females who show the reverse pattern, are referred to as sex-typed. They have incorporated the stereotype of the traditional male or female into their cognitive self-definition, and most likely into their role behaviors

(Bem, 1985, 1981). About a third of the typical college population falls into this category.

Women who describe themselves as significantly more masculine than feminine, and men who score as more feminine than masculine, are referred to as cross-sex-typed. This group comprises about 10 percent of the college population. A third group, about 25 percent of the college population, scores low on both masculinity and femininity, and is referred to as undifferentiated. The final 30 percent, those who score high on both masculinity and femininity, are androgynous, seeing themselves as possessing both masculine and feminine characteristics.

According to Sandra Bem, the androgynous man can not only show a range of masculine traits but can be gentle, warm, and affectionate when appropriate. He is as likely to stand his ground in an argument or competition as he is to cry openly at hearing of a friend's death. The androgynous woman can be tender, compliant, and supportive in appropriate situations, but would not hesitate to be assertive and independent when the situation called for it. Androgynous people should have a broader behavioral repertoire available to them, while the behavior of those who subscribe to traditional gender-role definitions should be less flexible.

Research findings have demonstrated that androgynous people are different from non-androgynous people in a number of important ways. In general they have higher levels of self-esteem (Orlofsky, 1977); tend to be better adjusted (Major, Deaux, & Carnevale, 1981); and are more nonconforming and nurturing (Bem, Martyna, & Watson, 1976). LaFrance and Carmen (1980) have demonstrated that androgynous people have a wider variety of nonverbal expressive behaviors, and several researchers have found that those who score high in androgyny have a different way of seeing *others* as well as themselves. For example, androgynous people are not as quick to judge others on the basis of their sex, and they are also less likely to describe people and their actions in terms of the categories *male* and *female* (Crane & Markus, 1982; Larsen & Seidman, 1986).

In addition, androgynous people seem to have an easier time in initial encounters with members of the opposite sex. For example, Ickes and Barnes (1978) performed a study in which they introduced male students to female students and then left them to converse for a few minutes, measuring the degree of attraction they felt for one another at the end of the encounter. One might predict that the best kind of match would be between a traditionally masculine male and a traditionally feminine female. Yet this was not the case. In fact, couples that had at least one androgynous partner reported more attraction for one another than those without an androgynous member.

Androgyny, however, is not without its critics, and several researchers have pointed to flaws and complications in its measurement and use (see Kelley & Worrell, 1977, and Lubinski, Tellegen, & Butcher, 1983, for

Although most people take on traditional sex roles, society has come to recognize the rights of nonmasculine males and nonfeminine females.

reviews and critiques). One particularly important issue involves the finding that psychological adjustment and behavioral adaptability are as highly associated with masculinity as with androgyny (Witley, 1983).

Do the findings associated with androgyny suggest, therefore, that each sex might adopt the positive qualities of the other? Or do they imply that there is greater value in women adopting male traits than vice versa? One recent study (Antill, 1983) is notable in that it demonstrates the value not only of androgyny but of femininity as well. In over 100 couples in Sydney, Australia, the single most important contributor to marital happiness was the ability of each partner to incorporate feminine traits. In particular, androgynous males, men who could express warmth and sensitivity, were more likely to be in happy marriages, especially when paired with feminine women.

In short, androgyny is a useful concept. It expands our understanding of how men and women can function and of how they relate to societally prescribed sex roles. Androgyny is not, however, a cure-all for effective functioning. As noted by Susan Basow (1980): "We need to go beyond merely broadening the sex role norms. Rather we need to transcend the norms themselves and help make sex roles less salient. When that occurs, people can just be people—individuals in their own right, accepted and evaluated on their own terms" (p. 301).

As we saw with Jean and Gene, gender-role stereotypes are hard to eliminate. As noted earlier in the chapter, such stereotypes appear to be widely accepted by members of both sexes and are expressed by youngsters well before they even reach school. We may hope that in school, however, Jean, Gene, and their classmates might be treated more equally and become more educated about these matters, and that stereotypes might begin to disappear, or at least grow weaker. Yet in school, stereotypes about boys and girls, and about men and women, seem to crystallize rather than to evaporate. Is there any way we can apply our theories of gender roles and our knowledge about the socialization process to undo these stereotypes?

Marcia Guttentag and Helen Bray (1976) attempted one such application, and their successes as well as their failures are informative. Guttentag and Bray selected three very different school systems in the greater Boston area and studied over 400 children in kindergarten, the fifth grade, and the ninth grade. The goal of their six-week intervention was to encourage nonsexist (i.e., nonstereotyped) thinking about play and sports activities as well as occupational and family roles among children at each of the three grade levels.

Consistent with the general orientation of cognitive theory, they chose materials that were appropriate to the level of understanding and interest of each grade. They encouraged the students to rethink their self-definitions and their images of others through discussion, role playing, and imaginative games. Consistent with social learning principles, they held training sessions for teachers to encourage them to serve as good role models, to teach them to avoid reinforcing boys and girls for different kinds of behavior, and to remind them to give direct and immediate reinforcement whenever a child acted in a nonstereotyped way.

Guttentag and Bray learned that children were least guided by stereotyped thinking when it came to themselves, were moderately stereotyped in relation to same-sexed peers, and were very biased in their gender-role stereotypes of the opposite sex. Kindergartners of both sexes were generally most open to new modes of thinking. For instance, prior to the intervention, kindergartners typically indicated that a given occupation could be filled by people of one sex or the other, but not both. Six weeks later, their occupational role judgments were more complex and flexible. Girls at both the fifth and ninth grade levels were quite open to considering lifestyles that integrated home with career, but older boys (especially ninth graders) were likely to disregard or reject nonstereotyped values of all types.

Would we consider this intervention a success? Only partially. But we can learn a good deal from it nonetheless. Why were the older boys so rigid about stereotyped behaviors and rejecting of nontraditional roles? Apparently they were concerned about the loss of power and status that is seen as part of the macho male stereotype, and believed that they had nothing to gain by loosening their stereotypes. This suggests that any future intervention with males, young or old, must emphasize the aspect of *complementarity* in gender roles. A loosening of gender-role stereotypes does not mean that women win and men lose, but that each sex will not be as tightly constrained or bound as it was before. For women, the gain seems more obvious. But for males, an undoing of stereotypes means that the sometimes stifling pressures to succeed can be lessened, that men need not fear expressing their emotions, and that fathers might find more time to spend with their children.

More generally, even though some changes did come about, why was the impact of the program so limited? Why were greater changes not accomplished? The answer to this lies in the scope and the duration of this project. The fact that any gains were accomplished by a program that lasted only six weeks and was limited to the classroom is actually quite impressive. Imagine the changes that could result if such programs were implemented in nursery schools and lasted throughout a person's school career? What would be the effect if this kind of treatment were expanded into the community and reached the home through the media? With the understanding we are gaining of where gender-role stereotypes come from and how they develop through the process of socialization, we are likely to develop even better and broader programs, both formal and informal; and this will prove to be one more useful application of social psychological knowledge.

SUMMARY

1. Socialization is an ongoing process by which people come to adopt the attitudes, behaviors, and ways of seeing the world of the groups to which they belong and relate. As part of the socialization process, individuals learn to follow the norms of society, the unwritten rules for acceptable behavior.
2. Roles refer to categories of people and the set of normative expectations for behavior among members of the category. Each role player has a role partner, such as teacher and student, parent and child. The

rights of any given role player are complementary to those of the role partner.

3. Role strain can occur under five different conditions: when there is a lack of clarity about proper behavior; when the obligations of two roles are incompatible and need to be fulfilled simultaneously; when there is a lack of consensus among role partners; when there is a poor fit between role expectations and the personal characteristics of the role player; and when there are so many obligations that the person feels overloaded.
4. The doctor-patient relationship represents an example of complementary roles. Talcott Parsons has noted that patients play the "sick role," in which they are exempted from normal duties and are expected to do what they are told in order to get well. Doctors are expected to use their expertise to help the patient, and are granted the right to tell the patient what to do. Some theorists, however, have suggested that there can also be much strain in this role relationship.
5. The term *sex* refers to the characteristics of men and women attributable to biology; *gender* refers to the characteristics attributable to learning and culture. The normative expectations society places on individuals for certain types of behavior by virtue of being male or female are known as gender roles.
6. Stereotypes are structured sets of beliefs about the personal attributes of a group of people. The traditional stereotype of masculinity focuses on competence and dominance, whereas the stereotype of femininity emphasizes warmth and expressiveness.
7. The considerable research on male-female differences indicates that few differences actually exist, and where they do they are small. Some characteristics do differentiate males from females, such as aggressiveness, dominance, and achievement. While there is some evidence for biological determination of certain traits, the majority of the evidence points to the critical role of learning and culture.
8. The two best-documented theories of gender-role socialization are social learning theory and cognitive theory. Social learning theory proposes that gender roles are learned through direct reinforcement and the imitation of models in the home, school, and media. Cognitive theory focuses more on what goes on in the child's mind and deals with the child's increasingly complex understanding of what it means to be masculine or feminine.
9. Great changes in attitudes toward women have taken place over the past 50 years. But significant psychological barriers such as unconscious ideologies, evaluation biases, and differential attributions for success continue to keep women from receiving greater recognition.
10. Two positions are held on the value of work outside the home for married women. Work may act as a buffer against stress, allowing an

outlet for self-expression and accomplishment. Or it may act as a source of stress when work is not done by choice, when it is not satisfying, and when there is little moral or material support in the home.

11. Current thinking suggests that an individual can possess both masculine and feminine traits. Such an individual is referred to as androgynous. Androgyny has been associated with high levels of self-esteem, nurturance, independence, and an ability to be flexible in behavior according to the needs of the situation.

CHAPTER 5
Attitudes

As Dave Atkins headed for the meeting with his old friend, he realized that his agenda was more serious than Bill Driscoll could possibly be expecting. This was to be an informal, friendly reunion, to be sure, but to Dave Atkins that was far from all it was. As soon as he had run into Bill, he knew that he could use the knowledge that Bill had. Dave needed someone who knew something about the technical side of attitudes—how to sample and survey and measure attitudes—but also someone who knew about how people's attitudes got to be what they were, what they meant, and perhaps how to change them. But first Dave Atkins had some attitude assessment and change of his own to do. He had to win Bill's interest and support.

Dave was about to turn his long-standing interest in the problems of the world and his community into a run for a seat in the state legislature. Having been a volunteer in several campaigns while he was in college just a few years ago, Dave felt he had a fair idea of what a campaign involved. He had done some telephone and door-to-door canvassing, helped with some campaign office work, watched some strategy being planned, and even given a few speeches to neighborhood groups. With this experience he knew that there is quite a bit to do in a political campaign. He would have to determine what issues were important to the voters and how they felt about the candidates. He needed to find out how best to present his position on the issues, to plan strategy, raise money, deliver flyers, canvass the neighborhoods, speak to groups of people, and make sure his supporters got to the polls on election day.

Most of these efforts required an understanding of attitudes. Because of Bill's work in college studying about and helping with research on attitudes, Dave hoped Bill would agree to work on the campaign. Since Dave Atkins was an unknown to the voters, he hoped Bill could ensure that the attitudes they formed about him would be favorable. Bill could advise him about which of his characteristics and beliefs would have the most impact on the voters' attitudes, and could point out other factors that determine the attitudes people come to hold toward candidates.

Another obvious need was to learn about the voters' attitudes toward issues and personalities in the campaign. How could they survey the district and measure the relevant attitudes in a useful way? Was there an important relationship between the groups people already belonged to and the attitudes they held? And what would their attitudes have to do with their willingness to contribute time or money to the campaign? Most important, on election day would they go to the polls and cast a vote for Dave Atkins? These questions must be addressed and answered by all prospective candidates. Yet, as we will see throughout this chapter, they really involve basic social psychological issues applied to the political arena. At the end of this chapter, we will return to Dave Atkins's concerns and see how the social psychologist's knowledge and methods can be of use.

THE CONCEPT OF ATTITUDE

By the term **attitude** social psychologists mean a general and enduring feeling, positive or negative, about social objects (Petty & Cacioppo, 1981). These social objects include people, physical entities, events, and abstract ideas. The positive or negative feelings are evaluative reactions to those objects, and they vary in degree. You may like someone or something a lot or just a little.

When we say the attitudes are "general," we mean that they are global reactions, rather than narrow and specific responses. And when we say they are "enduring," we mean that they remain largely unchanged over time and circumstance. This contrasts, for example, with moods, which may change easily and often. "I love new wave music"; "The government's nuclear arms policy is terrible"; and "I'm crazy about foreign cars" are all examples of attitudes.

Even with this definition, the exact nature of an attitude has been elusive to social psychologists. First of all, no one has ever seen one. Attitudes are psychological states that must be inferred from a person's verbal statements and overt behavior. As a result, even those psychologists who have studied attitudes most closely have not entirely agreed about them. Table 5.1 lists a number of definitions of attitudes that various

TABLE 5-1
Some Definitions of *Attitude*

An attitude is . . .
"A general and enduring positive or negative feeling about some person, object, or issue." (Petty & Cacioppo, 1980)
"A mental and neural state of readiness, organized through experience, exerting a directive or dynamic influence upon the individual's response to all objects and situations with which it is related." (Allport, 1935)
"A complex of feelings, desires, fears, convictions, prejudices or other tendencies that have given a set or readiness to act to a person because of varied experiences." (Thurstone & Chave, 1929)
"A tendency to act toward or against something in the environment which becomes thereby a positive or negative value." (Bogardus, 1931)
"An enduring organization of motivational, emotional, perceptual, and cognitive processes with respect to some aspect of the individual's world." (Krech & Crutchfield, 1948)
"The sum total of a [person's] inclinations and feelings, prejudice or bias, preconceived notions, ideas, fears, threats, and convictions about any specific topic." (Thurstone, 1928)

attitude theorists have proposed. These definitions reveal some differences in thinking about such aspects of attitudes as their stability, origins, and relationship to behavior. At the same time, the fundamental notions expressed in our basic definition seem to run through all of these definitions (Kiesler, Collins, & Miller, 1969; McGuire, 1968a).

It is helpful to distinguish attitudes from closely related concepts, namely, beliefs, values, and opinions. **Beliefs,** as social psychologists use the term, lack the evaluative or feeling component that is at the heart of the attitude concept. Beliefs are perceived relations among objects and events. They categorize objects, or combine them with a fact or attribute. In short, they are cognitive only. "New wave music combines elements of rock, jazz, and other forms that preceded it" or "Our arms policy contributes to the likelihood of nuclear war" are statements of belief. Although they differ from each other in a number of ways, they share one thing in common. They communicate the speaker's *cognitions* about the objects in question, but they do not directly convey the speaker's *evaluations* of these objects.

Values are evaluative, but are so abstract that they are tied to no particular social objects or classes of objects. Freedom, justice, beauty, comfort, and obedience are examples of values that people might subscribe to. People do subscribe to different values, and do ascribe varying degrees of importance to them, but the values as held are not combined with or connected to any objects (Rokeach, 1973; Allport, Vernon, &

In churches and temples of all religions, values are preached, opinions expressed, and attitudes formed. Just as these concepts are closely related, our own attitudes, beliefs, and values are often linked and agree with one another.

Lindzey, 1960). In some contexts, *values* may refer to positive or negative feelings toward a large abstract class of social objects.

Opinions and attitudes are so intimately related that they have been called "names in search of a distinction, rather than a distinction in search of a terminology" (McGuire, 1968a). Some have suggested that opinions be treated as more specific manifestations of attitudes, which are more general (Hovland, Janis, & Kelley, 1953). Others have suggested simply that an opinion be defined as the verbal expression of an attitude (Zimbardo, Ebbesen, & Maslach, 1977). These two terms come very close to being synonyms.

It is a widespread assumption that attitudes are critically important to the conduct of human affairs. Not only do political campaigners worry about people's attitudes, but so do governments in power, educators, propagandists, lobbyists, Madison Avenue advertisers, lawyers, promoters of rock groups, sellers of soapsuds, and all the rest of us. Table 5.2 presents a number of views that commentators throughout history have offered about the importance of attitudes and opinions.

Each of us has a nearly endless inventory of likes and dislikes pertaining to people we know and don't know, religion, politics, sports, music, foods, and so on. Contemporary life includes widespread efforts by politicians, businesses, and others to measure the attitudes people hold. To what uses are such measures put? The major illustration we have been employing

TABLE 5.2
Some Views on the Importance of Attitudes and Opinions

"The world is governed by opinion."—Thomas Hobbes

"Public opinion in this country is everything."—Abraham Lincoln

"We are all of us, more or less, the slaves of opinion."—William Hazlitt

"Few people are capable of expressing with equanimity opinions which differ from the prejudices of their social environment."—Albert Einstein

"Every revolution was first a thought in one [person's] mind. Every reform was once a private opinion."—Ralph Waldo Emerson

"Even despotism needs to rest, in the last resort, on public opinion."—Jean-Jacques Rousseau

"Let me write the people's songs, and I care not who makes the laws."—Eighteenth-century sage

is that of political use. Public opinion measurement has at least the potential to contribute to democratic processes by making the public's opinion more readily known. By knowing what the public feels about various issues and by knowing what the public thinks of them, political leaders can make more informed judgments. By keeping one eye on the polls, politicians are in essence yielding another degree of participation to the people.

The measurement of attitudes is equally important to the private sector. Indeed, the founders of political opinion polling got their start doing consumer research. The decision to launch a new product or to modify an old one (large cars to small, for example) and the timing of such decisions involve vast sums of money to be made or lost. Businesspeople increasingly include the findings of "market research" among the considerations that guide those decisions (Jacoby, 1975; Woodside, Sheth, & Bennett, 1977).

The step from measuring attitudes to predicting behavior is a short but precarious one. How stable are measured opinions? And even if attitudes are measured well, how closely related are they to the behavior they are intended to predict? It is, after all, the implications attitudes have for behavior that make them so important in the applied world.

Such issues are the focus of social psychology's interest in attitudes. Research has examined the nature and organization of attitudes as well as how attitudes are formed. Measurement techniques have evolved to facilitate not only the basic researcher's interest in attitudes but also the conduct of public opinion polls aimed at more practical ends. Finally, given the assumption that attitudes affect behavior, a good deal of research has been devoted to exploring that connection, which is not nearly so straightforward as one might assume.

HOW ATTITUDES ARE ORGANIZED

Structure and Balance

What does any single attitude "look" like? Social psychologists have long regarded attitudes as consisting of three major components: *affective, cognitive,* and *behavioral.* An attitude contains a large portion of positive or negative feelings (affect), which are joined by a series of beliefs and perceptions (cognition) toward a class of objects. These create a disposition to act in certain ways toward members of that class of objects. It is important to emphasize that the final component is not overt behavior itself but a plan, a policy of action. Attempts to verify this three-part structure empirically have found a close relation between the affective and cognitive components, but a relatively weak connection with the behavioral component (Ostrom, 1969).

Fishbein and Ajzen (1972) have suggested that the affective, or evaluative, component alone be designated by the term *attitude,* and that suggestion is reflected in the definition we have given. Beliefs, they propose, should be a separate construct. And the behavioral component should be designated a **behavioral intention,** that is, a plan of action, not the action itself. This foreshadows difficulties that we will encounter in linking attitudes to overt behavior.

The most well developed set of theories about attitudes involves cognitive balance. *Balance theories* rest on the assumption that attitudes are stable when a person's beliefs and feelings about an attitude object are consistent with each other (Abelson et al., 1968; Cacioppo & Petty, 1981; Heider, 1958; Rajecki, 1982). If my feelings toward various attributes of some object follow from one another, then my attitude is in a state of balance. But if I hold contradictory feelings toward different aspects of the object, my attitude is in a state of imbalance. A concrete example will make this clearer.

FROM THE FIELD
Martin Fishbein

Martin Fishbein (University of Illinois) has devoted his career to the study of the formation of attitudes and their influence on behavior. As we know from everyday life, attitudes seem to play a large part in many spheres of action; but as we see in this chapter, the relationship is by no means simple or direct. Fishbein and Ajzen's theory of reasoned action is an important step toward clarifying the link. Fishbein has applied this theory to a number of issues, particularly the prediction of voting preferences.

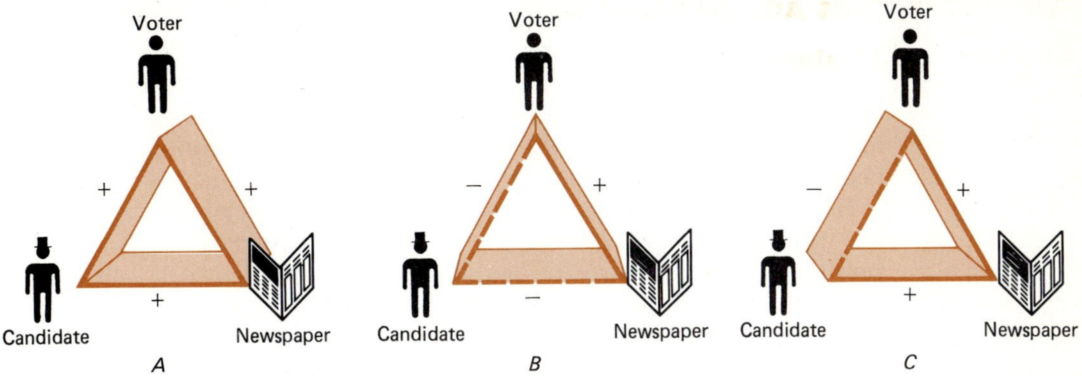

FIGURE 5.1
A Balance Theory View of a Voter's Attitudes Toward a Candidate (*A*) A newspaper that is respected endorses a candidate that a voter likes, producing a balanced state. (*B*) A newspaper that is respected comes out against a candidate that a voter dislikes, producing a balanced state. (*C*) A newspaper that is respected comes out for a candidate that a voter dislikes, producing an imbalanced state.

Imagine a voter who is trying to decide his or her attitude toward a candidate and who reads an editorial about the candidate in a newspaper. As noted by the solid line in Figure 5.1, part *A*, let us say that the voter has a positive feeling for the newspaper. If the paper endorses the candidate (a positive relation between the newspaper and the candidate) and the voter also adopts a positive attitude toward the candidate, then a balanced state will exist. If, instead of an endorsement, the newspaper comes out against the candidate, then the voter might also develop a negative attitude toward the candidate (part *B*) in order to maintain a balanced state. If the newspaper the voter respected endorsed a candidate the voter did not like (part *C*), however, then imbalance would result. It can be shown that balance exists whenever an even number of negative affective links (0 or 2) join a person, an attitude object, and the third person or object.

In a voter's real world, many sets of cognitions exist, some in competition with others. For instance, a respected newspaper may like a generally hated candidate; or a good friend may hate your favorite candidate. In an intuitive way, the voter has to weigh not only whether the cognitions and feelings are positive or negative, but also the intensity with which each is held. Was the newspaper's endorsement enthusiastic or only lukewarm? Is the voter's regard for the newspaper strong or mild?

Given that a state of imbalance exists, the theory suggests a way of restoring balance. In the case of Figure 5.1*C*, where a voter initially dislikes a candidate but respects a newspaper that endorses the candidate, balance would be restored by the voter's changing his or her assessment of either the candidate or the paper: "If the *Daily Bugle* thinks so highly of candidate Smith, perhaps I've judged the candidate rashly," or, "If the

Bugle can endorse that rat, perhaps it's not as good a paper as I've thought." This introduces the possibility of attitude change. It is even possible that the voter might try to convince the *Bugle* to change its endorsement, which would also restore balance. More complex versions of this simple balance theory will be discussed in the context of attitude change in the next chapter.

Balance theory has been subjected to a good deal of empirical research. For example, Jordan (1953) asked each participant in an experiment to rate the "inherent degree of pleasantness or unpleasantness" in a series of hypothetical situations. The situations were 64 vignettes representing all possible combinations of balanced and unbalanced, positive and negative, relationships among oneself, another person, and an attitude object. On the average, balanced states were rated as more pleasant than unbalanced states. In sum, balanced states are relatively pleasant and stable; imbalanced states are less pleasant and tend toward change.

Until quite recently, the theories and research of social psychologists were rarely applied to the arena of politics. Now, however, political campaigns are recognized as exercises in attitude formation and change, and social psychologists have begun to study them.

Interrelations Among Attitudes

Do attitudes about a range of objects exist as clusters with a high degree of interrelatedness? Or do they stand relatively independent of each other? Suppose you knew that a person was against abortion, against government regulation of business practices, and for the development of solar energy. Would you expect this person to favor capital punishment? To like flowers? To be for or against nuclear power plants?

Evidence exists attesting to the interrelatedness of various attitudes. For example, Prescott (1975) found that people with anti-abortion attitudes tended to favor harsh physical punishment for children, to be for capital punishment, and to feel that prostitution should be punished, that nudity within the family was harmful, that sexual pleasure weakened moral character, and that alcohol and drugs were more satisfying than sex. But attitudes do not always exist in clusters or necessarily predictable patterns. McConahay and McConahay (1977) found no relationship between attitudes toward sexual permissiveness and violence in a cross-cultural study.

What might we conclude about the interrelatedness of different attitudes? It is clear that attitudes do not occur at random. Something of a systematic nature is going on. But that something is social, not cognitive, in origin. The moment you acquire one strong attitude, all of your other attitudes do not fall into place like pieces in a puzzle. If you belong to groups that advocate certain attitudes, however, your attitudes on those issues are likely to be interrelated to the degree that you identify with those groups. If the bumper stickers on someone's car seem not to go together, they probably would if you knew what groups the owner belongs to.

This suggests, as many early attitude theorists proposed, that attitudes are social in their origins (Lewin, 1936, 1947; Sherif, 1936). Among some groups, as we have just seen, members will be found to oppose abortion and to favor capital punishment. These attitudes can fit within a syndrome that might be characterized as law-and-order-oriented or authoritarian. Among other groups members will be found to oppose abortion and to oppose capital punishment. These attitudes can be held together by the value of the sanctity of life. Though completely opposite in correlation to the other group members' attitudes, these two sets of views can be seen as logically organized and consistent.

A cognitive structure, or schema, may form for each group's members, holding their attitudes together by the values of "law and order" versus "life." These schemas may then impose more order on the attitudes, so that a new attitude inconsistent with this schema would be out of step with the others. Thus, some new attitudes may be adopted more easily than others. Over time, of course, groups and individuals do change their positions, and sometimes new schemas must be found to hold the new collection of attitudes and beliefs together in a coherent way.

The essential point to note is that the cognitive structure of attitudes does not compel them to fit together in certain ways, but rather that groups have the power to promote certain attitudes and certain clusters of attitudes. In a sense, the organization is imposed from the social exterior onto the cognitive interior. No clusters of attitudes hang together in an absolute sense. Attitudes will remain stable or change as one's groups remain stable or change.

HOW ATTITUDES ARE FORMED

How do the particular attitudes we hold come into being? In this section we will look at several different approaches to answering this question. We will begin with the way in which people perceive not only social objects but their own behavior in relation to those objects. Second, we will look at the role of beliefs, with their heavy emphasis on cognitive processes. Third, we will review learning theory approaches. Finally, we will consider the role of groups in the formation of attitudes.

The Effect of Perceptions

Mere Exposure Positive attitudes toward initially neutral things may be acquired merely by exposure to those things (Zajonc, 1968). It is not necessary that a person recognize the stimulus (Moreland & Zajonc, 1979) or even have meaningful beliefs about it (Zajonc, 1980). The more exposure, up to a point, the more positive one's attitude toward the object. No theory of attitude acquisition could be simpler.

Empirical research has demonstrated this effect with regularity. In various experiments it has been shown that novel stimuli presented frequently are better liked than other, virtually identical, stimuli presented less frequently. This has been done with Chinese characters (Zajonc, 1968), photographs of strangers (Zajonc, 1968), people (Saegert, Swap, & Zajonc, 1973), and music (Wilson, 1979), among other things. In one study, researchers showed people photographs of themselves that were either normal photographs or mirror images, and asked which they liked better. Close friends of the photographed person were given the same choice. As the mere exposure hypothesis would predict, people tended to like their mirror-image photographs, the version of their face they most frequently saw. Their friends tended to choose the normal images, the version they had seen most often (Mita, Dermer, & Knight, 1977).

The mere exposure effect implies that we not only become accustomed to objects—people, ideas, music, products—that we encounter frequently in our environment, but that we develop positive attitudes toward them as well. In studies of elections, it has been found that the candidate who is given the most mass media exposure usually wins (Grush, 1980). In a study of primary elections, the candidate receiving the most media exposure was the winner in 83 percent of the races (Grush, McKeough, & Ahlering, 1978).

Advertisers of products apply this principle in campaigns hoping to gain customers simply by presenting the product with a high frequency on television, in magazines, and in store displays (Cacioppo & Petty, 1980; also see Simon & Arndt, 1980). However, mere exposure works only up to a point. No doubt you have had the experience of tiring of a television advertisement. Above some frequency per unit time, or perhaps some absolute number of times, people tire of the stimulus and tune it out. Moreover, jokes seem not to get better at all with repeated hearings. Antagonistic processes—liking the familiar while seeking the novel—are undoubtedly at work (Jakobovitz, 1968; Maddi, 1968). But with the right spacing and variety, the mere exposure effect can be harnessed to produce quite positive attitudes.

Self-perception The idea that observers infer people's attitudes from their behavior seems obvious. But Bem's self-perception approach holds that the same process also occurs for each individual (Bem, 1967, 1972). He believes that we do not have direct introspective access to our own attitudes. Rather, we learn about our own attitudes the same way another person does—by observing our reactions to attitude objects.

The clearest examples may be those involving children. A child can readily experience liking or disliking without "knowing" his or her attitude toward the object. A child may enjoy various flavors of ice cream but ask for chocolate more frequently than other flavors. Eventually, the child will be asked what his or her favorite ice cream flavor is. According to **self-perception** theory, the way the child answers is to draw on memory about past behavior. The flavor that has been selected most often must be the favorite. This is just how an outside observer such as a parent would infer the child's preferences. According to this approach, the best way to know oneself, to find oneself, may not be by meditative, introspective contemplation, but by exposing oneself to a variety of experiences, places, and people, and thus learning about one's reactions to them.

The Link with Beliefs

The Theory of Reasoned Action A belief-based process of attitude formation is embodied in the "theory of reasoned action" (Ajzen & Fishbein, 1980; Fishbein & Ajzen, 1975). This theory will be discussed later in this chapter when we confront the complicated relationship between attitudes and action. For now, let us see what this theory can tell us about a more cognitive, as opposed to a perceptual, approach to attitude formation.

Recall that a belief is a cognition about the class membership of an object, person, event, or idea: Candidate Jones is a Republican. Candidate Jones is a businessman. Candidate Jones is a liberal. We may regard these things as *attributes* of Jones. We usually do not hold such beliefs in an all-or-nothing fashion, but rather we believe more or less strongly that an object possesses a given attribute. This reflects our sense of the probability that Jones is a member of particular classes: the class of persons who are Republicans, businessmen, and liberals. We may be certain that Jones is a Republican (belief strength = 1.00); pretty sure that he is a businessman, but heard it only from a friend who has been known to be wrong on occasion (belief strength = 0.70); and how liberal he is might be a matter of some confusion and dispute (belief strength = 0.40). These attributes hold different positive and negative values for you. Suppose you rated these values on a scale from −3 (most negative) to +3 (most positive). You are mostly indifferent about party affiliation, but you do prefer Democrats (your evaluation of Jones's party affiliation = −1). You are quite suspicious of businesspeople who seek public office (occupation = −3). And you prefer your politicians fairly liberal (+2). The values of these attributes are weighted by the probability that Jones has them, and they are added together to yield your overall attitude:

$$(-1 \times 1.0) + (-3 \times .70) + (+2 \times .40) = -2.3$$

Compare your attitude toward Jones with your attitude toward his opponent, Smith, summarized in Table 5.3. Because of your belief strengths about Smith's attributes and your evaluation of those attributes, your overall attitude toward Smith is more positive. Other people will value these attributes differently, will have different beliefs about the likelihood that each candidate has them, and may even regard different attributes as salient.

This simple mathematical model suggests how beliefs and value judgments combine to form attitudes by a kind of cognitive algebra. The theory does not argue that this is exactly what goes on in people's minds, but the model captures key features of the process: a selection of attributes salient to the person, a strength of belief, evaluation of the attribute, and

TABLE 5.3
Hypothetical Attitudes Toward Two Candidates As a Function of Belief Strength and Attribute Value

Candidate Jones		Candidate Smith	
Belief Strength times Value	Attribute		Belief Strength times Value
−1.0 = −1 × 1.00	Party: Republican	Party: Democratic	+1 × 1.00 = +1.0
−2.1 = −3 × 0.70	Occupation: businessman	Occupation: lawyer	+1 × 1.00 = +1.0
+0.8 = +2 × 0.40	Ideology: liberal	Ideology: liberal	+2 × 0.80 = +1.6
−2.3	Resulting Attitude		+3.6

a way of combining beliefs and values. If the model approximates the process well enough, it will account for and predict attitudes well. In fact, fairly high correlations have been found between attitudes measured directly and those predicted by the model. It has been used successfully to predict attitudes toward such things and people as birth control pills (Jaccard & Davidson, 1972), blacks (Fishbein, 1963), presidential candidates (Fishbein & Coombs, 1974), and energy proposals (Bowman & Fishbein, 1978).

Sources of Beliefs If beliefs lead to the formation of attitudes toward previously unknown or neutral people and issues, where do beliefs come from? Just as expressions of attitudes and efforts to produce various attitudes are all around us, so are efforts at producing beliefs, which will in turn produce attitudes. Are those who spread their beliefs interested only in your enlightenment, as many educators and journalists claim they are? Or are they interested in your attitudes, as advertisers and politicians obviously are? This is a subject of much debate. The sources of information and beliefs are all around us. Family, friends, teachers, and the media, as well as institutions such as business and government, all have a great impact. And we should not overlook our own direct personal experience with the world, or at least those portions of it with which we have contact. These and other sources of information build up the base of beliefs on which attitudes come to rest.

The Role of Learning

The three major kinds of learning, or conditioning—classical, operant, and modeling—are also important processes underlying the formation of attitudes.

Classical Conditioning **Classical conditioning** is the process by which previously neutral stimuli (the conditioned stimuli) come to elicit emotional, or attitudinal, reactions after they have been associated with stimuli that already have the power to elicit emotional responses (unconditioned stimuli). Let us consider an example.

A young mother of our acquaintance has two daughters, aged five and seven. Each night around bedtime she gets the children into their pajamas and sits with them in their bright and comfortable living room. Concertos by Beethoven or Vivaldi play on the stereo. The cold night is held back by a blazing fire. The daughters snuggle close beside their mother and they read to each other. This ritual began years before with the mother reading to them from children's books. Now the mother does not do all the reading, the books are not always for juveniles, and the language is not always English. In later years these children will find that they love to listen to classical music and to read. These things simply will feel good, and the children will enjoy them. Their mother will have conditioned them to feel that way. In short, they will have acquired strong positive attitudes toward reading and toward classical music. Let us analyze this instance of the classical conditioning of attitudes (see Staats, 1975; Lott & Lott, 1968).

From the perspective of classical conditioning, snuggling with Mother and the glow and warmth of the fire are unconditioned stimuli. They produce a variety of responses in the children such as relaxation, comfort, security, and well-being. Step 1 in Figure 5.2 depicts the situation. The classical music and the reading are the conditioned stimuli. Initially, they are neutral, eliciting no particular responses. Presented repeatedly along with the unconditioned stimuli (Step 2), a conditioned stimulus eventually acquires the capacity to elicit the same responses: relaxation, comfort, security, and feelings of well-being (Step 3).

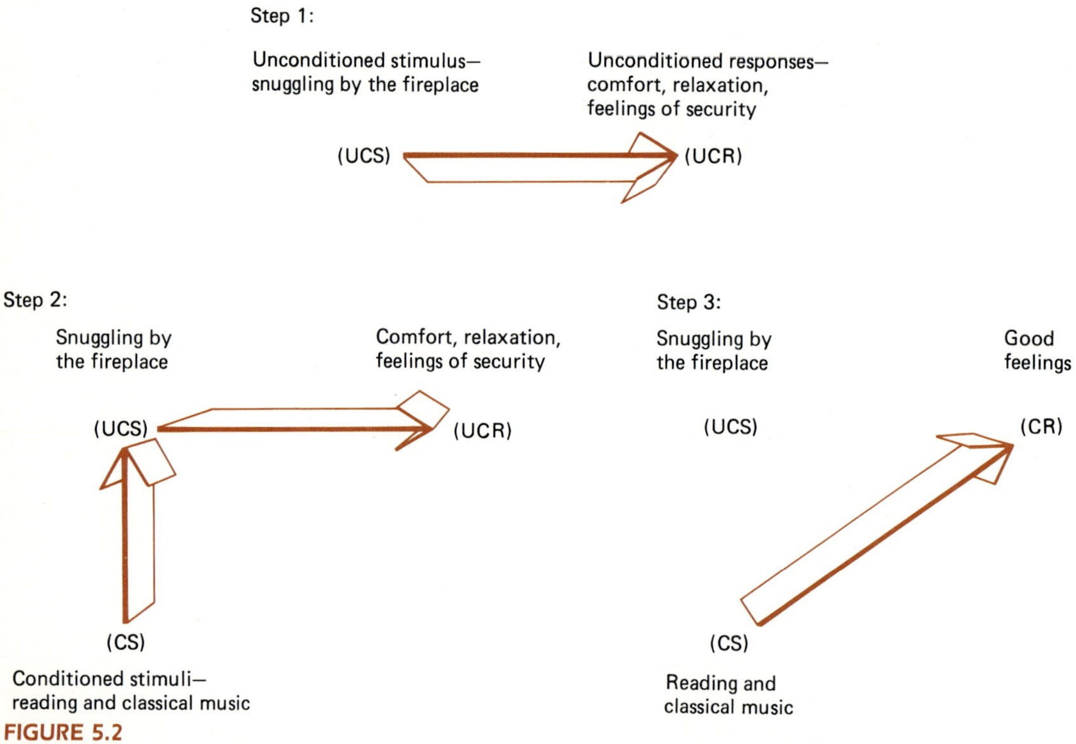

FIGURE 5.2

Classical Conditioning of Attitudes *Step 1.* Snuggling by the fireplace (unconditioned stimulus, UCS) is "naturally" associated with good feelings (unconditioned response, UCR). *Step 2.* Reading and classical music (conditioned stimuli, CS) are associated with snuggling by the fireplace (UCS). *Step 3.* By association with the snuggling (UCS), reading and classical music (CS) come to arouse good feelings (conditioned response, CR).

In this way, emotional responses toward these social objects (reading and music) have been conditioned; and positive attitudes toward these objects have been acquired. Of course, the attitudes learned could have been negative had the unconditioned responses been negative. And things other than books and music could have been the stimulus objects to which attitudes were conditioned, for example, cooking, doing mathematics problems, or playing with mechanical gadgets.

The conditioning of emotional reactions is a relatively easy and powerful way to acquire new attitudes, and they will be quite persistent. Parents do it all the time without realizing they are doing it. And we even do it to ourselves without realizing. No doubt when certain favorite old songs are played or certain places are visited, you may feel strong emotional reactions. Those stimuli—the songs, the places—have become conditioned to emotion-arousing experiences that you had in their presence.

Operant Conditioning Whereas classical conditioning is concerned with emotional responses that are developed in association with certain objects, **operant conditioning** is concerned with the reinforcement of overt behavior or thoughts. Responses that are reinforced will continue to occur; those not reinforced will decline in frequency and eventually become extinct (Skinner, 1938).

Children who express views similar to those of their parents are likely to receive some social reward: a smile, a compliment, in rare instances perhaps a raise in allowance. It is even more likely that a child who expresses a view contrary to the parent's will receive punishment, criticism, or at least disagreement. Thus, the child learns that certain attitudes are welcome and others are not. As a result, parents who are Muslim tend to produce children who are Muslim, and Democrats tend to have children who are Democrats (Stone, 1974).

Actually, the learning of political and other social attitudes occurs more powerfully in school and in peer groups than in families (Stone, 1974). The ability of peers, for example, to monitor and reinforce attitudes through acceptance or rejection, ridicule or respect, is considerable. Because so much communication between people is the direct expression of attitudes, the process of rewarding or punishing others in subtle and not so subtle ways for the views they express is a common mode of shaping the attitudes they will hold, or at least express.

Modeling **Modeling,** also known as vicarious or observational learning, is a "behavioral" process by which attitudes are acquired merely by observing the behavior of others (Bandura, 1965, 1977). Modeling is perhaps the most common means of learning for people of all ages. When people enter a new situation—new neighborhood, new job, first day at school—they look around carefully to see what everyone else in that setting is doing. They then learn just what behavior is appropriate and

It is no accident that the attitudes and behaviors of children often resemble those of their parents. Modeling, the learning of behavior from observation of those around us, is not only the most common but frequently the most subtle form of learning.

acceptable as the result of observing how the behavior of others is being received.

Modeling often works in conjunction with operant conditioning. A person in a new social environment usually is trying to fit in, to act "properly" (i.e., to obtain reinforcers), and to avoid looking foolish (i.e., to avoid punishers). This is a major part of the socialization process, whether we are talking about juvenile delinquents (e.g., Shaw, 1968), prostitutes (Bryan, 1965), military personnel (e.g., Merton & Lazarsfeld, 1950), or medical students (Merton, Reider, & Kendall, 1957). The effects of modeling are evident in the transmission of behavior from parents to children. For example, people who smoke tend to have children who smoke (Evans et al., 1978).

In addition to behavior, one also learns attitudes this way. The way people act toward various attitude objects allows an observer to infer the attitude they hold toward the object, event, or idea: admiration, respect, disdain, or hatred. As we enter new situations and join new groups, we tend to acquire the patterns of behavior of the people in them and to adopt their thoughts and feelings.

These three attitude-"conditioning" processes operate jointly in situations of actual attitude acquisition and change and, in fact, work along with other processes we will be discussing soon. An illustration of the way in which the processes of classical conditioning, operant conditioning, and modeling complement one another is provided by Zimbardo et al. (1977) in their analysis of the procedures used by the "Moonies" in making conversions to their cult:

> Potent social reinforcers are dispensed freely—smiles, approval, acceptance, praise, physical contact, and apparent love. Non-acceptable responses elicit an immediate uniform reaction from all members of the group; they are all saddened, never angered, by deviant acts or thoughts. . . .
>
> The intensity of the emotional and physical experience is exhilarating. . . . Attractive, similar peers model sincerity, happiness, vitality and the unconditional acceptance of the cult's ideas and of each other as followers. . . . Agreement is required not with "new" ideas or principles, but with familiar words and comfortable, nonobjectionable phrases. [pp. 184–185]

The reader might want to review this quotation and try to identify the various conditioning processes that appear in it. A further discussion of cult conversions can be found in Chapter 10, "Social Influence."

APPLICATION
INCULCATING ATTITUDES IN CHILDREN

Most likely you will want your children to be similar to yourself, to share your likes and dislikes for sports teams, politics, music, and religion. Perhaps you will even want them to be "better" than you are. You are sometimes extravagant when you know you should be frugal; sometimes lazy when you should be industrious; prefer to watch TV even though you think it would be better to read a good novel. You may find yourself, like generations of parents before you, telling your children, in essence, "Don't do as I do, do as I say."

But classical and operant conditioning of attitudes can be used for more than conditioning a fondness for books, music, or political attitudes. In fact, these processes go on all the time, even when parents have never heard of them. In such cases, however, conditioning is usually inadvertent and haphazard, and sometimes teaches the child something other than what the parent would like to be teaching.

Let's look at some examples. A parent suspects a child is secretly playing with matches and one day questions the child. The child reluctantly admits she has been doing so, and the parent proceeds to punish her. No doubt the parent intends the punishment to reduce the likelihood of the daughter's playing with matches. But it should not be hard to see that the child may have learned something additional, namely, that honesty was followed by punishment. Indeed, an operant analysis of the situation suggests that the likelihood of future honesty has been reduced more effectively than has future match playing, since punishment was the immediate outcome of the child's candor. A better solution might be to reward the child for honesty and to work out a suitable punishment with the child for breaking a rule against playing with matches. In that way the child is helped to associate rewards and punishments with the appropriate behaviors.

Let's take a less obvious example. Parents often ignore their children when the children are behaving themselves. But they pay attention to them (usually by hollering, or offering distractions such as candy or playing a game) when the kids begin to act up. An operant analysis of this arrangement suggests that the parent is reinforcing the undesired behavior (acting up) while tending to extinguish the desired behavior (behaving themselves). In these and a multitude of other ways, parents sometimes sabotage their own goals by conditioning the wrong behaviors. An examination of the process through the lenses of operant or classical conditioning can often make plain what is going wrong (Kazdin, 1977).

Perhaps the greatest enemies parents confront in trying to teach their children what they want them to be and to think are simply the parents themselves. Parents who smoke, drink too much, or fight frequently are teaching the child those things via modeling. An ironic example of such learning is when a parent tries to teach Johnny not to hit other children by spanking him. Given the threat of future punishment, Johnny is indeed less likely to do so—in the presence of the parent. But Johnny has also learned that hitting is thought to be an effective means of enforcing one's wishes, and Johnny will be more likely than before to hit other children—out of the presence of the parent (Sears et al., 1953). (For more on this issue, see Chapter 8.)

Sometimes, instead of modeling something bad, a parent fails to model something good. For example, owing to their sense of modesty, parents never use the toilet in a toddler's presence. When it is time to toilet-train the child, that strange object will seem frightening as well as cold, and the child will resist or sit on it anxiously, hardly knowing what to do there. The child's attitude toward the toilet quickly becomes negative. Had the child grown up observing the parents on it, the child would be eager to imitate the behavior of the parents and would have a more positive attitude toward the toilet (Azrin, 1974).

Finally, we should recall that social learning does not provide the only mechanisms by which attitudes develop in children. The mere exposure phenomenon tells us that simply growing up around certain things will produce positive attitudes toward them. Simply by being a member of the family, the child is exposed to certain stimuli and not others: bagels but not collard greens, baptisms but not choirs, factory workers but not systems engineers. The child will be exposed to a great deal of information that feeds into one set of attitudes but not others, and will become a member of certain groups (religious, educational, cultural, athletic) and not others, merely by virtue of the opportunities the parents make available.

The Influence of Groups

Most of the stimuli to which we are exposed, the beliefs we come to hold, and the conditioning we experience, though presented as individual psychological processes, are delivered to us by people in our social world. The power of other people to shape our attitudes is facilitated by their existence as groups. Thus, understanding attitude formation requires some understanding of this most social aspect of the social psychology of attitudes.

First of all, it is clear that our attitudes are strongly influenced by the groups of which we are a part. As we saw, children tend strongly to endorse the same attitudes as their parents, including political preferences, attitudes toward religion, and prejudices toward others (Hess & Torney, 1970; Epstein & Komorita, 1966; Stephan & Rosenfield, 1978).

Peers and others exert a powerful influence on our attitudes and beliefs, as we will see in more detail in Chapter 10. The most famous study of this process was reported by Theodore Newcomb (1943), who traced the change in attitudes held by students attending Bennington College, a small New England women's school. Bennington provided an interesting setting to study the group's effects because students generally came from conservative upper-class families into a school with a strongly liberal atmosphere.

By Thanksgiving break of their first semester, a shift in attitudes was already apparent. The new attitudes continued to form throughout the four years, but were strongest in students who became most involved in the life of the college. Those who maintained the closest ties to their families changed the least. After 25 years, the group-induced attitudes were still present, apparently because students selectively involved themselves with friends, mates, and organizations consistent with their new attitudes, those who would continue to support their attitudes (Newcomb et al., 1967).

The importance of groups to the formation of attitudes stems from a number of things. Most obviously, groups are a source of beliefs. Groups to which we belong (membership groups) or with which we identify (reference groups) guide us in learning what beliefs or attitudes we ought to hold in order to maintain the groups' acceptance or our own consistent identity. For instance, if you regard yourself as a Republican, when a new issue arises you will look to that group to find out what the "correct" attitudes are on that issue. In addition to information, groups are also able to deliver social influence, rewards, and punishments. Religious institutions spread their attitudes and beliefs by relying on parents who send their children for religious schooling, bring them to worship services, and transmit beliefs and condition attitudes at home. Friends we make at activities sponsored by religious groups further reinforce these attitudes. Therefore, the psychological processes that result in the formation of internally consistent groups of attitudes are applied in a wide range of times and places, by people linked together through social and institutional bonds. We ourselves, of course, are part of that social network, and give as well as receive influence. This reinforces our attitudes still further.

Groups usually do not attempt to promote their attitudes in a conscious or systematic way, but they accomplish this because they are ready-made networks that tend to touch and hold people. People refer to groups for attitudinal orientation, and groups provide a systematic flow of actions and information. The end result is that people share attitudes and beliefs more than would occur by chance exposure to such stimuli. In sum, the formation of attitudes involves a variety of psychological processes, but the one aspect they hold in common is that people, organized as part of a social process, help determine what we believe and what we do and do not like.

HOW ATTITUDES ARE MEASURED

In order to study the organization or formation of attitudes, or simply to find out what a person's attitudes are, it is necessary to measure them. At best, any measurement of an attitude reflects a small sample of it. Still, the importance we attach to attitudes and their measurement is seen by the attention we give to the results of public opinion polls. The In the News box on pages 186–187 offers the results of one such recent poll.

Reliable and valid measurement is essential to any science. We defined the concepts of reliability and validity in the context of personality measurement (Chapter 3). Their meaning in the measurement of attitudes is no different. By *reliability* we mean that if the same thing is measured repeatedly, it will always lead to the same conclusion about its nature or amount. By *validity* we mean a scale's ability to measure what it purports to measure. Many approaches to the measurement of attitudes have been developed. It is important to each of them that they have high reliability and validity. In the following sections we briefly describe and illustrate various techniques of attitude measurement. (For further information see Fishbein, 1967; Summers, 1970; and Scott, 1968.)

Direct Measures: Self-report

By far the most common approach to attitude measurement is simply to ask a person a question or a series of questions. The questions can be put verbally by an interviewer or can be presented on a written questionnaire (a "paper-and-pencil" measurement). Social psychologists use these **verbal measures of attitudes** widely because they are easy to construct, prepare, and administer, not because they have superior validity over other techniques. Owing to their popularity, these are also the most well developed and most studied attitude measurement techniques. We will examine several of the best-known and most widely used of the self-report techniques and illustrate them with sample measures of the important and much-debated social issue measured in the Gallup Poll on capital punishment.

Thurstone Scaling, or the Method of Equal-Appearing Intervals As you can see in Table 5.1 on page 167, Thurstone defined attitudes as the sum total of a person's feelings, biases, and beliefs about an attitude object. Accordingly, Thurstone wanted to sample the universe of a given person's feelings about the attitude (Thurstone & Chave, 1929). The first step, then, was to develop a pool of items, usually about 80 to 100, expressing as many views about the attitude object as possible.

By pretesting these items with a preliminary sample of people, the items' positions on an underlying attitude scale, their *scale values,* are determined. Each item also receives a score reflecting its ambiguity. To the extent that an item is seen differently by different raters, the item is undesirable as a measurement tool. About 20 items are then selected from the pool by choosing those that cover the whole range of possible positions and are relatively unambiguous. Table 5.4 shows a few items that might result from applying this procedure to the issue of capital punishment. To measure a person's attitude, the person is asked to check as many statements as he or she personally agrees with. The median scale value of the endorsed statements is the measure of the person's attitude; the scores range from 1.00 to 11.00, highly favorable to highly unfavorable.

Likert Scaling, or the Method of Summated Ratings An easier and faster method, which has approximately the same reliability and validity as Thurstone scaling, is Likert's Method of Summated Ratings (Likert, 1932).

TABLE 5.4
Examples of Thurstone Scale Items

(Check the statements with which you agree)

_____1. Capital punishment is no more effective a deterrent than life imprisonment (9.1)

_____2. Justice requires that a person who takes a life lose his or her own life. (2.0)

_____3. Only God has the right to end a human life. (6.9)

_____4. Executions cost taxpayers a lot less than lifetime imprisonment. (4.5)

_____5. If the state kills people, it teaches that killing is an acceptable means of solving problems. (8.3)

IN THE NEWS

DEATH PENALTY FOR MURDER

Question: *Do you favor or oppose the death penalty for murder?*

		January 10–13, 1986			
		Favor	**Oppose**	**No Opinion**	**Number of Interviews**
	NATIONAL	**70%**	**22%**	**8%**	**1,569**
Sex	Men	74	19	7	786
	Women	66	24	10	783
Age	Total under 30	70	24	6	326
	18–24 years	71	21	8	154
	25–29 years	68	28	4	172
	30–49 years	72	21	7	618
	Total 50 & older	69	20	11	620
	50–64 years	73	18	9	325
	65 & older	64	22	14	295
Region	East	64	26	10	404
	Midwest	73	17	10	393
	South	69	23	8	459
	West	76	20	4	313
Race	Whites	73	19	8	1,419
	Non-whites	50	41	9	150
	Blacks	47	43	10	132
	Hispanics	60	30	10	83
Education	College graduates	67	26	7	31
	College incomplete	73	20	7	386
	High school graduates	75	19	6	501
	Not high school grads.	63	23	14	363
Politics	Republicans	83	11	6	526
	Democrats	62	30	8	584
	Independents	69	22	9	404
Occupation	Professional & business	72	21	7	442
	Clerical & sales	78	16	6	102
	Manual workers	69	24	7	617
	Skilled workers	79	16	5	273
	Unskilled workers	61	30	9	344
Household Income	$50,000 & over	79	17	4	173
	$35,000–$49,999	78	16	6	182
	$25,000–$34,999	73	21	6	274
	$15,000–$24,999	72	22	6	359
	$10,000–14,999	66	22	12	228
	Under $10,000	60	27	13	264
	$25,000 & over	76	19	5	629
	Under $25,000	67	24	9	851
Religion	Protestants	72	20	8	905
	Catholics	70	22	8	438
Labor	Labor union families	74	20	6	310
	Non-union families	69	22	9	1,259

Design of the Sample

The design of the sample used by the Gallup Poll for its standard surveys of public opinion is that of a replicated area probability sample down to the block level in the case of urban areas and to segments of townships in the case of rural areas.

After stratifying the nation geographically and by size of community in order to insure conformity of the sample with the 1980 Census distribution of the population, over 350 different sampling locations or areas are selected on a mathematically random basis from within cities, towns, and counties which have in turn been selected on a mathematically random basis. The interviewers have no choice whatsoever concerning the part of the city, town, or county in which they conduct their interviews.

Approximately five interviews are conducted in each randomly selected sampling point. Interviewers are given maps of the area to which they are assigned and they are required to follow a specified travel pattern on contacting households. At each occupied dwelling unit, interviewers are instructed to select respondents by following a prescribed systematic method. This procedure is followed until the assigned numbers of interviews with male and female adults have been completed.

After the survey data have been collected and processed, the demographic characteristics of survey respondents are balanced to match the latest U.S. Census Bureau estimates of the adult population's demographic characteristics. The data are also weighted by the probability of finding individual respondents at home. These weighting procedures ensure the representativeness of the sample.

Since this sampling procedure is designed to produce a sample which approximates the adult civilian population (18 and older) living in private households (that is, excluding those in prisons and hospitals, hotels, religious and educational institutions, and on military reservations), the survey results can be applied to this population for the purpose of projecting percentages into numbers of people. The manner in which the sample is drawn also produces a sample which approximates the population of private households in the United States. Therefore, survey results can also be projected in terms of numbers of households.

Source: The Gallup Report (nos. 244–245), January–February 1986.

TABLE 5.5
Examples of Likert Scale Items

(Check your degree of agreement or disagreement with each of the following statements)

1. Civilized societies do not practice capital punishment.

+2	Strongly Agree
+1	Moderately Agree
0	Neutral
−1	Moderately Disagree
−2	Strongly Disagree

2. The state must retain the right to protect itself, even by taking a life.

+2	Strongly Agree
+1	Moderately Agree
0	Neutral
−1	Moderately Disagree
−2	Strongly Disagree

Once again, a large pool of items is collected, pared down to a workable number, and given to people to respond to. The people respond by indicating their degree of agreement on a five-point scale, as shown in Table 5.5. Total attitude scores are obtained by adding up the responses to the individual items. Each item is then correlated with the total score, and those that do not correlate highly are removed. Each person's total score is then recomputed for the items that remain, and that score represents the person's attitude. One of the features that makes Likert scales easier to construct and to administer is that the social psychologist can validate and measure the instrument using the same sample of people. This strongly agree–strongly disagree format is one that you have probably been called upon to answer in many a public opinion survey.

Semantic Differential The semantic differential method seeks to determine what a concept means to a person (Osgood, Suci, & Tannenbaum, 1957). The developers of this approach found that people perceived most things along three major dimensions: evaluation (positive or negative), activity (active or passive), and potency (weak or strong). Since the evaluative dimension is the attitude component, it was apparent that the semantic differential could be adapted to measure attitudes. By taking a variety of items that tap evaluation (for example, "good-bad" but not "fast-slow"), a person's attitudes can be assessed. The same criterion of correlation with a total scale score, as with the Likert scale, is used to exclude dimensions not contributing to valid measurement. The measure of the attitude would be the sum or average of the ratings of the various dimensions. Table 5.6 provides an example.

TABLE 5.6
Examples of Semantic Differential Items

(Rate your feelings about capital punishment on the scales below)

Capital Punishment

good	1	2	3	4	5	6	7	bad
harmful	1	2	3	4	5	6	7	beneficial
right	1	2	3	4	5	6	7	wrong
barbaric	1	2	3	4	5	6	7	civilized

One-Item Self-rating Scale The ultimate in simplicity is the single-item self-rating scale. In contrast to the burdensome preliminaries and computations of Thurstone scaling, the one-item scale requires only that the investigators ask the question, "Do you favor or oppose the death penalty?" (as used in the Gallup Poll), or, if they desire to know the extent of agreement, "How do you feel about capital punishment?" In this case, the two endpoints of the scale, representing the most extreme attitudes, are always clearly identified (see Table 5.7). The person gives his or her answer by choosing some point on the scale (Cox, 1980). The evidence is that this method is sometimes as reliable as the other techniques we have discussed (Taylor & Parker, 1964). Where people have a clear sense of what their attitudes are, and would be willing to reveal those attitudes candidly, the directness of the one-item technique appears to make up in brevity and simplicity whatever may be lost in reliability.

Techniques to Increase Validity When asked to state their attitudes, people may shade in one direction or another, camouflage their real feelings, or simply lie. This represents a major threat to the validity of these measures. For instance, people may try to cast themselves in a socially desirable light, and therefore fail to admit to an interviewer that they dislike certain ethnic groups or that they have changed their attitudes (Braver, Linder, & Corwin, 1977). The ease with which people may conceal or distort their true feelings is a major problem in the accurate measurement of attitudes, especially when dealing with sensitive issues.

TABLE 5.7
Example of One-Item Self-rating Scale

(Circle the *X* that indicates your position)

How do you feel about capital punishment?

favor X X X X X oppose

One attempted solution to this problem is the **bogus pipeline** (Jones & Sigall, 1971). This technique fights deception with deception. In the original bogus pipeline, electrodes were attached to the participants' wrists, and they were told that the electrodes could detect minute initial muscle movements. On a few practice trials, by using attitude information the researcher obtained previously, the people are made to think the apparatus "knows" what they think. Then, on subsequent trials, they will be afraid to lie, thinking that the apparatus will reveal their true attitudes. Since being found out to be a liar is more embarrassing to most people than admitting to harboring unpopular attitudes, people are often quite honest. Although it appears that the bogus pipeline gets people to be more candid about delicate issues, thereby increasing the validity of the attitude measurement (Sigall & Page, 1971; Quigley-Fernandez & Tedeschi, 1978), the deception involved in the technique has come in for criticism (Ostrom, 1973).

Quite a different solution to concealment of one's true feelings and beliefs is the method of randomized response (Shotland & Yankowski, 1982; Warner, 1965). This technique tries to provide so large a curtain of confidentiality that subjects should feel no need to lie. This is how it works. Suppose the attitude being measured involves the temptation to assassinate the president. The subject is asked two questions. The first might be, "Have you ever found yourself tempted to assassinate the president?"; the second might be, "Did you have breakfast today?" Respondents are told to flip a coin to determine which question to answer. If it's heads, the assassination question is answered; if tails, the breakfast question. Only they can know which question is being answered. By knowing the distribution of answers to the breakfast question in the population, the researcher can mathematically separate the distributions to come up with a distribution of answers to the assassination question. Thus, individuals get their privacy and researchers get their data.

Indirect Measures

Rather than putting a question directly to a person and asking for a self-report of an attitude, a variety of **indirect measures of attitudes** have been developed.

Error Choice This technique involves the construction of a multiple-choice attitude test in which no objectively correct answers are available or provided. For example, as "answers" to the question "What percentage of people executed in the United States were later determined to be innocent of the crimes for which they were executed?" the following options might be given: 0%, 2%, 5%, 10%, 15%. The error choice technique assumes that people will guess factual options that justify or are consistent with their attitudes. People opposed to capital punishment would tend to choose the higher figures; those favoring capital punishment would tend to choose the smaller figures (Hammond, 1948).

Behavioral Measures If attitudes are connected to behaviors, then we ought to be able to infer attitudes from how people behave toward objects relevant to their attitudes. A number of strategies based on this assumption have been developed. One category is that of *unobtrusive measures*, many of which have been described in a book by that title (Webb et al., 1981). Unobtrusive measures avoid getting in the way of the phenomenon they are studying. They may involve examinations of archival records, or discreet observation of behavior itself. For example, if you wanted to know which store window displays were most popular, you could measure the size of crowds gathering at them or the number of noseprints on the glass.

An unobtrusive measure well known to social psychologists is the *lost letter technique* (Milgram, Mann, & Harter, 1965). The assumption behind this technique is that people will assist causes they agree with, but not those with which they disagree. For example, if you came upon a stamped letter that was addressed and sealed, but appeared to have been lost on its way to a mailbox, would you pick it up and mail it? Your choice might depend upon where the letter was headed—for example, whether it was addressed to the Citizens' Committee to Outlaw Abortion or the Abortion Rights Organizing Office. In the lost letter technique, researchers leave a large number of letters around a community that are addressed to organizations on opposite sides of the issue of interest. To see which way the community leans on that issue, the researchers need only check their post office boxes to see which letters were more often mailed. The return rates correspond to the community's attitudes.

A third category of behavioral measures is that of nonverbal behavior and noncontent verbal behavior. As we noted in Chapter 2, *nonverbal behavior* includes postural cues, head nods, eye blinks, eye contact, body orientation, and other small, usually unnoticed, and generally uncontrolled movements. *Noncontent verbal behavior,* also known as *paralanguage,* includes volume, pitch, pause, tempo, and other such features of the voice (LaFrance & Mayo, 1978; Knapp, 1978; Mehrabian, 1972). The general idea behind using such behaviors as measures of attitude is that even if people try to distort their true feelings and beliefs, nonverbal "leakage" cues will give them away, provided one knows what to look for. Freud (1905/1959) suggested that "if his lips are silent, he chatters with his fingertips; betrayal oozes out of him at every pore."

People might try to misrepresent their true attitudes on many occasions: negotiators on opposite sides at a bargaining session; a witness at a trial; a president answering reporters' questions at a press conference. People have long wished they could open a window on the true feelings of others. And many people assume they can detect deception using such

TABLE 5.8
Nonverbal Indicators of Concealment of Attitudes and Belief

Liars engage in these behaviors:

- Appear less involved in their communications
- Appear less spontaneous and more rehearsed
- Exhibit more pupil dilation
- Commit more speech errors
- Speak in higher-pitched voice
- Show negative affect
- Exhibit verbal nonimmediacy
- Make more negative verbal statements
- Use more adaptors
- Smile less
- Speak more hesitantly

Observers think people are lying if the communicators

- Gaze less
- Smile less
- Exhibit more postural shifts
- Exhibit longer latencies
- Exhibit slower speech rate
- Commit more speech errors
- Speak more hesitantly
- Speak in higher-pitched voice

cues. Indeed, the law is sufficiently certain that jurors are able to do so that it guarantees that they can observe a witness's demeanor while giving testimony (e.g., McGuire et al., 1973).

As noted in Table 5.8, systematic studies show some support for this approach (Zuckerman, DePaulo, & Rosenthal, 1981). The best indicators of attempts to hide one's attitude are not behavioral, but verbal, such as speaking with less spontaneity, a greater number of speech errors (e.g., Mehrabian, 1971), increases in pitch (e.g., Ekman, Friesen, & Scherer, 1977; Krauss, Geller, & Olson, 1976), and increases in hesitation (e.g., Knapp, Hart, & Dennis, 1974). While observers do rely on many of these valid cues, they also look to cues that are not valid indicators of deception, such as gaze and postural shifting. Contrary to the assumption made by many people (and by the law), average observers are most able to detect deception by using their ears only (to detect paralinguistic cues), helped somewhat by access to body cues, and they actually are hindered in their accuracy by access to facial cues (Zuckerman et al., 1981).

Physiological Measures Nonverbal behavior includes the movement of skeletal muscles and the pitch of voice, over which a person has or could learn to have voluntary control. Physiological responses, except under the special conditions of biofeedback, are automatic and uncontrollable

(Shapiro & Crider, 1968). The most studied of such measures are electromyographic measures (muscle contractions measured by changes in electrical potential); galvanic skin response, or GSR (amount of electrical conductivity of the skin); and pupil diameter.

Polygraphs, or lie detectors, are based on the notion that people who are misrepresenting the truth experience stress which is manifested in physiological responses (Barland & Raskin, 1973; Saxe, 1983). Except for pupillary responses, these measures require attaching electronic apparatus to the person, which is not always feasible (for instance, at a presidential press conference). Neither GSR nor pupillary response has been found to be a valid measure of attitude. They measure the intensity of a response more than its direction (whether a person is positive or negative on the subject), and they are sensitive to factors other than the attitude toward the stimulus object (Petty & Cacioppo, 1981).

DO ATTITUDES PREDICT BEHAVIOR?

We have analyzed how attitudes are structured, seen how they are formed, and examined some of the ways in which they can be measured. We now turn to the topic that arouses most people's interest in attitudes, namely, the relationship of attitudes to behavior. Zimbardo (in Krupat, 1982) points out that the attractiveness of the concept of attitudes to early researchers was that it might afford a "quick and dirty" way of predicting behavior. And if attitudes could successfully predict behavior because they

Do attitudes have the power to predict behavior? In this situation, the two young men are likely to *believe* that they should help, but this does not necessarily mean that they will actually do so.

cause behavior, then perhaps we could even control behavior by controlling attitudes.

Ultimately, it is behavior that counts. Attitudes are important only if they tell us whether people associate with or exclude others of different races; whether they vote for candidate X or candidate Y; and whether they cheat on tests or spouses or income taxes. The easy assumption that people act in accord with their attitudes led to great interest in measuring, monitoring, and changing attitudes. But research designed to test that assumption brought it into doubt (Wicker, 1971; Brannon, 1976). And when it was found that a simple one-to-one correspondence between attitudes and behavior did not exist, considerable effort was put into trying to account for the failure of attitudes to account for behavior.

We will review attitude-behavior research to illustrate the nature of the problem, to examine some of its explanations, and to discuss a variety of proposed solutions. The best of the explanations, as we shall see, confirms the value of the attitude concept. Yet at the same time it points out the limitations of the concept and suggests ways of improving the correspondence between attitudes and behavior.

The attitude-behavior problem, as it has been called, might be viewed as a disappointment to the attitude theory enterprise. But its discovery and efforts at its solution have contributed much to understanding human behavior and to improving the conceptual and methodological tools of social scientists. The lessons learned might ultimately be viewed as important steps forward in the larger enterprise of understanding, predicting, and controlling behavior.

The Gap Between Attitudes and Behavior

Virtually every discussion of the attitude-behavior problem begins with an article by Richard LaPiere (1934) of a two-year trip he took in the early 1930s with a male Chinese student and the student's Chinese wife. LaPiere had long been concerned with the study of racial prejudice. He himself had collected considerable data, through attitude questionnaires, on its extent and nature in both the United States and Europe (e.g., LaPiere, 1928). Not only was racial prejudice widespread, but in many parts of the United States laws existed to compel the separation of races. LaPiere and his companions began their long journey, which would take them twice across the United States and up and down the Pacific coast, with understandable trepidation. They would have to rely on public accommodations such as hotels and restaurants and come into contact with many strangers. On the basis of attitudes that had been documented in surveys by questionnaires and interviews, LaPiere and his friends had reason to expect a difficult journey. Much to their surprise, however, only one of the 66 hotels and tourist homes they stayed at and 184 restaurants they entered refused to serve them. Indeed, LaPiere felt that they had been received pleasantly.

The contrast between the "intense" prejudice revealed by many attitude surveys and the reception they experienced must have been both a pleasant personal surprise and a theoretical shock to LaPiere. To test the apparent discrepancy further, he later wrote to many of the hotels and restaurants they had visited, asking "Will you accept members of the Chinese race as guests in your establishment?" In contrast to the actual behavior experienced, only one of the 79 hotels and one of the 177 restaurants replied that they would; all the rest said they would not. Thus the very establishments that in overwhelming numbers *said* they would not accept Chinese guests had, on an earlier occasion and in equally overwhelming numbers, actually welcomed them. LaPiere's study was somewhat primitive and suffered from a number of methodological flaws. For example, at each establishment the person who greeted the visitors was not necessarily the same person as the one who responded to the letter. Thus, the inconsistency was not necessarily between a given person's attitude and behavior, but between one person's attitude and another person's behavior. But LaPiere's study was provocative enough to begin a long line of studies that tried and failed to find much connection between what people say and what they do (Ajzen & Fishbein, 1977; Deutscher, 1973; Wicker, 1971).

Corey (1937) used a 50-item Likert scale to measure students' attitudes toward cheating and then constructed a testing situation wherein he was able to assess actual cheating over a series of weekly examinations. The correlation between attitudes expressed and cheating behavior was 0.02, virtually nonexistent. Saenger and Gilbert (1950) found no relationship between people's expressed attitude toward being waited on by black sales personnel and whether they actually did permit themselves to be served by blacks.

DeFleur and Westie (1958), in another effort to demonstrate a link between acts and sentiments, administered attitude scales to a large number of college students and then selected the most and the least racially prejudiced individuals for their experiment. The participants were each shown a series of color slides of interracial couples. They were then informed that additional photographs had to be made and were asked to volunteer. They were told that they would have to sign a separate authorization and release form for each of the eight possible uses of the photographs. The uses ranged from "laboratory experiments where it will be seen only by professional sociologists" to "a nationwide publicity campaign advocating racial integration." Participants were asked to sign forms for as many of the eight situations as they were willing to allow their interracial photograph to be used for. As they had anticipated, significantly more forms were signed by the low-prejudiced subjects, but the correlation between degree of prejudice and degree of commitment to be shown in an interracial photograph was only moderate. Only 16 percent of the variation in behavior was attributable even to these extreme differences in racial attitudes.

Evidence of the questionable relationship between attitudes and behavior comes not only from studies focused directly on the problem but also from studies of other issues. For example, Milgram's (1974) research on obedience found that most of his ordinary research participants inflicted what they thought were painful and even life-threatening electrical shocks on helpless victims. Yet the average person holds and expresses attitudes contrary to such cruelty. This apparent attitude-behavior discrepancy will be discussed at length in Chapter 10.

By the 1970s, it had become widely recognized that the relationship between attitudes and behavior was not the simple, causal, or even predictive relationship that was once dreamed about. While none of the studies found an inverse relationship between expressed attitudes and the behavior being predicted, even the most comforting of them found only a weak relationship. Wicker (1969), reviewing nearly three dozen studies of the relationship between attitudes and behavior, concluded that "little evidence [existed] to support the postulated existence of stable, underlying attitudes within . . . individual[s] which influence both [their] verbal expressions and [their] actions" (p. 75). Deutscher (1973) reported that by 1971 his bibliography on the subject had grown to 450 studies, and yet he was able to reiterate his earlier concern (1966, p. 29) that "we still do not know much about the relationship between what people say and what they do".

Explaining the Gap Between Attitudes and Behavior

The failure to find the expected relationship between attitudes and behavior has led to some important rethinking of the issue and has resulted in some important conceptual and methodological breakthroughs (see Ajzen & Fishbein, 1977, 1980; Warshaw & Davis, 1985; Jaccard & Becker, 1985). Following are some explanations that have been offered to account for the failure of attitudes to predict behavior:

1. We have not really been measuring "attitudes"; we have been measuring another kind of behavior. Attitudes are *psychological constructs;* responses to questionnaires are behavior. Thus, in actuality, we have been trying to predict one form of behavior from another, and finding they do not correlate highly (Kiesler, Collins, & Miller, 1969). For instance, concerning the concept of helping people in need, Darley and Batson (1973) found that most seminary students offered a positive verbal response on a questionnaire; yet, in reacting to an actual person in need, many who were in a hurry offered no assistance. Neither is the attitude; both are behavior. The real question, then, might be why two classes of behavioral responses to the same attitude object differ as often as they do.
2. These two kinds of responses differ in the consequences they have for the person expressing them. Brannon (1976) distinguishes between "attitude expressions" and behaviors. Attitude expressions, which we

usually just call attitudes, are behaviors that have, at most, only minor consequences for the person. The identical act may be an attitude expression in one context and a behavior in another. To say you favor capital punishment, as many people casually do, and then to say so when on a jury are reactions to the same issue, but they have very different consequences. As the attitude expression and the criterion behavior come to be more and more similar in their form and their consequences, as is the case in voting where each may be nothing more than an X marked on a piece of paper, the correlation between the two becomes higher.

3. To the extent that the reliability of the measurement of either the attitude or the behavior is imperfect, the observed correlation between the two will necessarily be smaller than the true correlation. For example, suppose we try to predict which sprinters will win a race by using times we collected during workouts with a stopwatch that had a somewhat loose hand. Although we surely can expect speed on one occasion to predict speed on a later occasion, the reduced reliability in one of the measures reduces the correlation between the predicted and the actual outcomes. This is simply a fact of life in measurement and prediction, and the low correlations may say more about the available tools than about the phenomenon being measured.
4. Even if measures of both attitude and behavior are perfect, differences in the "item difficulty" of the two can produce very low correlations. Kiesler, Collins, and Miller (1969) offer an analogy that illustrates this. Suppose a mathematics test had two items:

   a. $2 + 2 = ?$
   b. Differentiate the expression $\sin X^{-1/3}$.

   Ninety-nine percent of subjects might get the first item right and only 5 percent get the second right. We would not conclude that the low correlation between performance on these two mathematics-relevant behaviors casts doubt on a theory of underlying mathematical ability. We may, however, be making just this error in drawing conclusions from a low correlation between the verbal behavior of expressing an attitude and some other attitude-relevant behavior. To express on a piece of paper that one will not serve Chinese people and to say it to their faces are two different expressions of attitude whose consequences may be far from the same. "Inconsistency would be represented if those who refused face to face accepted by questionnaire, or if those who accepted by questionnaire refused face to face. There is no report that such cases occurred" (Campbell, 1963, p. 160).
5. Behavior is multiply determined. Even if attitudes are important causes of behavior, they are not the *only* causes of behavior. Many diverse factors from genetics to learned habits, personality, and motivations may be in competition with the relevant attitude to control the behavior that takes place. For example, people who abhor dishon-

esty act in accord with their attitudes overall. But they may still cheat on tests because the motivation to get high grades is strong, or they may cheat on taxes because they need the money. The Internal Revenue Service found that as economic conditions became tighter, more citizens tried to evade paying their taxes.

Another factor affecting behavior involves one's habits. Habits, by their automatic nature, may overwhelm any effect attitudes have on behavior (Triandis, 1977, 1980). For example, Smith (1977) found that employees' attitudes toward their work could not predict their attendance on an ordinary workday, when habits carried one to work almost "automatically." But on an unusual day, such as when a snowstorm occurred, work attitudes did predict attendance: the operation of habits was broken, giving people a reasonable excuse *not* to go to work. As a result, they had to make a conscious decision to go or not. In this conscious choice, their attitudes played a larger part than under the usual circumstances (Bagozzi, 1981).

6. The influence of situational constraints can override the influence of attitudes in determining behavior. A point made throughout this book is the power of situational, environmental, or structural influences on behavior. In any given situation where the behavior side of the attitude-behavior equation is measured, such constraints are certain to be operating. This is another of the determinants of multiply determined behavior.

   Situational constraints may take many forms. Sometimes the behavioral options are just not available. You may want to donate to a cause you believe in, but have no money. Sometimes we are placed in roles, and the expectations of others override our attitudes. A person in the Milgram obedience study, for example, is given a job to do and has an experimenter standing by issuing instructions. The discomfort of breaking out of that role and saying, "No, I won't," is unpleasant. Sometimes the desire to serve an attitude in one fashion interferes with the desire to serve it in another. The participants in Darley and Batson's helping experiment had people waiting for them and the clock ticking away. These are pressures that they succumbed to. One of the more important lessons of the attitude-behavior saga may be that the loftiest ideals as well as the most ignoble bigotry give way with disarming ease to mundane situational pressures.

7. Attitudes toward the class of objects under scrutiny are not the only attitudes that are relevant to the behavior. We may, in short, have competing attitudes. Negative attitudes toward people of other races may lead one to avoid associating with those people. But positive attitudes toward obeying the law or getting one's shopping done may lead even a person who is prejudiced against blacks to do business with black clerks. One might use this "other attitudes" possibility to reinterpret the situational constraints option discussed in Point 6 above. Perhaps one's attitudes toward "being on time" or "doing what

one is told" are held more intensely than one's attitudes toward helping people in need or rejecting those of other races. At first blush, this may appear astonishing. But our attitudes toward life's mundane rituals, encountered perhaps dozens of times each day, may grasp each of us more firmly than our attitudes toward the more profound—and more abstract, infrequent, and weak—of life's issues about which poets write and social scientists administer attitude scales.

Improving the Prediction of Behavior Through Attitudes

A number of theorists and researchers have exploited these very shortcomings to improve the prediction of behavior through knowledge of attitudes. They have done this by identifying certain conditions that promote the usefulness of attitudes in predicting behavior.

Similar Levels of Measurement If attitudes are measured on a diffuse and global level ("How do you feel about the French?"), but the behavior with which they are to be correlated is highly concrete and specific (your boss has asked you to meet with an important client at a French restaurant), a low correlation will result. On the other hand, if the attitudes and the behavior are measured at similar levels, they are likely to show a higher correlation.

In reviewing past research on the attitude-behavior problem, Ajzen and Fishbein (1977) found that those studies that measured specific attitudes and specific behaviors or those that measured broad global attitudes and a wide range of behaviors did, indeed, show higher attitude-behavior correlations than those that used dissimilar levels of measurement. Two studies illustrate this well. Davidson and Jaccard (1979) sought to predict the use of birth control pills over a two-year period by using attitude measures at four different levels of specificity, ranging from the most distant from the behavior (attitude toward birth control generally) to the closest (attitude toward using birth control pills during the next two years).

Table 5.9 shows the predicted effect: As the measures of attitude and behavior approached the same level, the correlation between attitude and behavior grew. Women who hold positive attitudes toward birth control may nonetheless choose not to use oral contraceptives. Some who hold negative attitudes toward birth control pills, perhaps because of their potential harmful side effects, may still use them over a relatively short span of time because they need an effective contraceptive. Clearly, the measure that predicted best was the one that came closest in specificity to the particular behavior of interest.

By contrast, Weigel and Newman (1976) used a broad general measure of people's attitudes toward the physical environment (pro-development versus pro-conservation) to predict specific behavior. General attitudes had only modest power to predict specific behaviors, such as signing

TABLE 5.9

Correlations Between a Specific Behavior, the Use of Birth Control Pills, and Attitudes Measured at Several Levels of Specificity[a]

	Attitude Measure	Correlation with Behavior
General	1. Attitude toward birth control	0.083
↓	2. Attitude toward birth control pills	0.323
	3. Attitude toward using birth control pills	0.525
Specific	4. Attitude toward using birth control pills during the next 2 years	0.572

[a] Based on a sample of 244 women.

Source: Data from Davidson & Jaccard (1979). Copyright by the American Psychological Association. Used with permission.

petitions concerning nuclear power plant construction or auto exhaust emission standards; obtaining additional signatures by circulating petitions; or participating in a roadside litter cleanup. When these single behaviors were combined into categories of similar behaviors, creating behavioral measures at a level of greater generality, each of the correlations became significant. And when these "categories of behavior" were further combined into a general "behavioral index" including all of the environment-relevant behavior, the general attitude–general behavior correlation reached its highest level.

Reduced Time Lapse The greater the time between measuring the attitude and measuring the behavior, the lower the correlation between them. The reason is probably obvious to you: the more time that passes, the more likely it is that the attitude governing the behavior has changed or that situational constraints have changed. The closer in time that we measure the attitude and the behavior of interest, the higher they will correlate. An example of this is voter polls used to predict election outcomes. The closer to election day a poll is taken, the more accurate is its prediction of the outcome (Petty & Cacioppo, 1981).

Self-monitoring At least one individual difference measure has been found that can distinguish those who show relatively high versus low attitude-behavior consistency, and that is a trait called self-monitoring. **Self-monitoring** is concerned with the tendency of some people to be more focused on inner states, while others are more focused on situational conditions (Snyder, 1979). Low self-monitors are more responsive to salient information about their internal states; high self-monitors are more reactive to situational stimuli. As we would expect, research on this trait indicates that the behavior of low self-monitors is more consistent with their attitudes (Snyder & Monson, 1975; Snyder & Tanke, 1976; Zanna, Olson, & Fazio, 1980).

Directing Attention to Inner States While self-monitoring is concerned with characteristic differences among people in their attention to inner and outer conditions, everyone's attention can be temporarily directed to the world outside or the world inside themselves. People who are made to focus on themselves (through such situational devices as having them fill out the attitude scale or perform the behavior with a mirror nearby) show higher attitude-behavior consistency than those who are not made as self-aware. Apparently, increasing people's self-awareness helps to increase the impact of their attitudes on their behavior. (Pryor et al., 1977; Scheier & Carver, 1980).

Direct Experience Attitudes formed through direct contact with attitude objects produce higher attitude-behavior correlations than attitudes formed without direct experience. Much of the time our attitudes are formed at a distance, based on secondhand or abstract information. For example, attitudes toward political candidates are often acquired by talking with friends or reading newspapers, rather than by interacting with the candidates themselves. Attitudes formed in this way are less likely to predict actual behavior than those that are formed as the result of a direct encounter with the candidate. This effect is due to several factors. In this case, for instance, the amount and salience of information about the candidate would be greater and more retrievable from memory, and greater contact with the situation surrounding the candidate would also exist (Fazio & Zanna, 1981).

A Revised View of the Attitude-Behavior Relationship: The Theory of Reasoned Action

Critical analysis and the findings of numerous research studies such as those we have discussed have led to a new theory linking attitudes and behavior in a more informed and sophisticated model. Ajzen and Fishbein's **theory of reasoned action** (1980) is perhaps the most comprehensive and thoroughly researched contemporary theory linking attitudes to behavior, and has made it possible to observe reliably a relationship between attitudes and behavior.

This theory assumes that people are rational and that they rely on information and attitudes to guide their behavior. Accurate prediction of behavior requires fitting together the correct variables (the ones that really do guide the behavior) in the correct order with the correct weights. Figure 5.3 depicts this model. The model identifies **behavioral intentions** as the most direct and powerful predictor of behavior. That is, instead of inquiring about a person's attitudes toward the object, ask about the person's intention to perform the particular behavior of interest. ("Which candidate do you *intend* to vote for? How confident are you that you will do so?") Behavioral intentions predict actual behavior with quite high

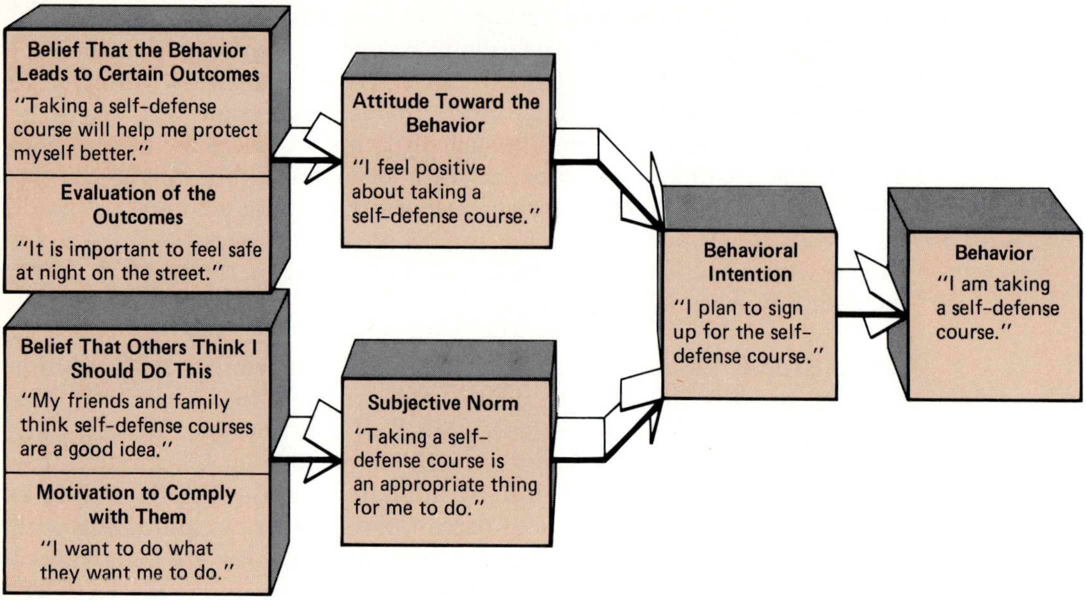

FIGURE 5.3
The Theory of Reasoned Action The theory of reasoned action connects attitudes to behavior. Behavior is caused by intentions. Intentions are caused by attitudes and subjective norms. The attitudes and the norms, in turn, are caused by beliefs about the action and perceptions of what others desire. *Source:* Adapted from M. Fishbein (1980). A theory of reasoned action: Some applications and implications. In H. Howe and M. Page (Eds.), *Nebraska Symposium on Motivation* (Vol. 27). Lincoln: University of Nebraska Press. Reprinted from 1979 *Nebraska Symposium on Motivation* by permission of University of Nebraska Press. Copyright © 1980 by the University of Nebraska Press.

accuracy. For example, Fishbein and Coombs (1974) were able to predict actual voting behavior using information about intentions to vote with correlations averaging in the 0.80s.

Behavioral intentions, in turn, are a product of two things. One is the person's *attitude toward the behavior*—that is, not toward the attitude object itself (e.g., the candidate) but toward the behavior (e.g., voting for the candidate). The second is *subjective norms.* Subjective norms are your belief about what other people in your life expect you to do with respect to the behavior in question. Thus even though you may hold a favorable attitude toward a particular issue or candidate, you may vote otherwise if you think all of your friends are going to vote that way.

Attitudes toward the behavior and the subjective norms are combined and then weighted for their importance to yield the behavioral intention. Attitudes toward the act and subjective norms have been shown to predict behavioral intentions well for such diverse behaviors as having babies (Davidson & Jaccard, 1979) and cheating in college (DeVries & Ajzen, 1971). This approach moves the measurement of attitudes closer to the measurement of behavior, and through subjective norms takes into account many other determinants of behavior besides attitudes.

Moving farther along in the process, Fishbein and Ajzen point out that attitudes toward behavior result from two sources: *beliefs that the behavior will lead to certain outcomes* and a person's *evaluation of those outcomes.* Similarly, subjective norms are the product of *beliefs that specific others think I should or should not perform the behavior* plus a person's *motivation to comply* with those social expectations. Public service announcements may tell you to quit smoking, but the motivation to comply is not likely to be very strong (i.e., it is likely to have a low weight). But if your doctor or closest friend were to say that you must quit to avoid serious health problems, then your motivation to comply would be higher. The various beliefs that different people hold about all of these things are presumed to be the product of individual experiences and personality, which are the product of *external variables.* This model also brings into the attitude-behavior picture the other variables that influence behavior, and sees those variables as exerting influence through the beliefs they foster.

Do these findings and theories solve the attitude-behavior problem? In a sense they do. They define conditions under which an attitude-behavior relationship regularly emerges. They do so, however, by putting attitudes in a more modest place. Recall that the earlier hope for attitudes was that they would replace other psychological constructs, such as habits, in predicting behavior; and that they would prove to be a powerful "quick and dirty" predictor, if not determinant, of behavior.

In summary, the Fishbein and Ajzen model makes clear that attitudes toward classes of objects are no longer the best predictors, but attitudes toward one's own behavioral options are. Most important, attitudes are only *one* element of an accurate and complete predictive model, and not even the most important one at that. Indeed, it is behavioral intentions that are the single best predictor. And behavioral intentions, unlike the general construct of attitudes, are specific and close in level and time to the behavior. Moreover, "behavioral *prediction* is *not* increased by assessing anything other than behavioral intentions. Knowing a person's attitude, subjective norm, or individual beliefs will not enhance prediction over that obtained solely by knowing the behavioral intention" (Petty & Cacioppo, 1981, p. 200). The recent breakthroughs in solving the attitude-behavior problem do not quite destroy the concept of attitudes in order to save it, but they certainly take it down a few pegs in its predictive and causal status and direct our attention to other factors.

APPLICATION
JURY SELECTION

Many people—including lawyers—believe that the attitudes a juror carries into the courtroom will play an important part in determining the verdict. Indeed, some commentators believe that this is "a very obvious fact: the people who constitute the jury can have as much or more to do with the outcome of a trial as the evidence and arguments'' (Kairys, Schulman, & Harring, 1975, p. 1). Most lawyers go so far as to believe that people's ethnic or national origin, occupation, sex, and other characteristics are correlated with their attitudes. For example, legal folklore advises lawyers to avoid having on their juries clergymen, schoolteachers, spouses of lawyers (because they know too much) (Simon, 1967), cabinetmakers (because they want things to fit together neatly), and Germans (because they are too exacting) (Mossman, 1973).

Taking seriously the possibility that basic attitudes may affect verdicts, the law allows lawyers to question potential jurors briefly about their attitudes, beliefs, and backgrounds in order to identify and exclude those who may be biased against a party to a case. During this procedure, called *voir dire,* lawyers on both sides question prospective jurors. They can reject any prospective juror if they can convince the judge that that person is biased. Each lawyer may even reject a limited number of people with no explanation.

In the past decade the notion that the attitudes of jurors strongly influence their verdicts has moved beyond an intuitive element of the trial lawyer's art (Saks & Hastie, 1978; Suggs & Sales, 1978). In a growing number of cases, lawyers have hired psychologists, sociologists, and market researchers to help select jurors by developing scales to measure attitudes relevant to issues in the case. These scales are then used to measure the attitudes in the population from which the jurors will be drawn. By correlating the attitudes to various attributes (race, sex, education, occupation, reading habits, etc.) of the population, lawyers believe that they can predict a potential juror's attitudes. In court, a person having an undesirable ''profile'' can be challenged off the jury (Bonora & Krauss, 1979; Schulman et al., 1973).

The advent of social scientists assisting in jury selection has naturally prompted more research on the subject (Penrod, 1979; Saks, 1976; Suggs & Sales, 1978). The first sobering discovery was that the survey findings varied from city to city, case to case, and time to time. Those few variables that emerged as effective predictors of attitudes in one survey were likely to be different on the next survey or a new case in a different city; and those few that reappeared might reverse direction. Females might turn out to have defense-oriented attitudes in Jacksonville, but prosecution-oriented attitudes in Seattle. Thus the generalized folklore of the legal community that certain kinds of people hold certain kinds of attitudes was found to be wrong. The second discovery was even more interesting. The pretrial attitudes themselves predicted verdicts only weakly, on the order of about 10 percent of the variance accounted for (Saks, 1976; Hans & Vidmar, 1982).

These findings parallel the experience of social psychologists with the attitude-behavior problem generally: a seemingly ''obvious'' relationship turns out to be weak, difficult to detect, and of dubious worth in pinpointing. The body of research on the attitude-behavior problem helps us understand why spending $25,000 on jury selection is not the most cost-effective way social psychologists can help lawyers win cases. If we refer to Fishbein and Ajzen's model

(Figure 5.3), we see that demographic variables do indeed play a part, but they are far removed from the target behavior of interest (i.e., the verdict). The attitudes of the jurors predicted from the demographic variables are rather broad and general, while the verdict is a specific response to the specific people, facts, and issues of the trial; thus the measures of the attitude and the behavior are at dissimilar levels.

The jurors' pretrial attitudes are weak influences on the verdict for several other reasons. Attitudes are in competition with powerful situational factors that exist in the courtroom: being impartial; doing a good, competent, honest job; submitting to the pressures of the other jurors; figuring out whether the defendant is or is not guilty by paying attention to the witnesses, exhibits, and other evidence during the trial. Finally, recall that the consequence of saying to an interviewer that you dislike a certain person or class of persons, or even that you would like to see them found guilty, is drastically different from the consequence of expressing the same attitude on a jury that is deciding an individual's fate. Thus the limited and complicated relationship between attitudes and behavior found in so many other areas has also been found among jurors.

What does determine verdicts? The research that has addressed or is relevant to the question (reviewed in Hans & Vidmar, 1982; Hastie et al., 1984; Saks, 1976) finds the evidence, arguments, and other information presented at a trial to be at least several times more powerful a determinant of the outcome than jurors' pretrial attitudes. Thus the specific attitudes formed *during* a trial, toward the role jurors are placed in and toward the people and events at issue, appear to determine jurors' verdicts—not the general biases with which they may arrive.

If the only thing Dave Atkins wanted Bill Driscoll to do for him was to survey the public and predict the outcome at the ballot box, that would be relatively easy. As long as he obtained a properly representative sample of registered voters, adjusted for different turnout rates among different groups, waited until well into the campaign, and then asked the prospective voters whom they intended to vote for, the prediction would come close to the actual election outcome. But that is of minor help to a candidate. What a candidate really needs to know are the determinants of peoples' votes and how they can be influenced so that the candidate can win. Let's look at some of the things this chapter teaches us about how to use knowledge of attitudes and behavior to help political campaigns.

Surveys of prospective voters early in the campaign could accomplish a number of things. The voters' attitudes toward the incumbent and possible challengers could be measured to find out what the chinks are in the incumbent's armor, and also to discover what your own candidate's perceived strengths and weaknesses are. The semantic differential might prove especially useful in discovering the electorate's perceptions of the candidates as well as their image of the most "ideal" candidate they can imagine. Information about group membership and loyalties can prove useful later in the campaign when you try to reach the voters by winning the support of leaders of groups to which people are loyal and responsive. By linking identifiable subgroups in the district with their past voting behavior and their attitudes toward issues, groups, and candidate characteristics, advertising efforts can be tailored for and targeted to the groups where they will have the most positive impact.

Actual persuasion attempts will be considered in the next chapter, but we already know that in forming attitudes, the views of important groups have a large impact on the development of positive or negative attitudes. We know that in building up attitudes on a base of beliefs, we can influence the attitude formed by influencing beliefs and evaluations. By knowing what the people find positive about a candidate, we can paint a public image to emphasize those attributes we know will be attractive and to play down those our survey tells us will be negative.

To the extent that the candidate's name and identity can be associated with stimuli that already elicit positive reactions, we can condition positive attitudes toward our candidate. A standard use of this principle is to associate a candidate's name with well-liked and respected endorsers or groups. Balance theory tells us that endorsements by the most widely liked people and institutions will be the most effective in forming positive attitudes toward our candidate. And the mere exposure effect tells us that the more the candidate's name is encountered by the voters in the media, on bumper stickers, or via word of mouth, the better they will like the candidate. As we shall see in the next chapter, however, the most effective techniques for producing positive attitudes will come less from the communication of information and more from the involvement of people and their behavior in activities favorable to the candidate.

SUMMARY

1. Attitudes are general and enduring feelings, positive or negative, about social objects. Because of their implications for behavior, attitudes are important to politicians, businesspeople, psychologists, and nearly everyone else.
2. Traditionally, attitudes were thought to have affective, cognitive, and behavioral components. Many social psychologists now hold the view that attitudes are restricted to the affective component. And rather than behavior itself, the behavioral component has become behavioral intention, a plan of action.

3. One of the fundamental ideas about attitudes is that they are structurally balanced. Imbalance leads to psychological discomfort and attitude change.
4. Many of the interrelationships among the attitudes a person holds are due to the coherence of the groups of which the person is a part.
5. In the mere exposure phenomenon, the more a person is exposed to a stimulus, the more positive an attitude that person develops toward it.
6. In self-perception, a person learns about his or her attitudes by observing and drawing inferences, just as an outside observer would.
7. The theory of reasoned action holds that attitudes are built up out of beliefs that vary in strength and that may have positive or negative values in varying degrees. The sources of beliefs include family, friends, school, news media, and many other sources.
8. Attitudes may be learned through classical conditioning, operant conditioning, and modeling. All three learning processes can combine to give people strong reactions to people, objects, and ideas.
9. The groups of which we are a part organize our attitude formation experiences in relatively coherent ways. They expose us to attitude objects, supply beliefs, and condition attitudes.
10. Attitude measures, like other psychological measures, must have adequate reliability and validity to be useful. Most attitude measures are direct verbal self-reports. These include Thurstone scaling, Likert scaling, the semantic differential, and the one-item rating scale.
11. Techniques to increase the validity of attitude measures, primarily to avoid distortion by subjects, include the bogus pipeline and the method of randomized response.
12. Indirect measures of attitudes include the error-choice technique, unobtrusive measures, nonverbal behavior, the lost letter technique, and physiological measures. While each has certain drawbacks, they allow us to assess attitudes that people might not be willing to express directly.
13. Much research has failed to confirm the expected relationship linking attitudes to behavior. A number of methodological and conceptual insights have evolved in an effort to explain the limited correlation between conventional measures of attitudes and behavior.
14. These insights have led to enhancements in methods for predicting behavior from attitudes. These refinements include using like levels of measurement, reduced time-lapse, self-monitoring, directing attention to inner states, and use of direct experience.
15. The theory of reasoned action has greatly clarified the attitude-behavior relationship. It introduces the concept of behavioral intentions as the best predictor of actual behavior; refocuses our interest from attitude objects themselves to attitudes toward the behavior; and moves attitudes to a less central position as a determinant of social behavior.

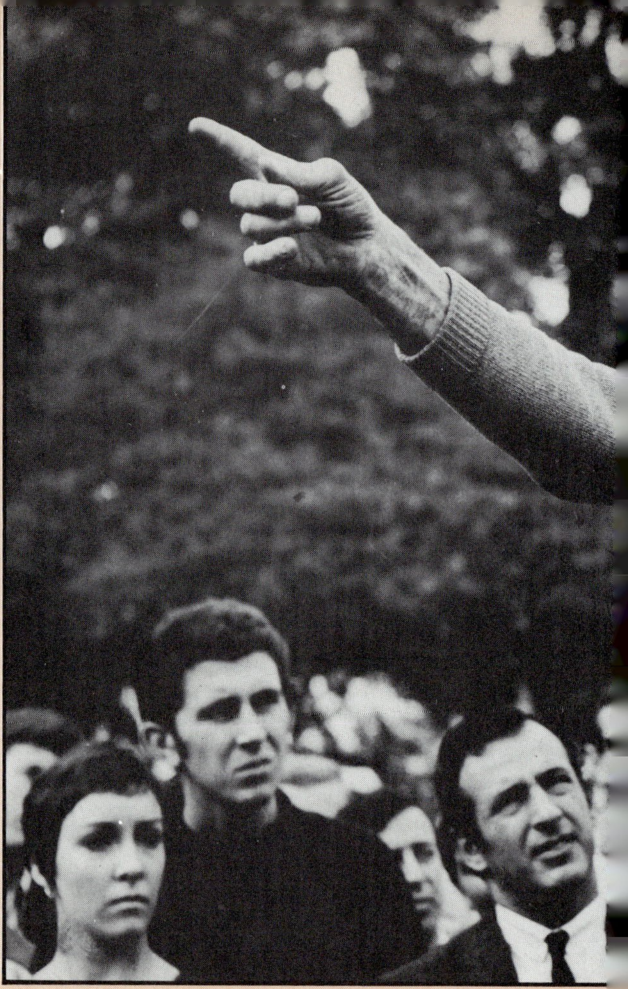

CHAPTER 6

Attitude Change

One bright, warm autumn morning, Evie Johnson finished breakfast, popped her lunch into her book bag, and headed out the front door on her way to a day of seventh grade. Her mother walked with her the few blocks to the corner where the school bus would pick her up for the ride to school. As the bus pulled up, Evie and her mother hugged goodbye more intensely than seventh-grade jitters normally required. Both knew that the trip she had been making for the three weeks since school began was a trip from the safety of her mother's embrace to a gauntlet of racism. They couldn't know it yet, but this day would end with Evie in a hospital emergency room.

The law said that cities could no longer segregate white and black children into separate schools, and Evie was one of the children caught in the middle of the process of change. Outside the formerly "white" schools waited angry crowds. The school days were punctuated by objects thrown at and into the school and occasional skirmishes between the noisy protesters and the police. At the end of the day the buses would begin to move out of the neighborhood with their load of frightened children, and the screaming protesters would throw beer cans, bottles, fruit, and rocks. Veterans of such attacks, the children would hit the decks to avoid a possible shower of splintered glass. This day Evie did not duck quickly enough.

How can we explain the behavior of the people who did such things and felt such hatred? For their part, the white parents and children felt their neighborhoods were being taken over by a federal court over which they had no control. Their schools were being invaded by black students, and their community was being invaded by armies of police. The local schools—their schools—had long been important to the residents as focuses of activity and community pride. Now it seemed that an alien government was taking all that away, and shipping their children away from their own beloved neighborhoods. All this was to be enforced, as needed, by police or soldiers. These angry and frightened people were determined to fight back.

In the end desegregation was to be accomplished forcefully: moving children around, and providing as many buses and police as the job required. Positive efforts at preparing the public, at changing their attitudes to tolerate, if not favor, desegregation were relatively few. They consisted of occasional news media editorials and taped TV and radio spots by politicians and sports heroes (especially black ones) urging citizens not to be violent, and to protect their children's safety.

The violence over several school years is testimony to the ineffectiveness of the attitude change techniques employed. What were the forces behind the attitudes held by the protesting parents? And why were the techniques used to change them so unsuccessful? At the end of this chapter we will return to this issue to consider what strategies of attitude change might have been applied using the basic principles of social psychological theories.

In the previous chapter we considered what attitudes are, how they are organized, formed, and measured, and their relation to behavior. In this chapter we look at the topic of attitude *change.* We will examine a variety of strategies for achieving attitude change, as well as several approaches to understanding the psychology of attitude change. Some of these approaches—such as the communication model, the social judgment model, and several newer cognitive models—view the person as a relatively passive target of influence. Other approaches—among them the cognitive dissonance model, the self-perception model, and the technique of role playing—see attitude change as a product of active behavioral involvement. In addition, we will examine obstacles to attitude change, and the part played by groups in producing or preventing attitude change.

THE PERSON AS RECIPIENT OF INFORMATION

The Communication Model

A group of social psychologists at Yale University in the 1940s and 1950s developed the basic concepts of the **communication model** of attitude change. They borrowed from the analysis of persuasion Aristotle proposed

This man clearly seeks to change people's attitudes about an issue that concerns him. According to the communication model of attitude change, he will successfully persuade his listeners only if they attend to his message, comprehend it, yield to it, and then retain it.

more than 2300 years ago in his *Rhetoric:* Who says what to whom and with what effect? They combined that analysis with a liberalized learning theory—"liberalized" because it made room for cognitive processes while holding on to the basic processes of conditioning and reinforcement (Hovland, Janis, & Kelley, 1953; Hovland & Janis, 1959; Hovland, Lumsdaine, & Sheffield, 1949).

Their perspective can be summarized simply: In order for persuasion to occur, a listener must *attend* to a communication, must *comprehend* it, then *yield* to it and, if the persuasion is to be more than only momentary, *retain* the message. To study this process their research generally fit the categories suggested by Aristotle's analysis. They asked about the impact of the *source* of a message, the *channel* by which it is communicated, the features of the *message* itself, and the characteristics of the *recipients* of the message.

Source Factors What are the characteristics of the person, group, or institution from which a message originates? Is the source credible or not, attractive or not, similar to the recipient or not, high or low in power, prestige, status? Does a change in any of these factors affect the amount of attitude change?

The **credibility** of a source is one of the most critical variables studied (Hass, 1981; Eagly, 1983). Credibility contains two components: expertise and trustworthiness. Highly credible sources can (1) be authoritative on the subject, and (2) be trusted to provide a relatively unbiased account of their understanding of the facts. For example, politicians around election time might not be seen as trustworthy sources because they may have ulterior motives for saying certain things. The local bartender may be viewed as entirely sincere in a discussion of nuclear strategy, but not credible because of a lack of knowledge.

To test the impact of a source's credibility, identical persuasive messages concerning how little sleep people can get by with were presented as coming either from a Nobel Prize–winning physiologist or a YMCA director (Bochner & Insko, 1966). These sources are about equal in trustworthiness; neither seems to have a vested interest in misleading. But one obviously seems more likely to be knowledgeable on the subject. As expected, the exact same message was more persuasive when it was seen as coming from the physiologist.

But the overall picture produced by the research is not so straightforward as in this example. A controversial aspect of the source-credibility effect is whether its immediate impact persists over time, or whether the impact of the low-credibility source catches up after a while. This catching up has been called the **sleeper effect.** Early researchers (Hovland & Weiss, 1951; Kelman & Hovland, 1953) found that as time passed, the persuasion produced by the high-credibility source decreased, but the persuasive impact of the low-credibility source actually increased. For example, after the passage of time, the people who heard messages from the YMCA director came to be nearly as persuaded as those whose source had been the physiologist.

Since these findings, considerable debate has taken place about the sleeper effect, and current evidence indicates that a detailed set of conditions must be just right for the effect to occur. These conditions require that (1) the message alone have a substantial impact on attitudes, (2) the attitude change be suppressed by its association with the source, (3) the identity of the source and the message's conclusion become dissociated, (4) the dissociation occur more quickly than forgetting the message, and (5) the identity of the source and the message content affect attitudes separately and do not affect each other. If these conditions are not met, the sleeper effect does not occur.

The *attractiveness* of a source shows a pattern similar to that of credibility. Attractive sources generally achieve greater acceptance of their message compared to unattractive sources (Chaiken, 1979). However, when the position advocated is a popular one, one that is likely to be acceptable to the audience, the attractiveness of the source makes little difference (Eagly & Chaiken, 1975).

Similarity is a trickier variable. First of all, similarity is never a feature of the source alone; it always involves a match or mismatch between the source and the audience. Also, what dimensions of similarity or difference are noticeable: one's sex, race, circumstances, experience, age, or education? The critical dimensions may vary with the attitude issue involved.

In any case, the positive persuasive effect of similarity seems to hold only for issues that center on unverifiable, nonfactual points. Where the issue involves matters that could be determined to be factually correct or incorrect, our attitudes are reinforced by dissimilar sources more than by similar sources (Goethals & Nelson, 1973). In matters of pure opinion, the consensus of similar others is critical; but in matters of fact, confirmation from similar others is largely redundant. On highly charged issues such as desegregation, sources such as sports heroes or politicians are unlikely to be effective. They are dissimilar sources. The most effective sort of source would probably be ordinary neighbors or people who previously opposed desegregation and busing, but who now believe that peaceful cooperation is the best route.

The effects of source factors seem to have been long and widely appreciated by persuaders. Lawyers choosing expert witnesses try to get the most prestigious experts possible, and try to promote the appearance of disinterest on the part of the experts—for example, by making the payment of a fee independent of the outcome of the trial. Advertisers use models who are either highly expert (e.g., doctors or scientists), attractive, or similar to the intended audience (e.g., young people, housewives, blacks, etc.).

Channel Factors By **channel** we mean the medium through which the message flows. Is the information transmitted to the recipient in writing, such as newspaper; by radio or TV; or through live, face-to-face communication? These are issues with which advertisers and other users of mass media must concern themselves (Werner, 1978). In general it appears that the closer a communication comes to a face-to-face encounter, the more persuasive it is (Cartwright, 1949; Katz & Lazarsfeld, 1955; Williams, 1975).

Some research has found, however, that more persuasion occurs over the "less likely" mediums (Keating & Latané, 1976). Also, the most effective medium may depend on the nature of the message. Complex or detailed communication can be comprehended better in writing, which people can read at their own pace (Chaiken & Eagly, 1976). For relatively simple messages, where source characteristics are likely to play a part, TV or face-to-face would be most effective (Andreoli & Worchel, 1978) because they emphasize visually conveyed features over message content.

Persuasion via video and audio channels also brings the viewer and listener images or sounds of the actual objects and events under discussion. More direct contact increases persuasive impact compared to only reading or being told about the issue (McGuire, 1969). In a trial, for example, presentation of the murder weapon itself or a bottle reeking of whiskey is expected to have more impact than a witness merely talking about those objects (Keeton, 1973).

Message Factors The heart of persuasive communication is the message itself. At a minimum, the audience must be told what position the advocate wishes them to adopt. But, as is evident in the discussion that follows, the salient features of a message have to do with its general structure and organization, not with the specific arguments that form its content. As we will see in a moment, few across-the-board effects hold; almost always the effects vary depending on other aspects of the communication.

Should the persuasive message concerning a subject be one-sided (presenting only the reasons that the audience should agree with the communicator), or should it be *two-sided* (including as well the arguments supporting an opposing view)? The motivation for some of the early research under the communication model was quite practical: aiding U.S. efforts in World War II. Fearing that the troops would be demoralized if the war lasted beyond their expectations, the U.S. government wanted to persuade them that a lengthier war would not be surprising. Two such messages were prepared and presented to several hundred soldiers, whose estimates of the war's duration were later obtained (Hovland, Lumsdaine, & Sheffield, 1949).

The results of these studies show that the one-sided and the two-sided messages did not differ in overall effectiveness, but interacted with certain other variables. Better-educated or more intelligent audiences were more influenced by two-sided messages; less well educated or less intelligent audiences were more persuaded by one-sided messages. Also, if an audience knew that another side existed or later learned of another side, then a two-sided message was more effective (Lumsdaine & Janis, 1953; Faison, 1961; Dipboye, 1977). Thus, the choice of one- or two-sided arguments depends upon what an audience is like and what it knows or soon will learn.

Several applications for this finding come to mind. For instance, since the opportunity for the other side to present its case is structured into the courtroom situation, lawyers in a trial would almost always be wise to offer a two-sided argument. Advertisers are faced with a less clear option. As Petty and Cacioppo (1981) have stated:

> Most advertisements list the benefits derived from the use of a product and ignore the cost involved in its use or the benefits of competitive brands. In other words, most advertisements are one-sided communication. This strategy is probably most effective when the product is well liked, widely consumed, has few competitors, and enjoys loyal customers. However, if the audience is well informed about its alternatives, the product is not widely preferred or the audience is likely to be exposed to advertisements for competitive products (which is the case for most products), then two-sided rather than one-sided advertisements may be more effective. [P. 75]

The power of words to move people is most evident when the words are used to arouse strong emotions and images. Poets, novelists, and politicians have long believed that the effective way to communicate a point is by presenting concrete images. A serious scientist, by contrast, presents abstractions, quantitative evidence, and studies. For example, in arguing for gun control, we could present the statistical evidence showing the number of deaths that would be avoided each year if handguns were banned. But a horrifying story about the night a father protected his family by chasing off a prowler at gunpoint might more readily persuade audiences to adopt the opposite viewpoint. Psychological research suggests that those who choose concrete and vivid images are right—audiences generally find anecdotes more persuasive than hard but pallid data (Nisbett & Borgida, 1975; Hamill, Wilson, & Nisbett, 1981; Saks & Kidd, 1980).

One of the most common kinds of emotion-arousing arguments is the kind that plays on the audience's fears, that is, **fear appeals.** Table 6.1 contains an example. By arousing the audience's fears, communicators hope to motivate their audience to seek refuge in the solutions they advocate. In spite of their intuitive appeal, fear-arousing arguments are effective only under certain conditions. The actions required to avoid the feared consequences must be clear enough and "do-able" enough for the recipient to carry them out. Otherwise the fear that has been aroused tends to produce what has been called "defensive avoidance" (Janis & Feshbach, 1953): The person will avoid the fear by not thinking about the issue at all, and therefore do nothing. Also, if the fear that is aroused is of too high a level, the person may not be able to attend to, recall, or carry out the recommended actions. As with many psychological variables, increasing fear works well, but only up to some optimal point. Beyond that, the arousal it produces interferes with responding (see Leventhal & Singer, 1966; Leventhal, Singer, & Jones, 1965; Beck & Davis, 1978). For example, a certain amount of fear before a test motivates studying; but if you are terrified of the exam you will not be able to turn your attention away from the fear and toward the books.

Another important issue related to the message involves timing, called **order effects.** For instance, if you are in a debate, would you be better off speaking first or last? This is a question of *external order effects* (Rosnow & Goldstein, 1967; Kiesler, Collins, & Miller, 1969; Thibaut & Walker, 1975). In the debate, would it be to your advantage to present your strongest arguments at the beginning (the anticlimax tactic) or the end of your presentation (the climax tactic)? This is a question of *internal order effects.*

Research indicates that the success of going first or last depends upon several matters of timing (see Figure 6.1, p. 218). The first communication prevails over the second (a primacy effect) when the messages immediately follow each other or the expressions of the attitude occur after a time delay of several days or more. A recency effect occurs when a time delay occurs between the presentation of messages and the attitude expression occurs immediately after the second message. Other arrangements—no time delays at all or time delays following both messages—enhance neither primacy nor recency (Miller & Campbell, 1959).

TABLE 6.1
Example of a Fear Appeal

The following is a letter from the Baker/Beech-Nut Corporation (as quoted in *Consumer Reports,* Summer 1976):

Baker/Beech-Nut Corporation
2 CHURCH STREET • CANAJOHARIE, N.Y., 13317

FRANK C. NICHOLAS
PRESIDENT

Dear Mother:

Much publicity has appeared recently which urges mothers to make their own baby food at home. Some of this publicity is distributed by manufacturers of food grinders, blenders and other implements to sell grinders and blenders. Some is well-intentioned. Much is misinformed.

We at Beech-Nut feel obliged to advise you that some potential dangers for your child exist in the home preparation of baby food. Much of the publicity has been self-serving and has ignored this fact. Beech-Nut would never want to sell its product at the expense of the health and well-being of babies. That is why Beech-Nut, as a responsible corporate citizen, feels compelled to speak out in the interest of safety and good nutrition for your baby.

You, as a mother, should know that some cases of methemoglobinemia have been reported in medical literature from the feeding of home-prepared spinach puree, carrot soup and carrot juice. Beets may also be a problem.

Nitrates in these products can be converted to nitrites during transportation, from bacterial contamination or in baby's stomach which contains less acid than an adult's stomach. Nitrites combine with red blood cell pigments in a manner which prevents these pigments from performing their job of transporting oxygen to the body. With too much methemoglobin, baby's skin turns blue and asphyxiation could result.

Commercial blanching and processing eliminates most of the nitrates, eliminates bacteria and inactivates enzymes to prevent any remaining nitrates from converting to nitrites, thus eliminating the risk.

You, as a mother, should know that babies are more sensitive to bacteria than

In line with this, a politician would probably prefer the first position to take advantage of primacy, since the arguments would be back-to-back but the voting would be days or weeks later. In a trial no advantage would exist from going first as opposed to last. We might note, however, that in a number of jurisdictions the prosecution goes first *and* last. As a result, the defendant is sandwiched in between, offering the advantages of both primacy and recency to the prosecution (Lana, 1972).

Recipient Factors Which characteristics of the recipient are important, and to what extent do they affect the attitude change process? As we have seen already, various effects of source, channel, and message are more or less effective depending upon some characteristic of the recipient. Certain recipient characteristics have been studied, among them intelligence, age,

adults, and there is significant risk of bacterial contamination and resultant food poisoning in home-made baby food. Most home-made baby foods are not sterile. Beech-Nut Baby Food is sterilized by heat and pressure cooking in hermetically sealed containers.

You, as a mother, should know that commercial baby food is adequate to the nutrition requirements of your baby. In contrast, do-it-yourself baby food loses nutrients four ways:

1. Through nutrient oxidation as a result of too much air inclusion, particularly when blenders are used.
2. Through pour-off of water-soluble nutrients.
3. Through use of raw foods of uncertain freshness.
4. Through freezing and thawing if food is made for subsequent meals.

The University of California, among others, has documented the greater loss of nutrients in home-prepared baby food compared to commercial products.

As a mother, you should know that Beech-Nut has dedicated over 40 years to making the purest, most nutritious baby foods using the best methods known to modern science and with the best medical advice available. Our standards in every case meet or exceed those established by federal and state regulatory agencies. Beech-Nut Baby Food contains no preservatives, artificial colors, artificial flavors or MSG. We assure you we will continue to make the best possible food for babies. We care.

Sincerely,

Frank C. Nicholas
President

P.S. If you would like to know more or have any questions, please send me a note with your questions, or send your phone number and I or our technical people will be happy to call you at whatever time you indicate is convenient.

Source: P. G. Zimbardo, E. B. Ebbesen, & C. Maslach (1977). *Influencing attitudes and changing behavior* (2nd ed.). Reading, MA: Addison-Wesley.

self-esteem, and sex. Recipient characteristics affect not only persuasibility but also the extent of attitude-behavior consistency (Zanna, Olson, & Fazio, 1980).

In most of the research on how personality factors affect persuasibility, simple relationships have not been found. For example, intelligent people are more persuaded by complex messages, while less intelligent people are more persuaded by simple messages (Eagly & Warren, 1976). Children become more persuasible as they mature, but after the age of about 8, the process reverses (McGuire, 1968). Similarly complex results were found for the relationship of a person's self-esteem to persuasibility (Gergen & Bauer, 1967; Nisbett & Gordon, 1967; Zellner, 1970).

The complex nature of these effects was clarified in an explanation suggested by McGuire (1968), as illustrated in Figure 6.2. Personality

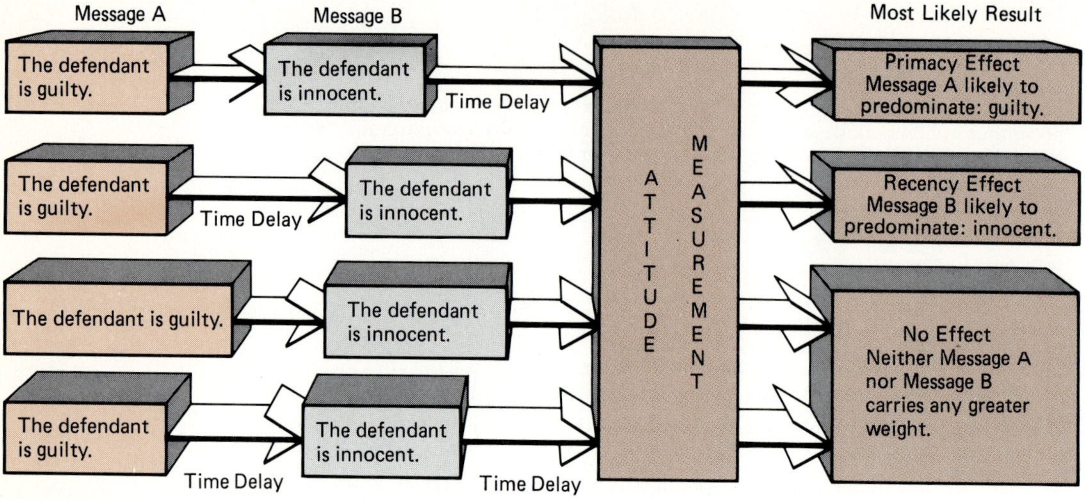

FIGURE 6.1

The Effects of Order of Presentation The effect of order of presentation—whether there is a primacy effect, a recency effect, or neither—depends upon the time that elapses between the two messages and the time from the last message to attitude measurement. *Source:* Adapted from N. Miller & D. T. Campbell (1959). Recency and primacy in persuasion as a function of the timing of speeches and measurements. *Journal of Abnormal and Social Psychology, 59,* 1–9.

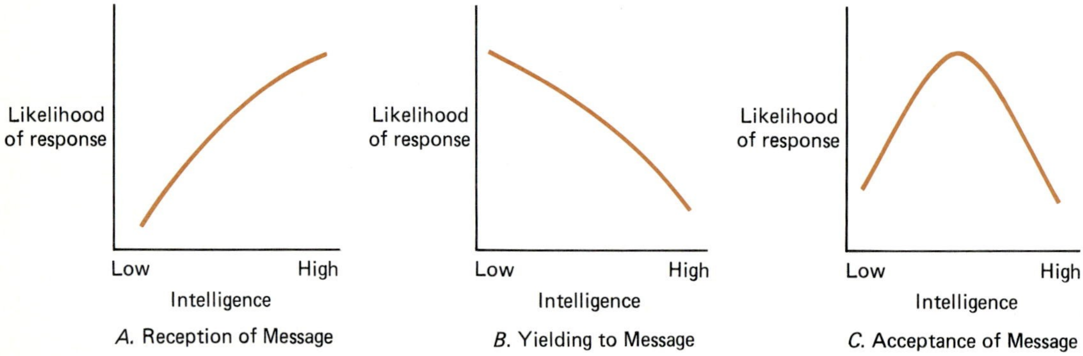

FIGURE 6.2

Factors Affecting Acceptance of Message, According to McGuire Since reception or comprehension of the message increases with intelligence (part *A*), but yielding decreases with intelligence (*B*), these factors cancel each other out. This leads to the prediction that the greatest acceptance of a message occurs for people at moderate levels of intelligence (*C*). *Source:* Adapted from W. J. McGuire (1968). Personality and susceptibility to social influence. In E. F. Borgatta & W. W. Lambert (Eds.). *Handbook of personality and research.* Skokie, IL: Rand McNally.

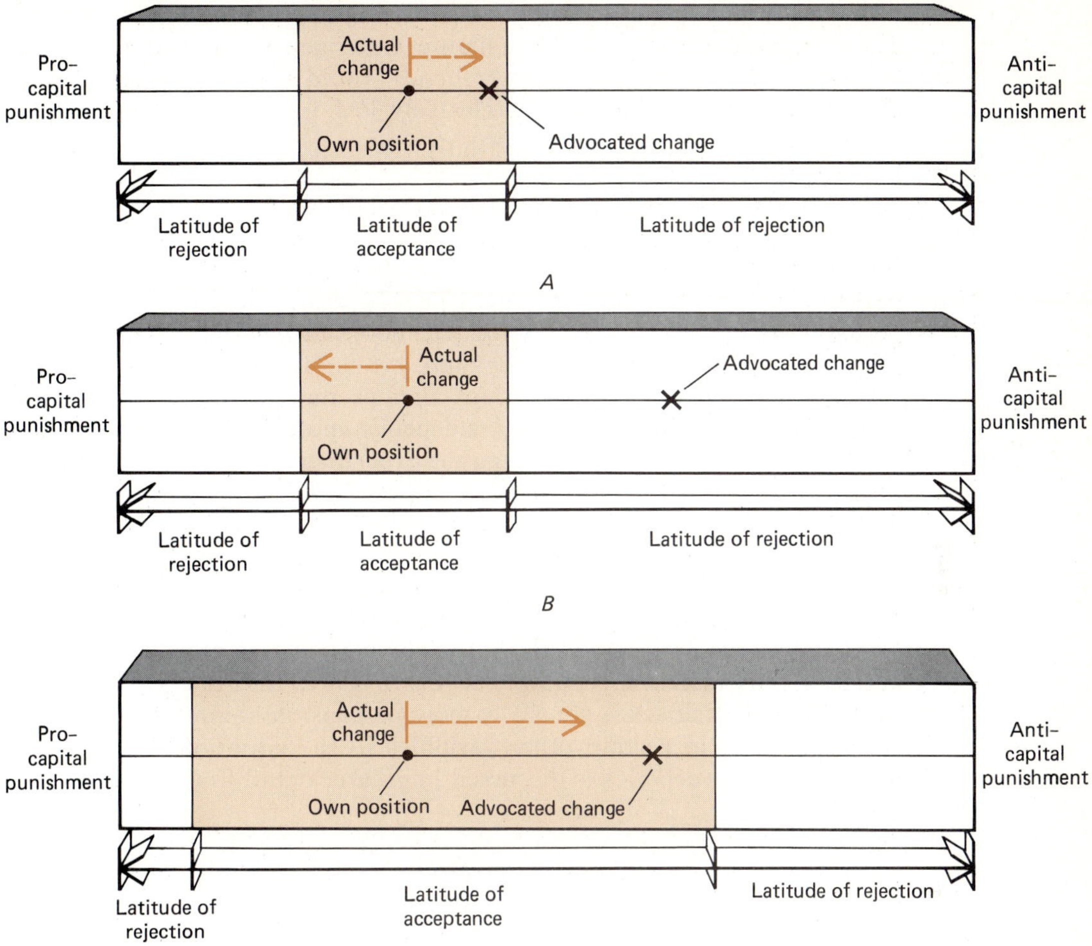

FIGURE 6.3
Results of Advocating Large or Small Amounts of Change for People Who Are More or Less Involved with an Issue In situation *A* the person is highly involved with the issue of capital punishment and therefore has a narrow latitude of acceptance. A small advocated change creates a small but positive change in the person's attitude. In situation *B* the same person is faced with a large advocated change (in the latitude of rejection). The result is a negative change, or boomerang effect. In situation *C* large change is advocated. Because this person is less involved with the issue and has a wider latitude of acceptance, significant positive change is generated.

variables produce effects that mediate attitude change, but they work in opposite directions. For example, while increased intelligence increases a person's ability to *understand* a message (see Figure 6.2, part *A*), it also decreases the tendency to *yield* to it (part *B*). These elements counterbalance one another to form the inverted U-shaped function seen in part *C*. Thus if the audience is relatively high in intelligence, a complex message (which is more difficult to comprehend) would produce more attitude change; but if the audience is relatively low in intelligence, an easily comprehended message would produce more attitude change (Eagly & Warren, 1976).

Sex is another characteristic that has received considerable attention in relationship to persuasion. Early studies showed women to be more persuasible than men (Cooper, 1979; Eagly, 1978), and it was suggested that this was due to some difference in their psychological makeup, that perhaps women were more intelligent, more harmonious, or more compliant (Eagly, 1978; Wood & Fishbaugh, 1981). The best current evidence suggests that these early conclusions were premature. Whether it is men or women who are more persuasible depends upon the subject matter and the gender of the person conducting the experiment. In those early studies the choice of subject matter had been "masculine," involving issues of greater interest to men than women. When the subject matter of the attitude issue was a topic about which females are more concerned and knowledgeable, then males were the more persuasible. Also, experimenters may be viewed as a source of the communication, and the experimenter's gender interacts with that of the recipient to produce different patterns of persuasibility (Eagly & Carli, 1981; Sistrunk & McDavid, 1971). Thus neither sex is generally more persuasible than the other. Both vary according to certain other variables in the situation. The specific nature of these variables is discussed in greater detail in Chapter 9.

Commentary on the Communication Model The communication approach has been one of the most comprehensive and influential of the major schools of attitude change research. It has identified a good many phenomena of attitude change, and has led to an understanding of the complex interactions among major variables in the attitude change process. And much later research in attitude change has sought to improve on these explanatory concepts.

The major problem of this model, especially from an applied viewpoint, is that it regards the target of persuasion largely as a passive recipient of information. Its findings are useful when the audience is in fact passive, cut off from social groups, and little affected personally by the issues under discussion. Examples of such situations include juries (which cannot discuss a case until it is over) and some consumers who want to know which is the best kind of product. But where the audience is an active part of the issue, where they behave and take action and are personally affected by the events in the messages being communicated, such as the racial conflict involved in school desegregation, we will find that other models provide a more powerful guide to attitude change.

APPLICATION
ADVERTISING

All of us are familiar with the Marlboro Man and his Marlboro Country: the rugged, hard-riding cowhand on the wide-open range. When we think of Marlboro cigarettes, we immediately think of this man and his way of life. The success of the classical conditioning of these associations in us can best be appreciated by realizing that Marlboro was first introduced years ago as a *woman's* cigarette, much as Virginia Slims are today. But Marlboro was ahead of its time and didn't find enough women smokers to make that market worth pursuing. Like many other products, tobacco is tobacco, so while the cigarette could not change much, its image could. As a result of years of pairing the cowboy image with the cigarettes, we have all become classically conditioned to associate Marlboros with cowboys and the West. Balance theory tells us that men who see (or want to see) themselves as strong, capable, and independent should form positive attitudes toward a brand that is positively linked with that image. And for those young and middle-aged men who identify with the cowhand, he models for them the behavior of smoking Marlboros. By repeating this same image over and over through the years, Marlboro also attracts customers through the mere exposure effect.

Courtesy of Ford Motor Company.

Look for the car in the Ford ad. It is one of the last things you notice, down at the darkened bottom of the picture. Far more prominent are the long, lonely stretch of desert the car has successfully traveled and the odometer reading of 60,000 miles. Here we have an implicit fear appeal: you don't want to own a car that cannot run reliably for years on end, that breaks down in godforsaken places. The ad suggests how to act on this fear: Buy a Ford. This ad is also working to change current beliefs that American cars are not particularly well built, beliefs that affect attitudes toward buying American cars. By emphasizing quality—both by saying Fords are of high quality and by offering an unusually long warranty—the reader's attitudes should begin to change, at least toward Fords. As in the theory of reasoned action, if quality and reliability are attributes of cars that rank high for the audience, this ad tells them that, in their cognitive calculus, Ford should come out with a better "score" than other American cars.

The Social Judgment Model

As we have noted several times already, the degree of a person's involvement with an issue interacts with many other variables in the attitude change process. The social judgment model addresses this issue directly (Sherif & Sherif, 1967; Sherif, Sherif, & Nebergall, 1965).

The Relativity of Judgment The judgments we make are not absolute; they rely upon comparisons with other available information. A 60° day is felt as "warm" if it occurs in December, but "chilly" in July. Lifting a typewriter feels like hard work after moving pillows, but seems like nothing if you have been moving pianos. The basis of comparison—in the preceding examples, the time of year or the kinds of objects carried—is known as an **anchor.** Sometimes we judge an object to be more unlike the anchor than it really is. For instance, the typewriters feel "light" because the pianos were "heavy." This tendency is known as **contrast.** The opposite may also occur. Sometimes we perceive an object to be more similar to an anchor than it really is. This is known as **assimilation.** For instance, temperatures and weights that are close to each other are often judged to be even more similar than they really are. What works for physical stimuli has been found to work for social stimuli as well. They can be assimilated toward or contrasted away from a comparison anchor.

Latitudes of Acceptance and Rejection A basic premise of the social judgment model is that your attitude, your own position, is a salient anchor in making judgments of other attitudinal positions. It argues that a range of positions close to your own position constitutes your **latitude of acceptance.** Within this latitude of acceptance, positions close to your own will be seen as more like yours than they really are; they will be assimilated. Those positions that are more distant from your own fall into the **latitude of rejection.** Such positions will be contrasted, that is, perceived as more discrepant with your own than they really are (Sherif, Sherif, & Nebergall, 1965). For instance, if your attitude toward racial integration is moderately negative, you are likely to see attitudes that are somewhat more negative than yours as close to your own (because they fall into your latitude of acceptance, you assimilate them); and to see moderately positive attitudes as quite far from your own (because they fall into your latitude of rejection, you contrast them).

The third important element of social judgment theory is that the widths of these latitudes vary according to your degree of "ego involvement," or attachment to your position. The more ego-involved people are, the wider their latitudes of rejection and the narrower their latitudes of acceptance. For example, two people may hold precisely the same attitude toward the notion of desegregating schools; that is, they may show exactly the same degree of agreement with or opposition to the issue. But one of these people may belong to several groups that advocate that position, and may be actively involved in trying to get this position adopted as official policy. According to social judgment theory, this more ego-involved person will more quickly reject views discrepant with his or her own (because of a narrower latitude of acceptance) than will the less ego-involved person (whose latitude of acceptance is wider).

This model explains what might otherwise make little sense. For example, two people with the same preferred attitude hear the same speech. One of them moves closer to the speaker's position, while the other "boomerangs" away from it. Why? This model tells us that identical communications will be perceived differently by people with different latitudes of acceptance and rejection, even if their own positions are the same. Communications falling within a person's latitude of acceptance will be assimilated to the person's own position, and attitude change in the direction of the communication is likely to occur. Within this range, the greater the discrepancy, the greater the attitude change. But when a communication becomes so discrepant as to fall into the latitude of rejection, it will be perceived as too discrepant, and attitude change is unlikely to occur. Indeed, if the communication is perceived as extremely discrepant, a change may occur in a direction opposite to that advocated by the communication; and the more extreme the message is, the greater this boomerang effect will be.

The lessons of this approach are fairly straightforward. To the most ego-involved people with the narrowest latitudes of acceptance and the widest latitudes of rejection, offer modest proposals for change close to their own position. For people who are less ego-involved (those with wider latitudes of acceptance and narrower latitudes of rejection), you can advocate more extreme positions in the hope that even greater change will occur. The predictions of this model are displayed in Figure 6.3 (p. 219).

Commentary on the Social Judgment Model Empirical research relevant to the social judgment model has supported some aspects of it, but raised doubts about others. People do seem to have varying latitude structures which affect their perception of and response to various messages (Sherif, Sherif, & Nebergall, 1965; Sherif & Sherif, 1967; Rhine & Severance, 1970). But the model does not allow us to specify with precision which messages will be persuasive and which will not (Eagly & Telaak, 1972). The size of latitudes might, instead, serve only as an index of general openness or closedness to persuasion (Eagly, 1981).

Finally, although social judgment theory deals well with the effect of involvement on attitudes, several studies have contradicted it or shown that, at least under some conditions, more involved people are more subject to persuasion (Apsler & Sears, 1968; Eagly, 1967; Petty & Cacioppo, 1979a, 1979b). This may be because their greater involvement may increase their attention so much that sound evidence and arguments overcome any tendency to reject discrepant arguments. As these findings suggest, the theory's major weakness may be that in focusing on the effects of involvement on latitude structures, it deals with few of the other attitude change processes considered by those who work with the communication model.

Cognitive Models

As opposed to the narrow focus of the social judgment model, other models of attitude change deal with a wide array of cognitive processes that explain how people process and respond to persuasive messages. The ones we will present include the theory of reasoned action and cognitive response analysis of persuasion.

Reasoned Action In the previous chapter we presented the basic outlines of the theory of reasoned action as part of our discussion about attitude-behavior inconsistency. The theory of reasoned action also has obvious implications for attitude change. If you recall, that theory is primarily concerned with the connection of beliefs to attitudes and subjective norms, and of attitudes and subjective norms to behavior (see Figure 5.3, p. 202). It follows from this theory that persuasive communications may change attitudes markedly, but intentions and behavior may not change at all because subjective norms are strong. For example, a person's attitude toward integration may be made more favorable. But if subjective norms against participating in integration are strong ("My friends will never speak to me again"), the person may continue to oppose integration. Similarly, a change in beliefs about what others think is desirable might produce little change if attitudes do not also change. Thus, in the case of white parents opposed to school desegregation, an attitude change program based on communicating information would be most effective if it were informed by some understanding of the beliefs, attitudes, and subjective norms on which the opposition rests.

Cognitive Response Analysis Cognitive response analysis proposes that the key to all persuasion lies in the individual's own cognitive responses to the message. If the cognitive responses are *pro-arguments,* a change toward the position will occur. In effect, you will actually end up convincing yourself. If the cognitive responses are *counter-arguments,* then no attitude change will take place, or, if strong enough, the counter-arguments will produce a **boomerang effect** (Greenwald, 1968; Love & Greenwald, 1978; Petty, Ostrom, & Brock, 1980, 1981), moving the individual away from the desired position. The goal of persuasion, according to this principle, is to control the content of those cognitive responses.

This approach offers us an increased understanding of some of the effects we have already discussed, and solves some problems that other theories had in accounting for those effects. For example, what is the effect of ego involvement on attitude change? Cognitive response analysis suggests that the more involved you are in an issue, the more thinking you will do about a message and the more cognitive responding will take place. If the message is close to your own attitude, pro-arguments are more likely to occur; and if the message is distant, counter-arguments will more likely occur.

Another issue that cognitive response analysis has addressed successfully is the effect of attentiveness versus distraction when being persuaded. In an old story, the famous lawyer Clarence Darrow is sitting in a courtroom and puffing on a cigar while his adversary gives a closing argument. Darrow had inserted a length of wire into his cigar so that it could burn down to the very end without the ash falling off. As the other lawyer's closing argument wore on, the ash grew longer and longer and the entire court, so the story goes, became so transfixed by wondering when Darrow's ash would fall that they paid no attention to the other lawyer. What Darrow apparently was trying to do was to distract the jury so much that they could not be persuaded by the other lawyer.

At high levels of distraction, such an act clearly works; you cannot be persuaded by something you haven't heard. But what is the effect at low or moderate levels of distraction? At the closing stage of a trial, jurors are well informed and probably highly motivated to listen and process what is being said. Suppose the cigar is distracting enough to take up only the cognitive capacity that would otherwise have been used for counter-arguing, but not so distracting that the jurors could not hear the other lawyer's arguments? Jurors who had already agreed with the opponent would be prevented from pro-arguing, but jurors whose attitudes at that point favored Darrow's case would be prevented from counter-arguing. Therefore, they would be less able to reject the opponent's arguments.

Empirical research on distraction effects does show that moderate levels of distraction facilitate attitude change, while high levels interfere with it (Petty, Wells, & Brock, 1976). Thus unless Darrow's distraction was either so mild that it distracted hardly at all or so distracting that it blocked message reception, his clever ploy was probably helping his opponent more than himself. Hecklers of political speeches are in the same position, and may do the speaker more good than harm (Petty & Brock, 1976; Petty, Brock, & Brock, 1978; Sloan et al., 1974).

Another technique of attitude change is the *rhetorical question*. Which do you suppose was more effective in getting an audience to mistrust former president Richard Nixon: a straightforward assertion that the man was not to be trusted, or the question "Would you buy a used car from this man?" When asking a rhetorical question, you do not expect a direct answer. Instead, you want to get the audience to think about the issue in a way that produces cognitive responses favorable to your position. Ads, bumper stickers, and political speeches all make use of this principle. When asked "Have you hugged your kids today?"; "What kind of man reads *Playboy*?"; or "Whose life is it, anyway?" each person generates a set of cognitions. Still, cognitive response analysis tells us that attitude change in a favorable direction will occur only if the rhetorical question generates pro-arguments, not if it elicits counter-arguments. And that depends upon the audience's involvement and the arguments available to them (Petty, Cacioppo, & Heesacker, 1981).

THE PERSON AS ACTIVE PARTICIPANT

The models of attitude change we have considered thus far have viewed the individual as an essentially passive recipient of messages which work their effects on the individual's attitude. The models we examine in this section pay special attention to the *behavior* of the person to be persuaded. While disagreeing on the psychological mechanisms involved, these theories do agree on the surprising conclusion that effective attitude change often is *preceded by* behavior change.

The Cognitive Dissonance Model

In the previous chapter we discussed balance theory (Heider, 1958) and its central postulate that people prefer or are more comfortable with balanced cognitions. Balance theory served as a general concept that was improved upon by a second generation of more refined theories, such as **cognitive dissonance.**

Cognitive dissonance theory suggests that humans have a built-in motivation to maintain consistency among cognitive elements, and that inconsistency produces psychological discomfort called *dissonance* (Fazio & Cooper, 1983). The novelist F. Scott Fitzgerald must have been talking about dissonance when he wrote, "The test of a first-rate intelligence is the ability to hold two opposed ideas in the mind at the same time and still retain the ability to function." Whenever cognitive dissonance is aroused, the person will act to reduce it. What are the "cognitive elements"? They are any and all thoughts, beliefs, or pieces of knowledge a person has, such as "Apples are red"; "I smoke cigarettes"; or "I like to smoke."

A pair of cognitive elements may stand in one of three relationships to each other: irrelevant, consonant, or dissonant. The beliefs that "apples are red" and "I smoke cigarettes" are *irrelevant* to one another, logically and psychologically. "I smoke cigarettes" and "I like to smoke" hold implications for each other. They are *consonant* cognitions. But suppose a person who smokes learns one day that researchers have found that smoking increases the likelihood of cancer. Assuming that the person is not suicidal, those cognitions are *dissonant*. The cognition "I smoke" and

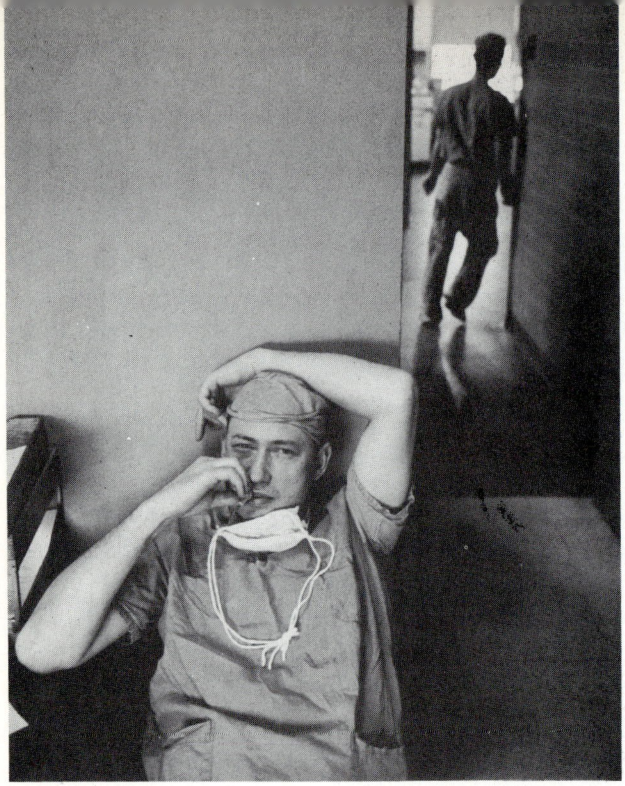

It seems to defy logic that a surgeon could remove a cancerous lung from a patient and then light up a cigarette to relax. The theory of cognitive dissonance tells us that people will feel motivated either to change their behavior or to alter their beliefs to make them more consonant with their actions.

the cognition "Smoking increases the likelihood of cancer" are incompatible. They do not coexist comfortably and, according to a traditional view of dissonance theory, are psychologically uncomfortable. This discomfort motivates people to change one of the conflicting cognitions to reduce the dissonance.

A surgeon once asked one of the authors how it could be that some of his colleagues could remove portions of a patient's diseased lungs, walk out of the operating room, and light up a cigarette. The theory of cognitive dissonance offers one major answer (Higgins, Rhodewalt, & Zanna, 1979; Sherman & Gorkin, 1980). Dissonance can be reduced in three ways: (1) the importance of certain cognitions can be changed; (2) new cognitions can be added or made salient; or (3) one of the dissonant cognitions can be changed to make it consonant. Thus smokers, even those who are thoracic surgeons, can either live with the psychological discomfort of dissonance or reduce it by giving up cigarettes. But these are not the only options. The surgeon might decide that the research is not conclusive and could turn out to be wrong, or might think about all the good things smoking does for him or her.

A study conducted shortly after the Surgeon General made the link between smoking and lung cancer widely known to the public in 1964 found that of a sample of smokers, 40 percent believed that the research was inconclusive. In contrast, only 10 percent of nonsmokers doubted the research findings. Still, only 9 percent of the smokers stopped smoking following release of the Surgeon General's report (Kassarjian & Cohen,

1965). Most smokers took the easier road to dissonance reduction: adjusting their attittudes instead of their behavior.

The dissonance produced by two strong and contradictory sets of cognitions creates psychological discomfort which can be tolerated only with difficulty. Indeed, the evidence is that people avoid getting into such crosscurrents in the first place or, once in them, work to extricate themselves. This should not be taken to mean that people work all day to bring their cognitions into consonance; other motives also operate. Dissonance theory argues only that, all other things being equal, people prefer psychologically consonant cognitions in order to maintain a positive self-image (Steele & Liu, 1983). Indeed, it does not suggest that our species is a *rational* animal; rather "it suggests that [we are] a *rationalizing* animal" (Aronson, 1978, p. 183).

Counter-attitudinal Advocacy and Induced Compliance Saying something in opposition to what you believe or feel is what social psychologists call *counter-attitudinal advocacy.* The process of being invited or seduced into such counter-attitudinal advocacy is called *induced compliance.* For example, suppose you believe fervently in the need for government-sponsored programs to aid the poor, and someone asks—to round out the sides on a debate or just for the fun of it—if you would argue in favor of reducing and replacing such programs.

In the classic experiment on this phenomenon (Festinger & Carlsmith, 1959), students were asked to perform a boring, monotonous task. Afterward they were asked if they would tell the next participant in the experiment that the task was interesting and fun (which it surely was not). Thus the students were invited to engage in counter-attitudinal advocacy, to say something that went counter to their attitudes. Half the students were offered $20 to mislead the next participant, and the other half were offered $1.

Dissonance theory would predict that the less the inducement to comply, the more attitude change would take place. For a student in this experiment, the dissonant cognitions are "I found the task boring" but "I told someone it was fun." Those who received $20, however, can add the cognition that they were paid handsomely for it, and continue to believe the task was boring ("I found the task to be boring, but told someone it was interesting because I was paid plenty to say so"). Students who were paid only $1 could not point to the inducement of the large sum of money, and could reduce the dissonance only by changing their attitude ("I told the person the task was interesting, but was paid only $1 to say so, so I must have found it not so boring"). The results showed that the $1 group did indeed rate the task as more interesting than did the $20 group. Thus we have the interesting confirmation of the phenomenon whereby the group that was paid less to express an attitude showed more attitude change in the direction of the expressed attitude than the people who were paid more.

Varela (1971) illustrates how clever salespeople can use dissonance processes to get customers to sell themselves on a product. By asking customers questions such as "How do you like the product?" they can get people to make positive statements about the product. These public statements cannot be undone; to some degree the customer has become committed to them. The person's attitude may change to bring it in line with the statement, or the person may have to behave consistently with the statement to avoid appearing inconsistent. The customer traps him- or herself. The same counter-attitudinal advocacy can occur in such spheres as politics, religion, or other matters of central importance to a person. Indeed, the more important the attitude, the easier it may be to arouse dissonance (Sherman & Gorkin, 1980).

Thus we see that when people are placed in a situation where dissonance is aroused, they seek a way to reduce that dissonance. When the situation is such that a change of attitude is the easiest or most effective way to reduce the dissonance, attitude change will result. This is most likely to occur under several conditions: when the behavior is clearly inconsistent with an existing attitude; when it was not coerced or accidental; when the behavior is "public"; and when the person's actions cause harm to someone (Wicklund & Brehm, 1976; Petty & Cacioppo, 1981).

Disconfirmed Expectations Another situation in which cognitive dissonance occurs is when one's expectations are disconfirmed by events. For example, what happens to members of a sect or cult who come to believe strongly in a prediction about the future that does not come true? Say they announce that the world will come to an end on July 23, and the fateful day comes and goes uneventfully. We might expect that they will

Common sense suggests that, when we predict something that fails to occur, we would tend to lose faith; yet very often the opposite happens and our faith is only intensified. Cognitive dissonance theory proposes that we try to convince ourselves and others that we were right in the first place to reduce the dissonance of a disconfirmed expectation.

recognize they were wrong and will abandon their former erroneous belief. Dissonance theory predicts, however, that under the proper conditions the opposite will occur; that is, people will come to believe even more strongly in the disconfirmed belief.

The dissonance conceptualization suggests that people's implicit thought processes operate something like this: I have believed that the world would end before now. It has not. (Dissonance is aroused.) I cannot reduce the dissonance by saying I was wrong; that would only produce more dissonance by contradicting my earlier, passionately held belief. I could reduce the dissonance in other ways, such as by believing that I was so right and took such proper action that I effected a change in the world that prevented the apocalypse. And since others around me believe the same thing, in spite of the seeming disconfirmation, my original belief must have been true after all.

Indeed, several studies of doomsday cults have found the dissonance theory prediction to hold. In one study, cult members gave away all their property and prepared to meet the end. When it did not come, they resolved the dissonance by congratulating themselves for having diverted the end through their faith, and some of them became even more ardent believers (Festinger, Riecken, & Schachter, 1956). In another study, an evangelical Christian group believed that the world would be destroyed in a nuclear holocaust on a certain date. After 103 members spent 42 days and nights in a bomb shelter, they recognized that the world had not come to an end, and reentered life believing more strongly than ever that God was in touch with them. After all, thanks to them God had postponed the holocaust (Hardyck & Braden, 1962).

Choices and Decisions When we say that a person has a difficult decision to make, we usually mean that choosing one alternative necessitates giving up desirable features of the other possible choices. People may encounter such conflicts in deciding which college to attend, which car to buy, or which job offer to accept. One job might involve work that is more satisfying; the second might pay more. If they both offer the same number of vacation days, or are equally far from home, conflict will not exist on those dimensions. Prior to making a decision, people experience *pre-decisional conflict,* in which they are drawn simultaneously toward all choices or drawn toward one choice but repelled by some of its unattractive features. Eventually, however, a choice gets made. Dissonance theory speaks to what happens after that choice is made.

After a decision is made, the recognition that the rejected alternative(s) had positive aspects is dissonant with rejecting it. Likewise, the recognition of negative elements in the chosen alternative is dissonant with selecting it. Thus, the person experiences *post-decisional dissonance* and seeks to reduce it. Four kinds of change could take place to reduce the dissonance: (1) changing the decision; (2) increasing the felt attractiveness of the chosen alternative; (3) decreasing the felt attractiveness of the unchosen alternative; or (4) perceiving the consequences of the alternatives as more similar than previously thought ("A and B are really much more alike than I used to think"). To the extent that the choices involve quite dissimilar options and the decision is difficult to undo, the most likely mode of dissonance reduction will be through changed attitudes toward the chosen and unchosen alternatives.

Those predictions of dissonance theory have been found in several laboratory and field studies. For example, Brehm (1956) gave students a choice among gifts they could receive as payment by manufacturers for having provided consumer ratings of products. Following a choice among gifts that were equally valued but dissimilar in features, the students greatly increased the favorableness of their attitudes toward the chosen alternative and decreased their favorableness toward the unchosen alternative. In field experiments, people were interviewed either before or after placing bets at a racetrack (Knox & Inkster, 1968), before or after placing bets at the Canadian National Exhibition (Younger, Walker, & Arrowood, 1977), and before or after casting their votes in an election (Frenkel & Doob, 1976). As shown in Figure 6.4, those people who were asked just

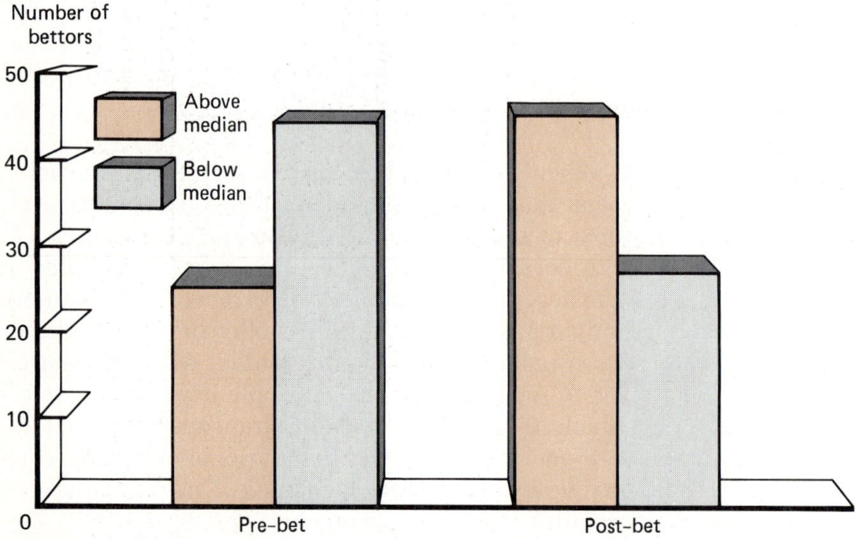

FIGURE 6.4

Number of Bettors Above and Below the Overall Median in Confidence Before and After Placing a Bet Before placing their bets, people are less confident about their chances of winning. The act of placing the bet increases the confidence of many people that they will win. *Source:* Adapted from R. E. Knox & J. A. Inkster (1968). Postdecision dissonance at post time. *Journal of Personality and Social Psychology, 8,* 319–323.

after making their behavioral commitment showed more favorable attitudes and greater confidence in their choices, compared with those people whose attitudes were measured just *before* placing their bets. Just before, they experienced conflict and uncertainty. But after, they "had to" feel more sure of their bets or else they would experience the dissonance of believing they had committed their money to a horse that would lose.

Selective Exposure Another implication of cognitive dissonance theory is that after making a decision, people tend to seek out supportive information and to avoid disconfirming information. Perhaps you recall that following the choice of a college or of a stereo, you were more interested in information praising your choice and you avoided sources that would commend the ones you did not choose. Although some early studies of this prediction failed to confirm its existence (Feather, 1963; Freedman & Sears, 1965; Rosen, 1961), more recent studies have found that if dissonance is aroused, selective exposure to information follows (Frey, 1982, 1981).

Insufficient Justification and Effort Justification Dissonance processes are a way of realigning one's cognitions and behaviors so that they are not at war with each other (Aronson, 1968). Actions already taken are irrevocable. Beliefs and attitudes, on the other hand, can be changed. Therefore, we may change our beliefs and attitudes in order to justify to ourselves the actions we have taken. Dissonance theory predicts that the less external **justification** for an act (the lower the reward, or the less the threat), the more dissonance will be aroused and the more attitude change will occur to reduce the dissonance. Thus if people can be induced to drive under the speed limit when no police car is in sight (a situation of "insufficient justification"), they are more likely to internalize attitudes supporting safe driving than they would if the police were present. This principle has been confirmed in studies ranging from children's evaluation of toys (Aronson & Carlsmith, 1963) to voters' evaluation of politicians (Cooper, Darley, & Henderson, 1974).

Similarly, when people must expend a great deal of effort to achieve something, they will value it more than if they achieve the same thing easily. Social psychologists term this phenomenon *effort justification.* In the classic study of this effect, women who sought to join quite ordinary discussion groups had to endure either an embarrassing "initiation" or an easy rite of passage to get into the group. In rating the same groups afterward, those whose entry was more difficult liked the groups more (Aronson & Mills, 1959). More recent research (Axsom & Cooper, 1985; Cooper & Axsom, 1982) suggests that desired personal changes can be achieved, such as gains in psychotherapy and loss of weight, using this principle. For example, Axsom & Cooper (1985) recruited overweight people for a weight-reduction clinic. As part of the program, half of these

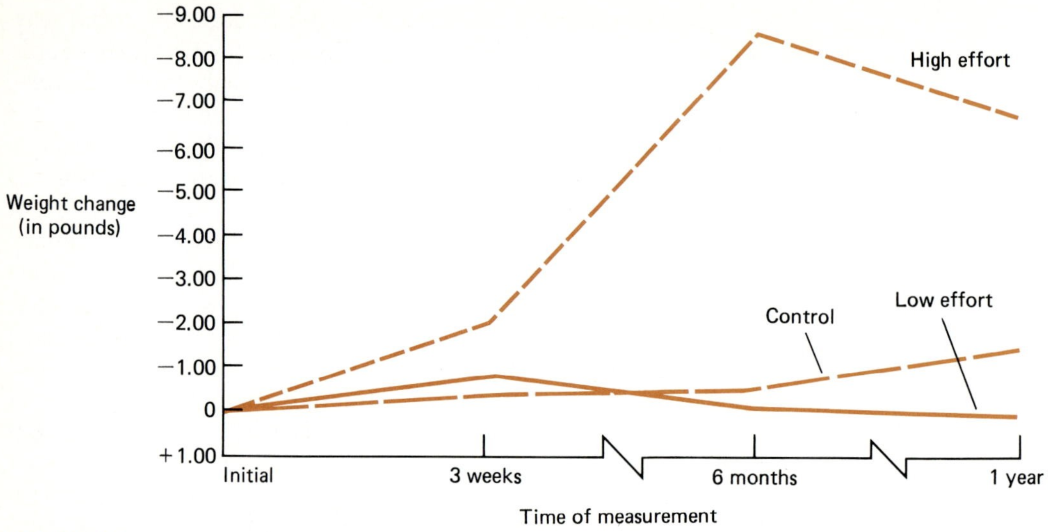

FIGURE 6.5
Weight Change as a Function of High and Low Effort Measured at Different Points in Time People in a weight-loss program requiring more effort lost more weight than people not in the program or in a similar program requiring little effort. And they kept more weight off as much as one year later.

people worked at a set of difficult and boring tasks during a five-session two-week period. The others were required to put out little effort. As Figure 6.5 shows, in comparison to both the low-effort and the control groups, the high-effort group produced dramatic results not only in the short run, but also as long as six months to one year later.

Many of society's institutions—the military, fraternities, the medical and legal professions—require extremely demanding efforts of people. Through the process of effort justification, "hazing" and other forms of excessive demands have the effect of increasing people's evaluation of the group they have been admitted to or the position they have achieved—simply to justify the effort they expended in getting in.

Overjustification What happens when a person is rewarded excessively for certain behavior? This provides *overjustification* for having performed the behavior. One situation in which this occurs is when people enjoy doing something for its own sake (that is, they gain intrinsic reinforcement from it) and are then paid (extrinsic reinforcement) to do the same thing. When the intrinsic reinforcement of a task is reduced or replaced by extrinsic reward, people's sense of their own liking for a task changes.

For example, athletes who love playing baseball may come to see it as "just another job" when they get paid very well for hitting home runs.

In one study, children who showed an intrinsic interest in drawing were divided randomly into three groups. One group was told they would receive a certificate for their artwork and did receive one; the second was not told of the award but received it anyway; and the third received no reward or promise of one. Two weeks later the children were again given an opportunity to engage in the art project, and their behavior was observed. The children who had been in the first group, those for whom external reward had been introduced into the activity, spent less time on the artwork and seemed to enjoy it less than did the two other groups (Lepper, Greene, & Nisbett, 1973).

This overjustification effect has also been referred to as "the hidden cost of reward." Apparently, if more justification is given for doing something than is needed—that is, the external reward is excessive—the perceived motivation for doing it shifts from the intrinsic rewards of the task itself to the extrinsic rewards, and the person's attitude toward the task becomes less positive. The implications of the overjustification effect touch many aspects of our lives. A society that heaps too much extrinsic reward on its people may be undermining the intrinsic rewards of doing things for their own sake, thereby "turning play into work" (Schwartz, Lacey, & Schuldenfrei, 1978).

The Self-perception Model

The attitude change phenomena we have described can be explained by psychological processes other than cognitive dissonance. A major alternative comes from attribution processes (discussed in Chapter 2), in particular the attributions we make about ourselves in the light of our own behavior. We discussed self-perception in the preceeding chapter under the topic of attitude formation. Let us see how it explains attitude change.

Daryl Bem (1965, 1967, 1972) has suggested that we come to know our own attitudes the same way an outside observer does, that we draw the same inferences in the same manner. Bem showed that individuals who have had dissonance studies described to them can correctly infer the attitudes that actual research participants came to hold. For instance, they inferred that a person who went through a difficult initiation must have valued the group greatly to have gone to that much trouble to join it. But if they heard that people had been compelled to join (e.g., by being drafted) they did not expect them to have such strong positive attitudes toward the group. In Bem's studies the process was clearly one of *inferring* attitudes from the observation of behavior and circumstances. This contrasts with the dissonance theory explanation that dissonant cognitions create a *motivational* pressure to reduce dissonance, often by changing attitudes.

Self-perception theory explains the major dissonance theory findings as follows: People subtly induced to act in a certain way will observe what they have done and conclude that they must hold the attitude that they expressed. This is because they cannot attribute the behavior to anything else (e.g., Salancik & Conway, 1975). In the overjustification paradigm, the salience of an excessive reward would lead a person to conclude: I must have acted the way I did because of this large reward for doing so, not because I intrinsically enjoy doing it (see Newman & Layton, 1984).

Which theory of attitude change is the correct one? There is no simple answer. In fact a series of experiments pitting dissonance theory against self-attribution theory has not been able to rule one convincingly out and the other in (Greenwald, 1975). A solution has been the suggestion that dissonance processes mediate attitude change in some domains (when behavior is opposite to a person's existing attitude and external justification for the behavior is insufficient) and self-perception processes operate in other domains (when the behavior is not seriously contradicted by an existing attitude) (Fazio, Zanna, & Cooper, 1977; Taylor, 1975). Both dissonance and self-perception occur, but they operate in different circumstances.

Role Playing

In this section we have referred a number of times to situations in which people say, write, or do something that supports a position with which they do not agree. This technique of role playing deserves special comment. In speaking out for a position you do not initially support, in taking on a role that is not really you, something happens psychologically. Your attitudes and beliefs tend to shift in a direction consistent with the role played. Indeed, role playing is one of the most potent and reliable attitude change techniques.

As we have seen, dissonance theory offers a possible explanation for the effect. People playing a role experience dissonant cognitions. Because attitudes are the least frozen, least publicly committed of their cognitions, attitudes change to become more consistent with the behavior to reduce the dissonance. Self-perception also can explain the role-playing phenomenon. At least under the conditions discussed above, people infer their attitudes from observing what they say or do.

Still other explanations have been offered to explain this phenomenon, notably *biased scanning*. When people search their memories for arguments in favor of the counter-attitudinal position, their search is "biased": They are likely to select only arguments consistent with the new position and to select only the best from the repertoire. In this process, the person becomes convinced that the counter-attitudinal position is correct, and attitude change results. Support for this self-persuasion interpretation comes from research showing that the more actively involved in the role playing a person is (compared to being a passive observer) and the more difficult it is (the more effort put into it or the more obstacles one encounters in doing it), the more attitude change results (Janis & King, 1954; King & Janis, 1956; Janis, 1959, 1968).

Consider the times you have found yourself role-playing. You began by participating in something you initially supported only slightly, but the more you occupied the role, the more you came to believe it was sensible and just. Or perhaps you found yourself in an argument with a friend over some issue that at first you believed only mildly, but the more you argued the more strongly you convinced yourself that your position was right. Politicians who assert politically attractive positions they do not personally believe in may well come to believe them after defending them for a time. Lawyers who happily represent either side of a case may end up believing in the side they find themselves on. When religious groups send their members out to proselytize, or political candidates get volunteers to make phone calls or to canvass neighborhoods, the helpers may or may not obtain converts. But what they certainly are doing as they carry out these roles is becoming increasingly convinced and committed themselves.

Commentary on the Active Participant Approaches

The wide array of situations we have discussed—disconfirmed expectations, decision making, role playing, selective exposure, and others—are in a sense all situations in which conflict between one's own attitudes and behavior is the central problem both for the person experiencing the conflict and the person studying it. We have reviewed a number of theoretical models proposed to explain these phenomena, the most extensively researched of which is cognitive dissonance theory. What all these approaches share is the importance they place on behavior as a prerequisite for attitude change, and this is in itself an important discovery that runs counter to our intuition. People generally think that most behavior change follows attitude change, but this approach suggests that the reverse is true.

Moreover, the findings and theories reviewed provide valuable clues to changing attitudes *and* behavior. In the real world of everyday lives, for instance, behavior changes probably precede attitude changes often and subtly, though not necessarily as a result of direct attempts made by others. A person takes a new job and finds herself agreeing with views she does not really espouse in order to get along with co-workers. Another person is invited to a meeting of a group whose views he did not really agree with, but the act of attending begins the shift of attitudes. Although not often used as conscious attitude change techniques (except perhaps by social psychologists), these techniques can, as we shall see, be put to work in organized programs of attitude change.

APPLICATION
CANVASSING FOR CAUSES

Different people are interested in different issues and different causes. But regardless of the issue and the side they are on, all have in common an interest in trying to win other people to their side. One strategy that is often employed by organizers of various campaigns is that of having volunteers canvass neighborhoods—visiting and speaking with residents, and leaving campaign literature with them.

You may feel that canvassing is not as glamorous as writing the editorials for newspapers or producing public service advertisements for prime-time television. But of the possible modes of attitude change, canvassing is the one most available to you, and, given its live, face-to-face quality, it has the potential to be more effective than editorials and television spots.

What advice can social psychology offer canvassers? In the early 1970s, Robert Abelson and Philip Zimbardo prepared a small book called *Canvassing for Peace* which applied social psychology to just this question. Their book was written to help the antiwar movement of that time bring an end to the Vietnam conflict. But the insights are applicable to canvassing for any issue.

The first piece of advice is to "be informed—get as much accurate, up-to-date, reliable information as you can. . . . You should be more expert on the issue than the people you will try to influence" (1970, p. 9). This serves several purposes. Having a wealth of information helps increase perceived source credibility, and that alone enhances the canvasser's effectiveness as a persuasive source. Also, encountering reasonable arguments from a supporter of the other side of an issue might shake a canvasser's confidence in his or her own attitudes. To learn a wide range of arguments and counterarguments helps canvassers to protect their own attitudes.

"Actively role-play with a friend the anticipated situation" (p. 10). By role-playing both parts, volunteers not only learn and prepare for their own role, but get some insight into how things will look from a target person's viewpoint. You can then see (or feel) what the person in the role of canvasser can do to help or hurt his or her own effectiveness.

"Be sensitive to the varied reasons underlying the attitude(s) in question" (p. 10). "Information by itself is probably the least effective way of changing attitudes and behavior! The presentation of facts must be part of a general approach which sees the individual as more than a rational consumer of information—as sometimes irrational, inconsistent, responding to social rewards, and concerned about how [s]he appears to [her]himself and to others" (pp. 10–11). A few minutes on a doorstep cannot change attitudes by changing fundamental beliefs, but it can have influence by altering the person's immediate social environment, needs for self-presentation, group identity, and so on.

In making the most effective use of peripheral route persuasion tactics, the organizer is advised to try to establish some "similarity with the source" (preferably by matching canvassers to neighborhoods populated by people of similar ethnic or other forms of identity), to increase credibility through expertise, to be introduced by or have the contact made by someone known in the community, and to be open-minded and pleasant.

The canvasser is advised not to "put the person on the defensive, or even encourage a public defense of (and thus commitment to) any position against you" (p. 15). To the contrary, it helps to get the person to engage in some kind of pro-attitudinal behavior, such as saying things sympathetic to the canvasser's position, signing a petition or a list to receive further information, or agreeing to contact a friend, for example, to notify the friend of a meeting. Such "behavioral commitment" is important to the process of attitude change, as we have noted earlier. Of course, the commitment must be made with minimal pressure, and it must be clear to the person that the choice is his or hers, free and voluntary, to support the cause or not, to sign up or not.

Though the front porch or living room chat lasts only a few minutes, and though its brevity will have only modest impact, some things can be said and done during those minutes to increase the span of the psychological situation. Obtaining some form of commitment for the cause, as just mentioned, is one way, especially if it involves some future act of involvement by the person. Another way is to arrange to come back on a later occasion, or to suggest the possibility of further contact. Even if you do not make it back, the expectation of future interaction keeps the influence alive; the contact is not "over" the moment you leave. Also, by your naming others in the neighborhood who are favorable to your position or candidate, the person is made aware of a social environment that contains support for what you've been advocating. People who will agree to do some canvassing themselves, to call friends about the time and place of a campaign speech, to deliver some pamphlets, or to allow a small meeting of neighbors to be held at their home will be more influenced by their own acts than by anything the canvasser could say to them.

These suggestions borrow a number of the principles we have discussed and apply them to a face-to-face, though brief, attempt at persuasion. Notice how the principles are adapted to make the most of both the strengths and weaknesses of the persuasion opportunity. Perhaps you can think of other steps that could be taken to make canvassing effective.

OBSTACLES TO ATTITUDE CHANGE

One person's attempts to persuade another are not always successful. Often attitude change does not occur because it is resisted actively. At other times attitude change fails to occur because of the sheer difficulty of altering the positions a person already holds. In this section we will discuss several obstacles to attitude change.

Resistance to Persuasion

Every person who wants to persuade also wants to prevent persuasion. Diplomats would like the minds of their allies not to be changed by the arguments of adversaries. A lawyer who is making a good case does not want the other side's lawyer to win the judge or jury away. A presidential candidate in a debate would like to do something to prevent the audience from being influenced by the other candidate, as well as try to win some favorable attitude change. Following are two important methods of producing resistance to attitude change.

Forewarning When audiences have a stake in an issue, two simple methods can be used to increase their resistance to counter-attitudinal persuasion. You can **forewarn** them about the content of the message they are about to hear, or you can simply ask them to think about the issue. Both tactics get them to generate counterarguments, what some have called *anticipatory cognitive responding.* This is the key to preventing persuasion.

Inoculation In medicine, **inoculation** is a technique that promotes resistance to disease by exposing people to a weakened version of the microorganism they must become resistant to. In the realm of attitude change, the approach is much the same. People are exposed to a weakened version of a set of arguments so that they will be resistant if later exposed to a stronger version of the same argument. This technique has been studied using some of the beliefs and attitudes most susceptible to change, cultural truisms.

Cultural truisms are attitudes and beliefs so strongly held and so widely shared within a society that people never hear them challenged. Common examples are attitudes toward personal health care: brush your teeth after each meal, see your dentist every 6 months, have a periodic chest X ray. Because cultural truisms are debated little, or not at all, people have few arguments favoring these beliefs. More important, people are unaware of the possible attacks on these beliefs and have no counterarguments with which to meet them (McGuire, 1964; McGuire & Papageorgis, 1961; Papageorgis & McGuire, 1961).

The problem, then, is how resistance to such persuasion can be produced. The key to producing successful resistance via inoculation is the provision of counterarguments. This is something debaters often do. They say, "My opponent will tell you X, Y, and Z, but here is what's wrong with those arguments. . . ." To the extent that the debater has correctly anticipated the opponent's arguments and provided counterarguments against them, the opponent's effectiveness will be lessened.

Complexity of Findings

The scientific approach to understanding persuasion confers obvious benefits, such as providing reliable information about what works and what does not work, and why. That may be especially helpful when the findings run counter to widely held myths. But at the same time that it helps separate the real from the unreal, systematic research complicates the life of anyone who wants to be a knowledgeable and effective persuader.

To make use of all the knowledge, one would probably need an on-line computer which is continually updated on the latest interactional effects and subtle discoveries. When we had some persuading to do, we would sit down at the computer terminal and let the computer conduct an "interview": Is the audience highly ego-involved in the issue, or not? What is the educational and intellectual level of the audience? Will the channel of communication be live, written, or televised? Is the message to be counter-attitudinal or consistent with the audience's attitudes? Has prior inoculation of the audience taken place? And so on. Then the computer would examine the entire situation in light of current empirical and theoretical knowledge, and recommend strategies and tactics that had the highest probability of producing effective persuasion. Since no such computer database yet exists, some people might throw up their hands in the face of the complexity and say, "What's the use of trying? I'll just keep on guessing." But strategies can be developed to help the translation from research to practice.

One strategy has been to take the various attitude change models that pertain to different domains of persuasion and to combine them into a comprehensive theory of attitude change by getting underneath the surface details to find the essence of what is going on. Petty and Cacioppo (1981, 1986) have taken an important step in that direction. They begin by suggesting that attitude change models pursue either a *central route* to attitude change, focusing on the processing of fundamental beliefs and arguments about the attitude issue itself; or a *peripheral route,* focusing on non-issue-relevant variables such as reinforcement, source attractiveness, or information about a speaker's motives (Eagly, 1983).

Whether a central or a peripheral approach will work best can be determined by examining variables such as involvement, which taps a person's motivation, or distraction, which taps a person's ability to pro-

FROM THE FIELD

John T. Cacioppo and Richard E. Petty

As much as anyone else in the field, John T. Cacioppo (University of Iowa) (shown at left) and Richard E. Petty (University of Missouri, Columbia) (right) have breathed new life into the study of attitude change. During the past decade, they have developed psychophysiological measures of attitude change; applied the cognitive response analysis of persuasion to such phenomena as forewarning, ego involvement, and distraction; and contributed to the unification of attitude change techniques through their theory of central and peripheral routes to attitude change. Their theory, discussed in this chapter, has been applied to such diverse fields as advertising and consumer behavior, clinical and counseling psychology, and health.

cess information. Change brought about through the central route is difficult and unlikely to occur, but the change that does occur will be enduring. Peripheral route change is easier to accomplish but shorter-lived.

Limitations to Mass Attitude Change Campaigns

One problem created by all this research is the impression that attitude change is easy to bring about. In virtually all of the experiments cited, *some* attitude change occurs, more under certain treatment conditions (e.g., high credibility) than others (e.g., low credibility). The problem, if it is one, is that laboratory settings make it relatively easy to produce attitude change in the short term (Cook & Flay, 1978). In the laboratory, people are captive audiences whose full attention is relatively easy to get; the issue studied is not usually a very involving one; and the changed attitudes need not endure long to be detected by the sensitive measures available to researchers.

By contrast, surveys looking for attitude change effects resulting from advertising campaigns among the public at large often find few reliable effects (Hovland, 1959). Only a subset of the population exposes itself to the communication, they may attend to only a fragment of it, and it may be only one weak communication among the many they hear. Still, not all mass media campaigns are doomed to failure. Calling upon several of the principles we have discussed, the Stanford Heart Disease Prevention Program did produce significant decreases in cardiovascular risk factors as well as a change in attitudes in three California towns (Maccoby et al., 1977). And, as we can see in the In the News box (pp. 244–245), some governments even believe that citizens of warring countries can be convinced by "paper bullets."

Attitude Change as a Phenomenon of Groups Any advertising, education, or propaganda campaign is weak in contrast to the immediate social environment of a person—the family, friends, work, and political and religious groups they belong to. These command more attention, convey information more vividly and vigorously, and control far more reinforcement than the mass media can. We should not forget the reality of the social context. Attitude change is a *social* phenomenon. Indeed, as we discussed in the previous chapter, attitude is a concept that really grows out of our lives as social animals, as creatures whose existence always involves other people.

Our most ego-involving attitudes derive from our group identities. The earliest research on attitudes paid explicit attention to the group setting. Sherif (1936) studied how group norms are acquired by individuals, and Lewin (1947) studied the attitude change effects of group participation and commitment. Even this early research recognized that the mere existence of a discrepancy between a group norm and an individual attitude set into motion processes on the part of both the group and the individual

As a means of integrating public schools in Boston, forced busing might have been successful in requiring people to change their behavior. Because of the measures used to enforce this strategy, however, it is unlikely that many attitudes about integration were changed at the time.

to reduce that discrepancy. Much of the later research tried to focus on those psychological processes, sometimes losing sight of the group processes that ignited and drove them.

Groups not only provide information, but, unlike written or electronically transmitted information, also set up the situations that bring about induced compliance. Since people derive important psychological and physical needs from membership in groups, the need to remain "in" is strong. Even in a modern urban society, where neighbors have little contact and perhaps no dependence on each other for survival needs, few people care to be at odds with their immediate neighbors. Although these influence processes are discussed under other chapter topics, their importance in attitude change, and attitude change as a central part of group dynamics, should not be overlooked.

Our discussion of attitude change phenomena and theories of the attitude change process should enable us to better understand why attitudes toward desegregation did not undergo immediate change in Evie's city and, indeed, why the attitudes of many probably became even more hostile to integration. We should also be able to devise some attitude and behavior change strategies that would have been more successful.

First, let us consider why attitudes did not change in a positive direction. School officials did not cooperate with the desegregation plan, and some even organized opposition to it. Coherent and decisive political leadership was absent, and citizens were not involved in the planning from the outset (Greenblatt & Willie, 1981). In the face of intense involvement and strong attitudes opposing desegregation, the communication of

IN THE NEWS

"PAPER BULLETS" WITH REAL TARGETS

In This Corner

During last year's Falklands war, British propaganda leaflets were ready to be dropped over Port Stanley, urging a peaceable surrender by the Argentinians. An intelligence officer, however, thought the leaflets were both crude and unconvincing.

Regardless of their quality, such sheets would undoubtedly interest members of the Psywar Society, an international association of psychological warfare historians and collectors of aerial propaganda leaflets.

Located in England, the organization has more than 300 members throughout the world, including a few dozen Americans. The members—who include teachers, surgeons, bankers and students—are fascinated by "paper bullets," relatively recent weapons of psychological warfare.

Aerial propaganda leaflets have an eventful history. Although a balloon dropped leaflets during the siege of Paris in 1870, it wasn't until World War I that aerial propaganda became an important element of war. At that time, the British showered millions of leaflets over German troops, which, some historians contend, helped undermine enemy morale. Paper storms flooded almost all the land battles on the war's Western Front. In Russia, Bolshevik pilots dropped Lenin's pronouncements for the benefit of the Russian masses.

Between the world wars, aerial propaganda sheets rained upon the Spanish Civil War, a Hungarian uprising and skirmishes in northwest India.

The outbreak of World War II created enormous demand for sophisticated psy-

peaceful information by the mass media had virtually no chance of prevailing. The order of a federal court, backed up by armed force, enabled people to attribute any behavior change to external pressures, ensuring that even positive behaviors would not lead to positive attitude change.

Altering strong attitudes requires strong strategies for change. As we have seen, some of the most effective techniques of attitude change involve engaging people in behavior that is consistent with the desired new attitudes (role playing, counter-attitudinal advocacy, or induced compliance), having them do so under their own volition, and keeping external pressures (both punishments and rewards) to a minimum. Acts of official coercion place the affected people in the position of acting out opposition, thereby reinforcing their anti-integration attitudes. The acts of compliance that did occur were made under pressure from high officials, so that no cognitive dissonance was likely to be aroused and any self-persuasion was likely to be against the efforts at integration. In short, official actions probably did more to promote boomerang effects than to induce positive attitude change.

A variety of solutions using what we know about attitude change can be found to this problem. Combining basic attitude principles with suc-

chological warfare. The British Royal Air Force and their allies dropped more than 2000 different types of propaganda, including newspapers and miniature magazines. Literally millions of leaflets flooded the Axis nations while the Germans hailed pamphlets on Allied Forces behind the Maginot Line. Propaganda designed to lower enemy morale also swamped Japan, New Guinea, Italy and North Africa.

In recent times, leaflets have been dropped over Korea, Vietnam and Afghanistan.

Peter Robb, the general secretary of the Psywar Society, has been collecting aerial propaganda for more than 50 years. His collection includes more than 10,000 items garnered from all over the world.

Organized in 1958, the Psywar Society publishes catalogues describing leaflets as well as a quarterly journal, aptly titled the "Falling Leaf." Recent issues feature articles on Japanese World War II propaganda and on war bond leaflets dropped by U.S. Army bombers over Long Beach, Calif., in 1943.

Robb points out that not all aerial messages deal with war. A French newspaper dropped leaflets over Paris in the 1920s, reporting the defeat of French boxer Georges Carpentier by Jack Dempsey. Last June, Indonesian planes dropped millions of leaflets in Java, warning villagers of blindness if they looked at a total solar eclipse.

Source: Donald Altschiller, *Boston Globe,* October 22, 1983, p. 1.

cessful desegregation plans from a variety of cities (Miller, 1980; Stephan & Feagin, 1980; Gerald & Miller, 1975), we can suggest the following:

Desegregation could proceed in a series of stages aimed at gradually shifting the student population to achieve the city's numerical goals. Each of the stages would seek to maximize parental and student voluntary choice to change schools, and would employ no coercive threats and minimal external inducements to bring about voluntary transfer. The first stage might simply invite volunteers to transfer. The next stage might offer free transportation to those willing to transfer. Schools could be modified to specialize in areas such as art, music, academics, aerospace, or computers to attract more volunteers.

By making each stage involve voluntary movement, no one would be forced to transfer, thereby defusing opposition and preventing the protests and other public actions that reinforce anti-integration attitudes. Anyone who adamantly did not want to change schools would not be forced to. Those who did transfer would know it was a personal choice, and attitude change in support of their act of desegregation would likely take place. If a neighbor were to question parents who consented to a transfer, the parents would find themselves generating arguments to defend their decision (thereby getting them to role-play). Because the inducement at each stage would be just enough to produce only a slightly greater amount of movement, the problem of overjustification would not occur.

What goes on in the classrooms themselves also affects interracial attitudes. The nature of intergroup contact affects the attitudes those groups' members will form for each other. This is another illustration of the finding that behavior change provokes attitude change. When classes are organized so that minority and majority groups compete against each other on unequal terms, antagonism increases. But when groups work together on an equal and cooperative basis, the opposite occurs (Weigel et al., 1975; Cook, 1984; Miller & Brewer, 1984). One example is the "jigsaw classroom," in which students are formed into small mixed-race groups. Each student learns a small part of the lesson. Then they combine their knowledge so that students learn the full lesson from one another. As a result of such cooperative behavior, students learn from each other and groups come to form more positive attitudes toward each other.

That the schools were to be desegregated was not in doubt. How that desegregation was brought about could make a considerable difference in people's lives. The strategies of gradual voluntary movement and citizen involvement over a period of years might seem a sluggish remedy to centuries of discrimination. But it might well have produced more cooperation, less violence, and more long-term positive attitude change than a judge's order to move children into schools and police onto streets. Different strategies do, indeed, lead to different outcomes. As Amir (1976) noted after reviewing 250 studies concerned with integration, "social planning can make the difference of whether one will like it, just accept it, or even fight against it" (pp. 293–294).

SUMMARY

1. Some approaches to attitude change view the person as a relatively passive target of informational influence. Other approaches see attitude change as the product of active behavioral involvement by the person.
2. The Yale communication model combines an analysis of the components of persuasive communication—source, channel, message, recipients—with a learning theory approach to psychology.
3. Major aspects of attitude change studied by the communication model include source credibility, one- versus two-sided messages, fear appeals, order effects, and the sex and intelligence of the audience.
4. The social judgment model applies the concepts of assimilation and contrast to reactions to persuasive communications that fall into a

person's latitudes of acceptance and rejection. The relative sizes of these latitudes are determined by a person's ego involvement in the attitude issue, and in turn affect whether attitudes change in a positive direction or boomerang.

5. The theory of reasoned action sees attitude change as a product of changes in beliefs. Beliefs influence not only attitudes but subjective norms as well.
6. Cognitive response analysis holds that most persuasion is self-persuasion. People generate pro- or counter-arguments in response to a persuasive message. It is the amount and nature of those cognitive responses that determine the direction and degree of attitude change.
7. Cognitive dissonance theory postulates that attitude change is prompted by an uncomfortable motivational state produced when a person holds cognitions that contradict each other. The most important of these situations occurs when a person's behavior is inconsistent with his or her attitudes. To reduce the dissonance, attitudes will change to become consistent with the behavior.
8. The greater the external justification for behavior inconsistent with an attitude, the less attitude change will take place. Most attitude change results from behavioral compliance that is induced by minimal external pressure.
9. Other phenomena explained by dissonance theory include attitude change following disconfirmed expectations, choices and decisions, insufficient justification, effort justification, and the tendency for people to expose themselves to information selectively.
10. The self-perception model interprets dissonance phenomena as resulting from inferences people draw about themselves from observation of their behavior and circumstances. Both dissonance and self-perception processes have been shown to operate, but each under different conditions of attitude change.
11. One of the most potent attitude change phenomena is role playing. The strength of role playing can be explained by cognitive dissonance theory, self-perception theory, and also by the concept of biased scanning.
12. Two important means of promoting resistance to change are forewarning and inoculation. Each method operates by exposing people to arguments that might follow, in order to allow them to avoid changing their positions when challenged.
13. Inducing attitude change in real-world situations is more difficult than in the laboratory. In natural settings any given persuasive message is less likely to be received or attended to, and is only one among many.
14. Attitude change is in part a phenomenon of groups. Group membership determines much behavior; affects ego involvement; and controls reinforcements, exposure to information, and many other of the critical elements of attitude change.

CHAPTER 7
Interpersonal Attraction and Romantic Relationships

To have and to hold from this day forward, for better for worse, for richer for poorer, in sickness and in health, to love and to cherish, till death do us part.
—Book of Common Prayer

According to the U.S. Census Bureau, in 1980 an estimated 2.4 million couples exchanged this vow to join their lives together in marriage. Typically, the bride and groom were young. In 1979, the average age for first marriage was 21.6 years for women and 23.4 years for men. At this young age, before many had settled on careers or even finished their education, these couples promised to work and live as partners and to love each other until one or both should die.

For many, that promise will not be kept. In 1980, nearly 1.2 million couples chose to dissolve their marriages through divorce—that works out to one divorce every 27 seconds. Half of those broken marriages, once framed to last 50 years or more, ended well before the couples' seventh wedding anniversary. The divorce rate in the United States has increased steadily since the late 1950s (Norton & Glick, 1976). The number of marriages per 1000 population increased by almost 25 percent from 1960 to 1980, a trend that largely reflects changes in the age composition of the country's population as the children of the post–World War II baby boom

---

This chapter was written by William DeJong.

reached their twenties. Over the same period, however, the divorce rate increased by 136 percent (*Statistical Abstract of the United States,* 1983). Roughly one-half of all marriages are now expected to end in divorce.

Does the growing divorce rate indicate that Americans are giving up on marriage? No. A 1980 survey conducted by the Institute of Social Research showed that 97 percent of the 18-year-olds questioned said they thought they would marry (*U. S. News and World Report,* June 20, 1983). Moreover, while it is true that the incidence of divorce has grown, the rate of remarriage is also high. For example, from 1975 to 1977, just under one-third of all marriages were remarriages. Clearly, most men and women in this country still aspire to be married, including those whose first marriages failed.

Nevertheless, this country's high divorce rate continues to be a significant social problem. Sadly, over 80 percent of divorces involve at least one child (Campbell, 1975). Children of divorce often feel responsible for the breakup, believing that their own less-than-perfect behavior led to discord between their parents. The confusion and distress they feel is compounded when one or both parents try to enlist them in the divorce battle or to compete for their loyalties.

The husband usually loses custody of the children. With his time limited to vacations and regularly scheduled visitations, he may lose touch with them. He may lose contact altogether if he or their mother moves away. The wife, unless she remarries, must raise the children alone, doing the work of two people to provide financial security and a good home. That divorced women with children who have not remarried report the lowest level of overall life satisfaction is not surprising (Campbell, 1975).

Can anything be done to reduce the incidence of divorce? Can people be helped to choose better marriage partners? Can they do more to hold their relationships together?

As social creatures, human beings have twin yearnings: to have a sense of group belonging and to be loved (Rubin, 1980). We want to be connected to a social network of friends. And we want a special, intimate relationship with a mate.

This chapter concerns the study of whom we like and love, how friendships and romances evolve, and what causes them to end. Friendships and romantic relationships obviously differ in significant ways. But social psychologists have learned that they share many features in common and involve similar processes.

FRIENDSHIP

For most of us, a life without friends is unimaginable. We depend on friends to help us understand our world, our reactions to events, and our own feelings (Schachter, 1959). We need friends to hear us out, console us, advise us, help us, teach us, and bolster us (Derlega & Chaikin, 1975). Friends who share our interests make our activities and daily experiences more fun (Weiss & Lowenthal, 1975).

Bell (1981) has argued that the importance that Americans place on friendships has increased in recent years. Our society is mobile, with almost 20 percent of the nation's population moving to a new home each year (Packard, 1972). In addition, an increasing number of Americans live alone. In 1960, 13.1 percent of the nation's households were one-person households; by 1980, this figure had increased to 22.6 percent. Such circumstances weaken our ties and reduce the support we receive from our extended families. In response, many of us have turned increasingly to friends to serve those functions that might have been filled by our extended families.

There are, of course, risks to establishing friendships with other people. Once we have become close to someone, we may someday experience the pain of loss when we or our friend moves away. Conflicts may arise, perhaps leading to the unhappy dissolution of the friendship. And friendship means vulnerability. Friends rely on each other; but friends sometimes let each other down. Friends share information about their feelings, ambitions, defeats, and hopes with each other; but friends sometimes violate the trust that has been placed in them (Rempel, Holmes, & Zanna, 1985). Still, our need for friends makes most of us willingly accept these risks.

Choosing Friends

Whom do we choose as friends? Social psychologists have found four factors that influence whether two people will become friends: (1) their physical proximity to one another, (2) the similarity of their interests and attitudes, (3) the complementarity of their personalities, and (4) their physical attractiveness.

Proximity An observation that is at once obvious and profound is that we tend to make friends with those who work or live near us. Several studies have demonstrated that geographical **proximity** has an enormous influence on friendship patterns (e.g., Nahemow & Lawton, 1975; Segal, 1974). Beyond that, any feature of our environment that brings people together can stimulate the process of making friends.

The best-known demonstration of the proximity-liking effect is a study conducted by Festinger, Schachter, and Back (1950). These researchers studied the pattern of friendships that developed in a large housing project for married graduate students. The several buildings in the project were of identical design; each apartment, except for those on the end of each building, faced onto a courtyard. It is important to note that residents were assigned to the apartments as they became available, not on the basis of preexisting friendships, educational interests, or background.

The process of forming friendships involves several factors. These two people have just met and seem to like each other. Can you name any of the variables that may account for their initial attraction?

Two aspects of the spatial arrangements of the dwellings were crucial determinants of the friendships made. The first was the actual distance between the apartments. Residents became friendliest with those who lived closest to them. In fact, friendships among residents separated by more than four or five apartments were extremely uncommon. The direction in which an apartment faced also had a crucial impact on the social life of the project's residents. Those who lived in units that faced the street rather than the courtyard had fewer than half as many friends as those who lived in the apartments facing the courtyard. Other architectural features that brought residents into contact with their neighbors tended to increase their popularity. For example, those who lived near stairwells or near the mailboxes were more popular than those living farther away from those areas.

One explanation for the proximity-liking effect is obvious. To become friends with other people, a person must have the opportunity to interact with them. The probability of chance encounters is greater for people who live or work near each other. As noted, even seemingly small differences in distance can have enormous impact.

Another explanation was suggested by Darley and Berscheid (1967). Because we want our interactions with others to be pleasant, it makes us uncomfortable to think that people we must spend time with are disagreeable. We can reduce our discomfort by playing up their good qualities and playing down their bad qualities. With our close neighbors, then, we may be motivated to see the good and ignore the bad, making us like them more. A final explanation for the effect of proximity on liking is suggested by the mere exposure effect, described in Chapter 5. As we see people again and again, and they become more familiar to us, our liking for them goes up (Brockner & Swap, 1976; Swap, 1977).

The effect of proximity on the process of friendship formation is greatest in the beginning. In the first days of the school year, for example, freshmen get to know the students who live near them. Later, as they exchange information and share experiences, proximity becomes a less important determinant of friendship than other factors, such as mutual interests and similar attitudes. Subtle aspects of our physical environment determine whom we meet. Then other factors determine who among our acquaintances will become our friends.

Similarity "Have no friends not equal to yourself." This ancient wisdom of Confucius, that the best friends are those who are similar to one another, continues to be common folk wisdom today. A large body of research in social psychology confirms that, in general, the greater the similarity between two people, the more attracted they are to each other.

Much of the research that has shown the similarity-liking effect has used the so-called "imaginary stranger" technique (Byrne, 1971). With this procedure, people are first given a questionnaire that measures their attitudes on a number of issues (e.g., belief in God, political party preference). Later, as part of a study on interpersonal judgment, people read about another person—the "stranger"—who has attitudes highly similar or dissimilar to their own. They are then asked to indicate their liking for that other person. As the proportion of similar attitudes increases, their attraction to the stranger increases. Apparent similarity also increases estimates of a stranger's liking for them (Gonzales et al., 1983).

The effect of attitude similarity has also been tested using more real-life procedures. In one study, investigators asked students to complete an attitude questionnaire. Opposite-sexed pairs were then formed, with some known to have highly similar attitudes and others known to be dissimilar. Each couple was introduced and then asked to talk to each other for half an hour at the student union. Subsequent questionnaire responses showed that similar pairs liked each other more (Byrne, Ervin, & Lamberth, 1970).

Similarity is important in long-term relationships as well. Kandel (1978) asked a large group of high school students to identify their best friend. These students also filled out an extensive questionnaire on their academic interests, leisure time activities, drug and alcohol use, religiousness, degree of involvement in extracurricular activities, attitudes, and so on. The similarity of student pairs who mutually identified one another as best friends was then examined.

Both male and female friendship pairs were found to be highly similar on a large number of variables. Highest similarity was found on three demographic variables—grade in school, sex, and race. Next highest was students' reported use or nonuse of marijuana and other illicit drugs. Other areas showing relatively high similarity between best friends included academic interests and participation in peer activities.

This observed similarity results in part from our selection of friends who share our backgrounds and interests. But in real ongoing friendships, similarity also emerges through our mutual influence on one another and our shared involvement in activities. Friends can change each other's attitudes, preferences, and behavior, and they thus become more similar over time (Newcomb, 1961).

Are people always more attracted to similar than to dissimilar people? Clearly not. For example, when a person is described to research subjects as being a former mental patient (Novak & Lerner, 1968) or a drug addict (Lerner & Agar, 1972), people express greater attraction when that person's attitudes are *dissimilar* to their own. In the same way, if people share characteristics with us that we do not especially like, similarity does not increase our attraction for them. For instance, people with positive self-concepts are more attracted to similar than to dissimilar others, but those with low self-concepts do not show this preference (Leonard, 1975; Goldman & Olczak, 1976).

Social psychologists have offered several possible explanations for the similarity-liking effect. First, our attitudes are often difficult to validate objectively; to find support for our beliefs, we must turn to other people (Festinger, 1954) (see Chapter 3). Given our uncertainty, we find agreement with our opinions to be rewarding, and we like people who reward us (Byrne & Clore, 1970). Similarity can also be rewarding because it promotes pleasant interaction and enjoyment in the same activities.

A second explanation for the similarity-liking effect is that, in general, people strive for consistency and balance in their social world (Heider, 1958; Newcomb, 1971, 1978) (see Chapter 5). A person who feels strongly, for example, that nuclear power plants should no longer be built will want friends to agree. Quite simply, their disagreement would be inconsistent with mutual liking. If the friends' opinions did not change, the continuing tension caused by the inconsistency might cause them eventually to dislike each other.

A third explanation for the similarity-liking effect has been studied by Wetzel and Insko (1982). They suggest that we are attracted to people who have the qualities and traits we want for ourselves. Thus, similarity to our *ideal* self, not our *actual* self, is the key. Studies showing a similarity-liking effect have confused the two, Wetzel and Insko argue, for most people do not perceive a wide gap between their ideal and actual selves. In one test of this idea, Wetzel, Schwartz, and Vasu (1979) measured college students' perceptions of their roommates' similarity to themselves and to their ideal selves. Similarity to the ideal self was the stronger predictor of how much these students liked their roommates.

Complementarity We prefer the company of people who agree with us and who share many of our characteristics. Do we also prefer the company of people whose personalities match our own? Or are we instead attracted to people whose personality traits complement ours? For example, if we like to have our own way about things, would we not be paired best with someone who is submissive to others' wishes? If we are the type of person who finds tremendous joy in comforting others, would we not be paired best with someone who needs such comfort?

Bermann and Miller (1967) tested this by asking student nurses whether they would prefer a roommate who was similar or complementary in terms of dominance/submissiveness. Most indicated they would prefer someone similar to themselves. The best relationships, however, were those between roommates whose personalities complemented one another (Bermann & Miller, 1967). If both roommates were domineering or both were submissive, their relationship was less satisfactory.

Wagner (1975) asked male summer camp counselors to rate how well they worked with each of their fellow counselors. It was found that counselors worked together better when one needed aid, comfort, and sympathy and the other provided it; when one was aggressive and the other was compliant, apologetic, and accepting of ridicule; and when one routinely sought praise, respect, and recognition and the other provided it.

Thus it is clear that a need for **complementarity** can sometimes play a role in interpersonal attraction. We will see later in the chapter, when the research on mate selection and marital adjustment is reviewed, however, that little is yet known about when complementarity plays a role and when it does not.

APPLICATION
COLLEGE ROOMMATE ASSIGNMENTS

Does a freshman roommate become a student's best friend or a bitter enemy? It depends on the luck of the draw. Most colleges collect little information about incoming freshmen to help the housing office match roommates. It is not surprising, therefore, that at many colleges students are unhappy with their assigned roommates. An incompatible roommate can make their introduction to college a nightmare. A student who just completed her first year at a large state university describes an experience that left her unhappy, badly affected her grades, and eventually resulted in her being assigned a new roommate:

> When I called Stacy before school started, she sounded very nice. We shared the same taste in music. Even our bedroom colors were the same! I thought she and I were going to become good friends. Unfortunately, things went badly from the start. Stacy stayed up until three in the morning listening to the same tape again and again. There was a rule for us to turn down our stereos and talk quietly after 10 P.M. so that our neighbors could study or sleep. Stacy kept saying that rooms are for living, not studying; there was always the library for that.

To investigate the factors associated with liking among college roommates, Hill and Stull (1981) conducted a study at the University of Washington. They found that approximately half of the roommates split up before the end of the school year. Unhappiness with the assigned roommate was not the only reason, but a major one: 28 percent of the males and 43 percent of the females who separated from their roommates indicated incompatibility as the reason. For males, those who stayed together were more likely to be in the same year of college and to have the same religious background. For females, only one variable was related to whether roommates stayed together: similarity of values.

Could a housing office do a better job of matching roommates by paying attention to the findings of social psychological research? The answer is yes. In addition to demographic characteristics (year of school, religious background, and so on) and values, schools could inquire about and match for attitudes (Byrne, 1971), extracurricular activities (Kandel, 1978), and behavior patterns (smoking, hours kept, study habits). They could match roommates who are similar to each other's "ideal self" (Wetzel, Schwartz, & Vasu, 1979). And they could measure key personality needs (e.g., dominance/submission) and assign roommates whose needs complement each other (Bermann & Miller, 1967).

Collecting and using this amount of information on several thousand incoming students each year would be a formidable undertaking. But depending on the magnitude of the roommate problem to administrators and students, it could well be worth the trouble and expense.

Physical Attractiveness Beautiful people are liked more than those who are not physically attractive (Adams, 1977; Berscheid & Walster, 1974a). This is not a surprising finding. It is important to recognize, however, that we also tend to assume that attractive people are more intelligent (Clifford & Walster, 1973); that they are more pleasant, more socially skilled, and of higher status (Adams & Huston, 1975); and that they are more sensitive and kind, more successful in their careers, and more happily married (Dion, Berscheid, & Walster, 1972). Attractive people are also seen as vain, materialistic, and more likely to have extramarital affairs (Dermer & Thiel, 1975), but on the whole, we seem to equate beauty with goodness (Dion, Berscheid, & Walster, 1972). As will be seen in the next section of this chapter, romantic attraction is greatly influenced by physical attractiveness.

The Process of Making Friends

Having become acquainted, how do people go on to become friends? Relationships between two people usually evolve, moving gradually from superficial to more intimate levels (Altman & Taylor, 1973). During a first meeting, people exchange basic facts about themselves—where they grew up, where they live, their line of work—and identify what they have in common. Later, they move on to more personal matters. Typically, one person moves on to a greater level of disclosure, and the other reciprocates

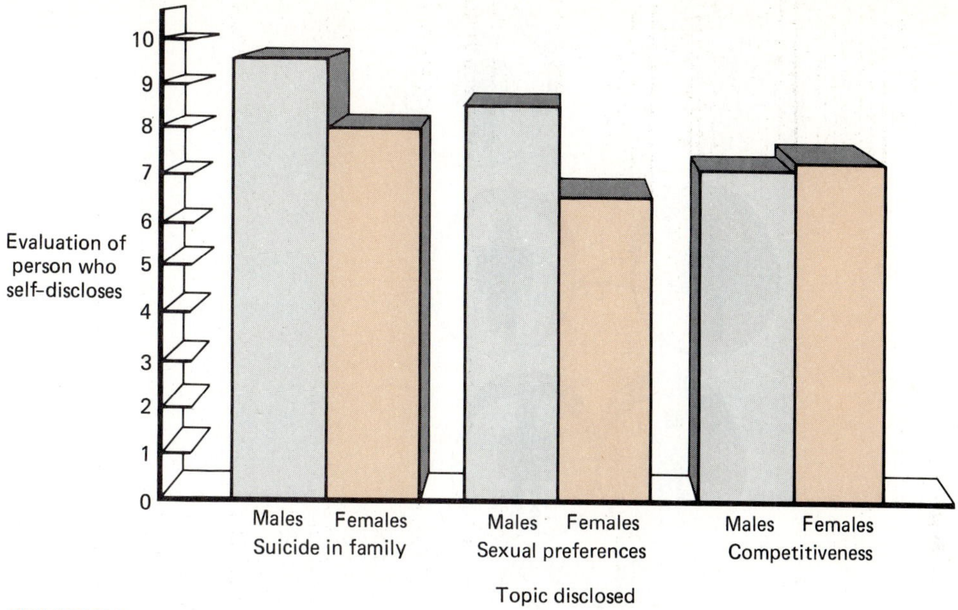

FIGURE 7.1

Reactions to Self-Disclosure How do men and women react to people who disclose intimate information about themselves? It depends on the topic of the disclosure. Some topics produce more favorable reactions than others. Women evaluate the discloser more favorably on some topics, but men and women react about the same to disclosures about competitiveness. *Source:* Based on C. L. Kleinke & M. L. Kahn (1980). Perceptions of self-disclosers: Effects of sex and physical attractiveness. *Journal of Personality, 48.2,* 190–205. Copyright © 1980 Duke University Press.

(Davis, 1977; Jourard & Friedman, 1970; Lynn, 1978). During the early stages of their interaction, people may begin to talk about their past experiences, people they know in common, or their reactions to political events. Disclosure does not automatically lead to liking. In fact, too much too soon can produce negative reactions. And, as Figure 7.1 demonstrates, women generally are evaluated more positively for disclosing information about themselves than men are, although the difference depends on the topic being disclosed (Kleinke & Kahn, 1980).

As they begin to know, understand, and trust one another, people talk about more intimate things—their ambitions, fears, romances, family or personal problems. If they spend sufficient time together, and if they continue to find the relationship rewarding, this mutual self-disclosure gradually moves their friendship to deeper and deeper levels (Derlega & Chaikin, 1975; Rubin & Shenker, 1980).

Finally, an interdependence between the two people may emerge. At this level, there is strong mutual attraction, trust, and openness. Because of intimate self-disclosure, each has knowledge of the other's feelings.

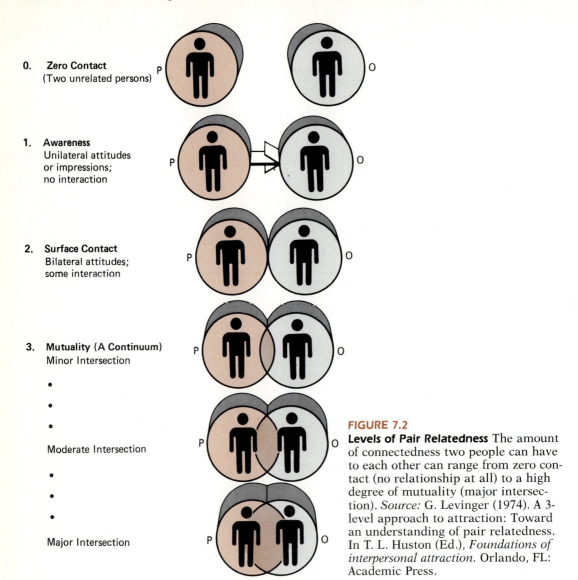

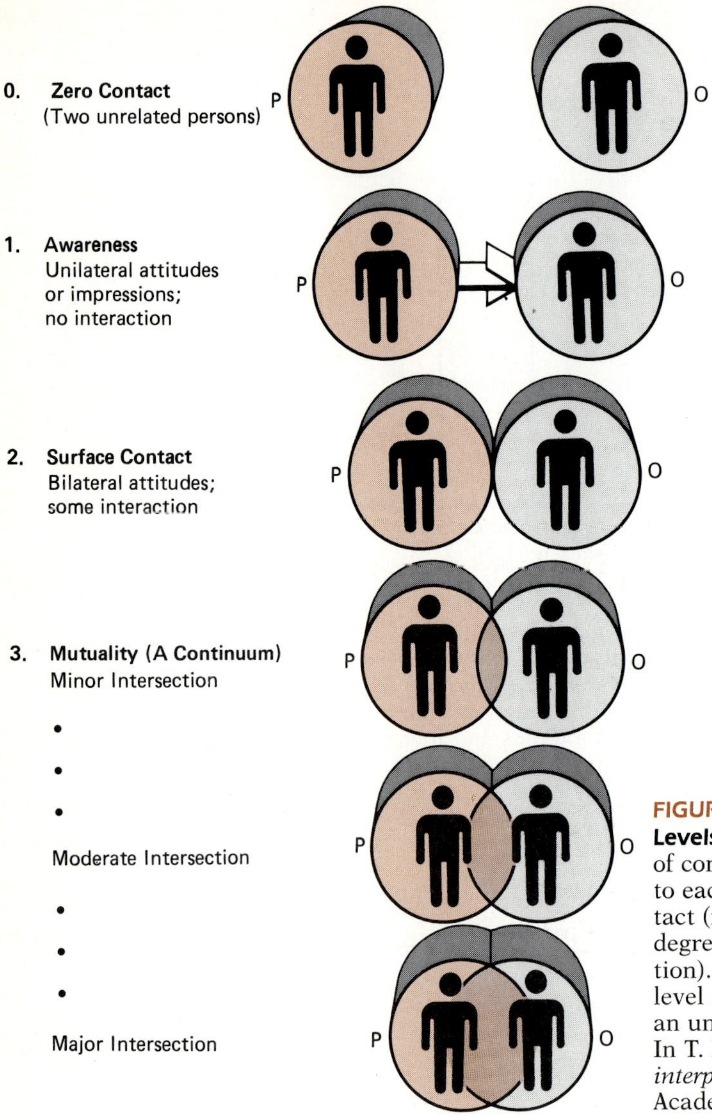

FIGURE 7.2
Levels of Pair Relatedness The amount of connectedness two people can have to each other can range from zero contact (no relationship at all) to a high degree of mutuality (major intersection). *Source:* G. Levinger (1974). A 3-level approach to attraction: Toward an understanding of pair relatedness. In T. L. Huston (Ed.), *Foundations of interpersonal attraction.* Orlando, FL: Academic Press.

They often equate the other's interests with their own; both their goals and actions become increasingly synchronized. But they also feel freer to express criticism and hostility.

In Figure 7.2, Levinger (1974) has illustrated the different levels of relatedness that can exist between two people. "Zero contact," the minimum state, describes the relationship between any person and most of the population of this planet. "Awareness" is unilateral; one person sees and assesses the other, but there is no interaction between them. "Surface contact" begins a process of interaction, which may grow in frequency and duration over time. At the last level, "mutuality," the overlap in their lives is large and continues to grow.

Assessment of Rewards and Costs As a relationship progresses, both people continually assess their level of satisfaction with it (Altman & Taylor, 1973). So long as satisfaction remains high, the relationship can continue to grow. But if one or both people become dissatisfied, the relationship may be discontinued. If interaction is unavoidable, as in the case of assigned roommates, or if disengagement might prove to be awkward or embarrassing, the relationship may be frozen at the current level of intimacy or regress to a lower level.

What determines the level of satisfaction we feel? Several social exchange theorists (e.g., Altman & Taylor, 1973; Homans, 1961; Thibaut & Kelley, 1959) have argued that satisfaction with a relationship remains high so long as its rewards exceed its costs. Rewards are the benefits that we receive from the relationship—the enjoyment of shared experiences and activities, valuable information, praise, admiration, help in time of need. Costs are the unpleasant aspects of interaction with another person—lack of responsiveness, excessive dependence, competitiveness. Our calculation of rewards and costs, these theorists argue, is not necessarily a conscious process, yet sizing up the net value of our friendships is something we do continually. In deciding whether to stay in the relationship, people sense the ratio of rewards to costs. They stay in a relationship if the ratio meets or exceeds what they would expect in alternative relationships.

Our tally of rewards and costs takes into account the apparent motives of the other person. For example, if we believe that other people hope to gain something from us, we are likely to view their praise or their agreement with us as ingratiation (Jones, 1964). We may have a similar reaction if their praise is too much at odds with our own opinion about ourselves (Berscheid & Walster, 1978). A person's ingratiating behavior may not cause us to dislike that person, but our positive feelings will be reduced at least somewhat (Byrne, Rasche, & Kelley, 1974). Interestingly, a person's honesty in the face of situational pressures to ingratiate appears to produce increased liking for that person (Drachman, de Carufel, & Insko, 1978).

Equity and Reciprocity The value of a friendship is also judged by rules of fairness and reciprocity. Both people may feel that, on balance, the rewards they receive from a relationship far exceed its costs. But if one person receives more rewards than the other or if that person is getting back more than he or she contributes, this too can create dissatisfaction. If both people perceive the imbalance, both will feel pressure to readjust

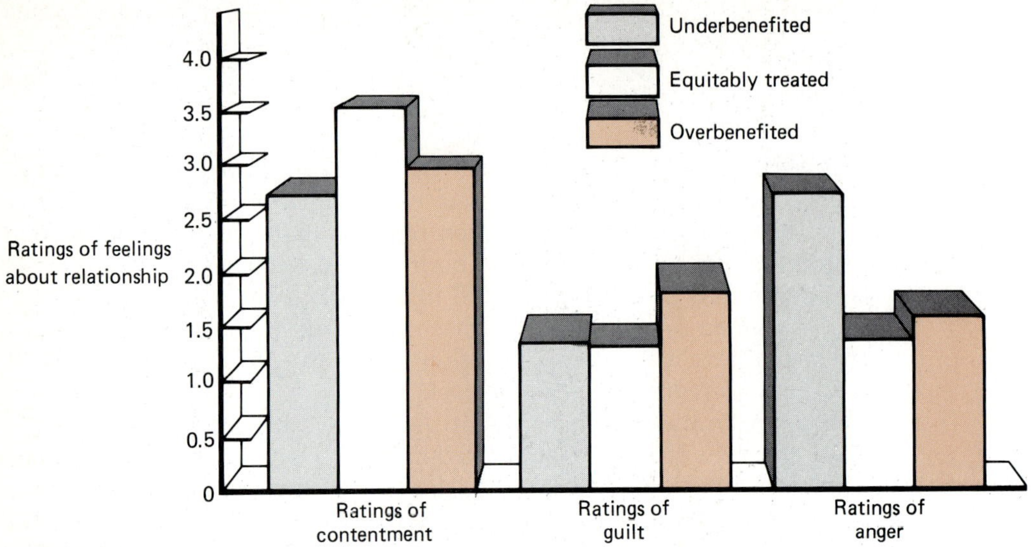

FIGURE 7.3
Equity in Dating Relationships The feelings people have about their dating relationships are greatly affected by the degree of equity experienced in the relationship. People who feel underbenefited by their relationship feel a high degree of anger. Those who feel overbenefited feel the most guilt. Those who feel equitably treated show the most contentment and the least guilt and anger. *Source:* E. Hatfield, G. W. Walster, & J. Traupmann (1979). Equity and premarital sex. In M. Cook & G. Wilson (Eds.), *Love and attraction: An international conference.* Oxford: Pergamon Press.

their relationship to eliminate the inequity. If one party fails to perceive the imbalance, or if the needed readjustment otherwise cannot be accomplished, the relationship may end. Thus, for a relationship between two people to be satisfactory, the rewards that relationship brings must be equitably distributed between them.

This idea is the basis of social equity theory, as described by Walster, Berscheid, and Walster (1973). Walster, Walster, and Traupmann (1978) asked several hundred students to evaluate their dating relationships in terms of how they felt about their relationships and what they put into and receive from the relationship. Those in equitable relationships were more content and less angry or guilty than those in relationships where they were either greatly underbenefited or greatly overbenefited from the relationship (see Figure 7.3).

One consequence of this preference for equitable relationships is that people are strongly motivated to treat others as they themselves have been treated, and to be treated as they have treated others. Gouldner (1960) has argued, in fact, that our social relations with others are guided by a norm of reciprocity, a code of behavior that dictates that we treat others in kind. This norm can guide relationships and, as we will see in Chapter 9, can also determine whether one person will help another or will appreciate help received.

ROMANTIC ATTRACTION

This country, with its emphasis on individuality and freedom, has long subscribed to the "romantic ideal"—that marriages should be based on love, rather than on economic or other practical considerations or on an arrangement by parents. This romantic ideal entails the view that love is fated, all-consuming, and beyond reason or control (Rubin, 1973). In contrast to popular stereotypes, the romantic ideal thrives more among men than women. Rubin (1969) asked people whether they agreed with several statements that embody the romantic ideal (e.g., "As long as they at least love one another, two people should have no difficulty in getting along together in marriage"). Men were more likely than women to endorse such statements. In addition, women report being more cautious when entering a new relationship, remaining more conscious of alternatives outside the relationship, and being more likely to end a relationship that is going badly (Rubin, Peplau, & Hill, 1981).

Of course, murmurings of the heart are not all that we attend to when dating and searching for a marriage partner. Even if we believe in the romantic ideal, we are not altogether impractical. The other person's age, social class, race, education, religious preference, personality, and attitudes about family, career, and other issues all enter into our choice. Thus selecting a marriage partner is to some extent a calculated decision. Courtship and marriage, like any other interpersonal relationships, are guided by the rewards and costs brought by each partner and by notions of equity. Romance may be an affair of the heart, but the rules of the "marketplace" still apply.

What Is Love?

What do we mean when we say that two people are in love? The topic of love has inspired great eloquence. "O lyric Love, half angel and half bird/ And all a wonder and a wild desire," wrote Robert Browning. Romantic love is a feeling, as Browning suggests, with both spiritual and physical elements. It involves a strong affection for another person, devotion, and caring, but also passion and desire.

Psychologists have distinguished between two basic types of love. Walster and Walster (1978) describe **passionate love** as "a state of intense absorption in another," often accompanied by physiological arousal. The loved one is an object of fantasy, longing, and desire. Such love typically diminishes over time (Berscheid & Walster, 1974b). In contrast, **com-**

As poets have always told us, love is a strange and wondrous thing. Recently, social psychologists have begun to develop and test theories about this elusive phenomenon. These two people appear to be in love, but do you think that they like each other, too? Is there really a difference?

panionate love is the deep, mature, and caring love we feel for family and longtime friends. It may be the type of love we feel for a romantic partner once our passionate love has cooled.

Rubin (1973), in a similar vein, differentiates between love as needing and love as giving, what the ancient Greeks called *eros* and *agape*. Eros involves a desire to be in the other's presence, to have physical contact, and to receive approval and comfort. Agape involves respect and caring for the other person; it is an altruistic love, guided more by reason than emotion. Rubin argues that eros and agape are best considered independent components of love, rather than as two different types of love. He identifies a third component, intimacy, which he defines as the bond or link between two lovers as reflected in their sharing and their close, confidential communication.

The Measurement of Love With these three components of love in mind, Rubin (1970) developed a self-report scale to measure the extent of romantic love. Students were asked to indicate their agreement or disagreement with each of 13 statements about their romantic partner. The following are some items from that scale:

1. If I were lonely, my first thought would be to seek ______ out. (Eros)
2. I would do almost anything for ______. (Agape)
3. I feel that I can confide in ______ about virtually anything. (Intimacy)

In addition to this "loving" scale, Rubin also developed a 13-item "liking" scale which measures how much the romantic partner is respected by the respondent, perceived to be similar, and thought to be intelligent, mature, and well adjusted. A sample item: "I would highly recommend ______ for a responsible job."

In a study of over 150 dating couples, Rubin (1970, 1973) found that dating partners who scored higher on the loving scale also reported being more likely to marry ($r=0.59$), but their liking scale responses were not as good a predictor of intended marriage ($r=0.35$). Also, as poets have suggested, couples who were strongly in love were more likely to gaze in each other's eyes during conversation than were those who were less strongly in love.

The Emotional Component of Passionate Love In Chapter 2, Schachter's two-factor theory of emotion was introduced. This theory postulates that a general state of physiological arousal is labeled as an emotional experience on the basis of cues in the environment (Schachter & Singer, 1962). Is the same true of passionate love? Berscheid and Walster (1978) have suggested that it is. They propose that if we are emotionally aroused and find ourselves in the presence of a potential romantic partner, we may label that arousal as sexual attraction or love. Very often that other person is the true source of arousal, but not always.

Support for this model is provided in a study by White, Fishbein, and Rutstein (1981). Men were first involved in a series of experiences, including hearing an audiotape that produced low arousal (a textbook description of a frog's circulatory system), high negative arousal (a gruesome description of a missionary being murdered and carved up), and high positive arousal (an excerpt from a Steve Martin comedy album). Next, they were told they would meet and talk to another participant, a woman, but would first see her on a brief videotape in another experimental room. The experimenters tried through various means (e.g., having people watch the monitor in a darkened room) to have the men focus entirely on their

FROM THE FIELD
Ellen Berscheid

To say that Ellen Berscheid (University of Minnesota) has created the subfield of interpersonal attraction would not be much of an exaggeration. Though her research centers on interpersonal attraction, it deals with various related aspects of this topic—why we choose to date whom we do; the question of equity in relationships; misattribution of arousal as an explanation for love at first sight; the role of physical attractiveness in judgments people make of others; the initiation of social relationships; and the nature and determinants of close relationships. Her research has important implications for what is both the most rewarding and the most painful aspect of our lives.

future meeting and to forget the earlier part of the experiment. The woman on the videotape was made up to appear either attractive or unattractive. When the woman looked attractive, romantic attraction increased with increasing arousal, whether positive or negative. When the woman was unattractive, and was therefore not viewed as a likely source of physiological arousal, interest in her declined with increasing arousal.

The Triangular Theory Brian J. Sternberg has proposed a "triangular" theory of love (Sternberg, 1986). The three sides of the triangle consist of commitment, intimacy, and passion. Commitment is the cognitive component of love; it consists of the decisions we make about the object of our liking or loving. Intimacy is the emotional component of love—closeness, sharing, support. And passion, which needs little definition, is the motivational component. Different kinds of relationships that we have with different kinds of people in our lives may consist of different amounts of these three ingredients. But only if all three ingredients are present, Sternberg's theory states, do we have complete, or "consummate," love. And only if the components are present in roughly equal amounts will the triangle have equal sides and therefore be "balanced" (see Figure 7.4).

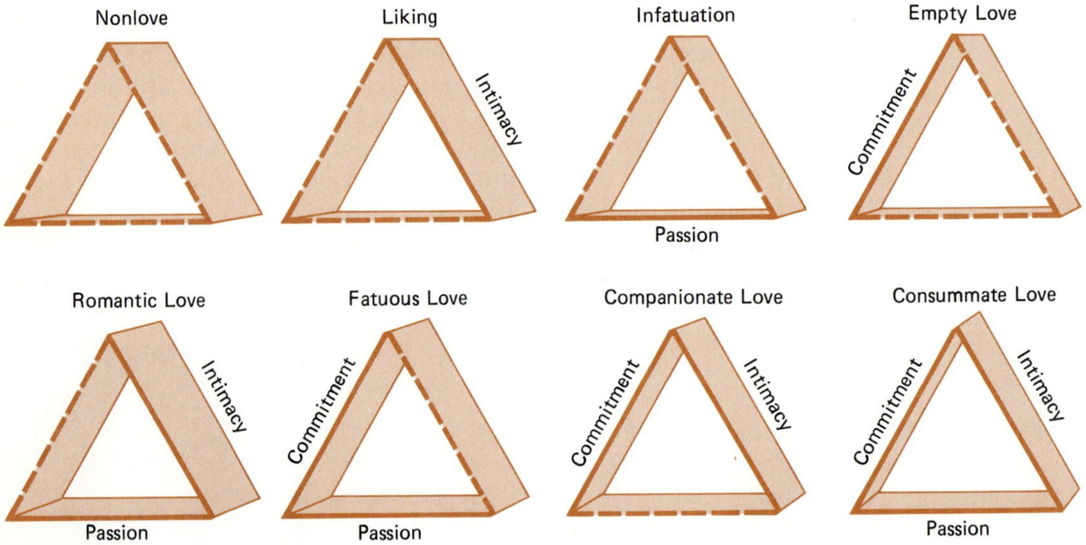

FIGURE 7.4
Kinds of Love Within the Triangular Theory The three ingredients of the triangular theory of love—commitment, passion, and intimacy—form the ingredients for eight different types of loving and liking, from nonlove (where none of the ingredients is present) to consummate love (where all three are present). *Source:* Adapted from R. J. Sternberg (1986). A triangular theory of love. *Psychological Review, 93,* 119–135. Reprinted from *Psychology Today* magazine. Copyright © 1968–1986 American Psychological Association.

For example, intimacy alone is what being friends, liking someone, is all about. Add commitment and you get companionate love, which is often what happens to romantic love whose passion has dried up. If you have passion without intimacy or commitment, that is mere infatuation. But all three together form a relationship of consummate love.

In one study that began the exploration of these issues, Sternberg and Grajek (1984) gave subjects the scales developed by Rubin and by Levinger (discussed elsewhere in this chapter) and asked that they be filled out in relation to various people in their lives: siblings, spouses, friends, parents, lovers. A variety of interesting findings were obtained. For example, it was found that men love and like their lovers the most and their siblings the least. Women like their lovers and their best friends about the same amount. But those earlier theories of love failed to account for all of the differences in relationships—that is, to distinguish one kind of relationship from another—that the triangular theory captures.

The Search for a Mate

Not so long ago, most dating couples adhered to the well-known "rules" of the dating game: the male approaches the female for a date and decides on the evening's entertainment; the date is planned in advance and is seldom spontaneous; the male pays all expenses. These traditional dating norms have given way to more flexible patterns. Frequently, a woman invites a man out, or they decide together to go somewhere. Costs are sometimes shared. Despite new styles of dating, however, exclusive male-female relationships are still just as prevalent as ever, with their primary purpose being the eventual selection of a spouse (Rubin, 1973).

Murstein (1971) has described three stages in the building of a romantic relationship. First is an initial attraction between two people based on their readily observable traits and attributes. Second, as the couple explore each other's attitudes, attraction is related to similarity in values and attitudes. In the third stage, attraction is related to the couple's ability to work as a cohesive unit and the extent to which their behavior matches the other's expectations for a spouse. When people are in the later stages of courtship, their relationship gradually becomes more and more exclusive (Milardo, Johnson, & Huston, 1983). Whom do we date and eventually marry? The answers provided by research on romantic attraction, dating, and marriage will seem familiar.

Proximity Choice of marriage partners, like choice of friends, depends on physical proximity. Bossard (1931) found, in examining over 5000 marriage applications, that one-fourth of the men and women lived within two blocks of their future spouses. In general, the likelihood of marriage declined steadily as distance between residences increased. This finding has been replicated in more recent studies (Ramsoy, 1966).

Similarity Ovid wrote, "If you would marry suitably, marry your equal." Most of us heed that advice. Murstein (1976) has noted that we tend to marry those of similar age, education, race, religion, and socioeconomic status.

Complementarity Familiar stereotypes—for example, the domineering wife who holds sway over her timid husband, the hard-driving businessman who is highly dependent on his wife's nurturance and support—suggest that people have at least some needs that are best met by spouses who are not similar, but who complement them (Winch, 1958). Research evidence on this hypothesis is inconclusive. Only Kerckoff and Davis (1962) have found evidence of need complementarity in mate selection. In their study, dating couples whose relationships had progressed over a seven-month period were more likely to have complementary needs. But other investigators have found that similarity of personality needs, not complementarity, is important in mate selection (Antill, 1983; Katz, Glucksberg, & Krauss, 1960; Murstein, 1961, 1967).

Reviewers of this research have noted a key methodological deficiency: investigators have measured general needs rather than needs that are tied to the specific relationship being studied (Levinger, 1964; Wagner, 1975). This is a crucial point, for our needs in friendships or work relationships may differ significantly from our needs in marriage. Clearly, more research on the importance of need complementarity in marital selection is needed.

Physical Attractiveness Several studies have shown that we are more eager to meet and date members of the opposite sex if they are good-looking. In one study, for example, women were told to expect to meet either an attractive or an unattractive man during the course of the experiment. Asked to provide a self-description that he could read before their meeting, they revealed many more intimate details about themselves when they expected to meet the attractive man (Brundage, Derlega, & Cash, 1977).

In a landmark study on dating preferences, a team of researchers organized a "computer dance" for the freshman class of a large university (Walster et al., 1966). The researchers had data on the attitudes, personalities, backgrounds, and academic records of these students, and they also had observers' ratings of the students' physical attractiveness. For the dance, male-female couples were paired randomly by a computer, with the single restriction that the male always be taller than his date. The students were asked, during the dance and again several weeks later, to rate their liking for their partner. By far the most important factor predicting liking for a partner was that person's physical attractiveness. Similar results were reported by Curran and Lippold (1975).

Marilyn Monroe embodied an ideal of physical attractiveness for women of the 1950s. Yet research suggests that physically attractive women may not have any more social interactions than women of average attractiveness, nor are they happier—as Monroe's suicide in 1962 may attest.

Are attractive individuals more socially successful? To explore this question, Reis, Nezlek, and Wheeler (1980) had college students of varying attractiveness complete a record of all interactions of ten minutes or longer they had had during four 10-day periods throughout the school year. From these entries, the investigators could note how long the interactions lasted, who initiated them, their intimacy, and how satisfying the students found them. Physically attractive males interacted with a greater number of females than did unattractive males, but attractive males had less interaction with other males. Surprisingly, attractive females did not have a higher number of interactions with either opposite- or same-sexed peers. Attractive women were, however, found to date more frequently, a result reported in earlier studies (Berscheid et al., 1971; Krebs & Adinolfi, 1975). Similar patterns of results were found in a second study conducted by the same research team (Reis et al., 1982).

The Matching Hypothesis All of us may prefer physically attractive dates. But in actually choosing our romantic partners, when rejection is a real possibility, we tend to select those who match us in physical attractiveness (Berscheid et al., 1971).

Folkes (1982) found evidence of such matching among clients of a Los Angeles dating service. In searching for potential dates, a client would first examine one-page fact sheets and then see five-minute videotaped interviews. When a client was interested in a particular person, that individual was notified, given information about the interested party, and asked whether a date was wanted. Dates were more often requested when the two clients were similar in physical attractiveness (Riggio & Woll, 1984; Woll, 1986).

Why does this kind of matching occur? Dating choices reflect both the attractiveness of the potential partner and the likelihood of that person's acceptance. To illustrate this, Shanteau and Nagy (1979) presented women with a choice between two potential dates who varied in attractiveness. A photograph of each male was accompanied by a verbal statement indicating the probability that he would agree to go out with her. Selection of the more attractive man was much more likely as the probability of his acceptance became more certain. A similar effect, though much smaller, was found for the less attractive men.

Evidence on the matching hypothesis illustrates that our decisions about whom to date and to marry are influenced by our calculation of what we "deserve." We are drawn to certain people, but we also fear rejection by them if what they can contribute to the relationship exceeds our own capacities. We try to maximize the rewards we receive, but pressures push us toward equitable relationships, where both partners derive from the relationship the same value they contribute.

APPLICATION
HELPING MEN AND WOMEN MEET

All societies must find a solution to the problem of helping men and women meet. In traditional cultures, marriages often were arranged, and matchmakers were useful in making the arrangements. A marriage, then, was not only a union of two individuals but also a linking of families and property. The goal was to bring about a reasonably stable pairing of two people, who until then may not even have known the other existed.

In modern cultures we have much the same fundamental goal. However, since the selection of a mate is usually left to the young lovers themselves, most people worry about how to find the "right" mate. We still use a number of old-fashioned techniques to find the right person, among them mutual friends to serve as informal matchmakers. But we also have invented a number of new technologies to serve that need, and the demand for these techniques grows as we grow older and our ability to find suitable companions diminishes. When the proximity afforded by school is over and we take jobs, the opportunity to meet potential mates is greatly reduced. Young adults turn to singles bars and other pickup spots (such as the supermarket or adult education courses), advertisements in personal columns, computer dating, video dating, and—the latest entry in the romance marketplace—software to evaluate your intended on your home computer (Medom, 1986). And, as you can see in the In the News box (pp. 270–271), the search gets even more trendy—and expensive—by the minute.

Let's look at the logic of some of these techniques in light of social psychological research on attraction. Most of these techniques begin with the recognition that in order for two people to get to like each other, they need to be placed in proximity with each other. That is the major barrier that every shopper and every "brokerage" tries to overcome.

Consider the recommendation that you ought to look for a potential partner not in bars but at the kinds of activities you like to engage in. If you like to read, visit the library; if you like the outdoors, join a hiking or biking club. The theory underlying these suggestions seems to be a reflection of the finding that people tend to marry people similar to themselves. But are hobbies the right variables? The research seems to indicate that the dimensions of similarity are on more fundamental grounds, such as education, socioeconomic status, race, religion—not that different from the old days.

Computer dating increases our opportunity to match ourselves with people who are right for us. But most computer dating still places us at the mercy of the programmer's theory of what makes for the right date. Research has revealed a number of dimensions on which similarity is important to attraction, other variables on which it is far less important, and at least some indication of other variables where complementarity is important. The degree to which computer dating services really do produce a good match probably depends on how aware they are of what characteristics really do lead to liking and loving. Video dating adds the dimension of physical attractiveness, which may be only skin-deep but, as we have seen, is important to the initial decision to become interested in a stranger (Riggio & Woll, 1984).

The newest entry in the romantic happiness market is a home computer program called IntraCourse. "Designed by a team of programmers, graphic artists, and clinical psychologists," this program allows a couple to explore their sexual makeup and compatibility, to compare the findings to statistical norms, and to assess the amount of "relationship disparity." We have to wonder whether this electronic means of determining compatibility is really an improvement over the old-fashioned method.

Sexual Intimacy

Recent years have brought striking changes in sexual attitudes and behavior (Sherwin & Corbett, 1985). Sex is now discussed more openly. Popular films, books, and advertisements are more sexually explicit. Even where opinions differ widely on such matters as pornography and premarital sex, it is noteworthy that the differences are readily discussed. As a result, a wide variety of sources of sexual knowledge are available to socialize young men and women (Strouse & Fabes, 1985).

IN THE NEWS

THE NEW MATING GAMES

Men and women who have spent years looking for love in all the wrong places are discovering new road maps to the altar. The old singles-bars routine has fallen victim to fears of AIDS, herpes and a lifetime of unfulfilling one-night stands. As the single population has grown older and more sophisticated, people are searching for spouses in "flirting" and "relationship" classes, exclusive (and expensive) dating services and singles nights at places like the Denver Art Museum. The quest has become more serious and up front; people are no longer afraid to use words like "commitment" and "family." But while singles today admit that they want what their mothers always said they *should* want, they're still having a devil of a time figuring out how to get it.

Hundreds of hopefuls are signing up for how-to workshops with names like "Fifty Ways to Meet Your Lover" or "Lover Shopping: How to Be Married One Year From Today." Gail Prince, who teaches courses in Chicago, tells women to carry conversation openers—like a feather boa or a copy of *Sports Illustrated*. Miami attorney Margaret Kent, whose course on "How to Marry the Man of Your Choice" costs $295 up front and another $1,000 after the wedding, has a four-step strategy: "Meet the man. Interview him for the job of husband. Audition for the job of wife. And tie the knot."

But a lot of women can't meet the man—and many men say they are having just as much trouble getting past step one. As a result, tony dating services have been attracting a special breed of lonely hearts. Gentlepeople, with offices from San Francisco to London, costs $950 a year and includes lawyers and doctors in its files. No computers or videotapes here. Gentlepeople's consultants act like executive recruiters, stalking prospective mates instead of CEO's. Those who need help with their image can sign up with Personal Profiles, a Chicago dating service that costs $1,250 a year. Overweight clients are urged to see a weight-loss consultant before they are accepted; blue-collar types are turned away. For $4,600, the service guarantees that you'll be engaged or married in three years.

Video dating still attracts a lot of cus-

Premarital Sex The clearest indication of the so-called "sexual revolution" is the increased frequency of premarital sex. In a review of several surveys on sexual behavior, Hopkins (1977) found that, between the late 1930s and the mid-1960s, about 55 percent of all males and 25 percent of all females reported having sex before marriage. After the mid-1960s, the incidence of premarital sex increased for both sexes, but especially for females. Incidence levels of over 60 percent for males and over 40 percent for females are now commonly reported. The AIDS epidemic may soon alter those trends. For public health reasons, it should; but it has not yet. So far, not only are more people of both sexes having premarital intercourse, but the sexes are also becoming more equal in this regard than they have been in the past.

Some people become sexually active at a very young age, while many others do not have their first sexual experience until college or later. Do

tomers. Joan Hendrickson, owner of the Georgetown Connection in Washington, D.C., says men and women size up prospective partners differently: "Women really read our profile forms, guys just look at the pictures." Even so, it's not always simple. When Denver advertising executive Diane Croce, 39, didn't get some responses from the men she had picked out at a video service, she was nonplussed. "I thought it was like ordering something from a catalog," she says. "I didn't know I could be rejected."

Upscale Clientele

The search has spilled over into the pages of mainstream newspapers and magazines. But the personals, once filled with descriptions of what Prince describes as "creeps, nerds and weirdos," now attract a more upscale and unabashed clientele. "Luscious and looking," is how one 40-year-old divorcée described herself in *New York* magazine recently. Drawing attention to the ad was a full-color head shot. The cost: $500 for a picture and 12 lines of copy.

Some singles prefer a more subtle scene. Singles nights at museums have become popular in several cities. At Washington's Smithsonian Institution, 150 singles—carefully selected so that there is an equal number of men and women—listen to a lecture and then sip champagne and nibble canapés while discussing such topics as high technology in Japan and American art. Janet Solinger, who runs the program, calls it "the squarest singles bar in town."

When all else fails, there's always that "nice boy Aunt Elsie knows." It's the oldest method of matchmaking, but, says New York marketing consultant Faith Popcorn, "we are seeing a return to traditional values and practices—people want to know the background of the next person they sleep with." Wait a minute, Mom. Did you say he's a doctor? And he likes kids? What's his number?

Source: Newsweek, June 2, 1986, p. 58.

people who become sexually active at a relatively young age differ in significant ways from people who do not? To answer this question, Jessor et al. (1983) randomly selected a sample of over 400 students from a small city in the Rocky Mountains region. From 1969 (when they were in junior high school) until 1979 (when they were young adults between the ages of 23 and 25 years), these students periodically filled out questionnaires on their sexual behavior. When had the respondents become sexually active? By 1979, only 8.4 percent of the males and 7.8 percent of the females had not had intercourse. For males, the average age for first intercourse was 18.0 years; for females, it was 17.6 years. Fully 60 percent of females, but only 40 percent of males, indicated that their first sexual partner was someone with whom they had had a steady dating relationship.

Several variables were related to the age at which the respondents became sexually active. Those who first had sexual intercourse at a younger age tended to place lower value on academic achievement, were less religious, and were more influenced by peer than by parental standards of behavior. They also placed greater value on being independent, and had more positive attitudes toward drug use.

Sex is now more often viewed as an inherent part of a dating or romantic relationship. In their study of over 200 dating couples, Hill, Rubin, and Peplau (1976) found that 82 percent of the couples reported they were having sexual intercourse; about 20 percent were living together all or most of the time. Fully 41 percent of these couples said that they had had intercourse within the first month after they started dating. These figures are not necessarily an accurate estimate for the population as a whole, because these participants had volunteered to participate in the study. Nonetheless, these data clearly illustrate that attitudes about premarital sexual behavior have changed dramatically since the mid-1960s.

Is sex a more important part of a dating relationship for men or for women? The answer found by Hill, Rubin, and Peplau (1976) was clear: for men. When asked to list the best things about their dating relationship, 16 percent of the men, but only 7 percent of the women, mentioned sex. Men were much more likely than women to list the "desire for sexual activity" as an important goal for their relationship. There is also some evidence that when couples abstain from sex, it is usually the woman who limits their sexual activity. Among the 42 abstaining couples, 64 percent of males but only 11 percent of females indicated that their abstinence was due to their partner's unwillingness to have sex (Peplau, Rubin, & Hill, 1977).

Does early sex help or hurt a romantic relationship? There is no clear-cut answer. Hill, Rubin, and Peplau (1976) compared those couples who had had sex during the first month of their relationship with those who had had sex after dating for more than a month. The couples who had waited presently had intercourse less frequently, but they scored higher on Rubin's (1970) love scale, more often said they were in love, and reported being closer. Generally, however, people in the two groups were equally satisfied with their romantic relationships. Interestingly, whether partners had sex early or late in their relationship, or had abstained entirely, was unrelated to whether they were still together.

Cohabitation According to the U.S. Census Bureau, in 1960 there were 17,320 unmarried couples living together; by 1981 this figure had climbed to nearly two million. A survey conducted by Macklin (1974) showed that the percentage of undergraduates living together varied from 9 percent at a small liberal arts college in the Midwest to 36 percent at the University of Texas. Macklin (1974) reported few differences between those students who had lived with a romantic partner and those who had not. Having cohabited was not related to religion at birth, parents' income level, or having come from a broken home. Students who identified themselves as practicing Catholics or Protestants, however, were less likely to report living together. Interestingly, no significant differences in academic performance existed between students who cohabited and those who did not.

Why are cohabitation and premarital sex more common now? First, improved contraceptive methods have greatly reduced the risk of unwanted pregnancy. But there are other reasons as well. Weiss (1974) points out that the age of the onset of puberty has been decreasing, while at the same time the duration of children's dependence on their parents until they can marry and establish their own households has been increasing. If sexual norms had not changed, young people would be expected to suppress their sexual drive for ten years or more.

Guttentag and Secord (1983), on the other hand, have argued that a society's sexual norms are related to the ratio of men to women in that society. On the basis of their historical and cross-cultural analysis, these researchers concluded that when there are more men than women, men prefer a relationship with only one woman, and conservative sexual attitudes prevail. In contrast, when there are more women than men, men are less willing to commit themselves to a relationship with one woman; as a result, sexual attitudes and behavior are more liberal.

Data from the United States illustrate this argument. According to the Census Bureau, in 1910 the ratio of males to females between the ages of 14 and 24 was 101.2, indicating a greater number of males. By 1970, when sexual attitudes and behavior were more liberal, that ratio had dropped steadily to only 98.7, indicating a greater number of females. In 1980, for persons between 15 and 24 years, the male-to-female ratio was reported to be 101.7. Is this higher ratio a sign that sexual attitudes will become more conservative? There is some evidence that the pendulum is starting to swing back again (Sherwin & Corbett, 1985).

Unsatisfactory Romances

Most romantic relationships do not result in marriage, but come to an end. This is to be expected, but it is surprising that social psychologists have devoted so little study to how and why relationships end. Only recently has this topic begun to receive the attention it deserves.

A longitudinal study of 231 dating couples conducted by Hill, Rubin, and Peplau (1976) provided the first good data on this issue. For their study, volunteer couples from schools in the Boston area were interviewed at six-month intervals over a two-year period. After two years, 55 percent of the couples were still dating, engaged, or married, and the remaining 45 percent of couples had broken up. In general, women reported a greater awareness of problems in the relationship, and they were more likely to break it off. Men reported being more emotionally affected by the termination of the relationship. As indicated in Table 7.1, typical reasons given

TABLE 7.1
Factors Contributing to the Ending of a Relationship (Percentage Reporting)

Factors	Women's Reports	Men's Reports
Dyadic		
Becoming bored with the relationship	76.7	76.7
Differences in interests	72.8	61.1
Differences in backgrounds	44.2	46.8
Differences in intelligence	19.5	10.4
Conflicting sexual attitudes	43.1	42.9
Conflicting marriage ideas	43.4	28.9
Nondyadic		
Woman's desire to be independent	78.7	50.0
Man's desire to be independent	46.8	61.1
Woman's interest in someone else	40.8	31.2
Man's interest in someone else	18.2	28.6
Living too far apart	28.2	41.0
Pressure from woman's parents	18.2	13.0
Pressure from man's parents	10.4	9.1

Source: C. T. Hill, Z. Rubin, & L. A. Peplau (1976). Breakups before marriage: The end of 103 affairs. *Journal of Social Issues, 32,* 147–168. Table 3.

for breaking up included boredom, a desire for independence, conflicting sexual needs, and the development of different interests. Notice that factors listed by men and women are generally similar. But in certain areas, such as "conflicting marriage ideas" and problems of "living too far apart," the two sexes report greatly differing percentages of these reasons for their breakup.

To some extent these breakups could have been predicted. Couples who reported less romantic involvement in the beginning of the study were more likely to break up, a result also reported by Levinger, Senn, and Jorgensen (1970). The woman's stated love for her partner was a better predictor of the course of their relationship than the man's. Reciprocation of affection was also a strong predictor. Of the couples who reported equal degrees of involvement in the relationship, only 23 percent broke up after two years. But when one partner's stated involvement was greater than the other's, 54 percent of the couples ended their relationship. And couples who were similar in age, educational aspirations, and physical attractiveness were more likely to stay together.

Certain types of people are more likely to be involved in romantic relationships that will break up. For example, men with a high need for power who tend toward an exploitive or derogatory view of women and who have more difficulty in relationships with women (McClelland, 1975; Winter, 1973) are more likely to be in relationships that will be terminated. In dating couples, such men express more dissatisfaction with their relationships and anticipate a greater number of problems in the future (Stewart & Rubin, 1976).

Assessment of Rewards and Costs Although many people deny that they consciously do so, partners continually assess how they are benefiting from their romantic relationships and what their alternatives are. Rusbult (1980) has defined four predictors of satisfaction within a romantic relationship:

1. Reward value, defined as a relationship's good attributes, plus the good traits and qualities of the partner.
2. Cost value, defined as a relationship's bad attributes, plus the bad traits and qualities of the partner.
3. Alternative outcome value, defined as the attractiveness of alternative relationships, measured in part by a respondent's interest in dating others and enjoyment of spending time alone.
4. Investment, defined as (a) the extent to which a partner has put resources (e.g., time, emotion) into the relationship; and (b) the total value of shared possessions, activities, and friends associated with that relationship but no other.

Rusbult found that when the reward value of a relationship was high and its cost value was low, people indicated much higher satisfaction. A strong commitment to the relationship was associated with not only high reward value and low cost value, but also high investment and low alternative outcome value.

Similar results were found when people were asked to report how they dealt with unsatisfactory romantic relationships (Rusbult, Zembrodt, & Gunn, 1982). When people had invested a great deal in the relationship, they were more likely to work for improvement and less likely simply to end it. This was also the case when their previous satisfaction with the relationship (rewards versus costs) had been very high. Also, if they had few or no alternatives outside the relationship, they were less likely to end it.

Abandoned romantic partners typically report that how rewarding their relationship was did not increase much over time, but that the attractiveness of alternatives for them had declined. As a result, they had continued to invest a great deal in the relationship until their partner chose to end it (Rusbult, 1983). The termination of a relationship, and the suspicion and jealousy that often attend it, can produce severe costs that we all have no doubt felt at some time (Mathes, Adams, & Davies, 1985).

Inequity There is evidence that inequitable romantic relationships are more troubled and perhaps more likely to fail. Walster, Walster, and Traupmann (1978) found that dating couples who said their relationship was equitable were relatively content and happy about their relationship, but those in inequitable relationships expressed greater anger or guilt. Couples in equitable relationships were more likely to be having sex and more likely to say their sexual activity was something they both wanted. Finally, more couples in equitable relationships predicted that their relationship would be stable in the future.

A specific source of inequity may be differences in physical attractiveness. White (1980) suggests that if a couple are dissimilar in attractiveness, this inequity creates tension which could result in the couple's eventual breakup. In a study of dating couples, White found that when the couple's attractiveness differed, the more attractive partner expressed a greater interest in dating others and reported having more opposite-sex friends, while the less attractive partner reported worrying more about the other person's wanting to start a relationship with someone else. These results were especially strong when the more attractive partner was male.

White did not find this same pattern of results for couples who were engaged or married. One explanation is that for couples who differ in attractiveness but who nonetheless get married, other compensations are offered by the less attractive partner that make the relationship equitable. For example, a man who is less attractive than his wife might be a good provider (Bar-Tal & Saxe, 1976), or be higher in power or status.

LONELINESS

All of us need and want companionship, and the effect of feeling lonely can be devastating. Lonely people are more often depressed (Weeks et al., 1980), anxious, tense, and bored (Perlman, Gerson, & Spinner, 1978;

Loneliness may be triggered by events ranging from the breakup of a relationship to the death of a relative to a move to a new location. To overcome loneliness, people can be helped to develop new social skills, and they can learn to attribute their problem to temporary and changeable aspects of their circumstances.

Russell, Peplau, & Cutrona, 1980), and more prone to drug use (Gorsuch & Butler, 1976) and even suicide (Gordon, 1976). When we say we are "lonely," we do not simply mean that we are alone, for we can feel lonely even when we are surrounded by other people. We usually mean that our relationships with other people are not what they should be; something is missing (Peplau & Perlman, 1982; Shaver & Rubenstein, 1979).

How pervasive is loneliness? In a national survey, Bradburn (1969) asked the following question: "During the past few weeks, did you ever feel very lonely or remote from other people?" Fully 26 percent of the respondents said that they had. Cutrona (1982) reports that two weeks after the school year began, 75 percent of UCLA freshmen said they had experienced occasional loneliness since arriving at school; 40 percent said that their feelings of loneliness had been of severe or moderate intensity. By the end of the spring term, 25 percent of the students still said they had experienced loneliness during the previous two weeks.

What triggers feelings of loneliness? First, the nature or extent of a person's social relationships can change, owing to a divorce, a romantic breakup, physical separation, the death of a loved one, unemployment, retirement, or extended hospitalization. Leaving family and friends to begin college is a major reason that many freshmen give for feeling lonely (Cutrona, 1982). Second, a person's needs for companionship or intimacy may change over time. For example, after their children have grown up and left home, a couple often has a renewed interest in cultivating new friendships (Peplau & Perlman, 1982).

Certain kinds of people may be predisposed to experience loneliness. Those who say they are lonely tend to be shy, self-conscious, introverted, unassertive, and have low self-esteem (Jones, Freemon, & Goswick, 1981; Russell, Peplau, & Cutrona, 1980). Lonely people report having difficulty introducing themselves, enjoying parties, participating in groups, and making friends (Horowitz & French, 1979). These characteristics may limit their opportunities for being with others and contribute to unsatisfactory patterns of interaction (Peplau & Perlman, 1982). (See the discussion of shyness in Chapter 3.)

What can be done to help lonely people? One possibility is *social skills training* to teach them how to initiate relationships. Lessons can deal with how to initiate conversations, how to pay attention to other people and respond appropriately to what they say, how to give and receive compliments, and how to handle silence (Jones, Hobbs, & Hockenbury, 1982). Other lessons can focus on nonverbal communications and how to enhance physical appearance (Rooks & Peplau, 1982). A variety of teaching techniques can be used—for example, self-observation (through the use of videotape), modeling, and role playing (Curran, 1977).

While this training may be an answer to social loneliness, Williams and Solano (1983) question whether it can really help those who suffer emotional loneliness from the absence of intimate relationships. To help with this type of loneliness, training should also focus on how to draw out other people by asking questions (Pilkonis & Zimbardo, 1979), strategies of self-disclosure, and general dating skills.

Another strategy for helping lonely people resembles the attributional approaches described in Chapter 2. Lonely people tend to ascribe their interpersonal failings to unchangeable defects in their personality, rather than to factors such as their mood, the effort they put out, or temporary situational variables (Anderson, Horowitz, & French, 1983). For instance, in Cutrona's (1982) study of UCLA freshmen, she compared students who continued to be lonely later in the school year with those who had started out lonely but no longer felt lonely after several months. Those who failed to recover more often cited their own shyness, a fear of rejection, and their inability to initiate relationships as the causes of their loneliness. Those who were no longer lonely more often blamed their earlier loneliness on the fact that they had just started college and were separated from their family and friends.

These results are suggestive. If lonely people can be led to view their loneliness as a result of situational forces, if they can be led to view it as temporary, it is likely that they will have greater success in establishing both social and intimate relationships. Cognitive-behavioral therapy, which applies basic attributional principles, may be capable of bringing about changes in people's explanations for their loneliness (Young, 1982), thereby helping to resolve their problem.

MARRIAGE

A good marriage—a working partnership based on love and mutual respect—can be an important source of happiness in people's lives. One survey of over 2000 adults found that, on the whole, married people—whether male or female, young or old, with children or childless—reported being more satisfied with their lives than did single, divorced, or widowed people (Campbell, Converse, & Rogers, 1976). This survey also revealed that the unhappiness experienced by most divorced people causes them eventually to seek remarriage.

How do marital relationships change over time? Levinger (1980) summarizes three general courses that a marriage can follow, as illustrated in Figure 7.5. Marriages seldom follow one of these paths exactly, and in fact other curves could be added to the figure, but Levinger's classification scheme is a useful model for thinking about marital relationships. The first possibility is that the mutual satisfaction a marriage brings will continue to grow until one partner dies. Such a marriage is rare. Most marriages show at least a leveling off and perhaps some decline in satisfaction over time. If the rate of decline is sharp enough, the marriage may eventually be terminated. This is the second of the three courses shown in Figure 7.5. The third possibility is that the marriage will be highly unstable—sometimes satisfying, but often disrupted by conflict.

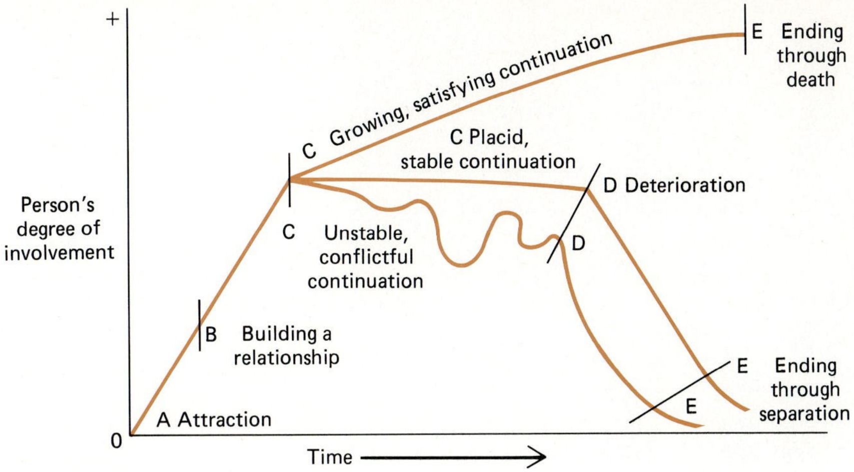

FIGURE 7.5
The Longitudinal Course of a Partner's Involvement in Three Contrasting Relationships The course of love beyond the early stages of attraction and building a relationship can take several different paths. One is continuing and growing satisfaction with the relationship. A second is placid, stable continuation, which may or may not lead to deterioration and separation. A third is an unstable and tumultuous continuation leading to deterioration and separation. *Source:* G. Levinger (1980). Toward the analysis of close relationships. *Journal of Experimental Social Psychology, 16,* 522.

The signs of a distressed marriage are unmistakable. Birchler, Weiss, and Vincent (1975) videotaped married couples as they talked about a topic of their own choosing and as they worked on a problem-solving task. Distressed couples smiled, laughed, and expressed agreement or approval less frequently, and more often criticized, interrupted, ignored, or disagreed with each other. These same couples reported a high number of day-to-day conflicts and spent little time in joint recreation.

Several factors are related to marital satisfaction and the course a marriage will follow: pressures created by the external environment, the characteristics of the marriage partners themselves, the couple's ability to communicate, and the rewards and costs the couple receive from the relationship. Let us consider the research evidence on each of these factors.

External Pressures

Marriages are less durable when a couple is faced with problems such as low income (Cutright, 1971) or unstable employment (Ross & Sawhill, 1975), or when the marriage was prompted by premarital pregnancy (Furstenberg, 1976). Large-scale surveys have also shown that couples with children are less satisfied with their marriages than younger couples

Marital relationships can change over time and become more or less satisfying. On the whole, though, marriage seems to supply couples with something of value, since surveys find that married people tend to be more content with their lives than are single, divorced, or widowed people.

who are childless or older couples whose children have left home (Campbell, Converse, & Rogers, 1976; Houseknecht, 1979). Similarly, Antill (1983) found that the more children were living at home, the less happy a married couple was.

Partners' Personal Charcteristics

As reported earlier, the research evidence is mixed on the role of need complementarity in mate selection. Is complementarity an important determinant of marital satisfaction? Meyer and Pepper (1977) asked 66 couples who had been married for a maximum of five years to fill out a questionnaire that measured their needs in 12 aspects of marital life. For example, those having a high "aggression need" reported being easily angered, being highly critical of their spouses, and finding enjoyment in arguments. Those having a high "nurturance need" described themselves as being responsive to requests for help from their spouses, sympathetic, and comforting. There was no evidence that complementarity led to higher marital adjustment. Well-adjusted couples were consistently more similar than poorly adjusted couples, especially in the needs for affiliation, aggression, autonomy, and nurturance.

Communication Ability

An ability to communicate with one's partner appears to be a major prerequisite for a happy marriage, and several researchers have noted that a breakdown in communication often accompanies distressed marriages. To study how well married couples communicate, Noller (1980) asked spouses from several couples to send an ambiguous message to their partners which could be given a positive, negative, or neutral interpretation depending on how it was said. Independent judges tried to guess which of the three meanings the participants had been asked to communicate. Thus two questions could be asked: Are the messages properly sent (encoded)? If so, are they then properly interpreted (decoded) by the spouses? High marital adjustment was associated with both better encoding and accurate decoding of correctly encoded messages.

Because females are generally quite good at both encoding (Rosenthal & DePaulo, 1979) and decoding such messages (Hall, 1978), the better performance by well-functioning couples was almost entirely due to differences among the males. In a follow-up study, Noller (1981) found that people from poorly adjusted marriages did just as well as those from strong marriages in decoding messages given by strangers. Thus this communication problem shown by distressed couples is not the result of a general deficit, but emerges from their troubled relationship.

One aspect of married life for which good communication is essential is decision making. A study by Falbo and Peplau (1980), conducted with dating, rather than married, couples, looked at the strategies couples use to influence their joint decision making. The investigators classified the listed strategies (see Figure 7.6) according to two dimensions: (1) strategies by which the person could take action alone (unilateral) versus those requiring action by both parties (bilateral); and (2) direct-active strategies versus indirect-passive strategies. As noted in Chapter 4, Falbo and Peplau found that men were more likely to use bilateral and direct strategies (e.g., bargaining, reasoning, talking). In contrast, women were more likely to use unilateral and indirect strategies (e.g., withdrawal, negative affect). Importantly, satisfaction with a romantic relationship was positively related to partners' use of direct strategies and negatively related to their use of indirect strategies. Unfortunately, a similar study has not yet been done with married couples, but we would expect a similar pattern of results.

Good communication between marriage partners also promotes successful conflict resolution. A survey of young married couples conducted by Levinger (described in Levinger, 1980) examined how they resolved important conflicts. Two approaches were more common among unhappy couples: avoiding the conflict, and attacking the other person through sarcasm or displays of temper. On the other hand, trying to work out a compromise was more common among couples reporting higher levels of marital satisfaction.

In another study, 33 married couples were videotaped while re-creating a previous conflict between them. They later watched the videotape individually and provided commentary on their discussion. Those couples who had a more accurate view of their partner's attitudes and perceptions were more likely to deal directly with their disagreement, to take their spouse's position into account, and to pay attention to their partner's feelings. If they were unsuccessful in resolving their conflict, they worked toward resolving their anger and reestablishing feelings of closeness. Those with less accurate perceptions of their spouse's attitudes and feel-

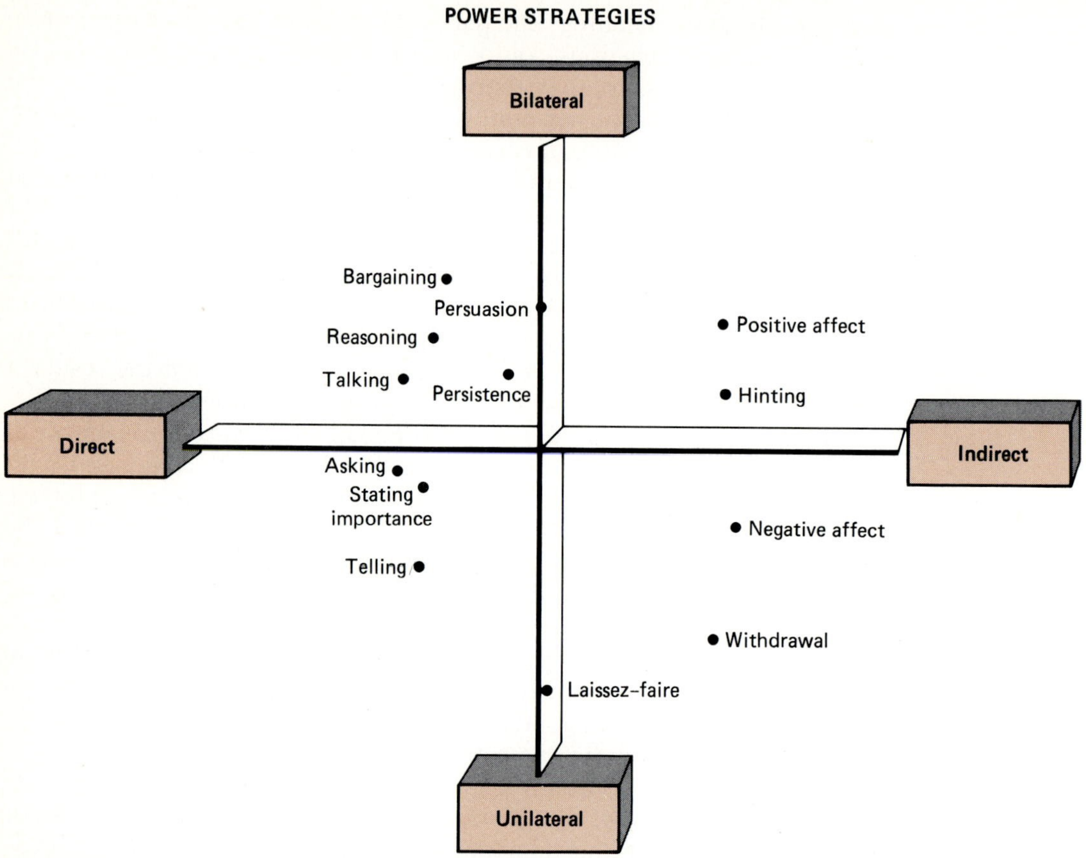

FIGURE 7.6
Power Strategies Used by Couples According to Their Degree of Directness and Mutuality People use a great many different strategies to try to influence their partner in a relationship. But Falbo and Peplau have found that all of them boil down to variations along two dimensions: the amount of mutuality (bilateral versus unilateral) and the amount of directness. *Source:* T. Falbo & L. A. Peplau (1980). Power strategies in intimate relationships, *Journal of Personality and Social Psychology, 38*, 623.

ings usually dropped the issue after their initial discussion had resulted in little progress. In addition, they gave little attention to the feelings that were generated during their argument (Knudson, Sommers, & Golding, 1980).

This research has shown that distressed couples do communicate less well than couples in satisfying relationships. But is poor communication the cause of their marital unhappiness, or is it just another sign that the marriage is in trouble? It is both. If the partners have poor communication skills, conflicts will remain unresolved and both partners will store up their hurt and anger. This further diminishes their capacity to take their partner's perspective, thus leading to further unresolved disagreements,

When a relationship starts to go sour, it changes in many ways. One of the most important causes and outcomes of a distressed marriage is a breakdown in communication.

suspicion, and recriminations. If there is no intervention, the quality of their marriage will continue to spiral downward until one or both decide to terminate the relationship (Miller, 1977).

Assessment of Rewards and Costs

As described earlier, the relative rewards and costs of a relationship, plus the perception of how rewarding potential alternatives will be, directly predict whether a romantic relationship will continue or end. Theorists have argued that marriages, too, should be analyzed in terms of social exchange or equity (e.g., Huston & Levinger, 1978; Walster, Walster, & Berscheid, 1978). Levinger (1976), for example, has noted that the decision to stay married is influenced not only by the rewards and costs of the marital relationship itself, but also by the costs of getting divorced. Compared to unmarried couples who live together, married couples report that a greater number of people would disapprove of their breakup and that the costs of their breaking up would be higher (Johnson, 1973). A major factor that many couples must consider is the hardship on the children that a divorce would bring. Religious constraints, the financial costs of dissolving a household, and the fear of living alone also weigh against a decision to divorce.

Direct tests of social exchange theory in the area of marital relationships are few, but there is some evidence to suggest that the theory does apply. Wills, Weiss, and Patterson (1974) report that unhappily married couples reward each other's behavior less frequently and that there is less reciprocity in their exchange of rewards. Howard and Dawes (1976) found that a simple reward/cost formula—the rate of a couple's sexual intercourse minus the rate of their fights—was predictive of marital satisfaction. Walster, Traupmann, and Walster (1978) found that men and women who felt they received fewer rewards and had greater costs than their spouses were more likely to have extramarital affairs than those who felt overbenefited by the inequity in their marriages.

Another factor to consider in thinking about the rewards and costs of a marriage relationship is people's motives for getting married. One survey showed that 57 percent of married women who said they had married primarily for love were very satisfied with their marriages, but of those who said they had married because they had been expected to, only 9 percent said they were very satisfied (Tavris & Jayaratne, 1976). Many reasons for marrying have nothing to do with the relationship itself—for example, to escape parental control, to avoid having an illegitimate child, to win financial security, to avoid the social stigma of being unmarried, or to escape loneliness. The results of this survey suggest that a marriage based on this type of reason is less likely to be rewarding.

Marriages, like other working partnerships, periodically come under strain. Pressure comes from money worries, in-law problems, and conflicting career demands, and a husband and wife will not always agree on how such pressures should be handled. Children, whose care and feeding require enormous energy, will necessarily crowd out the time a couple has for each other. Their sexual needs will not always be in tune. Over time, a husband and wife may grow in separate directions. Broad changes in the culture may affect how they define their relationship and the rewards they expect to receive from it.

What can help keep a marriage together in the face of all these obstacles? One answer is easy to say, but difficult to implement: good, open communication. The research reviewed in this chapter has suggested several rules of good communication:

1. Deal with problems as they come up; do not let hostility and resentment build by avoiding them (Levinger, 1980).
2. Do not attack the other person by saying hurtful or destructive things (Bienvenu, 1970; Levinger, 1980).
3. Make a conscientious effort to understand the other person's feelings, attitudes, and opinions (Knudson et al., 1980).
4. Do not overestimate the extent of mutual understanding that exists (Shapiro & Swensen, 1969).
5. Openly discuss feelings, worries, and concerns with each other (Hendrick, 1981).
6. In trying to influence the other person, use direct bilateral strategies such as reasoning and bargaining; avoid indirect unilateral strategies such as withdrawal and negative affect (Falbo & Peplau, 1980).
7. If the conflict cannot be resolved, work toward resolving the feelings of anger and reestablishing feelings of closeness (Knudson et al., 1980).

Implementing these rules requires that the partners drop a "win/lose" orientation. Rather than trying to gain a victory over the other, they should try to emerge as winners through compromise (Bach & Wyden, 1968).

Following these strategies can help a couple better resolve their conflicts. By reaching a settlement—and because the process of constructive confrontation increases understanding between the partners—their marriage can be strengthened. But how does a couple begin to use these rules if communication between them has broken down? How do they learn these rules well enough so that they become habitual? For almost all troubled couples, some kind of marriage counseling is necessary. Positive ways of interacting have to be modeled; the couple needs to rehearse what they have been shown; and the counselor needs to provide corrective feedback to guide their behavior. A number of counseling approaches draw on social psychological knowledge to help couples solve these problems.

One type of counseling that holds promise is "behavioral marital therapy" (Baucom, 1982; Lester, Beckham, & Baucom, 1980). First the counselor teaches the couple to be precise when defining a problem. For example, a wife may be hurt, confused, or resentful when her husband accuses her of being "insensitive," until he explains that he meant that when they go to parties, she talks only to her friends and never to him. Only when the specific problem behavior is identified can the problem be solved.

The next step is for the couple to list possible solutions, again in specific behavioral terms, and then to select a solution. For instance, this couple could agree that they would "check in" with each other every 30 minutes when they attend a party. Both partners would try to initiate contact; neither would wait for the other to make the first move. Once a solution is agreed upon, the therapist then helps the couple decide how the partner whose behavior is to change can be rewarded each time he or she acts appropriately.

Successful problem solving does, of course, require improved communication. With behavioral marital therapy, the therapist also monitors a couple's problem-solving discussions, stops them when they say something destructive, and suggests alternative ways to communicate. For example, one partner might say, "You shouldn't have yelled at me when I was late." "Well," the other partner replies, "I wouldn't have if you had been on time." Hearing this exchange, the counselor intervenes: "You're trying to decide who's at fault. It makes people angry to be blamed, and it prevents you from working together. Look for ways to handle the situation that will satisfy you both" (Lester, Beckham, & Baucom, 1980, p. 192).

What else can help keep a marriage together? A couple should give the highest priority to their time together. When taking their marriage vows, a couple declares that they want to work together as partners and to spend more time with each other than with anyone else. But the world seems to conspire against them so that they spend less and less time together. This problem is especially evident when both have jobs. They must do so much to keep the children, the household, and their careers afloat that they have little time left for each other.

Being aware of how much the demands in their lives split them apart, a couple can take several corrective steps. First, regular times should be set aside for them to talk and to go out. Second, as much as possible, they should develop shared interests, or should have some project that they work on together (Sherif, 1958, 1979). Third, they should consider whether a strict division of labor between them, though more time-efficient, may be unnecessarily contributing to their lack of time together. Similarly, as much as possible, decision making should be shared, not just divided according to expertise or interest.

These answers to the problem of divorce sound simple, but deceptively so. A happy marriage usually requires hard work, constant attention, and true commitment. Many couples are not up to the task. Others find that they are in the wrong marriage. For them divorce may still be the best alternative.

SUMMARY

1. Geographical proximity has an enormous influence on friendship patterns. Any feature of our environment that brings people together can stimulate the process of making friends.
2. The effect of proximity on the process of friendship formation is greatest when people are first brought together. As they exchange information and share experiences, other factors come into play, such as mutual interests and similar attitudes and values. The observed similarity between friends also results from their mutual influence on one another and their shared involvement in activities.
3. There is some evidence that we are attracted to people whose personality traits complement our own.
4. Beautiful people are liked more than those who are not physically attractive. Generally, we equate beauty with goodness.
5. Relationships between two people generally move from superficial to more intimate levels through a process of increasingly intimate self-disclosure.
6. As a relationship progresses, people continually assess their level of satisfaction with it. As long as satisfaction remains high, the relationship continues to grow. If it does not, the relationship may stay frozen at a lower level of intimacy or may even be terminated.
7. The value of a friendship is also judged by whether the relationship is guided by rules of fairness and reciprocity. If one person receives

more rewards than the other, relative to their investments in the relationship, this can create dissatisfaction with the relationship.

8. Psychologists have distinguished between two basic types of love: passionate love, which is a state of intense absorption in another, often accompanied by physiological arousal; and companionate love, which is deep, mature, caring love.
9. An evolving romantic relationship goes through three distinct stages: an initial attraction based on readily observable traits and attributes; an exploration of values and attitudes; an exploration of the couple's ability to work as a cohesive unit.
10. Choice of marriage partners, like choice of friends, depends on physical proximity, demographic similarity, and similarity of attitudes. Research on whether people select partners whose personality complements their own is inconclusive.
11. People are eager to meet and date attractive members of the opposite sex. But when they actually choose their romantic partners and rejection is a real possibility, they tend to select partners at about the same level of attractiveness as their own.
12. People who become sexually active at a relatively young age tend to place lower value on academic achievement, to be less religious, and to be more influenced by peer than by parental standards of behavior.
13. Sex is now more often viewed as an inherent part of a dating or romantic relationship. Over the past 50 years, an increasing percentage of young men and women have had premarital sex; that increase has been especially dramatic among women. AIDS is likely to alter this trend in the not-too-distant future. Virtually unheard of a generation ago, cohabitation is now much more common.
14. Romantic relationships are more likely to continue when they bring more rewards than costs to both partners, when both partners have a high level of investment in the relationship, and when alternative relationships are not perceived to be potentially more rewarding.
15. Women more often than men are aware of problems in a romantic relationship and are more likely to initiate a breakup.
16. Emotional loneliness, due to a lack of intimacy with others, and social loneliness, due to a small number of good friends, can have a devastating impact on a person. New treatment strategies for helping lonely people are being developed.
17. Several factors can contribute to marital dissatisfaction: pressures created by the external environment (e.g., low income, unstable employment); conflict of personality needs; poor communication and poor conflict resolution skills; a drop in the rewardingness of the relationship.
18. Open communication, constructive confrontation, and a resolve to give the relationship top priority can help marriage partners avoid divorce. Unfortunately, for many couples divorce may still be the best alternative.

GW

CHAPTER 8
Aggression and Violence

Every Saturday morning, while their parents are still in bed, millions of children flick on the television. They shop around the channels, choosing among "Mighty Mouse," "Superheroes," "The Three Stooges," and other shows. All of these programs show guns ablazing, monsters attacking, and punches delivered that send bad guys hurtling through walls and ceilings (*Pow! Bang!*). The children sit quietly and gaze blankly ahead, far more attentive to the mayhem on the screen than they ever are to their teachers at school.

Children are not the only ones who watch violent television programs. A number of years ago, a movie called *Fuzz* was released, about a gang of youths who poured gasoline over homeless people and set them on fire. Two days later a young woman in Boston was murdered in this way, and three weeks later a similar killing took place in Miami. Two weeks after the showing of a film about Charles Whitman and the so-called Texas tower murders, a man went to the top of a 24-story building in Toronto and began firing a rifle, injuring five people below. Over the objections of the Air Line Pilots Association, the movie *Doomsday Flight* has been shown on television a number of times. In it an extortionist demands money to disclose the location of a bomb on a passenger-filled plane. Each time the movie has been shown, in the United States, Canada, Australia, and France, a flurry of similar extortion attempts has taken place.

These dramatic examples suggest a number of important questions:

What are the effects of consuming a steady diet of violence and aggression on TV? Do the violent deeds that are dramatized daily on our television screens leave us untouched, or are we learning some important lessons about how, when, and why to hurt others? Or could it be that *watching* violence on television acts as a substitute for *doing* violence in real life? And to the extent that television does contribute to the development of violent attitudes and behavior in our society, what can social psychology contribute to reducing its impact?

THE NATURE OF AGGRESSION AND VIOLENCE

If we want to know about the prevalence of violence in our society, we have only to ask a single question: How safe would you feel walking home alone tonight through your local park? According to recent crime statistics (see Figure 8.1), we can see that in this country the rates of several types of violent crime have gone up steadily since 1972, and are only now on their way down again. Only about half of all crimes committed are ever reported, and less than 2 percent of suspects are actually convicted and sent to jail. During the twentieth century alone, nine assassination attempts have been made on U.S. presidents, two of them successful—and other public figures, among them Robert F. Kennedy and Martin Luther King, Jr., have been murdered.

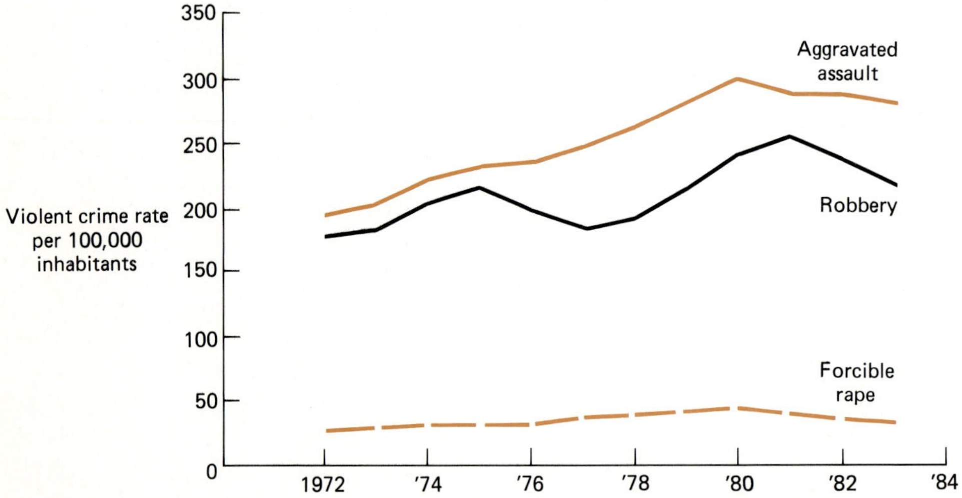

FIGURE 8.1

Selected Crime Rates: 1972 to 1983 Rates of crimes such as robbery, aggravated assault, and rape increased during the 1970s, but have leveled off or even dropped in the 1980s. *Source:* Adapted from *Statistical Abstracts of the United States* (1985).

Yet violence is hardly a recent invention, nor is it an American product. As Baron (1977) has noted, the Greeks who captured Troy in 1184 B.C. executed all males over the age of ten and sold the women and children into slavery. In the thirteenth century A.D., Genghis Khan invaded Asia and Europe and massacred millions of unarmed people. In more recent history, Adolf Hitler had at least 11 million innocent people executed during World War II. Today there are few areas of the globe that are untouched by large-scale violence. The Middle East, Central America, South Africa, and Northern Ireland are but a few perpetual hot spots.

So prevalent are violence and aggression in our lives that we often take the meanings of these words for granted. **Violence** is a term that we will utilize to refer only to harm doing that is *direct* and that causes injury through the use of *physical force,* whether on an individual or at a large-scale level. We speak of wars as acts of "massive violence," or of "violent prisoners" who are in jail for murder or assault. But harm doing is not always this clear and obvious, and we will therefore use the term **aggression** as a more general label that captures the many forms and elements of harm doing.

The most commonly accepted definition of aggression (Baron, 1977) states that it is (1) any form of behavior that is (2) directed toward the goal of harming or injuring another living being who is (3) motivated to avoid such treatment. The key elements are the first two: we must look for behavior, not just emotions; and this behavior must be motivated by a desire to inflict some form of harm or injury. According to this definition, then, daydreaming about getting even with the boss or kicking your car after it has broken down on the highway do not qualify as acts of aggression. These are merely "expressive acts." The third element, a requirement that the victim wants to avoid this harm, serves to distinguish aggression from those few instances of behavior where the "victim" actually wants to be on the receiving end, such as sadomasochistic acts or suicide.

The nature of the harm may take any number of different forms, from verbal to physical. As anyone who has ever been on the receiving end knows, a well-timed put-down can hurt just as much as a physical blow. In addition, harm can be inflicted in an indirect or even passive fashion. For example, spreading vicious rumors is clearly harmful, as is destroying a valued piece of an individual's or a group's property. A combination of all three of these dimensions is shown in Figure 8.2.

Intent and Anger

The second key element in our definition of aggression, *intention,* has been a challenge to philosophers and judges as well as to social psychologists. In order to be considered aggressive an act has to have as its goal the harming or injuring of another living being. This allows any purely accidental act to be ruled out, and rules in any act meant to harm regardless of whether it succeeds or fails. The person who drops a flowerpot and

	Physical: Active	Physical: Passive	Verbal: Active	Verbal: Passive
Direct aggression	Stabbing, punching, or shooting	Sit-in	Insults or put-downs	Refusing to speak or to answer questions
Indirect aggression	Hiring an assassin; setting a booby trap	Refusal to move from a sit-in	Spreading rumors or gossip	Failing to speak up in someone's defense

FIGURE 8.2
The Dimensions of Aggression According to Buss, aggression can be characterized along three dimensions: direct or indirect; active or passive; and physical or verbal. *Source:* Based on A. H. Buss (1961). *The psychology of aggression.* New York: Wiley.

breaks a friend's toe is clumsy rather than aggressive. But the person who tries to shoot a public figure is acting aggressively even if the shot misses and does no harm.

The problem with intention is that it cannot be seen; it must be inferred. And it is impossible to look inside another person's head and know whether an act was intentional or accidental. At first this issue might seem like just another academic exercise to complicate a simple point, but a look at our legal doctrines proves otherwise. When one person takes another's life, the punishment can vary—from a suspended sentence to the death penalty—depending upon the evidence concerning the person's intent.

Murder in the first degree is the most serious crime a person can be charged with. It involves killing a person "with malice aforethought," that is, with a direct plan or intention to cause "death or grievous bodily harm." Manslaughter also involves the taking of a life, but is regarded as a less serious crime because it is not a planned act. An example of manslaughter would be a family argument that resulted in someone being shot and killed. Negligent homicide means the loss of life resulting from carelessness, and is the least serious kind of homicide. Although all three acts result in a victim's death, the person convicted of negligent homicide receives a light sentence or none at all. Why? Because the act was considered unintentional or accidental.

Questions and decisions such as these come up fairly often in the courts. A few years ago a popular singer was accused of killing her lover by shooting him while he was showing her how to use his gun. Was this incident carefully planned to look like an accident, a case of an angry woman shooting her lover—or simply a tragic accident? This is the difficulty in considering intent. It demonstrates that prosecutors, judges, and juries must confront the very same issues as social psychologists, except in the former situation it could be a matter of life and death.

Angry Versus Instrumental Aggression

A different way of thinking about the issue of intent has to do with the specific reason an individual commits an aggressive act. A distinction made here (e.g., Buss, 1971; Feshbach, 1970) has to do with angry aggression versus instrumental aggression. *Angry aggression* deals with acts performed for the primary motive of doing harm. The person feels some strong emotion, often anger, and responds to that emotion by directing it against another person (Berkowitz, 1983; Averill, 1982). Zillmann (1979) has called this "annoyance-motivated aggression," pointing out that its goal is to reduce an unpleasant emotional state.

Instrumental aggression, or, as it has been called by Zillmann, "incentive-motivated aggression," also involves actions of intentional harm, but its primary purpose or motivation is to attain some form of material gain or advantage. The child who hits and takes toys away from a playmate and the storekeeper who shoots someone trying to rob the store are not primarily motivated to hurt the other person, but harm is intentionally caused to another with the objective of gaining or keeping material things. Similarly, people might perform instrumental aggression to achieve nonmaterial objectives, such as promoting their beliefs; for example, the Crusades, violent antigovernment demonstrations, and the bombing of abortion clinics.

Socially Sanctioned Harm Doing

In considering the examples above, we realize that certain forms of aggression, such as murder, are considered *antisocial* acts and are condemned by all; but other forms are referred to as *prosocial* aggression because they are sanctioned by society or even rewarded and praised (Sears, Freedman, & Peplau, 1985). Police officers and soldiers are sometimes called upon to injure or kill others as part of their jobs; they are praised for their efforts and called heroes. In the context of Vietnam War protests and ghetto rioting, Kahn and his colleagues (Kahn, 1972) surveyed the opinions of 1400 American men concerning their definitions of violence. As you can see in Table 8.1, the college students, white members of labor unions, and black Americans surveyed had very different concepts of violence. For instance, 91 percent of the union members felt that looting was violent, but only 23 percent of this same group felt that shooting looters was violent (Blumenthal et al., 1972). In sum, the matter of defining aggression is neither simple nor straightforward. Taking a closer look, we might say that, like beauty, aggression is in the eye of the beholder.

TABLE 8.1
Percentage of People in Selected Subgroups Defining Certain Acts as Violence

	College Students (n=63)	White Union Members (n=279)	Blacks (n=303)
Police beating students is violence	79%	45%	82%
Police shooting looters is violence	43	23	59
Looting is violence	76	91	74
Burglary is violence	47	67	70
Student protest is violence	18	43	23
Draft card burning is violence	26	63	51

Source: M. D. Blumenthal, R. L. Kahn, F. M. Andrews, & K. B. Head (1972). *Justifying violence: Attitudes of American men.* Ann Arbor, MI: Institute for Social Research, The University of Michigan. Reprinted by permission.

Instigations and Inhibitions

Aggression can take many forms from minor to major, interpersonal to international. We can study it using animals or humans, in the laboratory or in the field, via survey or experiment. In order to discuss all of these situations simultaneously, we will adopt a framework based upon Megargee's (1972) discussion of the role of instigations and inhibitions in aggression. **Instigations** are all those factors operating on an individual at any given moment to motivate him or her to act aggressively. Some instigations are internal (e.g., aggressive urges, biochemical factors, or personality dispositions), while others are external or situational (television violence, a crowd urging two people to fight, or the availability of a weapon).

Inhibitions represent the opposite side of the coin. They are all those factors, external and internal, that discourage an individual from acting aggressively. An example of an internal inhibitor is one's conscience or superego. External factors inhibiting an aggressive act might be the presence of a police officer or a warning from one's potential targets that they will strike back. In any given situation, all of these inhibitions and instigations, internal and external, must be balanced against one another. Depending upon their respective weights, the individual may attack verbally or physically, or may find that discretion is the better part of valor.

In the rest of this chapter, we will examine the various instigations to aggression. These include basic or fundamental causes, as well as immediate situational factors that can provoke aggressive acts. In addition, we will consider the various inhibitions to aggressive behavior and see how they can be translated into practical means for preventing aggression.

THE CAUSES OF AGGRESSION: LOOKING WITHIN THE PERSON

In searching out the causes of aggression, many social scientists have begun by looking at internal factors. In this section we will examine a number of classic and recent approaches that consider the effects of instincts, drives, genes, and personality.

The Psychoanalytic View

Sigmund Freud, whose life spanned the late nineteenth and early twentieth centuries, was influenced by the thinking of Charles Darwin. He developed a theory of human behavior that saw humans as guided by a set of innate animal-like drives or instincts. The key element of Freud's early theorizing was the life force, or *Eros,* which was at the biological root of all behavior. Yet Freud was terribly disturbed by the destruction he observed in World War I and the events leading up to World War II. He could not understand how this life force alone could account for war, which he saw as the greatest form of pathology on earth. As his theoretical ideas evolved, he reasoned that a second biologically determined driving force must be at work, a death instinct which he named *Thanatos.*

Freud believed that within each person aggressive energy is constantly produced, and that if allowed to build up, it will result in violent actions. The only checks against it are inhibitions, in the form of superego or conscience. Noting that fighting and even apparent cruelty go on between very young children, Freud believed that the superego is not inborn but develops during the middle childhood years (somewhere between the ages of 3 and 7). The strength of the superego, however, varies greatly from person to person. While Freud believed that aggression could be controlled somewhat, he did not believe it could ever be eliminated.

Ethological and Sociobiological Views

Another viewpoint on aggression that is rooted in the theory of evolution is that of the ethologists (Lorenz, 1966), who treat the behavior of all animals—including the species *Homo sapiens*—in terms of its genetic and biological bases. While most ethologists devote themselves to the study of animals, some have made sweeping generalizations about human aggression from the observation of animals in the wild. They believe that humans are born with a *fighting instinct* and therefore that aggression is built into our nature. One popularizer of ethology, Robert Ardrey (1966), has gone so far as to characterize the human animal as "a predator whose natural instinct is to kill with a weapon."

Although it is a highly dramatic approach that has captured much public attention, the ethological view of aggression has been the object of much criticism for being oversimplified and incomplete. The noted anthropologist Ashley Montagu (1973) points out that while much animal behavior may be based on instinct, human behavior is guided far more by learning and culture. He and others (e.g., Wilson, 1975; Rajecki, 1983) have pointed out that reasoning by analogy from animal to human aggression may be misleading. There is no available evidence to suggest that humans are "programmed to kill."

A more scientific and carefully documented approach that is also based on biological and genetic principles is that of the sociobiologists (Wilson, 1975; Barash, 1982). Sociobiologists also believe that aggression is a natural and inevitable part of life, but rather than attributing its existence to instinct, they believe that aggression is simply the result of competition for scarce resources and a desire for dominance. It is a fundamental condition that will always exist whenever two or more individuals or groups want access to something that only one can have.

According to this position, aggression is an instrumental behavior. It is performed for a specific purpose, such as gaining food or territory, or increasing one's status in the group. Those individuals who are most fit will gain access to resources and are also most likely to contribute to the gene pool of future generations by out-reproducing their competitors. Animals and people act aggressively not because of any fighting instinct, but because they are likely to benefit by it. Sociobiologists believe therefore that aggression is universal, and that it follows the same general principles whether we are talking about advanced technological societies vying for worldwide political influence, or about isolated tribes in the Amazon such as the Yanomamo, where the males attack other tribes for the primary purpose of capturing the women (Chagnon, 1979).

The sociobiological position focuses on three essential points: certain traits are universal; their universality comes from genetic coding; and the genetic coding is a result of evolutionary selection. Sociobiology has been criticized on several grounds: its generalizing from lower life forms (primarily insects) to humans; its treatment of metaphors as though they were reality (e.g., using the terms *royalty* and *slavery* to describe ant societies, and then equating them to human society); its data being highly correlational and thus subject to competing interpretations; and its dismissal of contradictory evidence (Lewontin, Rose, & Kamin, 1984).

For our purposes, the most important aspect of the debate is between the sociobiological idea that important behaviors such as aggression are preprogrammed and the idea that human behavior is largely determined by learned responses to various situations. From an applied viewpoint, some argue that whether or not sociobiology is right affects whether societies undertake to solve problems such as war and other violence, or whether they accept these things as unchangeable. Our own view is that the different viewpoints lead to differences in *how* we pursue change. The learning view, which suggests greater flexibility, implies one set of strategies for change; the more programmed view of sociobiology implies another set.

Physiological Causes of Aggression

The search for the causes of aggression within the person has taken other routes as well, one being the study of blood chemistry and the brain. Using lower animals, several classic studies have demonstrated the role of neurological factors in aggression. For instance, Smith, King, and Hoebel (1970) studied two groups of rats, one highly aggressive and the other nonaggressive. When a mouse was placed in the cage of an aggressive rat, the rat would kill it immediately, but members of the nonaggressive group never even attacked. Rats from both groups then had miniature tubes inserted into a specific area of their brains (the lateral hypothalamus), and either an activating or an inhibiting drug was introduced through the tubes. The results were dramatic. When the inhibiting drug was present, killer rats were absolutely peaceful. When the activating drug was injected, the former pacifists pounced upon their prey and killed. But when these chemicals were injected just one millimeter away from this specific site in the brain, no such changes occurred.

In spite of the findings of animal research that aggression has a physiological basis, no evidence exists to suggest that a simple "violence center" exists in the human brain (Simmel, Hahn, & Walters, 1983). Among higher animals, a variety of aggressive behaviors have been elicited from a number of separate portions of the brain (Delgado, 1969, 1970). In fact, Moyer (1971, 1975) has classified six distinct types of aggression, each with its own unique neural and endocrine pattern. Even among lower animals, simplistic models of brain and endocrine function in relationship to aggression have been challenged and ruled out (Simon, 1983; Miczek, 1983).

Genetic Abnormalities and Aggression

One fascinating direction that the search for internal causes of aggression has taken is the study of genetic abnormalities. In 1965 Jacobs and his colleagues reported that men who had an extra Y chromosome—XYY instead of the normal XY—were overrepresented in prison populations. They and other researchers proposed that perhaps for this unique group of individuals (XYY's occur about once in every thousand births), a tendency toward violence is genetically determined, just as height, eye color, and sex are.

In a large-scale survey conducted by Witkin and his colleagues (Witkin et al., 1976), however, this explanation was ruled out. Looking at personal and criminal data for their sample, the researchers found that XYY's were no more likely to engage in violent or criminal acts than were people with normal chromosome patterns. Instead, on the average, XYY men were found to be taller and somewhat less intelligent than average men, with the result that when they did commit crimes, they were more likely to be caught. Thus the examination of genetic abnormalities has so far proved to be a dead end.

The most recent work on genetic and other biological abnormalities and aggression has been put forward by Wilson and Herrnstein (1985) in *Crime and Human Nature.* Their theory is that some people are inherently more likely to engage in "street crime." They believe this is due either to genetic differences or to prenatal injuries which may result from a woman's drinking alcohol or smoking during pregnancy. Wilson and Herrnstein reviewed a large number of studies on these issues, among them studies of twins and adopted children, and concluded that the likelihood of engaging in violent or other criminal conduct is correlated in genetically related individuals.

As several reviewers (Kamin, 1986; Wales, 1985) have pointed out, the evidence offered by Wilson and Herrnstein suffers from the usual difficulties of imperfect correlational studies. For example, even the finding that the great proportion of violent crime is committed by males aged between 18 and 21 is open to the possibility that cultural forces rather than genetic and developmental forces are responsible. In addition, the evidence is inconsistent, with some of the data contradicting rather than supporting the theory.

Personality Factors and Aggression

A final avenue in the search for internal causes of aggression is the study of personality factors. One approach asks whether there is such a thing as a "violent" or "criminal" personality and, if so, what motivates people who habitually engage in violent behavior. Hans Toch (1980) conducted a series of intensive interviews with male prisoners who had a long record of criminal violence. On the basis of these interviews, he placed the men into either of two major categories. The first group contained those who used violence to show they were tough and to command respect among friends and gang members. Those in the second group also used violence instrumentally, as a means to an end, but they were less interested in image and more willing to use force to get what they wanted from others.

A second approach has been to look for individual and personality correlates of aggression among "normal" people. Among the variables discussed in Chapter 3, differences have been found between internals and externals. Internals, who feel they can actively control their fate, engage in aggression for instrumental purposes as well as to express anger. Externals, however, are likely to act aggressively *only* when they are angry (Dengerink, O'Leary, & Krasner, 1975). Type A's are more likely to engage in aggression than are Type B's, especially when they are not able to control a situation (Matthews et al., 1982); and, if ordered by an experimenter, authoritarians are more likely to deliver shocks to another person (Elms & Milgram, 1966; see Chapter 10 for details). In addition, males are generally more aggressive than females (see Chapter 4).

The search for personality factors associated with aggression, while different in emphasis from the psychoanalytic, sociobiological, or neurological approaches, shares with them one critical feature: each has looked *inside* the person. And while each has added to our understanding of aggression, we should not be surprised to find that situational factors can interact with or even counteract the personality tendencies of individuals to act aggressively. For a fuller understanding of aggression, we need to know how internal factors interact with external factors, and it is to the latter that we now turn.

THE CAUSES OF AGGRESSION: LOOKING AT THE ENVIRONMENT

Consistent with social psychology's interest in external determinants of behavior, the direction of much recent research and thinking has been toward a consideration of those factors in the current, past, and future environments of people that make them likely to act aggressively. The external variables that have been investigated vary widely. We shall look in some depth at the role of frustration as a cause of aggression, and also consider how the presence of aggressive cues can facilitate violent behavior. Then we will discuss the prevalence of models and rewards for aggression in our culture in considering the key role of learning in the development of aggression.

Frustration-Aggression Theory

If a person is engaged in some behavior meant to move toward a goal and something or someone gets in the way, this is what social psychologists term *frustration*. The encounter can be with a physical object such as a traffic jam that gets you to school 20 minutes late; or with a social one, such as finding out that the person you wanted to go to a party with is already going with your (former) best friend. We encounter frustrations of all sorts daily.

According to the theory proposed by John Dollard and his colleagues (Dollard et al., 1939), frustration is *the* major cause of aggression. As stated in their original **frustration-aggression theory,** the relationship is extremely simple and straightforward: Frustration always leads to aggression. And all aggression is caused by frustration.

This frustration-aggression connection is not difficult to demonstrate. For instance, Geen (1968) had college students work on a jigsaw puzzle that seemed quite solvable. In one condition, most students actually did solve the puzzle. In another condition, however, the experimenter's assistant kept interfering with the students and did not allow them to finish it. In a third condition, the puzzle was subtly changed so that it was actually not solvable. Geen found that people who were frustrated by not being able to complete the puzzle later gave more electric shocks to a third party than did those who had met no frustration.

This theory, which attempts to explain the root causes of aggression so simply, was greeted with great acceptance by many people in the field. It accounted for a complex phenomenon with a single concept, and it pointed to variables that were observable and understandable instead of to vaguely defined instincts or drives. Yet, after closer inspection, both components of the theory have been criticized and modified. First, all aggression is not caused by frustration; there can be many other causes, including direct attack (physical or verbal); the experience of pain; orders from others; or, as discussed earlier, a direct desire for personal gain at the expense of others. A soldier may shoot a person during a battle, but this cannot readily be traced to frustration. Therefore, the theory has been modified to suggest that frustration is *one* cause of aggression, but not the *only* cause.

The other half of the theory, that frustration always leads to aggression, has also been modified in light of the evidence. As noted by Neil Miller (1941), one of the originators of the theory, frustration can lead to many forms of behavior, only one of which is aggression. When we are frustrated, sometimes we do nothing, sometimes we sulk or blame ourselves, sometimes we dream of revenge, and sometimes we simply try harder to overcome the obstacle. Clearly, frustration can lead to many different responses. The question is, when does it lead to aggression?

Degrees of Frustration The first and most obvious factor relating frustration and aggression is the degree of frustration experienced. The greater the frustration, the greater the tendency to act aggressively. Worchel (1974) demonstrated this by giving experimental participants either their first, second, or third choice of reward for participating in a study. Those who got their third choice generally rated the experimenter more negatively than did those who received their second choice; and those who got their second choice were more negative than those who got their first. In a field study (Harris, 1974), experimental assistants barged into a line of people waiting for a movie, either right behind the first two people or much farther back. As in Worchel's findings, the intruders who cut in at the front of the line (thereby frustrating people who were closer to their goal) received a good deal more verbal and nonverbal abuse than those who pushed into line farther back.

The Displacement of Aggression While small, justifiable frustrations might lead to little aggression, even large and unjustified frustrations might not lead directly to aggression if strong inhibitions are present. If your boss tells you that she has decided against giving you that raise, you might swallow your anger and not tell her off for fear of being fired. Or, regardless of how frustrated you are by the 6-foot 9-inch, 280-pound fellow blocking your path, the odds are that you will merely ask him to step aside while emphasizing the word *please.*

When frustrations exist but inhibitions are strong, the tendency to be aggressive can be redirected or **displaced** toward another person or object

ior in all other realms. Aggression that is rewarded is more likely to be repeated; and aggression that is not reinforced will drop out. This view proposes that people act aggressively if and when they learn that aggression pays. If acting aggressively gets you tangible rewards such as money, or intangible rewards such as attention, approval, prestige, or social status, then you will continue to act in this manner (Zillmann, 1979; Bandura, 1973).

In addition to these reinforcement principles, classical conditioning can also account for aggression. For example, certain categories of people, who might otherwise be treated benignly, can become cues for aggression. If a particular ethnic group in a society is continually associated with (real or alleged) acts or symbols that arouse hostility, then any member of that group can elicit and be the target of aggression. This is the classical learning theory explanation for what we commonly call prejudice or bigotry. For instance, in a study by Berkowitz and Geen (1966), students watched a violent film starring the actor Kirk Douglas. Then they interacted with an experimental confederate who identified himself as either Kirk Anderson or Bob Anderson. In accordance with the classical conditioning view, angered participants later gave more electric shocks to "Kirk" than to "Bob."

The *social* learning approach to aggression places less emphasis on *direct* rewards and punishments, but stresses that much of what we learn about aggression, first as children and later as adults, is accomplished by *observation* (Bandura, 1973). We view others who are aggressive or not, who are successful or not, and they serve as *models* for our behavior. Parents, teachers, and friends, as well as adventurers, heroes, and villains in books, television, and movies—all allow us to learn in a way that is efficient and psychologically economical. They act; we observe and learn; and then, when appropriate, we imitate.

Bandura and his colleagues have performed a series of studies of the modeling phenomenon with children. In one of their earliest studies, Bandura, Ross, and Ross (1961) had two groups of nursery school children observe the behavior of an adult. In the first condition, the adult played with a large inflated Bobo doll, a clown with a weighted bottom that causes it to pop back up every time you hit it or push it down. The adult in this condition acted in an extremely aggressive manner, pushing, kicking, and yelling at the doll. In the course of this sequence, she engaged in unique aggressive acts that the children were not likely to have seen before. In the control condition the children merely watched an adult play constructively with tinker toys.

After observing the adults, all the children were mildly frustrated and were taken to a room containing a variety of toys, including many of those involved in the adult's aggression. Compared to the controls, the children who had witnessed the aggressive adult were more verbally and physically aggressive and specifically imitated more of the adult's unique aggressive behavior. In one of many follow-ups to this study, Bandura (1965) noted that children who observed an aggressive model who was *rewarded* later imitated the adult more than a control group did; and those who saw the model *punished* imitated her significantly less than those in the control group.

Bandura noted several points about the learning of the children in both the model-rewarded and model-punished conditions. Even though the children who observed the punished model did not perform many aggressive acts, they had acquired as much new information and new "skills" as the children in the other groups. When asked, they could reproduce the adult's behavior quite accurately even though they had chosen not to imitate it during the observation period. Those children who observed the model being rewarded did not approve of aggression any more than did the children who watched the adults who were punished. However, this hardly stopped them from imitating the aggression. As part of a separate study, one little girl watched a film in which a boy intimidated another and then walked off with his toys in a sack slung over his shoulder. She expressed her disapproval of the child's aggression, yet when later given the opportunity, she acted in the very same way as the model. She even went so far as to ask the experimenter whether there was a sack available for her (Bandura, Ross, & Ross, 1963).

APPLICATION
THE HOME AS THE CRADLE OF VIOLENCE: MODELING AND CHILD ABUSE

Research on modeling points out to us that some lessons children learn about aggression and violence are put into immediate action, while others, although equally well learned, are stored away for later use. For instance, what happens to children who grow up in homes in which their parents abuse them physically? When they become adults, how do they treat their spouses; and when they become parents, how do they treat their own children? While only a minority of abused children grow up to be abusing parents, numerous studies point to a clear correlation between being abused and being an abuser (Straus, Gelles, & Steinmetz, 1979; Gil, 1970; Lefkowitz et al., 1977).

Child abuse is a serious social problem, with estimates ranging from 30,000 to 1.5 million cases per year in the United States alone. In one study more than one-fourth of the mothers at a Los Angeles outpatient clinic reported spanking their children before they were six months old, and almost half were doing so before the child had reached its first birthday (Korsch et al., 1965). And Gelles and Straus (1979) report that 3 percent of the parents they interviewed admitted using a gun or a knife to threaten their children. Most child abusers are not crazy or sadistic, but are merely modeling the behavior of their own parents or have not learned other means of handling children. In fact, modeling may be the major factor in the intergenerational transmission of all kinds of behavior.

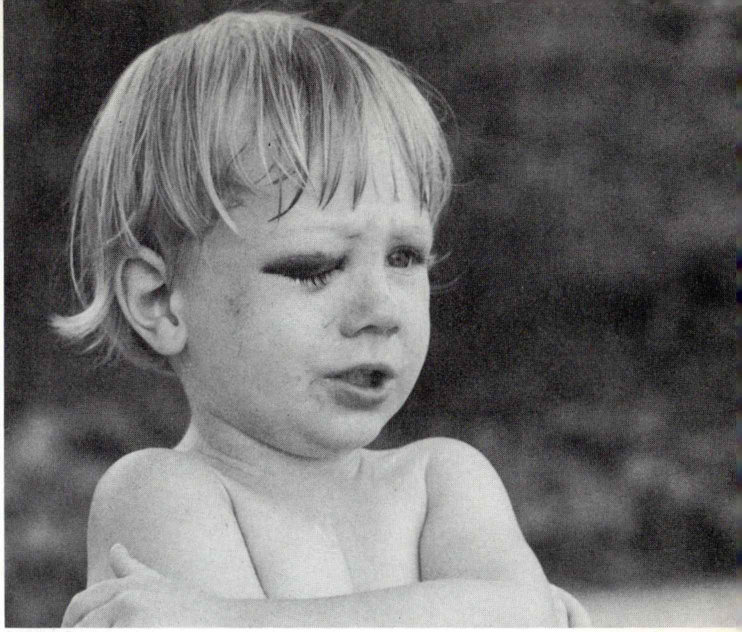

According to recent estimates, as many as 1.5 million cases of child abuse occur in the United States every year.

By recognizing the significant role of "faulty" social learning in the making of a child abuser, a number of practitioners have attempted to reduce or eliminate this social problem (Rosenberg & Reppucci, 1985). One technique, parent training, has been devised for parents who are judged to be potential abusers, and has been found effective in reducing the negative behaviors of both mothers and children (Reid & Taplin, cited in Resick & Sweet, 1979). It uses positive reinforcement and provides models of nonviolent means of discipline to help parents as well as children learn new skills. In short it teaches, and they learn to develop, ways of interacting with one another that are more adaptive.

Gray (1983) has provided parenting information to a variety of audiences using live and videotaped actors. The skits focus on assertive rather than aggressive problem-solving skills, and provide people with alternative methods of discipline, methods that avoid physical punishment. Attitude measures of viewers before and after viewing Gray's presentations show significant changes, especially for young people at high risk to be abusers. Long-term behavior changes, however, have not yet been assessed.

A final approach, Project Twelve Ways, aims at several possible causes of child abuse, as its title suggests. Offering child management and basic skills training, marital counseling, stress reduction, and self-control techniques, this program has resulted in significantly fewer incidents of child abuse and neglect among the families who have participated (Lutzker, Wesch, & Rice, 1984). For instance, 11 percent of the children in a control group were abused or neglected, as compared to only 2 percent in the Project Twelve Ways group.

Programs such as these have not eliminated child abuse. They demonstrate, however, that an understanding of the forces that instigate and inhibit aggression can be applied to an important social problem, and that the principles of social learning can be used to develop successful programs that reduce violence in the home.

TELEVISION AND AGGRESSION

The disciplining of a child by a parent is a *private* act, and therefore both social psychologists and policymakers have been hesitant to intervene unless there is clear evidence of abuse. Yet something else happens daily in the home that may have even greater impact on overall levels of aggression and violence. Violent television programs are watched by child and adult alike, and their content is a matter of *public* concern.

The amount of time children spend watching television is staggering. The average 12-year-old watches almost four hours of television per day (Liebert, Sprafkin, & Davidson, 1982), and 25 percent of the sixth and tenth graders in one study watched over eight hours of television on Sundays (Lyle & Hoffman, 1972). By the age of 16, the average television viewer is likely to have witnessed approximately 13,000 killings and numerous other acts of violence (Waters & Malamuth, 1975). Given these statistics, we must ask: What is the evidence concerning the effect of television violence? Does watching it increase, decrease, or have no effect upon the expression of violence among children and adults? Before going on, read the In the News box on pages 308–309 and see where you stand on these critical issues.

The Link Between Televised and Real-World Violence: The Case For

Bandura's studies at Stanford University and other laboratory research programs have received considerable attention and have led some observers to make sweeping generalizations about the dangers of watching aggressive models. These generalizations have been criticized on a number of grounds. For instance, the participants in Bandura's studies observed scenes that were unlike television programs, involving no plot, no dramatic value, and no justification for aggressive acts. The children were hitting a toy (the Bobo doll), not a person, and the situation was defined as play, not as harming. In order to overcome some of these criticisms, a number of researchers have shown children episodes of entire violent or nonviolent television shows and then compared the aggressive behavior of the children afterward. The results are fairly consistent: both immediately and some time after, the children who viewed the violent shows acted more aggressively (Liebert & Baron, 1972; Ross, 1972).

Another more comprehensive approach has been to offer children and adolescents a steady diet of aggressive or nonaggressive television in a systematic and controlled manner. In one such study, Stein and Friedrich (1972) consistently showed a group of approximately 100 preschoolers either prosocial TV programs (for instance, "Mister Rogers," who teaches sharing and caring), neutral shows (children's travelogues), or antisocial episodes (for instance, violent Batman and Superman cartoons). The children were observed for three weeks before, four weeks during, and two weeks after the showing of the programs. The results of this study as well as others in the United States and in Belgium (Parke et al., 1977) indicate that violent behavior went up with violent television, although in each of these studies the children most affected were those who were already judged to be aggressive.

A final approach has been to study truly long-term effects of TV viewing by correlating the viewing habits of children with various measures of aggressive behavior. The most notable of these long-term studies have been conducted by Leonard Eron and his colleagues at the University of Illinois at Chicago (Eron, 1980; Lefkowitz et al., 1977; Eron et al., 1972). In 1960 they began with the entire third-grade population of a town in the Hudson River Valley of New York State, 875 boys and girls. They examined a great number of behavioral and personal characteristics of these children, and also collected data on their parents and the home environments from which they came. A major finding of this initial study was that children who preferred violent television programs at age 8 were among the most aggressive in school.

Approximately ten years later, the researchers managed to contact and reinterview 427 of their original sample in order to look at the relationship between the learning conditions the 8-year-olds had been exposed to, their behavior at age 8, and their preferences and actions ten years later. They found that children who had been rated as aggressive by their 8-year-old peers tended to be rated as aggressive by the young adults who knew them at ages 18 and 19, indicating stability in aggressive behavior over ten years. Furthermore, the children who had been rated aggressive at age 8 were three times more likely to have generated a police record within the next ten years than those who had been rated as unaggressive (Lefkowitz et al., 1972). In fact, the single best predictor of the males' aggression at 19, even after controlling for a host of other factors, was the degree of violence in the television programs they had preferred to watch at age 8 (Eron, 1980).

Recently Eron and his colleagues (Eron et al., 1987; Huesmann et al., in press) have reported on a second follow-up of over 400 of the original participants, now approximately age 30. In accordance with earlier findings, aggressive behavior was very stable over the years of the study, with the most aggressive third graders not only getting into more trouble with the law, but also being more severe and punitive with their spouses and children 22 years later. The correlation between television violence at age 8 and aggressive behavior at age 30 was quite high, and the more youngsters watched television in the third grade, the more serious the offenses they committed at age 30. Eron (1987) acknowledges that the specific programs the children watched at age 8 hardly affected their behavior as adults, but he believes that the attitudes and norms generated by watching television violence allowed these people to learn, rehearse, and find acceptable the expression of aggression toward others.

IN THE NEWS

WHY TV WON'T LET UP ON VIOLENCE

"Violence is alive and well on television," Stephen Bochco, executive producer of "Hill Street Blues," said in a recent interview. Mr. Bochco, whose award-winning dramatic series has been praised for its sensitive, albeit gritty depiction of the world of urban police, was speaking partly in jest. But his words are as true as they have ever been.

Yet, there appears to be a difference in the quality, variety and pervasiveness of today's televised violence. Some observers believe that as a result of more than three decades of television, viewers have developed a kind of immunity to the horror of violence. "On the basis of the amount of exposure, certain things that initially would have been beyond the pale become more readily accepted," says David Pearl, director of the National Institute of Mental Health's project on television violence. . . .

On the one hand, more violent acts in television programs today occur with machine guns and other sophisticated weaponry than they once did, and even on critically acclaimed shows such as "Hill Street Blues" violence now occurs with a greater intensity and realism than in shows of a decade ago. In addition, more action series these days are laced with jokes or gags that occasionally crop up in juxtaposition with violent acts. There is also less distinction between heroes and villains, and more violent acts are committed by people with psychological problems. And on cable television, an increasing number of feature films intertwining sex and violence are finding their way into the home.

Moreover, a new form of television, the music video—rock music illustrated by video images—is also being examined by social scientists who say they detect a new form of violence without even the tenuous dramatic context of many standard television series. According to researchers, many such videos—largely seen on MTV Music Television, the 24-hour cable channel, but available on broadcast programs as well—are saturated with images of menace, cruelty and implied brutality as well as detached and often cold portrayals of violence against people and property. . . .

According to George Gerbner, dean of the Annenberg School of Communications at the University of Pennsylvania, the average level of violence in prime-time television has remained relatively consistent—at five or six violent acts per hour—in the 17 years he has been studying its incidence. Nevertheless, the networks acknowledge that viewers are likely to find more shows with violent content this year. "Because there are more action shows, there is a greater awareness and concern with respect to the volume of violence," said Alfred R. Schneider, vice president of policy and standards for ABC Inc.

More than actual volume, it is the kind of violence coming through the television screen that is gaining the attention of researchers and critics alike. One of the principal developments as revealed in the Media Institute's study is the increasing sophistication of the weaponry. The simple gunfight of the past has been augmented, according to Mrs. Lichter, by "high-tech crimes like terrorist bombings." To Mrs. Lichter, today's televised violence, "may be a lot meaner. A gunfighter shooting down a sheriff is one thing. When you have terrorist bombs, the potential is there for hundreds to die."

Programs in the past used the occasional machine gun, but such weapons as the M-60 machine gun and Uzi semi-automatic have become commonplace today on such shows as NBC's "The A-Team" and

"Miami Vice." On the same network's science-fiction series "V" earth-dwellers use military-style arms against the laser guns of alien invaders. And on CBS's "Airwolf" a supercharged helicopter packs enormous firepower. . . .

In Mr. Gerbner's view, the approach taken by "The A-Team" poses the problem of "an uninterrupted sequence of violence as a solution to almost any problem—an emotionless, sanitized violence." Network officials contend, however, that viewers are too sophisticated to tke shows such as "The A-Team" seriously. "It is recognized for what it is—a real 'Perils of Pauline' show," says Ralph Daniels, vice president of broadcast standards for NBC. "Sure it is militaristic, but who believes it? It is fantasy."

Another preliminary finding of the Media Institute study is that since the early 1970's more violence has been attributed to psychological problems. "Although it is still a small percentage, it is a big leap from before, when there was no psychological connection," says Mrs. Lichter. Moreover, she adds, "about the late 1960's the link between good guys and bad guys began to be blurred. Now we see more police being physically abusive or committing crimes. The public has been getting a more blurred image of what is good and what is bad."

Over the past several years, action shows have also begun to incorporate comedy as a means of stirring greater audience interest. "The audience wants the character to be more than a plain tough guy. They want to respond to the personal side," says Alice Henderson, vice president of program practices for the CBS Broadcast Group.

Network officials say they try to separate jokes from action sequences. "We have to be careful with the manner of humor so that we aren't making light of violence," says ABC's Mr. Schneider.

But sometimes comedic bits are intermingled with gunplay, as in a recent "Miami Vice" episode when an elderly denizen of the Everglades joked about using his alligator gun against some drug smugglers. After the weapon jammed repeatedly in the middle of a gun battle, it finally worked, and the man killed a smuggler. He gave a toothless grin and giggled when one of the show's lead detectives said, "Thanks, pal."

"Miami Vice" poses another variation on the nature of violence with its glamorous visual style and rock music video montages. "Does that style give you the ability or the scope to be able to deal with violence in a more heinous way than you ordinarily do in a straight action adventure?" says Mr. Schneider. "I don't know. I am trying to make up my mind."

Source: Sally Bedell Smith, *The New York Times,* January 13, 1985.

The Link Between Televised and Real-World Violence: The Case Against

Although numerous studies have demonstrated the link between television viewing and aggressive behavior, it would be misleading to suggest that no notable exceptions exist. As pointed out in a comprehensive review by Freedman (1984), a number of studies show no strong or consistent differences between groups exposed or not exposed to aggression, and a few studies even show that individuals were less aggressive after watching violent programs (Feshbach & Singer, 1971; Milgram & Shotland, 1973; Milavsky et al., 1982).

The possibility that viewing aggressive behavior can lead a person to act less rather than more aggressively comes from an idea originally expressed by Aristotle. He believed that spectators of a moving dramatic presentation were purged of the emotion presented on the stage, an experience he termed **catharsis.** As used by Freud and later by Dollard and his colleagues, catharsis involves a process by which a person either observes or experiences aggression in a mild form and is thereby "cleansed" of it. Within the context of the television violence question, the catharsis hypothesis suggests that angry people who see someone acting violently on the screen should experience satisfaction of their own violent urges vicariously, and as a result they should have less need to act aggressively themselves. If this is correct, parents should allow and even encourage their children to watch violence on TV in order to reduce their aggressive urges.

Social learning theorists disagree. They say just the opposite, that modeling aggressive behavior only leads to more. What is the evidence? The majority of the findings fail to uphold the cathartic effect of observing violence (Feshbach, 1984). In fact, when catharsis works, it reduces future aggression only to the extent that people engage in present aggression (Konecni, 1975). Therefore, even to the extent that some evidence does exist on behalf of this process, catharsis is hardly the safe alternative that some psychologists initially hoped for (Baron, 1977).

The Link Between Televised and Real-World Violence: The Reasons Why

The vast majority of the research evidence clearly supports the link between the viewing of violent television programs and aggressive behavior on the part of both children and adults. In reviewing the evidence for the National Institute of Mental Health (1982), a panel of social scientists pointed out four possible mechanisms for this connection:

1. Observational Learning When children see others act aggressively, the behaviors are noticed, stored, recalled, and imitated under the appropriate circumstances. These lessons, although quickly learned, are not quickly forgotten. As shown by Hicks (1968), children who saw an ag-

The vast majority of research suggests that viewing televised violence encourages both children and adults to act violently themselves.

gressive model acted more aggressively not only immediately after exposure, but eight months later they still exhibited 40 percent of the model's aggressive acts.

2. Disinhibition and Desensitization Not only do children learn to act on their instigations from watching violence on TV, but they may also come to lose their inhibitions. In an age when the good guys are likely to be just as violent as the bad guys, **disinhibition,** the reduction of restraints, may take place. As a result, children and adults may fail to see why they should hesitate to act upon their angry feelings.

Constant viewing of violence can also lead people to become **desensitized.** That is, they may no longer experience strong emotions at signs of suffering or other environmental cues that might inhibit their tendencies toward violence. In addition, children who watch a great deal of television violence come to think there is much violence in the world, and come to accept it as a mode of settling disputes and problems (Gerbner & Gross, 1974). Among the 19-year-olds studied in Eron's research, the more aggressive the people were, the more they thought that westerns and police dramas on TV showed the world as it really is.

3. Arousal and Labeling Proponents of this explanation point out that when people are strongly aroused, as they can be when watching violent television, they may come to act aggressively if they *label* their arousal as anger (Tannenbaum & Zillmann, 1975). For instance, at a rock concert people may be highly aroused for reasons having nothing to do with aggression. If, while the tension level is high, two people have a disagreement, the likelihood that it will lead to violence is significantly higher.

4. Reinforcement of Preexisting Tendencies The final explanation for the link between violence on TV and violence in reality is different from the others in that it reverses the direction of cause and effect. This explanation does not argue that TV viewing causes people to become violent, but rather that people who are violent or who have committed acts of violence will seek out TV programs with violent content. In an experimental test, Fenigstein (1979) arranged for one group of college students to make loud, unpleasant noises in front of another student, while a second group made no noise. He then gave both groups the opportunity to watch several films that previously had been rated either high or low in aggressive content. In accordance with this explanation, the group that had made the noises chose significantly more aggression-oriented films. Not surprisingly, and in line with this, Diener and DeFour (1978) found that the more men rated themselves as aggressive, the more they liked violent television programs. These various explanations combine to reveal a "reciprocal determinism": People who are inclined toward violence choose violent programs; having watched violent programs, they are more likely to be violent. The cycle continues.

CONDITIONS INSTIGATING AGGRESSION

The factors we have considered in the previous sections constitute *general* and *fundamental* determinants of aggression. Whether internal or external, they seek to explain the basic motives behind aggressive behavior. We will now turn our attention to more *specific* and *immediate* factors in the environment that provoke or allow aggression.

Anonymity and Aggression

When people become submerged in the identity and mentality of a large group, they become *deindividuated* and may end up committing acts that they would not dare do on their own (Le Bon, 1895; Festinger, Pepitone, & Newcomb, 1952). We will discuss this topic in greater detail in Chapter 13, on large groups, but it is important to mention here the strong effect that deindividuation can have on the reduction of inhibitions.

Zimbardo (1969), for instance, compared the behavior of two groups of students. The first had their individuality and identity made salient by wearing name tags and being called by their first names. The second never gave their names and wore hoods over their heads, making them faceless as well as nameless. Given the opportunity to deliver electric shocks to others, the duration of the shocks given by the deindividuated students was twice as long. It is easy to notice the parallels between Zimbardo's research and the violence and cross burnings of hooded Ku Klux Klansmen.

Alcohol, Marijuana, and Aggression

After a few drinks, most people loosen up and many of their inhibitions peel away. But does this lead them to be aggressive? While we have some correlational evidence relating alcohol to violent crime (Wolfgang & Strohm, 1956), not until the 1970s did systematic experimental evidence appear about the relationship between alcohol and aggression.

To test our popular notions about alcohol and aggression, Stewart Taylor and his colleagues at Kent State University began a program of studies on the effects of alcohol. Although Taylor could have made himself the only social psychology researcher in the country with lines of people waiting outside his office to volunteer, participants in his research were recruited without knowing that the study would involve alcohol. In one study (Taylor & Gammon, 1975) people were given either a high dose or a low dose of bourbon or vodka. Each drink contained alcohol and ginger ale, with two drops of peppermint oil added to disguise the taste so that the participants would not know what kind of alcohol they had drunk. After the drink, they were provoked and had the opportunity to administer electric shocks to another person as part of a competitive task.

In general, Taylor and Gammon found that people who had had a small dose of alcohol set lower levels of shock than a control group who had taken nothing; whereas those who had had a high dose were more aggressive than the control group. More recent research has added to our understanding of the alcohol-aggression link by suggesting that, when intoxicated, people are more responsive to acts of provocation (Pihl et al., 1981) and also less aware of their own behavior and the disapproval shown by others (Hull, 1981). In short, alcohol apparently works on both aspects of aggressive behavior, making people more likely to act on instigations and less responsive to sources of inhibition (Taylor & Leonard, 1983).

As he was confirming the notions people hold about how light and heavy drinkers act toward others, Taylor (Taylor et al., 1976) was also performing other research comparing the effects of alcohol and marijuana. Using much the same procedure as before, he found once again that drinkers were more aggressive after a large dose of alcohol than after a small dose. For marijuana smokers (actually, participants were given a dose of THC, the chemical in marijuana that produces the high) the results were different. Angered people who took a small dose of marijuana were slightly less aggressive than the control group. Those who had taken a high dose of marijuana were *least* aggressive of any of the groups (see Figure 8.3). This study and others like it (e.g., Myerscough & Taylor, 1985) lend support to the popular conception of marijuana as a substance that makes a person "mellow" rather than violent.

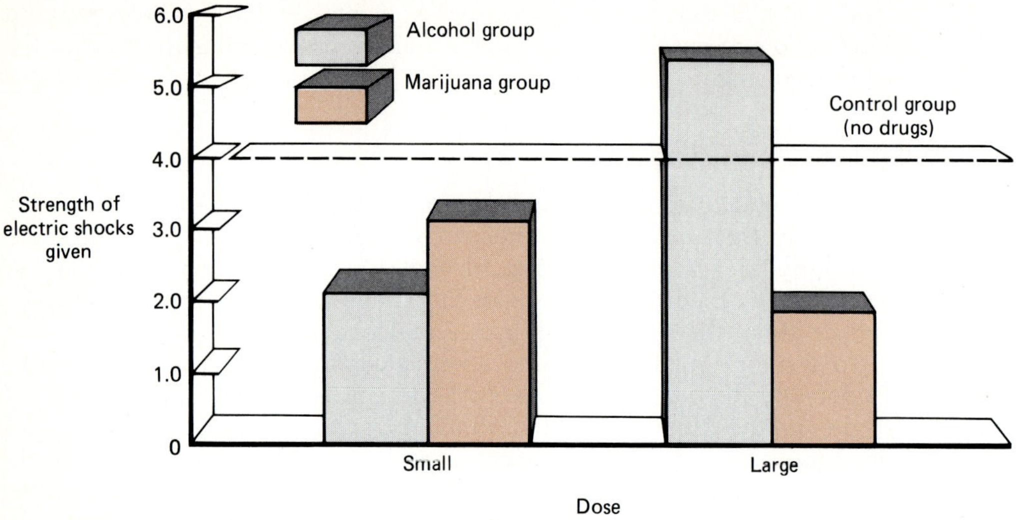

FIGURE 8.3
The Effects of Alcohol and Marijuana on Aggression Taylor and his colleagues found that the strength of electric shocks students gave when they had had small doses of alcohol and marijuana were weaker than those given by a control group. However, while larger doses made the marijuana group less aggressive, the alcohol group became even more aggressive with larger doses. *Source:* Based on S. P. Taylor, R. M. Vardaris, A. B. Rawtich, C. B. Gammon, J. W. Cranston, A. I. Lubetkin (1976). The effects of alcohol and delta-9-tetrahydrocannabinol on human physical aggression. *Aggressive Behavior, 2,* 153–161.

Environmental Stress and Aggression

Just as a good deal of alcohol may lower people's aggressive thresholds and make them likely to act on a provocation, it is also widely believed that environmental annoyances such as high levels of heat also lead people to be quick on the trigger. Reasoning from common sense that people who are hot and uncomfortable would be more likely to behave aggressively, Baron (1972) performed a study in which one group experienced cool temperatures while a second group roasted in temperatures above 90°. Much to his surprise, he found the opposite of what he had expected. Angered people who were very hot were *less* aggressive than the comfortable ones. To explain this, he interviewed people after the experiment. Those in the hot condition said that the heat was so stifling that they wanted to do everything they could to get out as quickly as they could (such as keeping the shocks as brief as possible).

As a result of this and another series of laboratory experiments (Baron & Bell, 1975, 1976; Bell & Baron, 1976), Baron has generated a theory about the relationship of aggression and any sort of discomfort or environmental stress, be it heat, noise, or crowding. He argues that aggression is mediated by the amount of negative emotion experienced. As the latter increases, so does aggression—but only up to a point. At some point the discomfort grows so great that it becomes a distraction. People then focus increasingly on themselves and on finding ways of avoiding discomfort. As a result they pay less attention to the person provoking their anger, and act less aggressively.

Having developed this notion in the laboratory, Baron and Ransberger (1978) attempted to test it by looking at the relationship between temperature and violence during the ghetto riots of the late 1960s and early 1970s. They found that more riots occurred when the temperature was high—in the mid- to upper 80s—while fewer occurred when the temperature was lower or higher than that. Carlsmith and Anderson (1979) have questioned their conclusions, however, citing the possibility that more riots occurred on medium-hot summer days simply because there *were* more medium-hot days. More recently, Anderson and Anderson (1984), using data on violent crime in Chicago, have shown that the rates of murders, rapes, and robberies continued to increase as the temperatures climbed. Therefore, the actual shape of the relationship of heat to violent behavior is still very much a subject of controversy.

Sexual Arousal, Violence, and Rape

Just as social critics have worried that viewing media violence may instigate people to act violently themselves, people have asked whether the increasing presence of sexual and erotic cues serve to provoke aggressive actions, especially sexually violent crimes such as rape. Early experimental work on this question provided conflicting evidence. Several studies showed that the viewing of erotic materials was followed by greater aggression (e.g., Zillmann, 1971), while others suggested that it led to reduced aggression (e.g., Baron & Bell, 1973).

Zillmann's theory of *excitation transfer* has helped clarify and explain these findings (Zillmann, 1983). According to the theory, the arousal produced by sexually stimulating pictures or films can persist and intensify a person's response to being provoked. If the arousal is pleasant, as when men look at moderately erotic materials such as *Playboy* photos, retaliation and aggression may actually be reduced. If extreme or deviant sexual practices are shown, however, the viewer is more likely to be annoyed than pleased, and the negative excitation may be transferred into the form of increased hostility and aggression. The results of an experiment in which male students saw either photos of nude women or films of bizarre sexual acts—a third group was not shown anything—are presented in Figure 8.4. The pleasing photos produced a small reduction in aggression compared to the control, but the extreme films (regardless of whether they included aggression) produced a significant increase in aggression (Zillmann, Bryant, & Carveth, 1981).

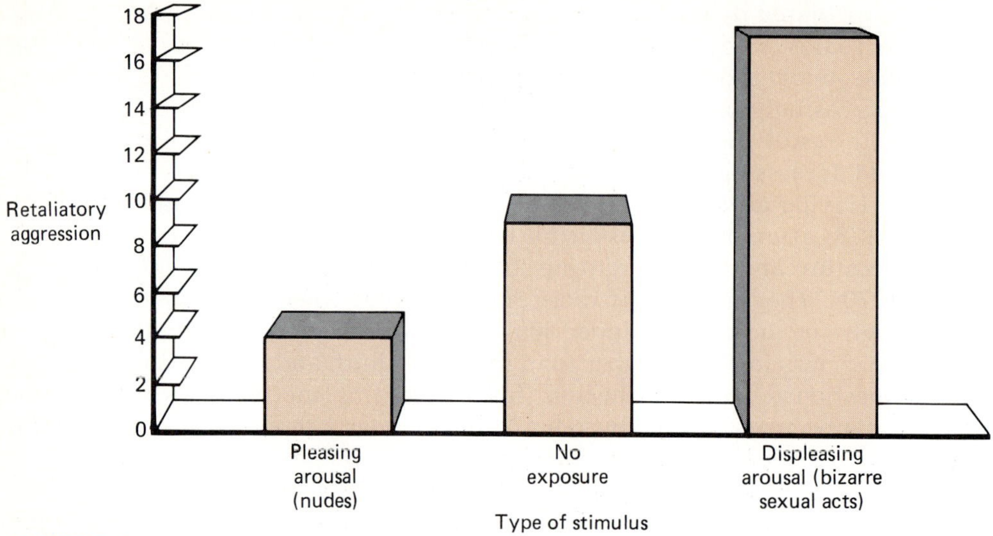

FIGURE 8.4
Retaliatory Aggression by Students After Viewing Pleasantly and Unpleasantly Arousing Material As Zillmann and his colleagues found, sexual arousal that is pleasant leads to less aggression, but sexual arousal that is unpleasant has the opposite effect. Based on D. Zillman, D. Bryant, & R. W. Carveth (1981). The effect of erotica featuring sadomasochism and bestiality on motivated intermale aggression. *Personality and Social Psychology Bulletin, 7,* 153–159.

But what about sexual violence in the real world, especially rape, which is becoming an increasingly visible social problem? First, we know from a number of studies that the acceptance of sexual violence, whether as rape or in other forms, is fairly prevalent among males. In a survey of high school students, for instance, over half of the males said they believed it was acceptable "for a guy to hold a girl down and force her to have sexual intercourse" under certain conditions, such as if "she gets him sexually excited or promises to have sex with him and then decides not to" (Goodchilds & Zillmann, 1984). And Malamuth (1981) reports a series of studies in which an average of 20 percent of "normal" men report a moderate likelihood (three or above on a five-point scale) that they might commit rape if they were assured of not being punished.

How do males come to develop such conceptions about sexual violence? Although there are many sources and models, experimental studies suggest that the combination of violent and sexual content in many R-rated and X-rated movies can have definite effects on the men who view them. A number of recent laboratory studies have shown participants neutral, purely sexual, or violent-sexual films and then studied their reactions (see Malamuth & Donnerstein, 1984, for an excellent review). In almost every study, watching erotic films with aggressive content led to more aggressive behavior than did exposure to neutral or to purely erotic films. Furthermore, this aggression does not have a random target but is directed toward females. When angered students could give electric shocks to a male, no differences were found after the viewing of purely erotic and aggressive-erotic films. But when the potential victim was female, the aggressive-erotic films generated significantly more aggressive behavior (Donnerstein, 1980).

In sum, the results of a growing research literature point in a clear direction. Following exposure to media with violent and sexual content, or even nonviolent matter that degrades women, many males may come to develop a set of attitudes about violence toward women that serve to reduce their sexual/aggressive inhibitions (Malamuth, Check, & Briere, 1986; Zillmann & Bryant, 1982). Such lowered inhibitions, combined with aggressive and sexual arousal and the presence of models and cues, may be not only increasing the number of rapes but encouraging mild forms of sexual aggression among "consenting adults." One positive note can be added, however. When people are exposed to depictions of rapes, as they sometimes are in the research discussed here, appropriate debrief-

FROM THE FIELD

Edward Donnerstein and Neil M. Malamuth

Ed Donnerstein (University of California, Santa Barbara) (shown above) and Neil Malamuth (UCLA Department of Communication Studies) (below) have been studying the effects of various types of pornography on attitudes about and behavior involving violence against women. Their research has been of particular importance ever since the attorney general appointed a commission on pornography to study the issue. Donnerstein and Malamuth have testified before the commission, and their findings are among the most informative modern data the commission has received about conditions under which pornography may or may not lead to harmful acts.

ing afterward can actually have the effect of educating them about myths associated with rape, making them less accepting of the idea that women somehow enjoy or invite sexual attacks (Malamuth & Check, 1984).

REDUCING AGGRESSION

With an understanding of the causes of aggression, we should now be ready to propose ways of eliminating, or at least reducing, aggression in our society. We shall discuss a variety of suggestions that have drawn the attention of social psychologists. In particular, we will consider the roles of threat and punishment, and take a close look at the ultimate punishment, the death penalty, to see whether it serves as an effective deterrent to violent crime.

The Role of Mitigating Circumstances

It seems inevitable that we will all experience some frustration in our everyday lives. If we could reduce the degree of frustration people faced, then we could also have a major impact on the amount of aggression in society. This, however, is easier said than done. A more practical suggestion is to help people to avoid misinterpreting the causes of frustration. For instance, if I push you, you might push me back—unless you realize that I myself was pushed, or that I tripped and pushed against you by accident. That is, when *mitigating circumstances* exist, when people attribute the causes of frustration to external or justifiable causes, they are more likely to be understanding than aggressive (Kremer & Stephens, 1983; Zillmann & Cantor, 1976).

In line with this notion, Caplan and Paige (1968) found that people who took part in the ghetto riots of the 1960s were no more violent or lawbreaking than nonrioters, nor were they the most frustrated. Rather, rioters were those people who not only felt frustrated but also attributed their frustrations to discrimination, a nonjustifiable cause. While the removal of injustice and discrimination (nonjustifiable frustration) remains the most effective long-term strategy to avoid racial violence, it is important that people are helped to recognize the existence of mitigating circumstances if and when they do exist. When frustrations are arbitrary or unfair, aggression may follow; but when they are recognized to be accidental or justifiable, anger can be reduced and aggression made less likely.

Incompatible Responses

Another approach to reduction of aggression has been to induce responses in people that are incompatible with aggressive behavior (Baron, 1983). The proposal is simple: People cannot experience two incompatible feelings simultaneously. You cannot be angry at the same time you are happy; you cannot be tense at the same time you are relaxed. Therefore, if people can be exposed to humor, feel empathy, or even experience mild sexual arousal when they otherwise would be angry, aggression could be reduced.

In a demonstration of this using empathy (Baron, 1977), one set of students was first angered by an experimental confederate with whom they were working, while a second group was not. Then all of the students were given the opportunity to deliver shocks to this person. In half the cases, the students were given an indication of how uncomfortable the shock recipient was, while in the other half no such information was made available. As shown in Figure 8.5, when the students were angry, seeing an indication of the other's pain was compatible with their feelings and increased the level of shock given. When the confederate had not angered the student, however, knowing of his pain produced empathy for him and therefore reduced the shock given.

Although this approach has been tested almost exclusively in the laboratory, Baron (1983) suggests several practical applications. In particular, he notes that people who have trouble controlling their tempers might be taught to self-generate incompatible responses when they begin to feel anger, therefore experiencing pleasant emotions instead of negative ones.

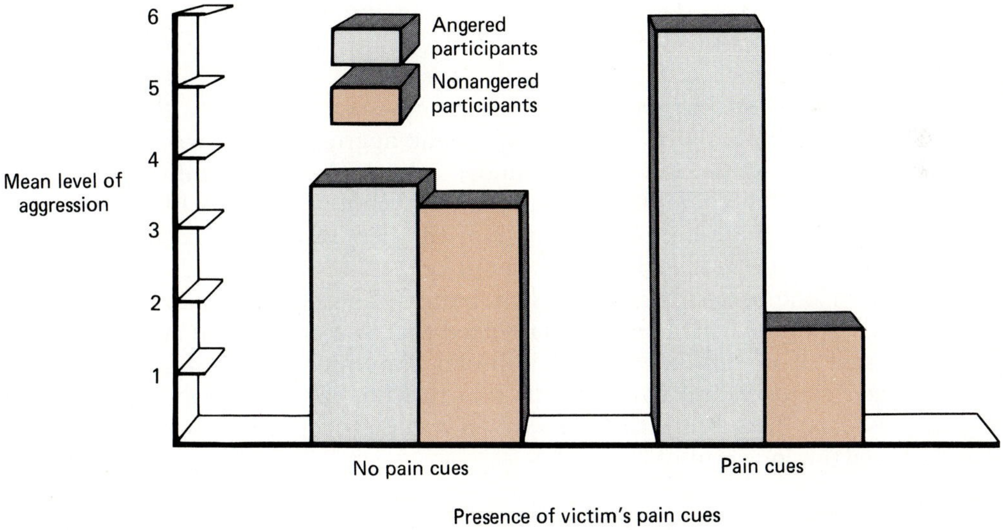

FIGURE 8.5
The Effects of Victim's Pain Cues and Prior Anger upon Aggression Baron found that nonangered students showed a slightly lower level of aggression when they observed the pain of the victim, but angered students showed much stronger levels of aggression when they could see the victim's pain. *Source:* R. A. Baron (1977). *Human aggression.* New York: Plenum Press.

Another suggestion, more controversial but potentially useful, is the use of incompatible responses to deter rapes. For example, women have actually reported throwing a potential attacker off track before he attacked by turning around and asking him for assistance, generating a set of feelings in him that were incompatible with his original intent (Baron, in Krupat, 1982).

Social Learning Approaches to Reduction

Since social learning theorists do not believe that aggression is inborn, they are the most optimistic about reducing or even eliminating it. They believe that through direct reinforcement and observational learning, children can learn that aggression is not the best (or the only) way to get what they want. Generally, the social learning school says that we should reward constructive or cooperative ways of dealing with frustration and conflict, and never reward aggressive behavior, but rather ignore or punish it (in nonviolent ways, lest we model violence). In fact, some have said that the simple *threat* of punishment may be enough to inhibit people from acting aggressively.

The Threat of Punishment People are not likely to do something that brings with it a strong likelihood of punishment. You would not be likely to hit someone who promised immediate and strong retaliation, and much of current U.S. defense policy is based upon discouraging aggression through a threat to deliver a punishing blow in return. Richard Walters (1966) has gone so far as to state: "It is only the continual expectation of retaliation by the recipient or other members of society that prevents many individuals from freely expressing aggression" (p. 69).

Yet threats will work only under a limited set of conditions (Baron, 1977): (1) the amount of threat and the likelihood that it will be delivered must both be extremely high; (2) if the person threatened has much to gain or little to lose, he or she is unlikely to be deterred; (3) threats work only if the person threatened is not angry. Therefore, if I am really angry or desperate, or if I am not convinced that you can or will carry out your threat, I am unlikely to be inhibited. Parents who constantly threaten their children and governments that rely on fear to keep their citizens in line face these limitations, and often find their repressive ways ineffective over the long run.

The Effectiveness of Punishment If the mere threat of punishment is not especially effective, then how about punishment itself? Once again a closer look points to its limitations. In order to be effective, punishment must be predictable and must follow aggression immediately (Baron, 1977). If it meets these conditions, the punishment will be connected to the crime and will be perceived by the wrongdoer as justified. However, when people do not see the connection or reason for their punishment, they can believe that they are being punished unfairly and may come to feel like victims themselves.

Another problem with punishment, as noted earlier in the chapter, is that it does not cause aggression to be "unlearned," but only inhibits it. Also, punishment often creates anger that may lead to aggression at a later point or be displaced onto another target. Most important, the parent who physically punishes a child by hitting, slapping, or spanking is teaching an unintended lesson—by serving as an aggressive model. In an old cartoon a father is shown spanking his son and saying, "Now this will teach you to go around hitting people." The father is unaware of the literal truth of what he is saying. Even when we are talking about acceptable levels of parental punishment rather than child abuse, it is not surprising that research in a number of different countries (e.g., the United States, Finland, and Poland) shows a correlation between parental use of physical punishment and the violence-proneness of their children, both boys and girls (Eron, 1982).

This suggests a final point on physical punishment involving a broader societal concern. Can a society itself effectively use threat and punishment as a means of reducing violence? Will stronger penalties deter violent crime or, as some have suggested, are these merely a form of public vengeance? These questions form the context for the debate that centers around the issue of capital punishment, the topic that we turn to next.

APPLICATION
THE ULTIMATE IN CRIME AND PUNISHMENT: THE DEATH PENALTY

An important public policy debate goes on everywhere from state legislatures to neighborhood bars. The issue is the constitutionality, the appropriateness, and the effects of the death penalty. Decisions about capital punishment are ultimately in the hands of judges and legislators, not social psychologists. But social psychological principles and research can help us make intelligent decisions concerning its use.

Opponents of capital punishment offer a number of arguments against it. They point out that an executed person might later be found innocent; that the death penalty tends to be invoked more often to punish blacks and other minorities; and that executions may desensitize people to violence and therefore lead to even more crime. Those in favor of capital punishment argue that the anger people feel toward those who have taken a human life should not be disregarded, and that people who murder should be dealt with in kind. They believe that the threat of death will make criminals think twice before they take a life, and thereby prevent murders.

The moral questions posed by the death penalty involve difficult philosophical issues—in many respects matters of *opinion*—that are beyond the realm of social psychology. What social psychologists can contribute to the debate, however, is *evidence* that will help us evaluate important assumptions about the effects of capital punishment. Is it an effective deterrent to crime? Does it somehow invite people to commit violent acts? Or does it have no effect either way?

Using a commonsense brand of psychology, the answer seems very simple. If the punishment for speeding is a three-month prison sentence, a person is more likely to think twice before hitting the accelerator than if the penalty were a $25 fine. By analogy, it seems reasonable to think that if the penalty for murder is what potential murderers fear most, death, then they will think twice before committing such an act. This is logical, but it fails to recognize the preceding discussion about the conditions under which threats and punishments are likely to succeed.

Given the way our judicial system works, the likelihood of receiving the death penalty in those states that allow it is hardly certain, nor is the punishment likely to follow swiftly after the crime. More important, the threat of punishment is more successful for instrumental aggression than for angry aggression. Yet most murders are acts of passion committed on impulse against people close to the murderer, not calculated acts. Therefore, it is incorrect to analyze them from a perspective of psychological costs and benefits (Bowers, 1984). Interviews with 83 men living on Florida's death row indicated that even for the rational killer, the death penalty was not consistently seen as more severe a punishment than life in prison (Lewis, 1979).

While many people argue that the death penalty will make criminals think twice before they take a life, much evidence suggests that the kind and the severity of the punishment have little effect on the decision to commit the crime.

The data on the deterrent effects of capital punishment are highly complex, and methodological debates abound. The majority of the evidence, however, has failed to uncover any deterrent effect (see Bowers, 1984, for a thorough review, and Ehrlich, 1975, for one notable exception). Phillips (1980), using British data over a period of 63 years, has suggested that well-publicized executions lead to a reduction in homicides for the following two weeks, but that this effect is canceled out by an equally large rise over the next five to six weeks. Others, however, have failed to find similar short-term reductions (King, 1978). Also, death penalty states do not have lower homicide rates than do neighboring non–death penalty states (Reckless, 1972).

Bowers (1984) has suggested that, just as adults serve as models of aggression when they spank a child, when society kills a killer it also serves as a model of violent behavior, which encourages rather than condemns violence. Labeling this encouragement a **brutalization effect,** he argues that the weight of the evidence is on the side of brutalization rather than deterrence, and that the end product of capital punishment is an increase rather than a decrease in homicides. Thus, because modeling may produce more violence than the threat of punishment deters, capital punishment may accomplish the opposite of what it intends.

While these issues still require a great deal more research and careful consideration, this discussion demonstrates the value of understanding basic issues such as the distinction between incentive-motivated (instrumental) versus annoyance-motivated (angry) aggression, and the problems of threat and punishment in controlling aggression.

Modeling Nonaggressive Behavior One limitation of punishment in general is that it tells the person what *not* to do, but it provides no information about alternative ways of acting. If a child is angry and knows that she should not hit, what else should she do to achieve her goals or to air her emotions? While much attention has been given to the role of imitation and modeling in the *learning* of aggression, less interest has been shown in providing nonaggressive or positive models in the *reduction* of aggressive behavior. Models provide alternative ways of acting for children to imitate. When children see others dealing constructively with conflict or frustration, they learn that successful outcomes can occur without resort to aggression.

The usefulness of positive models has been demonstrated in a number of experimental and naturalistic studies. For example, in one laboratory study, individuals were angered and then exposed to either an aggressive model who delivered strong shocks, a nonaggressive model who gave the weakest of shocks, or no model at all. As usual, the aggressive model produced the most aggressive responses. But those who watched the nonaggressive model gave significantly weaker and shorter shocks than even the control group (Baron & Kepner, 1970). This line of research suggests, first, that parents ought to be aware that their behavior, constructive as well as aggressive, can offer children new ideas about how to deal with anger and frustration. Second, it points out that we might place as much emphasis on providing positive models as we do on reducing the amount of violence when considering how to deal with the effects of television and other media. The possibility of reducing aggression in this way seems obvious and important. As we will note in the Application that follows, it is a recent but successful strategy.

At the beginning of this chapter we asked whether watching violence on television was associated with violent behavior, and now we see that the majority of the evidence says yes. At this point we can ask whether social psychological principles can help us reduce aggression among watchers of violence on television, and again the answer is yes. Let us look at three different intervention strategies and note how each one applies concepts from this and other chapters.

The first strategy follows directly from our discussion of positive modeling and imitation, and shows that positive models not only can reduce aggression but also increase helping. Imagine that you are watching a typical television action show in which the main characters get into trouble and manage to get out by violent means. Now imagine the same show, but with the script changed so that the actors accomplish their goals without resort to violence. This is just what Collins and Getz (1976) did in showing one or the other version to fourth, seventh, and tenth graders. When the researchers observed the children who had seen the constructive-model show, they found them to be not only less aggressive but also more helpful than either the aggressive-model group or a no-exposure control group. Other social psychologists (e.g., Liebert & Poulus, 1975) have actually made their own positive-model mini-tapes and used them with success as spot commercials on actual TV shows. On the basis of successes such as these, the major television networks have begun to design children's shows (such as "Fat Albert") to include positive models in each program for children to observe and imitate (Columbia Broadcasting System, 1977).

While it would be nice to have fewer aggressive and more constructive models on television, a second set of strategies takes television violence as a given, and tries to counteract it by putting negative labels on the aggressive action. For instance, can parents, by watching television alongside their children and commenting on it, *re*sensitize rather than *de*sensitize their children to the harm and suffering that violent acts can cause? To test this, Horton and Santogrossi (1978) took second through fifth graders and showed them a 12-minute excerpt from a violent police show. In one condition, the adult labeled the aggression in a negative way, using words such as *terrible* and *disgusting;* in other conditions the adult simply described some of the action in nonevaluative terms or made no comments at all. Later each child was asked to keep an eye on a group of preschoolers and to summon the adult if they "get into trouble." The children who had heard the anti-aggression commentary were less tolerant of the preschoolers' aggression and called the adult sooner than did those in the neutral group and the no-commentary control group.

Similarly, Huesmann and his colleagues (Huesmann et al., 1983) took first and third graders who watched a good deal of violent television, and presented information to them over several training sessions. In the sessions, they pointed out that most people don't solve their problems through aggression, and suggested that imitating the violence they saw was a bad thing. When compared to a control group, these children were rated as less aggressive by classmates and became more negative toward watching violent programs. These results suggest that by providing negative labels for acts of aggression, adults can reinforce children's inhibitions toward aggression, making them more sensitive to and less accepting of violence around them.

Finally, Leonard Eron (1982) has borrowed from the principles of role playing (see Chapter 6) in order to combat children's preferences for watching violent TV programs. He asked a group of 169 Chicago third graders to write a paragraph on "why TV violence is unrealistic and watching too much of it is bad," and to practice reading their paragraphs for videotaping to be shown to other Chicago schoolchildren. A control group went through the same procedure, but their public statements were about what they had done last summer. Eron reports that although the two groups were equal in aggressiveness a year before, four months after the session the experimental group showed significantly less aggressive behavior than the children in the control group.

While far more remains to be done in inoculating children against the effect of television violence, it seems clear that "we are not helpless in the face of that insidious teacher in our living room" (Eron, 1982, p. 209). Each of the interventions we have discussed has taken basic social psychological concepts and research findings and applied them effectively in reducing the impact of violent TV. There is every reason to believe that the future will bring more extensive and successful efforts.

SUMMARY

1. Aggression is any form of behavior that is directed toward the goal of harming or injuring another living being who is motivated to avoid such punishment. Violence is a form of aggression that is direct and that causes injury through the use of physical force.

2. Angry, or annoyance-motivated, aggression is a form of behavior directed against another person as a release of emotion, such as when two lovers quarrel. Instrumental, or incentive-motivated, aggression involves intentional harm, but here the idea is to gain or to keep something, as when one child knocks over another to take toys away.
3. Instigations are all the factors that motivate or encourage a person to behave aggressively. Inhibitions involve the factors that discourage aggression. People act aggressively only when instigations outweigh inhibitions.
4. The psychoanalytic perspective on aggression developed by Sigmund Freud suggests that a death instinct, *Thanatos,* is part of human nature. Therefore it suggests that aggression in one form or another is inevitable. The conscience, or superego, is the force that inhibits aggression.
5. Ethologists and sociobiologists also think of aggression as inevitable; however, sociobiologists believe that aggression is caused not by instinct but by competition for scarce resources.
6. Among lower animals such as rats, brain centers that activate and inhibit aggression have been identified, but no such simple "violence centers" exist among humans. In addition, the search for clear-cut personality and genetic characteristics associated with human aggression has met with only limited success.
7. Dollard and his colleagues initially proposed that frustration *always* leads to aggression, and that *all* aggression is caused by frustration. Currently, it is believed that frustration is but one cause of aggression, and that several factors determine whether frustration actually leads to aggression.
8. Cues in the environment act to set off aggressive behavior among those who are angry or frustrated. Controversial studies by Berkowitz and his colleagues suggest that the mere presence of guns sets off aggression, and conclusions about the effect of guns in the real world are equally controversial.
9. Social learning theorists believe that aggression is learned through the observation of others who serve as models. By seeing aggression rewarded, children learn that it is a successful mode of behavior. Even when they see adult aggression punished, children learn about new types of aggressive behavior, which they may display at a later time.
10. Extensive evidence on the relationship between watching violent television and displaying aggression points to a definite link between the two. The notion of catharsis, that watching media violence serves to purge an individual of the need to act aggressively, has received little empirical support. Television violence can cause a lowering of inhibitions, desensitize viewers to the suffering of victims, create

arousal which may be labeled as anger, and reinforce preexisting violent tendencies.

11. A number of specific and immediate environmental conditions can increase aggression. Alcohol in small doses appears to inhibit aggressive behavior, but does the opposite when taken in large doses. Unlike alcohol, marijuana leads to lowered levels of aggression when taken in large doses.
12. Arousal, whether in the form of heat, noise, or crowding, leads to aggression when it is at a moderate level. When arousal is extremely high, Baron believes that it becomes a source of distraction and leads people to reduce their discomfort rather than to act aggressively.
13. Exposure to media with violent and sexual content leads males to develop attitudes about violence toward women that reduce their aggressive inhibitions. Lowered inhibitions combined with aggressive and sexual arousal, models, and cues can contribute to higher rates of sexual violence.
14. A number of suggestions have been offered for reducing aggressive behavior in society. Among them are the provision of explanations for unavoidable frustrations so that people will recognize the existence of mitigating circumstances, and the generating of responses that are incompatible with anger.
15. Punishment as a deterrent for aggression has definite limitations. A particular problem with physical punishment is that people who punish serve as models of aggression themselves, and thereby justify rather than condemn violence.

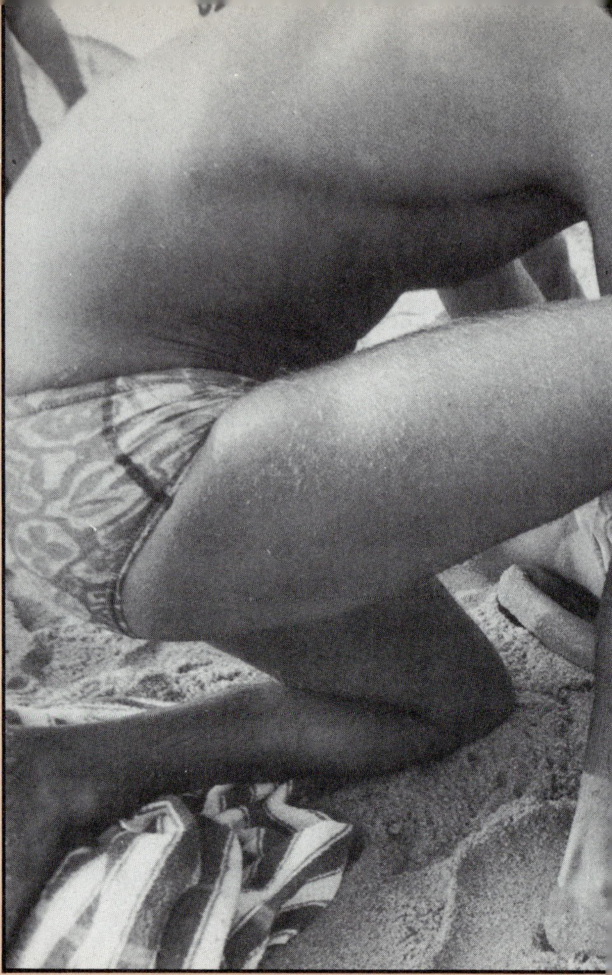

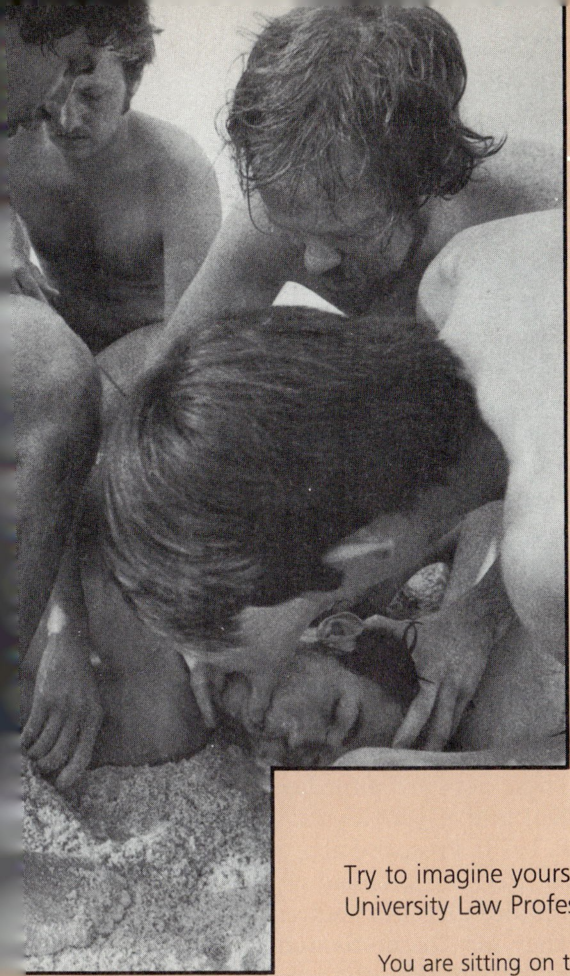

CHAPTER 9
Altruism and Helping Behavior

Try to imagine yourself in the following position, as described by Stanford University Law Professor John Kaplan:

> You are sitting on the edge of a pier, eating a sandwich, and watching the sunset when the fisherman next to you leans too far forward and falls in. He screams to you: "Help! I can't swim. Throw the life preserver." You make no effort to get up to throw the preserver, which is hanging only five feet from you, even though you could do this with absolutely no danger to yourself and with only the most minimal effort. Indeed, you sit chomping away on your sandwich and now, along with the sunset, you watch the fisherman drown. [1972, p. 291]

Question: has your action, or more accurately your inaction, put you in violation of any law, criminal or civil? By refusing to move a single muscle to help a man who could easily have been saved with no risk to you, have you done anything illegal? In 47 of the 50 U.S. states and most other English-speaking countries, the answer is a plain and simple no. You have not disobeyed any law, and you could not even be sued by the fisherman's widow for having refused to save him (Bohlen, 1908; Seavey, 1960).

Very few fishermen die this way and an equally small number of people appear to be this callous, but in everyday life we are called upon to help others. Sometimes the request is trivial and easily fulfilled: "Can you tell me how to get to Lexington Avenue?" Sometimes it involves more effort or commitment: "Would you donate $10 to the Heart Fund?" or "Would you volunteer four hours a week to tutor freshmen in math?" And on occasion, as with the drowning fisherman, the call may be one of life or death.

In Chapter 8 we pointed out that there is *too much* aggression and asked if social psychology could suggest ways to decrease it. In this chapter, we will note that there seems to be *too little* helping, and we will ask whether social psychology can point to ways of increasing it. For instance, is it possible for our legal system to influence people to do good? Can we provide penalties for those who don't help and incentives for those who do? In addition, can we find other ways to encourage people to help one another regardless of the legal sanctions involved?

In the previous chapter we noted that aggression is an act directed *against* another person, and therefore we referred to it using the term *anti*social. In this chapter we will use the term **prosocial behavior** to refer to acts that bring benefits to other people. These acts are aimed at producing, maintaining, or improving the physical and psychological welfare and integrity of others (Staub, 1978; Wispé, 1978). Prosocial acts can be heroic or mundane. They can involve actions that are planned and formal or spontaneous and informal; and may require direct or indirect aid giving (Smithson, Amato, & Pearce, 1983). They may be motivated by a desire to get something in return, or by nothing more than the personal knowledge of having helped. Prosocial acts can range from donating a dollar to the Girl Scouts to donating a kidney for a dying relative; helping a child to tie his shoes or risking one's life to help a person being attacked by a group of thugs. The only requirement for a behavior to be labeled prosocial is that it be "other-directed in a positive sense" (Wispé, 1978, p. xiv).

Altruism is a special form of prosocial behavior. Unlike instances of helping where a person might believe that the potential costs are low and the possibility for gaining rewards are high, altruistic behavior involves helping—sometimes even taking great risks—even though the act is not likely to be rewarded, recognized, or even appreciated. While some forms of helping may involve selfish motives, the altruistic act is selfless. It involves placing another person's interests above one's own, and acting in that person's behalf without a desire or expectation of being repaid in any form.

In this chapter we will consider the full range of helping acts and situations, both altruistic and not. We will seek to find out what motivates helping by looking internally, using genetic and personality explanations; then externally, by looking at the ways in which situational factors and decisions about benefits and risks determine helping. We will explore the role of factors such as moods, norms, and guilt, and then consider how children learn about helping others. At that point, we will change focus somewhat, considering helping from the opposite side of the coin, asking how people go about getting others to help them and how it feels to be on the receiving end. Finally we will consider how formal helping relationships are conceptualized and look at the advantages and disadvantages of each of these.

WHY PEOPLE HELP: INTERNAL FACTORS

Although the occurrence of heroic or self-sacrificing behavior is generally low, it is nonetheless puzzling for anyone who believes in the basic principles of reinforcement. The **altruistic paradox,** as it was first called in 1883 by sociologist Lester Ward (see Wispé, 1978), asks how it is possible for a behavior to be acquired or performed when it is not associated with a reward. Why would people perform an act that has the potential to put them at risk merely to help another?

The Evolution of Altruism

Implicit in this question about altruism is a view of human nature as competitive and self-centered that follows from Darwin's theory of the survival of the fittest. Those who are best adapted to their environment and act in their own behalf not only will survive but also will get to reproduce and to pass along their genes to future generations. According to such a view, altruistic individuals, brave but foolish, would not stand much chance of long-term survival and would soon become extinct.

Sociobiologists, however, recognize that altruism has not died, and can cite numerous examples of altruism throughout the animal kingdom (Wilson, 1975). Termites and ants protect their nests whenever an intruder enters, exposing themselves to great danger; honeybees sting intruders, thereby protecting the hive by killing themselves. Sociobiologists have attempted to explain the continued existence of altruism in evolutionary terms, reasoning that if it still exists it must have survival value for the group, if not the individual.

To account for the survival of this kind of self-sacrificing behavior, Wilson has expanded Darwin's concept of the fittest, suggesting the concept of *inclusive fitness* rather than *individual fitness.* By this he means that we should measure who and what survives not only on the basis of single individuals and whether they produce offspring, but also considering whether the survival of the larger group is enhanced. Thus if one individual dies protecting many close relatives (as in the examples cited), then (1) the family, group, or species benefits, and (2) the biological tendency toward altruism is maintained in the surviving relatives.

Social psychologists such as Donald Campbell (1972) have criticized such biological explanations. Campbell notes that while some basic and primitive forms of helping (such as in mother-child attachments) do exist and may have a biological basis, the complex forms of helping that exist among humans cannot be accounted for by this or other sociobiological examples (e.g., Trivers, 1971). Campbell believes that heroic behavior can be accounted for by *social* evolution better than by *biological* evolution, noting that people generate prosocial norms and values and pass them along from generation to generation just as certainly as they pass along their genes.

The Influence of Personality

While most social psychologists reject the idea that either altruism or helping in general is genetically determined, this has not kept them from looking within the person for other determinants of prosocial behavior. The question here is whether such a thing as a helping personality exists. Are there characteristics or traits that differentiate helpers, Good Samaritans, or altruists—whatever we choose to call them—from people who tend not to help others when they are in need?

Although some evidence exists on both sides of this question, the consensus is on the negative side. On the one hand, researchers have failed to find any significant relationship between helping and authoritarianism, Machiavellianism, social responsibility, need for approval (Latané & Darley, 1970), autonomy, submissiveness (Korte, 1971), independence, or trustworthiness (Yakimovich & Saltz, 1971). Other researchers, however, have found a positive relationship between helping and self-esteem (Walster & Piliavin, 1972), empathy (Fultz et al., 1986), and level of moral development (Morrison, Siegal, & Francis, 1984).

The explanation for this inconsistent pattern of results goes back to the basic Lewinian principle that behavior is a function of both personality and situation as discussed in Chapters 1 and 3. Each helping situation arouses slightly different interests, needs, and orientations. Each involves different risks, opportunities, and potential rewards. Therefore, the prediction of helping should be possible only from knowledge of the *interaction* between personality and situation, not from personality alone.

Satow (1975) has looked at the relationship between the need for social approval and helping. In accordance with an interactional hypothesis, he found that people who were high in the need for social approval donated more of their winnings to a university fund, but only when they felt that their behavior was being monitored by the experimenter (i.e., under conditions where their behavior could win them approval). Findings on sex differences and helping illustrate the same point. In general, males and females do not differ in helpfulness when minor requests for help are made, such as asking for change or directions (Latané & Darley, 1970). However, men typically help more often in emergency circumstances where the situation calls for the type of direct, assertive actions traditionally associated with the male role (Latané & Darley, 1970; Schwartz & Clausen, 1970). Likewise, women (because of their socialization) would probably offer more aid if the needed assistance involved comforting a lost child.

Gergen, Gergen, and Meter (1972) have provided the most direct test of the interactional hypothesis concerning helping. First they had students in their class take ten different personality tests, each of which might be associated with a predisposition to help. Later, all the students were asked if they would be willing to volunteer in any of five different capacities. The activities listed were especially chosen to represent a range of interests. Analyzing the data separately for males and females, they found that every one of the ten personality scales was related to some form of helping, but that the relationships differed from activity to activity and from sex to sex. Gergen and his colleagues summarize their findings by stating:

> Searching for the trait dispositions or individual differences that account for variability in pro-social behavior seems fruitless. Various types of pro-social activities will appeal to or motivate people for different reasons. The complex of payoffs for reporting a fire, rescuing the dying, sending lost letters, giving away candy, returning wallets, contributing to charities, helping people of other ethnic origins, and so on are all different. The types of persons who will choose to engage in such activities can be expected to differ in each case. [p. 117]

While few if any specific personality traits are related to helping in general, it should be noted that a person's broadly defined self-image may be an important factor. That is, regardless of all other dispositions or needs, those who are most likely to volunteer, to donate, or to take emergency action are the people who see themselves as helpers. This process of self-labeling begins with a positive first experience. People may find that giving blood did not hurt after all, or that others have praised them for their efforts on behalf of senior citizens. Such a positive experience is a critical first step, because it leads individuals to believe that they are people for whom this kind of activity is possible. This may then lead to further attempts at helping and, if they are successful, to a self-definition as a helper and a stronger commitment to action. Once acts of helping come to be attributed to intrinsic motivation rather than to external pressures (Deci & Ryan, 1985), people may even become "addicted" to good deeds (Piliavin, Callero, & Evans, 1982).

WHEN PEOPLE HELP: SITUATIONAL FACTORS

Although research in this area had been going on for many years, the upsurge in interest can be traced back to one dramatic event. In 1964 a murder took place in the Kew Gardens section of New York City. It was not the only murder that day, and thousands of murders have occurred in New York City since. The person who was killed was not famous; she was an ordinary 24-year-old woman by the name of Kitty Genovese. What is unique and sad about her death is that it was witnessed by 38 onlookers, none of whom helped directly or even raised a finger to call the police.

IN THE NEWS

THE NIGHT THAT 38 STOOD BY AS A LIFE WAS LOST

It flashes through Margaret Swinchoski's mind, each time she walks past the Kew Gardens, Queens, train station: This was where Kitty Genovese met her killer.

Even in the small town in Vermont where Miss Swinchoski grew up, Catherine Genovese's case became a shocking symbol of apathy.

Now Miss Swinchoski lives in the same quiet, middle-class neighborhood where Miss Genovese was slain 20 years ago as she tried to make her way from her car, parked in the train station lot, to her apartment on Austin Street.

"What Might Happen"

For more than half an hour that night, Miss Genovese's killer stalked and stabbed her, again and again, as 38 of her neighbors silently turned away from her cries.

"I walk here during the day but not at night," said Miss Swinchoski, a 25-year-old flutist, "because of what happened then and because of what might happen now."

The killer, Winston Moseley, had followed Miss Genovese into the parking lot at 3:20 A.M. on March 13, 1964.

Mr. Moseley, a 29-year-old machine operator and family man, was convicted after he confessed that he had been cruising around, planning "to rape and to rob and to kill a girl." He is serving a life sentence in Green Haven state prison, and was recently denied parole.

Mr. Moseley attacked Miss Genovese for the first time in front of the Austin Book Shop as she ran up the street, apparently toward a police call box. "Oh, my God, he stabbed me," she screamed into the early-morning stillness. "Please help me!" Windows opened and lights went on in the building across the street.

"Let that girl alone," yelled a man on the seventh floor. Mr. Moseley walked toward his car. As he later told the police, "I had a feeling this man would close his window and go back to sleep and then I would return."

Miss Genovese staggered around the

The lack of aid touched so sensitive a chord in the public that this incident was reported and debated throughout the United States, and the *New York Times* report of this incident was read into the *Congressional Record* (Milgram & Hollander, 1964). Twenty years later, the anniversary of this tragic event was the occasion for a symposium on helping (see the In the News box for some personal recollections of the event).

A public outcry came from editorial writers, politicians, and ordinary citizens. Words such as *apathy, alienation,* and *anonymity* were tossed about. Some people argued that "there ought to be a law," and others suggested that those who failed to act were probably satisfying some deep, evil urge by not intervening. Others condemned the city for robbing Kitty Genovese of friends, or for making them so cold and indifferent that not even they would help her. (See Chapter 11 for a discussion of the actual role of the city in this incident.)

As noted in Chapter 2, there is a tendency to try to find dispositional explanations for the behavior of others, especially when that behavior is

corner and fell inside the lobby of the first unlocked building she could find.

As witnesses watched from behind their curtains—one couple pulled up chairs to the window and turned out the light to see better—Mr. Moseley came back and calmly poked into doors until he found his victim. He stabbed her eight more times and sexually molested her.

First Call to Police

It was 3:50 A.M. when the police received their first call—from a man who said he did not want to "get involved."

Bernard Titowsky, owner of the Austin Book Shop, recalls coming in the next morning and finding blood near the door. "Time and rain washed most of it away," he said Saturday, sitting on a stool behind his antique cash register.

Mr. Titowsky and many other longtime residents remain sensitive about the case and say the residents were unfairly portrayed as callous. "No one wants to give the people that lived here any credit," he said. "They just want to use it as a sociology lesson."

A Woman Who Remembers

Most of the witnesses have moved away, or died. One who remembers is an 83-year-old woman, who lived next door to Miss Genovese. She was awakened at 3:30 A.M. that night when a friend called to say he had seen the attack but was intoxicated and did not want to deal with the police.

She put on a coat over her nightgown and went down the street to find a door ajar and Miss Genovese crumpled behind it. "She was dying," the woman recalled. "She was making noises like, 'Uh, uh, uh,' like she couldn't breathe." The woman then went to a neighbor, who called the police.

The woman said she wished people would forget. "We weren't apathetic," she said. "There are good people here. There's so much else bad in the world. Poor Kitty."

Source: Maureen Dowd, *The New York Times,* March 12, 1984, p. B1.

unpleasant. It allows us to differentiate ourselves from the "type of person" who does not help. Yet, as the discussion on personality and helping has suggested, helpers are not a special breed, nor are non-helpers evil. In fact, the 38 people who watched Kitty Genovese die were quite normal, decent people in every other way. But if they were not different or special, then why did they not help? More generally, what factors in that situation—or any situation—can account for why people do or do not help?

The Presence of Others: The Latané and Darley Model

Two young social psychologists who were teaching in New York City at the time of Kitty Genovese's murder, John Darley and Bibb Latané, were having dinner one night shortly after the incident. Like everyone else, they were discussing this issue and were attempting to explain the "unexplainable" behavior of those 38 people. They and others (see Milgram &

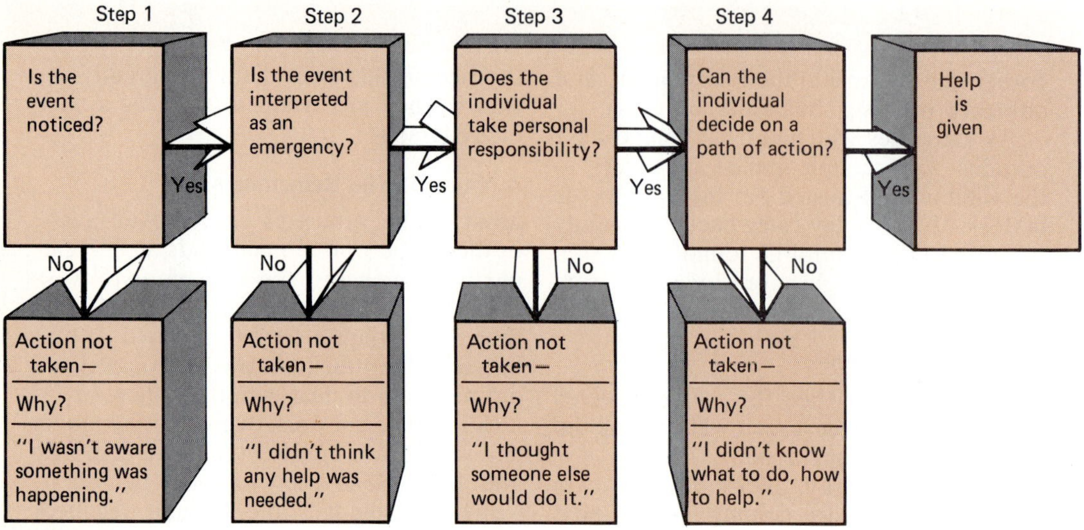

FIGURE 9.1
Latané and Darley's Decision Model of Emergency Intervention At each step of the model, potential helpers will not come to a person's aid if they answer no to the question. Only after they notice the situation, define it as an emergency, take personal responsibility, and decide on a course of action will they help. *Source:* Adapted from J. M. Darley & B. Latané (1968, December). When will people help in a crisis? *Psychology Today,* p. 57. Copyright © 1968/1986 American Psychological Association.

Hollander, 1964) realized that the full situation as later reported in the press was quite different from the actual situation as it unfolded. The onlookers saw only fragments of an event that was ambiguous and frightening; and they had to move from these confusing facts to personal action under a good deal of stress. Latané and Darley believed that through the use of some basic social psychological principles and concepts, they could build a model to explain this event and to account for the process of helping under any emergency situation. Their model, pictured in Figure 9.1, requires a person to move through each of four stages of choice. At each step, one decision will lead to a greater likelihood of helping, but the other will mean that the person will not help. The steps are as follows:

1. The bystander has to *notice* what is happening. Kitty Genovese was attacked at 3:20 in the morning. Many people who might have helped her were sound asleep and never even heard her cries for help. People who live in noisy, high-stimulation environments may narrow their range of attention and not even hear "extraneous noises" such as cries that might otherwise signal an emergency (Cohen, 1978). If people do not notice, they cannot help. If they do notice, then they are candidates to give aid.

2. The event must be *interpreted as an emergency.* The onlooker must decide that someone is in need of help. It was dark out when Kitty Genovese cried for help, and the people in this generally safe middle-class neighborhood were half asleep when they heard sounds coming from below. The probability that someone would be getting murdered right under their noses must have seemed extremely remote. Maybe a drunken person was yelling; maybe a husband and wife were having a quarrel.

   It is hard to know whether a person lying on the sidewalk is a drunk or has just suffered a heart attack. Does the smoke coming from a building three blocks away indicate that the building is on fire, or that someone is having a barbecue? Whenever people face such a decision, especially when it is ambiguous, they tend to believe that, as usual, nothing is wrong. If they decide there is no emergency, then no help will come. If they decide it is an emergency, they then move to step 3.
3. The individual must decide at this point that it is his or her *personal responsibility* to act. According to follow-up reports on the murder of Kitty Genovese, Emil Power, one of Kitty's neighbors, was about to call the police when his wife said, "Don't. Thirty people must have called by now." What if everyone had said the same thing? The responsibility for helping was so unfocused that no one individual felt the need to act. If people decide that someone else has dealt with it, or will deal with it, no help will be given. When they feel personal responsibility, they are more likely to help and can move on to step 4.
4. The person must now decide what form of assistance to give. Ideally the residents of this Kew Gardens neighborhood should have run out and chased the attacker away. But this and other forms of direct intervention obviously involve great risk. Still, indirect help, such as notifying someone, can seem like such a cowardly response that it is rejected. As a result, people might take no action at all. Only after this decision point has been passed do people reach the final step, the carrying out of the intervention. Only then will help be given.

A major contribution of the Latané and Darley model is in pointing out that the presence of other people can affect the amount of help that is given. First, other people help us to define and interpret the situation, and to decide whether it is an emergency. Second, the presence of other people can cause the responsibility for helping to be diffused among those present. Let us look at each of these points in more detail.

Defining the Situation As discussed in Chapter 3 on the self, whenever we are unsure of how to label an event or an emotion, other people serve an important function. We use them for social comparison (Festinger, 1954). That is, we observe how they are reacting, and use their responses as cues to how we should be interpreting the situation.

Imagine that you are in a packed theater, and you think you smell smoke. You think to yourself, "Perhaps there is a fire and we will all die. Maybe I should yell fire and save my life and everyone else's." But you suspect that you may be imagining the smoke, and that it's probably nothing. "I'd feel awfully stupid if I interrupted the performance and created a panic for no reason," you say to yourself. What to do? Stay cool, do not look upset, and look around ever so subtly to see what everyone else is doing. But what if everyone else is doing the same thing? If each person looks to the others in order to interpret the event and decide how to act, and sees them (1) looking unconcerned, and (2) doing nothing, a state of "pluralistic ignorance" develops in which everyone decides there is no emergency. As a result, each person is frozen in inaction by everyone else's collective inaction (Bar-Tal, 1976).

In order to investigate the manner in which others affect the labeling of a situation, Darley, Teger, and Lewis (1973) seated two people in a room and made sounds come from the next room as though someone were being seriously hurt. In one situation, the two were seated facing each other, while in the other condition they were back to back. When the pairs were face-to-face, the vast majority (75 percent) helped. Yet when the

FROM THE FIELD
John M. Darley and Bibb Latané

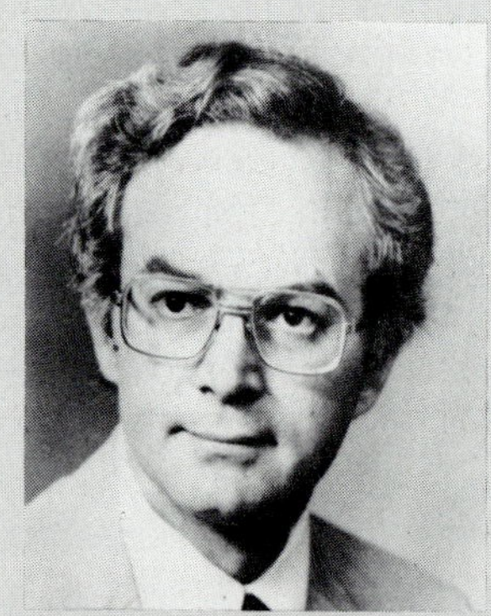

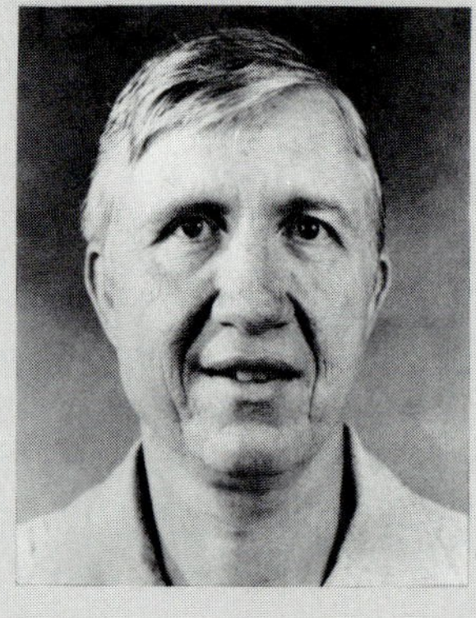

The social psychological study of emergency helping began one evening in New York City, while John M. Darley (shown above) and Bibb Latané (below) were discussing over dinner the murder of Kitty Genovese. They were dissatisfied with the explanations offered by news commentators because they did not take into account what was known about social behavior. The model of bystander intervention in emergencies that Latané and Darley sketched that evening on a napkin, which is described in this chapter, has influenced research on altruism—and our understanding of helping behavior—ever since. Professor Darley is on the faculty at Princeton University, and Professor Latané is now director of the Institute for Research in Social Science at the University of North Carolina.

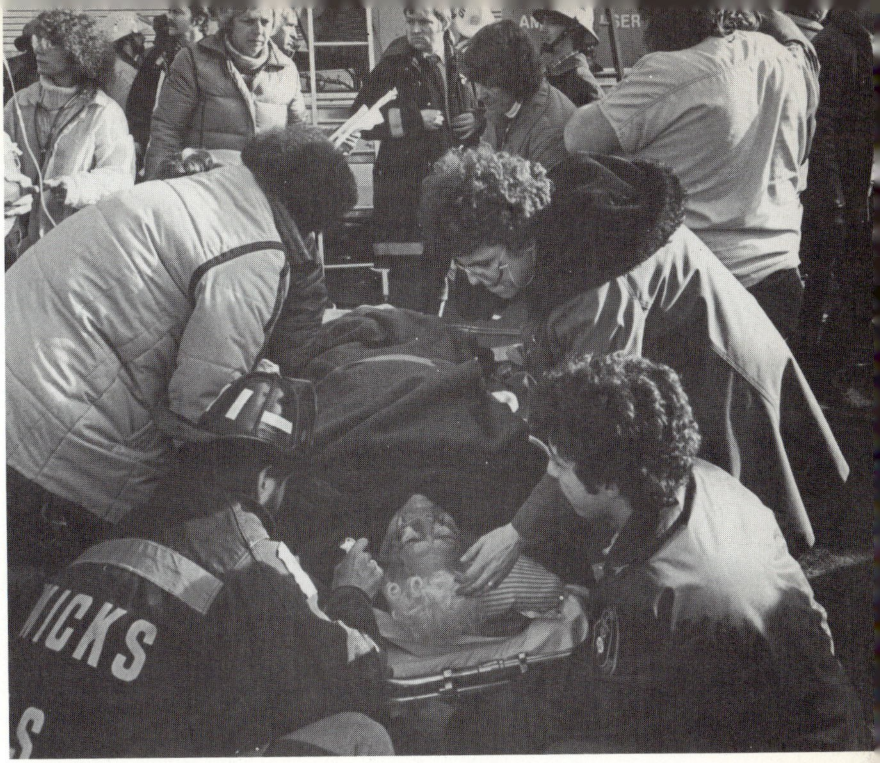

Volunteers join professional fire fighters in assisting an accident victim. According to Latané and Darley, the presence of other people can significantly influence whether an individual will offer to help in such a situation.

pairs were back-to-back, only 20 percent helped. The high level of helping among face-to-face people resulted because their spontaneous startle reactions provided a common definition of concern. The back-to-back people, however, could not use each other for *immediate* social comparison, and when they finally did communicate (verbally or nonverbally) they transmitted to each other the standard impassive posture of poise and composure.

From this study and a host of others (e.g., Shotland, 1985; Shotland & Huston, 1979) we can conclude that (1) when immediate social comparison is not possible, the presence of others leads us to define ambiguous situations as nonserious, and (2) in general, the more ambiguous the situation, the less help will be offered. Relating this back to the Kitty Genovese situation, note that the 38 people who observed the incident were themselves in separate apartments, each out of sight of the others and unable to communicate.

Diffusion of Responsibility Although social comparison often leads to a definition of nonemergency, let us assume that the people who witness an event do decide that action is necessary. Who is going to take responsibility and do something about it? The most notable contribution of the Latané and Darley model, if we can judge by the number of studies that have followed, is their concept of *diffusion of responsibility.* According to this concept, the greater the number of people who witness an emergency situation, the less any single individual feels the pressure to help. Responsibility is diffused, and so are guilt and blame. As a result, the presence of others *inhibits* rather than *encourages* helping. Although many people are shocked that Kitty Genovese received no help *in spite of* the presence of 38 people, the diffusion of responsibility principle implies that it would be more accurate to say that Kitty Genovese received no aid *because* of the presence of so many other people.

Numerous studies have been conducted to test whether there is a social inhibition of helping. According to Latané and Nida (1981), of 56 studies comparing group versus individual helping involving more than 2000 people, more than 85 percent confirmed the inhibition. In one early study (Latané & Darley, 1967), students were brought together to discuss the problems of adapting to a large urban college. In order to avoid the embarrassment of talking about personal problems with strangers face-to-face, they were told that each person was being placed in a separate room and that the experimenter would not even be listening. Each person was to speak in turn for about two minutes while the others listened.

In the first condition of the experiment, students believed the discussion group consisted of two people, themselves and one other; in a second condition, each student believed that a total of three people were present; and in a third condition each believed that a total of six people would be involved in the discussion. In reality, all the voices coming from the other cubicles were tape-recorded and controlled by the experimenter. The first (tape-recorded) person spoke about a number of adjustment problems and even admitted being prone to seizures. In the first round of discussion the "other people" spoke, and then the real participants took their turns. When the second round of discussion started, the first person began calmly but grew increasingly loud and incoherent, saying:

> I-er-um-I think I-I need-er-if-if could-er-er somebody er-er-er-er-er-er-er-er give me a little- er-give me a little help here because-er-I-er I'm-er- er h-h-having a-a-a real problem-er-right now and I- er-if somebody could help me out it would-it would- er-er s-s-sure be-sure be good . . . because-er- there-er-er-a cause I-er-I-uh-I've got a-a one of the-er-sei— er-er-things coming on and-and-and I could really-er-use some help so if somebody would-er-give me a little h-help-uh-er-er-er-er c-could somebody-er-er-help-er-uh-uh-uh (choking sounds). . . . I'm gonna die-er-er-I'm . . . gonna die-er-help-er-er-seizure-er (chokes, then quiet). [Darley and Latané, pp. 95–96]

In the first condition, subjects believed there was nobody else available to help. If they did not help, the victim would receive no aid. In the other two conditions, either one or four other potential helpers were available, thereby creating a diffusion of responsibility. Darley and Latané measured the percentage of people responding to the seizure in each condition as well as the time it took for a response. As Table 9.1 points out, the results confirmed their expectations. The more people believed to be present, the

TABLE 9.1
Effects of Group Size on Likelihood and Speed of Response

Group Size	Percent Responding by End of Fit	Percent Ever Responding	Time in Seconds
2 (Subject and victim)	85	100	52
3 (Subject, victim, and one other)	62	85	93
6 (Subject, victim, and 4 others)	31	62	166

Source: B. Latané & J. M. Darley (1970). *The unresponsive bystander: Why doesn't he help?* New York: Appleton-Century-Crofts, p. 97. Copyright © 1970. Reprinted by permission of Prentice-Hall, Inc., Englewood Cliffs, New Jersey.

smaller the percentage who helped, and the more time it took to get help. In follow-up studies in which people have been questioned about their reactions (e.g., Latané & Rodin, 1969), when others were present people were more likely to believe that emergency events were less serious, that intervention was not necessary or even wanted, and that if action was called for, someone else would take it.

APPLICATION
HELP! FIRE! POLICE! HOW TO GET HELP WHEN YOU NEED IT

The lessons learned from the Latané and Darley model have many important personal and practical applications. For instance, if you were being attacked, mugged, had fallen through the ice, or were in a burning building, does this model suggest particular things that you could do or say to bring others to your aid?

One technique, suggested by a student, focuses on step 1 of the Darley and Latané decision process model—noticing. This student said that if she thought someone were about to attack her, she would pick up the largest rock or other object she could find and throw it—not at her attacker, but through the nearest window of a house or apartment where a light was on. In this way there is no chance that the potential helper would fail to notice and to act by calling the police. She believed no matter whether the police had been summoned to arrest her or to protect her, what she needed was a police officer and this act would bring one. This suggestion recognizes that people are more likely to notice and to act upon threats to their own well-being than threats to others. It also reinforces the point made earlier that people often act for selfish rather than altruistic reasons.

Another technique that relies on the same general principle actually has been recommended in a number of college student handbooks. The suggestion is to call "Fire" rather than "Help." This method is likely to be successful because it provides an unambiguous definition of the emergency, enlists the self-interest and therefore focuses the responsibility of the helper, and suggests clearly a manner of providing help: call the fire department. Another advantage of this technique is that the perceived risk of doing something about a fire is likely to be a good deal less than dealing with a mugger.

A third suggestion may be useful for a person who is being followed and who has a choice about where an eventual confrontation will take place. If you can, arrange to be seen as well as heard. This proposal follows directly from a study performed by Shotland and Stebbins (1980). In it, college students were sent to a relatively deserted floor of a college building to be in an experiment. While waiting, half of the students saw a man and woman struggle at the end of the darkened corridor and then disappear into a room, while the other half saw nothing. Then all the students heard a very realistic tape recording coming from the room that sounded as if the woman were being raped. When the subjects had the evidence of their eyes as well as their ears, they helped 68 percent of the time, but when they only heard the struggle in the room, 13 percent helped. Apparently the visual evidence of the struggle clearly defined it as a rape, as many of those in the voice-only condition said they were not sure how to define the situation and whether to help. Some interpreted what was occurring as a quarrel between two people who knew each other, a personal matter they should keep out of, rather than a rape.

A final technique suggested by a social psychologist friend is an attempt to overcome diffusion of responsibility. This person, who lived in a midtown urban neighborhood with a high rate of robberies and muggings, was concerned about his safety at night while he walked his extremely unferocious dog. Noting that each building on the block had a doorman, he attempted to get to know each one and learn his name. In line with Latané and Darley, he realized that if he were attacked and yelled "*Someone* help me," responsibility would be diffused among all those hearing his cry, and there would be a strong chance that no single person would come forward to help. If instead he could yell "John" or "Joe, help me," this would focus responsibility on a single person.

Rewards and Costs: The Piliavin Model

The Latané and Darley model points out that various situational factors, especially the presence of others, can have a strong effect on how a person defines a potential emergency and whether that person feels sufficient personal responsibility and ability to act. Recently, Jane and Irving Piliavin and their colleagues (Piliavin & Piliavin, 1972; Piliavin, Piliavin, & Rodin, 1975; Piliavin et al., 1982) have proposed a fuller model of helping that not only deals with the presence of others, but also offers a glimpse into the head (and the gut) of a potential helper.

According to their model, the observation of an emergency is an emotionally arousing experience that is unpleasant and unsettling. This arousal increases with five factors: (1) the severity of the emergency; (2)

its clarity; (3) its physical closeness; (4) the degree of identification, similarity, or psychological closeness one feels with the victim; and (5) the length of time one observes the emergency. Given this state of arousal and discomfort caused by witnessing the need or suffering of others, the question then becomes what to do.

Assessing Rewards and Costs The Piliavins suggest that the person makes a decision based on an immediate assessment of the rewards and costs for helping and not helping. Will taking action entail serious risks? Are there risks to me and to the other person if I do nothing? What are the rewards if I do help? In short, they apply a basic reinforcement model to helping. When rewards outweigh costs, helping is likely. When costs outweigh rewards, it is not. And when rewards and costs are about equal, people experience a state of conflict.

Costs for helping, in the form of physical danger, effort, and time, can be minimal, life-threatening, or anything in between. In the course of helping you may have feelings of embarrassment, of disgust in dealing with someone who is bleeding or hurt, or even of inadequacy or guilt if your efforts fail. If you do not help, you may experience "personal costs" such as negative changes in your self-image, or blame and censure at the hands of others. In addition there are "empathy costs," knowing that someone else has continued to suffer as a result of your inaction.

As Figure 9.2 shows, when costs are low for not helping (the victim is not in great danger) and also for helping (little danger is involved in going to that person's aid), the response will be quite variable. The forces that might motivate or inhibit helping are both weak, and the outcome will be determined largely by other factors such as personality, norms, or specific aspects of the situation.

As long as the costs for helping are low, potential helpers face little conflict. They can reduce their arousal via action. When the costs are high, however, potential helpers face a dilemma. If the need of the victim is not great (as in the lower right-hand cell), the easiest response is to remove themselves from the scene. This can be accomplished physically, by leaving the situation and not having to face the victim; or it can be accomplished psychologically, by turning off and not thinking about or accepting the other person's need.

The Helper's Dilemma What happens in the typical emergency, the situation where both the need and the risks are great (the upper right-hand cell), such as the case of Kitty Genovese? The initial formulation of Piliavin and Piliavin (1972) argued that in this kind of severe emergency the most typical response would be to offer indirect rather than direct assistance. People would call the police or fire department rather than attempt to intervene themselves; they would summon others who were more able to do the job.

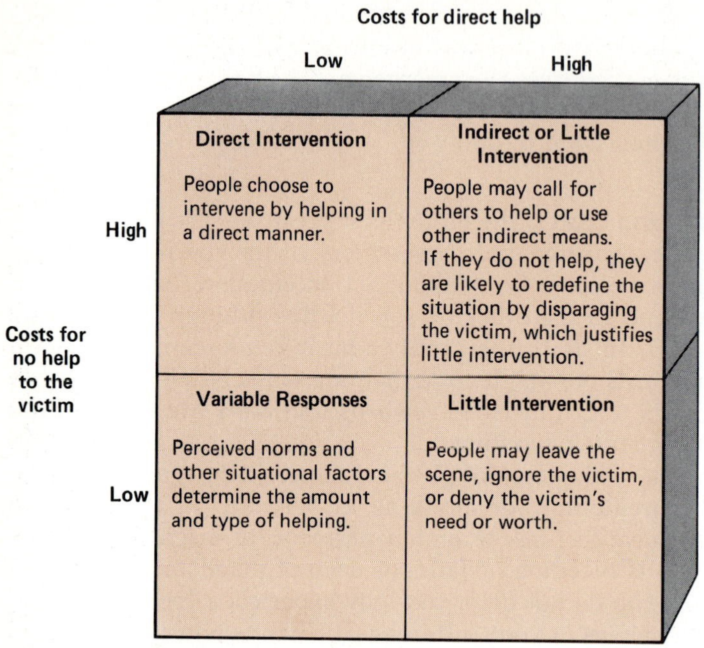

FIGURE 9.2
Typical Responses as a Function of Costs for Direct Help and for No Help When the costs for helping are low and the need for aid is great (upper left-hand cell), diret help is most likely given. When the opposite occurs (lower right-hand cell) little help is given. In the other two cases, the potential helper experiences some degree of conflict, and the amount of helping is affected by a range of other factors, such as personality and situation. *Source:* Adapted from Figure 12.1 of J. A. Piliavin, J. F. Dovidio, S. L. Gaertner, & R. D. Clark III (1982). Responsive bystanders: The process of intervention. In V. J. Derlega & J. Grzelak (Eds.), *Responsive cooperation and helping behavior: theories and research.* New York: Academic Press.

In light of research findings, however, the model was revised to suggest that the path of least resistance might be not a physical but a cognitive one (Piliavin et al., 1982). People reduce their conflicts about helping by reinterpreting and redefining the situation. They believe that the victim is not really in great need or did not want any intervention, as did those who heard the man and woman struggle in Shotland and Stebbins's research. In this way the situation *as perceived* moves into the lower right cell and allows people to be less concerned about not helping. In those situations where people cannot deny that help is wanted and needed, however, one cognitive resolution to the conflict is to believe that someone else will do it, as we have seen in the diffusion of responsibility. Diffusion of responsibility reduces the guilt (that is, part of the cost) associated with not helping.

This woman is being mugged in full view of several onlookers. Each of the bystanders is likely to be weighing the rewards and costs for intervention and nonintervention, and asking whether someone else will do anything to help.

Blaming the Victim Another kind of cognitive manipulation that people use to avoid helping involves disparaging or derogating the victim. If we can believe that the person in need is unworthy of our concern, or if we can attribute responsibility for the victim's state to some fault of his or her own, it is easier to explain to ourselves why we did not help. Melvin Lerner believes that we do this to maintain our belief in a "just world": People get what they deserve, so if they do not receive help it was probably because they did not deserve it (Lerner, 1980; Lerner & Simmons, 1966). Myers (1987) has noted a particularly vivid example of this phenomenon. A German civilian who saw the concentration camp at Belsen just after World War II could offer no explanation for what had been done to people there other than to say, "What terrible criminals these prisoners must have been to receive such treatment." Ryan (1971) has referred to this kind of thinking as **blaming the victim,** and has noted that it can inhibit the development of sympathy and keep us from providing aid to those who are in the greatest need.

Testing the Model The Piliavins' model has also generated much research. In one test of this model, a realistic emergency was enacted on a subway train in New York City. A male confederate of the experimenter staggered forward, collapsed, and fell on his back on the floor of a subway car while it was between stops. In one condition the person carried a white cane, while in the other he smelled of liquor and carried a bottle in a brown paper bag. In the white cane condition, the victim received help 95 percent of the time, whereas in the drunk condition, he was helped in only 50 percent of the cases.

Two explanations that derive from the Piliavins' model can be offered to account for this finding. First, the drunk is helped less because assisting him involves greater costs (e.g., the drunk smells, might vomit, etc.). A second explanation involves the lower level of "deservingness" of this kind of victim. A blind man deserves our help; it is not his fault that he cannot see. A drunken man seems to have brought his trouble on himself and is not worthy of the effort and risk to help him. A third possible explanation, not considered at length in the preceding models, is that we cannot identify with or feel for the drunk. This kind of explanation, involving empathy or other mediators of helping, is the next topic to be considered.

MOTIVATORS AND MEDIATORS OF HELPING

In our search for the answer to why and when people help, we have considered the importance of basic internal factors (i.e., genetics and personality), and then reviewed two models that emphasize the presence of others and our perceptions of rewards and costs. Yet a whole host of other factors, often more immediate or specific, also determine when we help, whom we help, and whether we help at all. In this section we will explore these factors, considering how empathy, moods, and feelings of

Empathy, or a strong cognitive or emotional identification with other people, may have motivated this rescue worker, here shown assisting a tornado victim, to select his line of work.

guilt can lead us toward or away from helping. Then we will deal with the extent to which norms affect helping, distinguishing between those norms that are held by society in general and those that are held by each individual personally.

The Role of Empathy

One factor that can lead a person to want to help another is a feeling of **empathy.** Empathy is defined as an emotional or cognitive identification with another person. It is different from sympathy in that sympathy implies that "I" feel sorry for "them." When people feel an empathic reaction, they experience a "we-ness" between themselves and others. They experience the other's distress as their own (Wispé, 1986); Hornstein, 1982).

As in the reward-cost approach, empathy theorists believe that the physiological arousal resulting from the distress of others motivates a person to help. But here the two approaches part ways. Reward-cost theorists emphasize self-centered motives, pointing out that people calculate how to best reduce *their own* levels of distress and arousal by helping. The focus of empathy theorists (Wispé, 1986; Batson et al., 1983) is just the opposite. They believe that empathic arousal leads people to take the perspective of the person in need and motivates them to help in order to reduce the *other's* distress rather than their own. Great debates have taken place over the degree to which helping is oriented toward self versus other rewards. Most likely, both motivations play a part.

Evidence suggests that empathy on a primitive level is present among even the youngest of children (Hoffman, 1982; Radke-Yarrow & Zehn-Wexler, 1984). For instance, infants less than two days old cry more intensely when they hear another infant's cry than when they hear other equally loud natural or computer-simulated sounds. Staub (1984) believes that the development of an empathic orientation begins with this kind of early emotional reactivity and combines with conditioning, role-taking ability, and the learning of values and beliefs as children grow older.

One important factor that affects empathy is the degree of similarity between the potential helper and the person in need. To demonstrate this, Suedfeld, Bochner, and Wnek (1972) had a young woman approach anti–Vietnam War demonstrators in Washington, D.C., asking help for a sick friend. When the person in need was next to a "Dump Nixon" sign, he received a good deal of help, but when he had a "Support Nixon" sign next to him he got far less. In addition to helping people with similar attitudes (Hornstein, 1982; Hornstein et al., 1971), people help others of the same race more than those of other races, and people who dress like they do more than those who dress differently (Dovidio, 1984). We are more likely to experience their needs as ours, and to help them as a result of feeling empathy.

The Effect of Mood

General emotional reactions, both positive and negative, can have a strong effect on helping. Alice Isen and her colleagues (Isen, 1984; Isen et al., 1978) have studied the relationship of mood on prosocial behavior using a variety of methods, settings, and subject populations. In one set of experiments, Isen (1970) looked at the effect of the "warm glow of success" on helping. In separate studies using both college students and young children, participants succeeded or failed on a task and were then given the opportunity either to donate money or to help pick up some fallen materials. Successful people were more helpful than controls or unsuccessful people. Isen has also induced positive moods in people by offering them a cookie, arranging for them to find a dime in the pay-phone coin return, or having them receive a free sample of stationery. In each case, good mood led to increased helping, although it should be noted that good feelings do tend to dissipate quickly and lose their effect on helpfulness (Isen, Clark, & Schwartz, 1976).

These findings are hardly surprising or complicated. The question that has fascinated helping researchers is *why* mood affects helping. Staub (1978) has proposed the concept of **hedonic balancing** to account for the effects of good mood. According to this concept, people weigh their own current state of well-being ("Am I better off than usual? About the same? Worse?") against that of the person in need. Feeling better than usual makes people attentive to the discrepancy between their own positive state and someone else's state of need, and this awareness leads them to feel benevolent. We might say that good mood disposes you to do unto others as others have done unto you.

The Power of Guilt

When people feel responsible for doing harm to another, they often feel guilty. Research on the effect of guilt has shown that people are more likely to help not only the person they have harmed directly but other people as well. Regan, Williams, and Sparling (1972) demonstrated this by asking shoppers at a mall to take a picture for them, using a camera that had been rigged so that it would not work. Half the shoppers were made to feel guilty, being told that they had broken the camera; the other half were told it was not their fault. Later, a confederate walked by and dropped groceries from her shopping bag. Of those who felt guilty, more than half helped; but of those who did not feel any guilt, only 15 percent offered help.

The Debate over Norms

Regardless of whether they are feeling guilty or are in a good mood, or whether they actually help or not, people still feel as if they *ought to* help. Why? As our initial discussion indicated, no law says that we must help.

But our obligation to help lies in the unwritten rules of conduct—social norms—that exist in every society.

Kinds of Helping Norms In just about every known culture, there are norms that say it is "good" to care about others and "bad" to hurt others or to act too selfishly. One potentially powerful force in guiding and directing helping is the **norm of social responsibility.** According to this norm, individuals should help those who depend upon them. When this norm is internalized, people "act on behalf of others, not for material gain or social approval, but for their own self-approval, for the self-administered rewards arising from doing what is 'right'" (Goranson & Berkowitz, 1966, p. 228).

In a series of experiments (e.g., Berkowitz & Daniels, 1964), this effect was demonstrated clearly. The more students thought that the evaluation given to their supervisor was based on how hard they themselves worked, the more their productivity rose. This was true even though they received no additional reward for the extra effort. We can see this norm utilized every Christmas season, when the local newspaper runs a list of the neediest cases or a radio station tells us about what the children at an orphanage want for the holiday. Such campaigns try to make the norm of social responsibility salient, realizing that people try to come through when they know others are relying on them.

The norm of reciprocity has also been shown to influence helping behavior (Gouldner, 1960). Reciprocity represents nothing more than a variant of the Golden Rule: Do unto others as they have done unto you. If someone has done something to help you, you should feel an obligation to reciprocate. Likewise, if you have helped someone else, the other person should feel a similar obligation to repay the favor. Reciprocity is closely related to the principle of **equity,** which deals with fairness in interper-

Several factors may be influencing this New Yorker's decision to give some change to a panhandler. Among them are likely to be his mood at the moment, as well as the norms of social responsibility and reciprocity.

sonal relations. It states that people expect to receive in proportion to what they give. Therefore, in an equitable relationship, people who have helped could expect that they will receive help in return.

Research on reciprocity has demonstrated that although this norm is strong, a number of situational factors determine whether behavior is guided by it. First, the desire to reciprocate depends upon the recipient's attribution of the helper's motives. People feel obligated to repay a favor only when the help given them was intentional and voluntary (Greenberg & Frisch, 1972). When help is either accidental or required, there is little reciprocity. Second, the tendency to reciprocate varies not so much with the absolute amount of help a person has received as with one's perception that the helper's efforts have incurred relative costs (Gergen et al., 1975). If the Rockefeller family sent you a $50 check to cover your hospital expenses, you would feel less gratitude than for the $10 collected on your behalf by a fourth-grade class.

While reciprocity is expected for many kinds of aid, sometimes it is inappropriate. In fact, in certain kinds of relationships the direct reciprocation of favors can almost be an insult (Clark, 1984). In an "exchange" relationship, such as that between business partners, when one person helps another there is an expectation that the favor will be repaid. In "communal" relationships, such as those between two close friends or between husbands and wives, giving is thought to be determined completely by the perception that the other person is in need. In this type of relationship, the sole idea behind giving is to make the other person feel good, not to get something in return. To reciprocate in kind devalues the gift of the first person. Clark and Mills (1979) demonstrated this by inducing either a communal or an exchange relationship between pairs of people. When individuals in an exchange relationship offered to reciprocate a favor, they were liked more; but when the relationship was seen as communal, people were liked better if they did *not* offer to reciprocate.

The Limitations of Norms Despite the widely acknowledged presence of norms as guides to social behavior, many researchers believe that norms have a very limited influence on actual helping. According to Latané and Darley (1970), one problem with norms is that they tend to be contradictory and vague. They are general, whereas each helping situation is specific. As a result, each instance may prove to be the exception to the rule. The mother who has taught her young child the virtues of charity is likely to be upset when she finds out that her son has given his piggy-bank savings to a panhandler. The norm says that "it is good to give"—but, then again, it is only good to give to some people under certain circumstances.

A second problem is that the norms in any given situation may conflict. The people who went to their windows at 3:20 A.M. to hear the cries of Kitty Genovese may not have been certain whether they were witnessing a quarrel or a murderer's attack. If they knew it to be an attack, the norm of social responsibility would lead them to intervene. But what if it was only a personal quarrel? If so, the norm of "mind your own business" might be more appropriate.

In summarizing their criticisms of the normative explanation, Latané and Darley state that "like the king of England, norms may reign, but not rule" (p. 27). By this they mean that everyone recognizes the symbolic power of norms, but their actual everyday power to regulate social behavior is small. Specific factors in each situation will determine behavior, so that norms, whether necessary or not, are hardly sufficient to explain helping.

Darley and Batson's (1973) study of help given by seminary students, described in Chapter 3, provides a vivid piece of research to demonstrate the limitations of a purely normative explanation of prosocial behavior. In that study, Darley and Batson created an ingenious situation in which highly moral young men were placed in a situation of great conflict. Rushing from one building to another while rehearsing a talk about the Good Samaritan, they were forced to decide whether to stop and help—to follow the norm—or to rush past the poor fellow so as not to disappoint the group of people who were waiting for them to deliver a talk. The results of this study show that the salience of the norm had only a slight effect on helping. The degree of hurry, a situational factor, had a strong effect that far outweighed the salience of the Good Samaritan norm.

Later, when questioned, many of the hurrying subjects who failed to help indicated their conflict and concern over what to do. Some said they planned to race through their talk and return to this poor fellow, while others said that they felt that the need of *many people* at the talk had to outweigh that of one needy person at the moment. To test whether this explanation was merely a rationalization for failing to help, Batson et al. (1978) varied the basic experiment somewhat. In this variation, one group of college undergraduates was told that they should hurry to another campus building, while the other group was told that there was no hurry. Within each group, half were made to believe that the need for their data was vital (the high importance condition) and half felt that it was not essential (low importance). As Figure 9.3 shows, the explanation offered by Darley and Batson's initial seminarians was supported. Those people who were late for a very important date helped only 10 percent of the time, whereas those for whom the data were less critical helped 70 or 80 percent of the time, regardless of whether they were in a hurry.

The criticism of the relationship of norms to helping bears a strong resemblance to the criticism brought against attitudes and their ability to predict behavior (as discussed in Chapter 5). In the case of norms, as in that of attitudes, we cannot expect vaguely stated, highly general norms to predict behavior in specific situations. In response to this, Shalom Schwartz (Schwartz & Howard, 1984) has developed an approach to

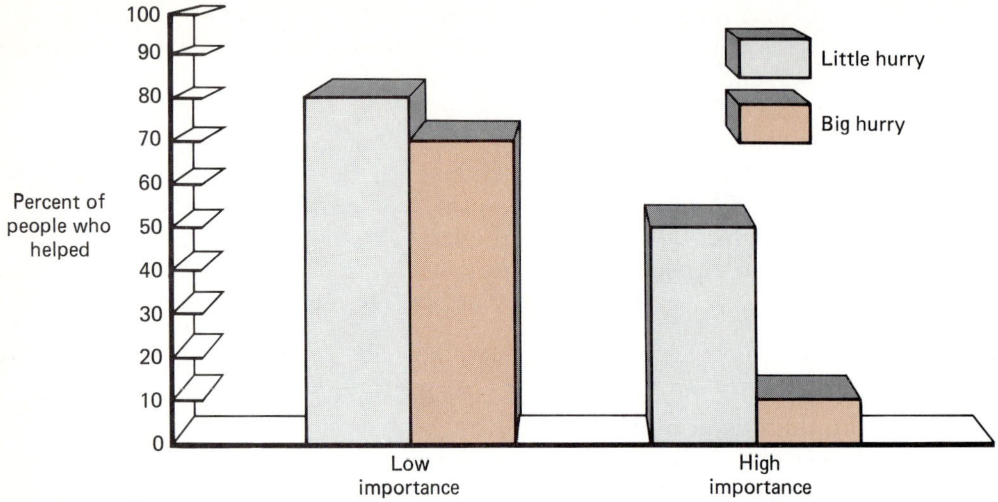

FIGURE 9.3

Percentage of People Who Offered Help to a Victim When people had something important to do and were in a hurry, very few (10 percent) stopped to help. *Source:* C. D. Batson, P. J. Cochran, M. F. Biederman, J. L. Blooser, M. J. Ryan, & B. Vogt (1978). Failure to help when in a hurry: Callowness or conflict? *Personality and Social Psychology Bulletin,4,* 99.

helping based on **personal norms.** Personal norms are "situation-specific behavioral expectations generated from one's own internalized values, backed by self-administered sanctions and rewards" (Schwartz & Howard, 1982, p. 329). According to Schwartz, the existence of personal norms accounts for why one person helps when another does not, even though both people are equally capable and the normative pressures in the situation are identical.

In summary, current research suggests that norms can play a role in determining helping behavior, but they are powerful only when defined at a personal level and when combined with situational factors. But where and how do people learn about these norms? In what way are they transmitted from person to person? In the next section, we investigate how children learn about helping, and consider the manner in which lessons about prosocial behavior are transmitted.

LEARNING TO HELP

Up until the age of 10, prosocial behavior seems to increase. A variety of reasons have been offered for this tendency, involving each of the motivating mechanisms discussed in this chapter. Aronfreed (1970) has suggested, for instance, that the capacity to feel empathy increases with age. Krebs, borrowing from Kohlberg's (1981) stage theory of moral reasoning, has pointed out that as children's ability to structure the world gets more complex, self-centered thinking becomes less common and children act in accord with higher-order moral principles (Krebs, 1982; Krebs & Gilmore, 1982). Others have pointed to the child's increasing awareness and internalization of norms involving social responsibility.

The Importance of Modeling

The power of *modeling* to influence behavior has received great attention in aggression research, but somewhat less in research on helping. Just as children model the aggressive content of television, children who watch programs that stress sharing and cooperation are more prosocially oriented (Rushton, 1980). Models remind us of the behavior that is appropriate in helping as well as harming. They show how to help, they inform us about the consequences of helping, and they reduce any inhibitions we may have against helping. The actions of a model may even show that helping can make us feel good.

The observation of helping models, especially parents, can have a strong effect on whether children grow up to be helpful adults. Hoffman (1975) has noted that fifth-grade children who were rated as highly altruistic had parents who rated altruism highly on their own personal hierarchy of values. Evidence is also provided by studies of adults who performed acts of great heroism or personal risk. Rosenhan (1970) interviewed young men and women who had spent a year or more in the American South working for the civil rights movement. He found that those who were most committed to this cause had warm, respectful relationships with at least one parent, and they reported that at least one of their parents had highly moral values.

London (1970) studied a very different group of helpers, Germans who risked their lives to shelter or rescue Jews during World War II. In a direct confirmation of Rosenhan's findings with civil rights workers, London found that all of these people also had a strong identification with at least one highly moralistic parent. One such rescuer from a family of poor farmers stated: "You inherit something from your parents, from your grandparents. My mother said to me when we were small, and even when we were bigger . . . 'regardless of what you do with your life, be honest. When it comes the day you have to make a decision, make the right one. It could be a hard one. But even the hard ones should be the right ones' " (p. 247).

Although the person just quoted emphasized what his mother told him to do, we may ask whether *preaching* altruism was sufficient to form her son's values, or whether she probably also provided a model for her son by *practicing* altruism. When the message parents relay to their children is "Do as I say, not as I do" (as when they warn us against the dangers of drug abuse with a second martini in hand), what is the effect?

Preaching Versus Practicing

What is more important in teaching children to be helpful, words or deeds? To investigate this question, Grusec and Skubiski (1970) had groups of third and fifth graders watch adults play a game and then donate to charity half of the marbles they had won. Other groups of students heard the models advocate that donating was a good idea, but they never had a chance to observe whether they actually gave or not. A third group did not observe a model at all. When the children then played the game themselves, those who had seen the model actually donate were themselves quite generous, but those who had only heard the model gave very little. In fact, these children gave no more on the average than did the control group.

Bryan and Walbek (1970) went one step further. In their research, young children watched a model who either verbally endorsed sharing, said that sharing was not good, or made a neutral statement. At the same time, half of the models in each of the three conditions actually donated and half refused. Thus some children observed a model who was either generous or stingy in word *and* deed, while others watched hypocrisy in action, a model who said that helping was important but did not help when asked. The results of this experiment indicate that the children's sharing *behavior* was affected far more by the models' deeds than by their words. Yet when the children had the opportunity to make a *verbal statement* to the next child, they repeated the model's rhetoric.

Therefore, if parents merely want their children to spout the norms, then they need only say that helping is important. If they want their children to act generously, then they need to act generously themselves. This research demonstrates that while children are capable of learning helping, they are also capable of learning hypocrisy. Parents who urge their children to share while they themselves do the opposite will most likely turn out children who do the same.

SEEKING AND RECEIVING HELP

Up to this point, our discussion of helping has been from the viewpoint of the helper. It is also important to consider helping from the point of view of the person in need. How does it feel to need help, to seek it, and to get it?

Gross and McMullen (1982) have generated a three-stage model of help seeking that resembles the Darley and Latané help-*giving* model as seen from the other side (see Figure 9.4). It begins with a set of events, conditions, or symptoms that a person recognizes. If they are seen to be normal or acceptable, then no help will be sought. Once they are defined as a problem, the individual has to weigh the possibilities. Will the problem go away by itself, can it be handled by self-help, or should help from

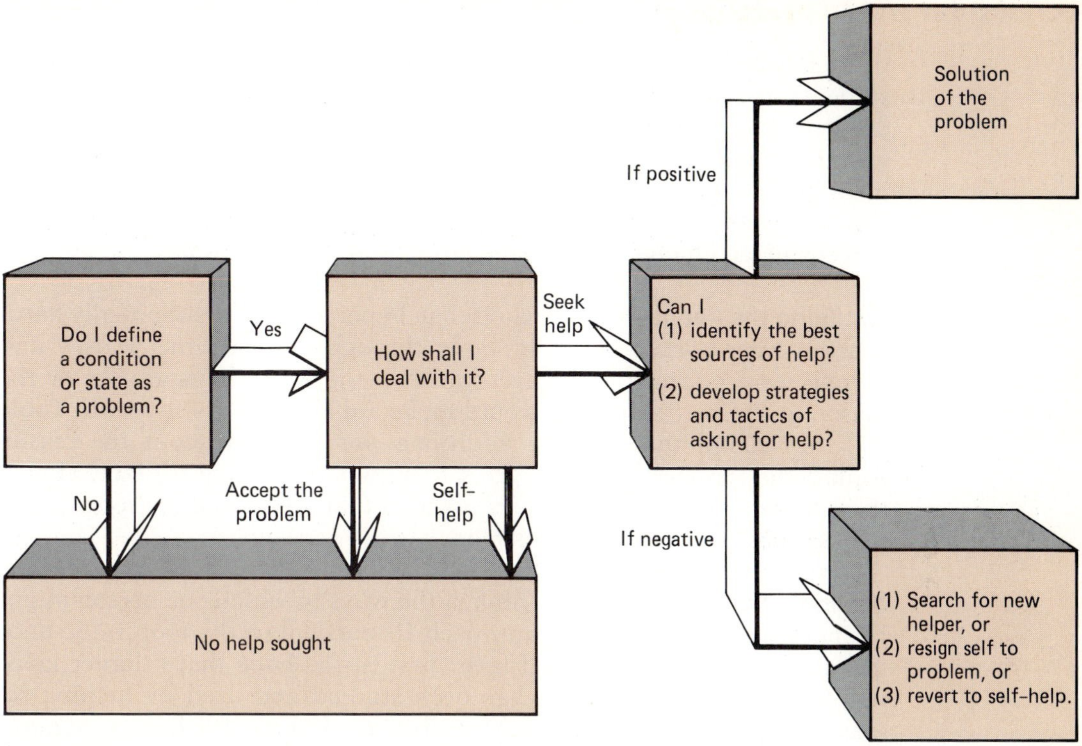

FIGURE 9.4
The Help-seeking Process The process of help seeking resembles the Latané and Darley model of help giving in several ways. In each, people must identify and define a need, choose to seek or give help, and then decide on a proper course of action to take. *Source:* Adapted from A. E. Gross & P. A. McMullen (1982). The help-seeking process. In V. J. Derlega & J. Grzelak (Eds.), *Cooperation and helping behavior: Theories and research.* New York: Academic Press, p. 312.

others be sought? Should I take some over-the-counter medication for that stomach pain that won't quit, or should I call my doctor? Should I go to a social service agency about my son's drug habit, or should I try to deal with it myself?

People may decide to deal with their problems by themselves for any number of reasons. They may believe in their own personal efficacy; they may feel that the costs of seeking help are too high; they may think that the available people or services are not suited to their needs; or any combination of these. Once they choose to seek help, they must decide *whom* to ask and *how* to ask. Both of these issues must be answered before help is sought and for help to be successful. In the next sections we will look at research done from the point of view of the help seeker, looking in particular at how to ask for help and how it feels to receive it.

Asking for Help

In their early research on helping, Latané and Darley (1970) had their students approach people in midtown New York City and ask for many different kinds of help, ranging from "What time is it?" to "Could you give me change for a quarter?" to "Excuse me, I wonder if you could give me a dime?" They found that the more effort or cost it took to help, the less help was given. Eighty-five percent of the people gave the time, 73 percent made change, and 34 percent actually gave a dime.

Justifying the Request Fascinated that 34 percent of the supposedly hard-hearted New Yorkers actually came through with a dime, Darley and Latané were curious to discover whether the way a person asks or the reason given for the request would make a difference. As shown in Table 9.2, they found that offering additional information about the reason behind the request produced great increases in helping. In fact, almost three-fourths of the New Yorkers asked actually gave a dime to someone who said his wallet had been stolen.

Getting a Foot in the Door Think of the ways in which one person might get help from another. One approach in particular, the foot-in-the-door technique—asking for a small favor first in the hope that a larger favor will be granted as a result—has been studied and used by helping researchers. In one foot-in-the-door study (Pliner et al., 1974), a large number of people in Toronto were asked to wear a lapel pin publicizing a cancer society drive, and were then approached the next day for a dona-

TABLE 9.2
Frequency of Response as a Function of Manner of Request

Manner of Request	Percent Helping
a. "Excuse me, I wonder if you could give me a dime?	34
b. "Excuse me, I wonder if you could give me a dime? I've spent all my money."	38
c. "Excuse me, I wonder if you could tell me what time it is? . . . and could you give me a dime?	43
d. "Excuse me, my name is ______. I wonder if you could give me a dime?"	49
e. "Excuse me, I wonder if you could give me a dime? I need to make a telephone call."	61
f. "Excuse me, I wonder if you could give me a dime? My wallet has been stolen."	72

Source: B. Latané & J. M. Darley (1970). *The unresponsive bystander: Why doesn't he help?* New York: Appleton-Century-Crofts, p. 11. Copyright © 1970. Reprinted by permission of Prentice-Hall, Englewood Cliffs, New Jersey.

tion. A control group was asked only to donate. While the rate of donating among the controls was 46 percent, among those who had agreed to the initial request—and all did—the rate was an impressive 74 percent.

Some people have suggested that the power of the foot-in-the-door technique is limited to helping acts that have few costs or are nonthreatening (Cialdini & Ascani, 1976; Foss & Dempsey, 1979). However, Carducci and Deuser (1984) have generated commitments of organ donations using this technique, and Schwartz (1970) has successfully demonstrated a refined version of this technique in getting students at the University of Wisconsin to agree to be bone marrow donors. Donating marrow is a painful and somewhat risky procedure calling for general anesthesia. Instead of asking for a simple favor and making the large leap to his critical request, Schwartz had people commit themselves to a series of graded requests that not only got a foot in the door but generated a psychological momentum that led to surprisingly high levels of commitment.

First, people were asked to give blood. All those who actually did were then asked to talk with a person about bone marrow donations for approximately 20 minutes. At the end of the discussion, they were asked whether they were willing to have the blood they had just donated tested for compatibility. Once they agreed to this, the interviewer said that it wasn't worth testing their blood unless there was a 50-50 chance that they would consider donating the marrow. After this, the key question was finally popped: Would they agree to be on call as donors? Although some people refused as the requests became more and more demanding, 80 percent of those approached agreed to this complex and potentially dangerous donation. Schwartz has therefore demonstrated that once a need has been justified, even complex and costly forms of aid can be generated using a step-by-step progression of requests. In the next section, we will see how these and other principles have been applied to an increasingly pressing need—getting people to donate blood.

APPLICATION
SEEKING HELP FOR A GOOD CAUSE: INCREASING BLOOD DONATIONS

Why do people give blood? There are certainly reasons not to: the procedure hurts a bit, it takes time, and few people like needles being placed in their skin. In addition to these costs, the rewards for donating are hardly immediate. Ninety-nine percent of the time, the donor does not even know how the blood is being used or for whom. Donating blood is, as Richard Titmuss (1971) has called it, "a free gift . . . to unnamed strangers" (p. 239). No wonder that hospitals and the Red Cross have so much difficulty in recruiting donors. Let us look at the ways that the social psychological principles relevant to prosocial behavior can be applied to understand blood donation and, as a result, to increase the number of people who become regular donors.

Piliavin, Evans, and Callero (1982) have suggested that many different pressures, both internal and external, lead people to donate blood. Personal norms concerning one's moral obligation and altruistic concern constitute the "pulls," the positive aspects of donating, that make people want to give. But they are usually not enough. There must also be "pushes," in the form of external pressures or the arousal of a sense of group or community responsibility. For instance, first-time donors typically come in with a friend who has given before.

According to Piliavin and her colleagues (Piliavin, Callero, & Evans, 1982; Piliavin & Callero, 1983), there is a series of three steps a person must go through to become a regular blood donor. The first is generating an *intention* to donate. The second step is getting the person to *act* on that commitment and actually show up to donate. Thirty-five to 40 percent of those who volunteer do not actually show up when it comes time to donate (Pittman et al., 1981; Foss & Dempsey, 1979). The third step involves getting people into the *habit* of donating, thereby making blood donation a regular, ongoing behavior for them.

Step 1: Getting a Commitment. Mass media campaigns often emphasize humanitarian concerns and appeal to people's altruistic motives in order to get them to donate blood. This is probably necessary to make people want and intend to help, but it is not sufficient. Donors and nondonors differ only slightly in their commitment to altruistic values, and not at all in social responsibility. The factors that differentiate these two groups are external, such as costs, social pressures, and incentives for donating (Condie, Warner, & Gillman, 1976). The use of modeling is another suggested technique; friends are likely to imitate one another when one agrees to donate.

Step 2: Getting the Donation. One way of getting people to show up involves neutralizing the constraints or inhibitions associated with giving. Since fear is the most mentioned reason for not donating (Oswalt, 1977), attitude change attempts can be made to convince people that the donation process is not painful or dangerous. A second recommendation is to reduce the amount of time between volunteering and donating. The closer the commitment is to the act itself, the less the dropoff from one to the other. Also, helping models can be effective in getting people not only to volunteer but actually to donate (Rushton & Campbell, 1977) by creating the impression that donating blood is common (i.e., normative). Foss (1983) found that on campuses with successful blood drives, students believed that a feeling of obligation to give was widespread among their peers.

Step 3: Getting the Habit. Whether we are concerned about maintaining an adequate supply of blood or about getting enough monetary donations to maintain a scholarship fund or a public television station, a supply of regular donors is needed. But how does a "rookie" donor come to be a "regular"? In their "blood, sweat, and fears" project, Piliavin, Evans, and Callero (1982) found that in order to become a regular, a donor's reasons had to become internalized. Regular donors seemed less concerned with pain and inconvenience, and were more motivated by an altruistic desire to give. After the first donation, instead of asking, "Why should I give?" those people who had become regulars changed the question to, "Why not?" What distinguishes the people who get hooked on donating is not any specific personality trait. Rather, as mentioned earlier, those who become regulars incorporate blood donating into their self-concepts, and come to label themselves as donors. More important than the approval or disapproval of others, they themselves would disapprove if they stopped giving.

Is it possible to affect people's self-images to lead them toward a "career" of helping? Although it would be difficult, research by Paulhus, Shaffer, and Downing (1977) suggests that it may be possible, especially with those who have given blood previously. These researchers led one group of blood donors to think about the altruistic component of helping, while another group thought only about the personal benefit involved. Veteran donors who were led to attribute their motives to an altruistic personal orientation expressed a stronger likelihood of donating in the future than those whose initial attribution involved personal gain. It would seem, therefore, that basic social psychological principles can be applied not only to the commitment and intention to donate, but in getting people to attribute altruistic motives to themselves, thereby making them committed to helping in the long run (Foss, 1986).

Receiving Help: The Hidden Costs

Although we have focused on how to get help when in need, we should recognize that not all needy people ask for help even when there are no great costs involved. For instance, according to the health belief model, whether patients seek out medical care depends on their perception of their susceptibility to disease, the seriousness of their condition, and the potential benefits and barriers they may encounter (Eraker, Kirscht, & Becker, 1984). Even when help is sought and given, some recipients may respond with appreciation and gratitude while others become angry and resentful. Negative reactions to receiving help have been observed among disabled war veterans (Nadler, Sheinberg, & Jaffe, 1982), the aged (Kalish, 1967), people on welfare (Goodwin, 1972), and Third World nations (Gergen & Gergen, 1974).

Why do people sometimes seek out help and other times avoid it, sometimes appreciate help and others times resent it? Jeffrey Fisher, Arie Nadler, and their colleagues (Nadler & Fisher, 1984; Fisher, Nadler, & Whitcher-Alagna, 1982), who have done extensive research on recipient reactions to aid, have proposed several possible explanations for why helping may not always be appreciated.

The first explanation focuses on the concept of *reactance*. As discussed in Chapter 2, people react negatively whenever someone else's behavior appears to limit their freedom (Brehm & Brehm, 1981). Therefore, whenever help comes with strings attached, people will resent it. For instance,

Briar (1966) found that many welfare families felt that receiving public assistance limited their freedom and put them at the whim of the system. Two-thirds of those interviewed believed that, because they were on welfare, their social workers could make surprise visits to their homes in the middle of the night.

A second explanation focuses on the concept of *equity*. As discussed in Chapter 7, people weigh the fairness of a relationship by comparing the ratio of what they get from it (outcomes) to what they brought to it (input). When people receive aid, their ratio of inputs to outcomes may seem unfair compared to those of the donor, and they may seek to avoid the inequity by refusing the aid. If they receive aid anyway and cannot restore equity physically (i.e., by repayment), they are likely to restore it psychologically. They may come to feel that the aid was already owed to them (Gergen & Gergen, 1974) or that the aid is worthless in the first place (Castro, 1974).

An attributional approach emphasizes the desire of recipients to understand the behavior and motives of the giver. It proposes that people ask not only why help was offered, but also why help was offered to *them*. When the attribution for one's own need is *internal*, (e.g., "I cannot help myself"), help is experienced as threatening and unpleasant. When the need for help can be attributed to *external* causes (e.g., bad luck), then the reaction is more positive. Liem (in press) has reported that unemployed workers often attempt to avoid receiving help in the form of personal counseling, because it is seen as an admission of self-blame and an acknowledgment that they are unable to handle their problems on their own.

Finally, the *self-esteem* approach suggests that help can be threatening if it implies that the donor is superior to the recipient. Welfare families and underdeveloped countries sometimes refer to being "robbed of their dignity" and resent the help they are given. They feel that help comes with the message that they cannot be counted on to be self-reliant and independent. Figure 9.5 summarizes the conditions that lead to supportive and nonsupportive helping and the reactions of recipients when help is perceived defensively and nondefensively. It shows that when help is offered voluntarily, involves "costs" to the helper, and allows the recipient a chance for repayment, it provides support for the recipient's self-esteem. Such help is seen as supportive rather than threatening, and those who offer it are usually liked and appreciated. This advice applies as much to foreign aid as to flood victims or the poor.

FORMAL HELPING RELATIONSHIPS

In discussing the costs as well as the benefits of giving and receiving aid, we have moved away from emergency situations and simple one-to-one assistance and toward help giving in more formal systems. Such help can

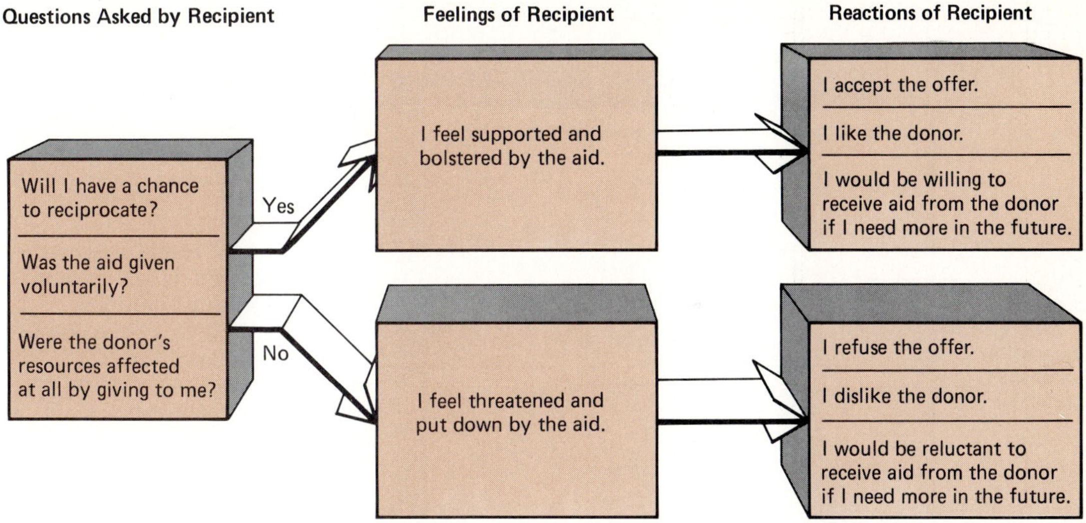

Questions Asked by Recipient
Feelings of Recipient
Reactions of Recipient
Will I have a chance to reciprocate?
Was the aid given voluntarily?
Were the donor's resources affected at all by giving to me?
Yes
No
I feel supported and bolstered by the aid.
I feel threatened and put down by the aid.
I accept the offer.
I like the donor.
I would be willing to receive aid from the donor if I need more in the future.
I refuse the offer.
I dislike the donor.
I would be reluctant to receive aid from the donor if I need more in the future.

FIGURE 9.5
Recipient Reactions to Aid When aid is given so that it provides support for the recipient's self-esteem, it is welcomed and appreciated. But when aid threatens self-esteem, it generates a defensive reaction. *Source:* Adapted from J. D. Fischer, A. Nadler, & S. Alagne (1982). Recipient reactions to aid. *Psychological Bulletin, 91,* 27–54.

be given by doctors, nurses, and pharmacists in hospitals or clinics, or by social workers or social service agencies in the community (as well as a host of other trained professionals).

Orientations to Problems and Solutions

When faced with a person in need, professional helpers must define the nature of the problem and, in doing so, decide on the best course of action to take. Is the person in need of treatment, education, and encouragement, or simply lacking in the means (e.g., money or tools) to overcome problems alone? Although the reasons for one course of action or another are not often recognized, Brickman et al. (1982) point out that this is determined by the answer to two basic questions: Who is responsible for the *problem;* and who is responsible for the *solution?* Restated in terms of attribution theory, these questions ask (1) whether we attribute the causes of the problem to the person or the situation; and (2) whether we attribute the responsibility for the solution to the person in need or to someone else. When we look at these two issues jointly, we generate four fundamentally different orientations toward people and their problems (see Figure 9.6). For each orientation, let us consider how the answers to these two questions lead a helper to take a different role and set of actions in assisting those in need.

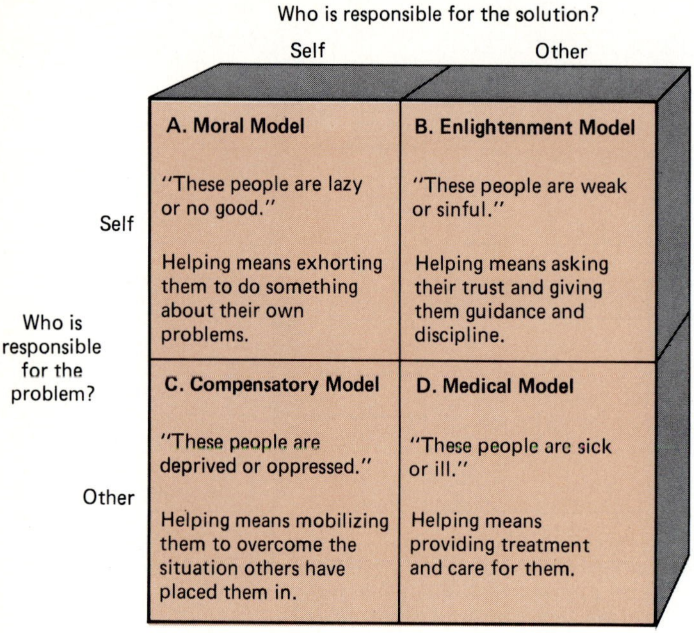

Who is responsible for the solution?
Self
Other
Who is responsible for the problem?
Self
Other
A. Moral Model
"These people are lazy or no good."
Helping means exhorting them to do something about their own problems.
B. Enlightenment Model
"These people are weak or sinful."
Helping means asking their trust and giving them guidance and discipline.
C. Compensatory Model
"These people are deprived or oppressed."
Helping means mobilizing them to overcome the situation others have placed them in.
D. Medical Model
"These people are sick or ill."
Helping means providing treatment and care for them.

FIGURE 9.6
Four Models of Helping According to Perceived Responsibility for Problems and Solutions
Whenever we face a situation in which people are in need of some sort of formal aid, the type of help given depends on how we come to answer two questions: Who is responsible for the problem, and who is responsible for the solution? *Source:* Adapted from P. Brickman et al. (1982). Models of helping and coping. *American Psychologist, 37,* 370.

Cell A, the moral orientation, is one in which people are thought to be responsible not only for their problems but also for the solutions. This is a view that has historically been held of alcoholics and criminals. The orientation here is: You did this to yourself, now get yourself out of it. The role of the helper is to encourage and exhort people to take responsibility, to bring them to face and solve their problems. The potential shortcoming of seeing people in this way is that it may not always be appropriate and may lead to victim blaming. For instance, victims of rape are often accused of having "chosen" to be raped, and victims of cancer may be told that they are "not trying hard enough" to recover. In the former case, we may be holding the person too responsible for the problem; in the latter, we may be holding the victim too responsible for the cure.

When helpers see others as in Cell B, the enlightenment model, they take the position that people are responsible for their problems but not for solving them. Those in need are seen as weak, guilty, or sinful and must submit to the sympathetic discipline supplied by helpers as authorities. This is the message of Alcoholics Anonymous: Admit that drinking is your fault, not someone else's, that you do not have the power to control it; and we will help you to cope with it. This kind of thinking has the benefit of placing the person in the midst of fellow sufferers who support and assist the person. But it may place too much authority and power in the hands of helping agents who may require complete allegiance, as

In this photo, a speech pathologist is helping a deaf child learn to speak by having him "feel" the vibrations of a certain sound. This is an example of a formal helping relationship.

when leaders of cult religions require their followers to trust them absolutely.

Cell C, the compensatory model, takes the stance that people are not responsible for their problems, but are responsible for overcoming them nonetheless. It is captured by the Reverend Jesse Jackson's statement to black people: "You are not responsible for being down, but you are responsible for getting up." Helpers who look at people in need from this viewpoint offer them a good deal of self-respect by not blaming them and by encouraging them to seek change rather than sympathy. A drawback of this orientation is that it seems inequitable to have to pull oneself out of a hole one did not dig. "If *they* caused the problem," such a person might ask, "then why don't *they* find the solution?" People who are helped according to this model may come to feel resentful and pressured.

Cell D represents the medical model, and is typical of the approach of the health care system in modern societies. According to this model, those in need are told they are not responsible for either their problems or the solutions to them. The helper says, "You are sick and I will make you better." This approach has the advantage of not blaming people for problems or circumstances that are beyond their control, but it has the potential disadvantage of fostering dependency. For instance, as we noted in Chapter 2, hospital patients and nursing home residents often come to feel a loss of control and sense of helplessness from being treated as passive objects who are not responsible for helping themselves get better (Taylor, 1986). Many people want and need a relationship that is more active, and want to be a part of caring for themselves or of effecting a cure.

Mental Illness: Whose Problem, Whose Solution?

The case of mental illness provides a perfect example by which to demonstrate that the model used to define the problem determines what kind of help will be given—and sometimes even whether help is given at all (Farina & Fisher, 1982). From the Middle Ages through the eighteenth century, people who acted in ways that were considered different or strange were thought to be possessed by evil spirits. Seen according to the moral model, they could be (and were) tried in a court of law and sentenced to die. During the Salem witch trials in seventeenth-century Massachusetts, people were tortured or hung because it was decided that they had chosen to practice witchcraft (i.e., were responsible for the problem) and refused to repent (would not assist in the cure).

Around the beginning of the nineteenth century, the medical model began to dominate our thinking about sanity and insanity. By stating that deviants were not evil, but rather sick, it absolved them of responsibility for their current state and entitled them to a course of *treatment* rather than *punishment*. This approach has been criticized in this century by those (e.g., Szasz, 1984) who believe that placing the label "sick" on those with problems discourages them from taking responsibility for their actions. Such critics suggest that we ought to use the compensatory model. That is, we should not blame those who have problems, but encourage them to cope actively with the stresses of everyday life.

To generalize from this discussion, we can see that the way in which potential helpers perceive their roles and the plight of those in need will determine the amount and type of help offered. When we believe that people are responsible for their problems, we often stigmatize, punish, or avoid them rather than help them. But when we believe their circumstances are not their fault, we are more likely to feel a sense of sympathy and empathy, and be willing to offer help.

At the beginning of this chapter, we asked whether the legal system could do anything to get people to help one another. Now, on the basis of our discussion of social psychological principles and research, we can look at what the law can and cannot do and consider ways in which person-to-person techniques might have advantages over a legal approach.

What can the law do? For one thing, it might provide penalties for not helping. Unlike most states in this country, duty-to-rescue laws exist in France, West Germany, and at least 11 other European countries. Had Kitty Genovese been attacked on the streets of Paris rather than New York, 38 people might have been found guilty of the "crime" of not helping. Yet according to the available evidence concerning legal penalties for not helping, such laws have had limited impact (Zeisel, 1966).

Still, the law can take other routes. In particular, laws can influence bystanders' perceptions of rewards and costs; they can affect the calculus of helping. First, legal inhibitions to helping might be removed. For instance, what happens if a person attempts to help and only makes matters worse? What would happen if the fisherman had fallen in, was struggling toward the shore, and in trying to help you hit him on the head with a life preserver and caused him to drown?

Doctors who come upon the scene of an accident often report a great deal of ambivalence over whether to stop. They feel a personal and professional obligation to render aid, yet they hesitate for fear that the victim or victim's family will sue them for negligence if their help is not successful (D'Amato, 1975). The response to this has been for many states to pass Good Samaritan statutes which shield physicians (and in some states anyone who offers aid in good faith) from liability for negligence when they voluntarily stop to help an accident victim. By reducing the potential costs while holding constant the rewards, laws can encourage helpers to get involved.

Rather than reducing costs, a second legalistic approach that can be taken is to encourage helping by increasing rewards. Although direct rewards are rarely provided, there are some notable exceptions. The Carnegie Hero Fund provides medals for acts of bravery and sacrifice, and sometimes even offers monetary compensation if a rescuer is injured or killed. Sometimes private organizations provide rewards for information leading to the capture of a criminal, such as the $140,000 offered in Los Angeles for information leading to the arrest of the Hillside Strangler. Although he recognizes that such a system might not be practical, Kaplan (1972) has suggested that we generate a "Good Citizens' Lottery" in which people who had helped others over and above the call of duty would be eligible for bonuses provided by the government.

These examples suggest that legalistic approaches might be effective by influencing individuals' reward-cost calculations. But what might account for the limits of their influence on helping? Three major factors argue against the effectiveness of helping laws. First, if help is needed in an emergency because no one in authority is present, then no one there can monitor the help giving either. Without monitoring, neither rewards nor costs can be imposed. Second, formal rules may invoke social norms, but they still cannot regulate or change the *internal* sense of obligation people feel toward one another. If people are not motivated by personal norms or empathy with another's plight to begin with, the power of external penalties or positive inducements cannot make up for that lack. Third, laws are powerless to influence the characteristics of situations in which the need for help occurs. They cannot reduce the ambiguity of a situation, nor can they keep responsibility in an emergency from diffusing among onlookers.

One simple piece of research (Moriarity, 1975) illustrates some things people could do to increase helping that laws cannot. At a crowded beach, an experimenter put down his towel and his portable radio. After putting on some rock music he turned to the person nearest him and either asked for a match or explained that he was going to the boardwalk. He then asked, "Would you watch my things?" After he left the scene, another member of the experimental team came along, snatched up the radio, and began to walk away with it. When no prior commitment to help was made, only 20 percent of the neighbors made any attempt to do something about the theft. When people had made a casual agreement to be responsible, 95 percent did something, often grabbing the thief by the arm and pulling the radio away from him.

How is it that a simple act of commitment accomplished something that no legislature could? By making his request, the person guaranteed that the potential helper would notice, focused responsibility on a single individual to help, made salient general (and perhaps personal) norms of social responsibility, and very likely encouraged a we-ness, or empathic feeling, between himself and the stranger. While getting help is not always this simple or successful, this experiment does make clear that the principles of social psychology can be directly applied to increasing the amount of helping people give. These principles, it should be noted, can be used not only by legislators or policymakers, but also by the average person who might need help or want to give it.

SUMMARY

1. Helping (or prosocial) behavior involves any act that is done on behalf of another person. Helping acts may be planned or unplanned, involve large risks or none at all, and may or may not be motivated by the hope of a reward.
2. Altruism is a special type of helping in which a person acts without any expectation or desire of reward or recognition. Sociobiologists suggest this tendency may be passed on genetically, but others believe it is a product of social rather than biological evolution.
3. Attempts to find a "helping personality" have not been successful. Instead, it is believed that different kinds of people are motivated to help in different situations.
4. Latané and Darley have devised a four-step model of helping. They believe that in order for help to occur, (1) an event must be noticed and (2) defined as an emergency. Then (3) an individual must take personal responsibility, and (4) find a satisfactory form of intervention.
5. The presence of others often leads a situation to be defined as a nonemergency and creates a diffusion of responsibility. According to the diffusion of responsibility principle, the more people who are

available to help, the less pressure there is on any single individual to help.

6. Helping can be analyzed according to the rewards and costs for intervention and nonintervention. According to a model devised by Piliavin and Piliavin, the most direct help is given when the need is high and costs are low. When both rewards and costs are high, indirect help may be given. Otherwise people may choose to avoid the situation physically or cognitively (by blaming the victim).
7. Several variables serve as immediate and specific predictors of helping. Empathy with the victim leads to a sense of a "we-ness" and increases the likelihood of helping. Guilt and good mood also serve as positive motivators.
8. Norms such as the norm of social responsibility and the norm of reciprocity may also increase helping. Research has demonstrated, however, that situational variables are often more important than norms. Schwartz has suggested that personal norms, which are situation-specific and internalized, serve as better predictors of helping.
9. One important way in which children learn to help is by modeling. Children especially imitate the deeds of models, so it is important to practice helping, regardless of what is preached.
10. Those in need of help do not always seek it. Instead they may accept their problems or try to deal with them on their own. If help is desired, it is best to focus attention on one's need and to offer a good explanation for one's need, or to ask for a smaller request first (the foot-in-the-door technique).
11. Help may not always be appreciated by the recipient. For instance, if there is no opportunity to repay a favor, people may resent the feeling of indebtedness. If helping comes with strings attached or is seen as a threat to self-esteem, it will be responded to in a defensive manner.
12. Formal helping relationships may be defined according to any of four models: moral, compensatory, medical, or enlightenment. These models vary according to who is responsible for the problem and who is responsible for the solution. Each model leads to a different perception of those in need, and results in the offering of different kinds of assistance.

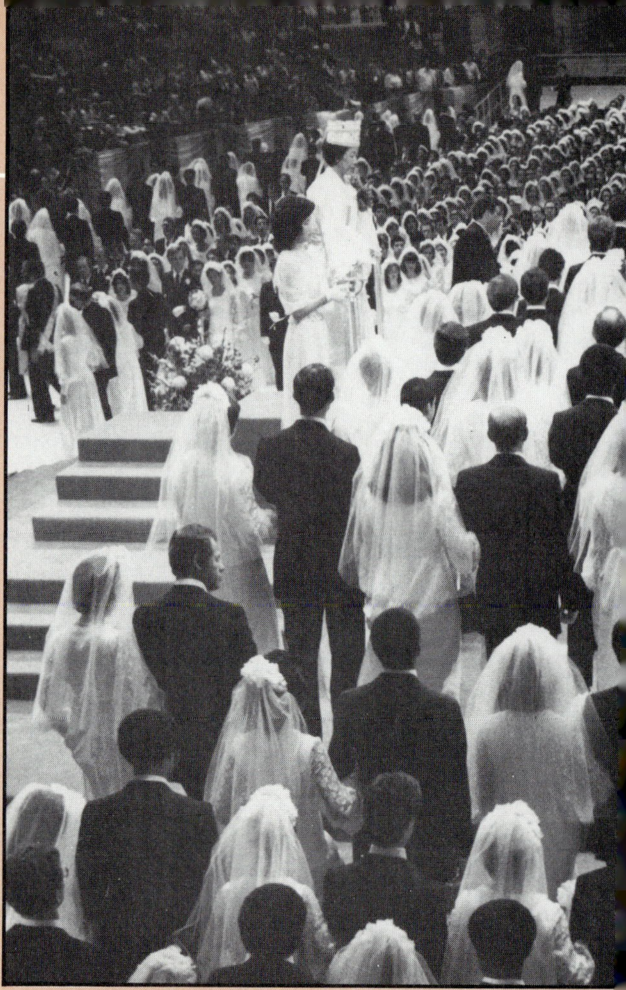

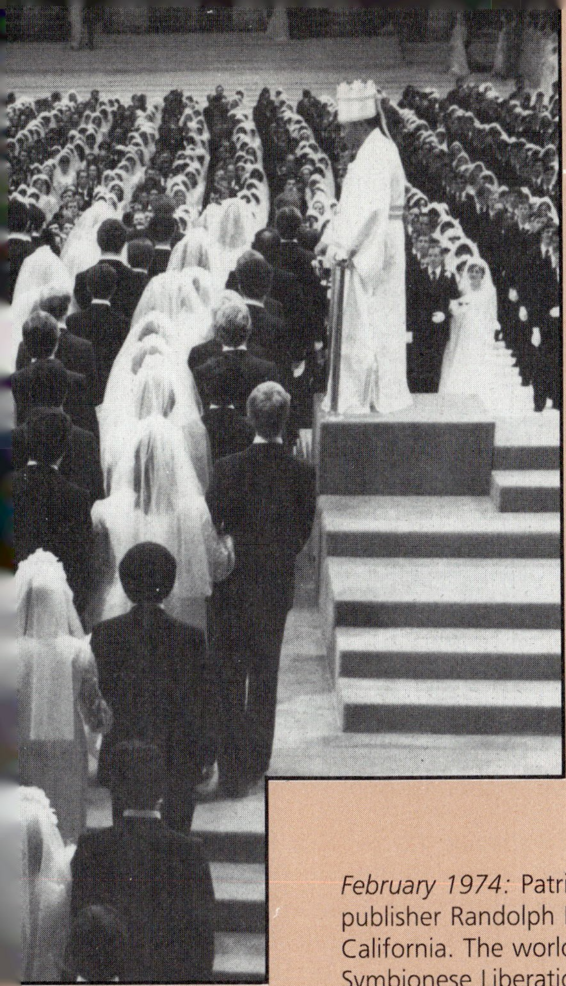

CHAPTER 10
Social Influence

February 1974: Patricia Hearst, the 19-year-old daughter of millionaire publisher Randolph Hearst, is kidnapped from her apartment in Berkeley, California. The world soon learns that her abductors are members of the Symbionese Liberation Army, a small, violent radical group. Less than two months later, Patty Hearst, reborn an urban guerrilla and newly named Tania, announces that she is staying with the SLA of her own accord. After having assisted in at least one bank robbery, she is finally captured by the police. Pleased that she is safe, but perplexed by her newly adopted radical values, her father wonders how she could have been so rapidly transformed except through brainwashing, drugs, hypnosis, or some other exotic influence technique.

April 1977: A California appeals court rules that the parents of five Moonies, followers of the Reverend Sun Yung Moon, cannot take custody of their children in order to remove them from the cult and change their attitudes. In spite of the court's findings, other parents who believe that their children have been changed through drugs and lack of sleep continue to hire professional "deprogrammers." They assert that they will use any means to recapture their children's minds from these "psychological kidnappers."

November 1978: Nine hundred and eleven people, all members of the People's Temple in Jonestown, Guyana, commit mass suicide. Their leader, the Reverend James Jones, calls them all together and directs them to swallow a cyanide-laced drink in the cause of "revolutionary suicide." Although a handful of people refuse and either escape or are killed, the vast majority commit the ultimate act of obedience. It is proposed that these followers must have been under the influence of mass hypnosis or some other unusual force to follow like sheep when the Reverend Jones ordered them to die en masse.

Most people are shocked and amazed to hear of such extreme and dramatic cases, and wonder how such changes and commitments could ever be accomplished. Could it be that the SLA, Reverend Moon, and James Jones have knowledge of bizarre techniques that are known to only a few? Did they accomplish their ends by means of drugs or the threat of bodily harm? Or could it be that the methods used by these "brainwashers," while applied more intensively, are basically no different from those that authorities use to influence citizens, and friends use to influence one another, every day? We will address the basic principles of social influence, and then we shall return to this issue to see how such principles can be applied to the understanding of brainwashing and conversion.

In this chapter we will discuss *social influence,* the process by which an individual's attitudes, beliefs, or behaviors are modified by the presence or actions of others. As we will see, change can come from many different sources and take many different forms. For instance, people may be influenced by another person's expertise; by the desire to be like, or to be liked by, someone else; or even through the use of threats. The changes that result may take the form of deep-seated conversion, or may occur only on the surface. One form of social influence, **conformity,** involves pressures that members of a *group* place on an individual to go along with them. We will see that groups can exert pressures on their members not only to act in accord with them but also to see the world as they do. A different form of social influence, **obedience,** involves pressures toward change that are exerted by a figure of authority. We will note just how difficult it is to resist authority, and discuss the factors that lead to greater or lesser obedience. Finally, we will balance our picture of social influence by noting that influence is a two-way street, and that sometimes successful pressure can be exerted on the many by the few or on the powerful by the weak.

THE DYNAMICS OF SOCIAL INFLUENCE

When people accept influence from one another, they may simply be going along, not really believing in what they are doing; or they may be true believers who fully believe everything they do and say. On a jury, a guilty vote carries as much weight whether the juror "truly" believes it or not.

But in thousands of other situations it matters greatly whether private acceptance accompanies public conformity. If your doctor or your friends try to pressure you to lose weight, you may tell them you will really try to do so, but mouthing the words and not the food may be two different things.

Processes of Social Influence

Herbert Kelman (1961) has pointed out that when we accept influence, three different processes can be involved. We may change for many different reasons, and, depending upon our relationship to the influencer, the nature of the situation, and a number of other factors, change can be surface and temporary or deep and long-lasting. For instance, during the Korean War some POW's collaborated with their captors to get better treatment, but reverted to their original beliefs as soon as they were free. But others, as we noted in the opening examples, really come to believe what they say and do under another's influence.

The first process Kelman talks about is **compliance.** Compliance involves accepting the influence of another person in order to receive social and material rewards or to avoid social and material punishments. People comply to get a favorable reaction, to be approved of by someone else. It matters little what they really believe as long as they sound sincere. For example, in a fraternity or a job interview, people are usually careful to express only the "correct" opinions, knowing they might get bounced out if they do not say what the other person hopes to hear.

We comply with people only when they have the ability to control rewards and punishments and when they can directly observe our behavior. If a supervisor at work walks up to a person with paycheck in hand, saying, "You like your job, don't you"? the answer *yes* is likely to be forthcoming regardless of what the person really believes.

Trying to influence people via compliance has definite limitations. First, the influencer truly must be able to deliver the rewards or punishments. A mugger holding a gun usually gains compliance, but if the victim finds out that the gun is not loaded, the need to comply is gone. Second, the influencer must be able to observe the behavior involved. A person's boss might promise to give him a promotion if he votes for her in the local election. There is no doubt about her ability to deliver on this promise, but can she exercise surveillance over the actual behavior? The employee could tell her he will vote for her, but once inside the privacy of the booth, he might do as he pleased.

A second type of influence, **identification,** differs from compliance in that it emphasizes accepting influence in order to *be like* or to *feel like*—to identify with—a person or group. The process of growing up involves identification with parents and acceptance of their values and ways of acting. As people get older and the sources of influence in their world broaden, they identify with and model their behavior after other students, teachers, celebrities, and public figures. For instance, many advertising campaigns take advantage of the desire to be like glamorous stars or famous athletes. People can also identify with groups ranging from a high school team to a local street gang to a political party. As we will note later, the feeling of belonging is critical for many people who get involved in social causes or cultist religions. The message takes some form of "if you believe in us, you can be like us."

Change that results from the process of identification differs from change via compliance. When people identify, they actually believe in the action or attitudes adopted, and the influencer does not have to be present. Still, social influence accepted via identification remains tied to an external source, and is not deeply tied to the individual's internal value system. This occurs only when people change via Kelman's third process, internalization.

Internalization occurs when individuals accept information or change their behavior because the new behavior is consistent with other beliefs and values that they already hold. In order to get someone to internalize, influencers need not be *powerful* as in compliance, or *attractive* as in identification; they need only be *credible.* When people internalize, the new behavior eventually becomes independent of the external source; it becomes a part of them that will be expressed regardless of the presence of the influencer. Internalized behaviors are those to which people are most committed, and are also the most resistant to further changes from outside influences. Compliance, identification, and internalization fall at three points from one end of a continuum to the other. Compliance-based behaviors are most in need of surveillance, most likely to change, most externally anchored, and most likely to involve a discrepancy between what is seen in public and what is felt in private. Internalization-based behaviors are just the opposite, and identification is in the middle of the two.

Kelman's framework points out that whether people accept influence in the first place and whether that acceptance is permanent depends upon the kind of relationship that exists between the influencer and the person being influenced. That is, it depends on whether the one has "power" over the other, and on what kind of power that is.

Bases of Social Power

Power is, most simply, the potential to influence (French & Raven, 1959). Parents exert power over their children, teachers over their students, doctors over their patients; but in more subtle ways, children influence parents, students exercise control over teachers, and patients also manipulate and affect their doctor's behavior (see Chapter 4 for a discussion of the rights and obligations of role partners). But what are the bases of power that people hold? How and why do some kinds of power work? And what are the consequences of using different kinds of power?

John French and Bertram Raven (French & Raven, 1959; Raven, 1965; Raven & Kruglanski, 1970), in considering the concept of power in great detail, refer to six different types of power that an individual may use. In many ways their types of power and Kelman's processes of influence resemble one another, and in other ways French and Raven's work augments and extends Kelman's scheme (see Table 10.1 for a comparison of their two systems). The six types of power identified are reward, coercive, referent, legitimate, expert, and informational.

Reward Power People have reward power over others if they have the resources to supply them with something they want in exchange for acting in a desired way. The reward may be concrete, in the form of a raise or the promise of a future favor, or it may be more general, in the form of approval or affection.

Coercive Power This basis for influence is the flip side of reward power. The person who uses coercive power holds out the stick rather than a carrot. As with reward power, the form of punishment may be quite immediate and concrete (e.g., a punch in the mouth or a $50 fine), or it may be indirect and intangible (e.g., disapproval or a feeling of guilt).

Taken together, reward and coercive power induce the kind of change

TABLE 10.1
Comparison of French and Raven's Bases of Power and Kelman's Processes of Influence

Type of Power	Process of Influence
Reward power: ability to deliver rewards Coercive power: ability to deliver punishments	Compliance
Referent power: ability to act as a reference source against which other people can judge themselves	Identification
Legitimate power: occupying a position in the social structure that makes people feel obligated to go along	Related to compliance in that rewards and punishments are implied, but differing in that none must be given and there is no need for surveillance
Expert power: possession of superior knowledge	Related to internalization in that the induced behavior is accepted at the level of true belief, but differing in that it is accepted more on faith or respect for expertise rather than on actual agreement or understanding
Informational power: possession of information that agrees with the person's beliefs or values	Internalization

Kelman refers to as compliance. They produce only surface-level change and require surveillance on the part of the rewarder or punisher. The distinction between the use of reward versus coercion is an important one, however. People who use reward power may themselves come to be rewarding. People like others who give them rewards and may even come to identify with them. As a result, the consistent use of reward power may eventually lead to identification, and the changes induced would then be less superficial. When coercive power is used consistently, however, it often arouses resentment and anger. Basketball coaches who use constant coercion in the form of threats and put-downs of their players may find that some of them will resist changing or even transfer to other colleges. Thus coercive power is not likely to be a successful strategy in the long run.

Referent Power People hold referent power when the target of influence has a desire to be like them. A person with referent power may be attractive in some way, or may be similar to the other person. The target therefore uses the influencer as a "frame of reference," as a standard against which to evaluate his or her own behavior. When this form of power is used, the change resembles Kelman's process of identification. An interesting variation on this theme is the use of negative referent power, which involves influencing someone to be just the opposite of what another person is like or stands for. One unusual use of negative referent power is revealed in a story about a close local election with many undecided voters. According to the story, candidate X hired actors to go into local bars and become drunk and obnoxious. Upon leaving, each actor crudely yelled out, "And remember to vote for Y." While we do not know the eventual result and do not recommend this particular application, it is likely that some people reasoned, "If that is the kind of person who is for Y, then I will support X."

Legitimate Power People who have legitimate power occupy positions in the social structure that say that *(a)* they have the *right* to tell another person what to do, and *(b)* the other person has the *obligation* to go along. People who are influenced by another person's legitimacy do not have to be rewarded or threatened; when the request is made, they feel they ought to do what is asked. Legitimate power has limits, however. Your social psychology instructor has the right to ask you to buy this and possibly other books, to require you to read so many pages per week, and to spend time preparing for exams. You are influenced to do all these things with little complaint because of his or her legitimacy. But if that same instructor asks you to buy him or her a ham sandwich, that would be going beyond the limits of legitimacy and you most likely would not agree.

Expert Power The person who has expert power has the ability to influence another by virtue of superior knowledge or expertise. Doctors have many years of training, and people most often accept their advice because of their greater knowledge. The same could be said of people in other professions or of any other person with greater expertise.

Informational Power Informational power involves the ability to influence someone else on the basis of reasoning and fact. Theoretically, informational power is independent of the source, because a person is convinced by the strength of the explanation rather than by the characteristics of the person doing the convincing. Informational power resembles expert power in that in both types people change on the basis of another's knowledge or ideas. But it differs in one important way. With expert power people accept influence based on the other's recommendation, even though they might not fully understand it. For informational influence to occur, the suggestion must not only make sense but must also fit into a person's system of beliefs and values. For example, a doctor might tell a middle-aged man to avoid pickles and canned soups in order to improve his health. Regardless of whether he understands the reason behind the advice, the man is likely to go along. This is because of the doctor's *expert power.* However, if the patient is informed and fully understands that salty foods can cause high blood pressure and that eating them can lead to heart attacks, he is likely to go along with the recommendation, not because of its source but because of the *informational power* behind it.

Raven and others have tested and applied this system in both real-world (Raven & Haley, 1980) and simulated (Litman-Adizes, Raven, & Fontaine, 1978) situations; and these notions of social power have been applied to relationships as mundane as friends influencing each other and as lofty as the power of the presidency. For example, as part of a large-scale project on reducing the incidence of unnecessary and dangerous infections that patients get in hospitals, Raven and Haley described each of the six types of influence to almost 850 doctors and nurses in charge of infection control. These medical practitioners were asked how likely they would be to use each type of power in order to convince either a staff nurse or an attending physician to act in accord with the prescribed hospital policy. Overall, they found a strong preference for the use of informational power, followed by expert power. Reward and coercive power were far less preferred, and were used most often when someone of high status was influencing someone of lower status.

In summary, both Kelman and French and Raven point out that we must consider the relationship of the influencer to the target of influence to gain a full understanding of social influence. In any given relationship, each person may possess a number of different types of power and must decide which to use in order to be most successful.

APPLICATION
SWALLOWING THE BITTER PILL: COMPLIANCE AND MEDICINE

When one of the authors of this text came to teach at a college of pharmacy, a topic he heard discussed by students and faculty alike was that of compliance. "How wonderful," he thought, "they've heard about Kelman's three processes of influence here." Instead, he found that to health professionals, compliance means "the extent to which a person's behavior (in terms of taking medication, following a diet, or executing lifestyle changes) coincides with medical or health advice" (Haynes, Taylor, & Sackett, 1979). In this context, compliance occurs when you take your medicine or follow doctor's orders; noncompliance is when you don't.

Every day, thousands of people take time off from their busy routines to visit their doctors. After missing work, traveling well out of their way, or sitting in a waiting room for an hour or more, they are examined, tested, and diagnosed. Then the doctor gives them advice (e.g., "Watch your weight"), makes recommendations (e.g., "Go on a low-sodium diet"), and often prescribes medication ("Take the little yellow pills three times a day"). The people pay their bills, return to work, school, or family, and in a great proportion of cases ignore what the doctor has told them.

The rate of noncompliance, the failure to comply with a doctor's recommendation, can be as high as 92 percent, and 50 to 60 percent is just about average (Stone, 1979; DiMatteo & DiNicola, 1982). While the consequences of not taking one's medications are many and potentially life-threatening (e.g., recurrence of an infection, continuation of hypertension), the pure waste in terms of help not received is staggering. After all, medicines that only sit in bottles serve no useful purpose.

If we think of the relationship between doctor and patient as one involving attempts at social influence (the doctor is trying to induce the patient to change his or her behavior or to take the proper medications), then the coincidence between the two uses of the term *compliance* may lead us to some insights about social influence in the medical arena. First, we can begin to understand how health professionals try to influence their patients and why people do or do not take their recommendations. Second, we can suggest ways in which doctors and health professionals might use social psychological principles to influence their patients more successfully.

To begin, we have to ask whether one important reason for much medical noncompliance is that doctors rely too much on appeals to authority (i.e., legitimate power) or superior knowledge (expert power) rather than giving their patients a full understanding of their recommendations (informational power). In addition, doctors also tend to use vague and immediate threats about health (coercive power) which lead to compliance in Kelman's terms. In such cases, it would not be surprising to find the attempt to influence unsuccessful once the patient leaves the doctor's office and there is no surveillance. One type of power that a health practitioner might utilize but rarely does is referent power. This is surprising because the establishment of a good doctor-patient relationship seems to be a key factor in determining whether people are cooperative and satisfied with their treatment in general (Krupat, 1983, 1986).

Judith Rodin and Irving Janis (1982), in noting that doctors should use themselves as a positive reference source, have demonstrated the use of referent power to induce change via identification in weight reduction programs. They describe three phases in which referent power can be developed, used, and maintained to influence patients.

Phase 1: Establishing referent power. Practitioners can gain referent power in many ways. One is to point out the similarities between themselves and the patient, especially concerning values and beliefs. Another way is to encourage patients to talk about themselves and to offer positive feedback. The doctor who is warm and accepting of the patient's doubts and concerns will develop a relationship of cohesiveness and trust. Knowing that the doctor also has trouble saying no to chocolate cake makes a patient feel more at ease and less guilty for having succumbed in the past to caloric temptation.

Phase 2: Using referent power. Once referent power has been established, the practitioner can use it to motivate patients' behavior. At this point, providing a rationale behind the recommendations to be followed (i.e., utilizing informational power) can also be useful in preparing the patient for the difficulties and discomforts that come with treatment. Patients can be taught methods of coping with temptation, such as planning in advance what to buy in the market or what to order in a restaurant before they are bombarded by glorious culinary sights and smells. Most important, once referent power is established, patients know they can fall back on the practitioner for assistance and advice if they are having trouble.

Phase 3: Maintaining referent power. All too often the role of the practitioner seems to stop once the patient leaves the office or has initial success. Periodic personal contact through follow-up visits or even by phone can help ensure that changes that were accepted initially via identification eventually become internalized.

CONFORMITY: HOW THE GROUP INFLUENCES THE INDIVIDUAL

Social psychologists have been greatly interested in the kinds of power that people exert over one another on an individual basis. But the one topic in social influence that has been of greatest interest is *conformity,* the influence of the *group* on the individual. Conformity involves (1) a recognition that there is a discrepancy between a person's opinion or behavior and that of the group, (2) a consideration of the group's position or behavior, and (3) an acceptance of or movement toward that position.

The primary motivation behind conformity may be *normative* or *informational* (Deutsch & Gerard, 1955). When people accept normative influence, they are conforming to meet the expectations of group members and to be approved of by them. Stated simply, they are going along to be part of the group, to be liked and rewarded for not being different. When conformity is normatively motivated, there is a strong chance that the person's *public* conformity is not accompanied by *private* acceptance (i.e., it is mere compliance). When conformity is informationally motivated, however, the person changes because the group's position is accepted as evidence about reality. There is little concern with what the group will think, and more concern with whether its position is correct or incorrect. As a result, public conformity and private acceptance are likely to coincide when the motivation to change is informational. Although normative and informational influence can operate as separate forces, in most situations it is difficult to separate them. People are typically concerned both with not being different and with not being wrong.

If conformity involves going along with the group, then what is its opposite? While many people would say independence, a closer look suggests that these two terms are not simple opposites (see Figure 10.1). As we have noted, conformity involves an active consideration of the group's position and then an acceptance of it. The opposite form of behavior involves an equally strong consideration of the group's position, but the end result is rejection—in the extreme case, an acceptance of just the opposite behavior. This form of behavior has been called *anticonformity* (Hollander & Willis, 1967; Willis, 1965). Another word for it might be *rebelliousness*. By way of example, imagine a person about to walk outside

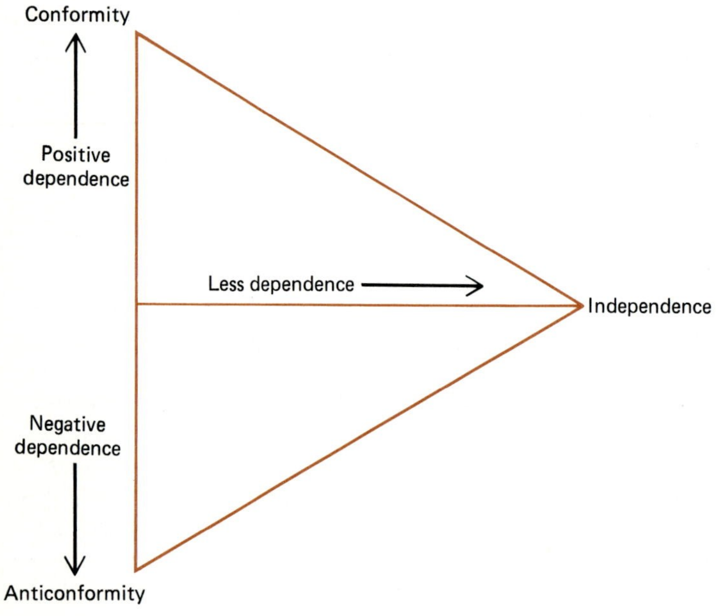

FIGURE 10.1

Conformity, Anticonformity, and Independence Conformity and anticonformity represent opposite ends of the scale because they both involve a reaction to the position of the group, either moving toward it (conformity), or away from it (anticonformity). An independent response gives no weight to opinion of the group either way. *Source:* E. P. Hollander (1981). *Principles and methods of social psychology* (4th ed.). New York: Oxford University Press, p. 230.

In spite of pressures to conform, there is usually at least one person in every crowd who manages to stand out.

a building when he or she notices that all the people in the street have umbrellas raised over their heads. To conform is to open the umbrella without even bothering to notice whether it is raining. To anticonform is to keep it closed no matter how much the rain is pouring down.

Conforming involves going along with the group, and anticonformity involves going against the group, but in both the person's response is tied to the others' behavior. **Independence,** on the other hand, means that the person is not automatically bound to the opinions or actions of others one way or the other. A more accurate term might be *non*dependence, because the person's final decision is nondependent on the opinions or actions of others. While the term *independence* is worth distinguishing from conformity and anticonformity, few of our actions are ever completely free of social influence. We are almost always affected in subtle or not so subtle ways by those around us, whether we realize it or not (Festinger, 1950; Latané & Nida, 1980).

If we think about the kinds of influence that take place when a jury hears a case, the three types of response—conformity, anticonformity, and independence—may all be represented at different points during a trial. While the trial is going on, the jurors are forbidden to talk to one another about the case. This is done so that each can come to an *independent* decision about the guilt or innocence of the defendant. Once the presentation is over and the deliberation begins, however, group pressures are exerted. Jurors then have the option of accepting the position of others (i.e., to conform), to consider the group's arguments but in the end to rely on their own judgment (to be independent), or to play devil's advocate (to anticonform).

Classic Studies in Conformity: The Research of Sherif and Asch

One of the most influential early researchers of conformity was Muzafer Sherif (1936). Making use of a phenomenon called the *autokinetic effect,* he began to study the way in which groups could affect the judgments of individuals. The autokinetic phenomenon is a visual illusion known among astronomers and experimental psychologists. If a person is placed in an absolutely dark room and is shown a stationary pinpoint of light, the light will appear to move (thus the name: *auto,* meaning self, and *kinetic,* meaning movement). The apparent motion occurs because people's eyes make small involuntary movements, and in a perfectly dark room they have no way to know that the movement is due to the seer and not the seen.

Sherif placed college students in a dark room either individually or in groups. He told them he would flash on a small light for a few seconds and it was their task to estimate the distance that the light moved. The correct answer, of course, was zero, but the light really did appear to move. "How much" was an ambiguous question because the students had nothing to judge the perceived movement against.

Sherif found that when individuals first gave their responses, their initial answers varied quite a bit. Over time, however, their answers were greatly influenced by one another and quickly converged around an average response, or "group norm." These results are directly in line with social comparison theory (see Chapter 3). When there is no obvious physical reality (i.e., the choice is ambiguous or unclear), people use others for comparison and are influenced by them. Other researchers (Jacobs & Campbell, 1961; Montgomery, Hinkle, & Enzie, 1976) followed Sherif's lead, sometimes using experimental confederates as members of the group. They showed that the group's effect could be demonstrated in other high-ambiguity situations such as the estimation of time (Montgomery and Enzie, 1971), and that as ambiguity grew so did the group's influence—sometimes to bizarre extremes. And even after those who had produced the influence were removed from the group, their influence often lingered.

A social psychologist who followed these studies with a sense of concern was Solomon Asch (1951). He believed that when put in a situation without any way of gauging the right answer, it was only natural to rely upon the responses of others. Yet many people were concluding from this kind of research that people were "conformers" in the most negative sense of the word. Therefore, in order to see whether people could disregard the group and rely strictly on themselves when it made sense to stick to their own opinions, he chose a clear-cut situation where right and wrong answers were obvious.

A participant in Asch's research arrives at a room along with six others for an experiment on the judging of lines. He (most of Asch's experiments

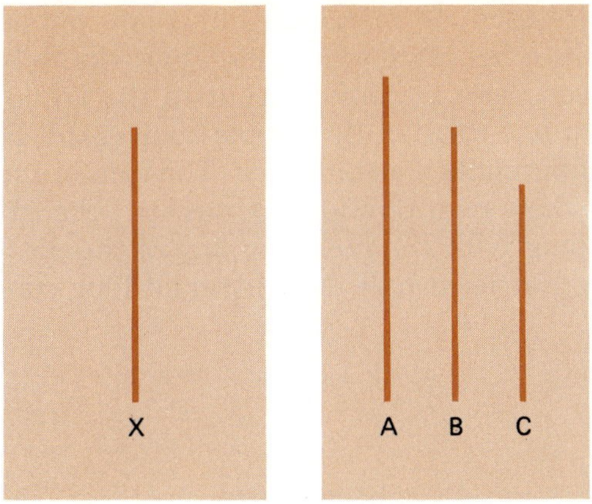

FIGURE 10.2
A Typical Set of Stimulus Lines Used by Asch
Participants in Asch's research were asked which of three lines, A, B, or C, was closest in length to line X. The experimenter's confederates gave obviously wrong answers—A in this case. Then the participants had to choose between the evidence of their eyes and the evidence of their ears.

involved males) sits down at a long table in the only available seat, which happens to be at the end of the table. The experimenter presents a card with a standard line (line X), and the participant's job is to decide which of three other lines, A, B, or C, is nearest in length to it, as in Figure 10.2.

The answer is obvious. Being at the end of the table, however, the person has to wait until all the others have given their answers before he can speak. The answer to the second card is equally obvious. When the third card appears, it is just as straightforward as the first two, but the first person quickly and casually gives an answer that is obviously incorrect. And then the next five respond the same way. Not knowing that the other six people are confederates of the experimenter and are giving the wrong answers on cue, the participant is placed in a difficult dilemma: to remain independent of the group and announce what his eyes tell him, or to go along with the group, thereby conforming to the unanimous majority.

Asch was asking the following question: Would people yield to the normative pressures ("I hate to appear so different from all the others. What will they think of me?") and the informational pressures ("They can't all be wrong; maybe I am"), or could they disregard the opinions of the group and remain independent, relying on their own perceptions? Although there was a wide range of reaction, Asch noted certain similarities between those who conformed and those who did not. Not one single person was indifferent to the confederates' responses. Some seemed confused and often asked the experimenter to repeat the instructions. All participants, even those who never conformed to the group's incorrect answers, expressed some measure of self-doubt, and many times they gave the correct answer with apologies.

Asch's experimental procedure has become a classic in the field because it is so simple and yet so powerful. It places people squarely between two forces—the group's opinion and their own senses—that are contradictory and irreconcilable, and it requires them to make an immediate public commitment in one direction or the other. Asch found that approximately one-third of all the responses given were in conformity with the group. This does not mean, however, that one-third of the people conformed. In fact, a wide range of individual differences was observed. Thirteen of the fifty students tested stayed with their own opinions throughout the experiment and never once went along with the group on any of the disagreement trials. Fifteen conformed at least half the time, and four conformed ten or more times.

Mediators of Conformity

As noted by Asch, not all people are equally subject to pressures from the group. In order to determine what factors affect conformity, social psychologists have studied numerous variables. In this section, we will consider how characteristics of the individual, task, group, and setting each act to increase or decrease conformity.

Characteristics of the Individual Just a few years after Asch conducted his experiments, Richard Crutchfield (1955) conducted similar research in which he investigated the relationship of personality to conformity. He placed 50 men in his own version of the Asch situation, gave them a whole battery of personality tests, and looked to see which scores were correlated with conformity. He found that those who conformed the most (referring to them as "overconformists") had less ego-strength, less ability to accept responsibility, less self-insight, less spontaneity, and more prejudiced and authoritarian attitudes.

While Crutchfield's early characterization of those who conform depicts them as weaklings, and is hardly flattering, subsequent research has shown that personality variables do a limited job of accounting for conformity over a variety of situations, issues, or groups (see Chapter 3). Although high self-esteem may be related to willingness to rely upon one's own opinions (Stang, 1972), conformity should not be seen as a characteristic of individuals, but as a joint function of the individual and the situation (recall social psychology's focus on both the person and the situation).

We might expect, for instance, that people who are authoritarian (see Chapter 3) would be closed-minded and rigid and therefore resistant to social influence. On the other hand, authoritarians are thought to be submissive to power and easily led by those in positions of authority. Should they, then, be conformers or not? Research has shown that in order to predict whether people will accept influence, we must know not only whether they are authoritarian but also the status of the influencer. When the person doing the influencing is high in status relative to the authoritarian, influence will be accepted; but when the influencer is relatively low in status, the influence is rejected (Moore & Krupat, 1971; Cherry & Byrne, 1977). Therefore it is not the personality of the individual that is related to conformity, but rather the interaction of the personality with the situation. (Again, see Chapter 3 for an extended discussion of the interactionist view.)

Another variable that has received a good deal of attention is gender. The stereotype of women as more submissive than men might lead us to suspect that females would be more subject than males to social influence, and early surveys of the literature (e.g., McGuire, 1969) concluded that women were in fact more susceptible. More recent reviews (Eagly, 1983), however, have come to a different conclusion. For instance, of 62 social influence studies conducted since 1940, Alice Eagly (1978) found that 82 percent reported no differences between males and females.

A closer look at those studies that do find male-female differences suggests that such differences may be more apparent than real. As we noted in Chapter 6, in some cases researchers have unwittingly chosen materials that favored men's areas of expertise and interest (Goldberg, 1974, 1975). Sistrunk and McDavid (1971) pretested opinion and factual items to determine whether men or women were more knowledgeable about each. Then they selected a set of feminine, masculine, and neutral items. They found that on masculine items, the women conformed more than the men; on the feminine items, men conformed more than women, and on neutral items there were no differences. More recently, this same effect has been replicated by Karabenick (1983), even though the areas in which the two sexes are knowledgeable have changed somewhat.

In addition, Feldman-Summers and her colleagues (Feldman-Summers et al., 1980) found that people of both sexes conformed more on male-related items when the influence source was male, and more on female-related items when the influence source was female. Finally, Eagly (1983, 1978) has argued that in many laboratory conformity experiments, women may comply (show public change without any private acceptance) in order to preserve social harmony, but their level of genuine change (internalization) is still no more or less than that of men.

One great limitation in drawing any general conclusions about conformity is that most of the studies reported have been conducted in North America. Would the same results hold in Japan or Norway or France? Although there has been relatively little cross-cultural research, existing studies do seem to demonstrate that choosing between oneself and the group arouses a universal set of emotions and concerns. Still, some national groups do show unique cultural patterns or degrees of conformity.

In Japan, for instance, Frager (1970) replicated Asch's line-judging research using students at Keio University in Tokyo. He found that 26 percent resisted the group's pressure and remained independent, a figure very close to Asch's earlier results with students in the United States. However, Frager also encountered a phenomenon that no previous American researchers had ever reported. On trials in which the confederates gave the *correct* answer and there was no conflict at all, a significant percentage of Japanese students anticonformed. That is, they went against the group and gave the wrong answer even though it disagreed with both the group and with the obvious perceptual evidence.

Although we cannot be sure why some of these students responded in this way, one explanation revolves around the concept of **reactance.** People experience reactance when they feel others are trying to control them (Brehm, 1966; Brehm & Brehm, 1981). They often react to perceived attempts to remove their freedom by behaving in a way that says, "you can't push me around." For example, compared to those who were politely asked not to write on the walls of a public restroom, people who were *ordered* not to write scribbled almost twice the graffiti (Pennebaker & Sanders, 1976). Frager's students may have felt as though their free will was being challenged, and they may have given the wrong answer in order to assert their freedom.

Milgram (1961) performed a number of variations of the Asch experiment in Norway and France. Norwegian culture is reported to place a high value on solidarity and group harmony; French culture is known for its fierce individualism on matters of opinion. In line with the images held of these two cultures, Milgram found consistent differences between them. The French had a strong tendency to stay with their own positions and were resistant to group pressures in general. The Norwegians, on the other hand, were attuned to group sentiment, concerned with avoiding public disagreement, and more often conformed to the opinion of others.

Characteristics of the Task The biggest difference between the research of Sherif and Asch is in the degree to which people had clear and certain sensory information in order to decide on an answer. When a great deal of ambiguity exists about the correct answer (as in the autokinetic situation), the certainty with which people hold their opinions should be low; and reduced certainty should lead to greater conformity.

This hypothesis has been tested directly in a number of ways. Coleman, Blake, and Mouton (1958) systematically varied the difficulty of counting the number of clicks that people heard by having the clicks come slowly or at a fast pace. They found that the harder the task was, the more people conformed. Deutsch and Gerard (1955) asked people to respond in an Asch-type situation either while the lines were in front of them or after they had been removed for a few seconds. They found that when people no longer had the evidence in front of them, they were less certain and conformed more. Finally, Luchins and Luchins (1961) made it possible for some people to be more certain by actually providing some of them with rulers in a line-judging experiment. Not surprisingly, when people were armed with the ability to validate their opinion by objective means, they were far less conforming to the group than people who had to rely on their vision alone.

Characteristics of the Group Asch attempted many variations on his basic experiment. Two issues that concerned him involved the size and unanimity of the majority facing the lone person. Imagine, for instance, that instead of a group of six people giving the wrong answer, now there was only one other college-age male present. When that person gave the incorrect answer, people looked at him as if he were crazy and went on to give the correct answer. Out of 12 disagreement trials with one naive participant and one confederate, the mean number of conforming responses was 0.33. No one conformed on more than one trial, and the majority of people never changed even once. Yet when Asch increased the majority to two, some people conformed as many as five times and the mean number of conforming responses went up to 1.53. With a majority of three, the effect bloomed, and one person even conformed on every trial. Out of a possible 12 trials, the mean number of conforming responses was 4.0.

Given the great impact of each person added, you might imagine that a unanimous majority of 8 or 10 or 15 would lead everyone to conform on every trial, but this was not the case. As Figure 10.3 indicates, Asch tested people against majorities that went as high as 15 but found that by the time a majority size of three was reached, the addition of more

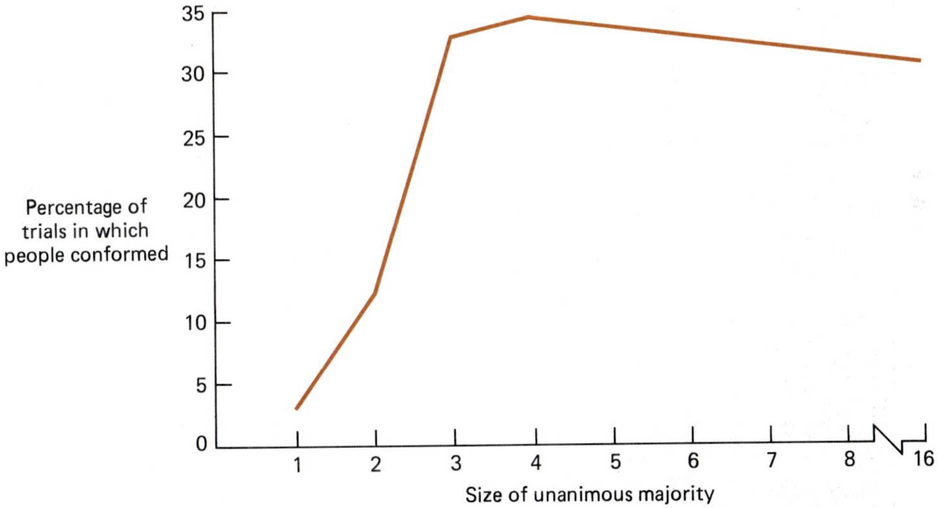

FIGURE 10.3
Group Size and Conformity The percentage of trials in which people conformed rose sharply as the size of the unanimous majority went from one to three. But beyond three, the addition of more group members did not effectively increase conformity. *Source:* Adapted from S. E. Asch (1951). Effects of group pressure upon the modification and distortion of judgment. In H. Gvetzkow (Ed.) *Groups, leadership and men: Research in human relations.* Pittsburgh: Carnegie Press, p. 188.

group numbers had no significant effect on conformity one way or the other. Gerard, Wilhelmy, and Conolley (1968) used a procedure similar to Asch's with majorities as high as seven. They found that the amount of conformity increased somewhat with larger group sizes, but that the absolute amount of conformity did not go higher than Asch's. Insko and his colleagues found more conformity with four confederates than with just one, but did not test group sizes that were larger or smaller (Insko et al., 1985).

Larger groups may fail to create greater conformity for a number of reasons. One recent important explanation is Latané's (1981) social impact theory, which will be discussed in some detail in Chapter 12. In essence, this theory argues that each additional person adds less to the group impact than the person who was added previously; the difference between two versus one is greater than three versus two, and so on. Before long, therefore, additional people add virtually nothing.

Another major explanation proposes that adding more people fails to offer a greater number of *independent* opinions. That is, once the first three or four people have stated their positions, all the others are seen as just following along, merely conforming themselves. As a result, the additional pressures are redundant with the pressures already present.

Wilder (1977) demonstrated this in an experiment in which people read the facts of a lawsuit and had to decide which party was to blame. A control group read the case and made their own decisions independently, not subject to any conformity pressures. Before making their decision, the experimental groups were first exposed to a tape recording of either one, two, three, four, or six people who urged an extreme position. In addition to the number of people urging the extreme position, the manner in which the opinions were presented also varied. In the case of six others, for instance, some people thought they were hearing the separate judgments of six, others the judgments of two groups of three, while some believed this was the opinion of one group of six. Wilder found that the opinion of six separate individuals led to more conformity than did two groups of three; and the opinion of two groups of three led to more conformity than one group of six. This demonstrates that the absolute number of different individuals was far less important than the number of separate or independent entities urging a position.

In real life we usually do not have to stand up to an absolutely unanimous group. Usually there is someone who disagrees with the group or supports our position. Asch next asked what would happen to the level of conformity if the group consensus was broken. For example, which would you find more difficult to face: eleven people, ten of whom disagree with you and one of whom agrees with you; or a smaller group of five, all of whom form a unanimous consensus? On this question all the research finds that the presence of one dissenter who breaks the unanimity of the group is a critical factor in reducing conformity, far more important than the number of people who oppose you.

When individuals are uncertain as to the proper course of action, they often look to others for direction. As these men communicate, it is likely that a group norm, or consensus opinion, will begin to develop.

The impact of a partner is great. In one of Asch's variations, the naive participant, who was put in the eighth position, heard all of the confederates—except the one in the fourth position—consistently give the incorrect answer. When this happened, instead of a conformity rate of nearly one-third, conforming responses dropped to less than 5 percent. Moreover, additional research has shown that the dissenter does not even have to be attractive, reliable, or correct, as long as the answer he or she gives is different.

In one experiment involving perceptual judgments (Allen & Levine, 1971), the dissenting partner wore thick glasses and had just failed a vision test before the experiment began. Still, compared to a unanimous group situation, the rate of conformity was lowered when this person dissented. Malof and Lott (1962) and Boyanowsky and Allen (1973) have demonstrated further that people will latch onto support wherever they find it, at least when the answer is one of fact rather than opinion. They found that highly prejudiced white participants were able to resist group pressures equally well, regardless of whether the person who agreed with them was black or white.

But why does it make so much of a difference when the group unanimity is broken? A study by Morris, Miller, and Spangenberg (1977) concerning *when* the dissenting opinion is expressed suggests two important reasons. In this research, all of the participants found themselves in the last position in a five-person group, and, depending upon the experimental condition, the person who broke with the majority and gave the correct answer was in the first, second, third, or fourth position. Conformity was reduced the most when the dissenter went either first or last.

From this we can infer that when the partner is in the first position, he or she neutralizes the group's informational influence by providing an immediate confirmation of reality. However, when the dissenter is in the fourth position and the first three confederates have all given the incorrect answer, people are likely to be feeling the group's normative pressures regardless of whether they think the group is right. When the confederate gives the answer just before the subject's turn, this reduces the fear of looking different and allows the subject to fall back on the partner for emotional support in resisting the group.

An important application for the legal system arises from our discussion of group size and group unanimity. When a jury is required to come to a unanimous decision, a great deal of group pressure is likely to be placed on the dissenting member or members to get them to conform. Is this pressure the same in a 6-person jury as it is in a 12-person jury? Anyone who has mastered fractions can tell that a 12-person jury split 10 to 2 is mathematically equivalent to a 6-person jury split 5 to 1. But are both splits equivalent in interpersonal dynamics and in pressure to conform? All of the available research evidence tells us that one person facing a unanimous majority of five is more likely to give in than two people facing ten. In this case, the evidence of social psychology goes beyond intuition and offers the legal system important insights into the jury process. In Chapter 12, "Small Groups," we will discuss this issue in greater detail.

Relationship to the Group As much as characteristics of the individual, the task, and the group are important in determining conformity, it is also important to consider the relationship of the individual to the group. One variable of interest involves the person's status or position of leadership within the group. People of high status have much power to pressure others to conform. They typically possess legitimate as well as reward and coercive power, and often have gained high status due to expertise. In juries, people of high general status (e.g., professionals and white-collar workers) are more likely to be chosen as foremen, to direct the discussion, and to influence the final vote than are people of lower status (Strodtbeck & Hook, 1961; Strodtbeck, James, & Hawkins, 1957).

High-status people not only influence others in areas related to their expertise, but also carry strong power to influence in areas that are completely unrelated. For instance, in one study it was found that people were more likely to conform to a physician than to a postal clerk on a simple perceptual task, even though there is no reason to believe that doctors can make these judgments better than anyone else (Moore & Krupat, 1971). Furthermore, Eagly (1983) has suggested that in instances where males have been shown to exert more influence than females, this is due to the fact that men typically occupy higher status positions than women.

Concerning the relationship of status to the acceptance of influence from group members, there is considerable disagreement. It has been hypothesized and demonstrated that leaders conform more than other group members in order to live up to and to model group norms (e.g., Homans, 1974); but also that this conformity allows them to build up "idiosyncrasy credit" (Hollander, 1960) which entitles them to deviate without suffering serious loss of standing with the group (see Chapter 12). Others have shown that those who are second in command conform the most (Harvey & Consalvi, 1960); and still others that those at the bottom of the ladder conform the most in order to gain status and to avoid total rejection by the group (Montgomery, 1971).

This set of conflicting findings suggests strongly that conformity is not a simple matter and that it occurs more or less depending upon the circumstances group members encounter. To summarize, three person-to-group factors play a major role in determining which individuals will yield to group pressure: (1) the degree of external status that the person brings to the group (e.g., a doctor as opposed to a plumber); (2) the degree to which a person's status is secure; and (3) the degree to which the person believes conformity or resistance is desired by the group and will help accomplish group goals. The lower the person's external status, the less secure the person's position in the group, and the more group consensus is valued, the more conformity we will find.

OBEDIENCE: HOW AUTHORITY INFLUENCES THE INDIVIDUAL

Conformity usually involves influence among members of a group who are roughly equal in terms of status. Typically the pressure is subtle rather than obvious, and most often we do not even realize the extent of influence that others have upon us. Even when we conform, we try to convince ourselves that our acts were really independent, and that we would have done the same thing anyway if others had not been present.

A form of social influence that differs from this is *obedience*. Obedience is a process that goes on between people who are unequal in formal status, such as teacher and student, doctor and patient. One has legitimate authority, and the other does not. The authority figure typically makes explicit and direct demands, and the person who carries them out often takes great pains to place the responsibility for the behavior on the demands of the other. Perhaps the one setting that comes to mind concerning obedience is the military, with its hierarchy of power and the concept of following orders. In this section we will review dramatic research on obedience and consider, as we did for conformity, why and when people obeyed. In addition, we will consider not only the findings but also the techniques of this research in considering the moral and ethical questions it has raised.

These young officers are in the process of willingly pledging their obedience to their superiors.

Milgram's Research on Obedience

Having carefully followed the research of Asch and tested the same principles in France and Norway, Stanley Milgram wondered whether the principles and methods of social psychology could be applied to understanding seemingly excessive obedience such as that shown by the German people during the Nazi era (Milgram, 1974, 1965). To get a cross-section of average adults, Milgram advertised in local newspapers in southern Connecticut. People of all ages and social and educational backgrounds answered the ad. When they appeared for the experiment at a building on the Yale University campus, they were greeted by a fellow participant in his mid- to late forties (actually a confederate of Milgram's) and a lab-coated experimenter. All participants were paid the promised fee and were told they were to participate in an experiment on the effect of punishment on learning.

Using a rigged drawing, the naive participant always became the "teacher" and the confederate the "learner." The teacher's job was to read a long list of word pairs that the learner was to learn. After each incorrect answer, the teacher supplied the correct answer and gave the learner an electric shock as punishment. The shock generator consisted of 30 switches going up in 15-volt steps to 450 volts, with written designations such as "Slight shock," "Intense shock," and "Danger: Severe shock." The last two switches (435 and 450 volts) were beyond the danger level and bore no label other than XXX. The teacher was to start with 15 volts for the first incorrect answer and to go up one level each time the learner made a mistake. The people in the experiment did not know that the confederate was an actor and that no actual shocks were received. If the participants hesitated, the experimenter (authority figure) reminded them that "the experiment requires that you continue" and that the experimenter would assume complete responsibility for whatever happened.

The teacher believed that the learner was in an adjoining room with his arms strapped to the chair "to avoid blisters and burns." He heard the learner ask about the shocks and mention that he had a mild heart condition. He also heard the experimenter respond that the shocks might be painful but were not dangerous. As the learner gave incorrect answers, the voltage level rose. When the 75-volt shock was delivered, the learner made a grunt; at 135, a pained groan; and at 150, he yelled "Experimenter, get me out of here! I won't be in the experiment any more! I refuse to go on!" These complaints continued throughout the session, indicating that the pain was great and his heart was bothering him. At 315 volts he let out a violent scream, saying he no longer would participate, and after 330 volts no further sound was heard at all. (Some students have described this as "dead silence.")

Simple question: If you were the teacher, how long would you continue to give shocks? Would you go until 450 volts if the experimenter insisted? If your answer is "no way," you are like the vast majority of others—psychiatrists, college students, and middle-class adults—who predicted that hardly a single person would continue to the end. The results of this study, however, were very different from the predictions. Although people were terribly anxious about pulling one switch after another, 65 percent of them obeyed, continuing to the 450-volt level rather than openly defying the experimenter.

Mediators of Obedience

How can it be that 65 percent of the people went on? How could they have been so callous or so cowardly? As teachers of psychology, we have presented this experiment to many different groups of students over a number of years, often accompanied by a film showing the reactions of

FROM THE FIELD
Stanley Milgram

Stanley Milgram died unexpectedly in 1984 at the age of 51. He had been one of the most creative social psychologists in the profession. Although this chapter discusses his controversial research on obedience to authority, you will see references to his other work throughout the book. In addition to his study of obedience, Milgram investigated the "small world" theory, the experience of living in a city, the effects of televised violence (using experimental variations of television programs that were actually broadcast), and a number of other topics to which he brought his genius for finding ways to cast new light on human concerns.

real teachers and learners. We are impressed that when students hear about the results, their very first tendency is to attribute the actions of the participants to *dispositional* causes. They believe that their obedience must tell us something about their personalities; that those who went along must have been aggressive, or submissive, or sadistic, or something. But whatever they were like, there is always the belief that "they are not like us." Females immediately assume that the obedient people were all male; black students notice that they were white; and students in their twenties usually point out that the people giving the shocks were of their parents' age.

To test whether personality variables could account for the degree of obedience, Elms and Milgram (1966) contacted 40 of the most obedient and 40 of the most defiant participants and gave them an extensive battery of personality tests. Although they found some differences in the personalities, prior experiences, and upbringing of defiant as opposed to obedient people, they concluded that no consistent or clear pattern emerged. In further studies conducted in Australia (Kilham & Mann, 1974) and Jordan (Shanab & Yahya, 1977), the results also indicated no important differences between obedient and defiant people. Similarly, the obedience levels of women (Milgram, 1974) and children (Shanab & Yahya, 1977) do not vary significantly from those of adult males. Just as we found in

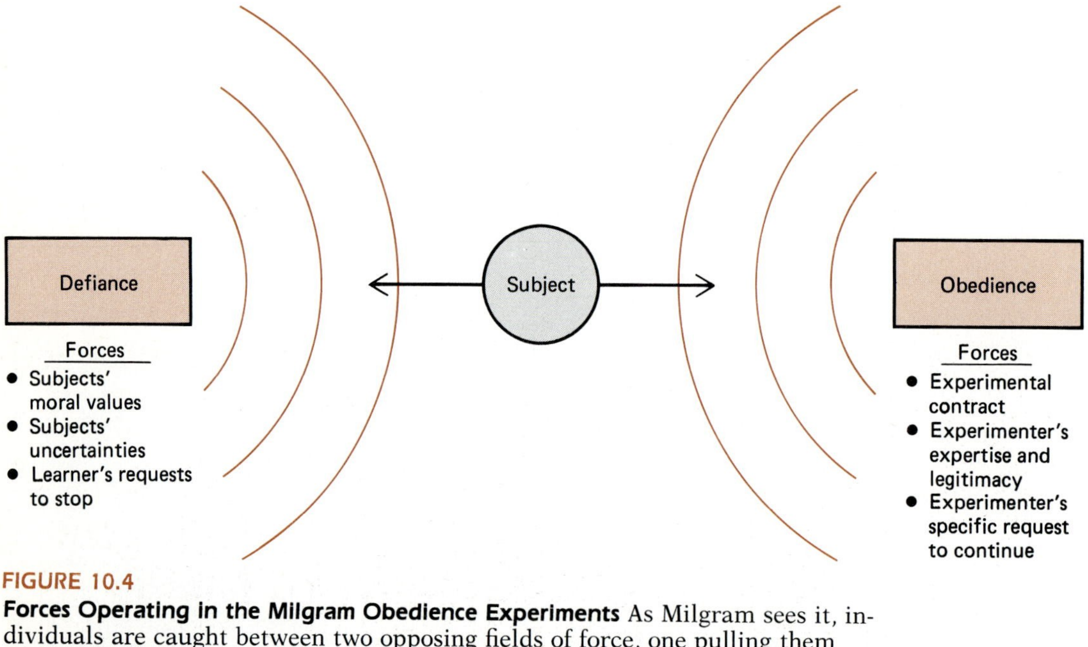

FIGURE 10.4

Forces Operating in the Milgram Obedience Experiments As Milgram sees it, individuals are caught between two opposing fields of force, one pulling them toward obeying the experimenter and continuing to give shocks, the other toward defying the experimenter and refusing to continue. *Source:* Adapted from S. Milgram (1963). *Obedience* [Film]. New York: New York University Film Library.

the case of conformity, it is not sufficient to try to explain obedience by looking to personality variables alone. Rather, we also ought to analyze the situational forces acting on people.

Even more than the participants in Asch's research, all of Milgram's seemed to experience extreme tension. All wanted to break off, to say no to the experimenter, but most were not able to take a firm stand and stick with it. Milgram believed that people were caught between two strong fields of force. On one side was a set of pressures pulling toward obedience. The unspoken experimental contract (see Chapter 1) as well as the payment called for people to cooperate; and the presence of the expert and legitimate experimenter provided explicit and strong pressure to continue. On the other side were a set of pressures against obedience: uncertainties, moral values, concerns for the health of the learner, and the learner's demands to be let out (see Figure 10.4). Milgram believed that by varying factors in the experimental situation, he could intensify the relative forces on one side or the other, thereby increasing or reducing the level of obedience.

Milgram first modified the basic experiment by varying the physical proximity of the learner to the teacher. In one condition the learner was in another room and could not be heard; in another, he was in the same room; and in another he was right next to the teacher. In fact, in this last condition the teacher had to force the learner's hand onto a shock plate to keep the experiment going. As shown in Figure 10.5, the maximum level of shocks decreased as the "force" pulling toward disobedience got closer and therefore stronger. When the teacher actually had to have physical contact with the learner for the shock to be delivered, 82 percent of them defied the experimenter. In another version of the experiment Milgram moved the experimenter farther from the teacher, and found

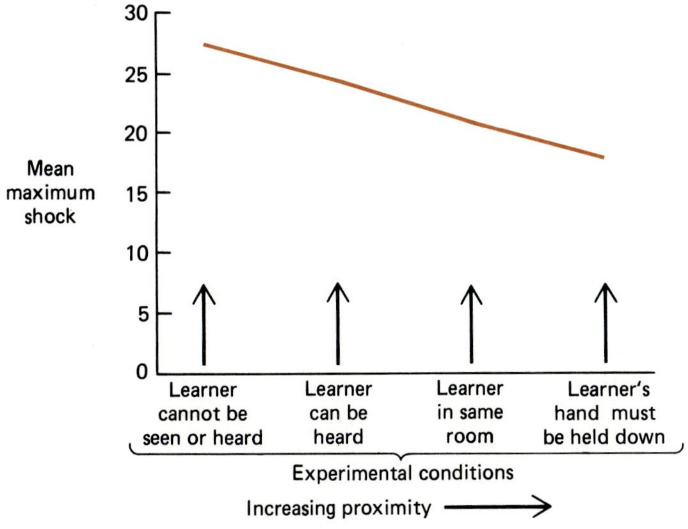

FIGURE 10.5
Mean Maximum Shock Levels as a Function of the Proximity Between Subject and Learner The closer the learner is brought to the teacher, the sooner the teacher quits the experiment by refusing to continue giving shocks. *Source:* Adapted from S. Milgram (1974). *Obedience to authority.* New York: Harper & Row, p. 36.

that when the experimenter was not in the room, obedience dropped sharply.

In yet another variation of the obedience experiment, Milgram (1965) asked whether group pressures could be used successfully to counteract the orders of an authority. In this case four males arrived at the lab, three confederates and one naive participant. In a rigged drawing, one confederate was chosen to read the words, one to note if the answers were correct, and the real participant was left in basically the same position as always—with the responsibility of delivering the shocks. The fourth confederate, of course, became the learner.

In this version the experiment continued as usual, except that at 150 volts, when the learner made his initial protest, the first confederate/teacher objected and refused to participate any longer. At 210 volts the second confederate/teacher did the same, leaving the real participant with the conflict of whether to *obey* the explicit pressures of the experimenter telling him to continue the experiment, or to *conform* to the implicit pressures of the others who had stopped.

Of all the variations Milgram attempted to see whether the experimenter's power could be undermined, this was by far the most successful. Only 10 percent of the participants in this condition continued to the end. This finding parallels Asch's findings concerning a nonunanimous majority. Whether an individual wants to oppose the demands of an authority or the expectations of a group, it is important to be able to find social support in defying the wishes of others. In fact, identification of factors that help people to stand up effectively against unjust authority may be one of the most important functions of Milgram's obedience research (see also Gamson, Fireman, & Rytina, 1982).

Milgram's Research Revisited

Milgram's obedience studies constitute one of the most newsworthy and controversial programs of research ever conducted in social psychology. It is difficult to avoid making a connection between his experimental setup and the situations of those who have committed terrible acts of violence only to claim they were merely following orders (see the In the News box). We can think of historical examples such as William Calley, who ordered the killing of over 100 Vietnamese villagers, or Adolf Eichmann, who oversaw the destruction of millions of Jews in the Nazi concentration camps. It is all too easy, however, to explain their behavior as a product of "warped minds" or "evil characters" (in strictly dispositional terms). We must also consider the powerful forces acting upon such people to obey, and be aware that strong pressures can and should be resisted when they lead us in ways that violate our moral principles.

Milgram's research has itself been the topic of much concern, both ethical and methodological (see Baumrind, 1964, 1985; Geller, 1982). The ethical questions have focused on three issues: (1) whether Milgram had

In November 1978 Jim Jones, the leader of a cult in the jungles of Guyana, persuaded hundreds of his disciples to commit mass suicide by drinking poison. This shocking incident was a graphic reminder of how strong the pressures to obey can be.

a right to expose people to a potentially stressful situation without any prior consent; (2) whether this experiment would cause people to lose trust in the truthfulness of researchers in general; and (3) whether the experience of obeying might not negatively influence the self-concept of people and cause them long-term psychological problems.

Sensitivity to the issue of informed consent has grown in recent years, and obedience studies have been part of the impetus for that. Obviously, had Milgram told people all about the experiment before inviting their participation, his findings would have been meaningless. The balance of interests—the value of the knowledge gained versus the participants' autonomy—remains a topic of debate. The second issue suggests that the more social psychologists use deception, the more they undermine the research enterprise in the long run. Again, this suggests that violations of the principle of dealing honestly with research participants should be reserved for only the most important work, if such violations are to occur at all. In response to the last of these issues, Milgram followed up on many of the participants by questionnaire and even by psychiatric interview. He reports that the vast majority of the people who participated in his research felt that it was a positive rather than a negative learning experience and valued their participation.

IN THE NEWS

CALLEY TAKES THE STAND

The scene was a small courtroom in a one-story brick building on a Georgia Army base, with a 27-year-old lieutenant in the dock. But at issue were agonizing questions of military expediency and morality, and of individual responsibility in the throat of war. This was the trial of Lt. William Calley, Jr., charged with murdering 102 men, women and children during the course of a rampage by his company through the tiny Vietnamese hamlet of Mylai nearly three years ago. Other men, including two generals, have been implicated in the event. Some may yet be tried. But Calley is the first officer actually to face a court-martial for what may be the worst battlefield atrocity ever committed in the name of the United States. . . .

Last week he finally took the stand to tell his story. He insisted that he was only following orders when he led the Mylai raid. "I felt then and I still do," Calley said, "that I acted as I was directed and that I carried out orders I was given." He had received his instructions, he told the court, from his company commander, Captain Ernest Medina. Calley admitted that he had personally decreed the mass execution of civilians, shot three men and a child himself and fired into a ditch full of villagers. He said Medina had led him to believe that everyone in Mylai was a Vietcong. Calley testified, "I never sat down and analyzed whether they were men, women and children. They were enemy, not people."

[Excerpts from Calley's testimony:]

A I started moving over to Sgt. [David] Mitchell's location to speed him up, find out what was over in that other part. When I broke out of the village on the southeastern trail, I at that time ran into Paul Meadlo who was there with a large—well, a group of people.

Q Did you have any conversation with Meadlo at that time?

A Yes, sir.

Q All right. Can you state what you said and what Meadlo said?

A In actual words, I can't really remember at this time. But I asked something to the effect if he knew what he was sup-

Methodologically, some researchers have argued that this research is flawed and cannot be generalized. For instance, Orne and Holland (1968) believe that the behavior of the subjects might have been due to experimental demand characteristics (see Chapter 1) that would not be as strong in the real world. Mixon (1971, 1979) has argued that while people such as Eichmann knew the exact consequences of their actions, Milgram's situation is not a good analogy because people might have convinced themselves that no harm was actually occurring. In addition, Gilbert (1981) has demonstrated that without the series of graded voltage levels that Milgram provided, the obedience levels of actual subjects is considerably lower. That is, Milgram's teachers were gradually eased along the path of obedience, or "shaped." Their extreme obedience was not instantaneous.

posed to be doing with those people. He said he did.

Q What was the substance of that [the next] conversation between you and Captain Medina?

A He asked me why I was disobeying his orders.

Q All right. Was anything else said by him?

A Well, I explained to him why—what was slowing me down, and at that time, he told me to waste the Vietnamese and get my people . . . in the position they were supposed to be. . . .

Q What did you do?

A I started over to Mitchell's location. I came back out. Meadlo was still standing there with a group of Vietnamese, and I yelled at Meadlo and asked him—I told him, if he couldn't move all those people, to get rid of them.

A I heard a considerable volume of firing to my north, and I moved up along the edge of the ditch and around a hooch and I broke out in the clearing, and my men had a number of Vietnamese in the ditch and were firing upon them, sir. . . .

Q What is your best impression of how many were there at the ditch?

A Four to five, sir. . . .

Q What did you do after you saw them shooting in the ditch?

A Well, I fired into the ditch also, sir.

Q Did you at any time direct anybody to push people in the ditch?

A Like I said, I gave the order to take those people through the ditch and had also told Meadlo, if he couldn't move them to waste them, and I directly—other than that, there was only that one incident, I never stood up there for any period of time. . . .

Q Now, why did you give Meadlo a message or the order that if you couldn't get rid of them to waste them?

A Because that was my order, sir. That was the order of the day, sir. . . .

Source: Life, 70 (8), March 5, 1971, pp. 22, 28.

Yet for all of its problems, this research has directed attention to an important theoretical and applied issue. Moreover, it has pointed out that obedience is not a characteristic of certain individuals, but that we are *all* potentially subject to the power that exists in the hands of authority.

TECHNIQUES OF INFLUENCE

Up to this point, we have focused our attention on the *why* of social influence, but not on the *how*. For instance, Asch's confederates did nothing more to produce conformity than state their opinions; Milgram's experimenter simply asserted that the teachers must continue. Yet, as we all know, influencing people usually is not as simple as this. We now turn to specific techniques that social psychologists have investigated, developed, and applied to influence people to change their behavior. We will consider two strategies, the foot-in-the-door and the door-in-the-face techniques, that are successful in generating compliance by making a smaller or larger request first. Then we will look at the effects of social models, and finally we will consider the role of incentives in producing social influence.

The Foot-in-the Door Technique

The **foot-in-the-door technique,** closely associated with the type of influence typical of salespeople (Freedman & Fraser, 1966), is based on a simple principle. In order to get a person to comply with a large request, the influencer should first make a smaller request. If a person wants a friend to lend him or her five dollars next week, that person ought to get the friend to lend a quarter (or to grant any small favor) this week (see Figure 10.6).

In Freedman and Fraser's initial foot-in-the-door study, the goal was to influence suburban homeowners to put a large, unattractive "Drive Carefully" sign right in the middle of their front yards. Half of the homeowners were first asked a small favor—to sign a petition to encourage safe driving—and then were asked to put up the big, ugly sign. The homeowners in the control condition were merely asked about the sign without a prior request. In the large-favor-only condition, very few (less than 17 percent) agreed, but of those who signed the petition first, over 55 percent agreed. This approach has been replicated successfully many times with a wide range of requests (DeJong, 1979, 1981; Snyder & Cunningham, 1975); although some have pointed out that it is less successful if the first request is too small (Zuckerman, Lazzaro, & Waldgeir, 1979) or if the second request is too large (Foss & Dempsey, 1979) or poorly timed (Beaman et al., 1983). However, with proper refinement, this strategy has been used to get people to give to charity (Pliner et al., 1974); to donate blood, kidneys, and bone marrow (see Chapter 9 and Saks, 1978); and to generate attachment to cult religions (see discussion at the end of this chapter).

A number of explanations have been offered for the success of the foot-in-the-door strategy. Gilbert (1981) has suggested that agreeing to a first request sets in motion a momentum of compliance, just as the graded shock levels did in Milgram's obedience research. Another explanation (Rittle, 1981) suggests that once people agree and actually offer help, they change their perception of helping, realizing that it is not difficult and can actually be satisfying. The most commonly offered explanation follows from Bem's (1972) self-perception theory (see Chapter 5). Agreeing to the first request generates a small but meaningful shift in the way people see themselves. As a result, they are likely to agree to the second request in order to be consistent with this newly changed self-perception.

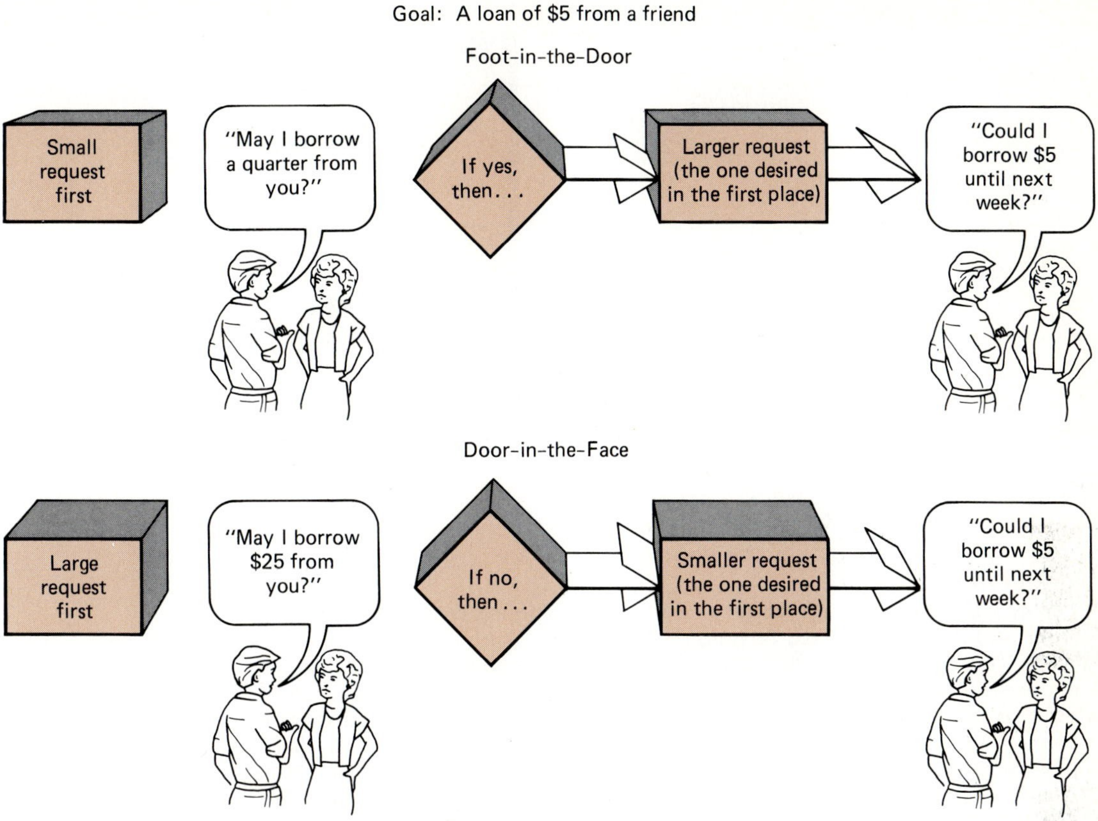
Goal: A loan of $5 from a friend
Foot-in-the-Door
Small request first
"May I borrow a quarter from you?"
If yes, then...
Larger request (the one desired in the first place)
"Could I borrow $5 until next week?"
Door-in-the-Face
Large request first
"May I borrow $25 from you?"
If no, then...
Smaller request (the one desired in the first place)
"Could I borrow $5 until next week?"

FIGURE 10.6

The Foot-in-the-Door and the Door-in-the-Face Techniques The foot-in-the-door technique starts with a small request and then graduates to a larger one. The door-in-the-face technique works in just the opposite way: the requester starts with an extremely large request and, after being turned down, moves to a smaller one. Both approaches have proven successful in a variety of situations.

The Door-in-the-Face Technique

The **door-in-the-face technique** is much the reverse of the foot-in-the-door. According to this strategy, the best way to get a request granted is first to ask for one so large that it will be refused. Then a second, more moderate request (the one the person really wanted all the time) is made (Cialdini, 1985). Let us take the same example used before, needing a five-dollar loan from a friend. Using the door-in-the-face technique, the person should ask a huge favor, one that the friend will surely refuse. Ask for $25 or to borrow the friend's new sports car for a week, and then lower the request to "a measly five dollars" (see Figure 10.6).

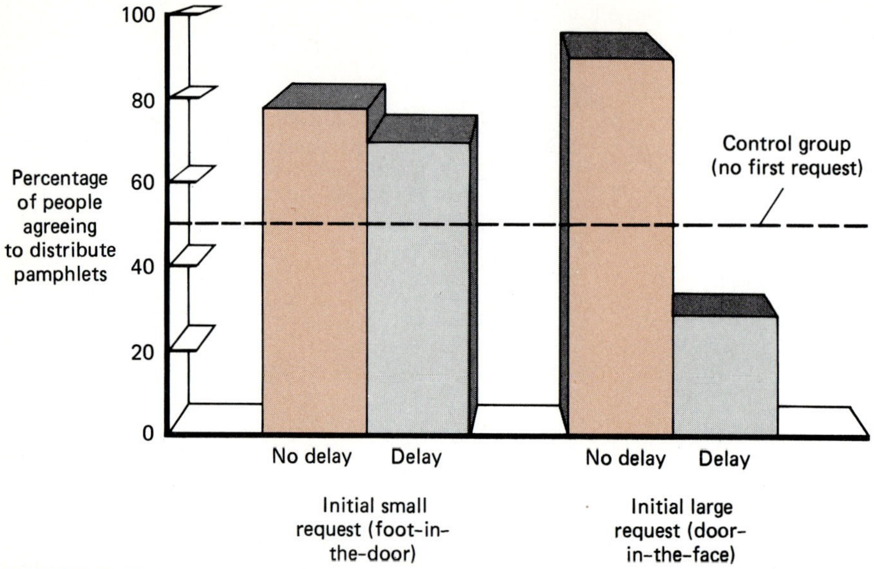

FIGURE 10.7

Percentage of People Agreeing to Distribute Pamphlets When Foot-in-the-Door and Door-in-the-Face Techniques Were Used Using the foot-in-the door technique, Cann and his colleagues found that they were just about equally successful whether or not there was a delay between the first and second requests. With the door-in-the face technique, the no-delay method was extremely successful; but with a delay, the second request was far less likely to be granted. *Source:* Based on A. Cann, S. J. Sherman, and R. Elkes (1975). Effects of initial size request and timing of a second request on compliance: The foot in the door and the door in the face. *Journal of Personality and Social Psychology, 32,* 777.

When Cialdini and his colleagues (Cialdini et al., 1975) asked people to work without pay for two hours a week over a period of two years for a local youth counseling program, not a single person agreed. Once turned down, however, the experimenter said, "Well, we also have another program you might be interested in," and asked if they would escort a group of children to the zoo one afternoon. The door-in-the-face proved to be just as powerful as the foot-in-the-door. Of those who were asked only to go to the zoo, 17 percent agreed; but among those who had refused the larger first request, half agreed to go.

Two explanations have been offered for the success of this method. The *self-presentation* view suggests that people do not like to be thought of as inconsiderate, and therefore tend to say yes to a lesser favor so as not to appear dispositionally unhelpful (Pendleton & Batson, 1979). The *reciprocal concessions* perspective suggests that when other people show an ability to compromise by reducing the request, there are pressures to reciprocate and meet them halfway (Cialdini, 1985). Therefore, while the foot-in-the-door technique involves an escalation of requests that people find acceptable, the door-in-the-face technique is a kind of bargaining-down procedure where the target of influence is pressured to say, "I'll be reasonable if you'll be reasonable."

While both of these techniques often are effective, research comparing the two has shown that sometimes one works better than the other (Harari, Mohr, & Hosey, 1980), and at times their success depends upon other variables. In comparing the foot-in-the-door with the door-in-the-face techniques, Cann, Sherman, and Elkes (1975) made either a small or large initial request and then followed it with a second, either immediately or seven to ten days later. As seen in Figure 10.7, the foot-in-the-door method was generally successful regardless of whether there was a delay. However, the door-in-the-face method generated the most success of all when followed by an immediate second request, but was even worse than a control group (no first request) when there was a delay.

The Use of Modeling

As discussed in Chapter 5, we often learn new behaviors or attitudes by observing the behavior of others. This process, known as **modeling,** is most typically a kind of "influence by accident" because the people who serve as models often are not aware that their behavior is being observed and imitated. For instance, many parents who smoke or drink to excess do not realize the extent of their influence over their children, and wonder why their children get into trouble with drugs.

Since modeling is potentially such a powerful force, a growing number of social psychologists have realized that social models can be used in a purposeful manner to affect people's behavior. For instance, Craig (1986) has demonstrated that people are able to tolerate higher levels of pain when provided with a model who seems to experience less pain. Jason and his colleagues (Jason, Zolik, & Matese, 1979; Jason et al., 1980) have had dramatic success in getting dog owners to scoop up their pets' droppings by providing models; and Jason (1977) has also helped to improve the verbal skills of young children with the same basic method. Many current attempts at getting people to donate blood, or not to drink and drive, have used peers or prestigious figures as models. Currently, E. Scott Geller and his colleagues are mounting a nationwide campaign to urge the producers of popular TV shows that feature automobile chases to show the stars buckling their seat belts whenever they get into their cars.

One particularly promising application of modeling is in the area of smoking prevention among adolescents. It has been found that over half of all young regular smokers pick up the habit between the seventh and ninth grades (Johnston, Bachman, & O'Malley, 1977) even though the vast majority of teenagers believe that cigarette smoking is dangerous to their health (Evans et al., 1981). Two reasons stand out in explaining why adolescents begin to smoke. First, many parents and other respected adults serve as models by smoking. Newspaper and magazine ads show happy, popular, and sexy people smoking, and teens imitate them. Second, other teens not only provide implicit (modeling) pressures when they smoke, but also apply overt pressures on their friends to follow along. Teenagers who do not conform fear group rejection and the loss of status among their peers. They are faced with questions such as, "Are you too scared to try?" and often have no response other than to give in to the pressure.

In order to overcome the overt and covert pressures to smoke that peers and adults provide, a number of research groups decided to fight fire with fire—or, more accurately, models with models. In Houston, over 3000 teenagers in 13 junior high schools were involved in the research program of Richard Evans and his colleagues (1984). The experimental groups received realistic and honest films and videotapes featuring teenagers who role-played situations in which others were tempting them to smoke. The teens were shown resisting and feeling quite good about it. Posters reinforcing these messages were put up in classrooms to emphasize the message that these "positive models" were offering.

Nathan Maccoby's group at Stanford used a slightly different approach (Telch et al., 1982). They relied even more directly on peer contact and provided direct and specific techniques to resist pressure. They trained local high schoolers to lead antismoking groups in nearby junior high schools. The high schoolers talked about their own problems of growing up, and "taught" via modeling how to handle pressure. For instance, they suggested that if called "chicken" for not smoking, the junior high school students could respond: "I would be more of a chicken if I smoked just to impress you."

The results of such programs appear quite promising. In a ten-week pilot study, Evans found that 18 percent of the seventh graders in a control group had begun smoking compared with 10 percent in the modeling groups. Even more promising are the results of a long-term follow-up of the Stanford program (see Figure 10.8). It shows that while those in the experimental and control schools did not differ at the beginning of the program, those who had been exposed to peer models learned to resist group pressure and were far less likely to begin smoking over a period of almost three years.

Incentives and Influence

Another straightforward and simple tactic is the use of incentives: In order to get people to change their behavior, offer rewards for acting in a certain way. The rewards can range from recognition and prestige and

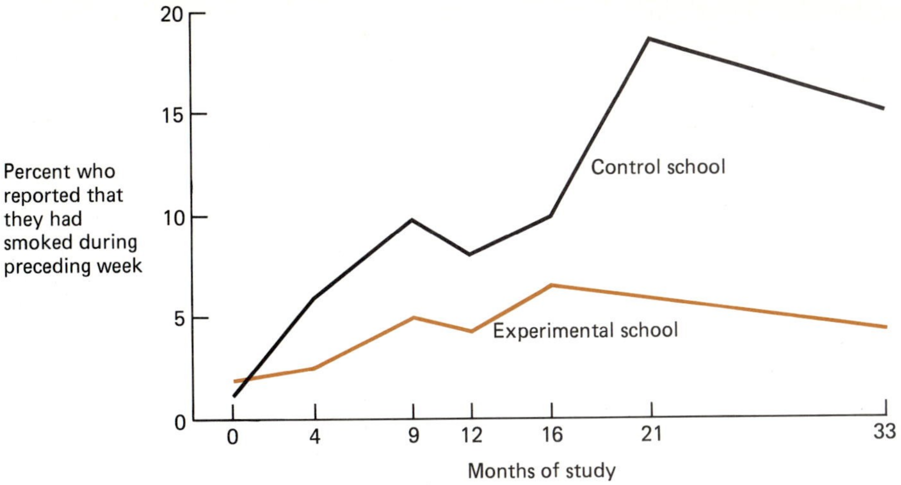

FIGURE 10.8
Reported Prevalence of Smoking Among Students Who Were Exposed to Anti-smoking Peers and Those Who Were Not As a result of the Stanford program, differences between the experimental and control schools appeared as early as four months later. The impact of the program continued to be strong well over two years later. *Source:* M. J. Telch, J. D. Killen, A. L. McAlister, C. L. Perry, and N. Maccoby (1982). Long-term follow-up of a pilot project on smoking prevention with adolescents. *Journal of Behavioral Medicine, 5,* 5.

increased comfort to cold cash. In fact, economic incentives have been the most used and studied form of reward (Cook & Berrenberg, 1981).

Economic incentives have been used with some success to curb littering in state parks (Clark, Burgess, & Hendee, 1972), movie theaters (Burgess, Clark, & Hendee, 1971), and zoos (Kohlenberg & Phillips, 1973). Geller and his colleagues have conducted an impressive series of social experiments using various kinds of incentives in activities ranging from littering (Geller & Lehman, 1986) to wearing seat belts (Rudd & Geller, 1985; Streff & Geller, 1986). In one study, seat belt usage went from a baseline level of approximately 20 percent up to 56 percent when drivers realized that seat belt wearers could win a prize (Geller, 1982).

Another area in which incentives have been used to influence behavior is in medicine. In an attempt to motivate patients to control their hypertension, researchers at the Peter Bent Brigham Hospital in Boston (Shepard et al., 1979) have offered patients the opportunity to receive up to $12 per visit—$4 for keeping their appointments and $8 for maintaining their blood pressure at an agreed-upon level through the proper use of medication. These patients were quite successful in controlling their blood pressure and, not surprisingly, always kept their appointments. At several medical centers, health professionals have begun to write contracts for patients in which they can receive prizes of their own choosing in return for meeting various medical goals (Quill, 1983; Steckel, 1982). Insurance companies have also provided incentives for positive health behavior in the form of reduced premiums for nonsmokers. Incentives can work not only on patients but on health providers as well. Among private physicians and especially in health maintenance organizations (HMO's), economic incentives are being provided to encourage preventive medicine. This results in a healthier population and reduces undetected conditions that would otherwise lead to unpleasant and expensive hospitalizations.

APPLICATION
SOCIAL PSYCHOLOGY AND ENERGY CONSERVATION

Up to this point, this chapter has focused on social influence on a small scale, on a one-to-one or group-to-individual level. Yet in some cases the target may be a large segment of the population, or even a whole country. How can people be influenced to change their driving habits to save gas, or to turn off lights when they are not in use? Can the principles and techniques of social influence be of any help to the problem of energy conservation when we approach it on such a large scale?

The major problem in changing people's behavior, whether we are talking about energy consumption or anything else, is that they must be motivated to change. People ask themselves, "Why should I be less comfortable [e.g., with the air conditioner off] or be inconvenienced [e.g., by having to leave when the car pool wants] if there is no immediate reward in sight to compensate me for changing?" In this case it is difficult to apply normative pressures, because people do not feel that they will lose face or risk disapproval by continuing their old ways. Nor do they see others around them making any changes in their behavior. Informational pressures—that carpooling saves gas, or that lowering the thermostat is important—are not very salient, nor in this context are they powerful.

Although they have deemphasized the role of reward power in small-scale group influence situations, many social psychologists have begun to realize that a program of incentives might be just the answer for changing people's conservation behavior on a large scale (see Cook & Berrenberg, 1981). Incentives can take many forms. The simplest and most direct are monetary. Winett, Kagel, Battalio, and Winkler (1978) offered families a substantial rebate to reduce their energy consumption and produced a 12 percent drop in use. McClelland and Belsten (1979–1980) conducted a "conservation challenge" in a large dormitory at the University of Colorado, offering students monetary prizes, and within two weeks energy consumption was down by 10 percent. In addition, Geller has noted that if incentives are offered to a *group* (e.g., a whole dormitory or a floor of a dorm) rather than to people on an individual basis, group members exert strong social pressures on one another to conform and thereby conserve.

Rewards do not have to be strictly financial. Social incentives in the form of recognition and approval have encouraged savings among heating oil consumers (Seaver & Patterson, 1976) and among truck drivers (Runnion, Watson, & McWhorter, 1978). Convenience and comfort have also been used as incentives by informed social planners to promote the use of car pools (Rose & Hinds, 1976). Every working day on the Bay Bridge connecting Oakland to San Francisco, thousands of commuters in buses or car pools whiz along in toll-free lanes while those who travel alone in their cars endure mile-long lines waiting to pay the 75-cent toll. When properly enforced, this has increased ride sharing considerably.

The use of incentives to change social behavior is not a perfect solution and has come under criticism from a number of directions (Seligman, 1985). Some have noted that the incentives required to maintain desired behaviors are not always cost-effective (Winett & Neale, 1979; McClelland & Canter, 1981). For instance, in the project at the University of Colorado, the savings in electricity amounted to $350, but $385 in prizes was awarded. Others have asked what happens when the incentives eventually are eliminated, suggesting that external rewards may actually inhibit internalization rather than encourage it (see Chapter 6 for the problem of overrewarding behavior). In Kelman's terms these criticisms suggest that long-term changes require internalization, whereas incentives create change only via compliance.

Advocates of the incentive-based techniques believe that once people actually get into the habit of doing something—for whatever reason—they may continue with that habit even after the initial reason is removed. Others point out that once consumers realize that by conserving they are saving themselves a good deal of money each month, conservation behavior will be *self-rewarding* and therefore permanent. For instance, a number of techniques giving consumers information in the form of feedback about the amount of electricity or money they have been saving have been successful even without additional financial incentives (Seligman, Becker, & Darley, 1981).

The application of basic principles from research in social influence to the problems of energy conservation has a short history. Yet the efforts we have reviewed demonstrate that even at this early stage, changes in behavior can be effected.

MINORITY INFLUENCE AND SOCIAL CHANGE

The emphasis throughout much of the work in social influence and conformity has been on how the majority (as in Asch's research) or those in power (as in Milgram's research) influence people who are in the minority or who have little power. Serge Moscovici, a highly respected French social psychologist, has argued that this is only a partial view (Moscovici, 1976, 1980). He points out that influence works *both* ways, and that the minority is not necessarily passive. All influence attempts cause conflict in *both* parties, and each party may force the other to reconsider its position.

Every new idea, Moscovici reminds us, begins with a minority of one. Great thinkers like Socrates and Galileo were "deviants"; their ideas were different from those of the majority. Still, a small, vocal minority can exert influence and bring about innovations in ways of thinking and acting. A glance back to the 1960s, when antiwar sentiments began with a few and grew to affect national elections and policies, reminds us of this point. Therefore, if we think of influence from this point of view, we think of it as a process that brings about *social change* rather than one that deals in *social control.*

Moscovici and his colleagues realize that the minority lacks most of the advantages of the majority. They are few in number and have few bases of social power. As a result, they have little ability to change others via normative or informational influence. What does the minority have going for it? First, Moscovici reminds us that in general people prefer consensus to dissent. By virtue of holding a different viewpoint, the minority forces the majority to direct its attention to their point of view. Simply by being different, the spotlight is thrown on them and their cause. Second, although those in the minority might not be liked, they tend to be respected and given a grudging recognition or admiration (Nemeth & Wachtler, 1974, 1983).

Moscovici and his colleagues believe that the key to creating change in the majority is the *behavioral style* of the minority, the way minority members orchestrate and pattern their behavior as they attempt to persuade (Moscovici & Nemeth, 1974; Wolf, 1985). Minority members must appear to be consistent, independent, and confident of their position. Yet they should not seem totally rigid and inflexible, to avoid completely alienating the majority. The majority must perceive that the minority has a viable position of which it is firmly convinced, but also that it is willing to compromise and make reciprocal concessions if necessary (Tanford & Penrod, 1984).

The type of experiment most often used to demonstrate minority influence is basically a reversal of the Asch situation (Moscovici, Lage, & Naffrechoux, 1969). Instead of hiring confederates to act the role of the majority, in this case two confederates consistently offer a minority position. The four real participants and the two confederates are asked to rate the color and brightness of 36 slides. Although the slides are all various shades of blue, in one condition the two confederates report green on all 36 trials, and in other conditions they report green on two-thirds or one-third of the trials. In the control condition, participants respond without confederates present. Almost none of the majority ever say "green" in the control condition or when the confederates are inconsistent in their responses. When the minority is perfectly consistent, however, green is reported at least 8 percent of the time and almost one-third of the subjects go along with the minority at least once.

The most fascinating contention of Moscovici (1980) is that the process of change created by **minority influence** is just the opposite of majority influence, and is potentially even more powerful. That is, Moscovici argues that much of the standard work on conformity shows that people change via *compliance;* they exhibit acceptance in public, but privately they do not really believe what they are saying or doing. He believes that minority influence generates *conversion;* many people privately change and accept the minority stance, but are afraid to state their new beliefs in public. Majority influence produces large changes, but they are more apparent than real because people are unlikely to internalize them. But when the minority produces influence, the change is small but real, and may eventually spread among the many.

In a sense we have come full circle. We began with a discussion of the differences among compliance, identification, and internalization, and reviewed the many ways by which powerful individuals and majorities influence minorities. In the end we have returned to these three kinds of influence and seen that along with obvious disadvantages, minorities enjoy certain unrecognized advantages to bring about internalization of their beliefs and practices. Therefore, the processes of top-down and bottom-up influence are not as different as we might have thought (Tanford & Penrod, 1984).

This chapter began with some seemingly astonishing examples of change. Now, in light of what we have learned about social influence, we return to them—and perhaps they will appear less astonishing. Having reviewed the processes, methods, and motives surrounding everyday social influence, we can now apply them to an understanding of extreme forms of change. The first thing we must recognize is that this kind of major change is not accomplished using coercive power or other compliance-based techniques. As Moscovici points out, threats get only collaboration—compliance at most—but they do not lead to conversion, or internalization, in our terms. We must look therefore to a number of other, more subtle approaches based on the principles of social influence to explain these "conversions of faith."

An important technique, common to all documented reports on political and religious conversion, is the use of paced demands. Potential converts are not changed all at once. Instead, just as people in Milgram's studies faced a series of escalating voltage levels, new recruits are asked to take small steps or to make small commitments at first, but each step leads to the need for greater commitment or change. This is clearly a highly refined version of the foot-in-the-door technique.

In John Lofland's work on the conversion techniques of the Unification Church (1981), he identified a series of steps used by Moon's followers to create new converts. The first stage he describes is the "pickup." Young Moonies spend much of their time initiating casual discussions in public places and even offering rides to hitchhikers in order to start a conversation. Potential converts might first be invited to dinner, then for a weekend retreat, and then for a more extended stay. Each step brings the potential convert closer to the fold and generates greater momentum for future change.

Once a person accepts an offer for dinner, this is the group's opportunity to "hook" the new recruit. Upon arriving, the prospect finds 50 or more active young people smiling and showing an extreme degree of friendliness and happiness. As described by one visitor, "They seemed to be circulating like sorority sisters during rush" (Lofland, p. 13). Members are instructed to reward the new visitors with compliments and approval and to present themselves as a happy, cohesive group with whom the recruits can identify (i.e., to use referent power). The principles of the religion introduced at this point are still vague and involve sharing, loving, and helping—values with which we all could agree—but at the same time, getting the group's collective foot in the door and paving the way for further cognitive changes (i.e., internalization).

The key element to all conversion experiences is getting control over the physical and social environment of the individual. The setting may be an SLA hideout in California, a weekend workshop on a farm outside of town, or the total isolation of a rural village in Guyana. The critical aspect is that the individual is separated from support for all prior ideas, much as the people in Sherif's autokinetic experiment were separated from all external frames of reference. People are engulfed in a group atmosphere of unanimity and absolute consensus. In such a situation, they become totally absorbed in the group and become highly susceptible to both normative and informational influences.

Normative influence takes the form of wanting to be accepted, and needing to belong and share everyone else's happiness. One prospect commented: "When I did hold back in some small way, and received a look of sorrowful, benevolent concern, I felt guilt and the desire to please as though it were God himself whom I had offended" (p. 16). In such an atmosphere, potential converts are open to informational influence, as they become unsure about just what is right and just what is wrong when their old values are challenged. Stark and Bainbridge (1980) point out that internal group ties can get so strong that they weaken ties to the outside world of family and friends. All ideas and feelings come to be defined by the group, independent of what those outside the group say. It is particularly important that the group or cult become the exclusive reference source for new converts so that they will be resistant to social influence (i.e., "deprogramming") once others find out about their conversion.

Not all people are equally subject to this form of social influence. Just as we pointed out that some personality variables are related to conformity in general, the people who are most likely to be attracted to and convinced about radical social, political, and religious groups are those who are young, alienated, or confused, or who feel they have reached a turning point in their lives. Yet we must recognize that these basic principles and methods apply to influence about all conventional religious and political movements as well. We would hardly refer to the changes students undergo in large fraternities or small colleges as "brainwashing" or "programming." But even though the extent of change and the intensity of pressure may differ in these more typical settings, the processes and the methods of change are the same in all of them.

SUMMARY

1. Social influence is the process by which any individual's attitudes, beliefs, or behaviors are modified by the presence or actions of others. The resulting change may be temporary or permanent, deep-seated or surface, depending upon the relationship of the person to the source of change.
2. Herbert Kelman has described three processes of social influence: compliance, in which change is motivated by the desire for a favorable reaction; identification, in which influence is accepted in order to be like or to feel like a person or group; and internalization, in which individuals accept new information or behaviors because they are consistent with their current values and beliefs.
3. To possess social power means to have the potential to influence. Types of power that have been identified are reward, coercive, referent, legitimate, expert, and informational. Medical practitioners often rely upon threats (coercive power), appeals to authority (legitimate power), and superior technical knowledge (expert power), rather than offering full explanations (informational power) or pointing out similarities between themselves and their patients (referent power).
4. Conformity involves the influence of the group on the individual. It may be primarily motivated by normative pressures (so as not to appear different) or informational pressures (because of the belief that the group is right). The opposite of conformity is anticonformity, an

active rejection of group influence. Independent behavior involves neither acceptance nor rejection, but implies that the person's actions were not affected by those of the group.

5. The classic studies of Muzafer Sherif have demonstrated that when people are highly uncertain about the correct answer, they compare their responses with one another, and their responses converge around a group norm. In such a situation, almost all people conform in some degree.
6. The research of Solomon Asch presented students with a situation in which the clear evidence of their eyes conflicted with the opinion of a unanimous group. Asch found that there was a great variation in response among individuals, but that one-third of all responses given were in conformity with the group's opinion.
7. A wide range of factors that affect conformity have been investigated. There appear to be no clear-cut personality or sex differences in conformity, although some cultural groups that value group harmony do show greater acceptance of group pressures.
8. Situational variables, such as the characteristics of the task, characteristics of the group, and position in the group, play an important role in affecting conformity. Of these, the presence of one or more supporters in the group seems to be a major factor in allowing people to resist conformity pressures.
9. Obedience differs from conformity in that it involves pressure from a legitimate authority rather than from a peer group. Stanley Milgram's dramatic research on obedience demonstrated that 65 percent of those told to deliver electric shocks to another continued to do so as long as the experimenter insisted.
10. As in conformity, there are no clear-cut individual difference patterns that differentiate between those who obey and those who do not. Situational variables, such as the proximity of the experimenter to the subject or the distance between the subject and the victim, do affect obedience. In addition, the presence of disapproving group members can reduce obedience significantly.
11. Two successful strategies of influence are the foot-in-the-door and the door-in-the-face techniques. In the former, the person first makes a small request and, if successful, escalates to a larger request (the one desired in the first place). In the latter, the opposite approach is taken. A person first makes an extremely large or unreasonable request and, once turned down, settles for making the smaller request that was desired all along.
12. Another successful technique of influence is modeling, by which people change their behavior by observing and then imitating the behavior of others. The application of this technique to the prevention of smoking among teenagers has shown positive results. Incentives,

whether material (e.g., money) or social (e.g., approval), have also proved useful in changing behaviors on a large scale, as with the use of seat belts and lowering energy consumption.

13. While most influence goes from the many (the majority) to the few (the minority), change can also go in the opposite direction. Serge Moscovici has argued and demonstrated that a minority viewpoint can be successful when those who hold it appear to be consistent, independent, and confident of their position.

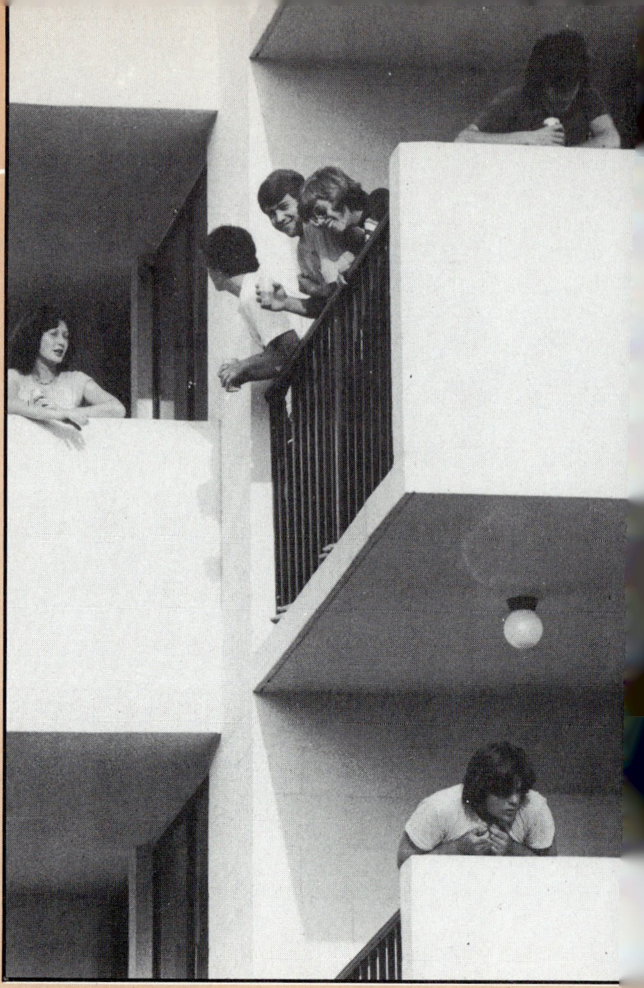

CHAPTER 11
Environment and Behavior

Tom Richardson had really looked forward to getting away from home and going off to college. Once out of the house he would finally have some privacy and be able to come and go as he pleased. No longer would he have to wait for his sister to get out of the bathroom or off the phone, nor would he have to endure his teenage brother's high-decibel fascination with the local punk-rock radio station. He would finally be able to exercise some control over his life. Now, having spent a semester in the freshman dorms, he realized that dorm life was indeed different. But in many ways it was worse, not better.

The dorm Tom lived in was fairly typical of those at the college. It was three stories high and housed a large proportion of the male freshmen. Each floor was dominated by a long central hallway with doors along both sides of the corridor leading to small, boxlike rooms. Each room contained two beds, two desks, and all the basic necessities of college life. At one end of the hall was a lounge, and a central bathroom was shared by all 34 people on the floor. Most of the people who lived in Tom's dorm called it "the zoo," and many were already planning to move out in their sophomore year.

The problem with the dorm was that it offered less privacy, less space, and less control than anything Tom had experienced before. There were people here, people there, people everywhere. They didn't just seem to meet, they collided—and it was not only in the touch football games that constantly took place in the 6-foot-wide corridor. Tom couldn't avoid running into familiar and unfamiliar faces, and it got to the point where he was sick and tired of people in general. Unless he hid in his room or went off to seek a quiet corner in the library, he had no privacy whatsoever. He wondered why he felt so crowded even when few people were around.

Tom's situation is fairly typical of the way many college freshmen experience dorm life, but does it have to be that way? Can dormitories be planned to help people feel less crowded? Can new dorms be built and old ones redesigned to offer people a sense of control and an interest in being with others rather than a feeling of helplessness and a desire to withdraw? In this chapter we will review the basic principles of person-environment relationships, and then we will return to consider ways in which social psychologists have applied them to the design of college dormitories.

As noted in Chapter 1, the focus of psychology historically has been on explaining behavior in terms of internal characteristics such as drives, motives, and instincts. One of the most basic contributions of social psychology as a field was to point out the value of *situationism,* to emphasize that behavior could be explained best by considering the interaction of the individual with various situational, environmental, and social structural factors. Yet throughout its brief history, the emphasis of social psychology has been on specific social pressures in the immediate situation; on the expectations, evaluations, and social pressures that people and groups placed on one another.

In the late 1960s, social psychologists "discovered" a number of pressing environmental issues such as crowding, noise, pollution, and urban slums. As a result, they broadened their definition of "external" or "environmental" factors to include the *physical* environment, and began to draw attention to the great reciprocal influence that people and their environments could have on each other. They began to interact more freely with anthropologists, sociologists, and criminologists, and brought their knowledge into the offices of architects and city planners.

In this chapter we will first provide an overview of environmental social psychology by clarifying the many different ways in which the environment can be conceptualized and described. Then we will discuss the relationship of people to the available space around them in considering three topics that have stimulated a great deal of research and application: personal space, crowding, and territoriality. Next, we will consider how one major physical setting, the city, leads people to adopt various modes of behavior to deal with the great numbers of people around them. Finally, we will consider how the principles of environmental-social psychology have been integrated into architectural planning, showing how good design can and does take into account the needs of people.

DESCRIBING THE ENVIRONMENT

Rudolf Moos (1973) has pointed out that there are many different ways in which we might conceptualize and describe various places:

1. According to their ecological, geographic, or physical design properties. For instance, a building could be described in terms of its height or its architectural style; a city in terms of its climate or its terrain; a college in terms of its size and location.
2. As "behavior settings." Roger Barker (Barker, 1968; Wicker, 1979), one of the few early social psychologists to study behavior in its true ecological context, used this term to refer to the fundamental units of public social life. Each behavior setting encourages a particular pattern of behavior as required or appropriate. For instance, libraries and churches call for one type of behavior, while gyms and bars call for very different kinds of activity and demeanor.
3. In reference to the personal or behavioral characteristics of the inhabitants. Places vary in the age, background, skills, and socioeconomic status of their inhabitants. For instance, Miami has many older people; Detroit, many auto workers; Beverly Hills, many movie stars. Two neighborhoods may vary in how involved their residents are in local politics and political action.
4. In terms of the social climate of the place. Places create different atmospheres for people to live and work (Moos, 1976; Krupat & Guild, 1980a). Some are open and friendly, others rigid and competitive. Anyone who has ever opened a guide to selecting colleges knows that the social climate of some schools is conducive to partying, while the atmosphere of others leads people to take a more serious approach to their studies.

Describing the environment is the first step in understanding how a given individual will experience it and behave in it. The environment as it physically exists will not be experienced the same by everyone because it must first pass through a set of filters (Rapoport, 1977; Wapner, Kaplan, & Cohen, 1973). First, members of different cultures or groups experience environments differently. Students, teachers, and administrators each relate to the college administration building differently. Atheists have different reactions to church than do true believers. People from one culture may misinterpret or be completely unaware of the meanings and significance that certain places hold for members of another culture. A holy burial ground for members of one group may be seen as an empty lot by outsiders.

Each individual has a differing set of needs, interests, roles, past experiences, and expectations. Depending on the unique configuration of these factors, each person is disposed to select separate aspects of the environment to pay attention to; to interpret the meaning of messages conveyed by the environment differently; to evaluate the environment against a unique set of personal standards; and to act in relation to the environment in a way that is personally idiosyncratic.

For instance, if a New Yorker and a student from a small rural high school both went to college in Madison, Wisconsin, the New Yorker would probably consider it a small town, while the other would consider it a big city. In comparison to his or her prior environment, the New Yorker would probably feel relatively safe and probably would not hesitate to go out at night alone. The small-towner, on the other hand, would probably perceive the campus differently and act in a way that was more cautious.

It would be a mistake, however, to go too far and assume that because each person's response to the environment has some idiosyncrasies, we cannot design and plan for large numbers of people at a time. We must realize that people have a great deal of shared reactions because of the things they hold in common. Therefore, it is only when we understand the *objective* characteristics of the environment in conjunction with the various *subjective* reactions people have to it that we can fully understand environmental behavior (Krupat & Guild, 1980b).

As we leave a person-centered focus and take a broader environmental view, the first set of person-environment issues to capture our attention deals with the relationship of individuals to their immediate spatial environment. How much space do people need around them to feel comfortable? Is it the same for all people or all interactions? Do people tend to claim the territory around them and are they willing to defend it against encroachment? How do people feel when they don't have enough space to carry out their day-to-day tasks, and what are the consequences of feeling too enclosed by others? Each of these questions touches upon matters of personal space, territoriality, or crowding, three important issues concerning spatial behavior.

PERSONAL SPACE

Personal space (see Figure 11.1) refers to an area that exists immediately around our bodies—some people have referred to it as an invisible bubble or a body buffer zone—into which others may not intrude (Dosey & Meisels, 1969; Hayduck, 1978, 1981). Although no one has ever seen this imaginary bubble, nor are we aware that we carry it around with us all the time, it is there as surely as a porcupine's quills. In fact, Robert Sommer (1969) has pointed out that personal space serves some of the same functions for humans as quills do for porcupines. It allows people to get just close enough for warmth and comradeship, but lets them know that they may not get too close.

Hall's Distance Zones

The one advantage that personal space has over quills is that it can expand or contract depending upon the situation. With some people and for some purposes we require more space, while at other times and other places

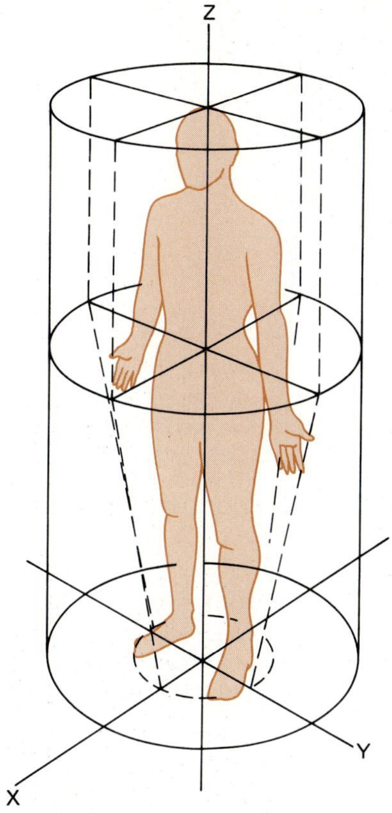

FIGURE 11.1

A Three-Dimensional Model of Personal Space In this artist's rendering, the individual's personal space bubble is of moderate size and equally large in the front and the back. However, personal space requirements of different people in different situations may change the size and shape of the bubble. *Source:* L. A. Hayduk (1978). Personal space: An evaluative and orienting overview. *Psychological Bulletin, 85,* 117–34. Copyright 1978 by the American Psychological Association.

we require less. Anthropologist Edward Hall, a keen observer of social-environmental behavior, has noted this tendency of people to maintain varying amounts of space between one another depending upon what their relationship is and what kinds of activities they are engaging in (Hall 1966). He has described four distance zones among North Americans, each with a closer and a farther phase.

Intimate Distance At the close phase of intimate distance people touch. This is the distance for lovemaking, comforting, fighting, or protecting. At this distance, we can also smell other people and even sense the heat from their bodies. Interactions at this phase are intense and reserved for a few. The far phase, 6 inches to 1½ feet, is used for intimate conversation or whispering.

Personal Distance This is the distance we use for activities with friends or acquaintances. From 1½ to 2½ feet is the distance we reserve for "close" friends, while others who are not as psychologically close usually do not get quite as physically close (about 2½ to 4 feet). Verbal exchanges rather than touch now take over as the medium of communication.

We can tell by the distance between these two men that they know each other. Still, notice how the crossed arms of the man in the plaid pants compensate for the encroaching position of the other.

Social Distance Ranging anywhere from 4 to 12 feet, this is the distance at which business transactions take place. The relationship between the two parties is impersonal and more formal. Touch is not possible or acceptable, and normal voice level must be maintained for effective communication. In an office, the visitor's chair is usually placed at this distance, and one's desk guarantees that others cannot get too close.

Public Distance Ranging from 12 feet to 25 feet or more, this is the distance maintained when people are of unequal status, or when dealing with important public figures, or in formal speaking arrangements. Notice how members of the jury must sit close to one another, while the judge is placed at a greater distance from everyone; or how the bubble around the president of the United States is physically maintained at a great distance by the members of the Secret Service.

A second important observation made by Hall is that people from different cultures require different amounts of space (Hall, 1966; Sussman & Rosenfeld, 1982). People from northern European (e.g., German) and British cultures typically prefer greater space for their interactions and are made more uncomfortable than are North Americans when they do not get the space they require. On the other hand, people from Arabic and Mediterranean cultures expect and require far less space. In the Arab world and in southern France, body contact—even pushing and shoving in crowded streets or marketplaces—occurs frequently, and people are not upset when touched by another or when they can sense the presence of others by body odor.

Because people are usually not aware that their own personal space requirements may differ from those of others, misunderstandings can arise when two individuals from differing cultures come together to interact. Each one may be surprised, confused, or annoyed when the other fails to maintain the "appropriate" distance. Take, for instance, Hall's description of what he termed the "UN Waltz," an informal meeting of an Arab and a British diplomat in the hallway of the United Nations. The British diplomat stops at a distance of 4 to 5 feet, a distance he would consider proper for conversing with a professional colleague. To his dismay, the Arab diplomat keeps advancing until he is only a foot or two away. Wondering why this fellow is being so "pushy" and feeling that it is impossible to carry on a conversation while staring into someone's eyes and feeling the heat of his breath, the Briton casually retreats a step or two as the conversation begins. The Arab diplomat, wondering how to speak across the void that has been created and wondering why this fellow is being so "distant," slowly advances to reestablish a proper distance—for him. The result is that each person is likely to be making negative attributions about the other as the couple "waltzes" around the hallway, the first going back-two-three while the other follows up-two-three in a pattern of retreat and advance across the diplomatic dance floor.

Considerable research indicates that personal space preferences vary not only among cultural groups but also among many other groups as well. Males seem to require more space than females (Wittig & Skolnick, 1978; Gifford, 1982); middle-class people require more than working-class people (Scherer, 1974); and adults require more than children (Aiello & Aiello, 1974; Smetana, Bridgeman, & Bridgeman, 1978; Tennis & Dabbs, 1975). In a comparison of violent and nonviolent prisoners, Kinsel (1970) found that the average amount of personal space needed by those with a history of violence was four times as great as those without a violent history. Not surprisingly, the violent prisoners required by far the greatest amounts of space protecting their backs (see Figure 11.2).

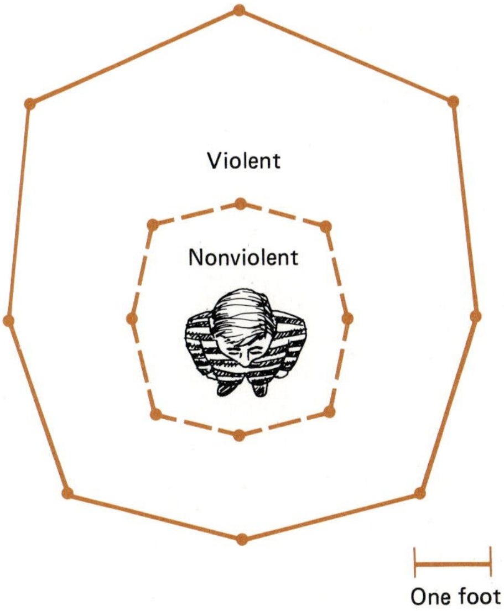

FIGURE 11.2

Personal Space Requirements of Violent and Nonviolent Prisoners The personal space requirements of violent prisoners were far greater than those of nonviolent prisoners. In particular, violent prisoners required more space behind them. *Source:* A. F. Kinzel (1970). Body buffer zone in violent prisoners. *American Journal of Psychiatry, 127,* 159–64. Copyright 1970, American Psychiatric Association.

When people share spatial norms and are acting appropriately for the setting and the activity, they are comfortable and relaxed. When they are too close or too far, however, they can be distracted, annoyed, or confused. Albert and Dabbs (1970) placed a person trying to be persuasive and a person to be persuaded at a distance of either 2 feet (too close for comfort), 5 feet (appropriate social distance), or 15 feet (too far for the circumstances). When the distance was just right, the target of persuasion paid more attention and thought the other person was more knowledgeable than when they were either too far or too close. In a follow-up, Dabbs (1971) found that the person who was too close was seen as pressuring and tended to be disliked.

The Functions of Personal Space

Personal space serves two major functions (Holahan, 1982; Fisher, Bell, & Baum, 1984). The first involves a defensive, or self-protective, function. People use the space around them to avoid becoming overloaded, to maintain privacy, or to reduce the stressfulness of the environment in general. When people feel in control, they are willing to maintain less space between themselves and others (Duke & Nowicki, 1972), but when they feel pressured, one reaction is to maintain greater space from others (Dosey & Meisels, 1969; Karabenick & Meisels, 1972).

When one's personal space is invaded, a number of reactions are possible. One typical reaction is flight. For instance, in one study (Konecni et al., 1975) experimental assistants walked up to people waiting to cross the street and stood anywhere from 1 to 10 feet away. The closer the assistants stood, the quicker the pedestrians crossed. Still, people often try means of adjusting to a spatial invasion rather than leave the scene. In a library, for instance, people may spread out notebooks and texts to defend against invasion, or suddenly turn away to face in the opposite direction (Patterson, Mullens, & Romano, 1971).

Michael Argyle and his colleagues (Argyle & Dean, 1965; Argyle & Cook, 1976) believe that people compensate for excessive physical closeness by creating psychological distance. We reduce eye contact, shift our posture by leaning back or facing away, or hold our arms in front. This reestablishes the equilibrium between ourselves and the physical and social environment that existed before the invasion.

Personal space functions in a second way as a regulator or indicator of attraction and liking. The first time that students enter a class for a new semester, it is easy to tell who knows whom and which people are friends outside of class. The seating pattern tells the story. Some people sit down alone or on the periphery. Others sit in pairs, often gazing into one another's eyes, as close to intimate distance as a public setting will allow. Still others sit in groups, perhaps members of a fraternity, sorority, or athletic team. As the semester progresses, new friendships evolve and seating patterns change to reflect the new "closeness" of class members. Research has confirmed that people maintain smaller distances when they are attracted to one another, when their activities are cooperative, when they are equal in status, and when they want to gain or express liking (Gifford, 1982; Mehrabian, 1968; Rosenfeld, 1965).

Just as liking and attraction are reflected in closer personal space, dislike or discomfort can go along with a maintenance of greater distances. A subtle indicator of the discomfort some people have when dealing with those who have a social or physical disability is the distance they maintain. In a study by Worthington (1974), a confederate of the experimenter was seated in either a regular chair or a wheelchair and asked passersby at an airport for directions. People stood farther away when the person was in the wheelchair. In another study, people with a facial disfigurement (an unattractive birthmark on one side of the face) interacted with others from one side or the other so that the birthmark could or could not be seen. When the birthmark could be seen, people tended to keep a greater distance (Rumsey, Bull, & Gahagan, 1982).

To summarize, while no one has ever seen a personal space bubble, the reactions of people to one another when they maintain too much or too little interpersonal distance suggests that personal space is very real. We require more or less space depending on cultural norms and the nature of the person and task involved. We use personal space to maintain control over the environment and to indicate attraction; and when our space is invaded, we respond physically or psychologically to reestablish the equilibrium that existed previously.

TERRITORIALITY

Just as we have strong commitments to the space immediately surrounding our bodies, we also have an interest in the places or geographic areas—the territory—that we occupy or use. This feeling of ownership, commitment, and willingness to defend a physical area is known as **territoriality.** Like personal space, territoriality can serve a number of functions. However, while personal space refers to a specific area immediately around one's body and involves an intense commitment, we may be attached to different territories in varying degrees.

Types of Territories

Territories vary according to the degree to which they are under complete or exclusive control of a single owner, as well as the relative duration for which people use them. *Primary territories* are owned or used completely by one person or group, and are occupied for lengthy periods. Your home or your room is the most obvious example. Primary territories afford their users privacy, security, and control. In fact, the inability to maintain control over a primary territory is a severe threat to a person's status and self-esteem. In their own homes, for instance, people feel free to post "keep out" signs, and reserve the right to tell someone to leave. They are likely to resent any unwanted intrusion and are ready to fight for their turf before they would think of leaving it.

Secondary territories are places that people share with others. They are used for briefer periods of time and are less critical than are primary territories to the lives and self-definitions of people. They represent places in which people feel *at* home although they are *not* home. A neighborhood bar, a local pharmacy, or the basketball court at the local park are places to which all people have access in a technical sense, although people who are recognized as regulars are far more likely to be approved of, greeted, and assisted. Although nobody claims to own such a place, the distinction between regular user and stranger in such a territory is an important one.

In contrast to secondary territory, which we might think of as semi-public space, *public territories* are those places that anyone can use with equal rights and freedom. Erving Goffman (1971) has referred to them as "free spaces." A large public beach or a city street are good examples. People come and go all the time and one person's claim to a given space is just as good as another's. Although people may claim spots for some duration, no lasting attachments are likely to form.

Functions of Territoriality

Territoriality serves a number of important functions. First, it plays an organizing role in everyday activity and promotes smooth group functioning (Edney, 1976). Imagine a world, if you can, in which no such thing as territoriality existed. Every space would be first come, first served;

When people feel territorial about a place, they personalize it, or place their own distinctive mark on it. This photo, for example, tells us a great deal about the person who occupies this bedroom. What do you feel you know about this person's sex, age, and interests just by looking at the way the room is decorated?

and you could not lay claim to a space and have someone respect it. You might leave home this morning and find that someone else had moved in by the time you got back. By allowing a sense of permanence or even temporary control, territoriality puts order in our lives, and therefore avoids arguments and conflicting claims to space. Among animals it allows for mating, food gathering, and the rearing of young. Among people it affords privacy (Altman, 1975), lends stability to our interactions, and can serve as a part of group and individual identity (Proshansky, Fabian, & Kaminoff, 1983).

In two very different settings, Irwin Altman and his colleagues have demonstrated this. In observations at home, Altman, Nelson, and Lett (1972) found that families typically had fixed seating arrangements at meals, and that things ran smoothly when people who shared a room (whether parents or children) established a system of claims to closets and drawers. In a second series of studies (Altman & Haythorn, 1967; Altman, Taylor, & Wheeler, 1971), the researchers observed pairs of U.S. Navy volunteers who were confined to tight quarters for eight to ten days in order to simulate undersea living conditions. When the two men established territorial claims over who used which chair and which bed and arranged a schedule for the use of items at different times, the pair functioned more smoothly.

A second function of territoriality is to symbolize dominant relationships. Most often, those who are more powerful or who hold higher status in a group get to express this by possessing more attractive items and areas or at least holding them first or longest. Esser (1973) and Sundstrom and Altman (1974) have reported this pattern in observational studies of young boys in institutionalized settings. They note, however, that clear territorial relationships take hold only when the group's membership is stable. When dominant people come and go, territorial relationships are often thrown up for grabs, and disobedience, fighting, or stealing may increase.

Territoriality and dominance can also be related in a slightly different way as expressed by the phrase "home team advantage." Research has confirmed that just as we have always guessed, people feel more confident and do better on their home turf than when they are away. Small dogs chase large ones from their own yards, chickens peck at others when in their own cages (Rajecki et al., 1977); students in their dorm rooms and apartments voice their opinions more strongly than visitors (Conroy & Sundstrom, 1977); and basketball teams win more games at home than on the road (Altman, 1975).

Territoriality also serves to promote personal and group identity through people's attachment to places. A number of researchers have noted that individuals and groups become personally involved not only in their homes but in their neighborhoods and even their cities as well. The territory that they live in or use actually seems to become part of them (Shumaker & Taylor, 1983; Stokols & Shumaker, 1980). While studying the effects of urban renewal, Fried and Gleicher (1961) noted that when their neighborhood was destroyed, many people in Boston's West End wept and grieved for their homes as they would for a close friend or relative.

Personalization

When people maintain control over a space, they usually want to let others know by adding some sort of distinctive mark to it. This sort of behavior is known as **personalization,** and may be done for positive, expressive reasons indicating pride and attraction; or for protective or aggressive motives in response to possible invasion. On the positive side, personalization expresses not only that "this is mine," but also that "this is me." It is an assertion of self and an expression of one's identity in the immediate physical environment. Freshman dropouts at the University of Utah (Vinsel et al., 1980) tended to decorate their rooms with posters and pictures from their precollege environment (e.g., photos of their parents or scenes of back home), while those who stayed in school personalized by putting up posters of Salt Lake City or the surrounding mountains.

Territorial displays serve a different purpose when they convey the message "This is mine—tread carefully," or sometimes simply "Keep out." Homeowners often place distinctive territorial markers such as hedges or fences to let others know that they are protective of their own property (Edney, 1972); and gangs often mark their territory with graffiti (Ley & Cybriwsky, 1974) as an indication of their strength. Among urban residents, especially the elderly, people who placed a number of territorial markers around their home were less fearful of the crime around them (Patterson, 1978; Taylor, Shumaker, & Gottfredson, 1985), demonstrating the symbolic power of territorial displays.

Therefore, territoriality also serves a set of important functions. It helps organize interaction, symbolizes dominance relationships, and encourages group identity. But does it make a difference if an environment fosters a sense of territoriality? What consequences might follow if public housing were designed to encourage or discourage it? As we will see, the consequences demonstrate an important application of the principles of social psychology to urban housing.

APPLICATION
TERRITORIALITY AND DEFENSIBLE SPACE

In the 1950s, many urban planners looked at the city's slum neighborhoods and decided they were beyond repair. The old three- to five-story buildings, most lacking elevators but not lacking roaches and rodents, would have to be torn down and replaced with clean and shiny high-rise apartment buildings. These products of urban renewal would provide healthy, comfortable, safe environments in which people would live happily. Unfortunately, the planners were wrong. While the old housing was badly in need of repair, its physical organization fostered a social system in which friends could congregate in various semipublic (secondary) territories, such as local establishments and the front steps of buildings; and a strong sense of local commitment (i.e., territoriality) existed (Gans, 1962; Jacobs, 1961).

In the place of these "slums" went up housing projects such as Pruitt-Igoe in St. Louis. Opened in 1954, it was almost a town in itself, consisting of forty-three 11-story buildings covering 57 acres and housing 12,000 people. Within 16 years Pruitt-Igoe was so vandalized, crime-ridden, and uninhabitable that the city government admitted its failure and demolished the entire tract.

While the problems with this project were numerous, one major contribution to the failures of this and many other large public housing projects was its form of design. The old lower-class neighborhood provided secondary territories in which social networks and social support could evolve, but the typical project had no place for such interaction. On the interior, the long, narrow corridors of the housing project building discouraged interaction and promoted anonymity. On the outside, the open space was too large, too undefined, and therefore unusable because it was too public (Jacobs, 1961). Yet the only alternative space to socialize in, one's apartment, was too private (i.e., primary territory). As a result, project dwellers had the choice (not unlike that of some dorm residents) of withdrawing into their apartments or trying to make contacts among others in the vast three-to-four-block expanses of purely residential buildings—and this was a difficult task.

Oscar Newman (1972) argued that while the large central areas and long, narrow corridors of urban projects provided aesthetically pleasing exterior space or efficient interior space, they also provided criminals with the ideal circumstances in which to operate. These public spaces belonged to no one, were watched by no one, and were defended by no one. In short, he believed that this form of design totally discouraged the development of territoriality.

Newman believed that the key ingredient lacking in these projects was **defensible space,** an environment in which territoriality and a sense of community lead people to work for, feel proud of, and be willing to defend *their* space. Design, he believes, can help create a feeling of shared ownership and responsibility for specific areas by subdividing space to create perceived zones of influence (see Figure 11.3).

Newman and his colleagues (e.g., Newman & Franck, 1982) as well as several others (Fowler & Mangione, 1981; Merry, 1981; Taylor & Gottfredson, 1986) have compared projects that are designed in line with defensible space principles against those that are not. They also have redesigned urban housing projects in cities such as Newark, New Jersey; Hartford, Connecticut; Baltimore; San Francisco; and elsewhere.

In Salt Lake City, Brown and Altman (1983) found that burglarized homes had fewer signs of territorial ownership than those that had not been burglar-

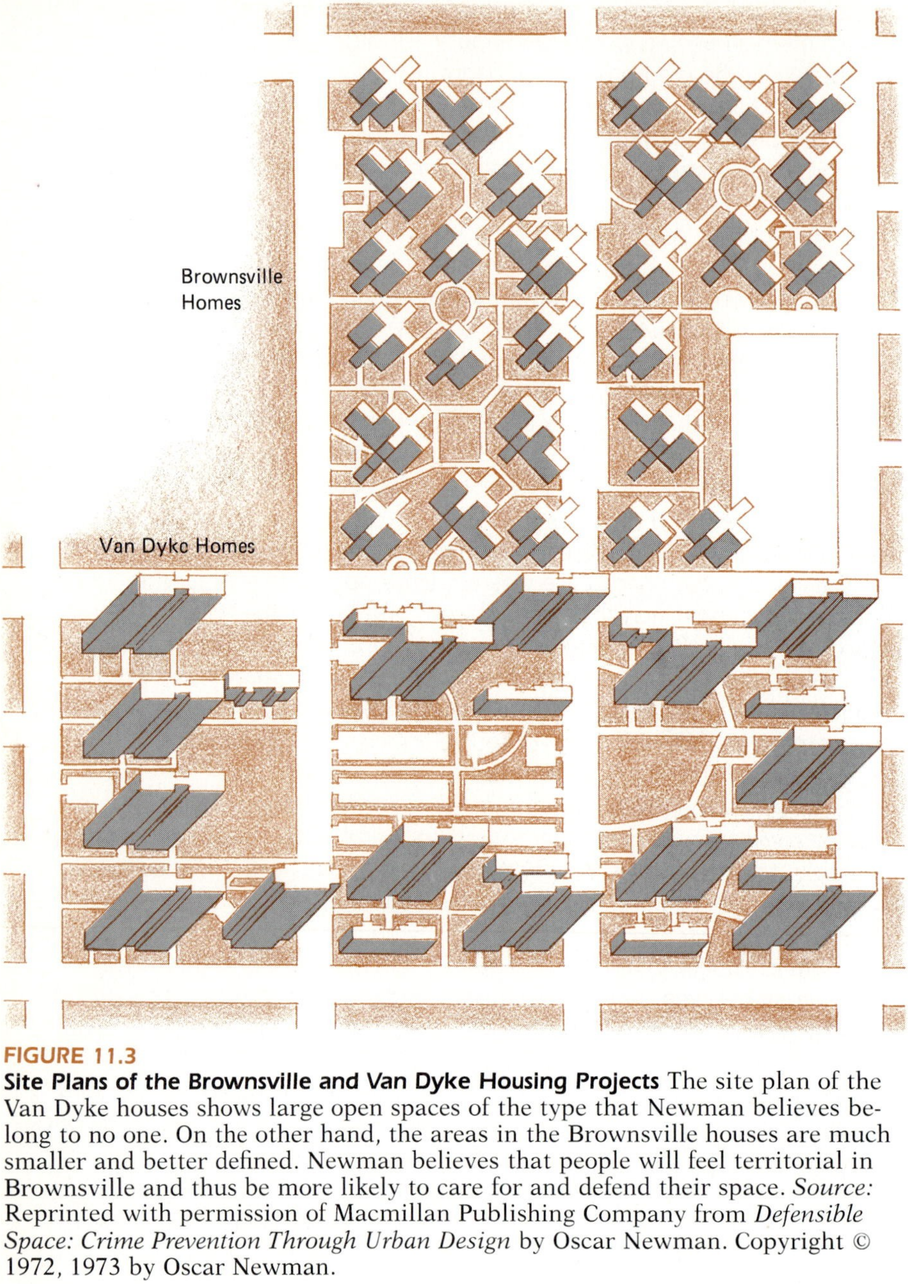

FIGURE 11.3
Site Plans of the Brownsville and Van Dyke Housing Projects The site plan of the Van Dyke houses shows large open spaces of the type that Newman believes belong to no one. On the other hand, the areas in the Brownsville houses are much smaller and better defined. Newman believes that people will feel territorial in Brownsville and thus be more likely to care for and defend their space. *Source:* Reprinted with permission of Macmillan Publishing Company from *Defensible Space: Crime Prevention Through Urban Design* by Oscar Newman. Copyright © 1972, 1973 by Oscar Newman.

ized. In Baltimore, Taylor, Shumaker, and Gottfredson (1985) reported that people who lived on blocks with real and symbolic barriers, where the residents felt responsible for what happened on their street, had less fear and less crime. And in Hartford, Connecticut, Fowler and Mangione (1981) actually made several physical changes in an urban neighborhood and generated significant social effects. By rerouting traffic and creating definable, defensible areas in the neighborhood, they reinforced the residential character of the area. Shortly after, and even three years later, the neighborhood was being used more, people felt more willing to report suspicious events, and an increased sense of optimism could be found there.

In spite of these confirmations of the theory and the reductions in crime and fear through increasing territoriality, not all defensible space projects have been able to achieve their goals. Crime and perceived safety depend on a large number of social and economic factors that design alone cannot overcome. Still, by demonstrating the way in which physical design can be used to stimulate territoriality and by showing that territoriality can lead to positive social consequences, Newman's ideas have clearly demonstrated the applicability of basic social psychological concepts to the solution of important social issues.

DENSITY AND CROWDING

Although personal space and territoriality have been of great interest to social psychologists, the topics of crowding and density have generated more interest and research than any other environmental matter. In this section, we will look first at the findings of animal research and consider whether these results can be generalized to humans. Then we will make a set of important distinctions about types of density and between the concepts of crowding and density themselves. We will then consider both experimental and field research on crowding to consider how and why crowding affects behavior.

Animal Research

Whereas one source of interest in population density flows from social psychology's concern with social issues such as urban crowding and overpopulation, a very different stimulus to considering how high-density living affects us is John Calhoun's research with mice and rats (1962). Calhoun's research was simple in design and dramatic in results. He began with a small group of rats housed in four pens that could accommodate about 40 to 50 rats comfortably. By closing the partition between pens 1 and 4 and making it more difficult to get to these pens by elevating the ramps, he encouraged an unequal distribution of rats (see Figure 11.4).

The rats quickly multiplied, reaching a density far greater than their environment was meant to hold. Throughout, but especially in the overpopulated middle pens, a general breakdown of individual, social, and sexual patterns of behavior occurred. In the middle pens, which he referred to as a *behavioral sink,* elaborate courting, nursing, and nest-building patterns became disorganized or disappeared altogether. Some rats became passive and withdrew completely; some became extremely ag-

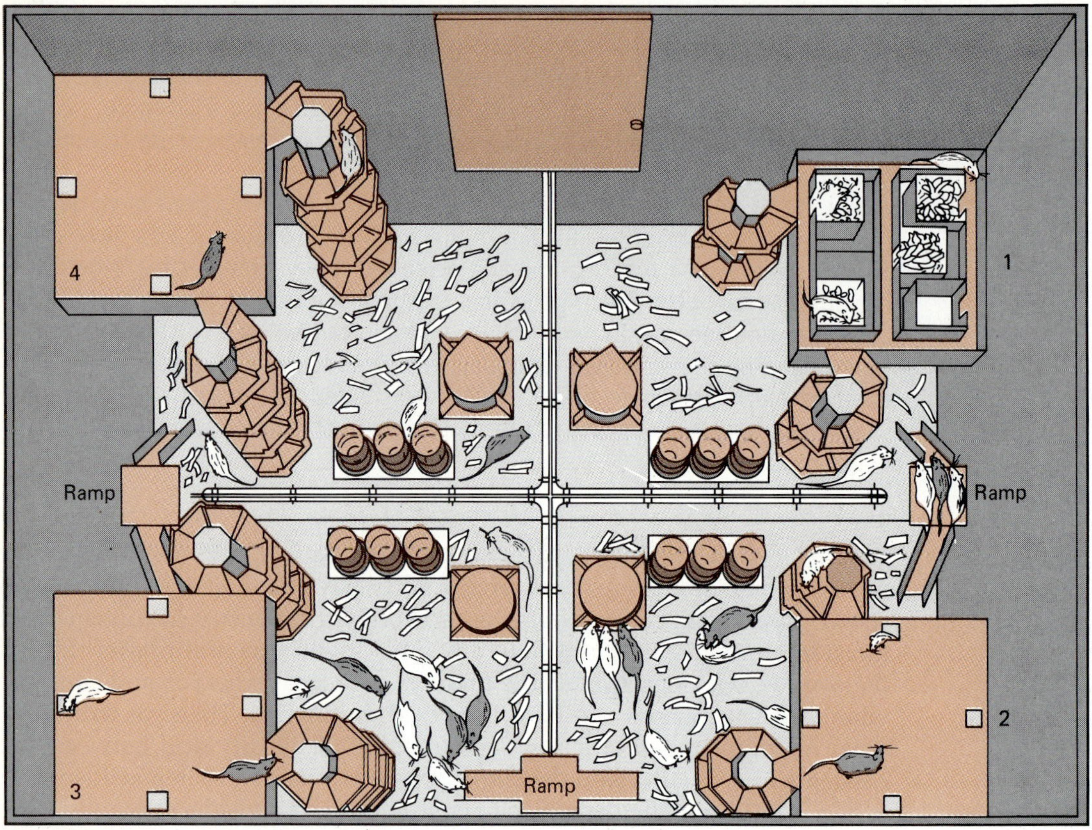

FIGURE 11.4
Physical Environment Designed by Calhoun to Study the Effects of High Density
In this "mouse universe" there was plenty of food and water, but limited space. Since no ramps existed between pens 1 and 4, density was greatest in pens 2 and 3. The breakdown of normal social and sexual patterns was greatest in these middle pens. *Source:* From J. Calhoun (1962, February). Population density and social pathology. *Scientific American,* pp. 140–141. Copyright © 1962 by Scientific American, Inc. All rights reserved.

gressive and hyperactive. Some males became sexually deviant, mounting males or females indiscriminately. Few females became pregnant, but among those that did the rate of miscarriage and infant mortality was very high.

In one of the many studies reported by Calhoun and his colleagues, a population that began with 8 mice rose sharply to 2200 in about one-and-a-half years' time. After that peak the population began a steady decline. A question of interest to many students is at what point the population leveled off, and whether it began to increase again once it got down to a reasonable level—thereby creating an unending cycle of ups and downs. While most students predict this sort of cyclic pattern, in actuality the population decline never leveled off. Subsequent generations were never able to correct their abnormal patterns. The last mouse, and this mouse society, died 1553 days after the experiment began (Marston, 1975).

These experimental results, together with reports of a massive die-off of deer on a densely populated island (Christian, 1975), suggest that once a population exceeds the capacity of its environment, it may never return to normal. On the basis of this research, some scientists have issued dire warnings about the future of the human race. Others, such as the noted biologist René Dubos (1970), have argued that humans are too complex socially and technically for us to draw any relevant inferences from such animal research. While the meaning of this research can be debated at length, the approach of most social psychologists instead has been to observe and test humans in experimental and field settings to discover firsthand just what the effects of crowding on people are.

Density Versus Crowding

When dealing with humans it is extremely important to make a distinction between **density** and **crowding**, and also among the kinds of high-density situations that can exist. Density is defined as an *objective* state, as the number of people per unit space. It tells us whether there is little or much room to move about, but nothing about the reaction of the people to it. Crowding is a *psychological* or *subjective* state (Stokols, 1972). For people to experience crowding they must (1) judge the amount of available space against their desired or typical level for accomplishing their goals, and (2) experience a sense of unpleasantness or dissatisfaction due to the constraints placed upon them. Therefore, high density is necessary to experience crowding, but it is not sufficient. At some times and for some purposes, we welcome and require high density. For instance, having a packed football stadium or busy dance floor makes these experiences more enjoyable. In many situations, however, such as traveling to work on a loaded bus or train, interaction at high density leads to the unpleasant feeling of crowding.

Social Versus Spatial Density High density can be created in either of two ways. The first, known as *social density,* involves adding more people to the same setting. Imagine, for example, a commuter train that picks up more and more passengers with each stop, or a museum or amusement park that becomes densely packed as the day goes on. The second, known as *spatial density,* involves the same number of people sharing a smaller space. Imagine a class of 40 people being moved from a lecture hall to a small seminar room.

Stokols (1976) and Loo (1978) have both pointed out that groups that experience increases in their number while remaining in a given space (social density) may experience particularly difficult problems. Not only do they have to deal with constricted space, but they also have to deal with new people and develop ways to accommodate and absorb them into the group. In addition, when spatial density increases, people may be upset with their space restrictions but have nobody in particular to vent their feelings toward. When social density increases, people may come to blame the newcomers for interfering, and problems of resentment as well as problems of social coordination can arise.

Inside Versus Outside Density A final distinction about types of density situations must be made. Place yourself in each of the following situations. In the first, you are in a Volkswagen Rabbit on an empty expressway driving at the speed limit. There are two passengers in front and three in the rear seat. You are the middle person in the back. In the other situation, you are the only person in the same car and the traffic is jammed for miles. You have moved about 50 yards in the last ten minutes. The odds are that you would feel crowded in both of these situations. But, depending on whether we measured the density inside the car or outside the car, we would get very different indications of density.

Figure 11.5 shows a set of profiles combining the varying levels of density both inside and outside (Zlutnick & Altman, 1972). Cell A represents a typical middle-class suburban setup in which the density is rela-

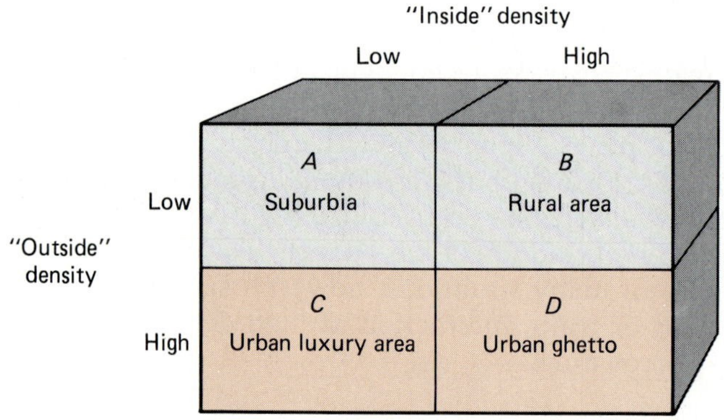

FIGURE 11.5
Four Different Types of High-Density Situations Zlutnick and Altman help us to recognize that the consequences of density may be very different, depending on whether it is measured and experienced on a macro level (on the outside, measured by people per square acre, for instance) or a micro level (on the inside, as measured by people per room, for instance). *Source:* S. Zlutnick and I. Altman (1972). Crowding and human behavior. In T. F. Wohlwill and D. Carson (Eds.), *Environment and the social sciences: Perspectives and applications.* Washington, D.C.: American Psychological Association.

tively low both within the home as well as outside. Cell B is best illustrated by rural poverty. Although it may be miles between homes (low outside density), many people might have to share bedroom or bathroom facilities. In a city setting where many high-rise buildings are packed right next to one another, outside density is high. City people who can afford spacious apartments, however, can escape into them where the density is low (cell C). But in the urban ghetto, densities are high no matter where we measure them. There is no escape from other people regardless of whether you are on the inside or out (cell D).

Reactions of People to Density and Crowding

The research on human density and crowding has gone in many methodological directions. We will review some of the laboratory and short-term experimental research, and also consider some of the correlational research on long-term effects of high density.

Experimental Evidence A first finding about density is that it is physiologically arousing, as indicated by a number of measures such as heart rate and blood pressure. Students participating in a relatively brief experimental study (Evans, 1979), shoppers in a heavily populated mall (Heshka & Pylypuk, 1974), busy commuters (Lundberg, 1976; Stokols & Novaco, 1981), prison inmates (Paulus, McCain, & Cox, 1978), and average people living or working under high densities all show evidence of increased physiological reactivity.

FROM THE FIELD
Daniel Stokols

Dan Stokols is one of the most prolific social psychologists studying the effects of the environment on human behavior. His research has been concerned with the impact of environmental stressors such as traffic congestion, crowding, and aircraft noise on human health and behavior, and with the application of research findings to the improved design of human environments. His latest work tests the effects of various environmental and social conditions on the health, motivation, and performance of workers in an experimental office set up in the Environmental Simulation Laboratory at the University of California, Irvine, where Dr. Stokols teaches social ecology.

Arousal can have many effects, some in the area of task performance and some in social behavior. The presence of many other people, for instance, can lead to increased performance on simple tasks but poorer performance on tasks that are complex or difficult (Paulus & Matthews, 1980; Evans, 1979). People who are crowded report more anxiety and other negative emotions than those who are not crowded (Saegert, MacKintosh, & West, 1975; Smith & Lawrence, 1978). In addition, those who are crowded—and even those who anticipate being crowded—are less attracted to the people around them (Baum & Greenberg, 1975; Worchel & Teddlie, 1976). Given the negative emotions that crowding seems to generate, it is not surprising that the level of helping is lower in high-density shopping centers and dormitories (Cohen & Spacapan, 1978; Bickman et al., 1973; Jorgenson & Dukes, 1976), and that levels of aggression are greater in high-density situations when resources are scarce (Rohe & Patterson 1974).

Another reaction noted among people who feel crowded is withdrawal, both physical and social. For instance, as the social density of play settings increases, children begin to play less with others (Hutt & Vaizcy, 1966; Loo, 1978; McGrew, 1970); and the more dense a setting becomes, the less willing students are to discuss personal or intimate topics (Sundstrom, 1975). When dorm residents feel crowded, they are less group-oriented and seek friends away from the crowded settings in which they live. In fact, this tendency to withdraw generalizes to other situations. While waiting for an experiment in another campus building, students who felt crowded in their dorms preferred not to sit close to a stranger; and in a dentist's waiting room, they were less comforted by the presence of another person than those who felt less crowded (Baum, Harpin, & Valins, 1975; Baum & Valins, 1977).

An important qualification concerning the effects of crowding is that high-density conditions apparently do not affect all people in the same way. In general, males react with more stress and discomfort than females in short-term situations, but when exposed to high densities that cannot be handled or modified over the long term, women appear to be more negatively affected. In a short-term experimental study, Yakov Epstein and Robert Karlin (1975) placed same-sex groups of six people in either small or large rooms (i.e., under high or low spatial density), and then observed their behavior in a game situation. While males reacted more competitively to those around them under high spatial density, the reverse was true of females (see Figure 11.6). Other researchers have found this same sort of effect in a variety of experimental settings (Schettino & Borden, 1976; Stokols et al., 1973).

Studies of college dormitories where three students had to be assigned to a room meant for two offer a different kind of finding (Aiello, Baum, & Gormley, 1981). Women living in triples spent more time in their rooms, worked at creating a homelike environment, and made an effort to coordinate activities with their roommates. But when they were not successful

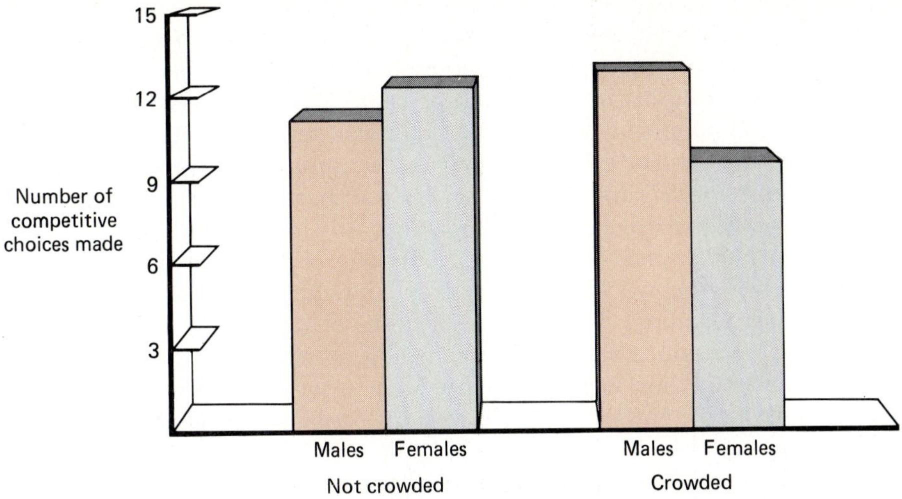

FIGURE 11.6
Competitive Choices Made by Males and Females When Crowded or Not Crowded This figure shows that males and females do not vary greatly in the number of competitive choices they make under normal conditions. When crowded, however, males become far more competitive, while females become far less competitive. *Source:* Adapted from Y. Epstein and R. Karlin (1975). Effects of acute experimental crowding. *Journal of Applied Social Psychology, 5,* 45.

it affected them quite negatively in terms of grades, health, and reported happiness. Males in triples, on the other hand, withdrew; they tended to avoid their rooms and their roommates. As a result, they "handled" the problem by staying away from it as much as possible, and consequently were not as affected by it in terms of grades and health.

Explanations for these sex differences vary. Jonathan Freedman (1975), who has posited the density-intensity hypothesis, believes that the major effect of density is to amplify a person's typical reaction. Males, who typically are more aggressive than females, become even more aggressive under high density. Females, who are more attuned to maintaining good social relations, work harder at that under high density, and benefit or suffer depending on how successful they are. Epstein and Karlin offer a slightly different explanation. They believe that social norms lead people to adopt different reactions to the same conditions. Women, who are allowed to show emotions, share their distress with others, and feel an increase in liking and cohesiveness when they are successful at coping. Males, on the other hand, are discouraged from sharing their distress, which leads them toward a more competitive, or individualistic, orientation when faced with high density.

Correlational Evidence Most of the research we have reviewed has been concerned with investigating the effects of relatively short-term crowding in specific settings. Another popular approach has been to study the correlation between census-type measures of density and statistical records of matters such as health, crime, and mental illness (see Kirmeyer, 1979).

In a study done in the Netherlands, Levy & Herzog (1974) found that the number of people per square kilometer was strongly related to juvenile delinquency, property crime, and births to unmarried women. In Honolulu, Schmitt (1957) found that as the number of people per acre increased, so did the rates of infant mortality, suicide, and tuberculosis. Yet Mitchell's (1971) research in Hong Kong, one of the most densely populated cities in the world, found hardly any differences attributable to density. In his sample, in which 28 percent of the people slept three or more to a bed and almost 40 percent shared their dwelling unit with people to whom they were not related, there were no major differences between high- and low-density areas on his measures of mental and physical illness.

With this and other evidence reported on both sides of the issue, a debate has been raging over whether people in densely packed cities are like Calhoun's rats (Krupat, 1985). Put simply, does high-density urban living lead to social pathology? The best answer that can be given at this point is as follows:

1. High-density living has the capacity to act as a source of stress and to intensify other sources of stress. Yet here the "people are not rats" perspective reminds us that humans can adopt complex modes of in-

Working and living in high-density conditions can contribute to stress and other problems, but we are not yet sure how severe these problems can be or why they occur.

dividual and collective action to coordinate and cope with their environment. Cultural norms and physical design solutions allow people to distinguish between public and private space, and allow for a maximum of privacy in a minimum of space (Michelson, 1976).

2. Density affects people differently depending on whether we are talking about great numbers of people inside or outside. When density is measured according to people per acre or kilometer (outside density), the findings have been weak or highly inconsistent. Yet inside measures (e.g., number of people per room) tap into the ways in which people disturb, distract, or annoy one another. When density is measured in this way (Galle, Gove, & McPherson, 1972), or when crowding is actually measured by asking people in their everyday living settings how they are reacting to density (Gove & Hughes, 1983), the results have been stronger and more consistent.
3. The relationship between density and social problems in the real world is often accounted for by a third factor—poverty. People who have good incomes simply do not choose to live more than one per room. People who are poor live in densely packed houses and apartments. Therefore it is difficult to tell, even by using complex statistical tests, to what extent social problems are related to feeling crowded and to what extent they are simply problems of poverty.

Explaining the Effects of Crowding

Assuming that the effects we have reviewed are due at least in part to crowding, we might begin to ask why crowding might have such consequences. A number of explanations for the effects of crowding have been offered. One position, the **overload** explanation, emphasizes that living in high-density settings places so many demands upon people that they can be overwhelmed (Simmel, 1950; Milgram, 1970). For instance, the dorm students that Baum and Valins studied were faced with so much noise, so many activities, and so many different demands on their time that their feeling of crowding might have resulted from overload. To reduce the demands on them, they withdrew into their rooms and stayed away from social interactions.

A second explanation points to the constraints that high density places upon us (Holahan, 1982). Schopler and Stockdale (1977), for example, suggest that density is experienced as crowding only when the number of people or the limits of space interfere with the accomplishment of certain important goals. The more important the goal, the more frustrated and negative people become toward others in their environment.

A third explanation revolves around the concept of *privacy.* According to Irving Altman (1975), privacy involves the desire to maintain just the right amount of contact—not too much and not too little—with the outside world. When people have too few others around them, they may come to

A commuter's daily trip to and from work can be both unpredictable and uncontrollable. When we begin to feel that we have lost control over the events around us, we may develop a sense of learned helplessness and may even give up and become depressed.

feel lonely or isolated. But when density gets high and people are not able to maintain the boundaries they want to have between themselves and others (i.e., they do not have enough privacy), then they may come to experience crowding.

A final explanation of crowding focuses on the *loss of control* that people experience when faced with too many others or too little space (Cohen, 1980; Sherrod & Cohen, 1979). For instance, what upsets dormitory students more than the number of people they have to deal with (overload) is not being able to determine when, where, or with whom they interact. They feel that they have lost their ability to control their surroundings and begin to develop a sense of **learned helplessness** (Baum & Valins, 1977).

As we discussed in Chapter 2, the concept of learned helplessness (Peterson & Seligman, 1984) involves a *generalized* belief that one's actions will not significantly affect the outcome of events. This belief results from one or more unsuccessful attempts to exert control over the environment. When people live among too many others, they begin to feel as if things are out of control—at least *their* control—and often they give up, even when they really could make a difference.

For instance, children who were similar except that some were from high-density and others from low-density homes were given a frustrating task: a puzzle that looked solvable but was not. Afterward, they were given one that could be solved with some effort. After failing on the first one, the low-density children continued to work hard at the second puzzle; but those children from high-density homes, being used to feeling helpless, did not try hard once they had failed the first time. They had learned too many times from past experience in their living circumstances that their actions were not likely to make any difference (Rodin, 1976).

Each of these explanations complements the other in that each describes a mechanism by which crowding can produce stress. It has been suggested, however, that loss of control is of critical importance because it carries important implications for the person's ability to carry out his or her goals (Krupat, 1985). That is, the presence of too many others has its strongest effects when it relays a symbolic message: You are helpless to exercise control over events as you would like. We shall see in the next section, when we talk about other sources of stress such as noise and pollution, that this message is also a critical mediator of stress.

THE CITY AND URBAN LIFE

A wide range of large-scale environments have been studied by environmental social psychologists, ranging from small towns (Barker & Wright, 1955) and suburbs (Gans, 1962) to areas that have experienced disasters, either natural ones such as floods and tornadoes (Burton, Kates, & White 1978) or technological ones such as nuclear plant accidents (Baum, Fleming, & Davidson, 1983). However, the setting of greatest interest to environmental and social psychologists has been the city, the place called home by approximately 70 percent of the population of the United States.

In this section we will review three very different perspectives on urban life. We will then compare the evidence for these perspectives by considering how urban life is similar to or different from life in small towns by comparing friendship patterns and helping behavior in each setting. Finally, we will discuss specific stressful aspects of the city such as noise, pollution, and commuting and consider the ways in which they, like crowding, can interfere with people's daily activities and make them feel a loss of control.

Perspectives on Urban Life

When people study the city, they are usually first struck by its large population size. But what does size imply? Does it lead to confusion and crowding, or does it provide opportunities? Does it overwhelm and harm people, or does it lead to adaptation and change? In this section, we will review three perspectives that begin with size, but interpret its effects in very different ways.

The Human Ecology Approach One of the earliest and most influential positions on urban life is that of human ecology (Park, 1926; Wirth, 1938). Sociologists such as Lewis Wirth, who subscribed to this view, took the principles of plant and animal ecology and tried to give them social equivalents. They believed that just as plants compete for space and light in a forest, people vie for scarce economic and social resources in the city.

Wirth believed that cities could be understood in terms of three variables: (1) size: cities are much larger in population than noncities; (2) density: not only is the population larger, but people in the city are also packed together much more tightly than in other places; and (3) heterogeneity: the people of the city are a diverse mix of racial, ethnic, class, and age groups.

Wirth's view of the city was a negative one. He felt that when so many people of different races, ethnic groups, and social classes are made to live in close proximity, they feel competitive, become indifferent to one another's needs, and are alienated from their environment. He believed that people in cities are pulled apart from one another and that common bonds and a sense of community cannot develop.

The Subcultural Approach While Wirth focused on the differences and friction that came with city life, another sociologist, Claude Fischer, took a much more positive view (Fischer, 1982). Looking at its opportunities rather than its constraints, Fischer's subcultural view points out that cities allow smaller communities to grow within them. He believes that cities encourage similar people to find and join one another, and they become as a result "mosaics of little worlds" (Park, 1926). Cities provide a *critical mass* so that people can form active subcultures. Not only do ethnic and racial enclaves such as Chinatown, Little Italy, and Harlem arise, where people can feel at home in their own "community," but "communities of interest" can form also—for example, among lovers of seventeenth-century Armenian dance, collectors of Indian-head pennies, and owners of poisonous snakes.

The Overload Approach One of the most popular social psychological approaches to understanding urban behavior is the overload model developed by Stanley Milgram (1970) from the early writings of Georg Simmel (1950). Milgram proposed that the way to understand urban life is to see the behavior of city people in terms of a series of adaptations to *overload.* Overload occurs whenever the physical or social environment provides too much stimulus for a person to process: too many sights, sounds, smells, people, and social demands to handle all at once.

To deal with overload, he believes that city people develop strategies of coping which characterize their overall behavior. One mode of adaptation, for example, is to give less time and attention to encounters with other people; urbanites seem to be in a perpetual rush. But city people are not in a hurry for everything and everyone. Another important coping mechanism for overloaded people is the setting of priorities. City people make distinctions between important and unimportant activities, and between the demands of friends and strangers. They may appear to be cool and callous on the outside (i.e., to strangers in public), but this does not mean that they will not be friendly and warm to others (i.e., to friends in private).

Unlike the social-ecological approach, which sees urbanites as competing with and alienated from one another, and unlike the subcultural approach, whose major emphasis is on the close group attachments that evolve in cities, the overload model points out that urbanites become close to certain people and certain aspects of the environment, but at the expense of becoming distant and alienated from other aspects of the city and its people.

Social Relations and Helping in the City

As we noted in Chapter 9, a young woman named Kitty Genovese was murdered in New York City in 1964, and not a single person of the 38 who witnessed the event came to her aid. A number of editorial writers took this event as an occasion for an attack upon the city, telling us that such an expression of public apathy could never have taken place in a small town. Is the failure to help an urban phenomenon? Are city people cold and indifferent to the needs of others? Do cities allow people to make close and lasting friendships? Let us evaluate some of the contrasting theoretical positions about cities in light of the available research evidence (Korte, 1980).

To look at the process of friendship development in city and town, Karen Franck (1980) followed newcomers to a small town and a big city during their first year. She noted that in the city the development of friendships was slower and harder at first, but within less than a year city people and small-towners had developed equally satisfying friendships (see Figure 11.7). A number of comprehensive reviews on this topic (Fischer, 1982; Korte, 1980; Krupat, 1985) conclude that the overall quality and quantity of social relationships does not vary between city and town. There is slightly less contact among neighbors in the city, but relationships with relatives and with friends do not differ according to the size of the place one lives in.

While the nature of urban and small-town friendships does not differ, however, the basis for their formation does. That is, small-town friendships are more likely to be based on *proximity,* the physical closeness of neighbor to neighbor. In the city, however, while the local neighborhood may be important to some (Riger & Lavrakas, 1982), friendships are more likely to be based on common interests and activities (a closeness of social interests that overcomes greater physical distances). Had Kitty Genovese's "close friends" been physically close when she called for help, they probably would have helped her. But in the city one's closest friends in a psychological sense are often quite distant geographically.

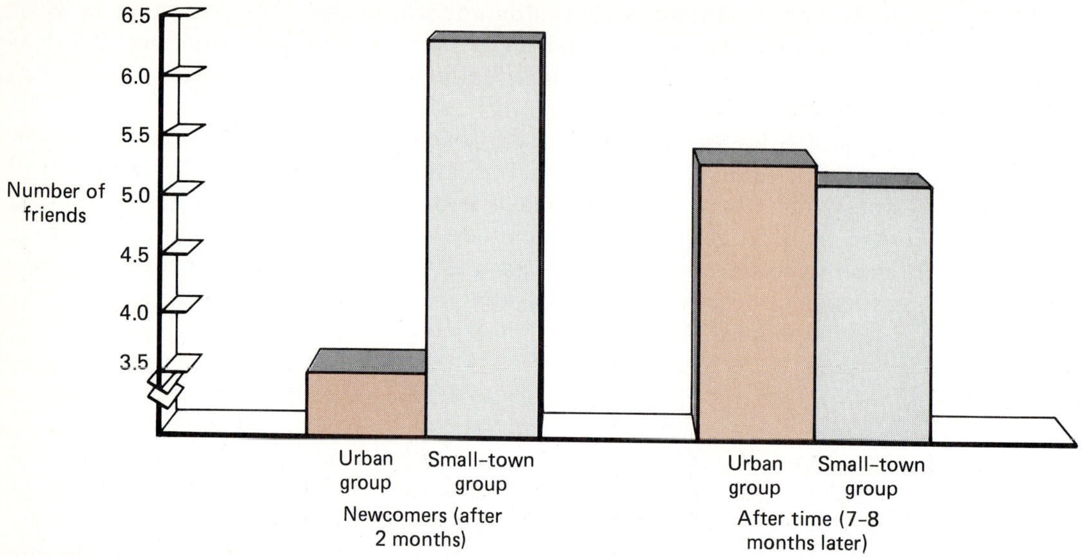

FIGURE 11.7
Friendships Among Urban and Small-Town People Newcomers to a small town made far more friends by the end of two months than newcomers to a city did. Within less than a year, however, the numbers of friends made by newcomers in both the city and the small town were almost identical. *Source:* Based upon data reported in K. A. Franck (1980). Friends and strangers: The social experi-52–71. Study conducted jointly by Karen A. Franck, W. R. Wentworth, and Charles T. Unseld with support from the National Science Foundation.

The more general question—are city people less helpful than those who live in small towns—has also been addressed, and the results are mixed (Amato, 1983). In a series of studies, people in cities were less likely to mail a lost letter (Korte & Kerr, 1975), to admit strangers to their homes in order to let them use the phone or conduct an interview (House & Wolf, 1978), or to be of assistance to someone who reaches them by dialing a wrong number (Milgram, 1970). However, some researchers have found no rural-urban differences, and others have found that other factors, such as the size of one's hometown, are even more important than the size of the city of current residence (Weiner, 1976).

It would appear that specific aspects of city dwellers' physical and social environments may discourage helping, even though they themselves are as concerned and interested as their small-town counterparts (House & Wolf, 1978). City residents may simply be more fearful of opening their doors and letting someone in. Or, as a result of stimulus overload, urbanites may narrow their focus of attention and be less likely to notice emergencies around them. (Cohen & Lezak, 1977; Sherrod & Downs, 1974). That is, when the social environment is highly demanding, people are less helpful—regardless of whether the actual setting is the city or the small town (Korte, Ypma, & Toppen, 1975).

The findings of research on both friendship and helping lead us toward two conclusions. First, little evidence exists to suggest that urbanites are generally alienated and without social support, as the human ecologists suggested. Second, city *people* are not that different from small-town *people*. Any differences that we note in the behavior of small-town and city people are more likely due to their adaptations to the differing environments than to any basic dispositional differences between the people who are found in these two places.

Urban Stress

One important difference between the two environments, city and town, has to do with the greater number of potential sources of stress found in the city. As we noted earlier, crowding can be one source of stress, but cities also bring with them noise (Cohen & Weinstein, 1982) and pollution (Evans, Jacobs, & Frager, 1982; Rotton, 1983), as well as an assortment of transportation and commuting problems (Stokols & Novaco, 1981).

Noise In a systematic attempt to relate laboratory research on noise to the stress of the urban environment, David Glass and Jerome Singer (1972) found that people who tried to perform a variety of tasks while

Urban stressors come in many shapes and sizes. Loud airplane noise is especially hard to adapt to because it is unpredictable and uncontrollable.

exposed to noise were not greatly affected in their performance. After completing the task, however, they were less tolerant of frustration and more likely to give up on an unsolvable puzzle. A particularly interesting finding was that the type and volume of noise was not nearly as important as other characteristics of the noise. People who felt they could predict and control when the noise started or stopped were not nearly as affected as those who could not (Sherrod et al., 1977; Sherrod & Downs, 1974). These findings for noise parallel the explanation of crowding effects earlier in the chapter. That is, loss of control and the resulting sense of learned helplessness can lead to a variety of negative consequences.

These laboratory findings have been subjected to a number of tests in the real world. Sheldon Cohen and his colleagues (Cohen et al., 1981) studied two matched groups of third and fourth graders in Los Angeles. One group of children lived in a quiet area, and the other lived directly under the flight path of the Los Angeles International Airport. The children from the noisy group not only had higher blood pressure, but were also more likely to give up on a difficult task. Bronzaft and McCarthy (1975) found as well that the reading achievement scores of two groups of New York City schoolchildren differed according to their exposure to noise. The better readers' classroom was on the side of the school that faced away from the elevated subway tracks. The poorer readers, although similar to the others in all other relevant ways, came from the noisier side of the school building.

Pollution Another element of urban life that seemingly cannot be avoided is foul air. Forty-three cities containing half of the American population have unhealthy air quality (see President's Council on Environmental Quality, 1978); and merely breathing the air in New York City is equivalent to smoking almost two packs of cigarettes a day (Rotton, 1978). Moreover, while the effects of crowding and noise on health are indirect, bad air can sometimes have direct and immediate effects on physical health and well-being, in the form of dizziness, headaches, and burning eyes.

Using research designs that often parallel those used in crowding and noise research, James Rotton and his colleagues (Rotton, 1983) have performed a series of laboratory experiments on the effects of unpleasant but nontoxic odors. In these experiments students are asked to perform various tasks either in a neutral-smelling room (control) or in a room in which the experimenter has "accidentally" spilled some awful-smelling stuff. Compared to the control group, students in the bad-smelling rooms reported feeling more aggressive, anxious, and fatigued, and less able to concentrate. They even found the bad-smelling rooms less pleasing visually. As in the research on crowding and noise, odors impaired performance on complex but not on simple tasks, and people who had been deprived of control were less likely to persist at an unsolvable puzzle that was given to them afterward.

Commuting At times one's surroundings are quiet and calm, at others the environment is noisy and hectic; some days the air is polluted, and other days it is quite acceptable. But one potential source of stress, the commute to work, is a daily occurrence. In a study of urban commuters, 38 percent of the people questioned reported transportation-related problems, congestion, and inconvenience as among their greatest problems (Quinn & Staines, 1979). In Salt Lake City, 18 percent of the female drivers and 12 percent of the males reported that at times they "could gladly kill another driver" (Turner, Layton, & Simons, 1975). People who travel to work in their cars during rush hour each day are more likely than others to have health problems such as chest pains and cardiac arrhythmias (Aronow et al., 1972); and urban commuters whose trip is particularly long (e.g., two hours) are subject to a variety of stress-related physiological imbalances (Bellet, Roman, & Kostis, 1969). Taking public transportation is beset with its own stress-related problems (Singer, Lundberg, & Frankenhaeuser, 1978).

Using the concept of *impedance* to indicate the degree to which commuters encountered situations that slowed or constrained their trip to work, Stokols, Novaco, and their colleagues (Stokols & Novaco, 1981; Novaco et al., 1979) surveyed 100 employees of two industrial firms. Dividing their sample into three groups that varied on the distance and time involved in their commutes, they found that the greater the impedance, the more the commute was seen as inconvenient, the less the employees were satisfied with their commute, and the more tense and nervous they reported feeling upon arrival at work.

The research on urban stress suggests that people who live in cities face a variety of conditions that may overload them and tax their ability to cope. Yet there is also evidence that some people may seek out and prefer high levels of stimulation, novelty, and challenge (Geller, 1980; Geller et al., 1982) and that urban residents are capable of developing and adopting successful coping strategies that insulate them from the potentially negative effects of urban life. In particular, the effects of the city—or any environment—seem to be most harmful when people feel a sense of learned helplessness. Conversely, people are most capable of adapting and even thriving when they feel in control. See the In the News box on pages 444–445 for one method of dealing with overload from noise. In the next section, we will see how the concept of gaining control has been studied and applied at the neighborhood level by social psychologists.

APPLICATION
GAINING A SENSE OF CONTROL IN THE CITY

As we have noted, one finding that pervades much research concerning problems in urban living has to do with a loss of control. A common theme among urbanites is "You can't fight City Hall." For instance, in a survey concerning air

IN THE NEWS

EARPLUGS: CURE FOR CITY NOISE

In much the same way that stereo headphones once began appearing on the ears of subway riders, replacing the screech of skidding steel wheels with Beethoven or the Rolling Stones, earplugs are now showing up in the ears of New Yorkers.

A small but fiercely competitive earplug trade has begun in New York City's subway system. Small plastic buckets filled with the tiny plugs hang in subway newsstands. Posters depicting a stick figure holding his ears and gritting his teeth are plastered to steel girders and walls. One earplug merchant says the competition in the new underground business has become "guerrilla warfare."

"I'm in competition with other people selling the same product," said Michael Groves. "It's become a jungle."

With the current construction boom in the city, the noise level has increased and with it the use of earplugs. Some people who wear earplugs say that, as their numbers have increased, they no longer draw the stares they once did. . . .

Mario D'Elia, chief dental technician at Memorial Sloan-Kettering Cancer Center, has been wearing earplugs during his daily subway ride from Bensonhurst to 68th Street in Manhattan for the last three years.

"Once I started to wear them," he said, "when I would forget them I couldn't stand the screeching. Every New Yorker is used to the noise, but once you wear earplugs you can't do without them."

Hearing specialists say that Americans have become increasingly aware that their ears are at risk in today's mechanized world. Citizens' groups have formed to combat noise. New York City adopted the nation's first antinoise code in 1972. Since then several American cities, including Chicago and San Francisco, have passed similar legislation.

Even the United Nations has taken up the issue. In a 1979 report entitled "The State of the Environment" the international organization singled out noise pollution, saying: "No one can escape the unwanted sound that is called noise, a disturbance to our environment escalating so rapidly as to become one of the major threats to the quality of human life."

Robert S. Bennin, the director of New

pollution, people were asked why they had never complained or taken action. Almost half responded that they had done nothing because they felt it would do no good (Rankin, 1969). However, to conclude either that all city residents are passive or that citizen involvement, when it occurs, does not have positive effects may be a serious mistake. In particular, social psychologists have studied and even become affiliated with local neighborhood groups, noting that involvement can overcome learned helplessness and make the city seem more responsive to one's needs.

An excellent example of research and application on how urban people attempt to exercise local control is the work of Abraham Wandersman and his colleagues in Nashville, Tennessee (Chavis, Stucky, & Wandersman 1983; Wandersman, 1984). They studied 17 block organizations in a large racially and economically mixed neighborhood, asking who participates and why, and what the effects of participation are.

York City's division of noise abatement in the Department of Environmental Protection, said that New York City, by its sheer physical size, is noisier than most other cities. Because there is more construction in the city now, it is noisier than it has been since the code was passed.

"The overall noise level in the city is higher, but it is more controlled," he said. "The code is probably the only barrier between the normal person and total insanity."

As an example of the increase in noise despite the code, he says, "You may have one air compressor that's legal, but by bringing in 10 legal air compressors, you still increase the noise by 10 times."

Mr Bennin said that with about one million cars in the city and 100,000 to 200,000 trucks the most pervasive noise is "vehicular traffic."

Dr. [Thomas H.] Fay, who is on the Environmental Control Board and helped write the city's antinoise code, said that in New York, "the public transit system noise is by far the most deleterious and hazardous noise source in the city to the largest number of people." His solution, though a temporary one, is earplugs.

"If I forget my earplugs or lose them, it makes the difference between a good day and a bad day," he said. "I'm willing to say that we could quiet New York overnight, temporarily, if we could get a pair of earplugs into the hand of every person."

Mr. Groves first began selling earplugs in 1978 after riding the subway every day from his home in midtown Manhattan to his job at Misericordia Hospital on 233rd Street in the Bronx.

During his first hour of work each day as an emergency-room receptionist, he says, he was "nasty" to the patients and he did not know why.

"I was riding on the subway and it dawned on me: I'm being bombarded by sound," he said. "I said, I'm going to wear earplugs."

Source: The New York Times, December 16, 1983, p. A28.

They found that the people who are most likely to join are those who are "rooted" to their home territories by long-term commitments (e.g., people who are older, married, and homeowners). These individuals perceive more problems on their blocks than others do, and they show a strong sense of civic duty and a firm belief that political action can accomplish their goals, rather than reflecting a feeling that problems cannot be overcome.

The results of neighborhood activism in this and other communities point to an interesting paradox. The development of citizen organizations has a relatively weak impact on the responsiveness of government and the actual provision of urban services (Warren, 1974). Yet in spite of this, people who participate experience an increase in satisfaction with the environment, a decrease in mistrust and apathy, an improvement in their relationships with neighbors, and a greater feeling of control over the environment (Rosener, 1977; Wandersman, 1984).

These findings have been interpreted to suggest that even when initial success is moderate, people who are brought together are likely to find common concerns and grounds for common action; and on this basis, their desire to try and try again is reinforced. In this way, the vicious cycle of learned helplessness (fail to control, then fail even to try) can be reversed, as "trying to control" and "exerting control" come to be more closely associated with one another. Whether we are talking about urban residents or any other group that is deprived of control (see the work of Langer and Rodin on nursing homes, as reported in Chapter 2), people can begin to feel "empowered" rather than helpless when they are encouraged to take an active rather than a passive role.

DESIGNING THE ENVIRONMENT

More often than not, we relate to our environment by taking it for granted, grumbling and complaining about it, or possibly even trying to do something about it (as discussed above). But rarely do we step back and ask just how a building, a neighborhood, or a city is planned. What considerations went into the building's design? To what extent and in what ways did the architects take into account the kind of people who would live or work there, the type of activities that would take place there, and the sorts of needs that the environment should satisfy? Only recently have social and environmental psychologists begun to bring their knowledge of social interaction to the fields of architecture and social planning. Their input has been growing in importance and has brought benefits to the people who use buildings or who live in cities designed by architects in collaboration with social scientists.

Design Considerations

When architects and designers plan a physical environment, whether a private home or a large apartment building, a small park or a whole city, they make certain basic assumptions about the needs of the people who will use it. Designers often focus on one of two aspects: *functional* or *aesthetic*. A strictly functional approach takes a mechanistic nuts-and-bolts view of people (Altman, 1973). It asks how tasks can best be accomplished, and pays close attention to things like controlling temperature and using materials that will hold up over time. Designs from this point of view are efficient but are often considered cold and sterile.

Purely aesthetic designs satisfy a different set of needs, while frustrating others. Aesthetic designs please the eye and inspire the spirit; they are seen as works of art, living sculpture. But they pay less attention to the functional needs of the occupants. An example is the Erich Lindemann Mental Health Center in Boston. The winner of architectural design

Architect Moshe Safdie's Habitat 67 in Montreal, shown here, is an innovative answer to urban design that is both functional and aesthetically pleasing.

awards for beauty, its circular pathways make finding one's way difficult. Considering that one problem of its users may be confusion and disorientation, a building that is made like a maze is likely to be frustrating no matter how beautiful it is.

John Zeisel (1975, 1981), a sociologist who has served as a consultant to architects and planners, has proposed a *behavioral* approach to design. This approach recognizes six universal human needs that an ideal environment satisfies:

1. Security—the ability to feel safe and secure.
2. Clarity—the ability to "read" the environment and find one's way from one place to another.
3. Privacy—the ability to regulate the amount of contact one has with others.
4. Social interaction—the ability to find places and spaces where one can have contact with other people.

5. Convenience—the ability to accomplish tasks easily.
6. Identity—the ability to feel a part of the setting and to make the setting a part of oneself.

He recognizes that it is sometimes impossible to satisfy all these needs simultaneously, and therefore that trade-offs often have to be made to satisfy some needs while giving less attention to others. Additionally, he and others point out that the means of satisfying these needs may vary from culture to culture (Rapoport, 1980; Brolin, 1972). Nonetheless, if a designer fails to consider all of these needs, the end product is likely to prove frustrating to the people who live or work in it.

Robert Sommer, one of the pioneers in the field of environmental psychology and behavioral design, has provided us with a simple and straightforward example of the way in which the arrangement of the physical environment can affect the pattern of activities in the social environment, thereby frustrating or satisfying the needs of residents (Sommer, 1969). Sommer was called into a state hospital in western Canada to discover why there seemed to be so little activity in a ward of elderly women. Several thousands of dollars had just been spent for new curtains, tiled floors, and brightly colored chairs. Yet the best-furnished ward in the hospital was still one of the most depressing places to be. Hardly anyone ever spoke. The women gazed blankly ahead or stared at the new furnishings.

But why? Sommer noticed that most of the chairs in the ward sat side by side along the walls. In the rear, several rows were arranged back to back, and next to each of the columns in the room sat four chairs, each facing in a different direction. With this physical arrangement of furniture, it was no wonder that Sommer thought that the women looked "like strangers in a train station waiting for a train that never came." He believed that the placement of the furniture discouraged social interaction. It oriented people *away* from one another. Just as a centrifuge pulls inanimate bodies apart, this kind of arrangement, which pulls people apart, can be described as *sociofugal.*

In place of this arrangement, which suited the needs of the staff for convenience and tidiness, Sommer and his colleagues rearranged the furniture to fit the needs of the residents for social interaction. They placed chairs in circles around the tables, arranged magazines and other materials around the room, and recorded the interactions two weeks later, once the residents had had a chance to become acclimated to their "new environment." Brief interactions such as exchanging greetings and asking questions increased by 55 percent, and conversations of a more sustained nature increased by 69 percent. Crafts activities increased, and the hoarding of newspapers and magazines virtually stopped once there were shared, secure spaces in which to leave them.

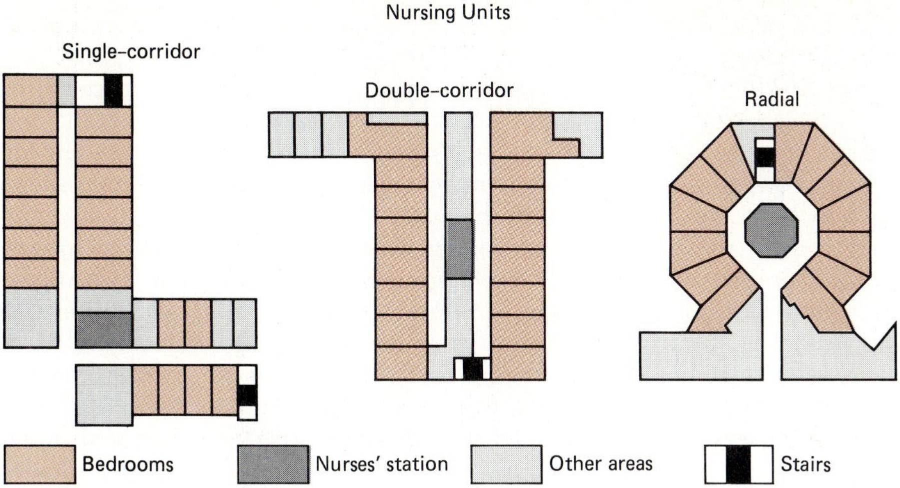

FIGURE 11.8
Hospital Design Layouts Studied by Trites and Colleagues In the radially designed wards at Rochester Methodist Hospital, more time was spent with the patients, and the nurses preferred to work there. Still, this type of setup was not without its faults. For instance, patients in the radial design felt that they had less privacy. *Source:* Redrawn from D. K. Trites, F. D. Galbraith, M. Sturdavant, and J. F. Leckwart (1970, December). Influence of nursing-unit design on activities and subjective feelings of nursing personnel. *Environment and Behavior, 2,* 303–334.

Improving Hospitals, Schools, and Offices

Following Sommer's lead, environmental psychologists have rearranged or designed a whole range of environments in an attempt to satisfy the needs of people. For example, Trites et al. (1970) compared three different types of hospital ward designs (see Figure 11.8) at Rochester Methodist Hospital. They found that in the radial design, travel time was less, time spent with patients was greater, and nurses preferred to be assigned to this unit. Follow-up studies have demonstrated, however, that designs that satisfy certain of the staff's needs are likely to frustrate some of the needs of patients. In radially designed areas, for instance, patients are more likely to complain about a lack of privacy (Reizenstein, 1982).

Another type of environment that has been redesigned with behavioral principles in mind is the office (Wineman, 1982). By removing floor-to-ceiling partitions and providing low movable barriers, the flexibility of task performance and work-related communication has been improved, and a sense of solidarity has also been created (Kubzansky, Porter, & Salter, 1980). Just as in the hospital, however, office workers often complain about visual and acoustical distractions in the open-plan office, and point out that without four walls surrounding them they have a reduced sense of privacy, territoriality, and control (Wineman, 1982, 1985).

Perhaps the most studied type of environment is that made for learning. Jeffrey Fisher and his colleagues (Fisher, Bell, & Baum, 1984) point out that the reason we sit at desks along straight rows goes back to medieval times, when students had to sit in rows near the windows to give them enough light. Yet we have not changed the basic design of classrooms even though the reason for arranging desks in straight rows no longer exists. Sommer and Olsen (1980) compared participation in two introductory psychology discussion groups at the University of California, Davis. In the traditional straight-row classrooms, fewer than half (48 percent) of the students participated, each making an average of 1.4 comments per person per class. In a "soft" classroom, one that was aesthetically pleasing and arranged in a circular style, not only did more students participate (79 percent), but there was also an increase in student-to-student as well as student-to-professor discussion.

In schools below the college level, the open classroom has been studied extensively (see Weinstein, 1981, 1982). The open classroom design creates a school without walls. It frees students from traditional architectural barriers and gives them a chance to move about and explore. It attempts to promote flexibility and to encourage interaction among students and between students and teachers (Gump, 1974).

Although the principle of less restrictive learning is a popular one, it is not without its critics. Many have argued that the open classroom merely moves us from one inflexible extreme to the other overly flexible end. Vast open spaces may overwhelm or confuse children, especially younger ones (Hurt, 1975). The use of space can be uneven, with certain places greatly underutilized (Rivlin & Rothenberg, 1976); and noise often acts as a source of distraction and stress (Weinstein, 1977).

Two differing routes have been taken in response to these criticisms. First, further modifications in materials and design have led to better results. For example, sound-absorbent partitions have been used to mark off boundaries and special use areas, with the result of increasing privacy and reducing noise (Evans & Lovell, 1979). In this way the classroom becomes more flexible; it is neither completely open nor completely closed, and it allows work and play, interaction and learning, to exist quite literally side by side. A second response has been to design schools that have a diversity of spaces, some open and some closed, to take into account different activities that go on in them as well as the differing needs and styles of both students and teachers (Krovetz, 1977).

It has been suggested by some that humans are capable of adapting to their surroundings no matter how well or poorly designed—and to a large extent they are probably right. On the other hand, as we have seen in this section, the environment as designed is capable of facilitating and encouraging certain behaviors while frustrating and discouraging others. As our knowledge of social behavior grows more sophisticated and more applicable to the real world, we should have less occasion to have to overcome the deficiencies of the buildings and cities we build. Instead, their design will be informed by the principles and concepts that social psychologists have developed and tested, and the resulting environment will be built to human specifications.

With a basic understanding of environmental-social principles, let us return to Tom Richardson's problems in dormitory living. Andrew Baum and Stuart Valins (1977) studied students who lived in the same sort of dorms at the State University of New York at Stony Brook and at a smaller private school, Trinity College. The floors in these dorms had a traditional setup of 16 or 17 double-occupancy rooms, a centrally located bathroom, and a lounge at the end of a long central hallway (see Figure 11.9).

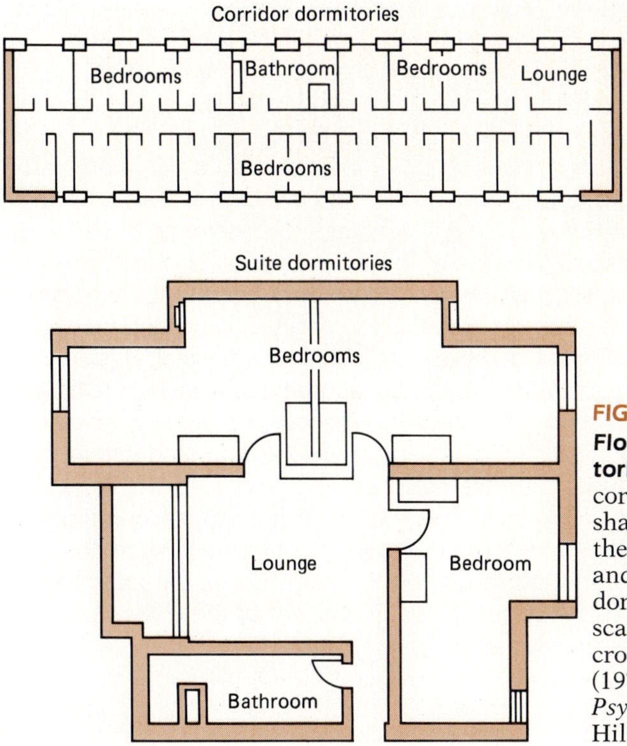

FIGURE 11.9

Floor Plans of Corridor and Suite Dormitories Studied by Baum and Valins In the corridor dormitories, many more students shared the same facilities, and as a result they came to feel crowded, overloaded, and not as satisfied. Students in the suite dorms experienced life on a much smaller scale and felt more in control and less crowded. *Source:* A. Baum and S. Valins (1977). *Architecture and social behavior: Psychological studies in social density.* Hillsdale, NJ: Erlbaum.

Each of these schools also had a second kind of dormitory whose design was also studied. These dorms were similar in that they were also three stories high and housed about 34 students per floor. They provided about the same amount of closet space, and generally their facilities were quite similar. Here the resemblance stopped. Instead of a *corridor* design, the physical arrangement of space in this dorm was a *suite* design. Each suite consisted of two or three double-occupancy rooms, a small lounge area, and a bathroom. Instead of sharing the bathroom and lounge areas with everyone else on the floor, students in this arrangement shared them with three to five others. The overall density of the two dorms was almost identical, but the scale at which students experienced each of the two environments was quite different. Suite residents "lived" among smaller groups of people, while corridor residents shared their living space with everyone on the floor.

Baum and Valins compared the behavior and attitudes of the residents of both dorm types. At the end of their first year, 58 percent of the corridor residents reported that the dorm felt crowded, and only 12 percent felt they could control what happened to them in the hallways. In comparison, only 10 percent of the suite residents reported feeling crowded—even though their buildings were identical in density—and 40 percent felt they could exert control over activities in their hallway. Also, while most social interaction in both dormitories occurred in the areas right around the dorm bedrooms, when suite residents just wanted to read or do something alone they could still use the lounge. Corridor residents had to withdraw physically into their rooms or head off to the library to gain privacy. As time passed, rather than being able to adapt to their environment, corridor residents showed increasing signs of withdrawal and learned helplessness (Baum, Aiello, & Calesnick, 1978).

Baum and Valins suggest that while all dormitories bring together large numbers of students, their design can either intensify or provide buffers against the problems of group living. Suites limit access to small clusters of people who know each other on a personal basis and allow residents to develop and share a sense of group *social* identity and group *physical* territory. Corridor designs provide an overload of individuals and interactions, thereby discouraging such feelings.

While the literature on crowding, territoriality, and personal control applies itself to accounting for differences between corridor and suite dorms, how might it be useful for people reading this right now in the room of a corridor dorm? Is the lesson to tear down 80 percent of the college dorms now built, or are there practical alternatives?

Andrew Baum and his colleague Glenn Davis (1980) tried an architectural intervention that was as simple as it was ingenious. Working with officials at Trinity College, they took a standard long corridor floor housing 40 students and bisected it, converting three bedrooms in the middle of the floor to lounge areas and erecting a wall with unlocked doors in the middle. In effect, the floor now consisted of two groups of 20 people rather than one group of 40. Incoming freshmen were randomly assigned to one of three settings: the standard long corridor design, the long corridor bisected design, or a short corridor in a different but comparable dormitory. The researchers watched and waited.

As anticipated, stress- and control-related problems were fewer in the two short corridor designs than in the long. Residents in all three settings tended to have similar feelings of control and patterns of behavior up through the first few weeks of class. By seven weeks into the term, however, the short corridor and bisected corridor floors had more local group interest and interaction, more usage of shared spaces for social purposes, and less withdrawal.

This approach of Baum and his colleagues highlights the way in which the physical environment can have a profound impact upon students' adaptation to college life. Moreover, while one popular way of dealing with stress has often been to treat *people* through personal counseling, relaxation techniques, or other such means, this suggests that by "treating" the *environment* it may be possible to prevent the experience of stress and problems of crowding in the first place.

SUMMARY

1. The physical environment can be described according to many different criteria. Four important ways of characterizing the environment are according to its ecological, geographic, or design properties; as a set of behavior settings (places that encourage specific patterns of behavior); according to the characteristics of its inhabitants; and according to the social climate of the place.
2. Personal space refers to an area immediately surrounding one's body into which others may not intrude. The amount of personal space required increases or decreases as a function of the characteristics of the individual, the task, and the relationship to the other in an interaction. Personal space serves a defensive function and is also a regulator and indicator of attraction.
3. Edward Hall describes four interpersonal distance zones that people maintain in their interactions: intimate, for comforting, lovemaking, or fighting; personal, for activities between friends; social, for business transactions; and public, for formal interactions or with those of high status.

4. Territories vary according to the degree to which they are under a person's exclusive control as well as the duration for which they are used. Primary territories, such as homes, are owned or used by one person or group for long periods. Secondary territories, such as a local pub or grocery, are spaces that people inhabit for shorter periods, but where regulars are known and welcomed. Public territories, such as a large urban street, are places in which people come and go constantly and no person can hold lengthy claim to any space.
5. Territoriality refers to a feeling of ownership, commitment, and willingness to defend a geographic area (territory). Territoriality plays an organizing function in allowing claims to space, symbolizes dominant relationships among people, and promotes group identity through attachment to places. An indication of territoriality is personalization, the process of making one's identity known in a place through distinctive markings or decorations.
6. Density refers to an objective state, the number of people per unit space. Crowding is a psychological or subjective state in which people experience dissatisfaction owing to a lack of space caused by the presence of too many others.
7. Experimental research has demonstrated that people who feel crowded experience greater physiological arousal, do more poorly in complex mental tasks, and tend to help others less. Women typically respond more positively to crowding, and attempt to coordinate their activities with others. Men typically react negatively and withdraw from interaction. The long-term effects of high-density living, however, present a mixed picture, with some studies indicating negative effects and other studies none.
8. A number of explanations have been offered to explain the effects of crowding. The overload explanation focuses on the high level of stimulation in a dense environment; the interference explanation points to the constraints that others create when working or living in high density; and the privacy explanation highlights the need to control the access that others have to you. The broadest model, learned helplessness, suggests that people feel a loss of control when in the presence of too many others and experience negative effects because they give up trying too easily.
9. Theories of urban behavior focus on different distinctive elements of the city. The human ecology perspective focuses on size, density, and population heterogeneity, and proposes that urban living leads to personal and social disorganization. The subcultural approach takes a more positive view, emphasizing the ways in which active and satisfying subcultures form in the city. The overload approach points to both positive and negative outcomes of urban life, but emphasizes that both are the result of active coping rather than passive responding.

10. Urban conditions such as noise, pollution, and commuting act as sources of stress. As with crowding, it has been suggested that each of these most taxes the ability of city people to cope when it leads to a loss of control and a feeling of learned helplessness.
11. Environmental designers often take a functional or an aesthetic focus—using a mechanistic view of people as task workers in the former, or seeing the environment as a work of art in the latter. Settings such via the application of environmental and social psychological principles.

CHAPTER 12
Small Groups

The assembly line moves parts into position and controls the speed with which cars are produced. You must stay at your post, interact as little as possible with other workers, and perform your specific task. That task may be to guide the body down onto the chassis, to push the seats into place, or to place a light bulb into the appropriate socket. Whatever it is, you have to repeat it every minute or so.

Production quotas are the major issue for U.S. management: turn out the specified number of cars each day; their condition is secondary. The greatest sin would be to stop the "line," and thereby slow the assembly of cars. You are a part of that line. If you see a defect in a car, you are supposed to let it go by, to be caught (it is hoped) by the quality control inspector.

To do such work is not much of a pleasure. Not only is it repetitive, but it also cuts you off from much of what makes work rewarding. On the assembly line, you are prevented from being involved with other people, you have no opportunity to improve the process or product in even the smallest way, and you have no real control over what is going on. Such a situation is not only boring, but also makes you feel that both you and the product are of little importance. You find that you have lost all interest in your job, and often you do not even show up for work. And you are not unique. Absenteeism in these kinds of jobs runs at about 15 percent. Many of the other workers are bored, alienated, and uninvolved in the well-being of the company on whose existence their own well-being depends.

When work takes this form, both the companies and their workers are in serious trouble. Without the benefit of the workers' ideas and motivation, the quality of American automobiles and other products was exceeded by that of foreign auto makers, especially the Japanese. As consumers came to appreciate the quality of Japanese automobiles, their sales rose to about one-quarter of the U.S. market (Byron, 1981). And as U.S. industry declined, U.S. workers began to lose their jobs.

What we have described is one way to organize workers. Actually, it describes a way *not* to organize people into work groups, but instead to keep them disconnected individuals. In this chapter we will examine what happens when people come together in groups, the properties of those groups, and the different ways the groups can be structured. In particular, we will ask: What is the effect of such processes on the people in the group and on their products? Then, at the end of the chapter, we will look at how the social psychologists' knowledge of behavior in small groups has been applied to improving the lives of workers and their industries.

Few of us appreciate the extent to which groups are central to our lives. We are born into families. We attend schools to which we are loyal against rival schools. Within our schools we are assembled into sections and classes, we cluster into cliques, and we join teams. We usually work in groups. Even seemingly solitary practitioners such as dentists and some doctors belong to professional associations which share information, provide group insurance, lobby for protective laws, and do many other things for their professional community. Some people receive psychotherapy in groups. Some people live in communes. Our wars are fought by groups. And our armed forces are organized into services: air force, army, navy. When it is time to bury us, that too is done by people coming together as a group.

GROUPS AND THE INDIVIDUAL

The word *group* is often used loosely to refer to virtually any collection of two or more persons. In this section we will discuss the types of groups that exist and the effect of being a group member.

What Is a Group?

A group implies more than a collection of isolated individuals. When social psychologists refer to a group, they usually mean a collection of people who are involved with one another. Group members interact with each other, care whether the group stays together or falls apart, influence each other's attitudes and behavior, and develop relatively stable relationships (see Shaw, 1981; Bales, 1950; Fiedler, 1967). Sometimes these are called psychological groups to emphasize the presence of characteristics that are typical of interacting, interconnected collections of people.

This list of characteristics may at first seem formidable, but it is typical of a vast array of groups with which we all are intimately familiar. The smallest and most common psychological group, the **dyad**—two people, a couple—is typically an interacting psychological group with all of the properties of a group we have mentioned (Thomas & Malone, 1979). The same is true of small families (Waxler & Mishler, 1978), surgical teams, volleyball teams, juries, and roommates.

Membership and Reference Groups Psychological groups can be distinguished further as being either **membership groups** or **reference groups.** A membership group is one to which we belong socially and physically. A reference group is one with which an individual identifies with and uses as a standard for self-evaluation (Krech, Crutchfield, & Ballachey, 1962). Any given psychological group may for a given person be a membership group, a reference group, or both. People may belong to a religious congregation but care little for the group's values and not care what the members think of them. Other people, such as students, may not yet have entered a particular profession; indeed, the members of that profession do not even know the student exists. Still, a student may aspire to belong to and strive to be like that group. If you hope to become a journalist, you are likely to adopt the styles of speech, thought, and manner of journalists and to use them as a standard against which to compare your own behavior. Sherif and Sherif (1969) have neatly summarized this distinction in noting that a person's membership groups are defined more by *social* connections; a person's reference groups are defined more by *psychological* connections.

Just as people can and do belong to many groups, they can also identify with many reference groups. The one that is most important to a person is called the primary group, while the less important are secondary groups. To be in one group implies being out of certain other groups. A group that is important to you and to which you belong constitutes an **in-group;** a group to which you do not belong or, indeed, which opposes your group is an **out-group.**

In this chapter we focus on small groups, although designating a group as "small" is fairly arbitrary. Most researchers in this area usually study groups of about four to eight people, but sometimes they are interested in groups as small as two to as large as twelve or sixteen. The meaningful limit to "small group" is often taken to be the size within which people can still have face-to-face contact.

Aggregates Versus Groups A collection of two or of sixteen people does not automatically constitute a psychological group. Sets of people who are merely in the same place at the same time, and may even be doing the same thing, are known as *aggregates* unless they have some degree of psychological and social connectedness. Fellow passengers on a bus or an elevator and patients in a waiting room are all merely aggregates. They have something in common, but interdependence and interaction are minimal or nonexistent.

The distinction between psychological groups and mere aggregates is not a hard line. Some groups may be difficult to classify. A religious congregation or a class in a school may be a mere aggregate or may be a psychological group, depending upon the relations among its members. Groups that are only aggregates at one point, such as bus passengers, can be transformed into a psychological group by, for example, a traffic accident. Principles that apply to psychological groups usually do not apply to aggregates. People in psychological groups behave differently toward each other than people in aggregates, as in the way they relate their self-interest to that of others. And yet mere aggregates of people are not without power to transform the behavior of individuals, as we shall see in this chapter.

Why do we join so many groups so often? Many possible explanations exist, all of which add up to the notion that groups enable us to do things we would not be able to do as individuals, including increasing our chances of survival. Sociobiologists, for example, hypothesize that our gregariousness is part of our own genes' "strategy" for survival (Barash, 1979).

The most primitive group is the family or kinship group, those people who are biologically related. The survival of that group ensured survival not only of individuals but of their shared genetic heritage. The sociobiological view holds that the great variety of contemporary groups is an outgrowth of the basic genetic strategy of our species to form into groups. In part, these groupings may be formed out of habit, as it were, but they often have an obvious survival value of their own. Small fish can turn away a predator by schooling and appearing to be a single large animal. Wolves (or humans) who cannot defeat game individually can attack as a group and succeed.

Most social psychologists believe that groups are so useful to individual well-being that they would form whether or not the sociobiological hypothesis is correct. If our environment—complete with the difficulties of nurturing young, avoiding predators, and accumulating venture capital—is such that forming into groups improves the chances of individual success, then individuals will form groups. And when the tasks to be performed are accomplished better by individuals working alone, then individuals will learn not to form groups for these purposes.

Compresence

Some social psychologists have been interested in the kinds of effects that are produced in the behavior of individuals by the merest gathering together of people and animals—that is, **compresence.** Individuals in the presence of others behave differently than they do when alone (Zajonc, 1980). Some of the effects are surprising.

When locusts and grasshoppers form into a swarm, their wings change shape, their thoraxes grow in size, at least one kind of wingless individuals grows wings, and another species changes color. The changes reverse when the individual is separated from the group. Chickens, puppies, and other animals eat more food when others are present (e.g., Harlow & Yudin, 1933; Tolman, 1965). Some species of ants, bees, and termites simply cannot survive without the continual presence of fellow members of their species—death occurs within hours even when the physical environment is kept ideal for survival (Zajonc, 1980).

For both humans (Schachter, 1959) and animals (e.g., Bovard, 1958; Davitz & Mason, 1955), the presence of at least one other individual during a stressful situation has a calming effect. When a woman is accompanied by a close and trusted companion, she can tolerate the physical discomforts of birth more easily (Colman & Colman, 1971). And at the far end of life, it is thought that deterioration and death are accelerated by the social isolation that usually accompanies old age in our society (Butler, 1975).

Social Facilitation

The first social psychologist to study the effects of the presence of others on a person's behavior was Norman Triplett. Triplett was a bicycle racing enthusiast, and he noticed that racers rode faster against another rider than when they raced against only a clock. He conducted the first laboratory experiment in social psychology when he had students wind fishing reels both alone and in groups (Triplett, 1897). Like the bicycle racers, they performed better in groups than when alone, and this phenomenon became known as **social facilitation** (Allport, 1924).

For the next 75 years, social psychologists explored variations of the basic social facilitation experiment, testing whether people in groups could also do better at solving puzzles, escaping from a shock apparatus, and performing other tasks. The accumulated results were inconsistent: sometimes doing a task in a group facilitated performance; sometimes it inhibited performance.

Robert Zajonc (1965) has proposed an elegantly simple explanation that makes sense of the confusion. His theory of social facilitation proposes that the presence of others produces a general arousal that heightens motivation. Behavior is then more energetic and faster. But which behavior? Zajonc further hypothesized that our responses fall along a dimension from well learned to poorly learned. If we are skilled at a task (i.e., if it is well learned), correct responses are high in our response hierarchy, and they are even more likely to be performed under conditions of arousal. If we are unskilled, errors are high on our response hierarchy, and they are more likely to occur when arousal is heightened. Thus the presence of others ought to facilitate well-learned responses and inhibit poorly learned responses.

After nearly a century and well over 200 studies of social facilitation, Bond and Titus (1983) report that Zajonc's explanation works best when talking about complex tasks, but less well concerning simple tasks. Other explanations have been offered as well for this phenomenon. A concern over being judged by others, **evaluation apprehension,** is another explanation that has received some support (Bray & Sugarman, 1980). In fact, in a field test of this explanation, Worringham and Messick (1983) showed that joggers speed up when they are watched by others in their path.

The implications of this phenomenon are all around us. It explains why the best athletes perform "in the clutch," when it counts most on national television during a championship contest; while lesser athletes put in their best performances during practices, when arousal and evaluation apprehension are both lower. It may also explain why the better-prepared students thrive on the tension of an examination. Less well prepared students would probably do better if they could take their exams alone—along with finding other ways to reduce arousal.

THE PROPERTIES OF GROUPS

In defining psychological groups, we noted that individuals belonging to such groups share considerably more than each other's presence. It is not surprising, therefore, that involvement in a group has profound effects on attitudes and behavior of participating individuals. What are the properties of groups that produce effects on people? Psychological groups are characterized by various properties such as cohesiveness, the existence of norms, and pressure to conform to those norms. In addition, groups vary in the number and type of individuals who compose them. In this section we will examine some of these properties more closely.

Cohesiveness

Cohesiveness deals with the issue of why people are in a group rather than out of it. Cohesiveness denotes the sense of closeness or "we-ness" that a group feels. It is typically defined as "the resultant of all the forces acting on all the members to remain in the group" (Cartwright & Zander, 1968, p. 74). From the intense dyad that is the couple to the loose collection of people who meet once a month to discuss a novel, something holds the group together or causes it to fall apart. What are these forces?

A group stays together because its members are attracted to each other more than they are to alternative relationships. Attractiveness may in part be interpersonal (the causes of which can be found in Chapter 7, "Interpersonal Attraction and Romantic Relationships"), but it is due also to the dynamics of the group. Group members share practical (task-oriented) goals and a concern for their members' psychological well-being (a social-emotional orientation). The group structure and process also provide satisfactions to individuals as well as sufficient alienation from out-groups (Cartwright, 1968; Thibaut & Kelley, 1959).

High cohesiveness affects group members in several other important ways. Groups that are highly cohesive obtain greater adherence to group goals and norms, greater uniformity, and greater influence over members. Indeed, group cohesiveness sets the upper limit on a group's power over its members (Thibaut & Kelly, 1959; Davis, 1969). Highly cohesive groups show high levels of communication and involvement, as well as greater willingness of individuals to defend and make sacrifices for the group (Cartwright, 1968). This is illustrated by the outstanding performance of highly cohesive sports teams and businesses as compared to the faltering achievement of groups that are well staffed and well financed but low in cohesiveness.

When under (social or physical) attack, highly cohesive groups usually become even more unified, rather than less. This runs counter to the assumptions or hopes of the attacker, who believes the attack will "demoralize" the group. Such attacks usually galvanize the unit into a more cohesive unit, whether the group is a political one facing opposition (Janis, 1982) or a city under siege during war (U.S. Strategic Bombing Survey, 1945).

Norms and Conformity Pressures

A second property of psychological groups is their tendency to create or to adopt norms. As discussed in Chapter 4, norms are "rules of behavior, proper ways of acting, which have been accepted as legitimate by a group" (Hare, 1976, p. 19). Norms often exist for the simple purpose of establishing the in-group's identity, such as when young schoolgirls all wear the same barrettes, when college students dress as preppies, or when bankers all wear the same kind of suit. The most salient and most enforced norms, however, are those related to the group's goals.

Goals of work groups commonly involve norms about the kind and amount of work that may be done. Norms concerning the members' allowable level of productivity are especially significant, as deviations of too little (a "chiseler") or too much productivity (a "rate-buster") usually draw the criticism of co-workers. Such "floors" and "ceilings" on output have been found among workers in many settings—the electronics industry, machine shops, and elsewhere (e.g., Taylor, 1903; Mayo, 1933; Zaleznik, Christiansen, & Roethlisberger, 1958). Some workers are capable of producing more and earning more, but they are held back by the group norm. Others might like to lag behind, but are pulled up to the norm. Some of the earliest studies of workers' norm enforcement found that individuals increased their output and earned an average of 60 percent more pay when freed from their group's influence (Taylor, 1911).

The work group's norms, however, evolve neither to punish members nor to undermine management. They arise to protect the group's perceived interests. In some cases, workers may fear cuts in pay rates as a consequence of increased output, so in effect they would earn less for doing more. Therefore, they protect themselves from this threat by placing a limit on output, and criticizing anyone trying to be a rate-buster (Sherif & Sherif, 1969).

At other times, group norms can enforce extremely high levels of work. One of the authors once worked for an organization in which a norm for hard work and high productivity arose among a subgroup of employees. Staff members (on fixed salaries) competed against each other to see who could put in longer hours and get more done. Since cars were parked in order of their arrival at the office's parking lot, everyone could see who had arrived first, second, and so on. Occupying a lead parking position became a badge of honor, sometimes won only by arriving hours before the official start of the workday.

In other kinds of groups, other norms become important. Members of religious sects enforce norms related to the group's theological beliefs. Street gangs reward "macho" talk and behavior. Academicians have norms for publishing research or being cited by peers. Physicians have norms for choices of treatment or ways of dealing with patients. To be accepted by the group, newcomers must learn the norms and comply with them. The norms change over time and vary from one subgroup to another. For example, the use of shock therapy was once more widespread than it is today, and is still used often in some mental hospitals but barely at all in others (Benedict, in press).

A person is always a member of several groups at once, perhaps a primary group of daily face-to-face contact and a more diffuse secondary group of larger size. Often the two groups conflict—for example, the profession says to treat with medication but one's immediate co-workers prefer surgery; or a religion advocates certain food taboos while a member's friends like to eat those foods. In cases of conflict, individuals typically behave more in line with the norms of the primary group (e.g., Dentler, 1961; Rosen, 1955).

It is the nature of psychological groups to establish norms automatically and to attack deviation from them. The result is conformity to the norms. If the group's pressure does not motivate a deviant to fall into line, the person will eventually be ignored or even rejected by the group, given up as a lost cause. Merely holding an opinion on an important issue that is not shared by the group can produce this effect (Festinger & Thibaut, 1951; Schachter, 1951; Allen, 1965).

Insulation from the group's pressure is possible. People who have been good, loyal group members have stored up what is called **idiosyncrasy credit.** It refers to the good will of the group that accrues—like money in a bank account—to group members who have been "good citizens" of the group. The more of a good citizen you are, the more credit you store up. As you deviate from the group's norms, you draw on that credit and may eventually use it up. How fast the idiosyncrasy credit is depleted will depend upon how much a person has to start with, how often one deviates, and how serious the deviations are. Violating minor norms is less costly than violating major ones.

Group Composition

The people composing a group may be similar to or different from each other in any number of ways. Individuals vary in terms of their personalities, attitudes, styles of behavior, abilities, and so on. How does the composition of the group affect its behavior?

We might suppose that some personality types make better group members, such as people who are more task-oriented or more socio-emotional, more extroverted, or low (or high) in authoritarianism. For example, one study found that people who are high in authoritarianism make slower progress and are less cooperative, but also show less disagreement and less competition compared with low authoritarians (Haythorn, 1956). The best summary of the effects of individual personalities on group behavior is that groups function best, are most productive and their members most satisfied, when their members are *similar* to each other—if they all prefer close interpersonal relationships, if they are all authoritarians, or if they are all introverted or extroverted (Shaw, 1960; Hare, 1976). Thus it is not the kind of personality itself that matters, but whether a group is homogeneous or heterogeneous. Therefore, individual differences among group members play a modest role in group performance (McGrath & Altman, 1966), certainly more modest than such variables as cohesiveness, norms, group structure, and task structure.

Group Size

Does the size of a small group make any difference in its process or its products? Some people believe size makes quite a difference, as is evident from the battles that are often fought over the proper size of courts and juries, legislative bodies, and governing boards of all kinds. Weick (1979)

We spend much of our time in small groups. These six people, for example, have gathered together to coordinate the various tasks in a project they are working on. How might the process and the product differ in a larger group? In a smaller group?

gives us some sense of the possible alterations in a group's structure and relations among its members that may result from changes in its size:

> The transition from one to two creates the basic unit of social behavior, the dyad. In a dyad there is interdependence, reciprocal behavior, and the necessity for accommodation to another person. The transition from two to three is significant because now there exists the possibility of an alliance between two members against the third one. The phenomena of control, cooperation and competition, and influence are produced by this transition. A triad also is less vulnerable than a dyad. If one person leaves, a social unit still remains. But if one person leaves a dyad, the social unit dissolves. The transition from three to four creates the possibility of two equal dyads or alliances, and this may perpetuate both the social unit and the problems of control. The significant feature of four is that an alliance between two members is not sufficient to gain control. The excluded pair may themselves form an alliance, in which case the possibility of a stalemate increases. [Pp. 24–25]

A variety of effects is regularly observed as a function of increased group size. First, as the size of the group goes up, the time available for each member to participate in the group unavoidably declines (Hare, 1952). Members feel more inhibited about participating (Gibb, 1951; Carter et al., 1951), they find their participation less satisfying, and disagreement increases (Bales & Borgatta, 1955; Slater, 1958; Berkowitz, 1958). At the same time, the likelihood of allies being present increases as do the human resources available to the group—an important matter to which we will turn later when we discuss group problem solving. Moreover, the group's reliability and accuracy tend to increase with increasing group size for the same reason that eight thermometers give a more accurate average temperature than two—namely, random errors are averaged out (Stroop, 1932).

The relationship of group size to psychological variables has been captured by Latané's *social impact theory* (Latané, 1981; Latané & Nida, 1980). According to this theory, the arrival of one other person in your otherwise empty life space has a greater impact on you than an increase from 99 to 100 people. The marginal impact (that is, the difference in impact due to the next additional person) decreases as group size increases. The result is that although the effect of the group on an individual increases as the size of the group increases, that effect grows more and more slowly. Latané and his associates have shown this relationship to account for such varied effects as the tension felt when speaking to a group (Latané & Harkins, 1976), conformity (Latané & Nida, 1980), and offering help (Latané & Dabbs, 1975).

An important related finding has been termed **social loafing**—the phenomenon whereby each individual puts out less effort as additional members are added to a group, even though the total group effort keeps increasing. In one study (Latané, Williams, & Harkins, 1979) students were asked to make as much noise as possible by shouting or clapping, either alone, in pairs, or in groups of six. When a member of a six-person group, each individual put out less effort (less noise), producing only 36 percent of the volume that six separate individuals were capable of generating. In a similar vein, a study of diners in Columbus, Ohio, showed that people eating alone tipped by almost 19 percent of their bill, while the percentage each person contributed to the tip decreased as the size of the dining party increased (see Figure 12.1). The form of this figure is consistent with the predictions of social impact theory.

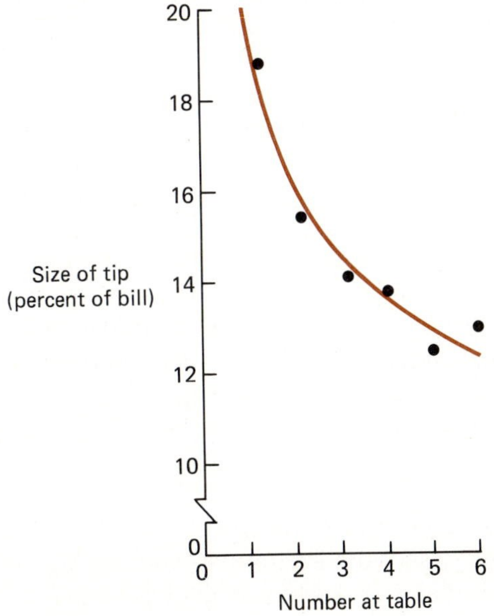

FIGURE 12.1
Size of Tip as a Function of the Number of People Eating Together When a group of people pay their dinner check as a group (rather than by separate checks), the size of the tip (as a percentage of the total bill) decreases as the number of people in the group increases. *Source:* B. Latané (1981). The psychology of social impact. *American Psychologist, 36,* 351.

APPLICATION
JURY SIZE AND THE SUPREME COURT

For more than six hundred years of English common law, *jury* meant a group of twelve people required to reach a unanimous verdict. And for nearly two hundred years of U.S. constitutional history, that is also what it meant.

But in 1970 the U.S. Supreme Court ruled that neither history nor tradition nor precedent must bind a jury to any particular size. The determination of proper jury size, said the court, must rest on a "functional analysis of the jury's purpose." That is, to find out the minimum allowable jury size, one had to look to the actual functioning of the jury, and how that was affected by reduction in size. If a smaller group engaged in the same process and reached the same decision as a group of twelve, then the smaller group was equivalent to the larger group and was therefore legal.

After conducting such an analysis, the Supreme Court in *Williams* v. *Florida* (1970) declared that juries of six people were the functional equivalent of twelve-person juries and were therefore constitutional. The court concluded that "the performance of this role is not a function of the particular number of the body that makes up the jury. . . . [W]e find little reason to think that those goals are in any meaningful sense less likely to be achieved when the jury numbers six, than when it numbers twelve" (*Williams,* pp. 100–101).

Not surprisingly, such a radical departure from tradition drew the close attention of legal scholars and social scientists. On what had the court based its conclusion of equivalence between twelve-person and six-person juries? The court cited several "studies" that in reality were no more than someone's assertions that smaller juries would behave the same as larger ones. The court also cited a number of actual empirical studies (e.g., Asch, 1952; Kalven & Zeisel, 1966) but, incredibly, interpreted them to mean the virtual opposite of what they actually implied. For example, those studies all agree that the existence of a single ally makes the greatest difference in a minority's ability to resist majority pressure, with additional allies adding less and less to the minority's strength in much the fashion described in Latané's social impact theory. The Supreme Court, however, erroneously took the studies to mean that minority resistance in a jury split 5 to 1 was the same as that in one split 10 to 2.

In this chapter we have noted some of the effects of group size. In addition to the effects on conformity, larger groups are also less cohesive, less satisfying to members, more contentious, and more likely to deliberate vigorously. In research studying juries specifically, larger juries were found more able collectively to recall the trial's evidence. Because larger groups bring more human resources to a problem and cancel out individual members' errors, they generally make more accurate decisions (Saks, 1977; Zeisel, 1971; Zeisel & Diamond, 1974; Grofman, 1976).

While researchers had been testing the Supreme Court's notions about juries expressed in the Williams case, state legislatures were testing how small the law would allow them to set their size. Eventually the issue again came before the

Supreme Court in a later case, *Ballew* v. *Georgia* (1978). But this time the court halted the decline at six (Sperlich, 1979; Roper, 1980). The Supreme Court's opinion in that case cited approximately 20 social science studies and discussions of the group size question "because they provide the only basis, besides judicial hunch, for a decision about whether smaller and smaller juries will be able to fulfill the purpose and functions of the Sixth Amendment" (p. 480). On the basis of these studies, the court concluded that further shrinkage would change the behavior of juries in ways that the legal system could not tolerate. Indeed, the most extensive use by the Supreme Court of social science findings to reach a decision occurred in that case.

We must note that almost all of the studies the opinion reviewed compared juries of six and twelve. But how could comparisons of six versus twelve showing changes in the jury's behavior lead to the conclusion that juries smaller than six were not as good? What we see here is that while research findings have been used extensively, they have not been used flawlessly or faithfully, nor has their use been without controversy. Thus the Supreme Court's use of social science in the jury size cases is both an important example of its relevance to decision making about legal policy, and an illustration of the danger of inadequate use of research to inform policy.

THE STRUCTURE OF GROUPS

Groups may take many forms, and members of the same group may each play different parts. As a result, power is distributed unevenly among group members, and the content and direction of communication can vary. To consider these issues, we now turn to a consideration of the systematic patterning, or structure, of behavior within groups.

Roles and Positions

An important structural feature of groups involves the roles and positions its members assume. Roles, those expectations for behavior of a person occupying a given position in a group, emerge even in unstructured work or discussion groups. Some people take on task-completion roles, working to move the group toward accomplishing its goals, and others take on socio-emotional roles, working to maintain the happiness of group members (Bales & Slater, 1955; Bales, 1958). When people change positions within a group or change groups, their roles can change and, accordingly, their behavior usually will change. In the space of a few minutes a middle manager can go from being subordinate at a meeting with the boss to dominant at a meeting with the workers. Thus some aspects of the behavior of people in groups can be accounted for through an analysis of the roles associated with given positions (see Chapter 4 for a fuller discussion of role theory).

Patterns of Communication

Perhaps the most familiar and fundamental thing that humans do in groups is to communicate. Accordingly, much of the early research on behavior in small groups concerned itself with trying to describe the amount, nature, and pattern of communication among group members; and later to identify the causes of these patterns and the consequences of different patterns.

Interaction Process Analysis Different kinds of groups systematically vary in the amount and distribution of communicative acts in which they engage. Of the many systems devised to capture and code the communications of group members (reviewed in Hare, 1976), the most influential has been **interaction process analysis** (IPA), developed by Bales (1950). This system enables observers to note and code who in the group communicates with whom, and it codes each communicative act into one of twelve categories, as seen in Figure 12.2.

The communication patterns that emerge for different kinds of groups vary greatly, as illustrated in Table 12.1. In some groups, the focus is on the socio-emotional element, addressing the interrelationships and feel-

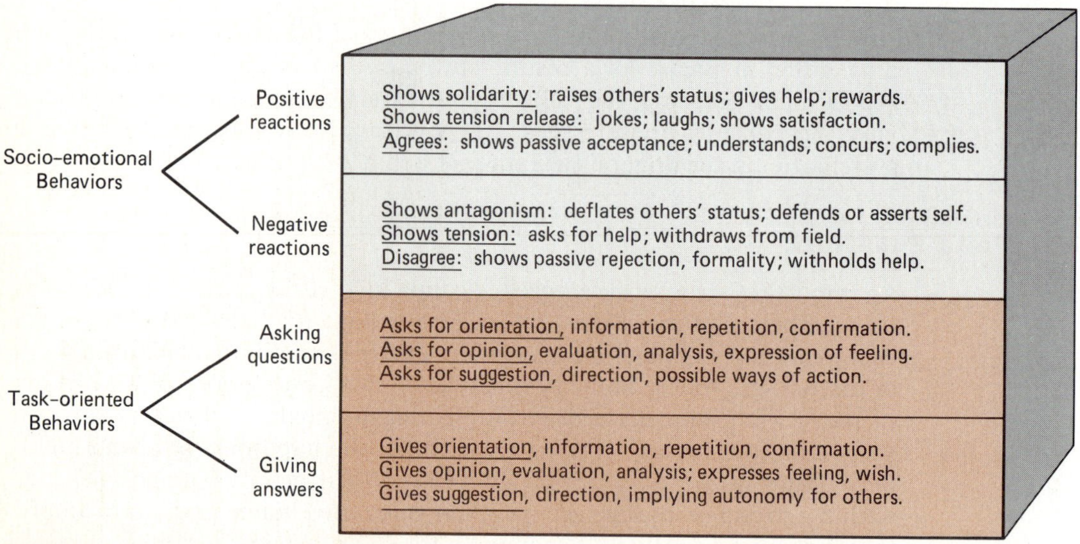

FIGURE 12.2
Interaction Process Analysis Categories These are the categories of behavior used in Bales's interaction process analysis of group behavior. They fall into two basic areas: socio-emotional and task-oriented. For each area, there are two sets of complementary behaviors, such as positive/negative reactions and asking questions/giving answers. *Source:* Based on R. F. Bales (1950). *Interaction process analysis.* Reading, MA: Addison-Wesley. Reprinted by the University of Chicago Press, 1976.

TABLE 12.1

Interaction Profiles for Different Kinds of Small Groups (in percentages)

Interaction Process Analysis Category	Social Conversation (Slater & Bales, 1957)	Playing Board Game (Olmsted, 1952)	Subjects Under Lysergic Acid (Slater, Morimoto, & Hyde, 1958)	Psychiatric Stress Interview (Hare et al., 1960)	Jury Deliberation (Strodtbeck & Mann, 1956)	Labor Mediation Sessions (Landsberger, 1955)
1. Shows solidarity	8.8	2.0	9.5	0.1	1.2	2.4
2. Shows tension release	17.7	6.1	30.4	0.5	3.0	1.2
3. Shows agreement	9.0	13.7	10.5	0.9	17.9	10.5
4. Gives suggestion	0.0	20.2	7.1	0.5	4.0	3.0
5. Gives opinion	17.4	25.7	16.7	16.7	26.1	24.5
6. Gives information	28.7	14.2	13.6	56.9	38.3	32.7
7. Ask for information	11.0	3.0	3.2	12.9	4.6	7.3
8. Ask for opinion	1.8	3.8	1.2	2.8	1.9	2.2
9. Ask for suggestion	0.0	1.8	0.6	0.0	0.2	0.3
10. Shows disagreement	2.1	7.7	5.3	0.6	2.0	7.5
11. Shows tension	3.0	1.0	2.0	6.1	0.6	1.7
12. Shows antagonism	0.0	0.2	0.4	1.8	0.2	4.7

Source: R. F. Bales and A. P. Hare (1965). Diagnostic use of the interaction profile. *Journal of Social Psychology, 67*, 240. Reprinted with permission of the Helen Dwight Reid Educational Foundation. Published by Heldref Publications, 4000 Albemarle St. N.W., Washington, D.C. 20016. Copyright © 1965.

IN THE NEWS

A FATAL ERROR OF JUDGMENT

My God, Thiokol, when do you want me to launch? Next April?

As Allan McDonald told it, that exasperated protest from NASA was the key moment. Under the gun, the managers of Morton Thiokol, Inc., overruled their engineers and signed approval for the space shuttle Challenger to blast off, sending six astronauts and a teacher to their immolation over the Atlantic four weeks ago. After McDonald's testimony to the presidential commission investigating the disaster was leaked to the press, the nature of the inquiry and the nation's view of the space program inexorably changed. Whatever technical problem caused the Challenger to blow up, it was clear that serious warning flags had been raised and, further, that they went unheeded by middle-level officials and evidently were never communicated to the top. "It's not a design defect. There was an error in judgment," Hank Shuey, a rocket-safety expert who has reviewed NASA data, told NEWSWEEK. In that case, the implication was as clear as it was disturbing: the astronauts and Christa McAuliffe didn't have to die. . . .

Perhaps most damaging to the fabric of public trust was the indelible image of the telephone conference call the night before the fatal launch, reconstructed by reporters. A caucus of Morton Thiokol engineers in Brigham City, Utah, concerned about the effect of abnormally low temperatures on the booster-rocket seals, produced an official recommendation: no go. "We all knew if the seals failed, the shuttle would blow up," one engineer later told National Public Radio. But NASA's solid rocket project manager, Lawrence Mulloy, argued that there wasn't enough proof that cold weather stiffens the seals; the agency's George Hardy said he was "appalled" at their insistence that the launch wait for warmer weather. From Cape Canaveral, engineer McDonald protested—"It's so damn cold and none of us are really sure of anything"—but as The Washington Post reconstructed it, NASA issued a blunt order: "We want a formal written recommendation" to launch. Thiokol, builder of the booster, gave in. The next morning one Thiokol engineer shakily watched the lift-off. "I thought, gee, it's going all right. It's a piece of cake. A friend turned to me and said, 'Oh, God, we made it. We made it.' Then . . . the shuttle blew up. And we all knew exactly what happened."

In that telling, McDonald and his colleagues were very nearly heroes. But had NASA really bullied Thiokol? Three members of the presidential commission, after nine hours of talks with Thiokol executives

ings of the people in the group. In others, the focus is more task-oriented, centering on the work the group exists to accomplish. A category such as "Gives information" can vary from a low of 13.6 percent of acts for people under the influence of LSD to a high of 56.9 percent for people in a psychiatric stress interview (Bales & Hare, 1965). While the IPA is useful in the general evaluation of group communication, some researchers (e.g., Roter, 1977) have adapted it to analyze special situations such as doctor-patient interactions.

at Brigham City, said they had found no coercion. "It looks like a professional engineering disagreement," said Washington attorney David Acheson. "We pried into it quite a lot." The prying will continue before the full commission this week. . . .

Human failures led to NASA's fatal error. Former Secretary of State William Rogers, the commission's chairman, said he was "appalled" to find out that at least three of the agency's key executives were never told of the engineers' revolt on the eve of the launch. The discovery prompted Rogers to declare that NASA's "decision-making process may have been flawed" and to exclude NASA officials who participated in the launch from taking part in the investigation. One of the three left in ignorance—Jesse W. Moore, head of the shuttle program—said that if he had known of the objections, "we would certainly have asked a lot of penetrating questions." Rogers impounded all records of the discussions (McDonald reportedly took copious notes).

In part, insiders say, NASA's executive style reflects the complexity of the decisions that must be made: with hundreds of people involved in a launching, no decisions would be possible if they all had to be made at the top. Thus NASA has evolved an almost Japanese system of consensus. Problems and discords are fully aired, says Moore; they "bubble up the line until they get resolved." If the issues can't be settled, the launch will be scrubbed. But Moore acknowledged that the top level for any decision "is hard to define," and he wouldn't speculate on how high knowledge of the weather dispute had bubbled.

Some critics, in fact, saw this vagueness as a subconscious goal of the NASA system. "They have a system set up so that no one is responsible," says one close observer. "No one wants to sleep with having killed somebody." After the Apollo investigation, no one was fired or even lost a promotion. The system did achieve reform: the investigators called for rough 5000 engineering fixes, and the rigorous process that went with them helped prevent another serious accident for nearly 20 years. But like all human systems, it can evolve for the worse. As a senior aerospace expert serving on the Rogers commission put it, "It's so structured that communication is inhibited. No matter how big a program is, there ought to be a top dog who is responsible."

Source: A fatal error of judgment. *Newsweek,* March 3, 1986, pp. 14–18.

In addition to varying in the content of communication, groups may also vary in the sheer amount of communication that takes place. That may be due not only to the nature of the group's purpose and the relationships in the group, but also to the role or position of people in the group or to the size of the group. In every group, some people talk more than others. As the size of the group increases, the gap between the most and the least talkative members grows larger (Bales & Borgatta, 1955; Slater, 1958).

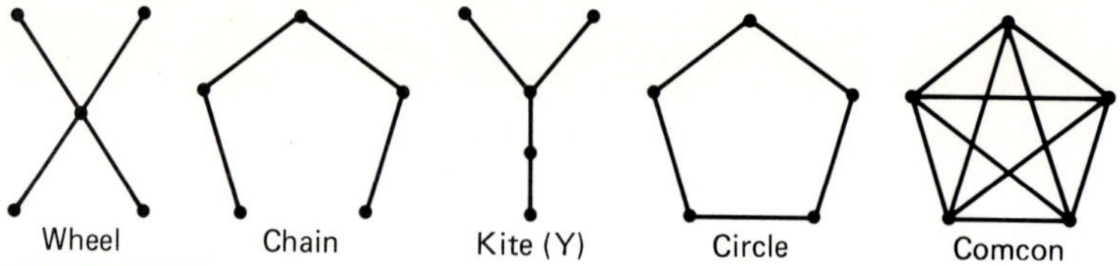

FIGURE 12.3

Communication Networks in a Five-Person Group Lines of communication among five people can be structured into a number of different forms. Different patterns have different effects on the ability of the group to solve problems and to be productive, and also on the morale of the people in the group.

Communication Networks In many groups the patterning of communication to and from group members is subtly regulated either physically or, more often, socially. In a small business firm, the chief executive may require that employees communicate with him or her only through the chief executive's assistants. In larger and more complex organizations the restrictions can be greater and the distance may grow between a decision maker and an individual who has vital information for that decision maker. This was noted, for instance, in the tragic case of the space shuttle Challenger that blew up in flight on January 28, 1986. Concerns held by several engineers never made it through channels to those at the top of NASA, who had responsibility for deciding whether the launch should go ahead (see the In the News box on pages 472–473).

Even in small face-to-face groups, communication may not be free to flow equally in all directions. Role or status structures subtly impose restrictions on communication. Consider the limitations on free communication in surgical teams, military units, and football huddles. Even people who in principle are free to communicate with all members of the group may tend to limit their paths of communication for reasons of physical arrangement. For example, people sharing offices or apartments along the same corridor usually speak to their immediate neighbors more than to those at greater distance (Festinger, Schachter, & Back, 1950; Nahemow & Lawton, 1975).

Figure 12.3 presents a variety of **communication networks.** A business with rules for communicating through "proper channels" resembles the kite, or Y, arrangement in which all communication flows through a central path. Army platoons, surgical teams, and football huddles resemble the wheel, wherein the leader can communicate with any given member of the group, but those other members are less able to communicate among themselves. People whose offices are along a corridor resemble the chain or the circle network. A group of equals meeting face-to-face or on a conference call fit the pattern known as all-channel, or "comcon" (that is, common communication).

Networks are categorized as being "centralized" when one person (or just a few members) has direct access to the group at large while others have little access. Networks are "decentralized" when all members have more or less equal access to each other. The wheel, the chain, and the Y are relatively centralized networks, and the circle and comcon are relatively decentralized.

The efforts of small group researchers have been aimed mostly at finding out the effect of such networks on accuracy and efficiency in solving problems, and on the morale of members. Do some networks facilitate while others inhibit problem solving? Do some networks promote efficiency and accuracy in solving problems more than others? A great volume of research has tried to answer these questions (Bavelas, 1950; Shaw, 1964; Collins & Raven, 1968). In a typical study a group of people are given a problem to solve and placed in an experimental situation that channels their communication into one or another of the networks under study. This is usually done by limiting the access of people to each other, such as by requiring that communication take place over intercoms that can contact only designated group members.

The pattern of findings of these studies is summarized in Table 12.2. We can see that in nearly all the studies, decentralized groups needed to send more messages in order to solve problems, regardless of whether the problems were complex or simple, but that satisfaction in decentralized

TABLE 12.2
Comparison of Centralized (Wheel, Chain, Y) and Decentralized (Circle, Comcon) Groups on Speed, Accuracy, Messages Sent, and Satisfaction

Factor	Simple Problems	Complex Problems
Time		
Centralized faster	14	0
Decentralized faster	4	18
Messages		
Centralized sent more	0	1
Decentralized sent more	18	17
Errors		
Centralized made more	0	6
Decentralized made more	9	1
No difference	1	3
Satisfaction		
Centralized higher	1	1
Decentralized higher	7	10

Source: M. E. Shaw (1964). Communication networks. In L. Berkowitz (Ed.), *Advances in experimental social psychology* (Vol. 1). New York: Academic Press.

groups was nearly always higher. Thus decentralization of communication has certain inefficiencies, but it makes people happier about their part in the group and may lead to better long-term productivity.

More interesting, however, is the effect of the network on speed and accuracy. We see that the type of network interacts with the type of problem. Simple problems were solved more quickly by centralized groups, and centralized groups made fewer errors. Complex problems were solved more quickly and more accurately by decentralized groups. Thus communication patterns affect the way people perform in groups and also play a part in determining their satisfaction with their work.

Power Distribution

Power is an important part of the patterning of behavior and relationships within groups. It refers to the ability of a group member to influence the direction of the group and the behavior of its members. Studies of groups in natural settings, including children in nursery school (e.g., Merei, 1949), groups of adolescents (e.g., Whyte, 1943), work groups (e.g., Whyte, 1948), mental health teams (e.g., Zander, Cohen, & Stotland, 1959), and the family (e.g., Strodtbeck, 1951), all show that some members have more influence over the group's behavior than others. Those with more power may be said to have higher status within a group. The forms of power—including referent power, coercive power, legitimate power, reward power, and expert power—vary and have been discussed in Chapter 10, "Social Influence." Power differentiation—that is, the fact that some members have more and some have less—seems to be a fact of life in groups.

Patterns of Relationships

The final aspect of group structure we will discuss is that of interpersonal choice. This refers to the pattern of relationships or the preferences for association among individuals in the group. Put simply, group members are closer to some people than to others. Coalitions often form in groups, and subgroups can consistently operate as a unit in some matters (Komorita & Moore, 1976). Isolates (those who choose and are chosen by no one) may be pushed out to the psychological fringes of the group, while other members may cluster at the group's psychological center. The pattern of relationships within the group has consequences for the group's cohesiveness, stability, communication networks, power distributions, and capacity for accomplishing its goals.

A sociometric diagram, or **sociogram**, is a device by which the social psychologist represents the pattern of relationships within a group (Moreno 1953). It is constructed by observing groups, or by asking individuals to rank which other members they would choose to be friendly with, to

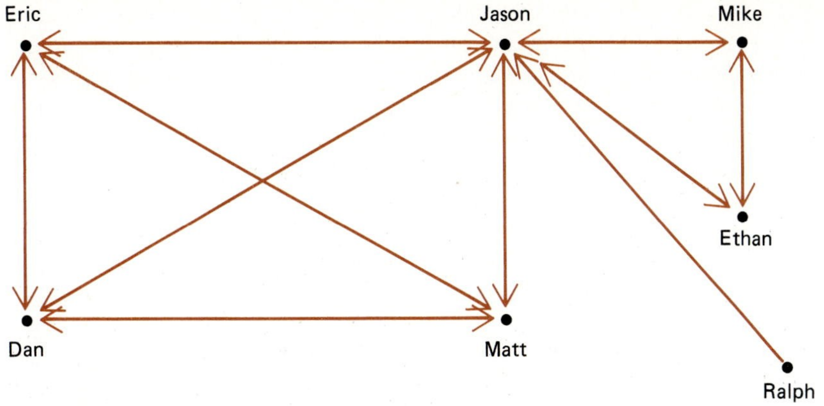

FIGURE 12.4
A Sociogram of a Seven-Person Group This sociogram illustrates friendship choices among seven people. Jason is a "star," being chosen by every other person in the group. Ralph is an "isolate," being chosen by no one. Mike and Ethan like each other, but don't have much interest in most of the other members of the group.

work with, or to reject as a friend or co-worker. Figure 12.4 contains a sociogram of a seven-person group, with some choices reciprocated and others not. We can see from this that one person, Jason, is the "sociometric star," choosing and being chosen by all others; while Ralph is an "isolate," being chosen by no one else. The reciprocated choices of Eric, Matt, Dan, and Jason identify them as a "clique." Similarly, Mike, Ethan, and Jason form a cohesive unit, with Jason serving as the link between the two subgroups.

APPLICATION
GROUP DYNAMICS IN T-GROUPS AND GROUP THERAPY

The knowledge about groups we have discussed thus far, particularly the effects of groups on their members, is often referred to as group dynamics. Almost from its inception, this knowledge was applied to groups formed to solve troubling individual and social problems. Kurt Lewin and the social psychologists with whom he worked were invited in 1946 by the Connecticut Interracial Commission to train community leaders to help reduce tension between racial groups. Lewin and his associates tackled the problem by applying what they knew of group processes. In so doing they established what has come to be known as sensitivity-training groups, training groups, or simply T-groups. A **T-group** is a small group that meets under the direction of a "facilitator" who takes the group through various exercises and experiences, using group dynamics principles to bring about various effects depending upon the goals of the participants.

The goals may include increasing the members' sensitivity to others; generating greater awareness of their impact on others; creating changes of attitudes, norms, or behavior; developing leadership skills; or learning about group dynamics itself. For example, people who are community leaders in places where tension between ethnic groups is high might want to gain a better understanding of the way norms emerge, and how they might be changed.

T-group members usually spend about 15 to 50 hours as a group, spread over several days or weeks. They emerge with an awareness of themselves and of others that is based not only on abstract knowledge, but also on the group-induced events they experienced. The use of T-groups to improve the functioning of organizations and to increase the sensitivity and effectiveness of individuals has met with widespread acceptance. The National Training Laboratory was formed in 1950 with headquarters in Bethel, Maine, where it holds summer institutes. Training sessions based on its principles are now held throughout the country and the world.

At about the same time that T-groups applied the principles of group dynamics for the solution of problems in communities and organizations, clinical psychologists began developing group therapy for the solution of problems on an individual level. Many people considered group therapy a poor substitute for individual therapy, and pointed out that its only advantage was economic. By combining ideas from group dynamics with those of personality dynamics and psychotherapy, however, group therapy has proved to be valuable in its own right (Korchin, 1976).

Group therapy and T-groups have important similarities and differences. Group therapy arose in the context of the traditional helping professions; it involved the treatment by psychotherapists of patients suffering from psychological disorder. The T-group arose in an educational and research context. It sought to make normal, healthy people more aware of themselves and more effective in relating to other people. T-groups are led by "facilitators" (rather than therapists), who are educators and social psychologists (rather than clinicians). Gradually, however, the T-group and group therapy have become less distinct from each other. Therapists think of their patients less as sick individuals, and facilitators are more likely to think of the T-group's effects as "therapeutic."

The most important similarities between group therapy and T-groups have to do with their shared use of the principles social psychology has discovered about what happens to people in groups (Korchin, 1976; Whitaker & Lieberman, 1964; Yalom, 1975). The pressure for positive change that can be mobilized by a cohesive group is potent; and it can often surpass that of a one-to-one patient-therapist relationship. This is because therapists can use the group to magnify their influence, while at the same time seeming less intrusive in a patient's life. Using knowledge about group dynamics, a skilled leader can promote group cohesiveness, guide the creation of group norms, establish boundaries within and between groups, stimulate and then resolve conflict. High group cohesion can facilitate therapy by increasing the sense of security, and promoting greater openness to influence and closer adherence to norms (Frank, 1957;

Psychotherapy conducted in groups is not only less expensive than individual sessions, but also uses the principles of group dynamics to accomplish its goals. Other people supply us with a basis for comparison, provide feedback, and offer social support for our views and actions.

Yalom & Rand, 1966; Goldstein, Heller, & Sechrest, 1966; Bednar & Lawlis, 1971). Thus, both in T-groups and in group therapy, many of the basic principles of group dynamics have been put to work to try to alleviate psychological discomfort and improve well-being, awareness, and effectiveness.

THE FUNCTIONING OF GROUPS: PROBLEM SOLVING, PERFORMANCE, AND DECISION MAKING

Earlier in this chapter we suggested that people come together into groups in order to achieve their goals more effectively than they could acting as individuals. We now examine how groups function in performing their tasks and achieving their goals.

Individuals Versus Groups

One of the oldest issues for social psychologists as well as for thinkers in other times and places has been the relative merit of working on a problem singly or in a group. Are two heads better than one? With regard to quality of performance but not efficiency, it is usually found that groups perform better than individuals (e.g., Davis, 1969; Shaw, 1981). Several reasons account for this. The first is mere statistical pooling: increased size reduces random error. Another reason is the increase in total information available to a group as compared to an individual. In addition, the probability of a group's having one highly competent individual is increased. Another advantage groups have over individuals is that they have the benefit of error-spotting by others: other people are better at finding our mistakes than we are alone. As a result, in some circumstances groups make better decisions than even the best individual in the group (e.g., Barnlund, 1959).

On the other hand, on some tasks groups do not do as well as individuals. Group superiority fades if the task does not lend itself to a division of labor, if organizational problems overwhelm the group, or if the group establishes norms of low performance. One study, for example, found that discussion groups lost 80 percent of the ideas contributed by the members (Lorge et al., 1955). Thus groups sometimes do better and sometimes do worse than individuals. The next question, then, is which factors favor the superiority of groups and which favor individuals. The heart of the answer is the nature of the task to be performed.

The Structure of the Task

Distinctions among task types provide important clues to predicting when groups will do better than individuals and whether certain kinds of groups will do better than others. We have already encountered one distinction among tasks, that of performance tasks versus learning tasks. Zajonc's findings indicate that groups facilitate performance tasks but inhibit learning tasks.

One of the most useful ways of distinguishing the **structure of tasks** was conceived by Steiner (1972). He proposed that tasks may be classified according to three dimensions. The first has to do with a task's divisibility. A *unitary* task is one that cannot be successfully divided into subtasks; a *divisible* task can be. Driving a car is a relatively unitary task. To have one person steering, another pressing on the pedals, and a third watching out for traffic would not improve the drive. Building a car is a divisible task. Once this distinction is noted, it is obvious that groups hold a considerable advantage over individuals in performing divisible tasks but not in performing unitary tasks.

The second dimension concerns quantity versus quality. *Maximizing* tasks are those requiring the most or fastest output for successful accomplishment, such as the output of widgets by a factory. *Optimizing* tasks call for quality rather than quantity in production. Examples of optimizing tasks include finding the correct solution to a problem such as navigating a space shuttle, or deciding whether to start a new product line.

The third factor looks at the kind of group process that is called for to accomplish the task. *Disjunctive* tasks are those where the strongest or best solution proposed by any one member is the solution adopted by the group. In these tasks, once the correct solution to a problem has been found, it is immediately recognized as correct by the group. Puzzles are a familiar example of this kind of task. Groups have an obvious advantage over individuals in performing disjunctive tasks, as do large groups over small groups, because the larger the group the greater the likelihood that it will have a member smart enough or skilled enough to come up with the solution (Lorge & Solomon, 1955; Davis, 1969).

In contrast to the kind of task in which the group is only as good as its best individual members, on some tasks the group is no better than its weakest link. This is the *conjunctive* task, and is illustrated by a mountain-climbing team that can reach the summit no faster than its slowest member. A third kind of task is the *additive* task, which requires that members combine their individual efforts to form the group product. A sales division's gross revenues reflect an additive task, because gross revenues represent the combined accomplishments of the entire sales staff. Finally, the *discretionary* task leaves the group free to adopt any of the other processes or a combination of them in performing the task.

Let us see how the performance of different kinds of groups is affected by the type of task they face. In dealing with the effects of group size, Steiner suggests that an increase in the number of members increases the human resources available to the group, thereby increasing its potential productivity. But the larger the group becomes, the more the difficulties of working together undercut the potential gains. These "process losses" detract from the group's potential productivity. If the potential productivity grows at a faster rate than the process losses, adding people to the group will improve its performance up to a point, beyond which process losses will overtake potential productivity gains. If the process losses grow at a faster rate than the potential productivity, then adding people will hurt the group's performance. Because they capitalize on increased resources, disjunctive tasks and additive tasks should be done better by larger groups than by smaller groups. Because conjunctive tasks entail process losses and little likelihood of gain from increased resources, larger groups should not be expected to perform these as well as smaller groups.

Badore (1979) put Steiner's theory to a test by having military personnel solve a variety of problems—and the theory was borne out. As we can see in Figure 12.5, disjunctive and additive tasks generally showed improvement with increased size (up to a point, and that point was reached at nine people for the additive task), and conjunctive tasks were performed worse by larger than by smaller groups.

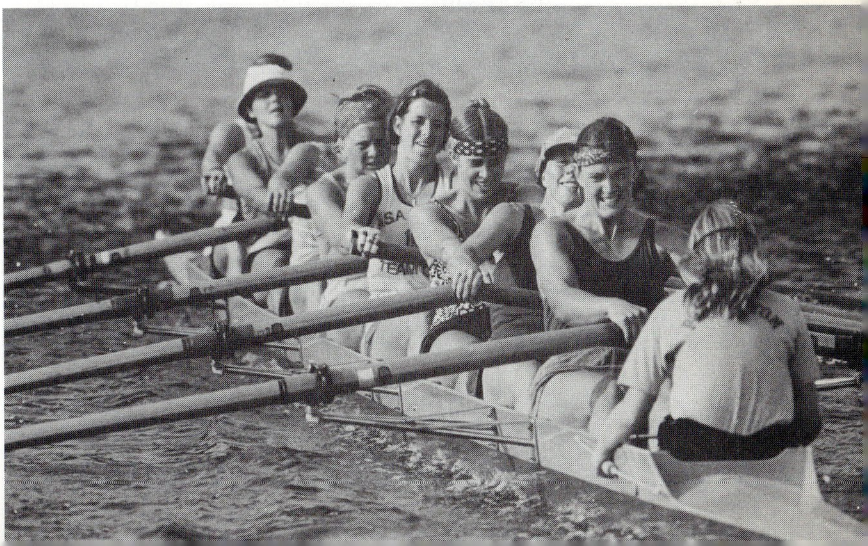

This crew team is engaged in what has been called an "additive" task. The output of the whole group depends on the coordinated efforts of each member, which sum up to a single product.

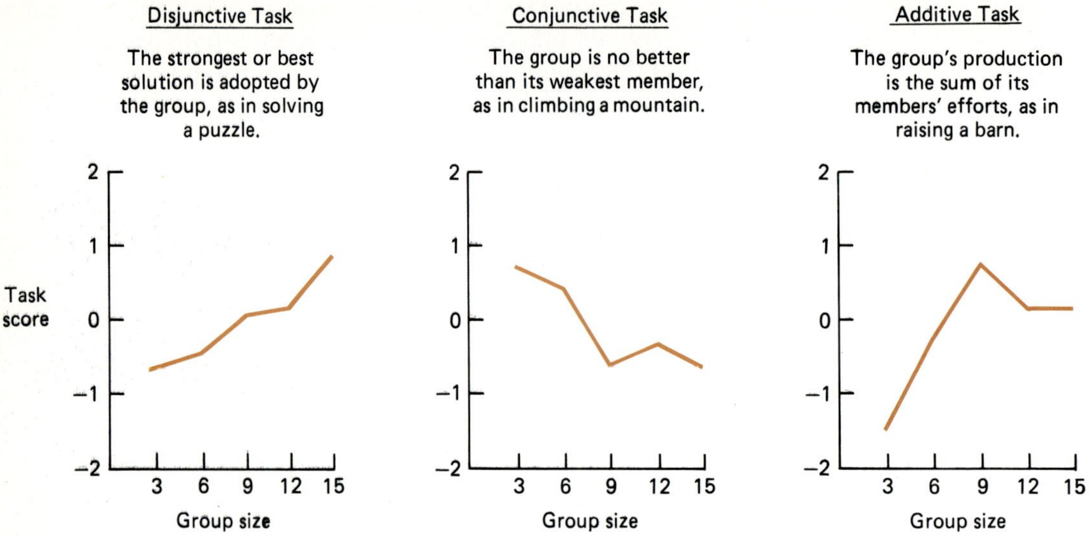
Disjunctive Task
The strongest or best solution is adopted by the group, as in solving a puzzle.
Conjunctive Task
The group is no better than its weakest member, as in climbing a mountain.
Additive Task
The group's production is the sum of its members' efforts, as in raising a barn.
Task score
2
1
0
−1
−2
3 6 9 12 15
Group size

FIGURE 12.5
Problem Solving as a Function of Task Type and Group Size Whether increasing size enables a group to perform better or interferes with the group's ability to solve problems depends upon the type of problem (and therefore the type of task the group must engage in). For disjunctive and additive tasks, more people do the job better. For conjunctive tasks, the more people there are, the poorer the group's performance. *Source:* N. L. Badore (1979). Group size and task effects on group problem-solving. Doctoral thesis. Chestnut Hill, MA: Boston College, p. 50.

Social Decision Rules

In order to come to decisions, groups use various kinds of **social decision rules.** By social decision rules we mean the scheme by which individual judgments are combined to form group decisions. Should a simple majority prevail? Or should a decision require a two-thirds or three-quarters majority? Or a unanimous decision? Each of these is a familiar social decision rule in one or another of the many decision-making groups in our society (Smoke & Zajonc, 1962).

In addition to the explicit or formal decision rule, Davis and his colleagues have noted that groups also appear to adopt implicit decision rules which govern their actual decisions (Davis, 1973, 1980; Stasser, Kerr, & Davis, 1980). For example, a jury of 12 people may be instructed to reach a unanimous verdict (the explicit decision rule), but in reality may be operating according to a tacit group norm that dictates a different (implicit) decision rule such as "If a strong majority favors a verdict, go along with it." Indeed, juries that start out being split 11 to 1 or 10 to 2 almost never result in hung juries (Kalven & Zeisel, 1966).

If we combine Davis's notion of implicit decision rules with Latané's social impact theory, we find a good account of how juries combine the individual preferences of their members into a group verdict (Saks, 1977).

As the size of one faction increases relative to the other, the probability that the majority will prevail of course increases. But each new person that faction wins to its side adds less to that likelihood than did the preceding person who was won over. In a 6-to-6 split the first person to change sides, making the distribution 7 to 5, shifts the probability more profoundly than any of those who will fall into line later.

Group Polarization

We have seen that a continuing theme in the social psychology of groups has been that behavior differs when people are in groups as compared to when they act as individuals. This holds also for the content of the decisions they make. Early findings comparing decisions made by individuals with those made by groups show that group decisions were riskier than those made by the separate individuals who constituted the group (Stoner, 1961; Kogan & Wallach, 1964). The phenomenon was dubbed the **risky shift.**

The problems presented involved dilemmas of choice: Should a person take a particular new job? Should the football team go for one or two points after the touchdown? In each case, the choice involved risk. In leaving a safe old job for an uncertain new one, a person faces the possibility of great success, but also faces the risk of failing completely. The football team behind by one point can easily achieve a tie with a one-point kick, or can try for the win with a two-point play. But if the two-point play fails, the team will remain one point behind and lose the game. Participants in these experiments were asked the minimum probability of success (one chance in ten that the new job would work out, two chances in ten, etc.) they felt necessary in order to choose the riskier option. The group consenus typically indicated a willingness to take a chance with a lower probability of success than the average probability acceptable to the individuals.

FROM THE FIELD
James Davis

Jim Davis is one of the leading authorities on decision making in small groups. In his earlier work he studied the differences between decision making by individuals and decision making by groups. More recently he has studied how groups move from individual differences and disagreements toward a group consensus. This research inevitably included the study of competition and cooperation, social influence, and social perception and judgment. Findings from Professor Davis's research have been usefully applied in shaping policies governing jury trials. Professor Davis is on the faculty of the University of Illinois.

Why did groups show a shift toward risk? An array of explanations was proposed and tested: (1) diffusion of responsibility in a group—the risk of failure fell on no one individual; (2) rhetoric of risk—arguments for risky choices were inherently more persuasive; (3) social decision schemes—the process of combining individual choices into group consensus magnified majority opinions (Cartwright, 1971; Clark, 1971; Pruitt, 1971a, 1971b; Vinokur, 1971).

As these explanations were tested, problems with the "riskiness" of the risky shift emerged. First, when individuals initially leaned in a conservative direction, the group decision shifted to a still more conservative position. A shift occurred, but it reflected an exaggeration of individual judgments in whichever direction the cultural norm pointed. Thus it was more appropriate to speak of a risk shift than a risky shift: decision making in groups produces changes in people's willingness to take risks, but the shift can go in either direction, more risky or more conservative (Myers & Bishop, 1970; Fraser, 1971).

Second, these shifts result only when certain conditions are met: group discussion must occur, a discrepancy must exist among individual opinions, and the decision must involve some issue on which group or cultural norms exist—that is, a normatively "correct" or "preferred" direction must exist (Moscovici & Doise, 1974). Third, issues that really involve no risk, but simply differences of judgment, also show group-induced shifts. Thus the effect is far more general than originally thought. Groups tend to magnify any judgmental trends that come into the group as the preferences of individuals. This tendency is now known by the more general title of the **group polarization phenomenon** (Myers & Lamm, 1976).

A group polarization study expanded to the area of decision making in juries showed that when the evidence leaned toward guilt, mock jury deliberations pushed the group judgment closer to guilty than did the average of individual judgments. When the evidence leaned toward innocence, group discussion magnified the predeliberation individual judgments to even less certainty of guilt. Moreover, the polarizing effect occurred only for those matters discussed in the deliberation; judgments on undiscussed matters did not change (Myers & Kaplan, 1976).

Two major explanations currently exist for the group polarization effect. The first is based on the concept of **social comparison,** according to which members compare themselves to others and try to come closer to the apparent norm than they each had been initially. That is, once individuals see which way the group is leaning, they try to outdo each other in going that way. The second explanation emphasizes informational influence processes which hold that the most favorable arguments in a group discussion accumulate on the side of the norm toward which individuals were originally leaning, thereby drawing them even farther in that direction (Myers & Lamm, 1976).

The implications of the group polarization phenomenon are significant for any decision making done by groups—as most decision making is.

This effect probably occurs for groups as diverse as boards of directors, cabinets of heads of state, juries, faculty meetings, the Joint Chiefs of Staff, and hospital ethics committees. The polarization effect will bring these groups to a more extreme position than the individuals comprising them, on average, were initially willing to go.

Groupthink

The group polarization phenomenon shows again that groups do something to individuals, in this case altering their judgments in the areas of certainty and risk. The phenomenon of **groupthink** illustrates how serious and even dangerous these effects can become. The groupthink concept, as proposed by Janis (1982), refers to a phenomenon in which members become so concerned with the group and its own processes that they stop focusing on the external demands they were meant to cope with. In such cases, there is greater concern with obtaining the approval of the group than with generating effective solutions. In addition, strong pressure develops for conformity to the group's norms, feelings of antagonism are generated toward out-groups, and a strong sense of cohesiveness emerges among group members. As a result, the group's critical judgment and reality testing deteriorate, and group pressure drives out even individual moral judgments.

Janis examined memoirs of participants in major fiascoes of American defense and foreign policy—the Bay of Pigs invasion, the attack on Pearl Harbor, the invasion of North Korea, and the Vietnam War. In each case he found the following group processes, which characterize groupthink:

1. Discussions were limited to few alternatives.
2. Initial decisions were rarely reexamined for overlooked flaws.
3. Options that had been dismissed early were rarely reconsidered for possible overlooked advantages.
4. The group exhibited a bias in responding to information and evaluations from outsiders, so that supportive views were sought and critical views were dismissed.
5. The group showed little recognition that people outside the group would disagree with the decision and try to block it, and consequently developed few strategies for dealing with opposition.
6. The group persisted in support of the favored policy even in the face of mounting evidence that it was a bad idea.

All people and groups have biases in favor of their own solutions, but Janis points out that when groupthink is operating, an unusual softheadedness takes over and critical appraisal declines.

Janis's data consisted of subjective reports of experiences by participants. Tetlock (1979) put the groupthink hypothesis to a test using more objective overt evidence: public statements made in speeches, the *Congressional Record,* and official documents and papers. Tetlock compared crises that were solved effectively to those that became fiascoes—those that presumably were reached under conditions of groupthink. Supporting the predictions were the findings that decision makers under groupthink made significantly fewer complex statements about the problem and evaluated the groups with whom they were aligned (e.g., the South Vietnamese government) significantly more positively than did those decision makers not operating under groupthink.

Janis suggests several steps to avoid groupthink:

1. Assign group members to be critical evaluators—devil's advocates—of the tentative decisions.
2. Invite people who are not members of the core group to react to the group's views and solutions.
3. Divide the group into independent subgroups to consider and propose separate solutions.
4. After a decision has been made, hold a meeting to give members a "second chance" to air doubts and reconsider the choice.

Features can be built into groups to promote contentiousness, which may produce less camaraderie but better decisions. Juries, for example, are supposed to "deliberate," to argue with each other over the correct decision. Saks (1977) found a tendency for members of larger juries (twelve people) to find each other "less reasonable" than did members of smaller juries (six people). But the larger juries were also more likely to recall more of the evidence (the "reality" which they had to analyze) and were more likely to reach the correct decision. Thus the stimulating of argument reduced error. Moreover, juries are structured so that groupthink is nearly impossible. They are shielded from any sense of antagonism from outside groups, their options are made explicit in advance, and they are under no pressure to decide hurriedly. If they are a contentious lot, they will stay at the task of deciding for a relatively long time. And if they are cohesive and enjoy interacting with each other, the only way the interaction can continue is to keep deliberating; as soon as they reach a decision, they will be disbanded.

Improving Group Performance

How can groups be constructed to produce the best solutions, to make the best decisions, and to produce the highest-quality products?

First, group performance can be improved by improving the task skill of individuals in the group, particularly when the tasks are difficult. In other words, train the individual members to perform the relevant tasks better. As we noted earlier, the characteristics of individual group members are more important when the task facing the group requires special skills. Thus, when the task is complex, modification of a group's composition to provide specially able members will improve the group's performance (e.g., Maier, 1972; Maier & Hoffman, 1960; Pryer & Bass, 1959).

A second way of improving group performance is to allow the members of the group to function as individuals when it is more appropriate or efficient. For example, when a task calls for individual thinking, a group can set aside time for that, rather than trying to reach a solution or make a decision by interacting constantly. This simple device increases the quality of the eventual group product (Gustafson et al., 1973). A third measure to improve group performance is to increase the size of the group or the heterogeneity of the group for dealing with additive or disjunctive tasks, but not beyond the point where process losses will undermine the increased potential.

Other kinds of adjustments involve modifying the group's structure or the process by which it functions. An example of a structural change would be to divide the group into subgroups to deal separately with individual parts of a problem and later combine their work into a whole. The technique of **brainstorming** provides an example of a change in process. When brainstorming, members of the group are asked to delay critical analysis of each others' suggestions until all ideas are "on the table"; only then will assessment leading to the final decision take place (Bouchard, Barsaloux, & Drauden, 1974; Lamm & Trommsdorff, 1973).

Another procedure, called the Delphi technique (Dalkey, 1969), has been used to generate good advice or projections from groups of experts. Using the Delphi technique, people offer their opinions and reasons in writing, and the responses and reasoning are circulated among all members to digest. Then a new round of opinions is solicited. Eventually the group will tend to converge on a shared opinion, having shifted toward the emerging group norm, and the consensus is assumed to be the best collective decision. Note that the influence is not so much social pressure as informational pressure—in a sense the reverse of groupthink.

LEADERSHIP

No discussion of the behavior of groups would be complete without a consideration of leadership. What is meant by leadership? What is a leader? *Leader* may be defined as one of the roles in a group. The role may be structured into a group as a formal position, such as president or chairperson. In these instances, the position of leader automatically brings with it greater power, even before any particular person is assigned to it. Not all groups need leaders or have a formal position for a leader, but the role often emerges, especially in groups tending toward hierarchical structure. The term *leader* may also refer to the person who fills the role. The leader of a group is the person who successfully influences the behavior of others in the group, initiates structure in the group, and, more than other members, helps the group progress toward its goals (Stogdill, 1950; Fiedler, 1967; Hollander & Julian, 1969). Understanding leadership, however, involves considerably more than explaining the role or position of leader.

Leadership involves fitting the right person to the needs of a given situation. Martin Luther King, Jr., who is pictured here, was a relatively young but charismatic leader who stepped forward to assume a key role as a spokesman for the civil rights movement of the early 1960s.

Theories of Leadership

Research in leadership and the development of a theory to explain the phenomenon have followed a course that we have seen repeated in the study of many other areas of human behavior. That course begins by looking for explanations in the individuals themselves, to see if leadership is determined by certain traits or other qualities of the individual. Failure to find any consistent evidence that leaders had specific characteristics or traits has led to an examination of situations and environments, and finally of the interaction between the individual and the situation. We will review each of these approaches in turn.

Leadership Traits Approach This approach is sometimes called the "great man" or "great woman" approach. It assumes that one or a few people, because of unique qualities, take charge of a corporation, a scientific field, or a nation, and by the force of their personalities or abilities carry it to glory. This approach assumes that without Thomas Jefferson, Benjamin Franklin, and their colleagues, the United States would not have come into existence, and that without Albert Einstein there would be no atomic age. Investigation into this approach has been conducted by historians, management researchers, and social scientists. It usually takes the form of observing leaders of existing groups in order to identify the characteristics that set them apart from other members of the group. Another method used involves measuring the traits of all members of the group and then trying to predict which kinds of people would be selected or would emerge as leaders.

The kinds of characteristics that were first suggested as traits of leadership are abundant: physical attributes such as size, strength, or appearance; personality traits such as good adjustment, extraversion, compulsiveness, empathy, charisma, high energy, and so on; and cognitive abilities such as intelligence or ability to analyze, synthesize, or organize ideas and viewpoints. By 1950 it had become apparent that this approach was leading nowhere (Stogdill, 1950; Gouldner, 1950; Yukl, 1981; Shaw, 1981). As more and more studies were done, the list of traits grew longer. In more than a few studies, almost no traits emerged as distinguishing leaders from nonleaders, and often the traits proved contradictory: in some studies the trait was associated with leaders, in other studies with followers (Cartwright & Zander, 1968). For example, dominance, aggressiveness, and freedom from paranoid tendencies are more characteristic of leaders in some groups but of followers in other groups. The few traits that appeared with even fair regularity were that, compared to nonleaders, leaders are more intelligent (but not too much more), bigger (but not too much bigger), more reliable, more active, participate more, and come from higher socioeconomic groups (Mann, 1959).

The failure of the trait approach to provide an adequate account of leadership may be due to technical shortcomings, such as problems in measurement and research design, or to its inherent inadequacy as a concept. The current majority opinion is that this approach is unsound and only leads up a blind alley.

Situational Approach The situational approach holds that whether a given person becomes a leader of a group has nothing to do with his or her personal characteristics and everything to do with the flow of events, the circumstances, and the structure of the physical and social world of the group. These elements, which are really external to the individual, sweep particular individuals into the leadership role. The leader is simply a person who is in the right place at the right time.

The notion conveyed by the situational approach is captured in the German word *Zeitgeist,* which means "the spirit of the times" and has been used to account for major historical events. It proposes that people play roles written by history and directed by circumstance. Rather than a great man or great woman causing great events to happen, the situational approach claims that great events are the product of historical forces that are going to happen whether specific leaders are present or not. For example, major discoveries in science are often made simultaneously and independently by several researchers or teams pushed along on the same tide (Simonton, 1979). Similarly, when a small group needs to accomplish something, it will find a leader to facilitate it. But why does one member emerge as leader rather than another? Why does one member provide better leadership in certain situations than a different member? Answers to these questions are provided by the situational approach's important relative, the interaction approach.

Interaction Approach The interaction approach proposes that both the characteristics of the individual and the situation in which the group finds itself account for who will become the leader. According to this approach, the success of a group under a particular person's leadership is a joint function of that person's characteristics and of numerous situational factors such as the group's structure and the task at hand. Supreme Court

Justice Sandra Day O'Connor expressed the essence of the interaction approach in a commencement address at Stanford University in which she quoted the ancient commentary known as the Talmud: "In every age there comes a time when leadership suddenly comes forth to meet the needs of the hour. And so there is no man who does not find his time, and there is no hour that does not have its leader."

Suedfeld and Rank's research (1976) illustrates the interaction approach as applied to important historical events. They examined the role of cognitive complexity in leaders of revolutions. Cognitive complexity is the tendency to categorize objects and events into many rather than few groupings, and to make judgments in shades of gray. Early in a revolution, the issues are relatively simple: the goal is for "us" to defeat "them." Successful revolutionary leaders display relatively simple cognitive styles. After the revolution is won, a leader must deal with the running of a government, which poses a more complex set of problems. Successful postrevolutionary leaders are those whose cognitive complexity is equal to the complexity of the tasks. Thus people who make effective revolutionary leaders often make poor heads of state following the revolution.

The dominant interaction theory is Fiedler's **contingency model of leadership** (1964, 1967). This theory identifies a major personality variable relevant to leadership behavior and several situational factors, and then studies the interaction between personality and situation. The personality variable pertains to *leadership style.* Leadership style is a reflection of the leader's values with regard to task accomplishment and interpersonal relations. At one extreme is the leader who values successful interpersonal relations to the exclusion of task accomplishment. The leader at the other extreme places the highest value on task accomplishment, even at the expense of interpersonal relations (Rice, 1978).

Fiedler developed a way of measuring this personality dimension called LPC (Least Preferred Co-worker). Operationally, the LPC is a paper-and-pencil test that measures a leader's perceptions and reactions to the least preferred co-worker with whom he or she has ever worked. The same instrument is used to measure the most preferred co-worker (MPC). The difference between the two profiles yields an ASo score (Assumed Similarity of opposites). Leaders who score very low on LPC, and also distinguish sharply between the most and least preferred co-workers (low ASo), are the leaders who value the task; leaders with high LPC and high ASo value interpersonal relationships.

Fiedler's model also identifies three situational factors. First is leader-member relations. Leaders may be liked, trusted, and supported, or, at the other extreme, disliked, mistrusted, and attacked. This is the most crucial of the situational factors with which leaders must deal. The second is task structure. A task is clearly structured when it has readily identifiable goals and only one possible solution, immediately recognizable as correct by the group members. The task structure is said to be unclear

Favorable	I	II	III	IV	V	VI	VII	VIII Unfavorable
Leader-member relations	Good	Good	Good	Good	Poor	Poor	Poor	Poor
Task structure	Structured		Unstructured		Structured		Unstructured	
Leader position power	Strong	Weak	Strong	Weak	Strong	Weak	Strong	Weak

FIGURE 12.6
The Contingency Model of Leadership and Group Performance These are the eight possible group situations a leader may face, according to Fiedler's contingency model of leadership. Different styles of leadership do best in different group situations. *Source:* F. E. Fiedler (1978). Recent developments in research on the contingency model. In L. Berkowitz (Ed.), *Group processes.* New York: Academic Press. Copyright 1978 by Academic Press, Inc.

when the goals are not readily identifiable, many possible solutions exist, and it is difficult to know a correct decision when one is found. The third factor is position power. How much power does the leader have? The position in which a leader finds him- or herself may afford great potential coercive power over members (e.g., a boss who can hire, fire, set vacation schedules, make work assignments) or virtually none (e.g., a boss who is basically a figurehead). These factors are combined into eight possible combinations of situations, as depicted in Figure 12.6. They are arranged from the most favorable situation (good leader-member relations, structured task, much power) to the least favorable situation (poor relations, unstructured task, little power).

The interaction theory of leadership is valuable in matching leader styles to group situations. It shows, for example, that task-motivated leaders (low LPC) do consistently better in some situations (the more "favorable" ones) and relationship-motivated leaders (high LPC) do better in others (the less "favorable" ones). Clearly, interaction models of leadership behavior are necessarily more complicated than trait models, but this cost pays dividends in improved accuracy and understanding of how leaders function. We can see from Fiedler's contingency model that there are no necessarily "good" or "bad" leadership styles or traits, but that their effectiveness depends on how appropriate they are to the group situation.

Training Leaders

The study of leadership, often sponsored by business, government, and military organizations, is one of the oldest areas of social psychological research and has offered some of the most practical payoffs. Many of these organizations wanted to determine how to select or train people to be leaders. One story has it that when Henry Ford wanted to hire new executives he would place a paper clip on the floor of his office and watch to see if the person coming in for an interview noticed the misplaced clip and returned it to its proper place. Ford's theory was that good executives showed attention to detail. While these "tests" were going on in Dearborn, Andrew Carnegie in Pittsburgh was conducting the same test, but he looked for applicants who *ignored* the paper clip. Good executives, he thought, knew how to separate the important from the trivial. Had the trait approach proved successful, effective leaders could be obtained by selecting people using the list of discovered leadership traits, with tests and paper clips at the ready. Or perhaps people could be taught how to behave "like a leader."

We have seen, however, that no one set of traits or behaviors is always the most effective in leading a group; which ones are best depends upon the group situation. We may conclude from this that leaders of different styles must either be matched to different situations or potential leaders taught how to modify the situation to bring it closer to one in which their particular style of leadership works best. That is what has been done in leader-match training. Leaders are classified for leadership style and then taught how to diagnose a situation according to the three factors discussed earlier: leader-member relations, task structure, and position power. If they are a good match to the situation, fine. If not, they are taught how to provide more or less task structure, how to alter leader-member relations, and so on. In this way, leader-match training seeks neither to form the leader according to a predetermined style of leadership nor to modify the situation without regard to the leader. Rather, its goal is to optimize the match of the leader to the group situation (Fiedler, Chemers, & Mahar, 1977).

This chapter began with a consideration of the assembly line. The **quality circle** (QC) is an application of group principles that was generated to solve production and quality problems that all companies face. Quality circles are small groups of workers who meet about once a week to identify problems that occur in their area of the company, to research and analyze those problems, and to devise solutions. If management approves the solution, the workers put the changes into practice. QCs are now found at Hughes Aircraft, Hewlett-Packard, Ford, Honeywell, and many other American companies.

QCs were begun in Japan in 1961, at the suggestion of Kaoru Ishikawa, a professor at Tokyo University. They are an integral part of most Japanese companies, and are considered an important reason for the continual improvement in the quality of that country's products. Ironically, this

"Japanese management import," Japan's "secret of success," was born in the United States. Ishikawa had drawn his ideas for QCs from the work of "many of the American organizational and behavioral scientists . . . whose writings were already well known in Japan" (Mohr & Mohr, 1983, p. 13; Byron, 1981).

The prototype of QCs was developed in the United States in the 1940s. Alfred Marrow, a student of Kurt Lewin and later his biographer, inherited the Harwood Manufacturing Corporation in rural Virginia. The performance and productivity of the plants were low. Being a newly trained social psychologist, Marrow wanted to see if any of the ideas or methods Lewin and his associates were developing could improve Harwood. He invited Lewin and several colleagues to use Harwood as an industrial social psychology laboratory. They conducted several successful experiments in the self-management of worker output, leadership training, changing stereotypes, and overcoming resistance to change. And at the heart of each of these innovations were discussion and decision in small groups.

The most famous example is a study by the social psychologist John French and Harwood's personnel manager, Lester Coch (French & Coch, 1948; French, 1950; see also Tornatzky & Solomon, 1982). They noticed that management usually introduced changes by calling a meeting and telling the workers about new assignments and methods. Workers, however, usually tried to resist rather than cooperate and change. Coch and French asked whether changes could be accomplished in a better way.

The two men tried three different ways of introducing change. One was the usual method, in which workers were simply told how things were going to be. This group of workers showed the familiar consequences of this approach: production immediately dropped 20 percent and never regained its earlier level, morale fell sharply, and hostility toward supervisors and complaints to the union increased. Nine percent of these employees quit the company. A second group of workers was asked to choose representatives to meet with management and work out the details of the changes together. This group reached its pre-change output in two weeks, showed no antagonism toward management, and no one quit. In the third method, all of the affected employees (not only representatives) participated in the planning of the change in all its aspects, and made suggestions in addition to those management had in mind. This group regained its output level in two days and kept improving, leveling off at a rate of productivity 14 percent above its pre-change output. No hostility arose, all worked well with their supervisors, and no one quit.

Today's QCs go beyond Coch and French's groups by having workers actually initiate change themselves. The advantages are numerous. The QC engages the people with the most intimate knowledge of a problem in the problem-solving process. Because the task of problem solving is disjunctive and optimizing, and because the workers stimulate each other's thinking, bring different insights to the group, and correct each other's errors, they produce better solutions than a manager or engineer working alone. For example, in 1980 Toyota received an average of 17.8 suggestions from each employee, the great majority from QCs, and 90 percent of them were adopted by the company (Cole, 1981). Each problem solved in Japan is believed to represent a savings of at least $5000—amounting to billions of dollars each year (Mohr & Mohr, 1983).

In addition to technical and financial benefits to the company, QCs confer important benefits on the employees who participate. Each group's members are continuously engaged in thinking about what they and the company are doing. Their daily work becomes more meaningful. Their awareness on the job translates into the discovery and eventual solution of new problems. The group develops norms of caring about and contributing to the improvement of the product. The group involvement produces cohesiveness. And in turn the workers feel more involved in the company. As at Harwood, employees become more satisfied, absenteeism and turnover decline, and productivity increases. In short, by applying basic group principles to industry, products have been made better, workers have become happier, and the economies of at least two countries have been improved.

SUMMARY

1. A great amount of human behavior is carried on in groups. Understanding social behavior requires an understanding of group processes.
2. Two or more people can be distinguished as being a mere aggregate or a psychological group. Psychological groups consist of members who interact with each other, influence each other, and develop stable relationships. The groups to which we belong are in-groups; opposing groups are out-groups. By small groups social psychologists usually mean face-to-face interacting groups of about two to sixteen people.
3. The effects of groups are illustrated by compresence (the effects of merely being together) in animals and insects, in which their physical appearance as well as their behavior varies according to whether they are alone or in groups.
4. Performance can vary, depending on the degree of preparation and on whether it takes place alone or in groups. The presence of others stimulates performance of well-learned tasks; performance of poorly learned tasks is likely to be worse in a group than alone.
5. One of the important properties of groups is cohesiveness, the result of all the forces acting on group members to keep the group intact.

As cohesiveness varies, the behavior of group members varies. Groups also evolve norms and apply pressure to group members to produce conformity to the norms.

6. The particular characteristics of group members are not so important to group functioning as the degree of heterogeneity or homogeneity of the characteristics in the group.
7. The size of the group has effects on the experience and behavior of group members. According to Latané's social impact theory, each additional member increases the influence of the group on its members, but as groups become larger each additional member adds less and less.
8. The structure of groups refers to their roles, communication patterns, power distribution, and patterns of relationships. Communication patterns or networks regulate who can communicate with whom. Centralized networks are more efficient and more accurately solve simple problems. Decentralized networks are faster and more accurate in solving complex problems. Satisfaction is higher in decentralized networks.
9. Groups perform better than individuals on tasks in which the work can be divided up, but only up to the point where the process losses associated with increasing size become so great that they cancel out the benefits of greater human resources. The nature of the task is an important determinant of whether groups will be better or worse.
10. Tasks can be distinguished according to whether they can be broken into parts (unitary or divisible); whether they involve quality or quantity of effort (maximizing or optimizing); and how the contributions of individuals are combined to form the group product (disjunctive, conjunctive, additive, or discretionary).
11. In decision-making groups, rules for combining individual preferences develop and are "understood," or they are imposed on the group explicitly—such as a unanimous verdict or a majority vote.
12. Participation in group decision making produces shifts in the risk judgments that people make. In general, the group process polarizes judgments.
13. Groupthink is a set of conditions and processes that reduces the critical judgment and reality testing of groups so that they sometimes make poor decisions. A number of ways to avoid groupthink have been developed.
14. Group performance can be enhanced by improving individual task skill, altering the group composition, structure, or process, or employing such devices as the Delphi technique.
15. Leadership has been approached from several perspectives: the trait approach, the situational approach, and the interaction approach. Fiedler's contingency model of leadership suggests leader-match training as the best way to improve leadership.

CHAPTER 13
Large Groups

The world's most continuous trouble spot is the Middle East. If World War III begins, the Middle East is a likely candidate for its starting point. Recent years have seen mutual slaughter by Iraq and Iran, the equivalent of civil war in Jordan and Lebanon, and, of course, the seemingly interminable conflict between Israel and her Arab neighbors.

In 1948, when the United Nations created the state of Israel, the Arab League, composed of 21 sovereign nations with a territory 600 times that of Israel and with 40 times the population, immediately declared war. During the fighting many Palestinian Arabs fled for their lives and have spent a generation trying to return home. During that generation Israel has been subjected to continued armed incursions, terrorist attacks, and political, economic, and diplomatic boycott. That period has seen five major wars between the Arabs and the Israelis, and a consistent refusal by virtually all of the Arab nations to abandon their hope of destroying Israel: "No reconciliation, no negotiation, no peace" (Tuchman, 1956, 1982; Moore, 1974).

As a result, Israel has built up its military power and expanded its borders in preparation for the next attack. That expansion, in turn, has made Arabs angrier. By creating refugees such as the Palestinian Arabs, the conflict has severely threatened Jordan's stability and destroyed Lebanon's. The United States and the Soviet Union jockey for influence, and carry out their own cold war through their Middle Eastern surrogates. The industrialized world wonders nervously about the fate of vast quantities of precious oil under the sand and sea of the volatile Middle East. And the tension is topped off by the gradual spread of nuclear weapons to small, angry nations.

At the heart of the Arab-Israeli conflict is what seems to be an insoluble dilemma. The Arab nations want Israel to be erased from the map, "driven into the sea." Israel wants the Arabs to accept her existence and leave her alone, and wants the displaced Palestinians to settle in other Arab countries and forget about turning Israel into their homeland. By now the hostilities are deeply entrenched. The disputing groups communicate little with each other, usually only to exchange threats and accusations. The people on either side maintain prejudices against each other, and spend little time developing workable solutions to the objective conflict that divides them. Time is spent, instead, justifying their own respective positions, threatening and sometimes killing each other.

Can we better understand the psychology of this social conflict? What perpetuates it, and how does it draw in new generations and peoples? Can our understanding help explain the thoughts and actions of the people and nations now trapped in costly and dangerous conflict? And, most important of all, can our knowledge show a way toward resolving or reducing the conflict, or at least keeping it within tolerable proportions?

The preceding chapter discussed the small "psychological" groups of which we are all a part. We also belong to and are profoundly affected by much larger groups, even though we never meet most of the other members of these large aggregates. In this chapter we will examine behavior in three major kinds of large group situations: collective behavior, behavior in organizations, and behavior of groups in conflict. *Collective behavior* takes place when a person is a member of a loosely structured and usually temporary group, such as a mob or a crowd. If the collection of people remains together over a longer period, we can refer to it as a social movement or a revolution. *Behavior in organizations* is the product of highly structured, enduring arrangements of people brought together to achieve planned goals. The most familiar examples of such organizations are corporations, governments, and other institutions. The social psychological study of the *behavior of groups in conflict* has tended to focus on ethnic conflict and international conflict, but includes various other group conflicts such as labor versus management, rival gangs, and political groups.

The groups we saw in the previous chapter were small enough to enable the members to have face-to-face contact, to engage in direct communication, to respond to each other as individuals, and to maintain group structure and process on an informal basis. The groups we examine in this chapter are dramatically different. Their goals must still be pursued and the members' needs for satisfying participation must be met if the group is to function. But the sheer size of the groups in this chapter makes it necessary that they operate by different processes.

The central problems of very large groups lie in creating and maintaining any social connections at all among members. People in a large group can be so numerous and far-flung that they personally know only a fraction of the other members of the group. Where is the interpersonal glue that binds large groups together? Just how connected are we to others? Consider all of the people in your hometown or city—better yet, all of the people in your nation. Are we generally isolated into relatively small subgroups, in touch with our own corner of the world but disconnected from all the others? Or does a chain of personal contacts join each of us to virtually every other person in the country? When we discover that a person we meet on a plane knows our Aunt Myrtle in Milwaukee, and we exclaim what a small world it is, is that a rare surprise or is it to be expected?

Stanley Milgram (1967) set about to answer this question empirically. He chose people at random from Wichita, Kansas, and asked them to try to reach the wife of a divinity school student at Harvard. The people in Wichita were given a packet containing the name and some background information about the target person. They were to try to reach her only by contacting people they knew on a first-name basis who would be able to advance them toward the target person. Each person they contacted was given a roster on which to list the names of each person who formed the growing chain, until the roster was finally placed in the hands of the target person. Also in the packet were postcards which served as tracers: each person receiving the packet would fill out a card and mail it to the researchers so that the developing chain could be followed. The study was replicated with people from Omaha, Nebraska, targeting a stockbroker in a suburb of Boston.

How many people would you guess it took to reach the target person? Unlike the predictions of some who believed these chains would go on endlessly, Milgram found the median number of intermediaries to be only five. Thus, the stranger who sits next to you on the bus, who cuts in front of you in line, who interests you at a party, and even the criminal who burglarizes your home are probably connected to you by a mere handful of intermediate friends. This is called the **small world phenomenon.** The reason we are unaware of the network in which we are embedded is that you and the stranger on the bus do not yourselves own the knowledge of who the five or so intermediaries are who connect you to each other. Even in this modern, far-flung world, we are more connected to each other than we realize.

APPLICATION
SOLVING A PERSONAL FINANCIAL CRISIS IN THE "SMALL WORLD"

A social psychologist of our acquaintance once found himself needing to move from Washington, D.C., to Boston. He placed his Washington home on sale and put a $10,000 deposit on a new one in Boston. The mortgage agreement for his new home required that before the loan would actually be made, the Washington home had to be sold, or at least had to be under contract with a buyer. Unfortunately, when the time came, it was not. One week before the move, a loan officer from the bank called and said that unless the Washington home was sold, they could not make the loan for the Boston home.

A chain reaction of personal disasters loomed. With no mortgage, there would be no new home to move into. The sellers of the Boston home would not have the money they needed to buy their new home, and they might get to keep the $10,000 deposit as partial damages. The social psychologist tried to persuade the loan officer to go forward with the loan anyway to avoid the impending catastrophe. "Surely there is some kind of arrangement we can make." The reply: "No. Find a buyer for the Washington home within the next few days or no loan."

The social psychologist believed that if he knew someone influential at the bank, the loan would not be denied. He further suspected that the small world technique could create such a connection.

He jotted down the names of several Boston friends who he thought had a chance of knowing someone in the banking community. The first friend he called said he knew no one at that particular bank, but was friendly with a vice president (VP1) at another bank. The friend called VP1, who, it turned out, had a good friend (VP2) who was a vice president at the target bank but had nothing to do with mortgages. That vice president, of course, was a colleague of the vice president responsible for mortgages (VP3). Each link along the chain—friend, VP1, VP2—made a telephone introduction of the social psychologist to the next friend in the chain until the critical person, VP3, was ready to talk to his friend's friend's friend's friend, the social psychologist. (Note: the chain had only three intermediaries; four if you count VP3 as an intermediary to the original loan officer.)

VP3 said he would be happy to help out any friends of his friend, and he instructed his staff to process the loan. The final call of the day was from the loan officer who had made the initial phone call that day, this time saying that the bank would be happy to go forward with the loan.

COLLECTIVE BEHAVIOR

The social connections that underlie collective behavior are even more tenuous than those that form "small world" chains. But still they exert a great influence on behavior. When people participate in crowds, mobs,

TABLE 13.1
Examples of Collective Behavior over a Three-Month Period, from the *Los Angeles Times,* 1982

Date		Headline
January	1	"1.42 MILLION EXPECTED AT 93RD ROSE PARADE"
	4	"SHANGHAI PEOPLE BRING REVOLUTION 'DOWN TO EARTH' "
	8	"MEXICAN TRUCKERS' STRIKE AGAINST HARASSMENT GROWS"
	10	"WHITES REVOLT OVER INDIANS' NO-TAX STATUS"
	15	"CROWD TESTS MARTIAL LAW"
	19	"INDIA ARRESTS THOUSANDS IN ATTEMPT TO CRUSH STRIKE"
February	1	"205 ARRESTED IN POLAND DURING GDANSK RIOTING"
	6	"INS RAIDS PANIC LITTLE TOKYO: 27 SEIZED; MANY SHOPS AND RESTAURANTS CLOSE"
	11	"REVOLT REPORTED IN SYRIAN CITY"
	16	"84 FEARED LOST AS STORM WRECKS ATLANTIC OIL RIG"
	17	"RESISTANCE TO MARTIAL LAW IN POLAND GROWS"
	18	"POLISH POLICE DETAIN 3,500"
March	11	"200 INDIAN VILLAGERS SLAIN IN GUATEMALA"
	11	"ANGRY OVER POPE'S VISIT, CROWD JEERS ARCHBISHOP"
	15	"INDIANA FLOOD WORST SINCE 1913; THOUSANDS FLEE AS STORMS HIT MIDWEST"
	24	"10,000 PROTEST AS REAGAN TELLS OF COMPASSION FOR NEEDY"

religious revivals, panics, emergencies, manias, riots, revolutions, and social movements, they are involved in what social psychologists call **collective behavior.** This form of behavior is more common than we might realize, as noted in Table 13.1, which lists headlines of collective behavior. These various forms of collective behavior share general elements in common. They are all departures from the normal structured channels of social existence, and they display a lack of planned organization along with a relatively high degree of unpredictability and spontaneity.

"Life as usual," if we think about it for a moment, is remarkably predictable. The repetition and well-known norms of conduct make it easy to foretell much social behavior. But on a day when a blizzard paralyzes the city, or a mass power outage occurs during rush hour, people are cut loose from their usual patterns and what they will do is less predictable. If you have ever been in a building during a bomb scare or in a city shut down in the aftermath of a snowstorm, you have had a taste of the temporary loss of norms, the uncertainty, and the heightened awareness of other people that characterizes collective behavior.

The Individual in a Crowd: Deindividuation

When people are highly identifiable as individuals, and therefore conscious of themselves, they generally behave in more conservative, cautious ways, more in tune with the belief they have about the kind of person they are or the way they "ought" to behave. This represents a high degree of individuation. The opposite end of the continuum is **deindividuation,** where people are unidentifiable as individuals, are highly aroused, are focused on a novel and unstructured situation, and "lose" themselves in their activities and surroundings. Deindividuation often leads to bizarre, violent, and destructive behavior: from behaving "like a wild man" at a party or sports event, to lynch mobs, riots, and massacres by soldiers.

Among the causes of deindividuation are anonymity, diffused responsibility, and active participation. For example, a person is more likely to feel anonymous in a crowd, and the larger the crowd, the greater the feeling of anonymity. (See Chapter 10 for a discussion of the relationship between anonymity and aggression.) The importance of reduced self-awareness in deindividuation has been confirmed in various settings (Diener, 1979; Beaman et al., 1979; Diener et al., 1976). For example, Diener and colleagues set up a situation in which Halloween trick-or-treaters would be tempted to steal. The researchers were able to reduce theft from 57.2 percent to 7.5 percent of the children by asking them their names and separating them out from their groups, thereby individuating them.

Zimbardo (1969) found that when people were placed in an experimental situation in which they were to give electric shocks to another person, deindividuated subjects gave more electric shocks over time and were insensitive to whether the victim was "nice" or "obnoxious." By contrast,

Prisons are among the many institutions that deindividuate people. Once inside, these inmates have their clothes taken from them, are given a number and a uniform, and are treated alike. Deindividuated people are more easily controlled, but they may also become less governable should a riot break out.

individuated subjects gave shorter shocks that declined over time for the "nice" victim and increased for the "obnoxious" victim. Similarly, Zimbardo (1969) noted that in a deindividuated urban setting, an old car was stripped in less than three days, left as a useless hulk of metal; but in a more individuated suburban setting, a nearly identical car stood for over a week without incident.

Although it may seem that deindividuation often leads to disorder, sometimes societies deindividuate people by placing them in their groups so as to impose order. Executioners are hidden or wear hoods to hide their identities, and they often operate as a group. In firing squads, one randomly selected rifle contains blanks so that individual responsibility is diffused, and any given member of the group can entertain the possibility of not being responsible for killing. Putting soldiers in uniforms reduces their individuation, thereby inducing them to conform more readily to the group's orders. But deindividuation need not always work to increase violent behavior. By wearing habits and praying in groups, for example, the individuality of nuns can more easily be subordinated to group norms for obedience and piety. Thus deindividuation can also promote highly moral behavior.

Processes of Collective Behavior

Gustave LeBon (1895) was the first to attempt to describe and explain mob behavior. He proposed that the members of a crowd give up their individual consciousness and take on a "collective mind," as though the mob has become a single organism. Few if any modern social scientists accept this notion, although many of LeBon's concepts have been incorporated into modern theories of collective behavior (Smelser, 1963; Wheeler, 1978). Let us examine the processes that transform a group of people into a lynch mob or into a panicked crowd charging toward the exits of a burning theater.

Contagion When a country is experiencing serious economic crises or food shortages; when the electricity is out; or when a natural disaster such as a flood or storm strikes, existing social organizing processes prove inadequate for people's needs. In their desire to comprehend what is happening, people try to fill the void, and **contagion** often occurs. In an analogy to an infectious epidemic, contagion refers to the spread of new ways of acting and thinking among the people affected by the social discontinuity. They mill about, make telephone calls, and otherwise contact each other to share uncertainties, feelings, and suggestions about the situation. Note how this process sounds very much like that of social comparison, as discussed in Chapter 3.

Through contagion, people become more and more unified in feelings about the situation. They may appear homogeneous, or of one mind, but they are really a collection of individuals with a heightened need to deal with a novel situation. Other people provide them with the best—indeed the only—account of what makes sense, and in their state of heightened suggestibility, they are likely to adopt the same feelings or actions. When Orson Welles's 1938 radio dramatization of H. G. Wells's "War of the Worlds" panicked a million people into believing there had been an invasion from Mars, their response was in part a result of contacting other people to see how they were interpreting the situation and what they were doing about it. Those who found that others thought it was a fictional broadcast did not panic or flee for their lives (Cantril, 1958).

An important component of emotional and behavioral contagion, then, is the spread of information, typically through rumors (Allport & Postman, 1947; Rosnow & Fine, 1976). Rumors are characterized by two related processes, leveling and sharpening. **Leveling** involves the shortening of a message, and the dropping of detail as it passes from person to person. **Sharpening** involves narrowing the message's focus to a few points, and it is characterized by increasing simplification. Finally, rumors are assimilated to the circumstances to make them appear to fit the needs of the situation.

For example, suppose a policeman has been accosted by a woman while making a routine arrest. He tries to calm her down, and, in the jostling of a tense crowd, the woman is slightly injured and taken to a hospital. A leveled and sharpened rumor that the police are "going around beating up women" may spread, assimilated to underlying community mistrust of and hostility toward the police. The rumor may help precipitate a riot. To the extent that rumors can be replaced with accurate and trusted information, contagion can be reduced and riots prevented. During the riots of the 1960s, a number of cities established rumor control centers to achieve just this purpose.

Another rumor transmission phenomenon involves casualty estimates. According to Quarantelli (1978), the estimate of killed and injured people increases directly with the distance from the site of the tragedy. Reporting the Alaskan earthquake of 1964, for example, newspapers in Columbus, Ohio, put the number killed in Anchorage alone at 1000. Chicago papers estimated 500; Seattle, 300; and Anchorage, 100. The actual number of deaths turned out to be 7. In the Chernobyl nuclear accident of 1986, one New York newspaper reported 2000 deaths; the Russian newspapers reported 2.

Convergence Another process of collective behavior is the tendency of people of similar concerns and interests to converge in a given time and place. Emergencies or disasters cause a convergence of people toward the site of the emergency—some to provide help, some out of curiosity, some returning to their homes for loved ones, some to exploit the situation. Such convergence effects regularly hinder official rescue efforts, and authorities would be delighted to find a way to reduce the tendency toward convergence (Fritz & Mathewson, 1957).

Emergent Norms If contagion and convergence are responses to a breakdown of familiar norms and patterns of social existence, we should expect that one of their most important consequences would be the generation of new norms. In a natural disaster, for example, many of the usual social arrangements that make life possible stop working, at least temporarily. People need to redefine what the situation is, whether the threat will continue, where food, water, and shelter will be coming from, and who will make the necessary decisions. Whether people will kill for a can of tuna fish or help rescue each other will depend upon the norms that emerge to govern their new situation. The more unstructured and frightening a situation, the more urgently people will seek out group norms and the more forcefully the group will press the emerging norms on group members.

Manifestations of Collective Behavior

We have noted a number of different kinds of collective behavior and the processes by which they operate. Crowds, mobs, panics, revivals, emergencies, manias, riots, revolutions, and social movements are all similar in that they involve a loss of self-awareness, a departure from conventional norms, and the emergence of new norms and collective group action. Some forms of collective behavior, such as mobs and panics, are short-lived; others, such as social movements and revolutions, have a longer life. Many of them are characteristically destructive, such as mobs and riots. Others are not.

Emergencies or disasters may involve panic, such as when too many people try to escape from a building through too few exits and trample

These workers are on strike—an instance of collective behavior. Their action may lead to constructive change by pressuring management to negotiate in good faith, or it may get out of hand and lead to violence and disruption.

each other. But it is a myth that, unless controlled by the authorities, people in disasters usually panic, loot, and become otherwise antisocial. Studies of disasters reveal that the redefined situations generally involve giving aid, rescue, and mutual support. In most disaster situations people become unusually prosocial (Dynes, 1970).

While some manifestations of collective behavior are short-term responses to crisis, others, notably revolutions and social movements, can have enduring effects on society. They aim at profoundly changing the status quo, and they are the least spontaneous and least disorganized of those mass actions we call collective behavior (Milgram & Toch, 1969). The **social movement** "represents an effort by a large number of people to solve collectively a problem that they feel they have in common" (Toch, 1965, p. 5). It is characterized by a loose organization, including slogans, symbols, agitation, rallies, and marches, and it draws large numbers of people together in collective feelings, beliefs, and actions. Well-known illustrations of social movements are the overthrow by colonial America, France, and Russia of their monarchical governments. The ayatollahs' Islamic revolution in Iran was an even more profound social movement—aimed not only at overthrowing a political order but also at radically altering the nation's economic, religious, and cultural life.

But social movements need not be so extreme; they can also aim at fine-tuning an existing society. Examples in the United States include the civil rights movement of the late 1950s and 1960s, the antiwar movement of the late 1960s and 1970s, and the women's movement, rekindled in the 1960s. Mass changes in life-style (clothes, music, living and working habits) are also social movements.

Collective behavior generated by emergency situations contrasts with that produced by social movements in several important ways (Sherif & Sherif, 1969). In an emergency, collective behavior is instigated by an unexpected disaster. It is sudden, spontaneous, short-lived, and nonrecurrent, and its consequences are limited mostly to the immediate victims of the crisis. Movement-instigated collective behavior arises out of simmering discontent, articulated in a "bill of gripes" (Sherif & Sherif, 1969) whose goals are stated in platforms and manifestos (be they written by Paine and Jefferson or Marx and Lenin). The collective actions they generate can be staged or primed to occur, and opportunities for collective expression are sought out. Each incident of collective behavior is more organized than emergency situations, but they need not involve violence—consider the movements led by Mahatma Gandhi and Martin Luther King, Jr. Social movements seek to, and often do, affect the lives of many or all members of the society. If the movement prevails, as did the American, French, Soviet, and Chinese revolutions, the revolutionaries become the new established order, with appropriate history, ideology, and ritual to support it.

Despite their differences, the various forms of collective behavior occur through similar processes: contagion, convergence, and emergent norms.

Compared to other manifestations of collective behavior, social movements are the most organized, least spontaneous, and most enduring.

BEHAVIOR IN ORGANIZATIONS

We now turn to the kind of large group that is by far the most deliberately planned, least spontaneous, most coordinated, and most structured: the organization. An organization is defined as "the planned coordination of activities for the achievement of some common, explicit purpose or goal, through division of labor and function, and through a hierarchy of authority and responsibility" (Schein, 1980, p. 15). Those who would form, repair, or reshape organizations must concern themselves with a wide array of matters all at once.

Types of Organizations

When most of us think of the typical business organization, we generate the following images: a board of directors selected by the owners (stockholders) sets long-term goals and hires managers to direct the day-to-day conduct of employees. Tasks are broken down into small units so that each employee has a specialized and often repetitious job. However, organizations that are dramatically different from this hierarchical or traditional model do exist. In the Israeli kibbutz, workers own the organization and elect their management, thereby employing a democratic model in the workplace as well as in the political system. In so doing, the workers ultimately control the organization's goals, tasks, and methods. In American cooperatives the consumers of the goods or services (rather than stockholders) elect a board of directors and share in the profits. But, like stockholders, they have no control over the details of the organization's work.

In Volvo assembly plants in Sweden, workers are organized into teams. Although the overall plant runs on an assembly line, the vehicles come off the line into semiautonomous work areas where teams have control over how they will accomplish the tasks they are responsible for. Each team of 15 to 20 workers decides how to go about their responsibilities and when to change their procedures. Their work cycle varies from 16 to 40 minutes, with each worker doing a greater variety of tasks than their North American counterparts, who perform a narrow range of tasks requiring only one or two minutes to complete (Katz & Kahn, 1978).

Structures of Organizations

Attempts to understand what makes organizations succeed or fail, and interventions to improve them, can be at any of three levels: the individual, the social structure, and the technostructure (see Katz & Kahn, 1978; Dunnette, 1983). *Individual*-level analysis concerns personnel selection and training, resolving problems by seeing how the individual can change or be changed or by replacing employees who are not performing satisfactorily. According to this view, people are the problem *and* the solution. This approach involves a difficult, time-consuming, and expensive strategy. Nevertheless, the attraction of fixing the organization by fixing its people is strong.

The **social structure** of the organization refers to the roles the members are to occupy, the flow of authority, and the communication channels available to them. It is also concerned with whether people work alone or in groups, how many levels exist from top to bottom, and how centralized or decentralized the organization is. Social structures are more difficult to "see" than are the people in them, especially for the members of the organization themselves. So if a problem arises, managers tend to see its causes and potential cures in the individual. But this may be an incorrect diagnosis, and many organization consultants look to change task or role structures or communication lines rather than personnel. Sharing the major perspective of social psychology, they believe that by changing the organizational structure they can change the behavior of the people.

When organization researchers and consultants look at the **technostructure** of an organization, they are concerned with the technological and physical aspects of the organization rather than with its social organization or its individuals. If employees are injuring themselves with equipment, a technostructural viewpoint suggests redesigning the machines rather than exhorting the workers to be more careful. The organization is also affected by the technologies that are its means of doing what it does. The invention of the telephone radically altered the way people in and between organizations dealt with each other, and made possible skyscraper office buildings and geographically far-flung corporations. The advent of computers and word processors, by reducing the need for the lowest level of office skills (performed by clerks and secretaries), is also changing the shape of the modern organization (Goleman, 1983).

The technostructure of an organization has a strong impact on its social structure (Woodward, 1965). This in turn has an impact on the behavior of the people who work in the organization. Some efforts at organizational improvement—often called the "socio-technical" approach—have aimed at creating an optimal fit among all these levels of the organization (Faucheux, Amado, & Laurent, 1982; Trist et al., 1963).

THEORIES OF ORGANIZATIONS

Theories of organizations were born in the latter part of the nineteenth century to guide and support the Industrial Revolution that gave rise to so many manufacturing organizations. These theories have evolved as new empirical knowledge and new philosophical ideas have developed, and organizations have evolved with them. They are important because they affect the way organizations are structured, their ability to function, and the quality of work life for the people they employ.

Three basic models can be identified: classical, human relations, and human resources. Each has not so much replaced as added to its predecessor (Hodgetts and Altman 1979). Similarities and differences among the three are presented in Table 13.2.

Classical Model

The classical theory of organizations reflects the totally rational, mechanistic mentality of its day. It sought to make organizations scientific, efficient, and smooth-running machines; and it viewed workers as mere extensions of the machinery. Scientific managers, usually mechanical engineers, conducted time and motion studies in order to specify the tasks, methods, and time allowed for workers to perform their tasks, and they set up reward structures that created strong incentives for achieving or exceeding the production quotas (Taylor, 1911). Such techniques were supplemented by the work of administrative theorists, who tried to specify firm rules for helping managers to direct the workers (e.g., Urwick, 1943).

Classical theorists attempted to combine scientific management and administrative theory by creating organizational structures that were strict, logical, and orderly. As a result, the people of the organization all had specialized jobs and worked according to specific rules and standards. They were oriented toward their duties and the organization in a manner that was both formal and impersonal (Hodgetts and Altman, 1979).

The classical theory of organizations has had considerable impact. It led to dramatic productivity increases, sometimes tripling what the prescientific organization had produced. But the organizational structures to which these principles gave rise were too rigid to adapt to changes in the organization's environment (new products, new markets, new demands), and the enforced formality could not take advantage of informal social structure or the creativity and insights of the workers. The workers were often unhappy because they were isolated from other people. They felt alienated from management and the organization as a whole, and pressured to produce a fixed amount in a rigid way.

One problem of classical managers is that they tended to reflect what McGregor (1960) has termed **Theory X.** Theory X managers believe that people are inherently lazy and that they dislike work, lack ambition, seek little other than financial security, and need direction, prodding, coercion, and even punishment in order to be productive. The alternative was **Theory Y.** Theory Y managers believe that work is as natural as eating, sleeping, or playing; that under the right circumstances people will seek responsibility and eagerly pursue organizational goals; and that most people thrive on the opportunity to be involved in the organization and to exercise their creativity and imagination in helping the organization to function better.

TABLE 13.2
Theories of Management

Classical Model	Human Relations Model	Human Resources Model
Assumptions	*Assumptions*	*Assumptions*
1. People inherently dislike work.	1. People want to feel important and useful.	1. People do not inherently dislike work; they want to contribute to meaningful goals which they have helped establish.
2. What people earn for doing the work is more important than the work itself.	2. People want to "belong" and at the same time be recognized as individuals.	2. Most people are capable of exercising a great deal more self-direction, self-control, and creativity than is required in their present job.
3. Few people either want or can handle work requiring self-direction, self-control, or creativity.	3. Social needs are more important than money in motivating people to work.	
Policies	*Policies*	*Policies*
1. The basic job of the manager is to supervise and control the subordinates.	1. The basic task of the manager is to make the workers feel useful and important.	1. The basic task of the manager is to make use of his/her "untapped" human resources.
2. In doing this, the manager needs to break the jobs down into simple, repetitive, and easily learned operations.	2. The manager should keep his/her people informed and listen to their objections to his/her plans.	2. The managers should create an environment in which everyone can contribute to the limit of his or her ability.
3. Finally, the manager should establish detailed work routines and procedures which are enforced firmly and fairly.	3. Subordinates should be allowed to exercise some self-direction and self-control on routine matters.	3. Full participation on important matters and continual broadening of subordinates' self-direction and control should be encouraged.
Expectations	*Expectations*	*Expectations*
1. People can tolerate work if the boss is fair and the pay is decent.	1. By sharing information with subordinates and getting them involved in routine decisions, the manager can help them satisfy their basic needs to belong and feel important.	1. The expansion of subordinate influence, self-direction, and self-control will bring about direct improvements in operating efficiency.
2. If the work is simple enough and people are closely controlled, they will produce up to standard.	2. By satisfying these needs, the manager can improve morale, reduce resistance to formal authority, and induce the subordinates to cooperate.	2. When subordinates make full use of their resources, work satisfaction may well improve.

Source: Adapted from R. E. Miles (1975). *Theories of management: Implications of organizational behavior and development.* New York: McGraw-Hill, p. 35. Copyright 1975. Reprinted with permission.

Human Relations Model

Human relations theory was concerned with applying the knowledge of postwar psychology to the behavior of people in organizations. While retaining the virtues of task specialization, logical structure, and control in the organization, this theory added an understanding of workers as *social beings*. The research and applications generated by the human relations approach were focused on small group processes, many of which we discussed in the preceding chapter.

The earlier scientific managers knew that people perform differently in groups than when working individually. The researchers of the human relations school found out why they did, and began to use that knowledge for the welfare of the organization and the workers. Human relations theorists helped develop the concepts of group norms and participatory management, promote the value of control over one's own work, and use other concepts that emerged from research on small groups. They appreciated, assessed, and improved organizational cohesiveness, loyalty to the organization, and commitment to its goals. Finally, in addition to enhancing the satisfaction and dignity of the workers, such techniques increased the productivity of organizations beyond what was achieved by the classical approach (Tornatzky & Solomon, 1982).

Human Resources Model

The human resources model combines attention to the human beings working in the organization with attention to the structure of the organization. Management controls the environment in which people work, and the nature of that organizational environment affects the experiences

The classical model of organizations proposes that these workers are not self-motivated and require firm and constant supervision. The human relations and human resources models give more credit to workers, focusing more on people's desire to be recognized and approved of and on their capacity to enjoy work and find it fulfilling.

and productivity of the workers. An important example of this general approach is provided by Katz and Kahn's (1978) *open systems theory.* Open systems theory is concerned with how the components of an organization interact with each other as a system. In addition, it views the organization as an **open system**—that is, one that interacts with its environment by importing people, energy, and materials into itself. Inside the organization are its tasks, technologies, structures, and human beings. All these must be geared toward achieving the organization's goals, and they must interact effectively together. Problems in any one subsystem can affect the performance of other subsystems (French & Bell, 1978; Raia & Margulies, 1979).

IMPROVING ORGANIZATIONAL EFFECTIVENESS

Research and theory about organizations are a part of social psychology that is very obviously applicable to the problems of society. Indeed, it has spawned a whole new subarea of psychology—organizational psychology—and consulting firms, whose business it is to assist organizations in improving their structure and functioning, have multiplied and prospered. Consultants draw up comprehensive plans for "organizational development" (OD) (Likert, 1961, 1967; Dimock, 1978; Blake & Mouton, 1969) which are too complex to consider in this chapter, but let us consider three discrete examples which will give you a sense of the kinds of interventions that have been tried.

Job Enrichment and Job Enlargement

The tasks included in a job and when or how they are performed can determine how enjoyable a job is. In studying the relationship between the nature of a person's job and long-term satisfaction with it, Kahn (1973) found that jobs with the greatest task variety and control are the most enjoyed. We might infer from this that the more control people have over the performance of their job tasks, the more they will like the job. Unsatisfying jobs can be "enlarged" or "enriched" by providing a greater variety of tasks, the opportunity to switch tasks from time to time, or the opportunity to choose which of the tasks to do and when to do them. One quite simple version of this is "flextime": In jobs where it makes sense to do so, the employee can decide when to report to work and when to leave (Raia & Margulies, 1979; see also Locke, 1976).

Sensitivity Training

T-groups, as discussed in the previous chapter, have been employed in organizational settings. Their purpose is to improve the ability of employees to understand themselves, especially in relation to others, and to learn how to better communicate and function in groups (French & Bell, 1978). By 1975 a majority of the 10 million people who had experienced some form of sensitivity training had done so under the auspices of the organization for which they worked (Benne, 1975).

The advent of T-group training brought with it grand hopes of creating broad changes by transforming the very nature of human institutions. Those who advocated T-groups hoped that by changing the people of the organization they could slowly but surely change the basic fabric of the organization itself (Katz & Kahn, 1978). Evaluations of the effects of T-groups on organizations have not met these high expectations. Most of the changes in individuals do not endure, and the organization does not change even when it saturates its management and supervisory staff with sensitivity training (Gibb, 1975; Bowers, 1973; Strauss, 1976; Beer, 1976).

The reason for this lack of impact may be that the individual is the wrong target of change. Even if change in individuals is achieved—and the immediate effects of sensitivity training can be dramatic—returning to the same structure, roles, and relationships, gradually restores the organization and its members to their previous state. Little is achieved by changing the individuals and leaving the organizational structure unchanged. Sensitivity training by itself is not enough.

Survey Feedback

Data on attitudes and perceptions of the organization can be collected from people in various levels and functions of the organization via survey and then "fed back" into the organization. Such information can be helpful in diagnosing problems, deciding on solutions, and assessing the impact of management actions. Several kinds of feedback are possible. The information can be fed back to management to monitor how the organization is functioning and to decide what changes need to be made. Or the feedback can go to employees throughout the organization who can meet within their own levels of the organization or in vertically integrated groups (managers and workers together) to discuss the problems and decide upon solutions. One such survey feedback device which is part of a company's regular annual report is the "social audit" (Abt, 1977). In this kind of audit employees rate the adequacy and importance of various benefits, working conditions, and professional growth opportunities. Such information can help management decide the most cost-effective way to spend the organization's energy and money, and can later be used to assess the success or failure of its moves.

Organizations, especially private businesses, have provided an apt and eager setting for the application of social psychology. As with any intervention or application, we must keep in mind that no technique is a panacea, and the impact of any method to change behavior needs to be evaluated to determine whether and how well it is working (e.g., Keller, 1978). Applications of social psychology that work well can result in not only a better quality of work life for employees but also more productivity for companies. Sometimes labor and management can both be winners (Lawler, 1982; Tornatzky & Solomon, 1982).

BEHAVIOR OF GROUPS IN CONFLICT

In contrast to organizational life, where conflict is regarded as a temporary aberration and research pursues even greater harmony, intergroup and international life seems to be characterized by permanent and often violent conflict.

Intergroup conflict exists whenever the goals, interests, and actions of one group are incompatible with those of another (Austin & Worchel, 1979; Turner & Giles, 1981). This usually means conflict among racial or ethnic groups, but can also mean the quieter clashes of interest between the sexes or the more focused conflicts within a community or between organizations. Racial conflict has long been and probably will long be one of the central problems of life in the United States. And it has long been an important focus of research by social psychologists, whose applied concerns have generally been directed at changing those features of society that give rise to this conflict (Katz, 1976). The history of race conflict spans U.S. history. The white majority has virtually exterminated the native Americans who once populated the continent, imported Africans and subjected them to slavery, and during World War II placed its citizens of Japanese ancestry into American concentration camps (Miyamoto, 1973). In evolved form, such conflicts continue today.

International conflict is more distant and abstract, but when its violence breaks out, it is more acute and unbridled (Kelman, 1965). Hardly a day passes that the front pages do not report a war somewhere or preparation for one almost everywhere. Preparations for war continue at a present cost to the world of well over one million dollars per minute.

Although violence is an undesirable product of conflict, conflict in and of itself is not necessarily bad. In fact, some people have argued that it is not only an inevitable component of social life (Simmel, 1955) but also a necessary, even desirable one (Bonoma & Milburn), 1977). Conflict between political candidates or parties is usually beneficial to a nation; indeed, in democracies such conflict is considered a central virtue of the political system.

Conflict can also be useful in maintaining cohesion within groups (Dion, 1979; Markides & Cohn, 1982). It helps maintain boundaries and can limit disruptive intrusions by out-groups. It allows opposing groups to test their strength in a way that can avoid the outbreak of violence. Conflict creates coalitions that otherwise would not form (Coser, 1956, 1967; Dion, 1979) and enables groups to bring about social change.

Our concern is probably best directed at avoiding *destructive conflict,* wherein "participants are dissatisfied with the outcomes and feel they have lost," and at trying to promote *constructive conflict,* wherein "participants all are satisfied with their outcomes and feel they have gained as a result of the conflict" (Deutsch, 1973, p. 17). In a "good" conflict there is not a winner and a loser, but a solution. In our discussion of conflict, we will look at the kinds of conflict that occur, the causes of conflict, and what is known about managing or resolving conflict.

Categories of Conflict

The Focus of Conflict The object of a conflict can vary. Katz (1965) has broadly distinguished three kinds of conflict: *economic,* where the groups are competing for scarce resources; *power,* where they are vying to dominate the course of the relationship; and *value,* in which people are upset over the differences in beliefs and attitudes between themselves and an out-group. Value conflicts may appear to be the least serious, since the fight is over nothing more than what is in another person's head, but recall from the chapters on the self (Chapter 3) and attitudes (Chapters 5 and 6) that certain values may be central to a person's identity and to the way in which he or she sees the world. The killing of nonbelievers by the tens of thousands was once a popular practice in several of the world's major religions.

Objective and Perceived Conflict While Katz's typology points to the focus of the conflict, Deutsch (1973) has noted that conflict can be of several types depending on whether its basis is an actual or a perceived incompatibility of interests. A *veridical conflict* is one that exists in reality and is accurately perceived, as is typical of disputes over money or territory. A *contingent conflict* is one that is real enough, but would disappear if the parties realized that a rearrangement of circumstances would allow them both to achieve their goals. For example, two cars come face-to-face on a narrow mountain road. If they try to pass simultaneously, they will have a very real conflict over resources (the road). But if they can agree that one will wait until the other has passed, the conflict will evaporate.

In a *displaced conflict* the parties are overtly fighting over one thing (the manifest conflict) while the real trouble between them is something else (the underlying conflict). When a couple argues over who will wash the dishes, but one is really angry that the other arrived home late, they have displaced the real conflict onto a false issue. A *misattributed conflict* occurs when two groups perceive each other as the cause of their problems when they are really the wrong parties to the dispute. An example of this is when a government deflects criticism from itself by setting subgroups of its people against each other. *Latent conflict* is when an objective basis for conflict exists, but is not experienced or acted upon by the parties.

When the women's movement encourages consciousness-raising activities, it is trying to bring to the surface latent conflicts such as unfair pay and limited opportunities that are nevertheless little protested against by many women.

Finally, *false conflict* is one in which a conflict between groups exists but has no objective basis, and thus involves misperceptions of the situation. Ralph White (1965, 1966, 1968) has argued, for example, that U.S. involvement in the Vietnam War was rooted largely in misperceptions. The Vietnamese sought independence while U.S. officials feared they wanted communism. A false conflict can become real if the process of conflict creates grievances of its own. As soon as one group harms the other, a real basis for conflict has been created.

Causes of Conflict

The typologies of conflict hint at the causes of conflict. These causes range from differences in race, culture, beliefs, or values through misperceptions of the situation or the other party's motives, to genuine competition over limited resources.

In-Group Bias How little does it take for conflict to erupt between groups of people? One ingredient, certainly, is the existence and perception of an *in-group* ("us") and an *out-group* ("them"), as discussed in the last chapter. We see ourselves as belonging to groups, and we set up boundaries that exist in our own cognitions as much as they do in any external world. These differences in perception and affect, as well as a willingness to act for or against people on the basis of our definition of them as members of an in-group or out-group, is known as **in-group bias.**

People who read about a war or watch it on the television news are likely to feel anxiety and tension over "our" group's losses and a sense of relief or even pride when learning of "their" losses. The same soldiers who can be loving and playful toward the children of their own national group can be indifferent or even murderous toward children of the out-group. In less dramatic areas of life, we see people cheering for the home team and donating more money to their own religious group's charities. When told their ethnic group's ability to tolerate pain is the issue in an experiment, people even show more pain tolerance than when only their individual tolerance is at stake (Lambert, Libman, & Poser, 1960).

The tendency of in-groups to devalue out-groups was first studied by Sumner (1906) and was termed **ethnocentrism.** Various facets of ethnocentrism are summarized in Table 13.3. Lewin (1948) suggested that this tendency stems from the "interdependence of fate" shared by members of the in-group. When national or ethnic groups with long histories and complex cultures find themselves cohesive for the purpose of their well-being if not survival, or in conflict with other groups for scarce resources,

TABLE 13.3
Facets of Ethnocentrism

Orientations Toward In-Group	Orientations Toward Out-Group
See selves as virtuous and superior	See out-group as contemptible, immoral, and inferior
See own standards of value as universal, intrinsically true	Rejection of out-group values
See selves as strong	See out-group as weak
Sanctions against theft	Sanctions for theft
Sanctions against murder	Sanctions for murder
Cooperative relations with other group members	Absence of cooperation
Obedience to authorities	Absence of obedience
Willingness to retain membership in group	Rejection of membership
Willingness to fight and die for group	Virtue in killing out-group members in warfare
	Maintenance of social distance
	Negative affect, hate
	Use as bad examples in training children
	Blame for in-group troubles
	Distrust and fear

Source: Adapted from M. B. Brewer (1979). The role of ethnocentrism in intergroup conflict. In W. G. Austin & S. Worchel, *The social psychology of intergroup conflict.* Monterey, CA: Brooks/Cole.

in-group bias may have survival value and is therefore a reasonable development.

But we know from a classic series of studies carried out at a boys' summer camp (Rohrer & Sherif, 1951; Sherif & Sherif, 1953; Sherif, White, & Harvey, 1955; Sherif & Sherif, 1956) that long cultural histories and survival needs are not necessary for in-group bias to develop. At the outset of this research, all the boys were housed in the same large bunkhouse, which allowed friendships to develop freely. Sherif and his fellow researchers gathered data on who the boys' best friends were. Later the boys were divided into two separate groups and housed in separate cabins. In particular, best friends were split up and put into different groups.

The two groups participated in most activities separately. Joint activities usually involved competitions in games and sports. Before long, each new group developed its own friendships, jokes, jargon, customs, nicknames, and hierarchies. In spite of the early friendships, the boys soon felt the most liking for members of their new group and showed little fondness for members of the out-group. In Figure 13.1, you can see the dramatic changes in friendship choices made before and after the two

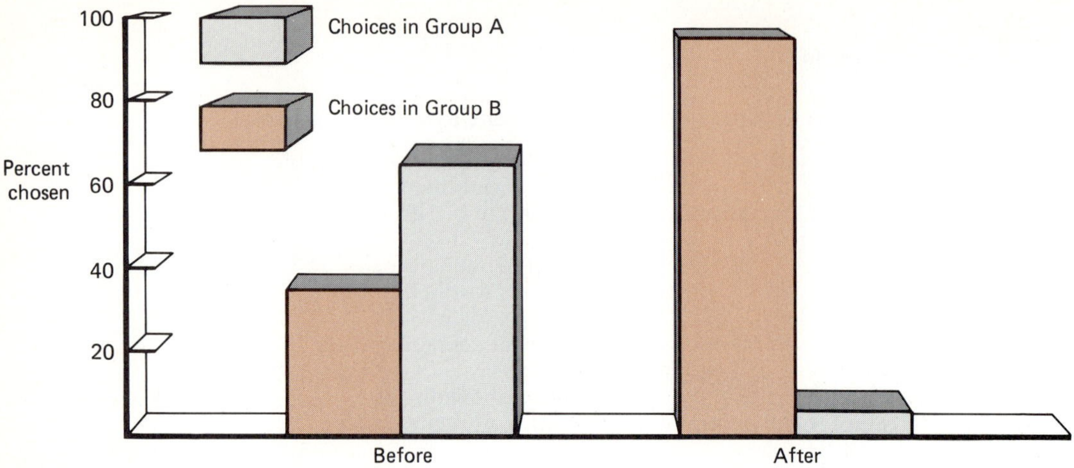

FIGURE 13.1
People Chosen in Each Group by Members of Group A In Sherif and Sherif's Robber's Cave research, children were assigned to groups. The "before" bars show that the children in Group A had more friends in Group B than in their own group. After forming into groups and becoming more cohesive, these friendship choices changed, so that almost every child in Group A chose a best friend in his own rather than in the other group. *Source:* Adapted from M. Sherif and C. W. Sherif (1969). *Social psychology.* New York, Harper & Row, p. 232.

groups were formed. When asked to judge achievement in games where performance was hard to evaluate, the boys consistently overestimated the performance of in-group members and underestimated that of out-group members. Later, with the introduction of competition between the groups, outright hostility emerged toward all members of the out-group, including aggressive competition at sports, ridicule, sabotage, and fighting. These demonstrations of in-group–out-group consequences do not stand alone. Many other kinds of perceptual and cognitive distortions of out-groups by in-groups have been found (Howard & Rothbart, 1980; Jones, Wood, & Quattrone, 1981; Linville & Jones, 1980; Park & Rothbart, 1982), several of which we will discuss later.

Perhaps Sherif's camp experiments seem to involve situations where in-group bias and rejection of out-groups seem "reasonable," given the campers' experiences over a few weeks. If conditions became still more short-term and minimal would the in-group bias effect still arise? How faint can the boundaries between groups become for the members of one group to continue to treat the members of another group unequally?

Rabbie and Horwitz (1969) set out to find these minimal conditions in an experiment with 112 Dutch teenagers. They took eight students at a time and divided them into two groups of four, labeling them the blue and the green groups. The two groups had no interaction of any kind.

Ratings of their impressions of each other's characteristics at this stage showed no in-group bias. Mere classification, then, was not enough.

In other conditions, the groups were to receive transistor radios as a gift for participation. The researchers said that they had only a limited number of radios and could give them away to only one of the groups. Which group got the radios was decided by (1) a vote by one of the groups, (2) an arbitrary choice by the experimenter, or (3) the toss of a coin. What did it take to produce in-group favoritism and hostility toward the out-group? Did it require selfish treatment of one group by the other? Unfair treatment by a third party for no reason? Or nothing more than random fate? All three of these conditions produced the in-group bias.

Thus even the chance allocation of a desired commodity to group members who never interacted and did not even know each other was sufficient to cause people to rate their own group as more worth belonging to, and the other group as less desirable. In short, it takes next to nothing to produce the phenomenon of people favoring "their" group and disliking and depriving an out-group. Little wonder that theologian William Inge once defined a nation as "a society united by a delusion about its ancestry, and by a common hatred of its neighbors."

Prejudice Social conflicts in the real world are, of course, produced by more than the bare minimum of in-group bias. As discussed in Chapter 6, attitudes are learned—passed along from generation to generation—and can prepare a person to have conflict with out-group members. In addition to attitudes, people learn **prejudice** and stereotypes about their own group and out-groups (see Table 13.4) which support and maintain the conflict (Crosby, Bromley, & Saxe, 1980; Hamilton, 1981).

As we discussed in Chapter 4 in reference to the sexes, **stereotypes** are simplified beliefs about characteristics thought to be common to all members of a group. The existence of stereotypes has several consequences. First, physical and social differences are used as the basis of categorization, and information is organized around these characteristics. Second, differences within groups tend to be overlooked, and differences between groups tend to be exaggerated. For instance, if members of two stereotyped groups interact and are later asked to describe the interaction, they can remember whether a given person was from the in-group or the out-group but not which individual it was. And if prejudiced people get to know a member of the out-group well, they can preserve the stereotype simply by concluding that "this person is an exception."

Part of the hostility between groups is based on assumed differences in beliefs and values: we believe in X; they believe in Y. In fact, a number of studies have found that race is not as important to people as shared values and beliefs are. Given a choice between associating with a person of one's own race who holds values in conflict with our own, or a person of a different race whose values and beliefs are in agreement with our

TABLE 13.4
Comparison of Stereotype Trait Frequencies of American Ethnic Groups, 1933–1967[a]

Ethnic Group	1933	1967		1933	1967
Germans			*Japanese*		
Scientific-minded	78	47	Intelligent	45	20
Industrious	65	59	Industrious	43	57
Stolid	44	9	Progressive	24	17
Extremely nationalistic	24	43	Ambitious	—	33
Efficient	16	46	Efficient	—	27
Irish			*Negroes*		
Pugnacious	45	13	Superstitious	84	13
Quick-tempered	39	43	Lazy	75	26
Witty	38	7	Happy-go-lucky	38	27
Very religious	29	27	Musical	26	47
Extremely nationalistic	21	41	Ostentatious	26	25
Jews			*Turks*		
Shrewd	79	30	Cruel	47	9
Mercenary	49	15	Very religious	26	7
Industrious	48	33	Treacherous	21	13
Ambitious	21	48	Physically dirty	15	14
Materialistic	—	46	Aggressive	—	17

[a] Percentage checking various traits.
Source: Adapted from M. Karlins, T. L. Coffman, & G. Walters (1969). On the faking of social stereotypes: Studies in three generations of college students. *Journal of Personality and Social Psychology, 13,* 4–5.

own, most people choose the latter (Rokeach & Mezei, 1966; Moe, Nacoste, & Insko, 1981). But owing to *autistic hostility,* most members of the conflicting groups do not get to learn what members of the out-group think. If we dislike certain people, we minimize our contact with them; the resulting silence ("autism") precludes the opportunity for the conflict to be resolved (Newcomb, 1947). As a result, the initial hostility is reinforced and perpetuated. In a study using black and white children, Epstein, Krupat, and Obudho (1976) found that neither group of children made choices based exclusively on race. Each assumed, however, that the *other* group made *its* choices according to race.

We can see that the social psychological study of prejudice is an application of the large body of research on attitudes (Chapters 5 and 6) and social perception (Chapter 2) to the problems of intergroup conflict. What people believe and feel affects how they respond to and behave toward out-groups. That in turn affects each group's beliefs and attitudes, and the processes of hostile thought and action can reinforce, deepen, and perpetuate the conflict.

Social Traps

Often the events that occur during the course of a conflict can themselves become objective bases of conflict. The more a party to a conflict has invested in a conflict—lives, wealth, lost alliances—the more it has to "lose" by not continuing. Only by going forward can it hope to recoup its investment in the conflict, though in doing so it runs a risk of still greater losses. This is known as a social trap. **Social traps** are situations of interdependence in which the behavior that will provide short-term gain ultimately will lead to greater losses (Rubin & Brockner, 1985; Teger, 1980; Rubin et al., 1980; Rubin, 1981). They reflect a mentality that says, "We will continue because we must. We've gone too far to back out now."

Alan Teger demonstrated the psychological power of social traps through the Dollar Auction. In this auction a group of people are invited to bid on a one-dollar bill. The highest bidder wins the dollar. The unusual feature of this auction is that payment must be made by the second highest bidder as well as by the highest. Bidders eagerly dive in, pursuing their dream of spending only eight cents and receiving a dollar. What they find, however, is that whoever is in second place does not want to spend seven cents to get nothing. The second person can forestall a loss by bidding nine cents. And upward it goes.

These bidders are trapped in a situation described as *negative interdependence:* if one wins, the other must lose. Even after the bidding goes *above* a dollar, so that even the "winner" will lose money—and Teger reports that the bidding always goes above the dollar mark—the bidding battle continues. The motivations then change from the pursuit of profit to the avoidance of loss to inflicting punishment on one's opponent. The Dollar Auction simulates the trap in which parties to larger conflicts eventually find themselves.

Teger reviews data on escalation in wars and strikes and finds that it follows the same pattern as in the Dollar Auction. For example, in the Vietnam War, the more lives and money the United States lost, the more lives and money the government wanted to commit to "winning." Additional losses were spent trying to make the old ones "worth" the cost. Thus, in addition to the objective losses, a party in such a trap also has to contend with such psychological risks as possible loss of face. We must not underestimate the power of such a motivator, especially when trying to fashion solutions that disputants will find acceptable (Brown, 1968).

Responses to Conflict: Cooperation Versus Competition

Groups in conflict can relate to each other via cooperation, an attempt to find mutually acceptable solutions, or competition, an attempt to beat or outdo the others. Social psychologists have studied these processes by using simulated conflict situations, usually games. They enable researchers to re-create essential elements of a conflict situation, to vary the conditions of conflict and strategies for its resolution, and to see what effects these changes have. The resulting theories are then compared to studies from natural situations, and conceptions of the causes of and solutions to conflict are fashioned.

One such technique is known as the **Prisoner's Dilemma Game** (PDG). Luce and Raiffa (1957) modeled the PDG after the situation in which two suspects are arrested and interrogated. If both remain silent, they cannot be convicted. But if one confesses, two things occur: The confession will be used as evidence against the other, who will be given a long sentence, and the confessor will get only a light sentence. If both confess, however, they will both get moderate sentences. Figure 13.3 presents a typical PDG matrix. The prisoners become players; each has the choice of either cooperating or competing, and the outcome is a joint product of the choices they make. If both cooperate, both win one point. If one cooperates and the other competes, the competitor gains two points and the cooperator loses two points. But if both try to gain an advantage by competing, both lose a point. Competing and cooperating can both be risky—*depending upon what the other person does.* The choices they make depend upon their trust for each other, their respective motivations, and their strategies.

The PDG has been used not only by social psychologists but by mathematicians, managers, political scientists, and students of international relations because it permits easy manipulation of important variables in conflict situations such as availability of communication opportunities, incentives, and relative sizes of rewards versus costs for cooperation and

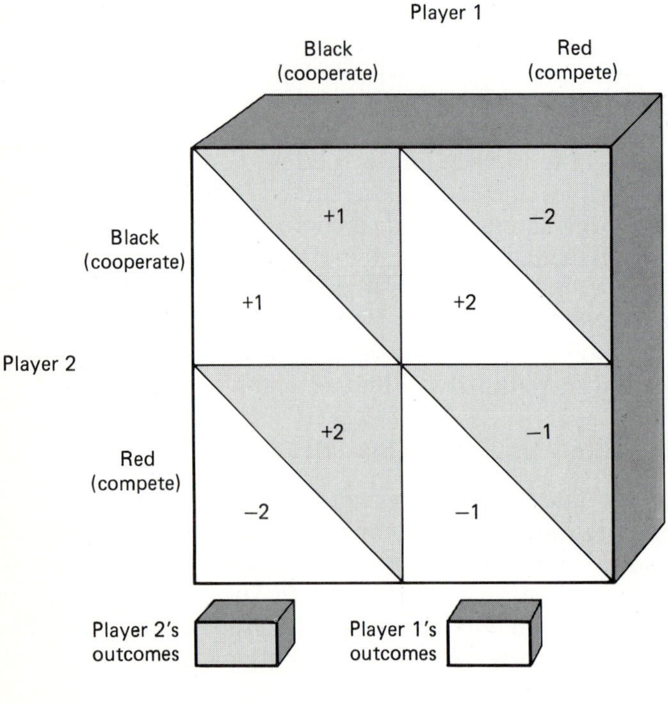

FIGURE 13.3
A Typical Example of a Prisoner's Dilemma Game Each player can choose red or black. The outcome for both players is determined by their joint choices. The amounts in the matrix indicate how many points, money, or other goods are won (or lost) by each player on each turn. Player 1 gets the lower-left amounts in each cell; Player 2 gets the upper-right amounts. For example, if Player 1 chose black and Player 2 chose red, Player 1 would lose 2 and Player 2 would win 2.

competition. From such research, many findings have emerged about the nature of behavior in conflict situations (Nemeth, 1972; Pruitt & Kimmel, 1977).

For example, different strategies produce varying outcomes. A strategy of pure competition (choosing the competitive option each time) leads to a high degree of competition from an opponent—about 80 percent competitive choices. The opposite extreme, pure cooperation, improves matters to about 50 percent cooperation from the opponent, but still leaves us being exploited half the time (Chammah, 1970; Rapoport, 1973) or, worse, mercilessly dominated by the opponent (Black & Higbee, 1973; Bixenstein, Potash, & Wilson, 1963; Solomon, 1960; Shure, Meeker, & Hansford, 1965). The most successful strategy is *contingent cooperation,* tit-for-tat responding. Every time our opponents are cooperative, so are we; every time they are uncooperative, so are we. That raises their level of cooperation to about 70 percent (Rapoport, 1973; Kuhlman & Marshello, 1975). Still, different strategies are most effective depending upon the level of competitiveness of one's opponents (Kuhlman & Marshello, 1975).

Over time, the choices made by opponents tend to stabilize and converge. Toward the end of a 300-trial PDG, the pairs of participants tend to make the same choices. They learn consistently to compete with each other or to cooperate. Most of them learn to cooperate, so over time the level of cooperation gradually increases. But some parties do stabilize at low levels of cooperation, continually inflicting and receiving damage (Rapoport & Chammah, 1965).

Attributions of our opponent affect whether we cooperate or compete. Expecting cooperation from the other side and believing that the other side can be trusted to cooperate increases cooperative choices. If we expect cooperation and receive competition, that violation of our expectations will abruptly alter our behavior. A former director of the U.S. Arms Control and Disarmament Agency has pointed out that the United States, having failed to ratify three consecutive arms control treaties, had the additional problem in later negotiations of convincing Soviet negotiators to take us seriously (Smith, 1983). Thus, in choosing negotiators, each side tends to send people who are perceived by the other side as trustworthy and who in their own styles are cooperative—not to the point of making unreciprocated concessions, but able and willing to be contingently cooperative—if they want to conclude a mutually satisfactory agreement (Zartman & Berman, 1982).

APPLICATION
A MATRIX ANALYSIS OF THE NUCLEAR ARMS RACE

Let us attempt to use the PDG matrix to shed light on the evolution of a social conflict such as the nuclear arms race (Brams, Davis, & Straffin, 1979; Schelling, 1975). Consider the situation faced by Superpowers A and B. Each side has

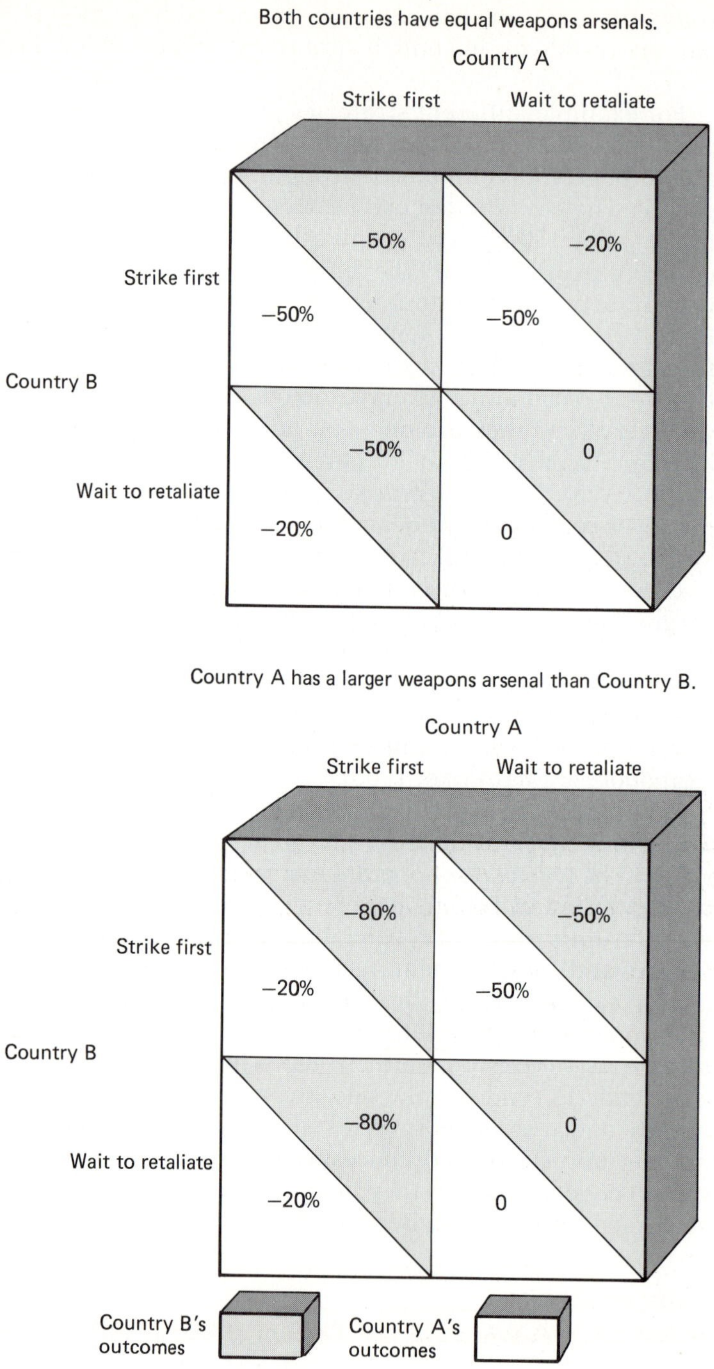
Both countries have equal weapons arsenals.
Country A
Strike first
Wait to retaliate
Country B
Strike first
Wait to retaliate
−50%
−50%
−20%
−50%
−50%
−20%
0
0
Country A has a larger weapons arsenal than Country B.
Country A
Strike first
Wait to retaliate
Country B
Strike first
Wait to retaliate
−80%
−20%
−50%
−50%
−80%
−20%
0
0
Country B's outcomes
Country A's outcomes

FIGURE 13.4

The Nuclear Arms Race as a Prisoner's Dilemma The arms race between the United States and the USSR can be seen as a Prisoner's Dilemma. As shown in the top matrix on the opposite page, they face identical risks, but whichever country waits to retaliate loses more of its population than the country that strikes first. To improve its security, Country A enlarges its arsenal so that, in the bottom matrix, it can do as much harm in retaliation as Country B can do on a first strike (the 50%/50% cell). But this makes country B far more vulnerable to a first strike from Country A (the 20%/80% cell). Country B can restore its own security only by enlarging *its* arsenal. As this process repeats itself, we have an escalation in nuclear arms.

about the same number of missiles. The leaders of each nation have the choice of launching a first strike against the other or of waiting to retaliate until attacked by the other. Figure 13.4 presents the consequences of their joint choices.

The side that attacks first (see top matrix) can expect to destroy 50 percent of the population of the other side. The retaliation by the victim will be effective enough to destroy only 20 percent of the enemy's population. Of course, if neither side attacks first, then neither side will have attacked at all and each loses 0 percent of its population. Thus it is best not to attack at all. But if one side is convinced that the other is going to attack, then it is best to attack first.

In an effort to make an attack by the other side less likely, Country A decides to strengthen its forces to the point where its retaliation will do as much harm to Country B as Country B's first strike will have done to it. So Country A deploys more missiles. The new situation is displayed in the bottom matrix of Figure 13.4. If B strikes first, it will still wipe out 50 percent of A's population, but A's retaliation will now destroy 50 percent of B's population. The leaders of Country A think this increases their security by making it less attractive to B to strike first. And since A knows that it will not start the war, both will be safe.

But B does not trust A's leaders, and sees that if it waits to retaliate, it will lose 80 percent of its population while being able to kill only 20 percent of A's population. B decides that it must increase its own arsenal to create a greater deterrent against the possibility that Country A will attempt a first strike.

In the pursuit of its own security, each side makes the other side see an increased threat against which it must defend. As a result, the number of missiles keeps rising. What may make sense from a one-sided viewpoint could produce a joint result that is anything but sensible. The PDG matrix helps us to analyze how our actions will affect the world an opponent faces, and to try to predict what the opponent's response will be.

The Management and Resolution of Conflict

In the international arena, a war seems always to be raging somewhere. Within nations, competing groups seem to be locked in continual conflict. Although conflict may be inevitable, we can still aim toward an improvement in how conflict is *managed* (that is, what form the conflict will take) and how it can be *resolved* (whether it results in dissatisfaction and destruction or in a mutually satisfying outcome) (Himes, 1980).

In many realms conflict is managed well. Where once a conflict may have meant a protracted feud or a settlement by six-guns, we now have well-established, even ritualized, procedures for bringing the conflict to a resolution so that life can move on. Three familiar illustrations are sports, politics, and litigation. Each is gamelike and rule-ridden. But in each, parties subject their conflict to an accepted process of resolution and accept a final recognized result. Sports may seem a curious example, because there conflict and competition in a rule-ridden situation are not a problem; it is what sport is all about. But it is a helpful place to begin. Consider football. It illustrates a conflict between two groups competing for a victory. Its means are physical, even violent. Yet the conflict is carried on within a highly structured process which confines the allowable behavior, and both sides accept its methods and results. Each time a whistle blows, the battle stops until the next play resumes it. When the final gun is sounded, the combatants return to their respective locker rooms, one for celebration, the other for commiseration. The conflict is understood to be at an end, and its result is accepted by all.

In the political process, when a bill is passed or a candidate elected, the disputants accept the result without violent objection. They know that the way to fight further is in the next election, the next session, or in the courts. For centuries litigation has brought an end to a vast array of disputes among individuals and organizations who, without it, might have resorted to violence. The legal process provides a period of time for settlement by negotiation or, failing that, trial. Both sides play by complex and detailed rules. When the verdict is in and the final appeals are complete, both sides accept the result and get on with life.

In each of these systems, society has invented ways to allow conflict to be carried on within a structured process that permits a resolution and an end without violence. The conflict that remains within and between societies might someday be resolved similarly. In the international sphere, we see the beginnings of such systems in the United Nations, the International Court of Justice, and even laws, such as the Geneva Conventions, that govern the conduct of war (Howard, 1979).

Strategies for Resolving Conflict

A number of strategies have been developed for resolving conflict, or at least preventing its outbreak into destructive action. Many of them have proved effective, although some are less effective than others, or even counterproductive.

Threat Deterrence Threatening to do our adversary harm if the adversary engages in behavior we dislike is a familiar strategy. Whether we are talking about arms races or threats by unions and management to take action against each other, threat is a high-risk strategy which shows little evidence of real success in resolving conflict. Where one party is clearly much stronger, a credible threat can coerce the vulnerable party into submission. This is the strategy of *threat-deterrence:* we seek to deter undesirable conduct by threatening to respond to such behavior by inflicting harm. This deters open violence, at least temporarily, but fails to deal with the causes of the conflict. In bargaining situations, "threats increase the likelihood of immediate compliance, and concession." But in the long run, "the use of promises tends to increase the likelihood of bargainers reaching a mutually favorable agreement, while the use of threats tends to reduce this likelihood" (Rubin & Brown, 1975, pp. 283, 286).

Deutsch and Krauss (1960) have studied threats in bargaining using the Acme-Bolt Trucking Game (see Figure 13.5). The object for each player is to move his or her truck to its destination and thereby deliver its load and earn its profit. Each player can take a long route by which it will

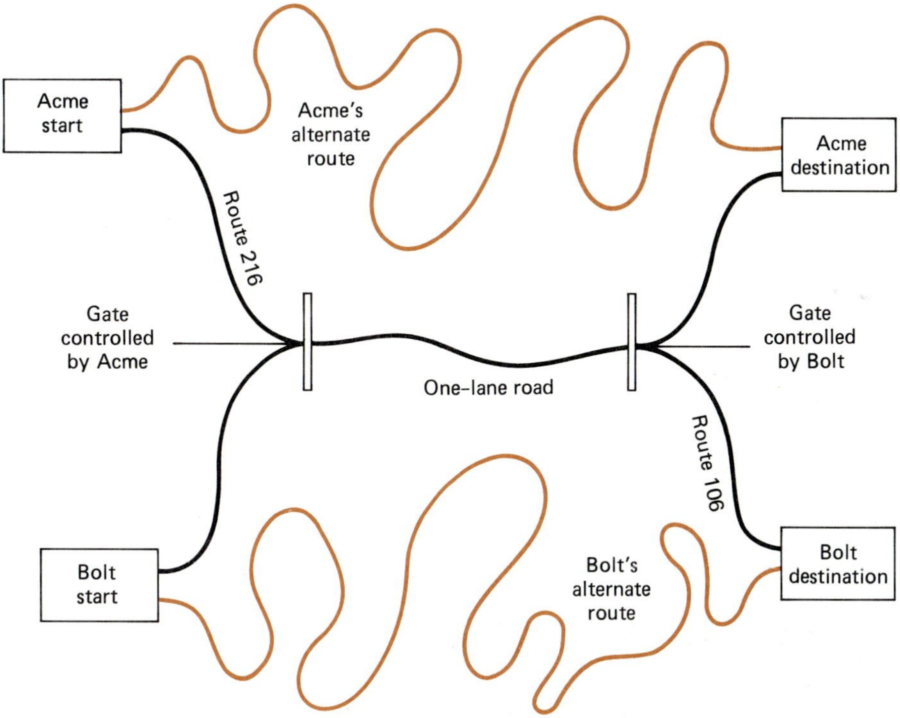

FIGURE 13.5
Participants' Road Map in the Acme-Bolt Trucking Game If Acme and Bolt take the long way around, they lose money. The most profitable route is the one-lane road. But to go that way, they need to find a way to cooperate with each other. *Source:* M. Deutsch and R. M. Krauss (1962). The effect of threat upon interpersonal bargaining. *Journal of Abnormal and Social Psychology, 61,* 183. Used with permission of the authors.

make only a little profit, or it can take a shortcut over a one-lane road and increase its profit. But only one truck at a time can pass over the one-lane road. If the players can find a way to cooperate over the use of the shortcut, they both gain; but if they compete over it, they may slow each other down and both make less money.

Threat was introduced by giving the power to one (unilateral) or to both (bilateral) sides to close a gate on the shortcut, making it impassable. When Acme had a weapon with which to threaten Bolt, they both achieved less than when neither had a weapon. When both had the weapon, they both did worst of all. Where both sides can match each other threat for threat and weapon for weapon, as in many international conflicts, threat often results not in deterrence but in escalation. Buildups increase the chances of war, rather than deterring it. Threat strategies usually accelerate rather than reduce conflict.

GRIT As we noted earlier, cooperation is maximized when each side's strategy is to make its behavior contingent on the other's. Osgood (1962) and Etzioni (1962) applied the notion of contingent cooperation to develop a method of reducing international tension and military threats through a series of unilateral initiatives. Osgood terms this strategy **GRIT** (*g*raduated *r*eciprocation *i*n *t*ension reduction). If mutual threat leads to escalation, they reasoned, mutual reduction might lead to de-escalation.

The opening moves consist of one side's planning, announcing, and carrying out a number of unilateral reductions, beginning with low-risk steps. Instead of building up its arms (so it can "negotiate from a position of strength"), it reduces them. If the other side reciprocates, a second set of more important tension-reducing moves is made. As the two sides gradually and alternately reduce their armaments and aggressive postures, each comes increasingly to believe the other side is interested in peace, which in turn makes possible progressively deeper reductions. If the opponent does not respond favorably early in the process, little has been risked and escalation can be resumed.

Evidence for the effectiveness of the technique has come from simulations (Lindskold, 1978, 1979; Lindskold & Collins, 1978; Crow, 1963; Pilisuk & Skolnick, 1968) as well as from the Kennedy Experiment (Etzioni, 1967, 1969). During the last months of his life, President John F. Kennedy was engaged in a GRIT strategy. For example, he banned further atmospheric nuclear tests by the United States and promised no resumption as long as other nations did not do so. His opening moves were quickly followed by some Soviet concessions, and there followed a series of U.S.-Soviet cooperative moves. Unfortunately, following JFK's assassination, U.S. policy turned aggressive again, in large part due to escalating U.S. involvement in Vietnam.

Superordinate Goals Sherif's experiments in intergroup conflict in boys' camps showed how easily conflict could erupt between competing groups, but Sherif also experimented with a number of techniques to replace the groups' conflict with cooperative relations. He found that conflict could be managed through the introduction of **superordinate goals.** A superordinate goal is a goal that both groups wish to achieve, but find they cannot without combining forces. They are not simply commonly desired goals, but goals where cooperation and common effort are required. For example, in one instance the camp's only truck broke down. Solving this problem—towing the truck—required the combined efforts of both groups working together. Sherif and Sherif (1953) found that the repeated experience of cooperation in the pursuit of superordinate goals progressively reduced the social distance and conflict between the groups.

The trouble with superordinate goals as a strategy for the deliberate resolution of conflict is that they can rarely be contrived; they must exist in the natural world of events experienced by the conflicting groups. Also, the most likely kind of superordinate goal is a common enemy. For example, the peoples of the earth might pull together to repel an invasion from an extraterrestrial enemy. But that particular superordinate goal provides no solution to conflict; it only expands it to a broader scope, with more groups aligned against other large coalitions.

The Contact Hypothesis As we noted, one of the consequences of conflict is a withdrawal from contact, resulting in autistic hostility. The contact hypothesis suggests that this process can be reversed, by providing opportunities for contact (Hill, 1982; Miller & Brewer, 1984). For example, sometimes assignments to schools, public housing, or military units separate or integrate people of different races. Several studies have shown positive change in the behavior and attitudes of members of different racial groups as the result of increased contact (Festinger, Schachter, & Back, 1950; Star, Williams, & Stouffer, 1965; Saenger, 1953).

Still, contact itself is not a magical cure (Sherif et al., 1961; Deutsch & Collins, 1951). It can be an occasion for confrontation, irritation, and escalation of conflict. Just being together is not enough. The conditions of the contact and the experiences that occur during it are important. Contact is more likely to reduce conflict when it takes place under conditions of equal status—intimacy as opposed to superficiality, and cooperation rather than competition (Amir, 1976; Cook & Selltiz, 1955; Worchel, 1979; Norvell & Worchel, 1981). If one group gives the orders and the other has to take them, if they are competing for scarce resources, or if they cannot get to know each other as individuals, contact will not reduce their conflict. Some integrated housing projects have combined low-income housing for poor minorities with more elegant housing for the middle class. The lack of equal status and superficiality of the contact probably dooms such efforts.

Negotiation **Negotiation** is the process whereby representatives of the disputing groups meet with each other directly to discuss whether some accommodation of their differences can be agreed upon (Strauss, 1978).

In Middle Eastern markets, all transactions are characterized by negotiation. Each party states its position on price, and then a compromise that is agreeable to both sides must be reached.

We are accustomed to seeing news stories about negotiations between representatives of disputing nations and between management and labor. Negotiation between less formally or legally organized groups, such as those involved in interracial conflict, is rarely attempted. Although the process of negotiation does not always go smoothly, bringing the parties face-to-face forces them to test their ideas about what a "good solution" is against the reality of the other party's position. As a result, the overly simple perceptions and solutions that sometimes arise out of what Janis (1982) describes as *groupthink* (see Chapter 12 for more detail) can often be avoided.

The most common orientation negotiations take is **conflictive bargaining,** in which each side adopts strategies and tactics for winning the most concessions while giving up the fewest. Much research in social psychology and other fields has sought to determine which strategies are most successful in concluding the most self-serving agreements. In general, such results are gained by the side that makes extreme initial demands, followed by concessions that are few, small, reciprocal, and rationalized to the opponent (Lawler & MacMurray, 1980).

To find out why some negotiations are more successful than others at producing resolutions, research has looked to a vast array of factors, including the number of parties and their historical and current relationship, physical settings, time limits, communication channels, and the personal characteristics of the bargainers (Morley & Stephenson, 1977; Zartman & Berman, 1982; Rubin & Brown, 1975; Druckman, 1977). Consider the single matter of whether a negotiation should be conducted in secret or in the open—with the negotiators' progress accessible to the constituents and the news media. Druckman has shown that less progress is made in open negotiations because the negotiators must posture more, are constrained not to try creative options, and must answer almost immediately for each move they make. President Carter's success in bringing about the Camp David accords between Egypt and Israel probably is attributable in part to the fact that the talks took place in a setting of enforced privacy (Rubin, 1981).

Despite the competitive orientations of most negotiations, it is possible to achieve cooperative solutions. In **integrative bargaining,** or *problem-solving negotiation,* parties engage each other not for the purpose of using the bargaining table as a place to win their dispute at the other's expense, but instead to fashion a mutually advantageous solution (Deutsch, 1973; Pruitt, 1981; Carnevalle, Pruitt, & Seilheimer, 1981; Pruitt & Lewis, 1977). Sometimes this is called a *win-win* strategy, as contrasted with conflictive bargaining, which starts out as win-lose and often ends up as lose-lose (Blake, Shepard, & Mouton, 1964). Consider a union and a company that go to the bargaining table, each seeking as complete a victory as possible. The result can be a delayed settlement or none at all, a prolonged strike, or eventually a bankrupt company. Instead of glorious victory, both the workers and the stockholders wind up with nothing. With integrative bargaining, both sides arrive looking for ways they can achieve many of their goals together.

Despite its frequent use, negotiation has been found a disappointing technique for reducing conflict. For this reason some researchers and theorists have looked, in one direction, to unilateral initiatives (e.g., GRIT), or, in the other direction, to third-party mediation. A primary cause of the difficulty with negotiations is the limited power representatives on both sides have to reach an agreement by which their respective

FROM THE FIELD
Irving L. Janis

Irving Janis's research covers so wide a range that he may be regarded as a social psychologist for all seasons. In this chapter we are most interested in his contributions to the understanding of intergroup conflict and the pervasive distortions that characterize decision making by political leaders—research for which he received the APA's Distinguished Scientific Contribution Award and the Kurt Lewin Memorial Award for integrating psychological research and social action. After spending most of his career at Yale, Janis is now at U.C. Berkeley doing research on errors made by top-level national leaders during international crises so that we may improve the management of crises in the future.

IN THE NEWS

SUPPORT GROWS FOR U.S. SCHOOL FOR PEACE

The idea surfaced for the first time in 1793, when Benjamin Banneker, a black philosopher, and Benjamin Rush, a signer of the Declaration of Independence, proposed a U.S. Department of Peace. It got nowhere.

On 139 more occasions since 1940, proposals for either a Department of Peace or a U.S. Academy for Peace have been introduced in Congress. None ever even reached the hearing stage. . . .

For the last six years, proponents have been raising money and wielding congressional support for a government-funded school in the Washington area that would train diplomatic and military personnel and other professionals in techniques for conflict resolution and peacemaking. . . .

Rep. Dan Glickman (D-Kan.), a strong supporter, said the academy's three-fold mandate would be to conduct research in peacemaking, to train individuals from government, private enterprise and voluntary associations in peacemaking skills, and to serve as an information clearinghouse in the field.

The proposal embraces some of the broad concepts that have been refined in the work of Roger Fisher, a Harvard Law School professor and an expert on the new negotiating techniques. He told the House committee [investigating the proposal] that "work at the Harvard Negotiation Project over the last few years has convinced us that there are some basic, common-sense concepts relevant to dealing with international conflict that are too often ignored, that can be learned and that can make a big difference."

These conflict-resolution techniques have begun to be used successfully in re-

groups will be bound. Negotiators often comment on the difficulty of deciding whether it was their opposites at the negotiating sessions or their superiors back home who were harder to deal with.

Still, many people feel that negotiations fail because we know too little about the process. As you can see in the In the News box, support for an Academy of Peace that would train negotiators has surfaced sporadically for almost 200 years. Although Congress finally did approve it, it has not been funded and therefore has not been active.

Third-Party Intervention The methods of conflict resolution discussed so far have involved only the principals to the dispute. An important alternative is the involvement of third parties in a variety of roles and serving a variety of functions (Rubin, 1981a; Grigsby & Bigoness, 1982). Typical third-party roles include adjudication and mediation. In *adjudication* the parties submit their dispute to judges who hear the facts and arguments and render a decision. In domestic disputes the government will enforce the judge's decision. In international disputes the parties are expected to comply but, of course, no international coercive power yet exists to compel compliance.

solving hostage-takings and calming prison riots, he said. Though "lawyers have spent a thousand years working on the litigation process," he said, "comparatively little work has been done on improving the negotiation process."

Fisher said there is an urgent need to start assembling all known materials on "the state of art" in the field of conflict resolution both for immediate use by negotiators and in preparation for the research and teaching functions of the proposed peace academy. . . .

Supporters point out that the start-up cost of $66 million to build and operate the academy for its first four years is one-fifth the cost of a B1 bomber. Beyond that, Milton C. Mapes, Jr., executive director of the National Peace Academy Campaign, stresses that "the first major effect of the Peace Academy would be its symbolism in establishing U.S. leadership in the field of creative peacemaking."

In arguing their case, advocates of the proposal like to quote General of the Army Omar Bradley, who said that "we have grasped the mystery of the atom and rejected the Sermon on the Mount. Ours is a world of nuclear giants and ethical infants. We know more about war than we do about peace. We know more of killing than we do of living."

Supporters believe that graduates of a future U.S. Academy for Peace, a fourth of whom would come from other countries, would make the world a safer place by helping nations find better and surer ways to wage peace rather than war.

Source: Robert Levey, *The Boston Globe,* August 4, 1982, p. 3. Reprinted courtesy of The Boston Globe.

In **mediation** an informal third party serves as a catalyst to help the parties reach a settlement. Henry Kissinger's "shuttle diplomacy" in the Middle East provides a prominent example of mediation. Mediators can suggest solutions and options the principals themselves may not be able to recognize, and can enhance communication by conveying information under conditions of less tension than if the parties communicated directly. Mediators promote integrative as opposed to conflictive bargaining and can work to increase the motivation and ability of the parties to reach agreement (Hamilton, Swap, & Rubin, 1981b; Rubin, 1980, 1981a).

To generalize about third parties is difficult because they can occupy a number of roles and serve a variety of functions. But experimental research as well as descriptive accounts of the effects of third parties suggest that they generally facilitate more rapid and effective resolution than two-party negotiations alone (e.g., Pruitt & Johnson, 1970; Podell & Knapp, 1969; Krauss & Deutsch, 1966). Knowledge of the role of third parties is increasingly being applied in a variety of settings, among them disputes among community groups (Fisher, 1976; McGillis, 1981), divorce (Spencer & Zammit, 1976), and international conflicts (Fischer, 1980; Kelman & Cohen, 1979).

Let us look at a specific application of social psychology aimed at reducing the conflict in the Middle East. The *problem-solving workshop* has evolved through the efforts of Australian diplomat John Burton and social psychologists Leonard Doob and Herbert Kelman (Kelman, 1965, 1981, 1982; Kelman & Cohen, 1979; Doob, 1970, 1974). It has been employed as part of the efforts to settle conflicts in places such as East Africa, Northern Ireland, and the Middle East.

Problem-solving workshops begin with a team of social scientist mediators who are committed to a peaceful solution. They are personally invested in the conflict, but they also are approximately evenly balanced between the conflicting groups. Thus, Kelman's Middle East team consists of several Jews and several Arabs. Members of each national group are understandably suspicious of the strangers, so time is required to build enough trust so they will seriously consider joining the workshop. Agreeing to sit down and talk with one's enemy is a large step that many people in an intense conflict are unwilling to take.

The ideal participant is considered to be a highly influential person who is not in a decision-making position. Official leaders are usually too constrained by political pressures to step away from the party line long enough to try new perceptions and create new options. Influential nonleaders, such as aides to or friends of the leaders, are in a position to do so, and then to communicate their views to the decision makers.

The next step is to hold separate pre-workshop meetings between the mediating team and representatives of each national group. A major purpose served by these meetings is to develop internal group cohesion, much as Sherif's campers did, as well as an agenda of issues. Also, strong assertions of out-group prejudice are more easily made at the pre-workshop meetings than at the workshop itself, and these shared prejudices further cement group cohesion. This helps ensure that the workshop will be a reflection of group, not individual, conflict; and that movement by a group member will not be dismissed as meaningless, since the in-group members have come to know and trust each other.

The workshop itself is situated in a context where pressures to adhere to entrenched views are reduced. It is typically held on a university campus, where free exploratory discussions are widely seen as acceptable, strictly unofficial, and without protocol. The meetings are kept isolated and confidential so that the participants are not continually influenced by and kept accountable to the larger groups to which they belong.

By the time the workshop begins, a number of important things have already inevitably occurred:

1. Autistic hostility has been overcome; the disputants are poised for face-to-face communication.

2. Whatever happens, they will see each other, perhaps for the first time, as human beings rather than as a forbidding national monolith.
3. A third party is present, which in itself tends to draw disputants out of hardened positions.
4. Although the groups are coming together, they are insulated from any official consequences of this act.
5. The usual norms that govern interaction between these groups are counteracted by the norms of the setting.

At the workshop, mediators present the goals and ground rules to the groups. They are encouraged to adopt a problem-solving focus, to collaborate on the analysis of the problem, and to try to invent solutions. In addition they are to analyze their perceptions of each other and their interactions with each other, on the assumption that the intergroup conflict will continually assert itself within the workshop. In short, the conflict is a "shared dilemma requiring some common effort for its solution" (Kelman & Cohen, 1979, p. 288). The goal of the workshop is to help the participants see the conflict and the people involved in a new light and from new angles.

The meetings are by no means academic conversation. They are intense interactions. The social scientist mediators do not promote harmony in the workshop, but try to generate analysis and new learning. They facilitate the interaction of the groups, guiding the discussion away from accusatory, legalistic, and conflict-expressive tracks and toward a task-oriented analysis of the conflict. The social scientists offer (1) theoretical input, to help distance the participants from the intensity of their larger conflict; (2) content observations, to draw out interpretations and implications of what has been said in the group and to fill in blind spots; and (3) process observations, to turn attention to here-and-now interaction.

This process breaks down the stereotyped, dehumanized, and distorted thinking about each other that is typical of intergroup conflict. It places the participants in direct contact with their adversaries under conditions where new perceptions are facilitated. Each group finds itself engaged in a process of cooperative analysis and problem solving with its adversary. If integrative solutions to the conflict are not found, the participants have at least acquired some new ways of thinking about the conflict and its eventual resolution.

SUMMARY

1. As groups increase beyond the size at which they can have face-to-face contact, group processes such as cohesiveness, communication, organization, and decision making become increasingly difficult to manage. Moreover, intergroup conflict becomes a serious problem.

2. Collective behavior takes place when a person is a member of a loosely structured and usually temporary group. Examples include mobs, riots, panics, emergencies, revolutions, and social movements.
3. The various kinds of collective behavior vary according to whether they are destructive or not, short- or long-lived, addressed to unique or to recurrent problems, and whether their impact is to fine-tune society or to have profound effects.
4. Deindividuation refers to the process of becoming lost or submerged in a group, and often results in bizarre, violent, or destructive behavior. Its causes include increased anonymity, diffused responsibility, and active participation in group activity.
5. Organizations are the most planned and structured of large group phenomena. These structures may vary from the typical hierarchical business organization familiar in the United States to the more democratic Israeli kibbutz; from Swedish assembly plants in which workers have a great deal of autonomy to cooperatives in which the consumers are also the owners.
6. Organizations may be analyzed at the levels of the individual, the social structure, and the technostructure. The way an organization is structured affects the way people interact with each other and perceive each other.
7. Classical organizational theory saw people as extensions of the equipment and tasks, and was used by scientific managers to improve the efficiency of organizations. Classical managers often subscribed to Theory X, a perspective that sees people as lazy and unmotivated.
8. Human relations theory, corresponding to Theory Y, added to organizational theorizing and understanding of workers by seeing them as social beings who would seek responsibility and exercise creativity given the proper circumstances.
9. Psychologists who apply knowledge of organizational behavior specialize in "organizational development." Examples of their methods include job enrichment and enlargement, sensitivity training, and survey feedback.
10. Intergroup conflict occurs when the goals, interests, and actions of one group are incompatible with those of another. The objects of a conflict may include economic competition, power, and value conflicts. Some conflict, such as that between political parties or competing theories, is constructive.
11. Conflicts may have objective material bases (veridical conflict) or may only be perceived (false). In some cases (contingent conflict), the parties do not recognize how easily the competition could be avoided, and in others (displaced conflict) battles may be generated over conflicts other than the real issues. Misattributed conflict is directed at the wrong group, and latent conflict exists when a real basis for disagreement exists but is not perceived by the two parties.

12. The minimum conditions for conflict include the existence of an in-group and an out-group. As people operate under a "we" versus "they" orientation, misperceptions, prejudice, and stereotyping of the out-group often occur.
13. Responses to conflict have been studied using a number of methods, among them the Prisoner's Dilemma Game. Responses to conflict may be cooperative or competitive. The kind of response varies depending upon each side's characteristic style and expectations and the other's behavior. The greatest amount of cooperation results from the strategy of contingent cooperation ("I'll cooperate if you do").
14. Strategies that have been tried to reduce conflict and whose effects have been studied include threat deterrence, GRIT, superordinate goals, equal status contact, negotiation, third-party intervention, and problem-solving workshops.

APPENDIX: RESEARCH METHODOLOGY

This appendix provides further details on the methods of research in social psychology introduced in Chapter 1.

Modes of Observation

In whatever setting research takes place, some way of observing the behavior under study must be devised. By *modes of observation* we mean the sorts of data collection instruments, devices, or channels of observation available to a researcher. Many of them will already be familiar to you because they are so widely used in modern society.

Questionnaires Written questionnaires are often given to people asking them to record their recollections, opinions, or beliefs about various matters. Questionnaires may be used in diverse research techniques such as surveys, where they can be mailed to people around the country or around the world, or as the means of collecting data at the conclusion of a laboratory experiment.

Interview Protocols Also known as interview schedules, these are almost identical to questionnaires except that instead of being filled out by research participants themselves, they form a script for an interviewer to ask and record an interviewee's responses. The interview can take place face-to-face or by telephone.

Objective Tests and Scales Some paper-and-pencil measuring instruments are designed to sample complex sets of behaviors such as personality traits or aptitude or intelligence, and have themselves been studied and validated. What makes them "objective" is that they contain a fixed assortment of response options. Typically they are multiple-choice options or a scale on which a person circles the extent to which he or she agrees with a statement.

Projective Tests Projective tests contrast with objective tests in that they provide people with a loosely structured stimulus and invite them to project their feelings or judgments onto it. The person's answers will then be reviewed by an expert scorer who interprets the responses according to the purposes of the test. The Rorschach inkblot test is a familiar example of a projective test.

Physiological Instruments For some social psychological research, physiological states or responses must be measured (Cacioppo & Petty, 1983). Methods include measures of electrical resistance of the skin (galvanic skin response), heart rate and blood pressure, and various chemical secretions in the blood that may, for example, be an index of stress.

Systematic Observation of Behavior One of the most straightforward ways of studying behavior is simply to observe it. Does a person go to the aid of another person in distress? How long does it take? What action does the person take? For any given study, the researcher knows exactly what behaviors to look for, and has data sheets on which to record them. But in other kinds of research, a participant-observer may take field notes on a great variety of things, and then try to sort them out carefully later.

Unobtrusive Measures Sometimes looking at or asking about behavior interferes with getting at a person's real responses. An alternative is the use of unobtrusive measures, in which a researcher can look at some artifact or residue of behavior (Webb et al., 1981). For example, noseprints on store windows or the degree of wear and tear on the floor near a museum exhibit can indicate the relative popularity of displays in ways that an interviewer may not be able to learn about. People might say they love the abstract Picasso, when they actually spend more time around the realistic nude by Eakins.

Archival Data All of the modes of observation discussed so far involve active data collection by the researcher. Another approach is to make use of "archival" data collected by others for other purposes. Police, court, school, and medical records are examples. Economists rely almost entirely on data collected by government and business and, unlike social psychologists, hardly ever collect original data (or need to).

Sampling

Whichever mode of data collection social psychologists use to study behavior, they have to question or observe some portion of the people rather than deal with everyone. A *sample* is a part of a population of people or things studied in order to understand the whole. Accordingly, the central issue is not size of the sample or whether it is drawn randomly, but rather its *representativeness.* A representative sample is one that faithfully reflects the population from which it is drawn. If you were doing a survey of voters' opinions, a properly selected representative sample of a few dozen people would be more informative than a survey of all 14,000 people attending one of the national party conventions. A representative sample provides a sound basis for generalizing about the population from which the sample is drawn. Unrepresentative (or "biased") samples can lead to erroneous conclusions. Consider the sampling problems involved in Freud's studies of small numbers of troubled well-to-do Victorian women in nineteenth-century Austria. Or consider the possibility of unrepresentativeness due to a heavy reliance on college students when the researcher is interested in generalizing to the adult population in general. Because of the importance of gaining representativeness in sampling, many specific techniques have evolved to fit particular research situations (see, for example, Kish, 1965; Rossi, Wright, & Anderson, 1983).

Measurement

Any research problem begins with *conceptual definitions* of what is under study. What is the study about? What are the concepts important to the phenomena being examined? We might be interested in attitudes, conformity, or the attribution of blame. We must first define what a concept means; that is, we must specify a conceptual definition.

In order to connect these abstract concepts to empirical data, they must be translated into *operational definitions.* An operational definition translates the concept to be studied into a set of procedures that will be used to measure it. One researcher's operational definition of aggression may be the voltage level of shocks one person is giving to another person in a laboratory experiment. Another researcher may operationally define aggression as the number of fights a married couple reports having had over the past year, or the number of arrests for murder that appear in a person's police record. Thus operational definitions are an important way of communicating just what a researcher means by a concept. They permit other researchers or consumers of the research to better assess a study's conclusions.

However we go about measuring variables, they may play different roles. The two most important of these roles are as independent and dependent variables. An *independent variable* is, essentially, the "cause," and the *dependent variable* is the "effect." In an experiment to discover whether an audience is more persuaded by an extreme or by a moderate statement of a position, the independent variable would be the extremity of the communication and the dependent variable would be the amount of attitude change that resulted.

Every device for measuring variables can be evaluated as to its reliability and validity. *Reliability* is the property of yielding consistent and stable measurements. If you weigh yourself twice on a scale, a reliable scale will give the same value both times. The *validity* of a measure is the extent to which it measures what it purports to measure. A bathroom scale may be sensitive and reliable. If it is used to measure weight it would also be valid. However, if we tried to use a bathroom scale as a measure of intelligence, it would not be a valid measure.

Research Designs and Inference

All of the foregoing features of a piece of research must be put together into an overall research design. The major kinds are case studies, correlational studies, true experiments, and quasi-experiments.

Which kind of design is best? That depends upon the research questions and the circumstances of the study. Each has characteristics that make it useful for some purposes but not for others. That is, some questions can be answered by a particular kind of study, but cannot be answered well by other kinds of studies. If a question can be asked from different angles using different methods, and the same answer results each time, our confidence that it is the right answer is increased (Campbell & Fiske, 1959). Before examining the advantages and disadvantages of several different kinds of studies, it is helpful to discuss two new kinds of validity: internal validity and external validity. Internal and external validity are two aspects of the design of a research study (Campbell & Stanley, 1963; Cook & Campbell, 1979).

Internal validity refers to the ability of the design to provide clear cause-effect inferences. Some studies are designed so that the research can unambiguously infer a cause-effect connection between the independent and dependent variables. With other designs, any inferences about causality are doubtful. Such barriers to strong inference are called "threats to internal validity," or "confounds."

External validity refers to generalizability. Are the people, techniques, and circumstances of a study representative of those to which we will want to apply the findings? An externally valid study is one that gives us results that can be generalized beyond the bounds of that single study. Let us turn to some specific designs and see how they stand up to threats to their validity.

Case Studies A case study is a research design in which one person or group is studied in depth. We learn a great deal, descriptively, about the person or group being studied, and can even observe changes over time. But any attempt to draw inferences about the causes of the observed changes will be highly speculative, because this design is riddled with threats to its internal validity.

For example, someone might look to a case study to try to determine why people take up smoking. The case study might show that the person under study was a normal, healthy 12-year-old. He became interested in Hollywood movies and acquired some heroes of the silver screen. The study might conclude that he smoked because they smoked, and therefore that people in general acquire the desire to smoke in essentially the same way. Such a study is a poor test of cause and effect because it cannot rule out the multitude of other possible causes. In this example, the other causes might be peer pressure, parents who smoked, or some kind of biological sensitivity to the chemistry of tobacco that makes a person especially likely to become a smoker. To single out any one variable as *the* cause of change in a dependent variable is impossible with a case study.

In terms of external validity, case studies also have limitations. The major problem with a case study is that it is as small a sample as one can collect. That is, even if the person in the case study engaged in the behavior for the reasons concluded by the study, there is no reason to believe that the same causes exist for people in general.

Correlational Studies Another way to study the causes of smoking would be to gather data on a larger sample of people and to look for patterns of relationships among variables such that certain ones are associated with smoking and others are not. This is the correlational method. In such a study we might find that the degree to which admired people (especially parents and celebrities) are perceived as being smokers correlates with whether the people in the study are smokers are not.

One of the most familiar kinds of correlational studies is the *survey,* typically used to gather information on public opinion, but also useful for inquiring about beliefs, experiences, and other kinds of information. A researcher could send questionnaires out to people, or conduct telephone or face-to-face interviews, and collect their responses. Then the researcher can analyze the results to see what correlational relationships emerge among the variables in the survey.

The pitfalls of correlational studies are so well known to social scientists that they have a saying about them: "Correlation does not prove causation." Two things may correlate, such as marital status and a host of other variables: life expectancy, income, health, criminal conduct, etc. Married men are healthier, wealthier, live longer, and commit fewer crimes than single men. Some commentators have concluded hastily that this means if more single men would get married, they and the world would be better off (Gilder, 1974). That may be, but it does not follow from the above data. Rather than marital status being the cause of all those other variables, the variables themselves may affect whether a given man stays single or marries. That is, men who are sickly, poor, or actively involved in crime may be less attractive to women, or for other reasons be less likely to marry.

Another aspect of correlation and causation is the "third variable" problem. Two things, such as number of televisions owned and grades in school, may correlate positively. But that may not mean that to raise your grades you should buy more television sets. More likely, the family's socioeconomic status (a third variable) is responsible for both the number of televisions and the children's performance in school.

In the example we have been considering, some other variable might be responsible for making the person smoke, and as a smoker the person tended to admire others who smoked. Thus, instead of taking up smoking because admired others smoked, it could be the other way around, and the real cause would remain undiscovered.

True Experiments Virtually all of the problems of internal validity are solved by the true experiment. The essence of the true experiment is random assignment of people to experimental and control groups. Experimental and control groups are groups of people identical to each other except that one receives a treatment and the other does not, or one receives one type of treatment (that is, one level of an independent variable) and the other receives a different treatment. "Control," in this context, means "comparison." A control group provides a basis for comparison so that we know what the effect of an independent variable is.

Note how this simple procedure eliminates most of the confounds. For example, imagine that a group of young people were randomly assigned to grow up in homes with parents who either did or did not smoke, or whose Hollywood heroes did or did not smoke. The smoking-hero and nonsmoking-hero groups, by virtue of having been randomly assigned to their groups, are alike in every way except the difference produced by the independent variable. Overall (or on the average) the groups will not differ in their biological or experiential backgrounds, or in the things that will happen to them during the experiment. The only thing that can account for any differing results is the independent variable. By thus eliminating the effects of confounds, the true experiment is a design with a high degree of internal validity, and it allows unambiguous cause-effect inferences to be made.

Note that the nature of the design has nothing to do with its setting. Although laboratory studies are almost always true experiments, true experiments can also be carried out in field settings. The practicalities of working in the field, however, sometimes make it extremely difficult and sometimes unethical to assign people randomly to conditions. It was for those situations where true experiments were not feasible that quasi-experiments were invented.

Quasi-Experiments A quasi-experiment is a study that lacks a true, randomly created control group, but whose control group can be shown nevertheless to be a good one (Campbell & Stanley, 1963; Campbell & Ross, 1968; Cook & Campbell, 1979). For example, we might be able to find groups of adolescents who are alike in all important respects except that they differ systematically according to some of the independent variables we are interested in. Or, if we are interested in how advertising affects smoking behavior, we could look at the effects that seem to result from different advertising campaigns that come along from time to time. In quasi-experiments we try to rule out confounds by logic or by additional data collection. Such studies are not as elegant as true experiments are, but researchers try to make them approximate true experiments so that they can generate some conclusions about cause and effect.

GLOSSARY

action research An approach to research and application in which the two are carried out simultaneously. Solutions to social problems are tested in real-world settings in ways that yield improved understanding at the same time social change is produced.

actor-observer effect The tendency for people to attribute the behavior of others to dispositional causes, while attributing their own behavior more to situational causes.

aggression Any form of behavior directed toward the goal of harming or injuring another living being who is motivated to avoid such harm.

altruism A special form of helping behavior in which a person acts without any expectation or desire of reward or recognition.

altruistic paradox The continued existence of altruism when there are no apparent rewards for its maintenance.

anchor The basis of comparison in social judgment, perception, and especially attitude change. A standard against which other positions are compared.

androgyny A condition or state whereby an individual incorporates in a flexible way characteristics that are considered both masculine and feminine.

anticonformity A process in which an individual is aware of the opinion or behavior of a group and then moves in the opposite direction in order to show rejection of that opinion or behavior.

applied research Research that is "problem-centered," addressed to finding or testing the validity of solutions to human problems. Compare *basic research.*

assimilation The process whereby objects or attitudinal positions are perceived to be more similar to an anchor than they really are.

attitude A general and enduring feeling, positive or negative, about a social object.

attribution theory A theory dealing with the processes by which people try to determine the causes of their own and others' behavior. The inferences made usually refer to causes that are dispositional (internal) or situational (external).

authoritarian personality A syndrome of attitudes that is characteristic of a pre-fascist personality type. The attitudes include prejudice against minority groups, political and economic conservatism, overconcern about social status, obedience to authority, and a belief in conventional conduct in all spheres of life.

Barnum effect In personality theory, the process whereby people presented with a personality profile consisting of generalities that fit nearly everybody tend to think that it describes them in particular, incorrectly concluding that the person or theory that produced the profile is able to produce a valid measurement of their personalities.

basic research Research aimed at building knowledge by testing the adequacy of theories. Compare *applied research.*

behavioral intention A product of attitudes; a plan of action, not the action itself.

beliefs Perceived relations among objects and

events that categorize objects, or combine them with a fact or attribute.

blaming the victim The act of placing blame on the very people who suffer from an injustice. It involves the assumption that people must be responsible for the bad things that happen to them.

bogus pipeline A device for increasing the candor in self-reports of attitudes; a complicated technique that involves making people believe that an electrical instrument can measure their true attitudes, which makes them reluctant to conceal these attitudes.

boomerang effect In attitude change, the process whereby persuasive arguments that are too extreme from the viewpoint of the audience produce attitude change in a direction opposite to that sought by the source.

brainstorming A group problem-solving technique in which members of the group are asked to delay critical analysis of each others' suggestions until all ideas are "on the table." Only then will assessment leading to the final decision take place.

brainwashing A process inducing massive or extreme change of a person's attitudes and/or values. Although brainwashing is linked to exotic techniques and the use of drugs, it can be effected by basic techniques of social influence, such as the removal of an individual from all other sources of social support.

brutalization effect A phenomenon believed to occur when acts of violence increase as a result of public awareness of the enforcement of the death penalty. It is suggested that society relays the message that retributive violence is acceptable, a message on which people then model their behavior toward others.

catharsis Psychodynamically derived notion proposing that aggression can be reduced when people are allowed to exhibit mild forms of it or to observe others acting violently.

central traits Those characteristics of a person (such as being warm or cold) that are related to many other traits, and which have the capacity to make a strong impact on the perception and evaluation of that person.

channel The medium through which a persuasive message travels.

classical conditioning The learning process by which previously neutral stimuli (the conditioned stimuli) come to elicit emotional, or attitudinal, reactions after they have been associated with stimuli that already have the power to elicit emotional responses (unconditioned stimuli).

cognitive dissonance A central feature of a theory by the same name which posits that humans have a built-in motivation to maintain consistency among cognitive elements and that inconsistency produces psychological discomfort, called dissonance. Whenever dissonance is aroused, the person will act to reduce it. Attitude change is one path of dissonance reduction.

cognitive theories Theories that focus on the processes by which human beings perceive, store, and process social information and the ways in which they use this information to guide their everyday interactions with others.

cohesiveness The sense of closeness, or "we-ness," that a group feels. The sum of forces that keep a group together.

collective behavior Behavior exhibited by crowds or mobs, such as religious revivals, panics, manias, riots, revolutions, and social movements.

communication model An approach to the study of attitude change, developed at Yale University. This perspective proposes that attitude change involves a process whereby in order for persuasion to occur, a listener must attend to a communication, comprehend it, yield to it, and then, if the persuasion is to be more than only momentary, retain the message.

communication networks Patterns of communication to and from group members. The various patterns are termed chain, kite (Y), wheel, circle, and comcon.

companionate love The deep, mature, caring love we feel for family and long-time friends. It may be the type of love we feel for a partner once our passionate love has cooled.

complementarity The condition in which two people have needs or characteristics that supply each other's lack. For example, if one likes to have his or her own way about things, a complementary person would be one who is submissive to the other's wishes.

compliance (1) A process in which an individual accepts social influence in order to receive social or material rewards or to avoid some form of punishment. (2) The process of following the advice or recommendation of a health professional.

compresence The merest gathering together of people and animals with members of their own kind.

conflictive bargaining A style of bargaining in which each side adopts strategies and tactics for winning the most concessions while giving up the fewest.

conformity A process in which an individual is aware of the opinion or behavior of a group and then moves in that direction in order to show acceptance of that opinion or behavior.

contagion In analogy to an infectious epidemic, a term referring to the spread of new ways of acting and thinking among the people affected by social discontinuity. It is one of the processes involved in collective behavior.

contingency model of leadership A theory of group leadership that takes into account situations, leadership style, and personality.

contrast The process whereby objects or attitudinal positions are perceived to be more unlike an anchor than they really are.

credibility The expertise and trustworthiness of the source of a persuasive communication. Highly credible sources can (1) be authoritative on the subject, and (2) be trusted to provide a relatively unbiased account of their understanding of the facts.

crowding A psychological or subjective state in which people experience dissatisfaction or discomfort owing to the presence of too many other people.

deductive Inferring particulars from general principles. In theory development, the phase in which a theory is subjected to empirical verification. Hypotheses based on the theory are derived and tested against new empirical observations. Compare *inductive.*

defensible space An environment in which physical spaces are subdivided and surveillance opportunities are created so as to encourage people to feel territorial and to care for and defend their surroundings actively.

deindividuation Condition where people are unidentifiable as individuals, highly aroused, focused on a novel and unstructured situation, and "lose" themselves in their activities and surroundings. Deindividuation often leads to bizarre, violent, and destructive behavior.

demand characteristics The expectations and perceptions of participants in experiments, whereby the participants successfully discern the expectations of the research and as a result confirm the experimental hypotheses.

density An objective state of the environment defined in terms of the number of people per unit space.

desensitization A process by which individuals' inhibitions to aggression become reduced as the result of repeated exposure to violence in the environment around them (especially in the media).

displaced aggression Aggression that is redirected at a target more convenient or less threatening than the original source because of the inhibiting characteristics of that source.

door-in-the-face technique A method of influence in which a large request is made, and then (once the large request has been rejected) a smaller, more reasonable request—the one desired in the first place—is made. Compare *foot-in-the-door technique.*

dyad A group composed of two persons.

empathy An emotional state that occurs when people identify with and actually attempt to place themselves in the perspective of someone in need of aid.

empirical A term describing the acquisition of knowledge through one's senses, through observation, and through experience.

equity The condition in which people receive benefits in proportion to their contributions.

ethnocentrism The tendency of in-groups to devalue out-groups, to see their own group's behavior as normal and correct and out-group behavior as abnormal and incorrect.

evaluation apprehension Concern or anxiety produced by being judged by others.

experimenter expectancy effect A problem of

interaction between experimenter and participant in which the researcher testing a hypothesis has an expectation about it that influences the outcome of the experiment.

fear appeals Messages that urge attitude change on the basis of fears held by the audience.

fear of success A concern that achievement in competitive situations could lead to negative consequences. Once thought to be a personality characteristic associated exclusively with females, it is now believed that fear of success can be experienced by anyone engaged in out-of-role competition.

field research Research that takes place in the setting in which the behavior of interest normally occurs. Settings can be workplaces, people's homes, police cars, etc.

field theory A theory conceiving of behavior as a joint product of all the forces acting on a person, both internal (psychological and biological) and external (social and physical environment).

foot-in-the-door technique A method of influence in which a small request is made, and then (once this small request has been granted) a second, larger request—the one desired in the first place—is made. Compare *door-in-the-face technique.*

forewarning A device that under certain conditions makes an audience resistant to persuasion, in which audience members are told in advance that they are going to hear a message intended to bring about attitude change.

frustration-aggression theory A theory positing that all frustration leads to aggression and that all aggression is caused by frustration. This theory has been revised to acknowledge the multiple possible causes of aggression as well as other outlets for frustration.

fundamental attribution error The tendency of people to attribute behavior to dispositional causes rather than to situational ones. People are especially subject to this error when explaining the behavior of others rather than their own behavior.

gender Those characteristics of males and females that are attributable to learning, culture, or experience.

GRIT *G*raduated *r*eciprocal *r*eduction *i*n *t*ension. A strategy applying the notion of contingent cooperation in order to reduce international tension and military threats. GRIT involves a series of unilateral initiatives leading to progressive de-escalation of conflict.

group polarization phenomenon The tendency among groups to magnify any judgmental trends that come into the group as the preferences of the individuals.

groupthink A phenomenon in which members of highly cohesive groups become so concerned with the group and its own processes that they lose sight of the external demands the groups were formed to cope with. In the case of groupthink, each member is more concerned with obtaining the approval of the group than with generating effective solutions. Such groups are likely to make disastrous mistakes.

halo effect The spread of positive response from one salient aspect of a person to all of his or her other characteristics.

hedonic balancing A process in which people weigh their own current state of well-being against that of another person in need. A positive discrepancy between one's own state and that of the other can lead to action on the other's behalf.

heuristics Cognitive shortcuts that help people make quick, efficient inferences. Heuristics can sometimes lead to biases and misattributions.

identification A process in which an individual accepts influence in order to be like or to feel like the source of influence.

idiographic approach An approach to personality theorizing that people have consistent patterns of responding, but that those patterns are highly individualized and do not lend themselves to measurement by a fixed set of underlying dimensions. Compare *nomothetic approach.*

idiosyncrasy credit Goodwill that accrues to the account of loyal group members. The more idiosyncrasy credit they have stored, the more they can successfully deviate from group norms.

implicit personality theory A set of beliefs held

by every person about interrelationships among personal characteristics. Most of the time people are not even aware of these beliefs and the assumptions they are based on.

impression management The manipulation of verbal and nonverbal information with the intent of affecting the impression or image others come to have of us.

independence A process in which a person chooses either to accept or to reject an opinion or behavior without giving any weight to the opinions or behaviors of other groups or individuals.

indirect measures of attitudes Those means of measuring attitude that do not seek direct self-reports, but rather obtain information that is correlated with attitudes. These measures include the methods of error choice, behavioral measures, unobtrusive measures, the lost letter technique, and measurement of nonverbal behavior.

inductive Inferring general principles from particular observations. In theory development, the phase in which concepts are proposed to explain observations. Compare *deductive.*

informed consent A principle of law and ethical philosophy which, in recognition of the principle of autonomy, requires that research be conducted only with participants who have intelligently agreed to take part. Before researchers may conduct research on a person, they must obtain that person's informed consent.

in-group The group to which we belong. "Us" as opposed to "them."

in-group bias The bias resulting from seeing ourselves as belonging to one group and not to another. The in-group bias causes differences in perception and affect, as well as a willingness to act for or against people on the basis of our classification of them as members of an in-group or out-group—"us" or "them."

inhibitions All those factors, both internal and external, that act to discourage the expression of aggression. Compare *instigations.*

inoculation A technique for increasing resistance to persuasion by exposing people to a weakened version of a set of arguments so that they will develop counter-arguments and be more resistant if later exposed to stronger versions of the same arguments.

instigations All those factors, both internal and external, that motivate or encourage a person to act in an aggressive manner. Compare *inhibitions.*

instrumental aggression Also called *incentive-motivated aggression.* Aggression in which the primary motive for doing harm to another is to gain some material end or advantage for oneself.

integrative bargaining Also known as *problem-solving* or *win-win negotiation.* A process in which parties engage each other not for the purpose of using the bargaining table as a place to win their dispute at the other's expense, but instead to fashion a mutually advantageous solution.

interactional experimenter effect The effect that results when a researcher unconsciously treats research subjects differently instead of treating them equally or randomly, thereby affecting the data.

interactionism An approach to the study of complex social behavior assuming that the best account of behavior will be provided by a theory that simultaneously takes into consideration both personal characteristics and situational variables.

interaction process analysis A method for measuring the amount and type of communication among group members.

intergroup conflict Conflict that exists whenever the goals, interests, and actions of one group are incompatible with those of another. Such conflict can be destructive, constructive, veridical, contingent, displaced, misattributed, or latent.

internal-external locus of control A test of personality based on the notion that people differ in the extent to which they believe they are in command of their lives (internal locus of control) rather than pawns in a world of random events (external locus of control).

internalization Process in which an individual accepts influence because the new behavior or attitude is consistent with current values or beliefs.

justification The reasons given to explain actions or beliefs. In cognitive dissonance theory, external justifications to which behavior change can be attributed affect the amount of dissonance produced and the consequent amount of attitude change. In effort justification, excessive effort expended in achieving something produces a need to exaggerate the value of the thing achieved. Rewards and punishments that are excessive can serve to overjustify behavior and may actually discourage attitude change.

laboratory research The most common kind of social psychological research. Laboratory research takes place in controlled settings in which social psychologists construct analogs of the social phenomena they wish to study.

latitudes of acceptance and rejection A basic premise of the social judgment model, in which one's attitude, one's "own position," is seen as a salient anchor in making judgments of other attitudinal positions. The range of positions close to one's own constitutes the latitude of acceptance. Positions falling within the latitude of acceptance will be seen as closer than they really are; they will be assimilated. Positions that are more distant from one's own fall into the latitude of rejection and are contrasted, seen as more unlike one's own than they really are.

learned helplessness A generalized feeling that one is unable to control events or outcomes. It is often accompanied by depression and a failure to try even when subsequent events are controllable.

leveling A process that involves the shortening of a message and the dropping of detail as it passes from person to person. Leveling occurs in rumor transmission and collective behavior. Compare *sharpening.*

looking-glass self A concept proposing that the primary way by which we come to know who we are is the reflection of ourselves provided by others.

Machiavellianism A personality type characterized by a willingness to manipulate other people and skill at doing so.

matching hypothesis A hypothesis holding that people tend to choose romantic partners who are of approximately equal physical attractiveness to themselves.

mediation A means of resolving disputes in which a third party assists the two disputing parties but exercises no control over the decision to accept or reject any given outcome.

membership group A group to which we belong socially and physically.

message In attitude change research, the persuasive communication; the content.

minority influence A process in which those who are smaller in number or power influence those who are greater in number or power.

modeling A "behavioral" process by which attitudes are acquired merely by observing the behavior of others. Also known as vicarious, or observational, learning.

"multiple selves" The notion that we are more flexible, adaptable, and changeable than has usually been supposed. The theory of multiple selves proposes that we adopt different styles of responding to different people in different situations, and that this reflects our ability to learn to cope with a multitude of situations.

negotiation A means of resolving disputes in which the parties to the dispute confront each other directly and try, through discussion and other nonviolent methods, to resolve their differences. When the negotiation is over the price of something that is being traded, it is called *bargaining.*

nomothetic approach An approach to personality assuming that the important underlying processes or structures of personality are the same for everyone, and theorizing that people vary according to where they fall along particular "trait" dimensions. Compare *idiographic approach.*

nonverbal behavior A person's visible characteristics and actions, such as facial expression and posture, as well as paralinguistic characteristics such as voice tone and rate. Nonverbal cues account for a large proportion of interpersonal communication and influence the formation of impressions.

norm of reciprocity A variant of the Golden Rule, this norm proposes that people should act to reciprocate past harm or favors done to them.

norm of social responsibility A norm stating that people should be helpful toward those who are dependent upon them in one way or another.

norms Unwritten rules of behavior, prescribing what is acceptable or approved in a given situation.

obedience A process in which a person accepts influence from an authority figure. The influencer is seen to have higher status and legitimate authority, and most often makes explicit demands that the person feels obligated to follow.

objective self-awareness A state of heightened attention to one's own self, usually brought about through some external means such as watching one's own behavior in a mirror.

observer effect Differences in observations made by different observers which result from differences in the observers' perceptual abilities, assumptions, behavior, etc.

open system In organizational theory, the view that organizations can be understood best as interacting with their environment, incorporating people, energy, and materials into themselves.

operant conditioning A form of conditioning concerned with the reinforcement of overt behavior or thoughts (as opposed to classical conditioning, which is concerned with emotional responses developed in association with certain objects). Responses that are reinforced will continue to occur; those not reinforced will decline in frequency and eventually become extinct.

opinion A term that is nearly synonymous with *attitude*. Some psychologists have suggested that opinions be treated as more specific manifestations of attitudes (which are more general). Others suggest that opinion be defined as the verbal expression of an attitude.

order effects Attitude change phenomena which occur as a result of the order in which certain information is presented.

out-group The group to which we do not belong. "Them" as opposed to "us."

overload A condition that exists when the amount of stimulation is too great for a person to process. Under such a circumstance, people must learn ways of adaptation or suffer negative effects.

paradigm A conceptual framework or set of assumptions that a researcher holds regarding the nature of the world within which his or her research takes place; a metatheory. The particular paradigm that scientists hold affects what they choose to study, how they study it, and what sense they make of their research findings.

passionate love A state of intense absorption with another person, often accompanied by physiological arousal. The loved one is an object of fantasy, longing, and desire.

personality The combination of traits and characteristics of an individual, as described by the person or an outside observer.

personalization The process whereby people put their own special claim on a territory they occupy by placing distinctive markings or decorations in or on it.

personal norms Situation-specific behavioral expectations that are internalized by an individual. The existence of such norms helps account for the differences in helping behavior of two people in the same situation.

personal space An area of space around a person's body into which others may not intrude. The amount of space may increase or decrease, depending on the circumstances. Also known as a body buffer zone.

prejudice Negative evaluation of people based on categorizing them as members of outgroups.

primacy effect The phenomenon whereby information that comes first exerts a stronger force or influence than that which comes later.

priming The process whereby thoughts and ideas are activated so as to make them more available in memory.

Prisoner's Dilemma Game A laboratory game for studying conflict. Two players are given the opportunity to make competitive or cooperative choices under a variety of conditions.

prosocial behavior Any act that is done on behalf of another person to produce, maintain, or improve that person's physical, social, or material well-being.

proximity Physical distance between people.

psychoanalytic theory A theory developed by Freud concerned chiefly with biological drives and early development.

quality circles Small groups of workers who meet about once a week to identify and analyze problems that occur in their areas of the company and to devise solutions to those problems.

reactance A state that people experience when they feel that another is trying to remove their freedom of choice or free will. This feeling is often followed by actions to reassert freedom and to exercise control.

reference group A group an individual identifies with and uses as a standard for self-evaluation.

reliability The ability of a test to measure like things and to see them as alike. A measurement that consistently produces the same result whenever it measures the same thing is reliable.

risky shift The finding that decisions made by groups are riskier than decisions made by individuals.

role A category of people and the set of normative expectations for people in that category. People occupy or play roles in which they and their role partners have complementary sets of privileges and obligations.

role playing Situations where people say, write, or do something that supports a position with which they do not agree or where they assume a role other than their usual role in life.

role strain A condition that occurs whenever role demands are unclear, incompatible with each other, not shared, inconsistent with the role player's personality, or simply too many in number.

role theory A theory of social psychology concerned with the impact on behavior of roles created by the society of which we are a part.

schemas Knowledge structures that simplify and organize complex information about others, ourselves, our roles, and events.

self A unique physical and psychological entity demonstrating continuity, yet capable of change. The way a person thinks of himself or herself and answers such questions as "Who am I?" and "What am I really like?"

self-centered bias The tendency to take more responsibility for oneself in a joint task than the other person believes you are accountable for.

self-disclosure Revealing information about the self which usually is not made available to others.

self-efficacy The perception of oneself as effective. Self-efficacy has been found to be an important determinant of one's actual success or failure at various tasks.

self-fulfilling prophecy The creation or confirmation of an event, experience, or behavior as a result of the mere expectation that it will occur.

self-handicapping A process that can occur when a person has favorably impressed others with the appearance of competence but thinks the performance that won the respect was due more to luck than ability. As a result, the person will tend to sabotage later performances so that a clear test of ability cannot be made and the initial favorable impression is protected because it cannot be tested further.

self-monitoring The tendency to be tuned in to—to "monitor"—our social surroundings and people's reactions to us. High self-monitors are more in touch with their surroundings and what people in various situations expect of them.

self-perception A theory of attitude formation proposing that we infer our own attitudes from observation of our own behavior in the same way that we observe others and infer their attitudes from their behavior.

self-serving bias The tendency for a person to take more credit for a successful task and less credit for an unsuccessful outcome than he or she actually deserves.

self-space The content that comes to mind when people think about themselves. In practice, the information a person gives when asked, in a general sense, "Tell us about yourself."

sex Those characteristics of males and females attributable to biology, physiology, or genetic influences.

sharpening A process that involves the narrowing of a message's focus to a few points; it is characterized by increasing simplification. Compare *leveling*.

sick role A role occupied by those who are labeled as being unable to fulfill their obligations. People in the sick role are exempted from their everyday duties, but are expected to make every effort to get well.

situated identities A concept holding that as people move from situation to situation, they bring forth those aspects of themselves that are most appropriate to each setting and that are most likely to achieve for them what they seek in each situation.

situationalism or **situationism** The view that behavior is a product of an organism's interaction with its environment. A central concept in social psychology's approach to the study of behavior, reflecting awareness of the importance of the situations in which behavior occurs.

sleeper effect A controversial aspect of the source-credibility effect, in which a source with low credibility is thought to become more influential over time as it becomes dissociated from the message.

small world phenomenon The finding that people are connected to other people through a chain of mutual friends made up of a surprisingly small number of links.

social comparison Comparing ourselves and our performance to that of others. A fundamental means by which we assess our own characteristics and abilities.

social decision rules The scheme by which the individual judgments of group members are combined to form group decisions.

social facilitation Improved performance due to the presence of other people as compared to performance when alone.

social factors Influences on behavior that include other people or the institutions, artifacts, situations, and social or physical structures people have created.

socialization An ongoing process by which people come to adopt the attitudes, behaviors, and ways of seeing the world of the groups to which they belong and relate.

social learning theory A theory of social psychology that is an outgrowth of the stimulus-response school of thought and encompasses classical conditioning, operant conditioning, and modeling.

social loafing A phenomenon whereby each individual puts out decreasing effort as additional members are added to a group, even though the total group effort keeps increasing.

social movement An effort by a large number of people to find a collective solution to a problem they believe is common to them all.

social self Those portions of a person's identity that have been learned from interaction with other people.

social structure When applied to an organization, the roles that organization members occupy, the flow of authority, and the channels of communication available.

social traps Situations of interdependence in which behavior that will provide short-term gain ultimately will lead to greater losses.

sociogram or **sociometric diagram** A device by which the pattern of relationships (among friends, co-workers, and so on) within a group can be described.

source The origin of a communication; the person, organization, or other entity from which a message emanates.

spontaneous self-concept An instance in which people define themselves as a result of a specific situation they find themselves in.

stereotypes Structured sets of beliefs about the personal attributes of a group of people. Stereotypes about racial, ethnic, and sex groups have been found to be extremely resistant to change.

subjective norms One's beliefs about what other people in one's life expect one to do with respect to particular behavior; part of the theory of reasoned action.

superordinate goals Goals that two groups wish to achieve but find they cannot achieve without combining their efforts. Subordinate goals are not simply commonly desired, but goals where cooperation and common effort are necessary for success.

symbolic interactionism An approach to the study of social behavior based on the idea that we can interact symbolically in the social world by imagining our behavior and how it will be responded to in a given social context.

task structure A way of classifying distinctions among task types according to three dimensions: divisibility, quantity versus quality, and group process. Tasks have been classified as unitary, divisible, maximizing, optimizing, conjunctive, and additive, among other designations.

technostructure The technological and physical aspects of an organization, as opposed to its social organization or its individuals.

temperament A generalized style of behavior. Some research suggests that four aspects of temperament are inherited genetically; activity, emotionality, sociability, and impulsivity.

territoriality A feeling of ownership, commitment, or willingness to defend an area that a person occupies.

T-group A small group that meets under the direction of a "facilitator" who takes the group through various exercises and experiences using principles of group dynamics. Also known as *sensitivity training*.

theory Explanations of empirical phenomena. Theories are not guesses that stand in for facts until the facts are found. They are explanations of observed facts.

theory of reasoned action A theory assuming that people are rational and that they rely on information and attitudes to guide their behavior.

Theory X and Theory Y Conflicting theories held by managers in organizations. Managers who subscribe to Theory X believe that people are inherently lazy; dislike work; lack ambition; seek little other than financial security; and need direction, prodding, coercion, and even punishment in order to be productive. Theory Y managers believe that work is as natural as eating, sleeping, or playing and that most people thrive on an opportunity to be involved in their organization and to exercise their creativity and imagination in helping the organization to function better.

threat deterrence Threatening to do our adversary harm if the adversary engages in behavior we dislike. The conventional way of trying to reduce the amount of conflict between nations.

unconscious ideology The set of beliefs and assumptions about people, their attributes, and their capabilities that are so basic individuals are not even aware that they hold them.

validity The ability of a test to measure what it purports to measure and not something else.

values Abstract concepts—such as freedom, justice, or beauty—that are tied to no particular social objects or classes of objects.

verbal measures of attitudes Means of measuring attitudes that ask people to provide a self-report, usually on a paper-and-pencil scale, such as Likert, Thurstone, semantic differential, or one-item rating scales.

violence A form of aggression in which harm is direct and is accomplished through the use of physical force. Violence can take place on any level from the interpersonal to the international.

BIBLIOGRAPHY

Abbey, A. (1982). Sex differences in attributions for friendly behavior: Do males misperceive females' friendliness? *Journal of Personality and Social Psychology, 42,* 830–838

Abelson, P. H. (1962). The need for skepticism. *Science, 138,* 175.

Abelson, R. P. (1981). The psychological status of the script concept. *American Psychologist, 36,* 715–729.

Abelson, R. P., Aronson, E., McGuire, W. J., Newcomb, T. M., Rosenberg, M. J., & Tannenbaum, P. H. (Eds.) (1968). *Theories of cognitive consistency: A sourcebook.* Chicago: Rand McNally.

Abelson, R. P., & Rosenberg, M. J. (1958). Symbolic psycho-logic: A model of attitude cognition. *Behavioral Science, 3,* 1–13.

Abelson, R. P., & Zimbardo, P. G. (1970). *Canvassing for peace: A manual for volunteers.* Ann Arbor, MI: Society for the Psychological Study of Social Issues.

Abrams, M. (1967). Political parties and the polls. In P. F. Lazarsfeld, W. H. Sewell, & H. L. Wilensky (Eds.), *The uses of sociology.* New York: Basic Books.

Abromitz, S. I. (1969). Locus of control and self-recorded depression among college students. *Psychological Reports, 25,* 149–150.

Abromitz, S. I. (1973). Internal-external control and social/political activism: A test of the dimensionality of Rotter's internal-external scale. *Journal of Consulting and Clinical Psychology, 40,* 196–201.

Abt, C. C. (1977). *The social audit for management.* Saranac Lake, NY: American Management Association.

Abt, C. C. (1980). Social science in the contract research firm. In R. F. Kidd & M. J. Saks (Eds.), *Advances in applied social psychology.* Hillsdale, NJ: Erlbaum.

Ackley, D. C. (1977). A brief overview of child abuse. *Social Casework, 58,* 21–24.

Adams, G. R. (1977). Physical attractiveness research: Toward a developmental social psychology of beauty. *Human Development, 20,* 217–239.

Adams, G. R., & Huston, T. L. (1975). Social perception of middle-aged persons varying in physical attractiveness. *Developmental Psychology, 11,* 657–658.

Adams, J. S. (1963). Toward an understanding of inequity. *Journal of Abnormal and Social Psychology, 67,* 422–436.

Adams, J. S. (1965). Inequity in social exchange. In L. Berkowitz (Ed.), *Advances in experimental social psychology* (Vol. 2). New York: Academic Press.

Adams, J. S., & Jacobsen, P. R. (1964). Effects of wage inequities on work quality. *Journal of Abnormal and Social Psychology, 69,* 19–25.

Adorno, T. W., Frenkel-Brunswick, E., Levenson, D., & Sanford, N. (1950). *The authoritarian personality.* New York: Harper & Row.

Aiello, J. R., & Aiello, T. D. (1974). Development of personal space: Proxemic behavior of children six to sixteen. *Human Ecology, 2,* 177–189.

Aiello, J. R., Baum, A., & Gormley, F. (1981). Social determinants of residential crowding stress. *Personality and Social Psychology Bulletin, 7,* 643–644.

Ajzen, I. (1971). Attitudinal versus normative

messages: An investigation of the differential effects of persuasive communications on behavior. *Sociometry, 34,* 263–280.

Ajzen, I., & Fishbein, M. (1977). Attitude-behavior relations: A theoretical analysis and review of empirical research. *Psychological Bulletin, 84,* 888–918.

Ajzen, I., & Fishbein, M. (1980). *Understanding attitudes and predicting social behavior.* Englewood Cliffs, NJ: Prentice-Hall

Albert, S., & Dabbs, J. M. (1970). Physical distance and persuasion. *Personality and Social Psychology Bulletin, 15,* 265–270.

Alexander, C. N., & Knight, G. W. (1971). Situated identities and social psychological experimentation. *Sociometry, 34,* 65–82.

Alexander, C. N., & Lauderdale, P. (1977). Situated identities and social influence. *Sociometry, 40,* 225–233.

Alexander, C. N., & Sagatun, I. (1973). An attributional analysis of experimental norms. *Sociometry, 36,* 127–142.

Alker, H. A. (1977). Beyond ANOVA: Psychology in the study of person-situation interaction. In D. Magnusson & N. S. Endler (Eds.), *Personality at the crossroads.* Hillsdale, NJ: Erlbaum.

Allen, R. B., & Ebbesen, E. B. (1981). Cognitive processes in person perception. *Journal of Experimental Social Psychology, 17,* 119–141.

Allen, V. L. (1965). Conformity and the role of deviant. *Journal of Personality, 33,* 584–597.

Allen, V. L., & Levine, J. M. (1971). Social support and conformity: The role of independent assessment of reality. *Journal of Experimental Social Psychology, 7,* 48–58.

Allioti, N. C. (1978). *Sex differences in reading: A biological explanation.* Paper presented at the Western Psychological Association convention, San Francisco.

Allport, F. H. (1924). *Social psychology.* Cambridge, MA: The Riverside Press.

Allport, G. W. (1966). Traits revisited. *American Psychologist, 21,* 1–10.

Allport, G. W. (1935). Attitudes. In C. Murchison (Ed.), *A handbook of social psychology.* Worcester, MA: Clark University Press.

Allport, G. W. (1937). *Personality: A psychological interpretation.* New York: Holt, Rinehart and Winston.

Allport, G. W., & Postman, L. (1947). *The psychology of rumor.* New York: Holt, Rinehart and Winston.

Allport, G. W., Vernon, P. E., & Lindzey, G. (1960). *Study of values* (3rd ed.). Boston: Houghton Mifflin.

Altman, I. (1973). Some perspectives on the study of man-environment phenomena. *Representative Research in Social Psychology, 4,* 109–126.

Altman, I. (1975). *The environment and social behavior: Privacy, personal space, territory and crowding.* Monterey, CA: Brooks/Cole.

Altman, I., & Haythorn, W. W. (1967). The ecology of isolated groups. *Behavioral Science, 62,* 169–182.

Altman, I., Nelson, P. A., & Lett, E. E. (1972). *The ecology of home environments.* Catalog of Selected Documents in Psychology. Washington, DC: American Psychological Association.

Altman, I., & Taylor, D. (1973). *Social penetration: The development of interpersonal relationships.* New York: Holt, Rinehart and Winston.

Altman, I., Taylor, D., & Wheeler, L. (1971). Ecological aspects of group behavior in social isolation. *Journal of Applied Social Psychology, 1,* 76–100.

Amato, P. R. (1983). Helping behavior in urban and rural environments: Field studies based on a taxonomic organization of helping episodes. *Journal of Personality and Social Psychology, 45,* 571–586.

American Anthropological Association (1971). *Principles of professional responsibility.* Washington, DC.

American Psychological Association, Committee for the Protection of Human Participants in Research (1982). *Ethical principles in the conduct of research with human participants.* Washington, DC.

Amir, Y. (1976). The role of intergroup contact in change of prejudice and ethnic relations. In P. A. Katz (Ed.), *Toward the elimination of racism.* New York: Pergamon.

Amrine, M. & Sanford, H. (1956). In the matters of juries, democracy, science, truth, senators and bugs. *American Psychologist, 11,* 54–60.

Anastasi, A. (1982). *Contributions to differential*

psychology: Selected papers. New York: Praeger.

Anderson, C. A. (1983). Motivational and performance deficits in interpersonal settings: The effects of attributional style. *Journal of Personality and Social Psychology, 45,* 1136–1137.

Anderson, C. A., & Anderson, D. C. (1984). Ambient temperature and violent crime: Tests of the linear and curvilinear hypothesis. *Journal of Personality and Social Psychology, 46,* 91–97.

Anderson, C. A., Horowitz, L. M., & French, R. de S. (1983). Attributional style of lonely and depressed people. *Journal of Personality and Social Psychology, 45,* 127–136.

Anderson, C. R. (1977). Locus of control, coping behaviors, and performance in a stress setting: A longitudinal study. *Journal of Applied Psychology, 62,* 446–451.

Anderson, J. R. (1980). *Cognitive psychology and its implications.* San Francisco: Freeman.

Anderson, K. O., & Masur, F. T., III (1983). Psychological preparation for invasive medical and dental procedures. *Journal of Behavioral Medicine, 6,* 1–40.

Anderson, L. A., & Arnoult, L. H. (1985). Attributional style and everyday problems in living: Depression, loneliness, and shyness. *Social Cognition, 3,* 16–35.

Anderson, N. H. (1965). Adding versus averaging as a stimulus combination rule in impression formation. *Journal of Experimental Psychology, 70,* 394–400.

Anderson, N. H. (1971). Two more tests against change of meaning in adjective combinations. *Journal of Verbal Learning and Verbal Behavior, 10,* 75–85.

Anderson, N. H. (1981). Integration theory applied to cognitive responses and attitudes. In R. E. Petty, T. M. Ostrom, and T. C. Brock (Eds.), *Cognitive processes in persuasion.* Hillsdale, NJ: Erlbaum.

Anderson, R., Manoogian, S., & Reznick, J. (1976). The undermining and enhancing of intrinsic motivation in preschool children. *Journal of Personality and Social Psychology, 34,* 913–922.

Andreoli, V., & Worchel, S. (1978). Effects of media, communicator, and position of message on attitude change. *Public Opinion Quarterly, 42,* 59–70.

Antill, J. K. (1983). Sex role complementarity versus similarity in married couples. *Journal of Personality and Social Psychology, 45,* 145–155.

Apsler, R., & Sears, D. O. (1968). Warning, personal involvement, and attitude change. *Journal of Personality and Social Psychology, 9,* 162–168.

Ardrey, R. (1966). *The territorial imperative.* New York: Atheneum.

Argyle, M., & Cook, M. (1976). *Gaze and mutual gaze.* New York: Cambridge University Press.

Argyle, M., & Dean, J. (1965). Eye contact, distance and affiliation. *Sociometry, 28,* 289–304.

Argyle, M., Furnham, A., & Graham, J. A. (1981). *Social situations.* Cambridge, England: Cambridge University Press.

Argyle, M., & Little, B. R. (1972). Do personality traits apply to social behavior? *Journal of the Theory of Social Behavior, 2* 1–35.

Argyris, C. (1976). Leadership, learning, and changing the status quo. *Organizational Dynamics,* Winter, 29–43.

Arkin, W., & Dobrofsky, L. R. (1979). Job sharing couples. In K. W. Feinstein (Ed.), *Working women and families.* Beverly Hills, CA: Sage.

Armistead, N. (1974). *Reconstructing social psychology.* London: Penguin Books.

Aronfreed, J. (1970). The socialization of altruistic and sympathetic behavior: Some theoretical and experimental analyses. In J. Macauley & L. Berkowitz (Eds.), *Altruism and helping behavior.* New York: Academic Press.

Aronow, W. S., Harris, C. N., Isbell, M. W., Rokaw, M. D., & Imparato, B. (1972). Effect of freeway travel on angina pectoris. *Annals of Internal Medicine, 77,* 669–676.

Aronson, E. (1968). Dissonance theory: Progress and problems. In R. P. Abelson, E. Aronson, W. J. McGuire, P. M. Newcomb, M. J. Rosenberg, & P. H. Tannenbaum (Eds.), *Theories of cognitive consistency: A source book.* Skokie, IL: Rand McNally.

Aronson, E. (1969). The theory of cognitive dissonance: A current perspective. In L. Berkowitz (Ed.), *Advances in experimental social* psychology (Vol. 4). New York: Academic Press.

Aronson, E. (1978a) *The social animal.* San Francisco: Freeman.

Aronson, E., & Carlsmith, J. M. (1963). Effect of severity of threat on the devaluation of forbidden behavior. *Journal of Abnormal and Social Psychology, 66,* 584–588.

Aronson, E., & Mills, J. (1959). The effects of the severity of initiation on liking for a group. *Journal of Abnormal and Social Psychology, 59,* 177–181.

Aronson, E., Stephan, C., Sikes, J., Blaney, N., & Snapp, M. (1978). *The jigsaw classroom.* Beverly Hills, CA: Sage.

Asch, S. E. (1946). Forming impressions of personality. *Journal of Abnormal and Social Psychology, 41,* 258–290.

Asch, S. E. (1951). Effects of group pressure on the modification and distortion of judgments. In H. Guetzkow (Ed.), *Groups, leadership and men.* Pittsburgh, PA: Carnegie Press.

Asch, S. E. (1952). Effects of group pressure upon the modification and distortions of judgments. In G. E. Swanson, T. M. Newcomb, & E. L. Hartley (Eds.), *Readings in social psychology* (rev. ed.). New York: Holt, Rinehart and Winston.

Asch, S. E. (1955). Opinions and social pressures. *Scientific American, 193,* 31–35.

Asch, S. E., & Zukier, H. (1984). Thinking about persons. *Journal of Personality and Social Psychology, 46,* 1230–1240.

Ashmore, R. D., & DelBoca, F. K. (1979). Sex stereotypes and implicit personality theory: Toward a cognitive-social psychological conception. *Sex Roles, 5,* 219–248.

Ashmore, R. D., & DelBoca, F. K. (1984). Gender stereotypes. In R. D. Ashmore & F. K. DelBoca, *The social psychology of female-male relationships: A critical analysis of central concepts.* New York: Academic Press.

Austin, W. G., & Worchel, S. (Eds.) (1979). *The social psychology of intergroup relations.* Monterey, CA: Brooks/Cole.

Averill, J. R. (1982). *Anger and aggression: An essay on emotion.* New York: Springer-Verlag.

Axsom, D., & Cooper, J. (1985). Cognitive dissonance and psychotherapy: The role of effort justification in inducing weight loss. *Journal of Experimental and Social Psychology, 21,* 149–160.

Azen, S., Snibbe, H., & Montgomery, H. K. (1973). A longitudinal predictive study of success and performance of law enforcement officers. *Journal of Applied Psychology, 57,* 190–192.

Azrin, N. H., & Foxx, R. M. (1974). *Toilet training in less than a day.* New York: Simon & Schuster.

Babad, E. Y., Birnbaum, M., & Benne, K. D. (1983). *The social self: Group influences on personal identity.* Beverly Hills, CA: Sage.

Bach, G., & Wyden, P. (1968). *The intimate enemy: How to fight fair in love and marriage.* New York: Morrow.

Back, K. W. (1972). *Beyond words: The story of sensitivity training and the encounter movement.* New York: Russell Sage Foundation.

Back, K. W. (1983). Teenage pregnancy: Science and ideology in applied social psychology. In R. F. Kidd & M. J. Saks (Eds.), *Advances in applied social psychology* (Vol. 2). Hillsdale, NJ: Erlbaum.

Badore, N. L. (1979). *Group size and task effects on group problem-solving.* Unpublished doctoral dissertation. Chestnut Hill, MA: Boston College.

Bagozzi, R. P. (1981). Attitudes, intentions,, and behavior: A test of some key hypotheses. *Journal of Personality and Social Psychology, 41,* 607–627.

Bales, R. F. (1950). *Interaction process analysis: A method for the study of small groups.* Cambridge, MA: Addison-Wesley.

Bales, R. F. (1958). Task roles and social roles in problem-solving groups. In E. E. Maccoby, T. M. Newcomb, & E. L. Hartley (Eds.), *Readings in social psychology* (3rd ed.). New York: Holt, Rinehart and Winston.

Bales, R. F., & Borgatta, E. F. (1955). Size of group as a factor in the interaction profile. In A. P. Hare, E. F. Borgatta, & R. F. Bales (Eds.), *Small groups: Studies in social interaction.* New York: Knopf.

Bales, R. F., & Hare, A. P. (1965). Diagnostic use of the interaction profile. *Journal of Social Psychology, 67,* 239–258.

Journal of Experimental Social Psychology, 18, 217–234.

Burton, I., Kates, R. W., & White, G. (1978). *The environment as hazard.* New York: Oxford University Press.

Burton, R. V. (1963). Generality of honesty reconsidered. *Psychological Review, 70,* 481–499.

Buss, A. H. (1961). *The psychology of aggression.* New York: Wiley.

Buss, A. H. (1971). Aggression pays. In J. L. Singer (Ed.), *The control of aggression and violence.* New York: Academic Press.

Buss, A. H. (1980). *Self-consciousness and social anxiety.* San Francisco: Freeman.

Buss, A. H., Booker, A., & Buss, E. (1972). Firing a weapon and aggression. *Journal of Personality and Social Psychology, 22,* 196–202.

Buss, A. H., & Plomin, R. (1975). *A temperament theory of personality development.* New York: Wiley-Interscience.

Butler, R. (1985). *Why survive?* New York: Harper & Row.

Bybee, R. W. (1979). Violence toward youth: A new perspective. *Journal of Social Issues, 35,* 1–14.

Byrne, D. (1971). *The attraction paradigm.* New York: Academic Press.

Byrne, D., & Byrne, L. A. (1977). *Exploring human sexuality.* New York: Thomas Y. Crowell.

Byrne, D., & Clore, G. L. (1970). A reinforcement model of evaluative responses. *Personality: An International Journal, 1,* 103–128.

Byrne, D., Ervin, C., & Lamberth, J. (1970). Continuity between the experimental study of attraction and real-life computer dating. *Journal of Personality and Social Psychology, 16,* 157–165.

Byrne, D. & Kelly, K. (1981). *An introduction to personality* (3rd ed.). Englewood Cliffs, NJ: Prentice-Hall.

Byrne, D., Rasche, L., & Kelley, K. (1974). When "I like you" indicates disagreement: An experimental differentiation of information and affect. *Journal of Research in Personality, 8,* 207–217.

Byron, C. (1981, March 30). How Japan does it. *Time,* pp. 54–60.

Cacioppo, J. T., & Petty, R. E. (1979). Attitudes and cognitive response: An electrophysiological approach. *Journal of Personality and Social Psychology, 37,* 2181–2199.

Cacioppo, J. T., & Petty, R. E. (1980). Persuasiveness of commercials is affected by exposure frequency and communication cogency: A theoretical and empirical analysis. In J. H. Leigh & C. R. Martin (Eds.), *Current issues and research in advertising.* Ann Arbor: University of Michigan Press.

Cacioppo, J. T., & Petty, R. E. (1981). Effects of extent of thought on the pleasantness ratings of P-O-X triads: Evidence for three judgmental tendencies in evaluating social situations. *Journal of Personality and Social Psychology, 40,* 1000–1009.

Cacioppo, J. T., & Petty, R. E. (Eds.) (1983). *Social psychophysiology: A sourcebook.* New York: Guilford.

Cacioppo. J. T., Petty, R. E., & Sidera, J. A. (1982). The effects of a salient self-schema on the evaluation of proattitudinal editorials: Top-down versus bottom-up message processing. *Journal of Experimental Social Psychology, 18,* 324–338.

Calhoun, J. B. (1962). Population density and social pathology. *Science, 206,* 139–148.

Campbell, A. (1975). Marriage, si, children only maybe. *Psychology Today, 8*(12), 37–43.

Campbell, A., Converse, P. E., & Rogers, W. L. (1976). *The quality of American life.* New York: Russell Sage Foundation.

Campbell, D. T. (1963). Social attitudes and other acquired behavioral dispositions. In S. Koch (Ed.), *Psychology: A study of a science.* New York: McGraw-Hill.

Campbell, D. T. (1969). Reforms as experiments. *American Psychologist, 24,* 409–429.

Campbell, D. T. (1972). On the genetics of altruism and the counter-balance components in human culture. *Journal of Social Issues, 28,* 21–38.

Campbell, D. T. (1975). Assessing the impact of planned social change. In G. M. Lyons (Ed.), *Social research and public policy.* Hanover, NH: Public Affairs Center, Dartmouth.

Campbell, D. T., & Fiske, D. W. (1959). Convergent and discriminant validation by the multitrait-multimethod matrix. *Psychological Bulletin, 56,* 81–105.

Campbell, D. T., & Ross, H. L. (1970). The Connecticut crackdown on speeding: Time-series data in quasi-experimental analysis. In N. E. Tufte (Ed.), *The quantitative analysis of social problems.* Reading, MA: Addison-Wesley.

Campbell, D. T., & Stanley, J. C. (1963). *Experimental and quasi-experimental designs for research.* Chicago: Rand McNally.

Cann, A., Sherman, S. J., & Elkes, R. (1975). Effects of initial request size and timing of a second request on compliance: The foot in the door and the door in the face. *Journal of Personality and Social Psychology, 32,* 774–782.

Cantor, N., & Kihlstrom, J. F. (Eds.) (1981). *Personality, cognition & social interaction.* Hillsdale, NJ: Erlbaum.

Cantor, N., & Mischel, W. (1977). Traits as prototypes: Effects on recognition memory. *Journal of Personality and Social Psychology, 35,* 38–48.

Cantril, H. (1958). The invasion from Mars. In E. Maccoby, T. M. Newcomb, & E. L. Hartley (Eds.), *Readings in social psychology.* New York: Holt, Rinehart and Winston.

Caplan, N. (1979). The two-communities theory and knowledge utilization. *American Behavioral Scientist, 22,* 459–470.

Caplan, N., Marson, A., & Stambaugh, R. (1975). *The use of social science knowledge in policy decisions at the national level: A report to respondents.* Ann Arbor, MI: Institute for Social Research.

Caplan, N., & Nelson, S. (1973). On being useful: The nature and consequences of psychological research on social problems. *American Psychologist, 28,* 199–212.

Caplan, N. & Paige, J. (1968). A study of ghetto rioters. *Scientific American, 219,* 15–21.

Caplan, P. J., MacPherson, G. M., & Tobin, P. (1985). Do sex-related differences in spatial abilities exist? *American Psychologist, 40,* 786–799.

Carducci, B. J., and Deuser, P. S. (1984). The foot-in-the-door technique: Initial request and organ donation. *Basic and Applied Social Psychology, 5,* 75–81.

Carlsmith, J. M., & Anderson, C. A. (1979). Ambient temperature and the occurrence of collective violence: A new analysis. *Journal of Personality and Social Psychology, 37,* 337–344.

Carnevale, P. J., Pruitt, D. G., & Seilheimer, S. (1981). Looking and competing: Accountability and visual access in integrative bargaining. *Journal of Personality and Social Psychology, 40,* 111–120.

Carter, L. F., Haythorn, W., Shriver, E., & Lanzetta, J. (1951). The behavior of leaders and other group members. *Journal of Abnormal and Social Psychology, 46,* 589–595.

Cartwright, D. (1948). Social psychology in the United States during the second world war. *Human Relations, 1,* 333–352.

Cartwright, D. (1949). Some principles of mass persuasion. *Human Relations, 2,* 253–267.

Cartwright, D. (1968). The nature of group cohesiveness. In D. Cartwright & A. Zander (Eds.), *Group dynamics: Research and theory* (3rd ed.). New York: Harper & Row.

Cartwright, D. (1971). Risk taking by individuals and groups: An assessment of research employing choice dilemmas. *Journal of Personality and Social Psychology, 20,* 361–378.

Cartwright, D. (1978). Theory and practice. *Journal of Social Issues, 34,* 168–180.

Cartwright, D. (1979). Contemporary social psychology in historical perspective. *Social Psychology Quarterly, 42,* 82–93.

Cartwright, D., & Zander, A. (Eds.) (1960). *Group dynamics: Research and theory* (2nd ed.). Evanston, IL: Row, Peterson.

Cartwright, D., & Zander, A. (Eds.) (1968). *Group dynamics: Research and theory* (3rd ed.). New York: Harper & Row

Cash, T. F., & Derlega, V. J. (1978). The matching hypothesis: Physical attractiveness among same-sexed friends. *Personality and Social Psychology Bulletin, 4,* 240–243.

Castro, M. A. (1974). Reactions to receiving aid as a function of cost to the donor and opportunity to aid. *Journal of Applied Social Psychology, 4,* 194–209.

Chagnon, N. (1979). Mate competition, favoring close kin and village fissioning among the Yanomamo Indians. In N. Chagnon & W.

Irons (Eds.), *Evolutionary biology and human social behavior.* North Scituate, MA: Duxbury Press.

Chaiken, S. (1979). Communicator physical attractiveness and persuasion. *Journal of Personality and Social Psychology, 3,* 1387–1397.

Chaiken, S. (1980). Heuristic versus systematic information processing and the use of source versus message cues in persuasion. *Journal of Personality and Social Psychology, 3,* 752–766.

Chaiken, S., & Eagly, A. H. (1976). Communication modality as a determinant of message persuasiveness and message comprehensibility. *Journal of Personality and Social Psychology, 34,* 605–614.

Chammah, A. M. (1970). Sex differences, strategy, and communication in a mixed-motive game. *Dissertation Abstracts International, 31*(2-B), 925–926.

Chavis, D. M., Stucky, P. E. & Wandersman, A. (1983). Returning basic research to the community: A relationship between scientist and citizen. *American Psychologist, 38,* 424–434.

Check, J. V. P., & Malamuth, N. M. (1984). Can there be a positive effect of participation in pornography experiments? *Journal of Sex Research, 20,* 14–31.

Cheek, J., & Zonderman, A. B. (1983). *Shyness as a personality temperament.* Paper presented at the annual meeting of the American Psychological Association, Anaheim, CA.

Cheek, J. M., & Buss, A. H. (1981). Shyness and sociability. *Journal of Personality and Social Psychology, 41,* 330–337.

Chemers, M. M., Hayes, R. B., Rhodewalt, F., & Wysocki, J. (1985). A person-environment analysis of job stress: A contingency model explanation. *Journal of Personality and Social Psychology, 47,* 628–635.

Cherry, F., & Byrne, D. (1977). Authoritarianism. In T. Blass (Ed.), *Personality variables in social behavior.* Hillsdale, NJ: Erlbaum.

Choo, T. (1964). Communicator credibility and communication discrepancy as determinants of opinion change. *Journal of Social Psychology, 64,* 1–20.

Christian, J. J. (1975). Hormonal control of population growth. In B. E. Eleftheriou & R. L. Sprott (Eds.), *Hormonal correlates of behavior* (Vol. 1). New York: Plenum.

Christie, R. (1954). *Authoritarianism re-examined.* In R. Christie & M. Jahoda (Eds.), *Studies in the scope and method of "The Authoritarian Personality."* New York: Free Press.

Christie, R., & Garcia, J. (1951). Subcultural variation in authoritarian personality. *Journal of Abnormal and Social Psychology, 46,* 457–469.

Christie, R., & Geis, F. L. (1970). *Studies in Machiavellianism.* New York: Academic Press.

Christie, R., & Jahoda, M. (Eds.) (1954). *Studies in the scope and method of "The Authoritarian Personality."* New York: Free Press.

Cialdini, R. & Ascani, K. (1976). Test of a concession procedure for inducing verbal, behavioral and further compliance with a request to give blood. *Journal of Applied Psychology, 21,* 206–215.

Cialdini, R. B. (1985). *Influence: Science and practice.* Glenview, IL: Scott, Foresman.

Cialdini, R. B., Borden, R. J., Thorne, A., Walker, M. R., Freman, S., & Sloan, L. R. (1976). Basking in reflected glory: Three (football) field studies. *Journal of Personality and Social Psychology, 34,* 366–375.

Cialdini, R. B., Vincent, J. E., Lewis, S. K., Catalan, J., Wheeler, D., & Darby, B. L. (1975). Reciprocal concessions procedure for inducing compliance: The door-in-the-face technique. *Journal of Personality and Social Psychology, 31,* 206–215.

Clark, M. S. (1984). Record keeping in two types of relationships. *Journal of Personality and Social Psychology, 47,* 549–557.

Clark, M. S., & Mills, J. (1979). Interpersonal attractions in exchange and communal relationships. *Journal of Personality and Social Psychology, 37,* 12, 24.

Clark, R. D., III (1971). Group-induced shift toward risk: A critical appraisal. *Psychological Bulletin, 76,* 251–270.

Clark, R. N., Burgess, R. L., & Hendee, J. C. (1972). The development of anti-litter behavior in a forest campground. *Journal of Applied Behavior Analysis, 5,* 1–5.

Clifford, M., & Walster, E. (1973). The effect of

physical attractiveness on teacher expectation. *Sociology of Education, 46,* 248.

Cline, V. H., Croft, R. G., & Courrier, S. (1973). Desensitization of children to television violence. *Journal of Personality and Social Psychology, 27,* 360–365.

Coates, D., Renzaglia, G. J., & Embree, M. C. (1983). When helping backfires: Help and helplessness. In J. D. Fisher, A. Nadler, & B. DePaulo (Eds.), *New directions in helping: Recipient reactions to aid* (Vol. 1). New York: Academic Press.

Cobb, S., & Rose, R. M. (1973). Hypertension, peptic ulcer, and diabetes in air traffic controllers. *Journal of the American Medical Association, 224,* 489–492.

Coch, L., & French, J. R. P. (1948). Overcoming resistance to change. *Human Relations, 4,* 512–533.

Cohen, C. E. (1981). Person categories and social perception: Testing some boundaries of the processing effects of prior knowledge. *Journal of Personality and Social Psychology, 40,* 441–452.

Cohen, J. (1977). *Statistical power analysis for the behavioral sciences.* New York: Academic Press.

Cohen, S. (1978). Environmental load and the allocations of attention. In A. Baum, J. E. Singer, & S. Valins (Eds.), *Advances in environmental psychology* (Vol. 1). Hillsdale, NJ: Erlbaum.

Cohen, S. (1980). After-effects of stress on human performance and social behavior: A review of research and theory. *Psychology Bulletin, 88,* 82–108.

Cohen, S., Evans, G. W., Krantz, D. S., Stokols, D., & Kelly, S. (1981). Aircraft noise and children: Longitudinal and cross-sectional evidence on adaptation to noise and the effectiveness of noise abatement. *Journal of Personality and Social Psychology, 40,* 331–345.

Cohen, S., & Lezak, A. (1977). Noise and inattentiveness to social cues. *Environment and Behavior, 9,* 559–572.

Cohen, S., & Spacapan, S. (1978). The aftereffects of stress: An additional interpretation. *Environmental Psychology and Nonverbal Behavior, 3,* 43–57.

Cohen, S., & Weinstein, N. (1982). Nonauditory effects of noise on behavior and health. In G. W. Evans (Ed.), *Environmental stress.* New York: Cambridge University Press.

Cole, R. E. (1981). The Japanese lesson in quality. *Technology Review, 83,* 28–33, 36–40.

Coleman, J. C., & Butcher, J. N. (1984). *Abnormal psychology and modern life.* Glenview, IL: Scott, Foresman.

Coleman, J. F., Blake, R. R., & Mouton, J. S. (1958). Task difficulty and conformity pressures. *Journal of Abnormal and Social Psychology, 57,* 120–122.

Collier, J. F. (1973). *Law and social change in Zinacantan.* Stanford, CA: Stanford University Press.

Collins, B. E., & Guetzkow, H. (1964). *A social psychology of group processes for decision making.* New York: Wiley.

Collins, B. E., & Raven, B. H. (1968). Group structure: Attraction, coalitions, communication, and power. In G. Lindzey & E. Aronson (Eds.), *Handbook of social psychology* (Vol. 4). Reading, MA: Addison-Wesley.

Collins, W. A., & Getz, S. K. (1976). Children's social responses following modeled reactions to provocation: Pro-social effects of a television drama. *Journal of Personality, 44,* 488–500.

Colman, A. D., & Colman, L. L. (1971). *Pregnancy: The psychological experience.* New York: Herder and Herder.

Columbia Broadcasting System (1977). Communicating with children through television. New York: CBS.

Condie, S. J., Warner, W. K., & Gillman, D. C. (1976). Getting blood from collective turnips: Volunteer donation in mass blood drives. *Journal of Applied Psychology, 61,* 290–294.

Conner, R. F., & Surette, R. (1980). Processing citizens' disputes outside the courts: A quasi-experimental evaluation. *Evaluation Review, 4,* 739–768.

Conroy, J., III, & Sundstrom, E. (1977). Territorial dominance in a dyadic conversation as a function of similarity of opinion. *Journal of Personality and Social Psychology, 35,* 570–576.

Cook, P. J. (1981). The effect of gun availability on violent crime patterns. *The Annals of the American Academy of Political and Social Science, 455,* 63–79.

Cook, R. F., Roehl, J. A., & Sheppard, D. I. (1980). *Neighborhood justice centers field test-final evaluation report.* Washington, DC: American Bar Association.

Cook, S. W. (1984). The 1954 Social Science Statement and school desegregation: A reply to Gerard. *American Psychologist, 39,* 819–832.

Cook, S. W., & Berrenberg, J. L. (1981). Approaches to encouraging conservation behavior: A review and conceptual framework. *Journal of Social Issues, 37,* 73–107.

Cook, S. W., & Selltiz, C. (1955). Some factors which influence the attitudinal outcomes of personal contact. *Acta Psychologia, 11,* 190–192.

Cook, T. D., & Campbell, D. T. (1979). *Quasi-experimentation: Design and analysis issues for field settings.* Chicago: Rand McNally.

Cook, T. D., & Flay, B. R. (1978). The temporal persistence of experimentally induced attitude change: An evaluative review. In L. Berkowitz (Ed.), *Advances in experimental social psychology* (Vol. 11). New York: Academic Press.

Cook, T. M., Novaco, R. W., & Sarason, I. G. (1980). *Generalized expectancy, life experience, and adaptation to Marine Corps recruit training* (AR-002). Seattle: University of Washington.

Cooley, C. H. (1922). *Human nature and the social order* (rev. ed.). New York: Scribner's.

Coombs, C. A. (1950). Psychological scaling without a unit of measurement. *Psychological Review, 57,* 145–158.

Cooper, H. (1979). Pygmalion grows up: A model for teacher expectation, communication, and performance influence. *Review of Educational Research, 49,* 389–410.

Cooper, H. M. (1979). Statistically combining independent studies: Meta-analysis of sex differences in conformity research. *Journal of Personality and Social Psychology, 37,* 131–146.

Cooper, J., & Axsom, D. (1982). Cognitive dissonance and psychotherapy. In G. Weary and H. Mirels (Eds.), *Emerging integration of clinical and social psychology.* New York: Oxford University Press.

Cooper, J., Darley, J. M., & Henderson, J. T. (1974). On the effectiveness of deviant and conventionally appearing communicators: A field experiment. *Journal of Personality and Social Psychology, 29,* 752–757.

Cooper, J., Zanna, M. P., & Taves, P. A. (1978). Arousal as a necessary condition for attitude change following induced compliance. *Journal of Personality and Social Psychology, 36,* 1101–1106.

Cooper, L. (1932). *The rhetoric of Aristotle.* New York: Appleton-Century-Crofts

Corey, S. M. (1937). Professed attitudes and actual behavior. *Journal of Educational Psychology, 28,* 271–280.

Coser, L. A. (1956). *The functions of social conflict.* Glencoe, IL: Free Press.

Coser, L. A. (1967). *Continuities in the study of social conflict.* New York: Free Press.

Cottington, E., Matthews, K., Talbott, E., Kuller, L., & Siegel, J. (1984). *Occupational stress, suppressed anger and hypertension: The Pittsburgh Noise-Hypertension Project.* Paper presented at the annual meeting of the Society for Epidemiological Research, Houston.

Cox, E. P. (1980). The optimal number of response alternatives for scale: A review. *Journal of Marketing Research, 17*(4), 407–422.

Craig, C. S., & McCann, J. M. (1978). Item nonresponse in mail surveys: extent and correlates. *Journal of Marketing Research, 15,* 285–289.

Craig, K. D. (1986). Social modeling influences on pain. In R. A. Sternbach (Ed.), *The psychology of pain.* New York: Raven Press.

Crane, M., & Markus, H. (1982). Gender identity: The benefits of a self-schema approach. *Journal of Personality and Social Psycholology, 43,* 1195–1197.

Crano, W. D., & Mellon, P. M. (1978). Causal influence of teachers' expectations on children's academic performance: A cross-lagged panel analysis. *Journal of Educational Psychology, 70,* 39–49.

Crocker, J., Hannah, D. B., & Weber, R. (1983). Person memory and causal attributions. *Journal of Personality and Social Psychology, 44,* 55–66.

Cromwell, R. L., Butterfield, E. C., Brayfield, F. M., & Curry, J. G. (1977). *Acute myocardial infarction.* St. Louis: Mosby.

Cronbach, L. J. (1975). Beyond the two disciplines of scientific psychology. *American Psychologist, 30,* 116–127.

Crosby, F., Bromley, S., & Saxe, L. (1980). Recent unobtrusive studies of black and white discrimination and prejudice: A literature review. *Psychological Bulletin, 87,* 546–563.

Crow, W. J. (1963). A study of strategic doctrines using the inter-nation simulation. *Journal of Conflict Resolution, 7,* 580–598.

Croxton, J. S., & Klonsky, B. G. (1982). Sex differences in causal attributions for success and failure in real and hypothetical sport settings. *Sex Roles, 8,* 399–410.

Crutchfield, R. S. (1955). Conformity and character. *American Psychologist, 10,* 191–198.

Curran, J. P. (1977). Skills training as an approach to the treatment of heterosexual-social anxiety: A review. *Psychological Bulletin, 84,* 140–157.

Curran, J. P., & Lippold, S. (1975). The effects of physical attractiveness and attitude similarity on attraction in dating dyads. *Journal of Personality, 43,* 528–539.

Cutright, P. (1971). Income and family events: Marital stability. *Journal of Marriage and the Family, 33,* 291–306.

Cutrona, C. E. (1982). Transition to college: Loneliness and the process of social adjustment. In L. A. Peplau and D. Perlman (Eds.), *Loneliness: A sourcebook of current theory, research, and therapy.* New York: Wiley.

Dabbs, J. M. (1971). Physical closeness and negative feelings. *Psychonomic Science, 23,* 141–143.

Dalkey, N. C. (1969). An experimental study of group opinion: The Delphi method. *Futures, 1,* 408–426.

D'Amato, A. (1975). "Bad Samaritan" paradigm. *Northwestern University Law Review, 70,* 798–812.

Danziger, K. (1985). The origins of the psychology experiment as a social institution. *American Psychologist, 40,* 133–140.

Darley, J. M., & Batson, C. D. (1973). From Jerusalem to Jericho: A study of situational and dispositional variables in helping behavior. *Journal of Personality and Social Psychology, 27,* 100–108.

Darley, J. M., & Berscheid, E. (1967). Increased liking caused by the anticipation of personal contact. *Human Relations, 20,* 29–40.

Darley, J. M., & Latané, B. (1968). Bystander intervention in emergencies: Diffusion of responsibility. *Journal of Personality and Social Psychology, 8,* 377–383.

Darley, J. M., & Latané, B. (1968, December). When will people help in a crisis? *Psychology Today,* pp. 54–57, 71.

Darley, J. M., Teger, A. I., & Lewis, L. D. (1973). Do groups always inhibit individuals' responses to potential emergencies? *Journal of Personality and Social Psychology, 26,* 395–399.

Darley, S. A. (1976). Big-time careers for the "little woman": A dual-role dilemma. *Journal of Social Issues, 32,* 85–98.

Darwin, C. (1872). *The expression of the emotions in man and animals.* London: John Murray.

Davidson, A. R., & Jaccard, J. (1979). Variables that moderate the attitude-behavior relation: Results of a longitudinal survey. *Journal of Personality and Social Psychology, 37,* 1364–1376.

Davidson, R. J., Schwartz, G. E., Pugash, E., & Bromfield, E. (1976). Sex differences in patterns of EEG symmetry. *Biological Psychology, 4,* 119–138.

Davis, J. D. (1977). Effects of communication about interpersonal process on the evolution of self-disclosure in dyads. *Journal of Personality and Social Psychology, 35,* 31–37.

Davis, J. H. (1969). *Group performance.* New York: Addison-Wesley.

Davis, J. H. (1973). Group decision and social interaction: A theory of social decision schemes. *Psychological Review, 80,* 97–125.

Davis, J. H. (1980). Group decision and procedural justice. In M. Fishbein (Ed.), *Progress in social psychology.* Hillsdale, NJ: Erlbaum.

Davis, R. C. (1982). Mediation: The Brooklyn Experiment. In R. Tomasic & M. M. Feeley (Eds.), *Neighborhood justice: Assessment of an emerging idea.* New York: Longman.

Davitz, J. R., & Mason, D. J. (1955). Socially facilitated reduction of fear response in rats. *Journal of Comparative and Physiological Psychology, 48,* 149–151.

Deaux, K. (1979). Self-evaluations of male and female managers. *Sex Roles, 5,* 571–580.

Deaux, K. (1984). From individual differences to social categories: Analysis of a decade's research on gender. *American Psychologist, 39,* 105–116.

Deaux, K., & Emswiller, T. (1974). Explanations of successful performance on sex-linked tasks: What is skill for the male is luck for the female. *Journal of Personality and Social Psychology, 29,* 80–85.

Deaux, K., & Lewis, L. L. (1984). Structure of gender components: Interrelationships among components and gender labels. *Journal of Personality and Social Psychology, 46,* 991–1004.

Deaux, K., & Taynor, J. (1973). Evaluation of male and female ability: Bias works two ways. *Psychological Reports, 32,* 261–262.

Deci, E. L. (1971). Effects of externally mediated rewards on intrinsic motivation. *Journal of Personality and Social Psychology, 18,* 105–115.

Deci, E. L. (1972). Intrinsic motivation, extrinsic reinforcement and inequity. *Journal of Personality and Social Psychology, 22,* 113–120.

Deci, E. L. (1975). *Intrinsic motivation.* New York: Plenum.

Deci, E. L., & Ryan, R. M. (1985). *Intrinsic motivation and self-determination in human behavior.* New York: Plenum.

Deffenbacher, K. A. (1984). Experimental psychology actually can assist triers of fact. *American Psychologist, 39,* 1066, 1067.

DeFleur, M. L., D'Antonio, W. V., & DeFleur, L. B. (1973). *Sociology: Human society.* Glenview, IL: Scott, Foresman.

DeFleur, M. L., & Westie, F. R. (1958). Verbal attitudes and overt acts: An experiment in the salience of attitudes. *American Sociological Review, 23,* 667–673.

DeFrancis, V. (1973). Testimony before the Subcommittee on Children and Youth of the Committee on Labor and Public Welfare. United States Senate, 93rd Congress, 1st session. On *S1191 Child Abuse Prevention Act.* Washington, DC: U.S. Government Printing Office.

DeJong, W. (1979). An examination of self-perception mediation of the foot in the door effect. *Journal of Personality and Social Psychology, 37,* 2171–2180.

DeJong, W. (1981). Consensus information and the foot in the door effect. *Personality and Social Psychology Bulletin, 7,* 423–430.

DeJong, W., Goolkasian, G. A., & McGillis, D. (1983). *The use of mediation and arbitration in small claims disputes.* Washington, DC: U.S. Department of Justice.

DeLeon, P. H., O'Keefe, A. M., Vanden Bos, G. R., & Kraut, A. G. (1982). How to influence public policy: A blueprint for activism. *American Psychologist, 37,* 476–485.

Delgado, J. M. (1969). *Physical control of the mind.* New York: Harper & Row.

Delgado, J. M. (1970). Modulation of emotions by cerebral radio stimulation. In P. Black (Ed.), *Physiological correlates of emotion.* New York: Academic Press.

Dembroski, T. (1980). Coronary-prone behavior. *National Forum, 60,* 5–9.

Dembroski, T. M., & MacDougall, J. M. (1982). Coronary-prone behavior, social psychophysiology, and coronary heart disease. In J. R. Eiser (Ed.), *Social psychology and behavioral medicine.* New York: Wiley.

Dengerink, H. A., O'Leary, M. R., & Krasner, K. H. (1975). Individual differences in aggressive responses to attack: Internal-external locus of control and field dependence-independence. *Journal of Research in Personality, 9,* 191–199.

Dennis, W. (1948). The new social psychology. In R. Patton (Ed.), *Current trends in social psychology.* Pittsburgh, PA: University of Pittsburgh Press.

Dentler, R. A. (1961). Political concern and opinion change in ten work groups. *Journal of Educational Sociology, 35,* 27–31.

Derlega, V. J., & Chaikin, A. L. (1975). *Sharing*

intimacy: What we reveal to others and why. Englewood Cliffs, NJ: Prentice-Hall.

Dermer, M., & Thiel, D. (1975). When beauty may fail. *Journal of Personality and Social Psychology, 31,* 1168–1176.

Deutsch, M. (1973). *The resolution of conflict: Constructive and destructive processes.* New Haven, CT: Yale University Press.

Deutsch, M. (1980). Socially relevant research: Comments on "applied" versus "basic" research. In R. F. Kidd and M. J. Saks (Eds.), *Advances in applied social psychology* (Vol. 1). Hillsdale, NJ: Erlbaum.

Deutsch, M., & Collins, M. E. (1951). *Interracial housing: A psychological evaluation of a social experiment.* Minneapolis: University of Minnesota Press.

Deutsch, M., & Gerard, H. (1955). A study of normative and informational social influences upon individual judgment. *Journal of Abnormal and Social Psychology, 51,* 629–636.

Deutsch, M., & Krauss, R. M. (1960). The effect of threat on interpersonal bargaining. *Journal of Abnormal and Social Psychology, 61,* 181–189.

Deutscher, I. (1966). Words and deeds: Social science and social policy. *Social Problems, 13,* 242.

Deutscher, I. (1973). *What we say/what we do.* Glenview, IL: Scott, Foresman.

DeVries, D. L., & Ajzen, I. (1971). The relationship of attitudes and normative beliefs to cheating in college. *Journal of Social Psychology, 83,* 199–207.

Dibiase, W., & Hjelle, L. (1968). Body-image sterotypes and bodytype preferences among male college students. *Perceptual and Motor Skills, 27,* 1143–1146.

Diener, E. (1979). Deindividuation, self-awareness, and disinhibition. *Journal of Personality and Social Psychology, 37,* 1160–1171.

Diener, E., & Crandall, R. (1978). *Ethics in social and behavioral research.* Chicago: University of Chicago Press.

Diener, E., & DeFour, D. (1978). Does television violence enhance program popularity? *Journal of Personality and Social Psychology, 36,* 333–341

Diener, E., Fraser, S. C., Beaman, A. L., & Kelem, R. T. (1976). Effects of deindividuation variables on stealing among Halloween trick-or-treaters. *Journal of Personality and Social Psychology, 33,* 178–183.

DiMatteo, M. R., & DiNicola, D. D. (1982). *Achieving patient compliance.* Elmsford, NY: Pergamon.

Dimock, H. G. (1978). The use of system-improvement research in developing a change strategy for human services organizations. *Group and Organization Studies, 3,* 365–375.

Dion, K., Berscheid, E., & Walster, E. (1972). What is beautiful is good. *Journal of Personality and Social Psychology, 24,* 285–290.

Dion, K. L. (1979). Intergroup conflict and intergroup cohesiveness. In W. G. Austin and S. Worchel (Eds.), *The social psychology of intergroup relations.* Monterey, CA: Brooks/Cole.

Dion, K. L., Baron, R. S., & Miller, N. (1970). Why do groups make riskier decisions than individuals? In L. Berkowitz (Ed.), *Advances in experimental social psychology* (Vol. 5). New York: Academic Press.

Dipboye, R. L. (1977). The effectiveness of one-sided and two-sided appeals as a function of familiarization and context. *Journal of Social Psychology, 102,* 125–131.

Doise, W., Csepeli, G., Dann, H. D., Gouge, C., Larsen, K., & Ostell, A. (1972). An experimental investigation into the formation of intergroup representations. *European Journal of Social Psychology, 2,* 202–204.

Dollard, J., Doob, L., Miller, N., Mowrer, O. H., & Sears, R. R. (1939). *Frustration and aggression,* New Haven, CT: Yale University Press.

Domino, G. (1968). Differential prediction of academic achievement in conforming and independent settings. *Journal of Educational Psychology, 59,* 256–260.

Domino, G. (1971). Interactive effects of achievement orientation and teaching style on academic achievement. *Journal of Educational Psychology, 62,* 427–431.

Donnerstein, E. (1980). Aggressive erotica and violence against women. *Journal of Personality and Social Psychology, 39,* 269–277.

Donnerstein, E., & Berkowitz, L. (1981). Victim reactions in aggressive-erotic films as a factor in violence against women. *Journal of Personality and Social Psychology, 41,* 710–724.

Donnerstein, M., & Donnerstein, E. (1977). Modeling in the control of interracial aggression: The problem of generality. *Journal of Personality and Social Psychology, 45,* 100–116.

Doob, L. W. (Ed.) (1970). *Resolving conflict in Africa: The Fermeda workshop.* New Haven, CT: Yale University Press.

Doob, L. W. (1974). A Cyprus workshop: An exercise in intervention methodology. *Journal of Social Psychology, 94,* 161–178.

Dosey, M., & Meisels, M. (1969). Personal space and self-protection. *Journal of Personality and Social Psychology, 11,* 93–97.

Dovidio, J. F. (1984). Helping and altruism: An empirical and conceptional review. In L. Berkowitz (Ed.), *Advances in experimental social psychology* (Vol. 17). New York: Academic Press.

Drachman, D., de Carufel, A., & Insko, C. A. (1978). The extra credit effect in interpersonal attraction. *Journal of Experimental Social Psychology, 14,* 458–465.

Druckman, D. (1968). Ethnocentrism in the inter-nation simulation. *Journal of Conflict Resolution, 12,* 45–68.

Druckman, D. (Ed.) (1977). *Negotiations: Social-psychological perspectives.* Beverly Hills, CA: Sage.

Druckman, D. (1983). Social psychology and international negotiations: Processes and influences. In R. F. Kidd & M. J. Saks (Eds.), *Advances in applied social psychology* (Vol. II). Hillsdale, NJ: Erlbaum.

Dubos, R. (1970). We can't buy our way out. *Psychology Today, 3*(10), 20–22, 86–87.

Ducett, J., and Wolk, S. (1972). Locus of control and extreme behavior. *Journal of Consulting and Clinical Psychology, 39,* 253–258.

Duke, M. P., & Nowicki, S. (1972). A new measure and social learning model for interpersonal distance. *Journal of Experimental Research in Personality, 6,* 119–132.

Dunnette, M. D. (Ed.) (1983). *Handbook of industrial and organizational psychology.* New York: Wiley.

Durkin, K. (1985). Television and sex role acquisition. *British Journal of Social Psychology, 24,* 101–114.

Dusek, J. B., Hall, V. C, & Neger, W. J. (1984). *Teacher expectancies.* Hillsdale, NJ: Erlbaum.

Dutton, D. G., & Lake, R. A. (1973). Threat of own prejudice and reverse discrimination in interracial situations. *Journal of Personality and Social Psychology, 28,* 94–100.

Duval, S., & Wicklund, R. A. (1972). *A theory of objective self-awareness.* New York: Academic Press.

Dweck, C. (1975). The role expectations and attributions in the alleviation of learned helplessness. *Journal of Personality and Social Psychology, 31,* 674–685.

Dynes, R. R. (1970). Organizational involvement and changes in community structure in disasters. *American Behavioral Scientist, 13,* 430–439.

Eagly, A. H. (1967). Involvement as a determinant of response to favorable and unfavorable information. *Journal of Personality and Social Psychology Monograph, 7,* (3, Part 2).

Eagly, A. H. (1978). Sex differences in influenceability. *Psychological Bulletin, 85,* 86–116.

Eagly, A. H. (1981). Recipient characteristics as determinants of responses to persuasion. In R. E. Petty, T. M. Ostrom, & T. C. Brock (Eds.), *Cognitive responses in persuasion.* Hillsdale, NJ: Erlbaum.

Eagly, A. H. (1983). Gender and social influence: A social psychological analysis. *American Psychologist, 38,* 971–981.

Eagly, A. H., & Carli, L. (1981). Sex researchers and sex-typed communications as determinants of sex differences in influenceability. *Psychological Bulletin, 90,* 1–20.

Eagly, A. H., & Chaiken, S. (1975). An attribution analysis of the effect of communicator characteristics on opinion change: A case of communicator attractiveness. *Journal of Personality and Social Psychology, 32,* 136–144.

Eagly, A. H., & Telaak, K. (1972). Width of the latitude of acceptance as a determinant of attitude change. *Journal of Personality and Social Psychology, 3,* 388–397.

Eagly, A. H., & Warren, R. (1976). Intelligence, comprehension, and opinion change. *Journal of Personality, 44,* 226–242.

Eagly, A. H., & Wood, W. (1982). Inferred sex differences in status as a determinant of gender stereotypes about social influence. *Journal of Personality and Social Psychology, 43,* 915–928.

Eagly, A. H., Wood, W., & Chaiken, S. (1978).

Causal inferences about communicators and their effect on opinion change. *Journal of Personality and Social Psychology, 36,* 424–435.

Eagly, A. H., Wood, W., & Fishbaugh, L. (1981). Sex differences in conformity: Surveillance by the group as a determinant of male nonconformity. *Journal of Personality and Social Psychology, 40,* 384–394.

Eden, D., & Shani, A. B. (1982). Pygmalion goes to boot camp: Expectancy, leadership, and trainee performance. *Journal of Applied Psychology, 87,* 194–199.

Edney, J. J. (1972). Property, possession and permanence: A field study in human territoriality. *Journal of Applied Social Psychology, 2,* 275–282.

Edney, J. J. (1976). Human territories: Comment on functional properties. *Environment and Behavior, 8,* 31–48.

Edwards, J. D., & Holmgren, R. L. (1979). Some prerequisites for becoming a "really" applied, non-academic social psychologist. *Personality and Social Psychology Bulletin, 5,* 516–523.

Ehrlich, I. (1975). The deterrent effect of capital punishment: A question of life and death. *American Economic Review, 65,* 397–417.

Eisen, S. V., & MacArthur, L. Z. (1979). Evaluating and sentencing a defendant as a function of his salience and the observer's set. *Personality and Social Psychology Bulletin, 5,* 48–52.

Ekehammar, B. (1974). Interactionism in personality from a historical perspective. *Psychological Bulletin, 81,* 1026–1048.

Ekman, P. (1971). Universals and cultural differences in facial expressions of emotion. In J. K. Cole (Ed.), *Nebraska symposium on motivation* (Vol. 18). Lincoln: University of Nebraska Press.

Ekman, P., & Friesen, W. V. (1975). *Unmasking the face.* Englewood Cliffs, NJ: Prentice-Hall.

Ekman, P., Friesen, W. V., & Bear, J. (1984). The international language of gestures. *Psychology Today, 18,* 64–69.

Ekman, P., Friesen, W. V., & Scherer, K. (1977). Body movements and voice pitch in deceptive interaction. *Semiotica, 16,* 23–27.

Ellis, G. T., & Sekyra, F. (1972). The effect of aggresssive cartoon on the behavior of first-grade children. *Journal of Psychology, 81,* 37–43.

Elmer, E. (1979). Child abuse and family stress. *Journal of Social Issues, 35,* 60–71.

Elms, A. C. (1975). The crisis of confidence in social psychology. *American Psychologist, 30,* 967–976.

Elms, A. C., & Janis, I. L. (1965). Counter-norm attitudes induced by consonant versus dissonant conditions of role playing. *Journal of Experimental Research in Personality, 1,* 50–60.

Elms, A. C., & Milgram, S. (1966). Personality characteristics associated with obedience and defiance towards authoritative command. *Journal of Experimental Research in Personality, 2,* 282–289.

Ember, C. R. (1973). Feminine task assignment and the social behavior of boys. *Ethos, 1,* 424–439.

Emery, F. E., & Trist, E. L. (1960). *Management science models and techniques* (Vol. 2). London: Pergamon.

Endler, N. S., & Magnusson, D. (1976). Toward an interactional psychology of personality. *Psychological Bulletin, 83,* 56–74.

Endler, N. S., & Okada, M. (1975). A multidimensional measure of trait anxiety: The S-R inventory of general trait anxiousness. *Journal of Consulting and Clinical Psychology, 43,* 319–329.

Epstein, R., & Komorita, S. S. (1966). Prejudice among Negro children as related to parental ethnocentrism and punitiveness. *Journal of Personality and Social Psychology, 4,* 643–647.

Epstein, S. (1973). The self-concept revisited: Or a theory of a theory. *American Psychologist, 28,* 404–416.

Epstein, Y. M., & Karlin, R. A. (1975). Effects of acute experimental crowding. *Journal of Applied Social Psychology, 5,* 34–53.

Epstein, Y. M., Krupat, E., & Obudho, C. (1976). Clean is beautiful: Identification and preference as a function of race and cleanliness. *Journal of Social Issues, 32,* 109–118.

Eraker, S. A., Kirscht, J. P., & Becker, M. H. (1984). Understanding and improving compliance. *Annals of Internal Medicine, 100,* 258–268.

Eron, L. D. (1980). Prescription for reduction of aggression. *American Psychologist, 35,* 244–252.

Eron, L. D. (1982). Parent-child interaction, television violence, and aggression in children. *American Psychologist, 37,* 197–211.

Eron, L. D. (1987). The development of aggressive behavior from the perspective of a developing behaviorism. *American Psychologist, 42,* 435–442.

Eron, L. D., Huesmann, L. R., Debow, E., Romanoff, R., & Yarmel, P. (1987). Aggression and its correlates over 22 years. In D. Crowell, I. Evans, & C. O'Donnell (Eds.), *Childhood aggression and violence: Sources of influence, prevention and control.* New York: Plenum.

Eron, L. D., Huesmann, L. R., Lefkowtiz, M. M., & Walder, L. O. (1972). Does television violence cause aggression? *American Psychologist, 27,* 253–263.

Esser, A. H. (1973). Cottage fourteen: Dominance and territoriality in a group of institutionalized boys. *Small Group Behavior, 4,* 131–146.

Etzioni, A. (1962). *A hard way to peace.* New York: Collier.

Etzioni, A. (1967). The Kennedy experiment. *The Western Political Science Quarterly, 20,* 361–380.

Etzioni, A. (1969). Social psychological aspects of international relations. In G. Lindzey & E. Aronson (Eds.), *Handbook of Social Psychology* (2nd ed.) (Vol. 5). Reading, MA: Addison-Wesley.

Etzioni, A. (1972, June). Human beings are not very easy to change after all. *Saturday Review,* pp. 3ff.

Etzioni, A., & Remp, R. (1972). Technological short-cuts to social change. *Science, 175,* 31–38.

Evans, G. W. (1979). Crowding and human performance. *Journal of Applied Social Psychology, 9,* 27–46.

Evans, G. W., Jacobs, S. V., & Frager, N. B. (1982). Behavioral responses to air pollution. In A. Baum & J. E. Singer (Eds.), *Advances in environmental psychology.* Hillsdale, NJ: Erlbaum.

Evans, G. W., & Lovell, B. (1979). Design modification in an open-school plan. *Journal of Educational Psychology, 71,* 41–49.

Evans, R. I., Rozelle, R. M., Maxwell, S. E., Raines, B. E., Dill, C. A., Guthrie, T. J., Henderson, A. H., & Hill, P. C. (1981). Social modeling films to deter smoking in adolescents: Results of a three-year field investigation. *Journal of Applied Psychology, 66,* 399–414.

Evans, R. I., Rozelle, R. M., Mittelmark, M. B., Hansen, W. B., Bane, A. L., & Havis, J. (1978). Deterring the onset of smoking in children: Knowledge of immediate physiological effects and coping with peer pressure, media pressure, and parent modeling. *Journal of Applied Social Psychology, 8,* 126–135.

Evans, R. I., Smith, C. K., & Raines, B. E. (1984). Deterring cigarette smoking in adolescents: A psychological-behavioral analysis of an intervention strategy. In A. Baum, S. E. Taylor, & J. E. Singer (Eds.), *Handbook of psychology and health* (Vol. 14). Hillsdale, NJ: Erlbaum.

Eysenck, H. J., & Nias, D. K. (1982). *Astrology: Science or superstition.* New York: St. Martin's Press.

Fairweather, G. W. (1967). *Methods for experimental social innovation.* New York: Wiley.

Fairweather, G. W. (1972). *Social change: The challenge to survival.* Morristown, NJ: General Learning Press.

Faison, E. W. J. (1961). Effectiveness of one-sided and two-sided mass communications and advertising. *Public Opinion Quarterly, 25,* 468–469.

Falbo, T., & Peplau, L. A. (1980). Power strategies in intimate relationships. *Journal of Personality and Social Psychology, 38,* 618–628.

Farina, A., & Fisher, J. D. (1982). Beliefs about mental disorders: Findings and implications. In G. Weary and H. Mirels (Eds.), *Integrations of clinical and social psychology.* New York: Oxford University Press.

Faucheux, C., Amado, G., & Laurent, A. (1982). Organizational development and change. In M. R. Rosenzweig & L. W. Porter (Eds.), *Annual Review of Psychology, 33,* 343–370.

Fazio, R. A., Zanna, M. P., & Cooper, J. (1977). Dissonance and self-perception: An integrative view of each theories' proper domain of application. *Journal of Experimental Social Psychology, 13,* 464–479.

Fazio, R. H., & Cooper, J. (1983). Arousal in the dissonance process. In J. T. Cacioppo & R. E. Petty (Eds.), *Social psychophysiology: A sourcebook* (pp. 122–152). New York: Guilford Press.

Fazio, R. H., & Zanna, M. P. (1981). Direct experience and attitude–behavior consistency. In L. Berkowitz (Ed.), *Advances in experimental social psychology* (Vol. 14). New York: Academic Press.

Feather, N. T. (1963). Cognitive dissonance, sensitivity, and evaluation. *Journal of Abnormal and Social Psychology, 66,* 157–163.

Feather, N. T., & Simon, J. G. (1973). Fear of success and causal attribution of outcomes. *Journal of Personality, 41,* 525–542.

Feldman-Summers, S., Montano, D. E., Kasprzyk, D., & Wagner, B. (1980). Influence attempts when competing views are gender related. *Psychology of Women Quarterly, 5,* 311–320.

Felstiner, W. L. F. (1975). Avoidance as dispute processing: An elaboration. *Law and Society Review, 9,* 695–706.

Fenigstein, A. (1979). Does aggression cause a preference for viewing media violence? *Journal of Personality and Social Psychology, 37,* 2307–2317.

Ferguson, T. J., & Wells, G. L. (1980). Priming on mediators in causal attribution. *Journal of Personality and Social Psychology, 38,* 461–470.

Feshbach, S. (1970). Aggression. In P. H. Mussen (Ed.), *Carmichael's manual of child psychology* (Vol. 2). New York: Wiley.

Feshbach, S. (1984). The catharsis hypothesis, aggressive drive, and the reduction of aggression. *Aggressive Behavior, 10,* 91–101.

Feshbach, S., & Singer, R. D. (1971). *Television and aggression.* San Francisco: Jossey-Bass.

Festinger, L. (1950). Informal social communication. *Psychological Review, 57,* 271–282.

Festinger, L. (1954). A theory of social comparison processes. *Human Relations, 7,* 117–140.

Festinger, L. (1957). *A theory of cognitive dissonance.* Stanford: Stanford University Press.

Festinger, L. (1964). *Conflict, decision, and dissonance.* Stanford: Stanford University Press.

Festinger, L., & Carlsmith, J. M. (1959). Cognitive consequences of forced compliance. *Journal of Abnormal and Social Psychology, 58,* 203–210.

Festinger, L., Pepitone, A., & Newcomb, T. (1952). Some consequences of deindividuation in a group. *Journal of Abnormal and Social Psychology, 47,* 382–389.

Festinger, L., Riecken, H. W., & Schachter, S. (1956). *When prophecy fails.* Minneapolis: University of Minnesota Press.

Festinger, L., Schachter, S., & Back, K. (1950). *Social pressures in informal groups: A study of human factors in housing.* New York: Harper & Row.

Festinger, L., & Thibaut, J. (1951). Interpersonal communication in small groups. *Journal of Abnormal and Social Psychology 46,* 92–99.

Fidell, L. S. (1976). Empirical verification of sex descrimination in hiring practices in psychology. In T. Inger & F. Denmark (Eds.), *Women: Dependent or independent variables?* New York: Psychological Dimensions.

Fiedler, F. E. (1967). *A theory of leadership effectiveness.* New York: McGraw-Hill.

Fiedler, F. E., Chemers, M. M., & Mahar, L. (1977). *Improving leadership effectiveness: The leader match concept* (rev. ed.). New York: Wiley.

Fincham, F. D. (1983). Clinical applications of attribution theory: Problems and perspectives. In M. Hewstone (Ed.), *Attribution theory: Extensions and applications.* Oxford, England: Blackwell Publishers.

Firth, M. (1982). Sex discrimination in job opportunities for women. *Sex-Roles, 8,* 891–901.

Fischer, C. (1982). *To dwell among friends: Personal networks in town and city.* Chicago: University of Chicago Press.

Fishbein, M. (1963). An investigation of the relationships between beliefs about an object and the attitude toward that object. *Human Relations, 16,* 233–240.

Fishbein, M. (Ed.) (1967). *Attitude theory and measurement.* New York: Wiley.

Fishbein, M., & Ajzen, I. (1972). Attitudes and opinions. *Annual Review of Psychology, 23,* 487–544.

Fishbein, M., and Ajzen, I. (1975). *Belief, attitude, intention, and behavior: An introduction to theory and research.* Reading, MA: Addison-Wesley.

Fishbein, M., & Coombs, F. S. (1974). Basis for decision: An attitudinal analysis of voting behavior. *Journal of Applied Social Psychology, 4,* 95–124.

Fisher, B. A. (1980). *Small group decision mak-*

ing: Communication and the group process (2nd ed.). New York: McGraw-Hill.

Fisher, J., Nadler, A., & Whitcher-Alagna, S. (1982). Recipient reactions to aid. *Psychological Bulletin, 91,* 27–54.

Fisher, J. D., Bell, P. A., & Baum, A. (1984). *Environmental psychology* (2nd ed.). New York: Holt, Rinehart and Winston.

Fisher, J. L. (1984). *Power of the presidency.* New York: Macmillan.

Fisher, R. (1980). Touchstones for applied social psychology. In R. F. Kidd & M. J. Saks (Eds.), *Advances in applied social psychology* (Vol. 1). Hillsdale, NJ: Erlbaum.

Fisher, R. J. (1976). Third-party consultation: A skill for professional psychologists in community practice. *Professional Psychology, 7,* 344–351.

Fisher, R. J. (1980). A third-party consultation workshop on the India-Pakistan conflict. *Journal of Social Psychology, 112,* 191–206.

Fisher, R. J. (1982). *Social psychology: An applied approach.* New York: St. Martin's Press.

Fiske, S. (1980). Attention and weight in person perception: The impact of negative and extreme behavior. *Journal of Personality and Social Psychology, 38,* 889–906.

Fiske, S. T., & Cox, M. G. (1979). Person concepts: The effect of target familiarity and descriptive purpose on the process of describing others. *Journal of Personality, 47,* 136–161.

Fiske, S. T., & Linville, P. W. (1980). What does the schema concept buy us? *Personality and Social Psychology Bulletin, 6,* 543–557.

Fiske, S. T., & Taylor, S. E. (1984). *Social cognition.* Reading, MA: Addison-Wesley.

Fitz, D. (1976). A renewed look at Miller's conflict theory of aggression displacement. *Journal of Personality and Social Psychology, 33,* 725–732.

Flanagan, T. J., Van Alstyne, D. J., & Gottfredson, M. R. (1982). *Sourcebook of criminal justice statistics.* Washington, DC: U.S. Department of Justice.

Foa, U. G., & Foa, E. B. (1974). *Societal structures of the mind.* Springfield, IL: Charles C. Thomas.

Folkes, V. S. (1982). Forming relationships and the matching hypothesis. *Personality and Social Psychology Bulletin, 8,* 631–636.

Fong, G. T., & Markus, H. (1982). Self-schemas and judgments about others. *Social Cognition, 1,* 191–205.

Fontana, V. J. (1973). *Somewhere a child is crying: Maltreatment causes and prevention.* New York: Macmillan.

Foss, R. D. (1983). Community norms and blood donation. *Journal of Applied Social Psychology, 13,* 281–290.

Foss, R. D. (1986). Using social psychology to increase altruism: Will it help? In M. J. Saks & L. Saxe (Eds.), *Advances in applied social psychology* (Vol. 3). Hillsdale, NJ: Erlbaum.

Foss, R. D., & Dempsey, C. B. (1979). Blood donation and the foot-in-the-door technique. *Journal of Personality and Social Psychology, 37,* 580–590.

Fowler, F. J., & Mangione, T. W. (1981). *An experimental effort to reduce crime and fear of crime in an urban residential neighborhood: Re-evaluation of the Hartford neighborhood crime prevention program.* (Draft executive summary.) Boston: Harvard/M.I.T. Center for Survey Research.

Fox, L. H., Tobin, D., & Brody, L. (1979). Sex role socialization and achievement in mathematics. In M. A. Wittig & A. C. Peterson (Eds.), *Sex related differences in cognitive functioning: Developmental issues.* New York: Academic Press.

Frager, R. (1970). Conformity and anti-conformity in Japan. *Journal of Personality and Social Psychology, 15,* 207–210.

Franck, K. A. (1980). Friends and strangers: The social experience of living in urban and nonurban settings. *Journal of Social Issues, 3,* 52–71.

Frank, J. D. (1957). Some determinants, manifestations and effects of cohesion in therapy groups. *International Journal of Group Psychotherapy, 7,* 53–62.

Fraser, B. G. (1976). The child and his parents: A delicate balance of rights. In R. E. Helfer & C. H. Kemp (Eds.), *Child abuse and neglect: The family and the community,* Cambridge, MA: Ballinger.

Fraser, C. (1971). Group risk-taking and group polarization. *European Journal of Social Psychology, 1,* 493–510.

Fraser, S. C., Beaman, A. L., Diener, E., & Kelem,

R. T. (1977). Two, three, and four heads are better than one: Modification of college performance by peer monitoring. *Journal of Educational Psychology, 69,* 109–114.

Fredericksen, N. (1972). Toward a taxonomy of situations. *American Psychologist, 27,* 114–123.

Freedman, J. L. (1975). *Crowding and behavior.* San Francisco: Freeman.

Freedman, J. L. (1984). Effect of television violence on aggressiveness. *Psychological Bulletin, 96*, 227–246.

Freedman, J. L., & Fraser, S. C. (1966). Compliance without pressure: The foot-in-the-door technique. *Journal of Personality and Social Psychology, 4,* 195–202.

Freedman, J. L., & Sears, D. (1966). Selective exposure. In L. Berkowitz (Ed.), *Advances in experimental social psychology.* New York: Academic Press.

Freeman, H. E., & Solomon, M. A. (1979). The next decade in evaluation research. *Evaluation and Program Planning, 2,* 255–262.

Freeman, H. E., & Solomon, M. A. (1981). Evaluation and the uncertain '80s. In H. E. Freeman & M. A. Solomon (Eds.), *Evaluation studies review annual* (Vol. 6). Beverly Hills, CA: Sage.

Freeman, S., Walker, M., Borden, R., & Latané, B. (1975). Diffusion of responsibility and restaurant tipping: Cheaper by the bunch. *Personality and Social Psychology Bulletin, 1,* 584–587.

Freidson, E. (1970). *Profession of medicine.* New York: Dodd, Mead.

French, J. R. P. (1950). Field experiments: Changing group productivity. In J. G. Miller (Ed.), *Experiments in social process.* New York: McGraw-Hill.

French, J. R. P., Jr., & Coch, L. (1948). Overcoming resistance to change. *Human Relations, 1,* 512–532.

French, J. R. P., & Raven, B. (1959). The bases of social power. In D. Cartwright (Ed.), *Studies in social power.* Ann Arbor, MI: Institute for Social Research.

French, W. L., & Bell, C. H., Jr. (1978). *Organization development: Behavioral science interventions for organization improvement* (2nd ed.). Englewood Cliffs, NJ: Prentice-Hall.

Frenkel, O. J., & Doob, A. N. (1976). Post-decision dissonance at the polling booth. *Canadian Journal of Behavioural Science, 8*, 347–350.

Freud, S. (1933). *New introductory lectures on psycho-analysis.* New York: Norton.

Freud, S. [fragment of an analysis of a case of hysteria] (Joan Riviere, Trans.) (1959). In *Collected papers of Sigmund Freud* (Vol. 3). New York: Basic Books (originally published 1905).

Frey, D. (1981). Postdecisional preference for decision relevant information as a function of the competence of its source and the degree of familiarity with this information. *Journal of Experimental Social Psychology, 17,* 51–67.

Frey, D. (1982). Different levels of cognitive dissonance, information seeking, and information avoidance. *Journal of Personality and Social Psychology, 43,* 1175–1183.

Fried, M., & Gleicher, P. (1961). Some sources of satisfaction in an urban slum. *Journal of American Institute of Planners, 27,* 305–315.

Friedman, H. S. (1979). Nonverbal communication between patients and medical practitioners. *Journal of Social Issues, 35,* 82–99.

Friedman, M., & Rosenman, R. H. (1974). *Type A behavior and your heart.* New York: Knopf.

Frieze, I. H., Whitley, B. E., Hanusa, B. H., & McHugh, M. C. (1982). Assessing the theoretical models for sex differences in causal attributions for success and failure. *Sex Roles, 8,* 333–334.

Fritz, C. E., & Mathewson, J. H. (1957). *Convergent behavior in disasters: A problem in social control.* Washington, DC: National Research Council Publication 476.

Frodi, A. (1975). The effect of exposure to weapons on aggressive behavior from a cross-cultural perspective. *International Journal of Psychology, 10*, 283–292.

Frodi, A., Macaulay J., & Thome, P. R. (1977). Sexual arousal, situational restrictiveness, and aggressive behavior. *Journal of Research in Personality, 11,* 48–58.

Fuller, L. (1971). Mediation—its forms and functions. *Southern California Law Review, 44,* 305–339.

Fuller, L. (1979). The forms and limits of adjudication. *Harvard Law Review, 92,* 353–409.

Fultz, J., Batson, C. D., Fortenbach, V. A., McCarthy, P. M., & Varney, L. L. (1986). Social evaluation and the empathy-altruism hypothesis. *Journal of Personality and Social Psychology, 50,* 761–769.

Funder, D. C., & Ozer, D. J. (1983). Behavior as a function of the situation. *Journal of Personality and Social Psychology, 44,* 107–112.

Furstenberg, F. E. (1976). Premarital pregnancy and marital instability. *Journal of Social Issues, 32,* 67–86.

Galle, O., Gove, W., McPherson, J. (1972). Population density and pathology: What are the relations for man. *Science, 176,* 23–30.

Gamson, W. A., Fireman, B., & Rytina, S. (1982). *Encounters with unjust authority.* Homewood, IL: Dorsey.

Gans, H. (1962). Urbanism and suburbanism as ways of life: A reevaluation of definitions. In A. M. Rose (Ed.), *Human behavior and social processes.* Boston: Houghton Mifflin.

Gans, H. J. (1962). *The urban villagers.* New York: Free Press.

Geen, R. G. (1968). Effects of frustration, attack, and prior training in aggressiveness upon aggressive behavior. *Journal of Personality and Social Psychology, 9,* 316–321.

Geller, D. M. (1980). Responses to urban stimuli: A balanced approach. *Journal of Social Issues, 36,* 86–100.

Geller, D. M. (1982). Alternatives to deception: Why, what, and how. In J. E. Sieber (Ed.), *The ethics of social research: Surveys and experiments.* New York: Springer-Verlag.

Geller, D. M., Cook, J., O'Connor, M., & Low, S. (1982). Perception of urban scenes by small town and urban residents: A multi-dimensional scaling analysis. In P. Bart, A. Chin, & G. Francescato (Eds.), *Knowledge for design: Proceedings of the 13th International Conference of the Environmental Design Research Association,* College Park, MD.

Geller, E. S. (1982). *Corporate incentives for promoting safety belt use: Rationale, guidelines, and examples.* Washington, DC: National Highway Safety Traffic Administration.

Geller, E. S., & Lehman, G. R. (1982). Motivating desirable waste management behavior: Applications of behavior analysis. *Paper delivered at the Second Penn Workshop on Litter Management,* Santa Barbara, CA.

Gelles, R. J., & Straus, M. A. (1979). Violence in the American family. *Journal of Social Issues, 35,* 15–39.

Gerard, H., & Miller, N. (1975). *School desegregation.* New York: Plenum.

Gerard, H. B., Wilhelmy, R. A., & Conolley, E. S. (1968). Conformity and group size. *Journal of Personality and Social Psychology, 8,* 79–82.

Gerbner, G., & Gross, L. (1974). *Violence profile No. 6: Trends in network television drama and viewer conceptions of social reality, 1967–1973.* Unpublished manuscript, University of Pennsylvania.

Gerbner, G., & Gross, L. (1976). Living with television: The violence profile. *Journal of Communication, 26,* 173–199.

Gerbner, G., & Gross, L. (1976). The scary world of TV's heavy viewer. *Psychology Today, 9,* 41–45.

Gergen, K. J. (1972). Multiple identity. *Psychology Today, 5,* 31–35, 64–66.

Gergen, K. J. (1973). Social psychology as history. *Journal of Personality and Social Psychology, 26,* 309–320.

Gergen, K. J. (1976). Social psychology, science and history. *Personality and Social Psychology Bulletin, 2,* 373–383.

Gergen, K. J. (1977). The decline of character: Socialization and self-consistency. In G. DiRenzo (Ed.), *We, the people: American character and social change.* Westport, CT: Greenwood Press.

Gergen, K. J. (1978). Toward generative theory. *Journal of Personality and Social Psychology, 36,* 1344–1360.

Gergen, K. J. (1982). From self to science: What is there to know? In J. Suls (Ed.), *Psychological perspectives on the self* (Vol. 1). Hillsdale, NJ: Erlbaum.

Gergen, K. J., & Basseches, M. (1980). The potentiation of social knowledge. In R. F. Kidd & M. J. Saks (Eds.), *Advances in applied social psychology* (Vol. 1). Hillsdale, NJ: Erlbaum.

Gergen, K. J., & Bauer, R. A. (1967). Interactive effects of self-esteem and task difficulty on social conformity. *Journal of Personality and Social Psychology, 6,* 16–22.

Gergen, K. J., Ellsworth, P., Maslach, C., & Spiegel, M. (1975). Obligation, donor resources and reactions to aid in three cultures. *Journal of Personality and Social Psychology, 31,* 390–400.

Gergen, K. J., & Gergen, M. (1974). Foreign aid that works. *Psychology Today, 8,* 54–58.

Gergen, K. J., Gergen, M. M., & Meter, K. (1972). Individual orientations to pro-social behavior. *Journal of Social Issues, 28,* 105–130.

Gergen, K. J., Greenberg, M. S., & Willis, R. H. (Eds.) (1980). *Social exchange: Advances in theory and research.* New York: Plenum.

Geschwind, N., & Galaburda, A. M. (1985). Cerebral lateralization: Biological mechanisms, associations, and pathology: A hypothesis and a program for research. *Archives of Neurology, 42,* 500–504.

Gibb, J. R. (1951). The effects of group size and of threat reduction upon creativity in a problem-solving situation. *American Psychologist, 6,* 324.

Gibb, J. R. (1971). The effects of human relations training. In A. E. Bergin & S. L. Garfield (Eds.), *Handbook of psychotherapy and behavior change: An empirical analysis.* New York: Wiley.

Gibb, J. R. (1975). The training group. In K. D. Benne, L. P. Bradford, J. R. Gibb, & R. O. Lippitt (Eds.), *The laboratory method of changing and learning: Theory and application.* Palo Alto, CA: Science and Behavior Books.

Gifford, R. (1982). Projected interpersonal distance and orientation choices: Personality, sex, and social situation. *Social Psychology Quarterly, 45,* 145–152.

Gil, D. G. (1970). *Violence against children: Physical child abuse in the United States.* Cambridge, MA: Harvard University Press.

Gilbert, S. J., (1981). Another look at the Milgram obedience studies: The role of the graduated series of shocks. *Personality and Social Psychology Bulletin, 7,* 690–695.

Gilder, G. S. (1974). *Naked nomads: Unmarried men in America.* New York: New York Times Books.

Gillie, O. (1976). *Who do you think you are?: Man or Superman—the genetic controversy.* New York: Saturday Review Press.

Gillig, P. M., & Greenwald, A. G. (1974). Is it time to lay the sleeper effect to rest? *Journal of Personality and Social Psychology, 29,* 132–139.

Gilmour, R., & Duck, S. (Eds.) (1980). *The development of social psychology.* London: Academic Press.

Ginosar, Z., & Trope, Y. (1980). The effects of base rates and individuating information on judgments about another person. *Journal of Experimental Social Psychology, 16,* 228–242.

Glaser, B. G., & Strauss, A. L. (1967). *The discovery of grounded theory.* Chicago: Aldine.

Glass, D. C., Contrada, R., & Snow, B. (1980). Stress, type A, and coronary disease. *Weekly Psychology Update, 1,* 2–7.

Glass, D. C., & Singer, J. E. (1972). *Urban stress.* New York: Academic Press.

Goethals, G. R., & Nelson, R. E. (1973). Similarity in the influence process: The belief-value distinction. *Journal of Personality and Social Psychology, 25,* 117–122.

Goffman, E. (1959). *The presentation of self in everyday life.* Garden City, NY: Doubleday.

Goffman, E. (1967). *Interaction ritual.* Chicago: Aldine.

Goffman, E. (1971). *Relations in public.* New York: Basic Books.

Goldberg, C. (1974). Sex roles, task competence and conformity. *Journal of Psychology, 86,* 157–164.

Goldberg, C. (1975). Conformity to majority as a function of task type and acceptance of sex-related stereotypes. *Journal of Psychology, 89,* 25–37.

Goldberg, P. (1968). Are women prejudiced against women? *Trans-Action, 5,* 28–30.

Goldman, J., & Olczak, P. (1976). Psychosocial maturity and interpersonal attraction. *Journal of Research in Personality, 10,* 146–154.

Goldstein, A. P., Heller, K., & Sechrest, L. B. (1966). *Psychotherapy and the psychology of behavior change.* New York: Wiley.

Goldstein, J. H. (1975). *Aggression and crimes of violence.* New York: Oxford University Press.

Goleman, D. (1983). The electronic Rorschach. *Psychology Today, 17* (February), 36–43.

Golub, S., & Canty, E. (1979). *Sex role expectations and the assumption of leadership by college women.* Paper presented at Eastern

Psychological Association convention, Philadelphia.

Gonzales, M. H., Davis, J. M., Loney, G. L., Lukens, C. K., & Junghans, C. M. (1983). Interactional approach to interpersonal attraction. *Journal of Personality and Social Psychology, 44,* 1192–1197.

Good, P., Simon, G. C., & Coursey, R. D. (1981). Public interest activities of APA members. *American Psychologist, 36,* 963–971.

Goodchilds, J. D., & Zillman, G. L. (1984). Sexual signaling and sexual aggression in adolescent relationships. In N. M. Malamuth & E. Donnerstein, *Pornography and sexual aggression.* New York: Academic Press.

Goodwin, L. (1972). *Do the poor want to work? A social-psychological study of work orientations.* Washington, DC: The Brookings Institution.

Goranson, R. I., & Berkowitz, L. (1966). Reciprocity and responsibility reactions to prior help. *Journal of Personality and Social Psychology, 3,* 227–232.

Gordon, S. (1976). *Lonely in America.* New York: Simon & Schuster.

Gormley, J. (1983). Predicting behavior from personality trait scores. *Personality and Social Psychology Bulletin, 9,* 267–270.

Gorsuch, R., & Butler, M. (1976). Initial drug abuse: A review of predisposing social psychological factors. *Psychological Bulletin, 83,* 120–137.

Gotlib, I. H., & Robinson, L. H. (1982). Responses to depressed individuals: Discrepancies between self-report and observer-rated behavior. *Journal of Abnormal Psychology, 91,* 231–240.

Gottman, J., Notarius, C., Markman, H., Bank, S., Yoppi, B., & Rubin, M. E. (1976). Behavior exchange theory and marital decisionmaking. *Journal of Personality and Social Psychology, 34,* 14–23.

Gouldner, A. (1960). The norm of reciprocity: A preliminary statement. *American Sociological Review, 25,* 161–178.

Gouldner, A. W. (Ed.) (1950). *Studies in leadership.* New York: Harper & Row.

Gove, W. R., & Hughes, M. (1983). *Overcrowding in the household* New York: Academic Press.

Graham, W. K., & Dillon, P. C. (1974). Creative supergroups: Group performance as a function of individual performance on brainstorming tasks. *Journal of Social Psychology, 93,* 101–105.

Gray, E. B. (1983). *Final report: Collaborative research of community and minority group action to prevent child abuse and neglect, vol. III: Public awareness and education using the creative aids.* Chicago: National Committee for the Prevention of Child Abuse.

Gray, J. D. (1983). The married professional woman: An examination of her role conflicts and coping strategies. *Psychology of Women Quarterly, 3,* 235–243.

Greenberg, J., & Cohen, R. L. (1982). *Equity and justice in social behavior.* New York: Academic Press.

Greenberg, M. S., & Frisch, D. M. (1972). Effect of intentionality on willingness to reciprocate a favor. *Journal of Experimental Social Psychology, 8,* 99–111.

Greenblatt, S. L., & Willie, C. V. (1981). School desegregation and the management of social change. In C. V. Willie & S. L. Greenblatt (Eds.), *Community politics and educational change: Ten school systems under court order.* New York: Longman.

Greenwald, A. G. (1968). Cognitive learning, cognitive response to persuasion, and attitude change. In A. G. Greewald, T. C. Brock, & T. M. Ostrom (Eds.), *Psychological foundations of attitudes.* New York: Academic Press.

Greenwald, A. G. (1975). On the inconclusiveness of "crucial" tests of cognitive dissonance versus self-perception theories. *Journal of Experimental Social Psychology, 11,* 490–499.

Greenwald, A. G. (1980). The totalitarian ego: Fabrication and revision of personal history. *American Psychologist, 35,* 603–618.

Greenwald, A. G. (1982). Is anyone in charge? Personalysis versus the principle of personal unity. In J. Suls (Ed.), *Psychological perspectives on the self* (Vol. 1). Hillsdale, NJ: Erlbaum.

Greenwald, A. G., & Runis, D. L. (1978). Twenty years of cognitive dissonance: Case study of the evolution of a theory. *Psychology Review, 85,* 53–57.

Griggs v. *Duke Power Company,* 401 US 424 (1971).

Grigsby, D., & Bigoness, W. (1982). Effects of mediation and alternative forms of arbitration on bargaining behavior: A laboratory study. *Journal of Applied Psychology, 87,* 549–554.

Grofman, B. (1976). Not necessarily twelve and not necessarily unanimous: Evaluating the impact of *Williams* v. *Florida* and *Johnson* v. *Louisiana.* In G. Bermant, C. Nemeth, & N. Vidmar, *Psychology and the law.* Lexington, MA: Lexington Books.

Grofman, B. (1977). Jury decision-making models. In S. Nagel (Ed.), *Modeling the criminal justice system.* Beverly Hills, CA: Sage.

Gross, A. E., & Fleming, I. (1982). Twenty years of deception in social psychology. *Personality and Social Psychology Bulletin, 8,* 402–408.

Gross, A. E., & McMullen, P. A. (1982). The help seeking process. In V. J. Derlega & J. Grzelak (Eds.), *Cooperation and helping behavior: Theories and research.* New York: Academic Press.

Gross, N., Mason, W. S., & McEachern, A. W. (1958). *Explorations in role analysis: Studies of the school superintendency role.* New York: Wiley.

Gruder, C. L., Cook, T. D., Hennigan, K. M., Flay, B. R., Alessi, C., & Halamaj, J. (1978). Empirical tests of the absolute sleeper effect predicted from the discounting cue hypothesis. *Journal of Personality and Social Psychology, 36,* 1061–1074.

Grusec, J. W., & Skubiski, S. L. (1970). Model nurturance, demand characteristics of the modeling experiment, and altruism. *Journal of Personality and Social Psychology, 14,* 352–359.

Grush, J. E. (1980). The impact of candidate expenditures, regionality, and prior outcomes on the 1976 Democratic presidential primaries. *Journal of Personality and Social Psychology, 38,* 337–347.

Grush, J. E., McKeough, K. L., & Ahlering, R. F. (1978). Extrapolating laboratory research to actual political elections. *Journal of Personality and Social Psychology, 36,* 257–270.

Gulliver, P. H. (1973). Negotiation as a mode of dispute settlement: Towards a general model. *Law and Society Review, 7,* 667–691.

Gump, P. W. (1974). Operating environments in schools of open and traditional design. *School Review,* August, 574–593.

Gurin, P., Gurin, G., Lao, R. C., & Beattie, M. (1969). Internal-external control in the motivational dynamics of Negro youth. *Journal of Social Issues, 25,* 29–53.

Gustafson, D. H., Shukla, R. K., Delbecq, A. & Walster, G. W. (1973). A comparative study of differences in subjective likelihood estimates made by individuals, interacting groups, Delphi groups, and nominal groups. *Organizational Behavior and Human Performance, 9,* 280–291.

Guttentag, M., & Bray, H. (1976). *Undoing sex stereotypes: Research and resources for educators.* New York: McGraw-Hill.

Guttentag, M., & Secord, P. F. (1983). *Too many women? The sex ratio discussion.* Beverly Hills, CA: Sage.

Guttmacher (Alan) Institute. (1976). *11 million teenagers: What can be done about the epidemic of adolescent pregnancy in the U.S.* New York.

Guttmacher (Alan) Institute. (1981). *Teenage pregnancy: The problem that hasn't gone away.* New York.

Guttman, L. (1950). The basis for scalogram analysis. in S. A. Stouffer, L. Guttman, E. A. Suchman, P. F. Lazarsfeld, S. A. Star, & J. A. Gardner (Eds.), *Measurement and prediction.* Princeton, NJ: Princeton University Press.

Haley, W. E., & Stricklund, B. R. (1977). *Locus of control and depression.* Paper presented at Eastern Psychological Convention, Boston.

Hall, D. T. (1972). A model of coping with role conflict: The role behavior of college educated women. *Administrative Science Quarterly, 17,* 471–486.

Hall, E. T. (1966). *The hidden dimension.* New York: Doubleday.

Hall, J. (1978). Gender effects in decoding nonverbal cues. *Psychological Bulletin, 85,* 845–857.

Hall, J. A., Roter, D. L., & Rand, C. S. (1981). Communication of affect between patient and physician. *Journal of Health and Social Behavior, 22,* 18–30.

Hamill, R., Wilson, T. D., & Nisbett, R. E. (1981).

Insensitivity to sample bias: Generalizing from atypical cases. *Journal of Personality and Social Psychology, 39,* 578–589.

Hamilton, D. L. (1981a). *Cognitive processes in stereotyping and intergroup behavior.* Hillsdale, NJ: Erlbaum.

Hamilton, D. L. (1981b). *Organizational processes in impression formation.* In E. T. Higgins, C. P. Herman, & M. P. Zanna (Eds.), *Social cognition: The Ontario Symposium* (Vol. 1). Hillsdale, NJ: Erlbaum.

Hamilton, D. L. (Ed.) (1981). *Cognitive processes in stereotyping and intergroup behavior.* Hillsdale, NJ: Erlbaum.

Hamilton, D. L., Katz, L. B., & Leirer, V. O. (1980). Organizational processes in impression formation. In R. Hastie, T. M. Ostrom, E. B. Ebbeson, R. S. Wyer, D. L. Hamilton, & D. E. Carlston (Eds.), *Person memory: The cognitive basis of social perception.* Hillsdale, NJ: Erlbaum.

Hamilton, D. L., & Zanna, M. P. (1974). Context effects in impression formation: Changes in connotative meaning. *Journal of Personality and Social Psychology, 29,* 649–654.

Hamilton, T., Swap, W., & Rubin, J. (1981). Predicting the effects of anticipated third party intervention: A template matching approach. *Journal of Personality and Social Psychology, 41,* 1141–1152.

Hammond, K. R. (1948). Measuring attitudes by error-choice: An indirect method. *Journal of Abnormal and Social Psychology, 43,* 38–48.

Haner, C. E., & Brown, P. A. (1955). Clarification of the instigation to action concept in the frustration-aggression hypothesis. *Journal of Abnormal and Social Psychology, 51,* 204–206.

Haney, C., Banks, C., & Zimbardo, P. (1973). Interpersonal dynamics in a simulated prison. *International Journal of Criminology and Penology, 1,* 69–97.

Hans, V., & Vidmar, N. (1982). Jury selection. In N. L. Kerr & R. M. Bray (Eds.), *The psychology of the courtroom.* New York: Academic Press.

Hansen, R. D., & O'Leary, V. E. (1983). Actresses and actors: The effects of sex on causal attributions. *Basic and Applied Social Psychology, 4,* 209–230.

Hapkiewicz, W. G., & Roden, A. H. (1971). The effect of aggressive cartoons on children's interpersonal play. *Child Development, 41,* 1583–1585.

Haque, A., & Lawsen, E. D. (1980). The mirror image phenomenom in the context of the Arab-Israeli conflict. *International Journal of Intercultural Relations, 4,* 107–116.

Harackiewicz, J. M. (1979). The effects of reward contingency and performance feedback on intrinsic motivation. *Journal of Personality and Social Psychology, 37,* 1352–1363.

Harari, H., Mohr, D., & Hosey, K. (1980). Faculty helplessness to students: A comparison of compliance techniques. *Personality and Social Psychology Bulletin, 6,* 373–377.

Hardin, G. (1968). The tragedy of the commons. *Science, 162,* 1243–1248.

Hardin, G., & Baden, J. (1977). *Managing the commons.* San Francisco: Freeman.

Hardyck, J. A., & Braden, M. (1962). Prophecy fails again: A report of a failure to replicate. *Journal of Abnormal and Social Psychology, 65,* 136–141.

Hare, A. P. (1952). A study of interaction and consensus in different sized groups. *American Sociological Review, 17,* 261–267.

Hare, A. P. (1976). *Handbook of small group research.* New York: Free Press.

Harlow, H. F., & Yudin, H. C. (1933). Social behavior of primates. I. Social facilitation of eating in the monkey and its relation to attitudes of ascendance and submission. *Journal of Comparative Psychology, 16,* 171–185.

Harrigan, J. A., & Rosenthal, R. (1983). Physician's head and body position as determinants of perceived rapport. *Journal of Applied Social Psychology, 13,* 496–509.

Harris, M. B. (1974). Mediators between frustration and aggression in a field experiment. *Journal of Experimental Social Psychology, 10,* 561–571.

Hartley, R. E. (1957). Personal characteristics and acceptance of secondary groups as reference groups. *Journal of Individual Psychology, 13,* 45–55.

Hartshorne, H., & May, M. A. (1928). *Studies in the nature of character* (Vol. 1) *Studies in deceit.* New York: Macmillan.

Harvey, O. J., & Consalvi, C. (1960). Status and conformity to pressures in informal groups.

Journal of Abnormal Social Psychology, 60, 182–187.

Hass, R. G. (1981). Effects of source characteristics on the cognitive processing of persuasive messages and attitude change. In R. Petty, T. Ostrom, & T. Brock (Eds.), *Cognitive responses in persuasion.* Hillsdale, NJ: Erlbaum.

Hastie, R. (1981). Schematic principles in human memory. In E. T. Higgins, C. P. Herman, & M. P. Zanna (Eds.), *Social cognition: The Ontario Symposium* (Vol. 1). Hillsdale, NJ: Erlbaum.

Hastie, R. (1984). Cause and effects of causal attribution. *Journal of Personality and Social Psychology, 46,* 44–56.

Hastie, R., Penrod, S., & Pennington, N. (1983). *Inside the jury.* Cambridge, MA: Harvard University Press.

Hayduck, L. A. (1978). Personal space: An evaluative and orienting overview. *Psychology Bulletin, 85,* 117–134.

Hayduck, L. A. (1981). The permeability of personal space. *Canadian Journal of Behavioral Science, 13,* 274–287.

Hayes-Bautista, D. E. (1976). Modifying the treatment, patient compliance, patient control and medical care. *Social Science and Medicine, 10,* 233–288.

Haynes, R. B., Taylor, D. W., & Sackett, D. L. (1979). Introduction. In R. B. Haynes, D. W. Taylor, & D. L. Sackett (Eds.), *Compliance in health care.* Baltimore, MD: Johns Hopkins University Press.

Haythorn, W. (1956). The effects of varying combinations of authoritarian and equalitarian leaders and followers. *Journal of Abnormal and Social Psychology, 53,* 210–219.

Heider, F. (1958). *The psychology of interpersonal relations.* New York: Wiley.

Heller, K., & Monahan, J. (1977). *Psychology and community change.* Homewood, IL: Dorsey Press.

Helmreich, R. L., Spence, J. T., & Gibson, R. H. (1982). Sex-role attitudes: 1972–1980. *Personality and Social Psychology Bulletin, 8,* 656–663.

Hendrick, S. S. (1981). Self-disclosure and marital dissatisfaction. *Journal of Personality and Social Psychology, 40,* 1150–1159.

Henley, N. M. (1977). *Body politics: Power, sex and nonverbal communication.* Englewood Cliffs, NJ: Prentice-Hall.

Hennig, M., & Jardim, A. (1977). *The managerial woman.* New York: Anchor Press.

Henry, J. H., & Galvin, K. S. (1984). Clinical implications of attribution theory and research. *Clinical Psychology Review, 4,* 15–33.

Herman, J. B., & Gyllstrom, K. K. (1977). Working men and women: Inter- and intra-role conflict. *Psychology of Women Quarterly, 1,* 319–333.

Heshka, S., & Pylypuk, A. (1975). *Human crowding and adrenocortical activity.* Paper presented at the annual meeting of the Canadian Psychological Association, Quebec.

Hess, R. D., & Torney, J. V. (1970). *The development of political attitudes in children.* Garden City, NY: Doubleday.

Hicks, D. J. (1968). Short- and long-term retention of affectively varied modeled behavior. *Psychonomic Science, 11,* 369–370.

Higgins, E. T., Bargh, J. A., & Lombardi, W. (1985). Nature of priming effects on categorization. *Journal of Experimental Psychology: Learning, Memory and Cognition, 11,* 59–69.

Higgins, E. T., Herman, C. P., & Zanna, M. P. (Eds.) (1981). *Social cognition: The Ontario Symposium* (Vol. 1). Hillsdale, NJ: Erlbaum.

Higgins, E. T., & King, G. A. (1981). Accessibility of social constructs: Information-processing consequences of individual and contextual variability. In N. Cantor & J. F. Kihlstrom (Eds.), *Personality, cognition and social interaction.* Hillsdale, NJ: Erlbaum.

Higgins, E. T., Klein, R., & Strauman, T. (1985). Self concept discrepancy theory: A psychological model for distinguishing among different aspects of depression and anxiety. *Social Cognition, 3,* 51–76.

Higgins, E. T., Rhodewalt, F., & Zanna, M. (1979). Dissonance motivation: Its nature, persistence, and reinstatement. *Journal of Experimental Social Psychology, 15,* 16–34.

Hilgard, E. R. (Ed.) (1978). *American psychology in historical perspective.* Washington, DC: American Psychological Association.

Hill, C. T., Rubin, Z., & Peplau, L. A. (1976). Breakups before marriage: The end of 103 affairs. *Journal of Social Issues, 32,* 147–168.

Hill, C. T., & Stull, D. E. (1981). Sex differences in effects of social and value similarity in same-sex friendship. *Journal of Personality and Social Psychology, 41,* 488–502.

Hill, G. (1982). Group versus individual performance: Are N + 1 heads better than one? *Psychological Bulletin, 91,* 517–530.

Hillson, J. (1977). *The Battle of Boston.* New York: Pathfinder Press.

Hilton, J. L., & Darley, J. M. (1985). Constructing other persons: A limit on the effect. *Journal of Experimental Social Psychology, 21,* 1–18.

Himes, J. S. (1980). *Conflict and conflict management.* Athens: University of Georgia Press.

Hodgetts, R. M., & Altman, S. (1979). *Organizational behavior.* Philadelphia: Saunders.

Hoferek, M. J., & Hanick, P. L. (1985). Woman and athlete—toward role consistency. *Sex Roles, 12,* 687–696.

Hoffman, L. R. (1959). Homogeneity of member personality and its effect on group problem-solving. *Journal of Abnormal and Social Psychology, 58,* 27–32.

Hoffman, M. (1977). Moral internalization: Current theory and research. In L. Berkowitz (Ed.), *Advances in experimental social psychology* (Vol. 10). New York: Academic Press.

Hoffman, M. L. (1975). Altruistic behavior and the parent-child relationship. *Journal of Personality and Social Psychology, 31,* 937–943.

Hoffman, M. L. (1982). Development of prosocial motivation: Empathy and guilt. In N. Eisenberg (Ed.), *The development of prosocial behavior.* New York: Academic Press.

Hofstadter, D. R., & Dennett, D. C. (1981). *The mind's eye.* New York: Basic Books.

Hofstatter, P. R. (1957). *Gruppendynamik: Die kritik der Massenpsychologie.* Hamburg, Germany: Rewohlt.

Hoge, V. (1964). Hospital facilities should fit the patient. In L. E. Weeks and J. R. Griffith (Eds.), Progressive patient care. *Bulletin of the Administrative Research Services, 3.*

Holahan, C. J. (1982). *Environmental psychology.* New York: Random House.

Hollander, E. P. (1958). Conformity, status, and idiosyncrasy credit. *Psychological Review, 65,* 117–127.

Hollander, E. P. (1960). Competence and conformity in the acceptance of influence. *Journal of Abnormal and Social Psychology, 61,* 365–369.

Hollander, E. P., & Julian, J. W. (1969). Contemporary trends in the analysis of leadership process. *Psychological Bulletin, 71,* 387–397.

Hollander, E. P., & Willis, R. (1967). Some current issues in the psychology of conformity and nonconformity. *Psychological Bulletin, 68,* 62–76.

Holsti, O. R. (1972). *Crisis, escalation, war.* Montreal: McGill-Queens University Press.

Holton, G. (1982). *Science and the discontinuity of history.* Address to the Duke University Roundtable on Science and Public Affairs, March 31. Cited in W. Bevan (1982). A sermon of sorts in three plus parts. *American Psychologist, 37,* 1303–1322.

Holtzworth-Munroe, A., & Jacobson, N. S. (1985). Causal attributions of married couples: When do they search for causes? What do they conclude when they do? *Journal of Personality and Social Psychology, 48,* 1398–1412.

Homans, G. C. (1961). *Social behavior: Its elementary forms.* New York: Harcourt, Brace, & World.

Homans, G. C. (1974). *Social behavior: Its elementary forms* (2nd ed.). New York: Harcourt Brace Jovanovich.

Hopkins, H. (1973). *The numbers game.* Boston: Little, Brown.

Hopkins, J. R. (1977). Sexual behavior in adolescence. *Journal of Social Issues, 33,* 67–85.

Horner, M. S. (1970). Femininity and successful achievement: A basic inconsistency. In J. M. Bardwick, E. Douvan, M. S. Horner, & Gutman (Eds.), *Feminine personality and conflict.* Belmont, CA: Wadsworth.

Horner, M. S. (1972). Toward an understanding of achievement-related conflicts in women. *Journal of Social Issues, 28,* 157–176.

Hornstein, H. A. (1982). Promotive tension: Theory and research. In V. J. Derlega & J.Grzelak (Eds.), *Cooperation and helping behavior.* New York: Academic Press.

Hornstein, H. A., Mason, H. N., Sole, K., and Heilman, M. (1971). Effects of sentiment and completion of a helping act on observer helping: A case for socially mediated Zeigarnik effects. *Journal of Personality and Social Psychology, 17,* 107–112.

Horowitz, L. M., & French, R. de S. (1979). Interpersonal problems of people who describe themselves as lonely. *Journal of Consulting and Clinical Psychology, 47,* 762–764.

Horton, R. W., & Santogrossi, D. A. (1978). The effect of adult commentary on reducing the influence of televised violence. *Personality and Social Psychology Bulletin, 4,* 337–340.

House, J. S., & Cottington, E. M. (1986). Health and the workplace. In L. H. Aiken & D. Mechanic (Eds.), *Applications of social science: Clinical medicine and health policy.* New Brunswick, NJ: Rutgers University Press.

House, J. S., Strecher, V., Mentzer, H. L., & Robbins, C. A. (1986). Occupational stress and health among men and women in the Tecumseh community health study. *Journal of Health and Social Behavior, 22,* 62–77.

House, J. S., & Wolf, S. (1978). Effects of urban residence on interpersonal trust and helping behavior. *Journal of Personality and Social Psychology, 36,* 1029–1043.

Houseknecht, S. K. (1979). Childlessness and marital adjustment. *Journal of Marriage and the Family, 41,* 259–266.

Hovland, C. I. (1959). Reconciling conflicting results derived from experimental and survey studies of attitude change. *American Psychologist, 14,* 8–17.

Hovland, C. I., & Janis, I. L. (Eds.), (1959). *Personality and persuasibility.* New Haven, CT: Yale University Press.

Hovland, C. I., Janis, I. L., and Kelley, J. J. (1953). *Communication and persuasion.* New Haven, CT: Yale University Press.

Hovland, C. I., Luchins, A. S., Mandell, W., Campbell, E. H., Brock, T. C., McGuire, W. J., Feierabend, R. L., & Anderson, N. H. (Eds.) (1957). *The order of presentation in persuasion.* New Haven, CT: Yale University Press.

Hovland, C. I., Lumsdaine, A. A., & Sheffield, F. D. (1949). *Experiments on mass communication.* Princeton, NJ: Princeton University Press.

Hovland, C. I., & Weiss, W. (1951). The influence of source credibility on communication effectiveness. *Public Opinion Quarterly, 15,* 635–650.

Howard, J., & Dawes, R. (1976). Linear prediction of marital happiness. *Personality and Social Psychology Bulletin, 2,* 478–480.

Howard, J. W., & Rothbart, M. (1980). Social categorization and memory for in-group and out-group behavior. *Journal of Personality and Social Psychology, 38,* 301–310.

Howard, M. (Ed.) (1979). *Restraints on war: Studies in the limitation of armed conflict.* New York: Oxford University Press.

Huesmann, L. R., Eron, L. D., Dubow, E. F., & Seebauer, E. (in press). Television viewing habits in childhood and adult aggression. *Child Development.*

Huesmann, L. R, Eron, L. D., Klein, R., Brice, P., & Fisher, P. (1983). *Journal of Personality and Social Psychology, 44,* 899–910.

Hull, J. (1981). A self-awareness model of the causes and effects of alcohol consumption. *Journal of Abnormal Psychology, 90,* 586–600.

Hunt, J. McV. (1965). Traditional personality theory in the light of recent evidence. *American Scientist, 53,* 80–96.

Hurt, N. J. (1975). How to keep kids from getting lost in the open school. *Phi Delta Kappan, 56,* 345–348.

Huston, T. L., & Burgess, R. L. (1978). The analysis of social exchange in developing relationships. In R. L. Burgess & T. L. Huston (Eds.), *Social exchange in developing relationships.* New York: Academic Press.

Huston, T. L., & Levinger, G. (1978). Interpersonal attraction and relationships. In M. R. Rosenzweig & L. W. Porter (Eds.), *Annual review of psychology* (Vol. 29). Palo Alto, CA: Annual Reviews.

Hutt, C., & Vaizey, M. J. (1966). *Differential aspects of group density on social behavior. Nature, 209,* 1371–1372.

Huttman, B. (1981). *The patient's advocate: The complete book of patient's rights.* New York: Penguin.

Hyman, H. H., & Sheatsley, P. B. (1954). "The authoritarian personality" —A methodological critique. In R. Christie & M. Jahoda (Eds.), *Studies in the scope and method of*

"*The Authoritarian Personality.*" New York: Free Press.

Ickes, W., and Barnes, R. D. (1978). Boys and girls together—and alienated: On enacting stereotyped sex roles in mixed-sex dyads. *Journal of Personality and Social Psychology, 36,* 669–683.

Insko, C. A., Smith, R. H., Alicke, M. D., Wade, J., & Taylor, S. (1985). Conformity and group size: The concern with being right and the concern with being liked. *Personality and Social Psychology Bulletin, 11,* 41–50.

Isen, A. M. (1970). Success, failure, attention, and reaction to others: The warm glow of success. *Journal of Personality and Social Psychology, 15,* 294–301.

Isen, A. M. (1984). Toward understanding the role of affect in cognition. In R. S. Wyer, Jr., & T. K. Srull (Eds.), *Handbook of social cognition* (Vol. 3). Hillsdale, NJ: Erlbaum.

Isen, A. M., Clark, M., & Schwartz, M. F. (1976). Duration of the effect of good mood on modeling: "Footprints on the sands of time." *Journal of Personality and Social Psychology, 34,* 385–393.

Isen, A. M., Shalker, T. E., Clark, M., & Karp, L. (1978). Affect, accessibility of material in memory and behavior: A cognitive loop? *Journal of Personality and Social Psychology, 36,* 1–12.

Israel, J., & Tajfel, H. (Eds.) (1972). *The context of social psychology.* London: Academic Press.

Jaccard, J., & Becker, M. A. (1985). Attitudes and behavior: An information integration perspective. *Journal of Experimental Social Psychology, 21,* 440–465.

Jaccard, J. J., & Davidson, A. R. (1972). Toward understanding of family planning behaviors: An initial investigation. *Journal of Applied Social Psychology, 2,* 228–235.

Jacobs, J. (1961). *The death and life of great American cities.* New York: Random House.

Jacobs, P. A., Brunton, M., & Melville, M. M. (1965). Aggressive behavior, mental subnormality, and the XYY male. *Nature, 208,* 1351–1352.

Jacobs, R. C., & Campbell, D. T. (1961). The perception of an arbitrary tradition through several generations of a laboratory microculture. *Journal of Abnormal and Social Psychology, 62,* 649–658.

Jacoby, J. (1975). Consumer psychology as a social psychological sphere of action. *American Psychologist, 30,* 977–987

Jakobovitz, L. A. (1968). Effects of mere exposure: A comment. *Journal of Personality and Social Psychology, 9,* 30–32.

James, W. (1890). *The principles of psychology.* New York: Henry Holt and Company.

James, W. H. (1973). James' locus of control scale. In J. P. Robinson & P. R. Shaver, (Eds.), *Measures of social psychological attitudes.* Ann Arbor, MI: Institute for Social Research.

Janis, I. L. (1958). *Psychological stress.* New York: Wiley.

Janis, I. L. (1959). Motivational factors in the resolution of decisional conflicts. In M. R. Jones (Ed.), *Nebraska symposium on motivation* (Vol. 6). Lincoln: University of Nebraska Press.

Janis, I. L. (1968). Attitude change via role playing. In R. Abelson, E. Aronson, W. McGuire, T. Newcomb, M. Rosenberg, & P. Tannenbaum (Eds.), *Theories of cognitive consistency: A source book.* Chicago: Rand McNally

Janis, I. L. (1982). *Groupthink* (2nd ed.). Boston: Houghton Mifflin.

Janis, I. L., & Feshbach, S. (1953). Effects of fear-arousing communications. *Journal of Abnormal and Social Psychology, 48,* 78–92 .

Janis, I. L., & Gilmore, J. B. (1965). The influence of incentive conditions on the success of role playing in modifying attitudes. *Journal of Personality and Social Psychology, 1,* 17–27.

Janis, I. L., & King, B. T. (1954). The influence of role-playing on opinion change. *Journal of Abnormal and Social Psychology, 49,* 211–218.

Janis, I. L., & Rife, D. (1959). Persuasibility and emotional disorder. In C. I. Hovland & I. L. Janis (Eds.), *Personality and persuasibility.* New Haven, CT: Yale University Press.

Janoff-Bulman, R. (1979). Characterological versus behavioral self-blame: Inquiries into depression and rape. *Journal Personality and Social Psychology, 37,* 1798–1809.

Janoff-Bullman, R., & Lang-Gunn, L. (in press). Coping with diseases and accidents: The role of self-blame attributions. In L. Y. Abramson (Ed.), *Social-personality inference in clinical psychology.* New York: Guilford.

Janowitz, M., & Bettleheim, B. (1950). *Dynamics of prejudice.* New York: Harper & Row.

Jason, L. A. (1977). A behavioral approach in enhancing disadvantaged children's academic abilities. *American Journal of Community Psychology, 5,* 413–420.

Jason, L. A., McCoy, K., Blanco, D., & Zolik, E. S. (1980). Decreasing dog litter: Behavioral consultation to help a community group. *Evaluation Review, 4,* 355–369.

Jason, L. A., Zolik, E. S., & Matese, F. (1979). Prompting dog owners to pick up dog droppings. *American Journal of Community Psychology, 7,* 339–351.

Jessor, R., Costa, F., Jessor, L., & Donovan, J. E. (1983). Time of first intercourse: A prospective study. *Journal of Personality and Social Psychology, 44,* 608–626.

Joe, V. C. (1971). Review of the internal-external control construct as a personality variable. *Psychological Reports, 28,* 619–640.

Johnson, J., Petzel, T., Zarantonello, M., & Johnson, H. (1985). Self-other attribution of responsibility for outcome by depressed and nondepressed college students in problem solving dyads. *Journal of Social and Clinical Psychology, 3,* 283–292.

Johnson, J. E. (1983). Psychological interventions and coping with surgery. In A. Baum, S. E. Taylor, & J. E. Singer (Eds.), *Handbook of psychology and health,* (Vol. 4). Hillsdale, NJ: Erlbaum.

Johnson, M. P. (1973). Commitment: A conceptual structure and empirical application. *Sociological Quarterly, 14,* 395–406.

Johnson, P. B. (1982). Sex differences, women's roles, and alcohol use: Preliminary national data. *Journal of Social Issues, 38,* 93–116.

Johnston, L. D., Bachman, J. G., & O'Malley, P. M. (1977). Drug use among American high school students: 1975–77. Rockville, MD: National Institute of Drug Abuse.

Jones, E. D. (1981). The District of Columbia's "Firearms Control Regulations Act of 1975": The toughest hand-gun control law in the United States—or is it? *The Annals of the American Academy of Political and Social Science, 455,* 138–149.

Jones, E. E. (1964). *Ingratiation: A social psychological analysis.* New York: Appleton-Century-Crofts.

Jones, E. E., & Davis, K. E. (1965). From acts to dispositions: The attribution process in person perception. In L. Berkowitz (Ed.), *Advances in experimental social psychology* (Vol. 2). New York: Academic Press.

Jones, E. E., Davis K. E., & Gergen, K. J. (1961). Role playing variations and their informational value for person perception. *Journal of Abnormal and Social Psychology, 63,* 302–310.

Jones, E. E., & Gerard, H. B. (1967). *Foundations of social psychology.* New York: Wiley

Jones, E. E., & Harris, V. A. (1967). The attribution of attitudes. *Journal of Experimental Social Psychology, 3,* 1–24.

Jones, E. E., & Nisbett, R. E. (1972). The actor and the observer: Divergent perceptions of the causes of behavior. In E. E. Jones, D. E. Kanouse, H. H. Kelley, R. E. Nisbett, S. Valins, & B. Weiner (Eds.), *Attribution: Perceiving the causes of behavior.* Morristown, NJ: General Learning Press.

Jones, E. E., & Pittman, T. S. (1982). Towards a general theory of strategic self-presentation. In J. Suls (Ed.), *Psychological perspectives on the self* (Vol. 1). Hillsdale, NJ: Erlbaum.

Jones, E. E., & Sigall, H. (1971). The bogus pipeline: A new paradigm for measuring affect and attitude. *Psychological Bulletin, 76,* 349–364.

Jones, E. E., Wood, G. C., & Quattrone, G. A. (1981). Perceived variability of personal characteristics in in-groups and out-groups: The role of knowledge and evaluation. *Personality and Social Psychology Bulletin, 7,* 523–528.

Jones, E. E., & Wortman, C. (1973). *Ingratiation: An attributional approach.* Morristown, NJ: General Learning Press.

Jones, W. H., Freemon, J. R., & Goswick, R. A. (1981). The persistence of loneliness: Self and other rejection? *Journal of Personality, 49,* 27–48.

Jones, W. H., Hobbs, S. A., & Hockenbury, D. (1982). Loneliness and social skills deficits.

Journal of Personality and Social Psychology Bulletin, 42, 682–689.

Jordan, N. (1953). Behavioral forces that are a function of attitudes and of cognitive organization. *Human Relations, 6,* 273–287.

Jorgensen, D. O. (1981). Locus of control and the perceived causal influence of the lunar cycle. *Perceptual and Motor Skills, 52,* 864.

Jorgenson, D. O., & Dukes, F. O. (1976). Deindividuation as a function of density and group membership. *Journal of Personality and Social Psychology, 34,* 24–39.

Jourard, S., & Friedman, R. (1970). Experimenter-subject "distance" and self-disclosure. *Journal of Personality and Social Psychology, 25,* 278–282.

Judd, C. (1983). Research methods in social psychology. In D. Perlman & P. C. Cozby (Eds.), *Social psychology.* New York: Holt, Reinhart and Winston.

Judd, C. M., & Johnson, J. T. (1981). Attitudes, polarization and diagnosticity: Exploring the effect of affect. *Journal of Personality and Social Psychology, 41,* 26–36.

Jurek v. *Texas,* 96 S.Ct. 2950 (1976).

Kagan, J., & Moss, H. A. (1962). *Birth to maturity: A study in psychological development.* New York: Wiley.

Kahn, R. L. (1972). The justification of violence: Social problems and social solutions. *Journal of Social Issues, 28,* 155–176.

Kahn, R. L. (1973). The work module. *Psychology Today, 6* (February), 35–39, 94–95.

Kairys, D., Schulman, J., & Harring, S. (Eds.) (1975). *The jury system: New methods for reducing prejudice.* Philadelphia: National Lawyers Guild.

Kalish, R. A. (1967). Of children and grandfathers: A speculative essay on dependency. *The Gerontologist, 7,* 185ff.

Kalven, H., & Zeisel, H. (1966). *The American Jury.* Boston: Little, Brown.

Kamin, L. (1986). Is crime in the genes? The answer may depend on who chooses what evidence. *Scientific American* (January), 22–27.

Kandel, D. B. (1978). Similarity in real-life adolescent friendship pairs. *Journal of Personality and Social Psychology, 36,* 306–312.

Kantor, R. M. (1977). *Men and women of the corporation.* New York: Basic Books.

Kaplan, J. (1972). A legal look at prosocial behavior: What can happen for failing to help or trying to help someone. *Journal of Social Issues, 28,* 219–226.

Kaplan, M. F. (1973). Stimulus inconsistency and response dispositions in forming judgements of other persons. *Journal of Personality and Social Psychology, 25,* 58–64.

Kaplan, M. F. (1974). Context induced shifts in personality trait evaluation: A comment on the evaluative halo effect and the meaning change interpretations. *Psychological Bulletin, 81,* 891–895.

Kaplan, M. F. (1975). Evaluative judgments are based on evaluative information: The weighted average versus the meaning change formulation. *Memory and Cognition, 3,* 375–380.

Kaplan, R. M., & Singer, R. D. (1976). Television and viewer aggression: A reexamination of the evidence. *Journal of Social Issues,* 35–70.

Karabenick, S. A. (1983). Sex-relevance of content and influenceability: Sistrunk and McDavid revisited. *Personality and Social Psychology Bulletin, 9,* 243–252.

Karabenick, S. A., & Meisels, M. (1972). Effects of performance evaluation on interpersonal distance. *Journal of Personality, 40,* 275–286.

Karlins, M., Coffman, T. L., & Walters, G. (1969). On the fading of social stereotypes: Studies in three generations of college students. *Journal of Personality and Social Psychology, 13,* 1–16.

Kasl, S. V. (1982). Chronic life stress and health. In A. Steptoe & A. Matthews (Eds.), *Health care and human behavior.* London: Academic Press.

Kassarjian, H. H., & Cohen, J. B. (1965). Cognitive dissonance and consumer behavior: Reactions to the Surgeon General's Report on Smoking and Health. *California Management Review* (Vol. 8), 55–64.

Kassin, S. M. (1979). Consensus information, prediction and causal attribution: A review of the literature and issues. *Journal of Personality and Social Psychology, 37,* 1966–1981.

Kassin, S. M. (1985). Eyewitness identification: Retrospective self-awareness and the accuracy-confidence correlation. *Journal of Personality and Social Psychology, 49,* 878–893.

Katz, D. (1960). The functional approach to the study of attitudes. *Public Opinion Quarterly, 24,* 163–204.

Katz, D. (1965). Nationalism and strategies of international conflict resolution. In H. C. Kelman (Ed.), *International behavior: A social-psychological analysis.* New York: Holt, Rinehart and Winston.

Katz, D., & Kahn, R. N. (1978). *The social psychology of organizations* (2nd ed.). New York: Wiley.

Katz, E., & Lazarsfeld, P. F. (1955). *Personal influence.* Glencoe, IL: Free Press.

Katz, I., Glucksberg, S., & Krauss, R. (1960). Need satisfaction and Edwards PPS scores in married couples. *Journal of Consulting Psychology, 24,* 205–208.

Katz, J., Capron, A. M., & Glass, E. S. (1972). *Experimentation with human beings.* New York: Russell Sage Foundation.

Katz, P. A. (Ed.) (1976). *Towards the elimination of racism.* New York: Pergamon.

Kazdin, A. E. (1977). *Behavior modification in applied settings.* Homewood, IL: Dorsey.

Keating, C. F, Mazur, A., Segall, M. H., Cysneiros, P. G., Divale, W. T., Kilbride, J. E., Komin, S., Leahy, P., Thurman, B., & Wirsing, R. (1981). Culture and the perception of social dominance from facial cues. *Journal of Personality and Social Psychology, 40,* 615–626.

Keating, J. P., & Latané, B. (1976). Politicians on TV: The image is the message. *Journal of Social Issues, 32,* 116–132.

Keeton, R. E. (1973). *Trial tactics and methods.* Boston: Little, Brown.

Keller, R. T. (1978). A longitudinal assessment of a managerial grid seminar training program. *Group and Organizational Studies, 3,* 343–355.

Kelley, H. H. (1950). The warm-cold variable in first impressions of persons. *Journal of Personality, 18,* 431–439.

Kelley, H. H. (1967). Attribution in social interaction. In E. E. Jones, D. E. Kanouse, H. H. Kelley, R. E. Nisbett, S. Valins, & B. Weiner (Eds.), *Attribution: Perceiving the causes of behavior.* Morristown, NJ: General Learning Press.

Kelley, H. H. (1967). Attribution theory in social psychology. In D. Levine (Ed.), *Nebraska symposium on motivation* (Vol. 15). Lincoln: University of Nebraska Press.

Kelley, H. H. (1973). The processes of causal attribution. *American Psychologist, 28,* 107–128.

Kelley, H. H., & Stahelski, A. J. (1970). Social interaction basis of cooperators' and competitors' beliefs about others. *Journal of Personality and Social Psychology, 16,* 66–91.

Kelley, J. A., & Worrell, J. (1977). New formulations of sex roles and androgyny: A critical review. *Journal of Consulting and Clinical Psychology, 45,* 1101–1115.

Kelly, G. A. (1955). *The psychology of personal constructs.* New York: Norton.

Kelman, H. C. (1958). Compliance, identification, and internationalization: Three processes of attitude change. *Journal of Conflict Resolution, 2,* 51–60.

Kelman, H. C. (1961). Processes of opinion change. *Public Opinion Quarterly, 25,* 57–78.

Kelman, H. C. (Ed.) (1965). *International behavior: A social-psychological analysis.* New York: Holt, Rinehart and Winston.

Kelman, H. C. (1967). Human use of human subjects: The problem of deception in social psychological experiments. *Psychological Bulletin, 67,* 1–11.

Kelman, H. C. (1982). Creating the conditions for Israeli-Palestinian negotiations. *Journal of Conflict Resolution, 26,* 39–75.

Kelman, H. C. (1983). Conversations with Arafat: A social-psychological assessment of the prospects for Israeli-Palestinian peace. *American Psychologist, 38,* 203–216.

Kelman, H. C., & Cohen, S. P. (1979). Reduction of international conflict: An interactional approach. In W. G. Austin & S. Worchel, *The social psychology of intergroup relations.* Monterey, CA: Brooks/Cole.

Kelman, H. C., & Hovland, C. I. (1953). "Reinstatement" of the communicator in delayed measurement of opinion change. *Journal of Abnormal and Social Psychology, 48,* 327–335.

Kenrick, D. T., & Stringfield, D. O. (1980). Personality traits and the eye of the beholder: Crossing some traditional philosophical boundaries in the search for consistency in all of the people. *Psychological Review, 87,* 88–104.

Kerckhoff, A. C., & Davis, D. E. (1962). Value consensus and need complementarity in mate selection. *American Sociological Review, 27,* 295–303.

Kessler, R. C., & McRae, J. A., Jr. (1982). The effect of wives' employment on the mental health of married men and women. *American Sociological Review, 47,* 216–227.

Kidd, R. F., & Saks, M. J. (Eds.) (1980). *Advances in applied social psychology* (Vol. 1). Hillsdale, NJ: Erlbaum.

Kiesler, C. A., Collins, B. E., & Miller, N. (1969). *Attitude change.* New York: Wiley.

Kilham, W., & Mann, L. (1974). Level of destructive obedience as a function of transmitter and executant roles in the Milgram obedience paradigm. *Journal of Personality and Social Psychology, 29,* 696–702.

King, B. T., & Janis, I. L. (1956). Comparison of the effectiveness of improvised versus non-improvised role-playing in producing opinion change. *Human Relations, 9,* 177–186.

King, D. R. (1978). The brutalization effect: Execution publicity and the incidence of homocide in South Carolina. *Social Forces, 57,* 683–387.

Kinsel, A. S. (1970). Body buffer zone in violent prisoners. *American Journal of Psychiatry, 127,* 59–64.

Kirmeyer, S. L. (1979). Urban density and pathology: A review of research. *Environment and Behavior, 10,* 247–270.

Kirp, D. L. (1976). Race, politics, and the courts: School desegregation in San Francisco. *Harvard Educational Review, 46,* 572–611.

Kish, L. (1965). *Survey sampling.* New York: Wiley.

Kleinke, C. L., & Kahn, M. L. (1980). Perceptions of self-disclosers: Effects of sex and physical attractiveness. *Journal of Personality, 48,* 190–205.

Klemesrud, J. (1979, March 11). Women executives: View from the top. *The New York Times,* p. 50.

Knapp, M. L. (1978). *Non-verbal communication in human interaction* (2nd ed.). New York: Holt, Rinehart and Winston.

Knapp, M. L., Hart, R. P., & Dennis, H. S. (1974). An exploration of deception as a communication construct. *Human Communication Research, 1,* 15–29.

Knox, R. E., & Inkster, J. A. (1968). Post-decision dissonance at post time. *Journal of Personality and Social Psychology, 8,* 310–323.

Knox, R. E., & Safford, R. K. (1976). Group caution at the racetrack. *Journal of Experimental Social Psychology, 12,* 317–324.

Knudson, R. M., Sommers, A. A., & Golding, S. L. (1980). Interpersonal perception and mode of resolution in marital conflict. *Journal of Personality and Social Psychology, 38,* 751–763.

Koffka, A. (1935). *The principles of Gestalt psychology.* New York: Harcourt Brace Jovanovich.

Kogan, N., & Wallach, M. A. (1964). *Risk-taking: A study in cognition and personality.* New York: Holt, Rinehart and Winston.

Kohlberg, L. (1966). Cognitive-developmental analysis of children's sex-role concepts and attitudes. In E. E. Maccoby (Ed.), *The development of sex differences.* Stanford, CA: Stanford University Press.

Kohlberg, L. (1969). Stage and sequence: The cognitive-developmental approach to socialization. In A. Goslin (Ed.), *Handbook of socialization theory and research.* Chicago: Rand McNally.

Kohlberg, L. (1981). *The philosophy of moral development: Moral stages and the idea of justice.* San Francisco: Harper & Row.

Kohlenberg, R., & Phillips, T. (1973). Reinforcement and rate of litter depositing. *Journal of Applied Behavior Analysis, 6,* 391–396.

Kolbe, R., & LaVoie, J. C. (1981). Sex-role stereotyping in pre-school children's picture books. *Social Psychology Quarterly, 44,* 369–374.

Komarovsky, M. (1946). Cultural contradictions and sex roles. *American Journal of Sociology, 52,* 182–189.

Komarovsky, M. (1982). Female freshmen view their future. *Sex Roles, 8,* 299–314.

Komorita, S. S., & Moore, D. (1976). Theories and processes of coalition formation. *Journal of Personality and Social Psychology, 33,* 371–381.

Konecni, V. J. (1975). Annoyance, type and duration of post-annoyance activity, and aggression: The "cathartic" effect. *Journal of Experimental Psychology: General, 104,* 76–102.

Konecni, V. J., Libuser, L., Morton, H., & Ebbeson, E. B. (1975). Effects of violation of personal space on escape and helping responses. *Journal of Experimental Social Psychology, 11,* 288–299.

Korchin, S. J. (1976). *Modern clinical psychology.* New York: Basic Books.

Kornfeld, D. S. (1972). The hospital environment: Its impact on the patient. *Advances in Psychosomatic Medicine, 8,* 252–270.

Korsch, B. M., Christian, J. B., Gozzi, E. K., & Carlson, P. V. (1965). Infant care and punishment: A pilot study. *American Journal of Public Health, 55,* 1880–1888.

Korte, C. (1971). Effects of individual responsibility and group communication on help-giving in an emergency. *Human Relations, 24,* 149–159.

Korte, C. (1980). Urban-nonurban differences in social behavior and social psychological models of urban impact. *Journal of Social Issues, 36,* 29–51.

Korte, C., & Kerr, N. (1975). Responses to altruistic opportunities under urban and rural conditions. *Journal of Psychology, 95,* 183–184.

Korte, C., Ypma, I., & Toppen, A. (1975). Helpfulness in Dutch society as a function of urbanization and environmental input level. *Journal of Personality and Social Psychology, 32,* 996–1003.

Krauss, R. M., & Deutsch, M. (1966). Communication in interpersonal bargaining. *Journal of Personality and Social Psychology, 4,* 572–577.

Krauss, R. M., Geller, V., & Olson, C. (1976). *Modalities and cues in the detection of deception.* Paper presented at the meeting of the American Psychological Association, Washington, DC.

Kraut, R. E., & Poe, D. (1980). Behavioral roots of person perception: The deception judgments of customs inspectors and laymen. *Journal of Personality and Social Psychology, 39,* 784–798.

Krebs, D. (1982). Altruism—a rational approach. In N. Eisenberg (Ed.), *The development of prosocial behavior.* New York: Academic Press.

Krebs, D., & Adinolfi, A. A. (1975). Physical attractiveness, social relations, and personality style. *Journal of Personality and Social Psychology, 31,* 245–253.

Krebs, D., & Gilmore, J. (1982). The relationship among the first stages of cognitive development, role-taking abilities, and moral development. *Child Development, 53,* 877–886.

Krech, D., & Crutchfield, R. S. (1948). *Theory and problems in social psychology.* New York: McGraw-Hill.

Krech, D., Crutchfield, R. S., & Ballachey, E. L. (1962). *Individual in society.* New York: McGraw-Hill.

Kremer, J. F., & Stephens, L. (1983). Attributions and arousal as mediators of mitigation's effects on retaliation. *Journal of Personality and Social Psychology, 45,* 335–343.

Kreps, G. L., & Thornton, B. C. (1984). *Health communication.* New York: Longman.

Kriesberg, L. (1978–1981). *Research in social movements, conflicts, and change* (Vols. 1–4). Greenwich, CT: J. A. I. Press.

Krovetz, M. L. (1977). Who needs what when: Design of pluralistic learning environments. In D. Stokols (Ed.), *Perspectives on environment and behavior: Theory, research, and applications.* New York: Plenum.

Kruger, W. S. (1973). Education for parenthood and the schools. *Children Today, 2,* 4–7.

Kruglanski, A. W. (1977). The place of naive contents in a theory of attribution: Reflections on Calder's and Zuckerman's critiques of endogeneous-exogenous partition. *Personality and Social Psyuchology Bulletin, 3,* 592–602.

Kruglanski, A. W., Freedman, L., & Zeevi, G. (1971). The effects of extrinsic incentives on some qualitative aspects of task performance. *Journal of Personality, 39,* 606–617.

Kruglanski, A. W., & Freund, T. (1983). The freezing and unfreezing of lay inferences: Effects on impressional primacy, ethnic stereotyping, and numerical anchoring. *Journal of Experimental Social Psychology, 19,* 448–468.

Krupat, E. (1982). *Psychology is social* (2nd ed.). Glenview, IL: Scott, Foresman.

Krupat, E. (1983). The doctor-patient relationship: A social psychological analysis. In R. F. Kidd & M. J. Saks (Eds.), *Advances in applied social psychology* (Vol. 2). Hillsdale, NJ: Erlbaum.

Krupat, E. (1985). *People in cities: The urban environment and its effects.* New York: Cambridge University Press.

Krupat, E. (1986). Physicians and patients: The delicate imbalance. *Psychology Today, 20,* 22–26.

Krupat, E., & Guild, W. (1980a). Defining the city: The use of objective and subjective measures for community description. *Journal of Social Issues, 36,* 9–28.

Krupat, E., & Guild, W. (1980b). The measurement of community social climate. *Environment and Behavior, 12,* 195–206.

Kubzansky, P. E., Salter, L. R., & Porter, G. (1980). "Ideology" of open office design: Issues and remedies. Paper presented at the Environmental Design Research Association Convention, Charleston, SC.

Kuhlman, D. M., & Marshello, A. (1975). Individual differences in game motivation as moderators of preprogrammed strategy effects in Prisoner's Dilemma. *Journal of Personality and Social Psychology, 32,* 922–931.

Kuhn, T. S. (1962). *The structure of scientific revolutions.* Chicago: University of Chicago Press.

Kuiper, N. A., & Higgins, E. T. (1985). Social cognition and depression: A general integrative perspective. *Social Cognition, 3,* 1–15.

Kulik, J. A. (1983). Confirmatory attribution and the perpetuation of social beliefs. *Journal of Personality and Social Psychology, 44,* 1171–1181.

LaFrance, M. (1985). The school of hard knocks: Nonverbal sexism in the classroom. *Theory into Practice, 24,* 40–44.

LaFrance, M., & Carmen, B. (1980). The nonverbal display of psychological androgyny. *Journal of Personality and Social Psychology, 38,* 36–49.

LaFrance, M., & Mayo, C. (1978). *Moving bodies: Non-verbal communication in social relationships.* Monterey, CA: Brooks/Cole.

Lambert, W. E., Libman, E., & Poser, E. G. (1960). The effect of increased salience of a membership group on pain tolerance. *Journal of Personality, 28,* 350–356.

Lamm, H., & Trommsdorff, G. (1973). Group versus individual performance on tasks requiring ideational proficiency (brainstorming): A review. *European Journal of Social Psychology, 3,* 361–388.

Lana, R. E. (1972). Persuasion and the law: A constitutional issue. *American Psychologist, 27,* 901.

Langer, E. J., & Rodin, J. (1976). The effects of choice and enhanced personal responsibility for the aged: A field experiment in an institutional setting. *Journal of Personality and Social Psychology, 34,* 191–198.

Lao, R. C., Upchurch, W. H., Corwin, B. J., & Crossnickle, W. F. (1975). Biased attitudes toward females as indicated by ratings of intelligence and likeability. *Psychology Reports, 37,* 1315–1320.

LaPiere, R. T. (1928). Race prejudice: France and England. *Social Forces,* 102–111.

LaPiere, R. T. (1934). Attitudes vs. actions. *Social Forces, 13,* 230–237.

Larsen, R. J., & Seidman, E. (1986). Gender schema theory and sex role inventories: Some conceptual and psychometric considerations. *Journal of Personality and Social Psychology, 50,* 205–211.

Larson, K. S. (Ed.) (1980). *Social psychology: Crisis or failure.* Monmouth, OR: Institute for Theoretical History.

Latané, B. (1981). The psychology of social impact. *American Psychologist, 36,* 343–356.

Latané, B., & Dabbs, J. M., Jr. (1975). Sex, group size and helping in three cities. *Sociometry, 38,* 180–194.

Latané, B., & Darley, J. M. (1970). *The unresponsive bystander: Why doesn't he help?* New York: Appleton-Century-Crofts.

Latané, B., & Harkins, S. (1976). Cross-modality matches suggest anticipated stage fright as multiplicative power function of audience size and status. *Perception and Psychophysics, 20,* 482–488.

Latané, B., & Nida, S. (1980). Social impact theory and group influence: A social engineering perspective. In P. B. Paulus (Ed.), *Psychology of group influence.* Hillsdale, NJ: Erlbaum.

Latané, B., & Nida, S. (1981). Ten years of research on group size and helping. *Psychological Bulletin, 89,* 308–324.

Latané, B., & Rodin, J. (1969). A lady in distress: Inhibiting effects of friends and strangers on bystander intervention. *Journal of Experimental Social Psychology, 5,* 189–202.

Latané, B., Williams, K., & Harkins, S. (1979). Many hands make light the work: The causes and consequences of social loafing. *Journal of Personality and Social Psychology, 37,* 822–832.

Lau, R. R., & Russell, D. (1980). Attributions in the sports pages: A field test of some current hypotheses about attribution research. *Journal of Personality and Social Psychology, 39,* 29–38.

Lawler, E. E. (1982). Strategies for improving the quality of work life. *American Psychologist, 37,* 486–493.

Lawler, E. J., & MacMurray, B. K. (1980). Bargaining toughness: A qualification of level of aspiration and reciprocity hypotheses. *Journal of Applied Social Psychology, 10,* 416–430.

Lawson, E. (1971). Hair color, personality and the observer. *Psychological Reports, 28,* 311–322.

Leahy, P. J. (1977). *The whistle blowers: A report on federal employees who disclose acts of govermental waste, abuse and corruption.* Washington, DC: U.S. Senate.

Leary, M., Knight, P., & Barnes, D. (1986). Ethical ideologies of the Machiavellian. *Personality and Social Psychology Bulletin, 12,* 75–80.

Le Bon, G. (1895). *The crowd: A study of the popular mind.* New York: Viking Press, 1960.

Lefcourt, H. M. (1982). *Locus of control: Current trends in theory and research* (2nd ed.). Hillsdale, NJ: Erlbaum.

Lefcourt, H. M., Lewis, L., & Silverman, I. W. (1968). Internal versus external control of reinforcement and attention in a decision making task. *Journal of Personality, 36,* 663–682.

Lefkowitz, M. M., Eron, L. D., Walder, L. O., & Huesmann, L. R. (1977). *Growing up to be violent: A longitudinal study of the development of aggression.* New York: Pergamon.

Lemke, S., & Moos, R. H. (1980). Assessing the institutional policies of sheltered care settings. *Journal of Gerontology, 35,* 96–107.

Leonard, R. (1975). Self-concept and attraction for similar and dissimilar others. *Journal of Personality and Social Psychology, 31,* 926-929.

Lepper, M. R., Greene, D., & Nisbett, R. E. (1973). Undermining children's intrinsic interest with extrinsic reward: A test of the overjustification hypothesis. *Journal of Personality and Social Psychology, 28,* 128–137.

Lerner, M. J. (1980). *The belief in a just world: A fundamental delusion.* New York: Plenum.

Lerner, M. J., & Agar, E. (1972). The consequences of perceived similarity: Attraction and rejection, approach and avoidance. *Journal of Experimental Research in Personality, 6,* 69–75.

Lerner, M. J., & Simmons, C. H. (1966). Observers' reactions to the "innocent victim": Comparison or rejection? *Journal of Personality and Social Psychology, 4,* 203–210.

Lester, G. W., Beckham, E., & Baucom, D. H. (1980). Implementation of behavioral marital therapy. *Journal of Marital and Family Therapy, 6,* 189–199.

Leventhal, G. S. (1980). What should be done with equity theory? New approaches to the study of fairness in social relationships. In K. J. Gergen, M. S. Greenberg, and R. H. Willis (Eds.), *Social exchange: Advances in theory and research.* New York: Plenum.

Leventhal, H., Singer, R., & Jones, S. (1965). Effects of fear and specificity of recommendation upon attitudes and behavior. *Journal of Personality and Social Psychology, 2,* 20–29.

Leventhal, H., & Singer, R. P. (1966). Affect arousal and positioning of recommendations in persuasive communications. *Journal of Personality and Social Psychology, 3,* 137–146.

Levinger, G. (1964). Note on need complementarity in marriage. *Psychological Bulletin, 61,* 153–157.

Levinger, G. (1974). A 3-level approach to attraction: Toward an understanding of pair-relatedness. In T. L. Huston (Ed.), *Foundations of interpersonal attraction.* New York: Academic Press.

Levinger, G. (1976). A social psychological perspective on marital dissolution. *Journal of Social Issues, 32,* 21–47.

Levinger, G. (1980). Toward the analysis of close relationships. *Journal of Experimental Social Psychology, 16,* 510–544.

Levinger, G., Senn, D. J., & Jorgensen, B. W. (1970). Progress toward permanence in courtship: A test of the Kerckhoff-Davis hypothesis. *Sociometry, 33,* 427–433.

Levinger, G., & Snoek, J. D. (1972). *Attraction in relationships: A new look at interpersonal attraction.* Morristown, NJ: General Learning Press.

Levy, J. (1976). Cerebral lateralization and spatial ability. *Behavior Genetics, 6,* 171–188.

Levy, L., & Herzog, A. N. (1974). Effects of population density and crowding on health and social adaptation in the Netherlands. *Journal of Health and Social Behavior, 15,* 228–240.

Lewicki, P. (1982). Social psychology as viewed by its practitioners. *Personality and Social Psychology Bulletin, 8,* 409–416.

Lewin, K. (1936). *Principles of topological psychology.* New York: McGraw-Hill.

Lewin, K. (1947). Group decision and social change. In T. M. Newcomb & E. L. Hartley (Eds.), *Readings in social psychology.* New York: Holt, Rinehart and Winston.

Lewin, K. (1948). *Resolving social conflicts.* New York: Harper & Row.

Lewin, K. (1951). *Field theory in social science.* New York: Harper & Row.

Lewin, K., Lippitt, R., & White, R. K. (1939). Patterns of aggressive behavior in experimentally created "social climates." *Journal of Social Psychology, 10,* 271–299.

Lewis, P. W. (1979). Killing the killers: A post-*Furman* profile of Florida's condemmed: A personal account. *Crime and Delinquency, 25,* 200–218.

Lewontin, R., Rose, S., & Kamin, L. (1984). *Not in our genes.* New York: Pantheon.

Ley, D., and Cybriwsky, R. (1974). Urban graffiti as territorial markers. *Annals of the Association of American Geographers, 64,* 491–505.

Leyens, J. P., & Parke, R. E. (1975). Aggressive slides can induce a weapons effect. *European Journal of Social Psychology, 5,* 229–236.

Lieberman, M. A., Yalom, I. D., & Miles, M. B. (1973). *Encounter groups: First facts.* New York: Basic Books.

Liebert, R. M., & Baron, R. A. (1972). Some immediate effects of televised violence on children. *Developmental Psychology, 6,* 469–475.

Liebert, R. M., & Poulos, R. W. (1975). Television and personality development: The socializing effects of an entertainment medium. In A. Davids (Ed.), *Child personality and psychopathology: Current topics* (Vol. 2). New York: Wiley.

Liebert, R. M., Sprafkin, J. N., & Davidson, E. S. (1982). *The early window: Effects of television on children and youth.* New York: Pergamon.

Liem, R. (in press). Unemployed workers and their families: Social victims or social critics. In P. Voydanoff & L. Majka (Eds.), *Families and economic distress: Coping strategies and social policy.* Beverly Hills, CA: Sage.

Likert, R. (1932). A technique for the measurement of attitudes. *Archives of Psychology, 140.*

Likert, R. (1961). *New patterns of management.* New York: McGraw-Hill.

Likert, R. (1967). *The human organization.* New York: McGraw-Hill.

Lindbloom, D. E., & Cohen, D. K. (1979). *Usable knowledge: Social science and social problem solving.* New Haven, CT: Yale University Press.

Lindskold, S. (1978). Trust development, the GRIT proposal, and the effects of conciliatory acts on conflcit and cooperation. *Psychological Bulletin, 85,* 772–793.

Lindskold, S. (1979). Conciliation with simultaneous or sequential interaction: Variations in trustworthiness and vulnerability in the prisoner's dilemma. *Journal of Conflict Resolution, 23,* 704–714.

Lindskold, S., & Collins, M. J. (1978). Inducing cooperation by groups and individuals: Applying Osgood's GRIT strategy. *Journal of Conflict Resolution, 22,* 679–690.

Linville, P. W., & Jones, E. E. (1980). Polarized appraisals of out-group members. *Journal of Personality and Social Psychology, 38,* 689–703.

Lippitt, G., & Lippitt, R. (1978). *The consulting process in action.* La Jolla, CA: University Associates.

Litman-Adizes, T., Raven, B., & Fontaine, G. (1978). Consequences of social power and causal attribution for compliance as seen by powerholder and target. *Personality Social Psychology Bulletin, 4,* 260–264.

Locke, E. A. (1976). The nature and causes of job satisfaction. In M. D. Dunnette (Ed.), *Handbook of industrial and organizational psychology.* Chicago: Rand McNally.

Lockheed, M. E. & Hall, K. (1976). Conceptualizing sex as a status characteristic: Applications to leadership training strategies. *Journal of Social Issues, 32,* 111–124.

Lofland, J. (1981). *Doomsday cult: A study of conversion, proselytization, and maintenance of faith.* New York: Irvington.

Loftus, E. F. (1983). Silence is not golden. *American Psychologist, 38,* 564–572.

Loftus, E. F., & Palmer, J. C. (1974). Reconstruction of automobile destruction: An example of the interaction between language and memory. *Journal of Verbal Learning and Verbal Behavior, 13,* 585–589.

London, P. (1970). The rescuers: Motivational hypotheses about Christians who saved Jews from the Nazis. In J. Macauley & L. Berkowitz (Eds.), *Altruism and helping behavior.* New York: Academic Press.

Loo, C. (1978). Density, crowding, and preschool children. In A. Baum and Y. M. Epstein (Eds.), *Human response to crowding.* Hillsdale, NJ: Erlbaum.

Loo, C. M. (1978). The effects of spatial density upon children: "Fishing with a net rather than a pole." In A. Baum & Y. M. Epstein (Eds.), *Human response to crowding.* Hillsdale, NJ: Erlbaum.

Lorber, J. (1979). Good patients and problem patients: Conformity and deviance in a general hospital. In E. G. Jones (Ed.), *Patients, physicians and illness.* New York: Free Press.

Lorenz, K. (1966). *On aggression.* New York: Harcourt Brace Jovanovich.

Lorge, I., & Solomon, H. (1955). Two models of group behavior in the solution of eureka-type problems. *Psychomtrika, 20,* 139–148.

Lott, A. J., & Lott, B. E. (1968). A learning theory approach to interpersonal attitudes. In A. G. Greenwald, T. C. Brock, & T. M. Ostrom (Eds.), *Psychological foundations of attitudes.* New York: Academic Press.

Lott, B. (1985). The devaluation of women's competence. *Journal of Social Issues, 41,* 43–60.

Love, R. E., & Greenwald, A. C. (1978). Cognitive responses to persuasion as mediators of opinion change. *Journal of Social Psychology, 104,* 231–241.

Lowery, L. R., Denney, D. R., & Storms, M. D. (1979). Insomnia: A comparison of the effects of pill attributions and nonpejorative self-attributions. *Cognitive therapy research, 3,* 161–164.

Lubinski, D., Tellegen, A., & Butcher, J. N. (1983). Masculinity, femininity and androgyny viewed and assessed as distinct concepts. *Journal of Personality and Social Psychology, 44,* 428–439.

Luce, R. D., & Raiffa, H. (1957). *Games and decisions: Introduction and critical survey.* New York: Wiley.

Luchins, A. S., & Luchins, E. H. (1961). On conformity with judgments of a majority or an authority. *Journal of Social Psychology, 53,* 303–316.

Lumsdaine, A. A., & Janis, I. L. (1953). Resistance to "counter-propaganda" produced by one-sided and two-sided "propaganda" presentations. *Public Opinion Quarterly, 17,* 311–318.

Lundberg, V. (1976). Urban commuting: Crowdedness and catacholemine excretion. *Journal of Human Stress, 2,* 26–32.

Lurigio, A. J., & Carroll, J. S. (1985). Probation officer's schemata of offenders: Content development and impact on treatment decisions. *Journal of Personality and Social Psychology, 48,* 1112–1126.

Lutzker, J. R., Wesch, D., & Rice, J. M. (1984). A review of "Project 12-Ways": An ecobehavioral approach to the treatment and prevention of child abuse and neglect. *Advances in behavior research and therapy, 6,* 63–73.

Lyle, J., & Hoffman, H. R. (1972). Children's use of television and other media. In E. A. Rubinstein, G. A. Comstock, & J. P. Murray (Eds.), *Television in day-to-day life: Patterns of use.* Washington, DC: United States Goverment Printing Office.

Lynn, S. J. (1978). Three theories of self-disclosure exchange. *Journal of Experimental Social Psychology, 14,* 466–479.

MacArthur, L. Z. (1972). The how and what of why: Some determination and consequences of causal attribution. *Journal of Personality and Social Psychology, 22,* 171–193.

MacArthur, L. Z. (1981). What grabs you? The role of attention in impression formation and causal attribution. In E. T. Higgins, C. P. Herman, & M. P. Zanna (Eds.), *Social cognition: The Ontario Symposium* (Vol. 1). Hillsdale, NJ: Erlbaum.

MacArthur, L. Z. & Baron, R. (1983). Toward an ecological theory of social perception. *Psychological Review, 90,* 215–238.

MacArthur, L. Z., & Ginsburg, E. (1981). Causal attribution to salient stimuli: An investigation of visual fixation mediators. *Personality and Social Psychology Bulletin, 7,* 547–553.

Maccoby, E. E., & Jacklin, C. (1974). *The psychology of sex differences.* Stanford, CA: Stanford University Press.

Maccoby, N., Farquhar, J., Wood, P., & Alexander, J. (1977). Reducing the risk of cardiovascular disease: Effects of a community-based campaign on knowledge and behavior. *Journal of Community Health, 3,* 100–114.

MacFarlane, J. W. (1963). From infancy to adulthood. *Childhood Education, 39,* 336–342.

MacFarlane, J. W. (1964). Perspectives on personality consistency and change from the guidance study. *Vita Humana, 7,* 115–126.

Mackay, C. (1841, reissued 1932). *Extraordinary popular delusions and the madness of crowds.* New York: Page.

Macklin, E. (1974). Going very steady. *Psychology Today, 8*(6), 53–59.

Maddi, S. R. (1968). Meaning, novelty and affect: Comments on Zajonc's paper. *Journal of Personality and Social Psychology, 9,* 28–29.

Magnusson, D. (1974). The individual in the situation: Some studies on individual's perception of situations. *Studia Psychologica, 16,* 124–131.

Magnusson, D., & Endler, N. S. (Eds.) (1977). *Personality at the crossroads: Current issues in interactional psychology.* Hillsdale, NJ: Erlbaum.

MaGuire, J. M., Weinstein, J. B., Chadbourn, J. H., & Mansfield, J. H. (1973). *Evidence* (6th ed.). Mineola, NY: The Foundation Press.

Maier, N. R. F. (1972). Decision-making in three versus four person groups. *Personnel Psychology, 25,* 531–534.

Maier, N. R. F., & Hoffman, L. R. (1960). Using trained "developmental" discussion leaders to improve further the quality of group decisions. *Journal of Applied Psychology, 44,* 247–251.

Major, B. (1980). Informative acquisition and attribution processes. *Journal of Personality and Social Psychology, 39,* 1010–1024.

Major, B., Deaux, K., & Carnevale, P. J. (1981). A different perspective on androgyny: Evaluations of masculine and feminine personality characteristics. *Journal of Personality and Social Psychology, 41,* 988–1001.

Malamuth, N. M. (1981). Rape fantasies as a function of exposure to violent sexual stimuli. *Archives of Sexual Behavior, 10,* 33–47.

Malamuth, N. M., & Check, J. V. P. (1984). Debriefing effectiveness following exposure to pornographic rape depictions. *Journal of Sex Research, 20,* 1–13.

Malamuth, N. M., Check, J. V. P., & Briere, J. (1986). Sexual arousal in response to aggression: Ideological, aggressive, and sexual correlates. *Journal of Personality and Social Psychology, 50,* 330–340.

Malamuth, N. M., & Donnerstein, E. (Eds.) (1984). *Pornography and sexual aggression.* New York: Academic Press.

Malof, M., & Lott, A. J. (1962). Ethnocentrism and the acceptance of Negro support in a group pressure situation. *Journal of Abnormal and Social Psychology, 65,* 254–258.

Malpass, R. S., & Devine, G. (1981). Guided memory in eyewitness identification. *Journal of Applied Psychology, 66,* 343–350.

Mann, R. D. (1959). A review of the relationships between personality and performance in small groups. *Psychological Bulletin, 56,* 241–270.

Markides, K. C., & Cohn, S. F. (1982). External conflict/internal cohesion: A reevaluation of an old theory. *American Sociological Review, 47,* 88–99.

Markus, H. (1977). Self-schemata and processing

information about the self. *Journal of Personality and Social Psychology, 35,* 63–78.

Markus, H., & Sentis, K. P. (1982). The self in social information processing. In J. Suls (Ed.), *Psychological perspectives on the self* (Vol. 1). Hillsdale, NJ: Erlbaum.

Marriage: It's back in style (1983, June 20). *U. S. News & World Report,* 44–47, 50.

Marrow, A. J. (1969). *The practical theorist: Life and work of Kurt Lewin.* New York: Basic Books.

Marrow, A. J., Bowers, D. G., & Seashore, S. E. (1967). *Management by participation.* New York: Harper & Row.

Marsh, S. H. (1962). Validating the selection of deputy sheriffs. *Public Personnel Review, 23,* 43–44.

Marshall, G. D., & Zimbardo, P. G. (1979). Affective consequences of indequately explained physiological arousal. *Journal of Personality and Social Psychology, 37,* 970–988.

Marston, H. M. (1975). Crowding and animal behavior. In E. Krupat (Ed.), *Psychology is social.* Glenview, IL: Scott, Foresman.

Maslach, C. (1979). Negative emotional biasing of unexplained arousal. *Journal of Personality and Social Psychology, 37,* 953–969.

Mathes, E. W., Adams. H. E., & Davies, R. M. (1985). Jealousy: Loss of relationship rewards, loss of self-esteem, depression, anxiety, and anger. *Journal of Personality and Social Psychology, 48,* 1552–1561.

Matthews, K. A., Weiss, S. M., D'etre, T., Dembroski, T. M., Falkner, B., Manuck, S. B., & Williams, R. B., Jr. (1982). *Handbook of stress, reactivity, and cardiovascular disease.* New York: Wiley.

Mayo, E. (1933). *The human problems of an industrial civilization.* New York: Macmillan.

McClelland, D. C. (1975). *Power: The inner experience.* New York: Irvington.

McClelland, L., & Belsten, L. (1979–1980). Promoting energy conservation in university dormitories by physical, policy, and resident behavior changes. *Journal of Environmental Systems, 9,* 29–38.

McClelland, L., & Canter, R. J. (1981). Psychological research on energy consumption: Context, approaches, methods. In A. Baum & J. E. Singer (Eds.), *Advances in environmental psychology* (Vol. 3). Hillsdale, NJ: Erlbaum.

McClintock, C. C. & Hunt, R. C. (1975). Non-verbal indicators of affect and deception in an interview setting. *Journal of Applied Social Psychology, 5,* 54–67.

McConahay, S. A., & McConahay, J. B. (1977). Sexual permisiveness, sex-role rigidity and violence across cultures. *Journal of Social Issues, 33*(2), 134–143.

McCord, J. (1979). Some child rearing antecedents to criminal behavior in adult men. *Journal of Personality and Social Psychology, 37,* 1477–1486.

McEwen, C. A., & Maiman, R. J. (1981). Small claims mediation in Maine: An empirical assessment. *Maine Law Review, 33,* 237–268.

McEwen, C. A. & Maiman, R. J. (1984). Mediation in small claims court: Achieving compliance through concent. *Law and Society Review, 18,* 11–49.

McGillis, D. (1981). Conflict resolution outside the courts. In L. Bickman (Ed.), *Applied Social Psychology Annual* (Vol. 2). Beverly Hills, CA: Sage.

McGillis, D., & Mullen, J. (1977). *Neighborhood justice centers: An analysis of potential models.* Washington, DC: U.S. Government Printing Office.

McGrath, J. E., & Altman, I. (1966). *Small group research.* New York: Holt, Rinehart and Winston.

McGregor, D. (1960). *The human side of enterprise.* New York: McGraw-Hill.

McGrew, P. L. (1970). Social and spatial density effects on spacing behavior in preschool children. *Journal of Child Psychology and Psychiatry, 11,* 197–205.

McGuire, W. J. (1964). Inducing resistance to persuasion: Some contemporary approaches. In L. Berkowitz (Ed.), *Advances in experimental social psychology* (Vol. 1). New York: Academic Press.

McGuire, W. J. (1968). Personality and susceptibility to social influence. In E. F. Borgatta & W. W. Lambert (Eds.), *Handbook of personality and research.* Chicago: Rand McNally.

McGuire, W. J. (1969). The nature of attitudes and attitude change. In G. Lindsey & E. Aronson (Eds.), *Handbook of social psychology* (Vol. 3, 2nd ed.). Reading, MA: Addison-Wesley.

McGuire, W. J. (1969). Theory-oriented research in natural setting: The best of both worlds for social psychology. In M. Sherif & C. W. Sherif (Eds.), *Interdisciplinary relationships in the social sciences.* Chicago: Aldine.

McGuire, W. J. (1973). The Yin and Yang of progress in social psychology. *Journal of Personality and Social Psychology, 26,* 446–456.

McGuire, W. J., & McGuire, C. V. (1982). Significant others in self-space: Sex differences and developmental trends in the social self. In J. Suls (Ed.), *Psychological perspectives on the self* (Vol. 1). Hillsdale, NJ: Erlbaum.

McGuire, W. J., McGuire, C. V., & Winton, W. (1979). Effects of household sex composition on the salience of one's gender in the spontaneous self-concept. *Journal of Experimental and Social Psychology, 15,* 86–90.

McGuire, W. J., & Papageorgis, D., (1961). The relative efficacy of various types of prior belief-defense in producing immunity against persuasion. *Journal of Abnormal and Social Psychology, 62,* 327–337.

Mead, G. H. (C. W. Morris, Ed.) (1934). *Mind, self and society.* Chicago: University of Chicago Press.

Medom, M. (1986, March). Move over, Dr. Ruth. *PC World, 81.*

Meehl, P. E. (1954). *Clinical versus statistical prediction.* Minneapolis: University of Minnesota Press.

Meehl, P. E. (1965). Seer over sign: The first good example. *Journal of Experimental Research in Personality, 1,* 27–32.

Megargee, E. I. (1966). Undercontrolled and overcontrolled personality types in extreme anti-social aggression. *Psychological Monographs, 80*(No. 611).

Megargee, E. I. (1972). *The psychology of violence and aggression.* Morristown, NJ: General Learning Press.

Mehrabian, A. (1968). Relationships of attitude to seated posture, orientation and distance. *Journal of Personality and Social Psychology, 10,* 26–30.

Mehrabian, A. (1971). Non-verbal betrayal of feeling. *Journal of Experimental Research in Personality, 5,* 64–73.

Mehrabian, A. (1972). *Non-verbal communication.* Chicago: Aldine-Atherton.

Mellor, E. F. (1985). Weekly earnings in 1983: A look at more than 200 occupations. *Monthly Labor Review,* January, 54–59.

Menges, R. J. (1973). Openness and honesty versus coercion and deception in psychological research. *American Psychologist, 28,* 1030–1034.

Merei, F. (1949). Group leadership and insititutionalization. *Human Relations, 2,* 23–39.

Merry, S. E. (1981). Defensible space undefended: Social factors in criminal control through environmental design. *Urban Affairs Quarterly, 16,* 397–422.

Merry, S. E. (1982). The social organization of mediation in non-industrial societies: Implications for informal community justice in America. In R. L. Able (Ed.), *The politics of informal justice: Vol. 2: Comparative studies.* New York: Academic Press.

Merton, R. (1948). The self-fulfilling prophesy. *Antioch Review, 8,* 193–210.

Merton, R. K. (1960). The ambivalences of Le Bon's "The Crowd." *Introduction to G. Le Bon, The Crowd.* New York: Viking Press.

Merton, R. K., & Lazarsfeld, P. F. (Eds.) (1950). *Continuities in social research: Studies in the scope and method of the "American Soldier."* New York: Free Press.

Merton, R. K., Reider, G. G., & Kendall, P. L. (Eds.) (1957). *The student physician.* Cambridge, MA: Harvard University Press.

Meyer, C. B., & Taylor, S. E. (1986). Adjustment to rape. *Journal of Personality and Social Psychology, 50,* 1226–1234.

Meyer, J. P., & Pepper, S. (1977). Need compatibility and marital adjustment in young married couples. *Journal of Personality and Social Psychology, 35,* 331–342.

Michelson, W. (1976). *Man and his urban environment: A sociological approach.* Reading, MA: Addison-Wesley.

Michelson, W. (1977). *Environmental choice, human behavior, and residential satisfaction.* New York: Oxford University Press.

Miczek, K. A. (1983). Ethopharmacology of aggression, defense, and defect. In E. C. Simmel, M. Eittahn, & J. K. Walters (Eds.), *Aggressive behavior: Genetic and neural approaches.* Hillsdale, NJ: Erlbaum.

Midlarski, E. (1971). Aiding under stress: The effects of competence, dependency, visibility, and fatalism. *Journal of Personality, 39,* 132–149.

Miell, D., & LeVoi, M. (1985). Self-monitoring and control in dyadic interactions. *Journal of Personality and Social Psychology, 49,* 1052–1061.

Miell, D. E., & Duck, S. (1983, July). Communicative strategies in the development of personal relationships. Paper presented at the Second International Conference on Language and Social Psychology, Bristol, England.

Milardo, R. M., Johnson, M. P., & Huston, T. L. (1983). Developing close relationships: Changing patterns of interaction between pair members and social networks. *Journal of Personality and Social Psychology, 44,* 964–976.

Milavsky, J. R., Stipp, H. H., Kessler, R. C., & Rubens, W. S. (1982). *Television and aggression: A panel study.* New York: Academic Press.

Miles, R. E. (1975). *Theories of management: Implications of organizational behavior and development.* New York: McGraw-Hill.

Milgram, S. (1961). Nationality and conformity. *Scientific American, 205,* 45–51.

Milgram, S. (1967). The small-world problem. In J. V. McConnell (Ed.), *Readings in social psychology today.* Del Mar, CA: C.R.M.

Milgram, S. (1970). The experience of living in cities. *Science, 167,* 1461–1468.

Milgram, S. (1974). *Obedience to authority.* New York: Harper & Row.

Milgram, S., & Hollander, P. (1964). The murder they heard. *The Nation, 198,* 602–604.

Milgram, S., Mann, L., & Harter, S. (1965). The lost-letter technique: A tool of social science research. *Public Opinion Quarterly, 29,* 437–438.

Milgram, S., & Shotland, R. L. (1973). *Television and anti-social behavior: Field experiments.* New York: Academic Press.

Milgram, S., & Toch, H. (1969). Collective behavior: Crowds and social movements. In G. Lindzey & E. Aronson (Eds.), *The handbook of social psychology* (Vol. IV). Reading, MA: Addison-Wesley.

Miller, A. G., Jones, E. E., & Hinkle, S. (1981). A robust attribution error in the personality domain. *Journal of Experimental Social Psychology, 17,* 586–600.

Miller. D. T., & Turnbull, W. (1986). Expectancies and interpersonal processes. *Annual Review of Psychology, 37,* 233–256.

Miller, M. (1977). Intimate terrorism. *Psychology Today, 10*(10), 79–82.

Miller, N. (1965). Involvement and dogmatism as inhibitors of attitude change. *Journal of Experimental Social Psychology, 1,* 121–132.

Miller, N. (1980). Making school desegregation work. In W. G. Stephan & J. R. Fagin (Eds.), *School desegregation.* New York: Plenum.

Miller, N., & Brewer. M. B. (Eds.) (1984). *Groups in contact: The psychology of desegregation.* San Diego: Academic Press.

Miller, N., & Campbell, D. T. (1959). Recency and primacy in persuasion as a function of the timing of speeches and measurements. *Journal of Abnormal and Social Psychology, 59,* 1–9.

Miller, N. E. (1941). The frustration-aggression hypothesis. *Psychological Review, 48,* 337–342.

Miller, N. E. (1948). Theory and experiment relating psychoanalytic displacement to stimulus-response generalization. *Journal of Abnormal and Social Psychology, 43,* 155–178.

Minard, R. D. (1952). Race relationships in the Pocahontas Coal Field. *Journal of Social Issues, 8,* 29–44.

Mischel, W. (1968). *Personality and assessment.* New York: Wiley.

Mischel, W. (1969). Continuity and change in personalty. *American Psychologist, 24,* 1012–1018.

Mischel, W. (1973). Toward a cognitive social learning reconceptualization of personality. *Psychological Review, 80,* 252–283.

Mischel, W. (1976). *Introduction to psychology* (2nd ed.). New York: Holt, Rinehart and Winston.

Mischel, W. (1977). On the future of personality measurement. *American Psychologist, 32,* 246–254.

Mita, T. H., Dermer, M., & Knight, J. (1977). Reversed facial images and the mere-exposure hypothesis. *Journal of Personality and Social Psychology, 35,* 597–601.

Mitchell, R. E. (1971). Some social implications of high density housing. *American Sociological Review, 36,* 18–29.

Mixon, D. (1971). Behavior analysis treating subjects as actors rather than organisms. *Journal for the Theory of Social Behavior, 1,* 19–31.

Mixon, D. (1979). Understanding shocking and puzzling conduct. In G. P. Ginsburg (Ed.), *Emerging strategies in social psychological research.* New York: Wiley.

Miyamoto, S. F. (1973). The forced evacuation of the Japanese minority during World War II. *Journal of Social Issues, 29,* 11–31.

Mnookin, R. H. (1973). Foster care—in whose best interest? *Harvard Educational Review, 43,* 599–638.

Moe, J. L., Nacoste, R. W., & Insko, C. A. (1981). Belief versus race as determinants of discrimination: A study of southern adolescents in 1966 and 1979. *Journal of Personality and Social Psychology, 41,* 1031–1050

Mohr, W. L., & Mohr, H. (1983). *Quality circles.* Reading, MA: Addison-Wesley.

Monahan, J. (1981). *Predicting violent behavior: An assessment of clinical techniques.* Beverly Hills, CA: Sage.

Montagu, A. (1973). Introduction. In A. Milgram (Ed.), *Man and aggression.* New York: Oxford University Press.

Montgomery, R. L. (1971). Status, conformity and resistance to compliance in natural groups. *Journal of Social Psychology, 84,* 197–206.

Montgomery, R. L., & Enzie, R. F. (1971). Social influence and the estimation of time. *Psychonomic Science, 22,* 77–78.

Montgomery, R. L., & Haemerlie, F. M. (1986). The "talking platypus phenomenon" in sex-biased performance evaluation research. Paper presented at the Southeast Psychological Association, Kissimmee, Florida.

Montgomery, R. L., Hinkle, S. W., & Enzie, R. F. (1976). Arbitrary norms and social change in high- and low-authoritarian societies. *Journal of Personality and Social Psychology, 33,* 698–708.

Moore, B., & Underwood, B. (1981). The development of prosocial behavior. In S. S. Brehm, S. M. Kassin, & F. X. Gibbons (Eds.), *Developmental psychology.* New York: Oxford University Press.

Moore, J. C., Jr., & Krupat, E. (1971). Relationships between source status, authoritarianism and conformity in a social influence setting. *Sociometry, 34,* 122–134.

Moore, J. N. (1974). *The Arab-Israeli conflict.* Princeton, NJ: Princeton University Press.

Moos, R. H. (1973). Conceptualizations of human environments. *American Psychologist, 38,* 652–665.

Moos, R. H. (1976). *The human context.* New York: Wiley-Interscience.

Moos, R. H. (1980). Specialized living environments for older people: A conceptual framework for evaluation. *Journal of Social Issues, 36,* 75–94.

Mordkoff, A., & Parsons, O. (1968). The coronary personality: A critique. *International Journal of Psychiatry, 5,* 413–426.

Moreland, R. L., & Zajonc, R. B. (1979). Exposure effects may not depend on stimulus recognition. *Journal of Personality and Social Psychology, 37,* 1085–1089.

Moreno, J. L. (1953). *Who shall survive?* Boston: Beacon House.

Moriarty, T. (1975). Crime, commitment, and the unresponsive bystander: Two field experiments. *Journal of Personality and Social Psychology, 31,* 370–376.

Morley, I., & Stephenson, G. (1977). *The social psychology of bargaining.* London: Allen & Unwin.

Morris, W. N., Miller, R. S., & Spangenberg, S. (1977). The effects of dissertive position and task difficulty on conformity and response conflict. *Journal of Personality, 45,* 251–266.

Morrison, D., Siegal, M., & Francis, R. (1983). Control, autonomy, and the development of moral behavior: A social-cognitive perspective. *Imagination, Cognition and Personality, 3,* 337–351.

Morse, S. J., & Gergen, K. J. (1970). Social comparison, self consistency, and the concept of self. *Journal of Personality and Social Psychology, 16,* 148–156.

Moscovici, S. (1976). *Social influence and change.* London, England: Academic Press.

Moscovici, S. (1980). Toward a theory of conversion behavior. In L. Berkowitz (Ed.), *Advances in experimental social psychology* (Vol. 13). New York: Academic Press.

Moscovici, S., & Doise, W. (1974). Decision making in groups. In C. Nemeth (Ed.), *Social psychology: Classic and contemporary intergration.* Chicago: Rand McNally.

Moscovici, S., Lage, E., & Naffrechoux, M. (1969). Influence of a consistent minority on the responses of a majority in a color perception task. *Sociometry, 32,* 365–379.

Moscovici, S., & Nemeth, C. (1974). Social influence III: Majority vs. minority influence in a group. In C. Nemeth (Ed.), *Social psychology: Classic and contemporary integrations.* Chicago: Rand McNally.

Moscovici, S., & Zavaloni, M. (1969). The group as a polarizer of attitudes. *Journal of Personality and Social Psychology, 12,* 125–135.

Mossman, D. (1973). Jury selection: An expert's view. *Psychology Today, 6*(12), 78–79.

Mosteller, F. (1981). Innovation and evaluation. *Science, 211,* 881–886.

Moyer, K. E. (1971). *The physiology of hostility.* Chicago: Markham.

Moyer, K. E. (1975). A physiological model of aggression: Does it have different implications? In W. S. Fields (Ed.), *Neural bases of violence and aggression.* St. Louis: Green.

Murphy, G. L., & Medin, D. L. (1985). The role of theories in conceptual coherence. *Psychological Bulletin, 92,* 289–316.

Murphy, J. J. (1972). Current practices in the use of psychological testing by police agencies. *Journal of Criminal Law, Criminology and Police Science, 63,* 570–576.

Murphy, T. (1980). *Michigan risk prediction: A replication study.* Final Report, Department of Corrections Program Bureau, Lansing, Michigan.

Murray, J. P., & Kippax, S. (1979). From the early window to the late night show: International trends in the study of television's impact on children and adults. In L. Berkowitz (Ed.), *Advances in experimental social psychology* (Vol. 12). New York: Academic Press.

Murstein, B. I. (1961). The complementarity need hypothesis in newlyweds and middle-aged couples. *Journal of Abnormal and Social Psychology, 63,* 194–197.

Murstein, B. I. (1967). Empirical tests of role, complementarity needs, and homogamy theories of marital choice. *Journal of Marriage and the Family, 29,* 689–696.

Murstein, B. I. (1971). A theory of marital choice and its applicability to marital adjustment. In B. I. Murstein (Ed.), *Theories of attraction and love.* New York: Springer.

Murstein, B. I. (1976). *Who will marry whom? Theories and research in marital choice.* New York: Springer.

Myers, D. G. (1987). *Social psychology* (2nd ed.). New York: McGraw-Hill.

Myers, D. G., & Bishop, D. G. (1970). Discussion effects on racial attitudes. *Science, 169,* 778–789.

Myers, D. G., & Kaplan, M. F. (1976). Group-induced polarization in simulated juries. *Personality and Social Psychology Bulletin, 2,* 63–66.

Myers, D. G., & Lamm, H. (1976). The group polarization phenomenon. *Psychological Bulletin, 83,* 602–627.

Myerscough, R. P., & Taylor, S. P. (1985). The effects of marijuana on human physical aggression. *Journal of Personality and Social Psychology, 49,* 1541–1546.

Nader, L. (Ed.) (1969). *Law in culture and society.* Chicago: Aldine.

Naditch, M. P., & DeMaio, T. (1975). Locus of control and competence. *Journal of Personality, 43,* 541–559.

Nadler, A., & Fisher, J. (1984). Effects of donor-recipient relationships on recipient's reactions to aid. In E. Staub, D. Bar-Tal, J.Karylowski, and J. Reykowski (Eds.), *The development and maintenance of pro-social behavior: International perspectives on positive developments.* New York: Plenum.

Nadler, A., Sheinberg, O., & Jaffe, Y. (1981). Coping with stress in male paraplegics through help seeking: The role of acceptance of physical disability in help seeking. In C. D. Spielberger, I. G. Sarason, & N. A. Milgram (Eds.), *Stress and anxiety,* (Vol. 18). Washington, DC: Hemisphere.

Nahemow, L., & Lawton, M. P. (1975). Similarity and propinquity in friendship formation. *Journal of Personality and Social Psychology, 32,* 205–213.

Nash, S. C. (1979). Sex role as a mediator of intellectual functioning. In M. A. Wittig & A. C. Peterson (Eds.), *Sex related differences in cognitive functioning: Developmental issues.* New York: Academic Press.

Nathanson, G. A. (1980). Social roles and health status among women: The significance of employment. *Social Science and Medicine, 141,* 463–471.

National Center for State Courts (1979). *State court caseload statistics.* Washington, DC: U.S. Department of Justice.

National Commission on the Causes and Prevention of Violence (1970). *To establish justice, to insure domestic tranquility.* New York: Award Books.

National Institute of Mental Health (1982). *Television and behavior: Ten years of scientific progress and implications for the eighties* (Vol. I, Summary Report). Rockville, MD.

National Research Act, PL 93–348 (July 12, 1974).

Nelson, E. A. , Grinder, R. E., & Mutterer, M. L. (1969). Sources of variance in behavioral measures of honesty in temptation situation: Methodological analyses. *Developmental Psychology, 1,* 265–279.

Nelson, S., D. & Caplan, N. (1983). Social problem solving and social change. In D. Perlman & P. Cozby (Eds.), *Social psychology.* New York: Holt, Rinehart and Winston.

Nemeth, C. (1972). A critical analysis of research utilizing the prisoner's dilemma paradigm for the study of bargaining. In L. Berkowitz (Ed.), *Advances in experimental social psychology* (Vol. 6). New York: Academic Press.

Nemeth, C., & Wachtler, J. (1974). Creating the perceptions of consistency and confidence: A necessary condition for minority influence. *Sociometry, 37,* 529–540.

Nemeth, C., & Wachtler, J. (1983). Creative problem solving as a result of majority and minority influence. *European Journal of Social Psychology, 13,* 45–55.

Newcomb, T. M. (1943). *Personality and social change.* New York: Holt, Rinehart and Winston.

Newcomb, T. M. (1947). Autistic hostility and social reality. *Human Relations, 1,* 69–86.

Newcomb, T. M. (1961). *The acquaintance process.* New York: Holt, Rinehart and Winston.

Newcomb, T. M. (1971). Dyadic balance as a source of clues about interpersonal attraction. In B. I. Murstein (Ed.), *Theories of attraction and love.* New York: Springer.

Newcomb, T. M. (1978). The acquaintance process: Looking mainly backward. *Journal of Personality and Social Psychology, 36,* 1075–1083.

Newcomb, T. M., Koenig, K., Flacks, R., & Warwick, D. (1967). *Persistence and change: Bennington College and its students after twenty-five years.* New York: Wiley.

Newman, J. F., Whitmore, K., & Newman, H. (1973). Women in the labor force and suicide. *Social Problems, 21,* 220–231.

Newman, J., & Layton, B. D. (1984). Overjustification: A self-perception perspective. *Personality and Social Psychology Bulletin, 10,* 419–425.

Newman, O. (1972). *Defensible space.* New York: Macmillan.

Newman, O., & Franck, K. A. (1982). The effects of building size on personal crime and fear of crime. *Population and Environment, 5,* 204–220.

Nicholson, J. (1984). *Men and women: How different are they?* New York: Oxford University Press.

Nieva, V. F. (1985). Work and family linkages. In L. Larwood, A. H. Stromberg, & B. A. Gutek, *Women at work* (Vol. 1). Beverly Hills, CA: Sage.

Nieva, V. F. & Gutek, B. A. (1981). *Women at work: A psychological perspective.* New York: Praeger.

Nisbett, R. E., & Borgida, E. (1975). Attribution and the psychology of prediction. *Journal of Personality and Social Psychology, 32,* 932–943.

Nisbett, R. E., Borgida, E., Crandall, R., & Reed, H. (1976). Popular induction: Information is not necessarily informative. In J. S. Carroll & J. W. Payne (Eds.), *Cognition and social behavior.* Hillsdale, NJ: Erlbaum.

Nisbett, R. E., & Gordon, A. (1967). Self-esteem and susceptibility to social influence. *Journal of Personality and Social Psychology, 5,* 268–276.

Nisbett, R. E., & Ross, L. (1980). *Human inference: Strategies and shortcomings of social judgment.* Englewood Cliffs, NJ: Prentice-Hall.

Noller, P. (1980). Misunderstandings in marital communication: A study of couples' nonverbal communication. *Journal of Personality and Social Psychology, 39,* 1135–1148.

Noller, P. (1981). Gender and marital adjustment level differences in decoding messages from spouses and strangers. *Journal of Personality and Social Psychology, 41,* 272–278.

Norton, A. J., & Glick, P. C. (1976). Marital instability: Past, present, and future. *Journal of Social Issues, 32,* 5–20.

Norvell, N., & Worchel, S. (1981). A reexamination of the relation between equal status contact and intergroup attraction. *Journal of Personality and Social Psychology 41,* 902–908.

Novaco, R. W. (1977). Stress inoculation: A cognitive therapy and anger and its application to a case of depression. *Journal of Consulting and Clinical Psychology, 45,* 600–608.

Novaco, R. W., Stokols, D., Campbell, J., & Stokols, J. (1979). Transportation stress and community psychology. *American Journal of Community Psychology, 4,* 361–380.

Novak, D., & Lerner, M. J. (1968). Rejection as a consequence of perceived similarity. *Journal of Personality and Social Psychology, 9,* 147–152.

Nuclear Regulatory Commission (1978). *A survey of policies and procedures applicable to the expression of differing professional opinions.* Washington, DC: Office of Management and Program Analysis, U.S. Nuclear Regulatory Commission.

Oakley, A. (1974). *The sociology of housework.* New York: Pantheon.

O'Connell, A. N., & Perez, S. (1982). Fear of success and causal attributions of success and failure in high school and college students. *Journal of Psychology, 11,* 141–151.

Orlofsky, J. (1977). Sex-role orientation, identity formation and self-esteem in college men and women. *Sex Roles, 3,* 561–575.

Orne, M. T. (1962). On the social psychology of the psychology experiment: With particular reference to demand characteristics and their implications. *American Psychologist, 17,* 776–783.

Orne, M. T., & Holland, C. C. (1968). On the ecological validity of laboratory experiments. *International Journal of Psychiatry, 6,* 282–293.

Ornstein, R. E. (1977). *The psychology of consciousness* (2nd ed.). New York: Harcourt Brace Jovanovich.

Orwell, G. (1949). *1984.* New York: Harcourt Brace Jovanovich.

Osgood, C. E. (1962). *An alternative to war or surrender.* Urbana: University of Illinois Press.

Osgood, C. E., Suci, G. J., & Tannenbaum, P. H. (1957). *The measurement of meaning.* Urbana: University of Illinois Press.

Osgood, C. E., & Tannenbaum, P. H. (1955). The principle of congruity in the prediction of attitude change. *Psychological Review, 62,* 42–55.

Ostrom, T. M. (1968). The emergence of attitude theory: 1930–1950. In A. G. Greenwald, T. C. Brock, & T. M. Ostrom (Eds.), *Psychological foundations of attitudes.* New York: Academic Press.

Ostrom, T. M. (1969). The relationship between affective, behavioral, and cognitive components of attitude. *Journal of Experimental Social Psychology, 5*(1), 12–30.

Ostrom, T. M. (1973). The bogus pipeline: A new *Ignis Fatuus? Psychological Bulletin, 79,* 252–259.

Ostrom, T. M. (1977). Between theory and within theory conflict in explaining context effects in impression formation. *Journal of Experimental Social Psychology, 13,* 492–503.

Oswalt, R. M. (1977). A review of blood donor motivation and recruitment. *Transfusion, 17,* 123–135.

Packard, V. (1972). *A nation of strangers.* New York: McKay.

Page, E. B. (1980). Operations research and social research: A two-way street for implementation of research findings. In C. C. Abt (Ed.), *Problems in American social policy research.* Cambridge, MA: Abt Books.

Paludi, M. A., & Bauer, W. D. (1983). Goldberg

revisited: What's in an author's name? *Sex Roles, 9,* 387–390.

Papageorgis, D., & McGuire, W. (1961). The generality of immunity to persuasion produced by pre-exposure to weakened counterarguments. *Journal of Abnormal and Social Psychology, 62,* 475–481.

Park, B., & Rothbart, M. (1982). Perception of out-group homogeneity and levels of social categorization: Memory for the subordinate attributes of in-group and out-group members. *Journal of Personality and Social Psychology, 42,* 1051–1068.

Park, R. E. (1926). The urban community as a spacial pattern and a moral order. In E. W. Burgess (Ed.), *The urban community.* Chicago: University of Chicago Press.

Park, R. E. (1950). *Race and culture.* Glencoe, Il: The Free Press.

Parke, R. D., Berkowitz, L., Leyens, J. P., West, S., & Sebastien, R. J. (1977). Some effects of violent and nonviolent movies on the behavior of juvenile delinquents. In L. Berkowitz (Ed.), *Advances in experimental social psychology* (Vol. 10). New York: Academic Press.

Parks, G. A. (1973). *Personal communication.*

Parsons, T. (1951). *The social system.* Glencoe, IL: Free Press.

Patterson, A. H. (1978). Territorial behavior and fear of crime in the elderly. *Environmental Psychology and Nonverbal Behavior, 2,* 131–144.

Patterson, M. L., Mullens, S., & Romano, J. (1971). Compensatory reactions to spatial intrusion. *Sociometry, 34,* 114–121.

Paulhus, D. L., Shaffer, D., & Downing, L. L. (1977). Effects of making blood donor motives salient upon donor retention: A field experiment. *Personality and Social Psychology Bulletin, 3,* 99–102.

Paulus, P. B., & Matthews, R. W. (1980). When density affects task performance. *Personality and Social Psychology Bulletin, 6,* 119–124.

Paulus, P. B., McCain, G., & Cox, V. C. (1978). Death rates, psychiatric commitments, blood pressure, and perceived crowding as a function of institutional crowding. *Environmental Psychology and Nonverbal Behavior, 3,* 107–116.

Pearson, J. C. (1985). *Gender and communication.* Dubuque, IA: William C. Brown.

Pendleton, M., & Batson, C. D. (1979). Self-presentation and the door-in-the-face technique for inducing compliance. *Personality Social Psychology Bulletin, 5,* 77–81.

Pennebaker, J., & Sanders, D. Y. (1976). American graffiti: Effects of authority and reactance arousal. *Personality Social Psychology Bulletin, 2,* 264–267.

Pennington, D. C. (1982). Witnesses and their testimony: Effects of ordering on juror verdicts. *Journal of Applied Social Psychology, 12,* 318–333.

Penrod, S. (1980). Practicing attorneys' jury selection strategies. Paper preseented at American Psychological Association meeting, Montreal.

Pepitone, A. (1981). Lessons from the history of social psychology. *American Psychologist, 36,* 972–985.

Peplau, L. A., Miceli, M., & Morasch, B. (1982). Loneliness and self-evaluation. In L. A. Peplau & D. Perlman (Eds.), *Loneliness: A sourcebook of current theory, research, and therapy.* New York: Wiley.

Peplau, L. A., & Perlman, D. (1982). Perspectives on loneliness. In L. A. Peplau & D. Perlman (Eds.), *Loneliness: A sourcebook of current theory, research, and therapy.* New York: Wiley.

Peplau, L. A., Rubin, Z., & Hill, C. T. (1977). Sexual intimacy in dating relationships. *Journal of Social Issues, 33,* 86–109.

Perlman, D., Gerson, A. C., & Spinner, B. (1978). Loneliness among senior citizens: An empirical report. *Essence, 2,* 239–248.

Perloff, L. S. (1983). Perceptions of vulnerability to victimization. *Journal of Social Issues, 39,* 41–62.

Peterson, C., & Seligman, M. E. P. (1984). Causal explanations as a risk factor for depression: Theory and evidence. *Psychology Review, 91,* 347–374.

Pettigrew, T. F. (1979). The ultimate attribution error: Extending Allport's cognitive analysis of prejudice. *Personality and Social Psychology Bulletin, 5,* 461–476.

Petty, R. E., & Brock, T. C. (1976). Effects of responding or not responding to hecklers on audience agreement with a speaker. *Journal of Applied Social Psychology, 6,* 1–17.

Petty, R. E., Brock, T. C., & Brock, S. (1978). Hecklers: Boon or bust for speakers? *Public Relations Journal, 34,* 10–12.

Petty, R. E., & Cacioppo, J. T. (1979a). Effects of forewarning of persuasive intent and involvement on cognitive responses and persuasion. *Personality and Social Psychology Bulletin, 5,* 173–176.

Petty, R. E., & Cacioppo, J. T. (1979b). Issue involvement can increase or decrease persuasion by enhancing message-relevant cognitive responses. *Journal of Personality and Social Psychology, 37,* 1915–1926

Petty, R. E., & Cacioppo, J. T. (1981). *Attitudes and persuasion: Classic and contemporary approaches,* Dubuque, IA: William C. Brown.

Petty, R. E., & Cacioppo, J. T. (1986). *Communication and persuasion: Central and peripheral routes to attitude change.* New York: Springer.

Petty, R. E., Cacioppo, J. T., & Heesacker, M. (1981). Effects of rhetorical questions on persuasion: A cognitive response analysis. *Journal of Personality and Social Psychology, 40,* 432–440.

Petty, R. E., Ostrom, T. M., & Brock, T. C. (Eds.) (1981). *Cognitive responses in persuasion.* Hillsdale, NJ: Erlbaum.

Petty, R. E., Wells, G. L. & Brock, T. C. (1976). Distraction can enhance or reduce yielding to propaganda: Thought disruption versus effort justification. *Journal of Personality and Social Psychology, 34,* 874–884.

Phares, E. G. (1976). *Locus of control in personality.* Morristown, NJ: General Learning Press.

Philips, D. P. (1980). The deterrent effect of capital punishment: New evidence on an old controversy. *American Journal of Sociology, 86,* 139–148.

Phillips, G. (1981). *Help for shy people.* Englewood Cliffs, NJ: Prentice-Hall.

Pierce, G. L., & Bowers, W. J. (1981). The Bartley-Fox gun law's short-term impact on crime in Boston. *The Annals of the American Academy of Political and Social Science, 455,* 120–137.

Pihl, R. O., Zeichner, A., Niaura, R., Nagy, K., & Zacchia, C. (1981). Attribution and alcohol-mediated aggression. *Journal of Abnormal Psychology, 90,* 468–475.

Piliavin, I. M., Piliavin, J. A., & Rodin, J. (1975). Costs, diffusion, and the stigmatized victim. *Journal of Personality and Social Psychology, 32,* 429–438.

Piliavin, J. A., & Callero, P. (1983). Developing a commitment to blood donation: The impact of one's first experience. *Journal of Applied Social Psychology, 13,* 1–16.

Piliavin, J. A., Callero, P., & Evans, D. E. (1982). Addiction to altruism? Opponent-process theory and habitual blood donation. *Journal of Personality and Social Psychology, 43,* 1200–1213.

Piliavin, J. A., Dovidio, J. F., Gaertner, S. L., & Clark, R. D. III (1982). Responsive bystanders: The process of intervention. In V. J. Derlega & J. Grzelak (Eds.), *Cooperation in helping and behavior: Theories and research.* New York: Academic Press.

Piliavin, J. A., Evans, D. E., & Callero, P. (1982). Learning to "give to unnamed strangers": The process of commitment to regular blood donation. In E. Staub, D. Bar-Tal, J. Karylanski, & J. Reykowski (Eds.), *The development and maintenance of prosocial behavior: International perspectives.* New York: Plenum.

Piliavin, J. A., & Piliavin, I. M. (1972). Effects of blood on reactions to a victim. *Journal of Personality and Social Psychology, 23,* 353–361.

Pilisuk, M., & Skolnick, P. (1968). Inducing trust: A test of the Osgood proposal. *Journal of Personality and Social Psychology, 8,* 121–133.

Pilkonis, P. A., & Zimbardo, P. G. (1979). The personal and social dynamics of shyness. In C. E. Izard (Ed.), *Emotions in personality and psycho-pathology.* New York: Plenum.

Pittman, T. S., Cooper, E. E., & Smith, E. W. (1977). Attribution of causality and the overjustification effect. *Personality and Social Psychology Bulletin, 3,* 280–283.

Pittman, T. S., Pallak, M. S., Riggs, J. M., & Gotay, C. C. (1981). Increasing blood donor pledge fulfillment. *Personality and Social Psychology Bulletin, 7,* 195–200.

Pliner, P., Hart, H., Kohl, J., & Saari, D. (1974). Compliance without pressure: Some further data on the foot-in-the-door technique. *Journal of Experimental Social Psychology, 10,* 17–22.

Podell, J. E., & Knapp, W. M. (1969). The effect of mediation on the perceived firmness of the opponent. *Journal of Conflict Resolution, 13,* 511–520.

Polit, D. F. (1979). Nontraditional work schedules for women. In K. W. Feinstein (Ed.), *Working women and families.* Beverly Hills, CA: Sage.

Prescott, J. W. (1975). Body, pleasure and the origins of violence. *The Futurist,* 64–74.

President's Council on Environmental Quality, Environmental Protection Agency (1978). Washington, DC: U.S. Government Printing Office.

Proshansky, H. M., Fabian, A. K., & Kaminoff, R. (1983). Place-identity: Physical world socialization of the self. *Journal of Environmental Psychology, 3,* 57–83.

Prothro, E. T. (1952). Ethnocentrism and anti-Negro attitudes in the deep South. *Journal of Abnormal and Social Psychology, 47,* 105–108.

Pruitt, D. G. (1971a) Choice shifts in group discussion: An introductory review. *Journal of Personality and Social Psychology, 20,* 339–360.

Pruitt, D. G. (1971b) Conclusions: Toward an understanding of choice shifts in group discussions. *Journal of Personality and Social Psychology, 20,* 495–510.

Pruitt, D. G. (1981). *Negotiation behavior.* New York: Academic Press.

Pruitt, D. G., & Insko, C. A. (1980). Extension of the Kelley attribution model: The role of comparison-object consensus, target-object consensus, distinctiveness, and consistency. *Journal of Personality and Social Psychology, 39,* 39–58.

Pruitt, D. G., & Johnson, D. F. (1970). Mediation as an aid to face saving in negotiation. *Journal of Personality and Social Psychology, 14,* 239–246.

Pruitt, D. G., & Kimmel, M. J. (1977). Twenty years of experimental gaming: Critique, synthesis and suggestions for the future. *Annual Review of Psychology, 28,* 363–392.

Pruitt, D. G., & Lewis, S. A. (1977). The psychology of integrative bargaining. In D. Druckman (Ed.), *Negotiations: A social-psychological analysis.* New York: Halsted.

Pryer, M. W., & Bass, B. M. (1959). Some effects of feedback on behavior in groups. *Sociometry, 22,* 56–63.

Pryor, J. B., Gibbons, F. X., Wicklund, R. A., Fazio, R. H., & Hood, R. (1977). Self-focused attention and self-report validity. *Journal of Personality and Social Psychology, 45,* 514–527.

Pyszczynski, T., Greenberg, J., Mack, D., & Wrightsman, L. S. (1981). Opening statements in a jury trial: The effect of promising more than the evidence can show. *Journal of Applied Social Psychology, 11,* 434–444.

Quarantelli, E. L. (Ed.) (1978). *Disasters: Theory and research.* Beverly Hills, CA: Sage.

Quattrone, G. A. (1982). Overattribution and unit formation: When behavior engulfs the person. *Journal of Personality and Social Psychology, 442,* 593–607.

Quattrone, G. A., & Jones, E. E. (1980). The perception of variability within in-groups and out-groups: Implications for the law of small numbers. *Journal of Personality and Social Psychology, 38,* 141–152.

Quigley-Fernandez, B., & Tedeschi, J. T. (1978). The bogus pipeline as lie-detector: Two validity studies. *Journal of Personality and Social Psychology, 36,* 247–256.

Quill, T. E. (1983). Partnerships in patient care: A contractual approach. *Annals of Internal Medicine, 98,* 228–234.

Quinn, R. P., & Staines, G. E. (1979). *The 1977 Quality of Employment Survey.* Ann Arbor, MI: Survey Research Center.

Rabbie, J. M., Benoist, F., Oosterbaan, H., & Visser, L. (1974). Differential power and effects of expected competetive and cooperative intergroup interaction upon intragroup and outgroup attitudes. *Journal of Personality and Social Psychology, 30,* 46–56.

Rabbie, J. M., & Horwitz, M. (1969). Arousal of

ingroup-outgroup bias by a chance win or loss. *Journal of Personality and Social Psychology, 13,* 269–277.

Rabbie, J. M., & Wilkens, G. (1971). Intergroup competition and its effect on intragroup and intergroup relations. *European Journal of Social Psychology, 1,* 215–234.

Radke-Yarrow, M., & Zehn-Wexler, C. (1984). Roots, motives, and patterns in children's prosocial behavior. In E. Staub, D. Bar-Tal, J. Karylowski, & J. Reykowski (Eds.), *Development and maintenance of prosocial behavior: International perspectives on positive development.* New York: Plenum.

Raia, A. P., & Margulies, N. (1978). *Conceptual foundations of organizational development.* New York: McGraw-Hill.

Rajecki, D. W. (1982). *Attitudes: Themes and advances.* Sunderland, MA: Sinauer Associates.

Rajecki, D. W. (1983). Animal aggression: Implications for human aggression. In R. G. Geen & E. I. Donnerstein (Eds.), *Aggression: Theoretical and empirical reviews* (Vol. I). New York: Academic Press.

Rajecki, D. W., Suomi, S. J. Scott, E. A., & Campbell, B. (1977). Effects of social isolation and social separation in domestic chicks. *Developmental Psychology, 13,* 143–155.

Ramsoy, N. R. (1966). Assortative mating and the structure of cities. *American Journal of Sociology, 31,* 773–786.

Randall, T. M., & Desrosiers, M. (1980). Measurement of supernatural belief: Sex differences and locus of control. *Journal of Personality Assessment, 44,* 493–498.

Rankin, R. E. (1969). Air pollution control and public apathy. *Journal of Air Pollution Control Association, 19,* 565–569.

Rapoport, A[mos] (1977). *Human aspects of urban form: Toward a man-environment approach to urban form and design.* Elmsford, NY: Pergamon.

Rapoport, A[mos] (1980). Environmental preference, habitat selection and urban housing. *Journal of Social Issues, 36,* 118–134.

Rapoport, A[natol] (1973). *Experimental games and their uses in psychology.* Morristown, NJ: General Learning Press.

Rapoport, A[natol] & Chammah, A. M. (1965). *Prisoner's Dilemma.* Ann Arbor: University of Michigan Press.

Rappaport, J. (1977). *Community psychology: Values, research, and action.* New York: Holt, Rinehart and Winston.

Raven, B. (1965). Social influence and power. In I. D. Steiner & M. Fishbein (Eds.), *Current studies in social psychology.* New York: Holt, Rinehart and Winston.

Raven, B., & Haley, R. W. (1980). Social influence in a medical context. In L. Bickman (Ed.), *Applied social psychology annual* (Vol. 1). Beverly Hills, CA: Sage.

Raven, B., & Kruglanski, A. W. (1970). Conflict and power. In P. Swingle (Ed.), *The structure of conflict.* New York: Academic Press.

Reckless, W. C. (1972). Use of the death penalty. In J. A. McCafferty (Ed.), *Capital punishment.* New York: Random House.

Rector, M. (1973). Who are the dangerous? *Bulletin of the American Academy of Psychiatry and the Law, 1,* 186–188.

Regan, D. T., Williams, M., & Sparling, S. (1972). Voluntary expiation of guilt: A field experiment. *Journal of Personality and Social Psychology, 24,* 42–45.

Reid, D., & Ware, E. E. (1974). Multidimensionality of internal versus external control: Addition of a third dimension and non-distinction of self versus others. *Canadian Journal of Behavioral Science, 6,* 131–142.

Reilly, M. E. (1978). A case study of role conflict: Roman Catholic priests. *Human Relations, 31,* 77–90.

Reis, H. T., Nezlek, J., & Wheeler, L. (1980). Physical attractiveness in social interaction. *Journal of Personality and Social Psychology, 38,* 604–617.

Reis, H. T., Wheeler, L., Spiegel, N., Kernis, M. H., Nezlek, J., & Perri, M. (1982). Physical attractiveness in social interaction: II. Why does appearance affect social experience? *Journal of Personality and Social Psychology, 43,* 979–996.

Reis, H. T. & Wright, S. (1982). Knowledge of sex-role stereotypes in children aged 3 to 5. *Sex Roles,* 8, 1049–1056.

Reisenzein, R. (1983). The Schachter theory of emotion: Two decades later. *Psychological Bulletin, 94,* 239–264.

Reizenstein, J. E. (1982). Hospital design and human behavior: A review of the recent literature. In A. Baum & J. E. Singer (Eds.), *Advances in environmental psychology. Vol. 4. Environment and health.* Hillsdale, NJ: Erlbaum.

Rempel, J. K., Holmes, J. G., & Zanna, M. P. (1985). Trust in close relationships. *Journal of Personality and Social Psychology, 49,* 95–112.

Resick, P. A., & Sweet, J. J. (1979). Child maltreatment intervention: Directions and issues. *Journal of Social Issues, 35,* 140–160.

Reston, J. (1975, March 14). Proxmire on love. *New York Times.*

Reyes, H., & Varela, J. A. (1980). Conditions required for a technology of the social sciences. In R. F. Kidd & M. J. Saks (Eds.), *Advances in applied social psychology* (Vol. 1). Hillsdale, NJ: Erlbaum.

Rhine, R. J., & Severance, L. J. (1970). Ego-involvement, discrepancy, source credibility, and attitude change. *Journal of Change and Social Psychology, 16,* 175–190.

Rice, R. W. (1978). Construct validity of the Least Preferred Co-workers Score. *Psychological Bulletin, 85,* 1199–1237.

Riger, S., & Lavrakas, P. J. (1982). Community ties: Patterns of attachment and social interaction in urban neighborhoods. *American Journal of Community Psychology, 9,* 55–62.

Riggio, R. E., & Woll, S. B. (1984). The role of nonverbal cues and physical attractiveness in the selection of dating partners. *Journal of Social and Personal Relationships, 1,* 347–357.

Ring, K. (1967). Experimental social psychology: Some sober questions about some frivolous values. *Journal of Experimental Social Psychology, 3,* 113–123.

Rittle, R. H. (1981). Changes in helping behavior: Self vs. situational perceptions as mediators of the foot in the door effect. *Personality and Social Psychology Bulletin, 7,* 423–430.

Rivlin, L. G., & Rothenberg, M. (1976). The use of space in open classrooms. In H. M. Proshansky, W. H. Ittelson, & L. G. Rivlin (Eds.), *Environmental psychology: People and their physical settings.* New York: Holt, Rinehart and Winston.

Robinson, J. P., & Shaver, P. R. (1973). *Measures of social psychological attitudes.* Ann Arbor, MI: ISR.

Rodin, J. (1976). Crowding, perceived choice and response to controllable and uncontrollable outcomes. *Journal of Experimental Social Psychology, 12,* 564–578.

Rodin, J. (1980). Aging, stress and the immune system. In S. Levine & H. Ursin (Eds.), *Coping and health.* New York: Academic Press.

Rodin, J., Bohm, L. C., & Wack, J. T. (1982). Control, coping, and aging: Models for research and intervention. In L. Brickman (Ed.), *Applied social psychology annual* (Vol. 3). Beverly Hills, CA: Sage.

Rodin, J., & Janis, I. L. (1982). The social influence of physicians and other health care practitioners as agents of change. In H. S. Friedman & M. R. DiMatteo (Eds.), *Interpersonal issues in health care.* New York: Academic Press.

Rodin, J., & Langer, E. (1980). Aging labels: The decline of control and the fall of self-esteem. *Journal of Social Issues, 36,* 12–29.

Rodin, J., & Langer, E. J. (1977). Long-term effect of control-relevant intervention. *Journal of Personality and Social Psychology, 35,* 897–902.

Rohe, W., & Patterson, A. H. (1974). The effects of varied levels of resources and density on behavior in a day care center. Paper presented at Environmental Design Research Association meeting, Milwaukee, WI.

Rohrer, J. H., & Sherif, M. (Eds.) (1951). *Social psychology at the crossroads.* New York: Harper & Row.

Rokeach, M. (1973). *The nature of human values.* New York: Free Press.

Rokeach, M., & Mezei, L. (1966). Race and shared belief as factors in social choice. *Science, 151,* 167–172.

Roll, S., & Virinis, J. S. (1971). Sterotypes of scalp and facial hair as measured by the semantic differential. *Psychological Reports, 28,* 975–980.

Rooks, K. S., & Peplau, L. A. (1982). Perspectives on helping the lonely. In L. A. Peplau & D. Perlman (Eds.), *Loneliness: A sourcebook of current theory, research, and therapy.* New York: Wiley.

Roper, R. (1980). Jury size and verdict consistency: "A line has to be drawn somewhere." *Law and Society Review, 14,* 977–995.

Rose, H. S., & Hinds, D. H. (1976). South Dixie Highway contraflow bus out care-proof lane demonstration project. *Transportation Research Records, 606,* 18–22.

Rose, T. L. (1981). Cognitive and dyadic processes in intergroup contact. In D. L. Hamilton (Ed.), *Cognitive processes in stereotyping and intergroup behavior.* Hillsdale, NJ: Erlbaum.

Rosen, B. C. (1955). Conflicting group membership: A study of parent-peer group cross pressures. *American Sociological Review, 20,* 155–161.

Rosen, S. (1961). Post-decision affinity for incompatible information. *Journal of Abnormal and Social Psychology, 63,* 188–190.

Rosenbaum, D. (1970). The natural socialization of altruistic autonomy. In J. Macauley & L. Berkowitz (Eds.), *Altruism and helping behavior.* New York: Academic Press.

Rosenberg, M. J. (1965). When dissonance fails: On eliminating evaluation apprehension from attitude measurement. *Journal of Personality and Social Psychology, 1,* 28–42.

Rosenberg, M. J. (1968). Hedonism, inauthenticity, and other goals toward expansion of a consistency theory. In R. Abelson, E. Aronson, W. McGuire, T. Newcomb, M. Rosenberg, & P. Tannenbaum (Eds.), *Theories of cognitive consistency: A source book,* Chicago: Rand McNally.

Rosenberg, M. S., & Reppucci, N. D. (1985). Primary prevention of child abuse. *Journal of Clinical and Consulting Psychology, 53,* 576–585.

Rosenberg, S., Nelson, C., & Vivekananthian, P. S. (1968). A multidimensional approach to the structure of personality impressions. *Journal of Personality and Social Psychology, 9,* 283–294.

Rosener, J. (1977). Citizen participation: Tying strategy to function. In P. Marshal (Ed.), *Citizen participation certification for community development.* Washington, DC: National Association for Housing and Redevelopment Officials.

Rosenfeld, H. M. (1965). Effect of approval-seeking induction on interpersonal proximity. *Psychological Reports, 17,* 120–122.

Rosenhan, D. (1970). The natural socialization of altruistic autonomy. In J. Macauley & L. Berkowitz (Eds.), *Altruism and helping behavior.* New York: Academic Press.

Rosenman, R. H., & Friedman, M. (1974). Neurogenic factors in pathogenesis of coronary heart disease. *Medical Clinics of North America, 58,* 269–279.

Rosenman, R. H., & Friedman, M. (1977). Modifying type A behavior pattern. *Journal of Psychosomatic Research, 21,* 323–331.

Rosenthal, R. (1966). *Experimenter effects in behavioral research.* New York: Appleton-Century-Crofts.

Rosenthal, R. (1967). Covert communication in the psychological experiment. *Psychological Bulletin, 67,* 356–357.

Rosenthal R., & DePaulo, B. (1979). Sex differences in eavesdropping on nonverbal cues. *Journal of Personality and Social Psychology, 37,* 273–285.

Rosenthal, R., & Jacobson, L. (1968). *Pygmalion in the classroom.* New York: Holt, Rinehart and Winston.

Rosenthal, R., & Rosnow, R. L. (Ed.) (1969). *Artifact in behavioral research.* New York: Academic Press.

Rosenthal, R., & Rosnow, R. L. (1984). *Essentials of behavioral research: Methods and data analysis.* New York: McGraw-Hill.

Rosenthal, R., & Rubin, D. B. (1978). Interpersonal expectancy effects: The first 345 studies. *Behavioral and Brain Sciences, 3,* 377–415.

Rosenthal, R., & Rubin, D. B. (1979). A note on percent variants explained as a measure of the importance of effects. *Journal of Applied Social Psychology, 9,* 395–396.

Roskies, E. (1979). Considerations in developing a treatment program for the coronary-prone

(Type A) behavior pattern. In P. Davidson (Ed.), *Behavioral medicine: Changing health life styles.* New York: Bruner/Mazel.

Roskies, E., & Avard, J. (1982). Teaching healthy managers to control their coronary-prone (type A) behavior. In K. Blankstein & J. Polivy (Eds.), *Self-control and self-modification of emotional behavior.* New York: Plenum.

Roskies, E., Kearney, H., Spevack, M., Surkis, A., Cohen, C., & Gilmans, S. (1979). Generalizability and durability of the treatment effects in an intervention program for coronary-prone (type A) managers. *Journal of Behavioral Medicine, 2,* 195–207.

Roskies, E., Seraganian, P., Oseasohn, R., Hanley, J. A., Collu, R., Martin, N., & Smilga, C. (1986). The Montreal Type A intervention project: Major findings. *Health Psychology, 5,* 45–70.

Roskies, E., Spevack, M., Surkis, A., Cohen, C., & Gilman, S. (1978). Changing the coronary-prone (type A) behavior pattern in a non-clinical population. *Journal of Behavioral Medicine, 1,* 201–216.

Rosnow, R., & Goldstein, J. (1967). Familiarity, salience and the order of presentation of communications. *Journal of Social Psychology, 73,* 97–110.

Rosnow, R. L., & Fine, G. A. (1976). *Rumor and gossip: The social psychology of hearsay.* New York: Elsevier.

Rosnow, R. L., & Robinson, E. J. (Eds.) (1967). *Experiments in persuasion.* New York: Academic Press.

Ross, H. L., & Sawhill, I. V. (1975). *Time of transition: The growth of families headed by women.* Washington, DC: Urban Institute.

Ross, L., Amabile, T. M., & Steinmetz, J. L. (1977). Social roles, social control, and biases in person-perception processes. *Journal of Personality and Social Psychology, 35,* 485–494.

Ross, L., Greene, D., & House, P. (1977). The "false consensus effect": An egocentric bias in social perception and attribution processes. *Journal of Experimental Social Psychology, 13,* 279–301.

Ross, L. B. (1972). *The effect of aggressive cartoons on the group play of children.* Doctoral dissertation, Miami University.

Ross, M. (1975). Salience of reward and intrinsic motivation. *Journal of Personality and Social Psychology, 32,* 245–254.

Ross, M., & Fletcher, G. (1985). Attribution and social perception. In G. Lindsey & A. Aronson (Eds.), *The handbook of social psychology* (3rd ed.). Reading, MA: Addison-Wesley.

Ross, M., & Sicoly, F. (1979). Egocentric biases in availability and attribution. *Journal of Personality and Social Psychology, 37,* 322–337.

Rossi, P. H., Wright, J. D., & Anderson, A. B. (1983). *Handbook of survey research.* New York: Academic Press.

Roter, D. L. (1977). Patient participation in the patient-provider interaction. *Health Education Monographs, 5,* 281–315.

Rotter, J. B. (1954). *Social learning and clinical psychology.* Englewood Cliffs, NJ: Prentice-Hall.

Rotter, J. B. (1966). Generalized expectancies for internal versus external control of reinforcement. *Psychological Monographs, 80* (1, whole no. 609).

Rotter, J. B., & Mulry, R. C. (1965). Internal versus external control of reinforcement and decision time. *Journal of Personality and Social Psychology, 2,* 598–604.

Rotton, J. (1978). The psychological effects of air pollution. Unpublished manuscript, Florida International University.

Rotton, J. (1983). Affective and cognitive consequences of malodorous pollution. *Basic and Applied Social Psychology, 4,* 171–191.

Royce, J. R., & Powell, A. (1983). *Theory of personality and individual differences: Factors, systems, and processes.* Englewood Cliffs, NJ: Prentice-Hall.

Ruback, R. B., & Greenberg, M. S. (1986). Ethical and legal aspects of applied social psychological research in field settings. In M. J. Saks & L. Saxe (Eds.), *Advances in applied social psychology* (Vol. 3). Hillsdale, NJ: Erlbaum.

Rubin, J. Z. (1980). Experimental research on third-party intervention in conflict: Toward some generalizations. *Psychological Bulletin, 87,* 379–391.

Rubin, J. Z. (Ed.) (1981). *Third party intervention in conflict: Kissinger in the Middle East.* New York: Praeger.

Rubin, J. Z., & Brockner, J. (1985). *Entrapment in escalating conflicts.* New York: Springer-Verlag.

Rubin, J. Z., & Brown, B. R. (1975). *The social psychology of bargaining and negotiation.* New York: Academic Press.

Rubin, J. Z., Provenzane, F. J., & Luria, Z. (1974). The eye of the beholder: Parents' views on sex of newborns. *American Journal of Orthopsychiatry, 44,* 512–519.

Rubin, Z. (1969). *The social psychology of romantic love.* Unpublished doctoral dissertation, University of Michigan.

Rubin, Z. (1970). Measurement of romantic love. *Journal of Personality and Social Psychology, 16,* 265–273.

Rubin, Z. (1973). *Liking and loving: An invitation to social psychology.* New York: Holt, Rinehart and Winston.

Rubin, Z. (1980). *Children's friendships.* Cambridge, MA: Harvard University Press.

Rubin, Z. (1981, May). Does the personality really change after 20? *Psychology Today,* 18–27.

Rubin, Z., Peplau, L. A., & Hill, C. T. (1981). Loving and leaving: Sex differences in romantic attachments. *Sex Roles, 7,* 821–830.

Rubin, Z., & Shenker, S. (1980). Friendship, proximity, and self-disclosure. *Journal of Personality, 46,* 1–22.

Rudd, J. R., & Geller, E. S. (1985). A university-based incentive program to increase safety belt use: Toward cost-effective institutionalization. *Journal of Applied Behavior Analysis, 18,* 215–226.

Rumsey, N., Bull, R., & Gahagan, D. (1982). The effect of facial disfigurement on the proxemic behavior of general public. *Journal of Applied Social Psychology, 12,* 137–150.

Runnion, A., Watson, J. D., & McWhorter, J. (1978). Energy savings in interstate transportation through feedback and reinforcement. *Journal of Organizational Behavior Management, 1,* 180–191.

Rusbult, C. E. (1980). Commitment and satisfaction in romantic associations: A test of the investment model. *Journal of Experimental Social Psychology, 16,* 172–186.

Rusbult, C. E. (1983). A longitudinal test of the investment model: The development (and deterioration) of satisfaction and commitment in heterosexual involvement. *Journal of Personality and Social Psychology, 45,* 101–117.

Rusbult, C. E., Zembrodt, I. M., & Gunn, L. K. (1982). Exit, voice, loyalty, and neglect: Responses to dissatisfaction in romantic association. *Journal of Personality and Social Psychology, 43,* 1230–1242.

Rushton, J. P. (1980). *Altruism, socialization, and society.* Englewood Cliffs, NJ: Prentice-Hall.

Rushton, J. P., and Campbell, A. C. (1977). Modeling, vicarious reinforcement and extraversion on blood donating in adults: Immediate and long-term affects. *European Journal of Social Psychology, 7,* 297–306.

Russell, D., Peplau, L. A., & Cutrona, C. E. (1980). The revised UCLA Loneliness Scale: Concurrent and discriminant validity evidence. *Journal of Personality and Social Psychology, 39,* 472–480.

Ryan, W. (1971). *Blaming the victim.* New York: Random House.

Saegert, S. C., MacKintosh, E., & West, S. (1975). Two studies of crowding in urban public places. *Environment and Behavior, 7,* 159–184.

Saegert, S. C., Swap, W., & Zajonc, R. B. (1973). Exposure, context, and interpersonal attraction. *Journal of Personality and Social Psychology, 25,* 234–242.

Saenger, G. (1953). *The social psychology of prejudice: Achieving intercultural understanding and cooperation in a democracy.* New York: Harper's.

Saenger, G., & Gilbert, E. (1950). Customer reactions to the integration of Negro sales personnel. *International Journal of Opinion and Attitude Research, 4,* 57–76.

Saks, M. J. (1976). The limits of scientific jury selection: Ethical and empirical. *Jurimetrics Journal, 17,* 3–22.

Saks, M. J. (1977). *Jury verdicts.* Lexington, MA: Heath.

Saks, M. J. (1978). Social psychological contributions to a legislative subcommittee on organ and tissue transplants. *American Psychologist, 33,* 680–690.

Saks, M. J. (1980). Social psychological perspectives on the problem of consent. In G. P. Melton, G. P. Koocher, & M. J. Saks (Eds.), *Children's competence to consent.* New York: Plenum.

Saks, M. J., & Hastie, R. (1978). *Social psychology in court.* New York: Van Nostrand Reinhold.

Saks, M. J., & Kidd, R. F. (1980). Human information processing and adjudication: Trial by heuristics. *Law and Society Review, 15,* 124–160.

Saks, M. J., & Van Duizend, R. (1983). *The use of scientific evidence in litigation.* Williamsburg, VA: National Center for State Courts.

Salancik, G. R., & Conway, M. (1975). Attitude inferences from salient and relevant cognitive content about behavior. *Journal of Personality and Social Psychology, 32,* 829–840.

Sampson, E. E. (1975). On justice as equality. *Journal of Social Issues, 31,* 45–64.

Sampson, E. E. (1981). Cognitive psychology as ideology. *American Psychologist, 36,* 730–743.

Sander, F. (1982). Varieties of dispute processing. In R. Tomasic & M. Feeley (Eds.), *Neighborhood justice: Assessment of an emerging idea.* New York: Longman.

Sanford, N. (1970). Whatever happened to action research? *Journal of Social Issues, 26,* 3–23.

Sarason, I. G., Smith, R. E., & Diener, E. (1975). Personality research: Components of variance attributable to the person and the situation. *Journal of Personality and Social Psychology, 3,* 199–204.

Sarnoff, D. (1960). Reaction formation and cynicism. *Journal of Personality, 28,* 129–143.

Sarnoff, D. (1965). The experimental evaluation of psycho-analytic hypotheses. *Transactions of the New York Academy of Science, 28,* 272–290.

Satow, K. (1975). Social approval and helping. *Journal of Experimental Social Psychology, 11,* 501–509.

Saxe, L. (1980). *The efficacy and cost-effectiveness of psychotherapy.* Washington, DC: Government Printing Office.

Saxe, L. (1983). The perspective of social psychology: Toward a viable model for application. In R. F. Kidd & M. J. Saks (Eds.), *Advances in applied social psychology* (Vol. 2). Hillsdale, NJ: Erlbaum.

Saxe, L., & Fine, M. (1980). Reorienting social psychology toward application. In L. Bickman (Ed.), *Applied social psychology annual* (Vol. 1). Beverly Hills, CA: Sage.

Saxe, L., & Fine, M. (1981). *Social experiments: Methods for design and evaluation.* Beverly Hills, CA: Sage.

Schachter, S. (1951). Deviation, rejection, and communication. *Journal of Abnormal and Social Psychology, 46,* 190–207.

Schachter, S. (1959). *The psychology of affiliation.* Stanford, CA: Stanford University Press.

Schachter, S. (1964). The interaction of cognitive and physiological determinants of emotional state. In L. Berkowitz (Ed.), *Advances in experimental social psychology* (Vol. 1). New York: Academic Press.

Schachter, S. (1971). *Emotion, obesity, and crime.* New York: Academic Press.

Schachter, S., & Singer, J. E. (1962). Cognitive, social, and physiological determinants of emotional state. *Psychological Review, 69,* 379–399.

Scheier, M. F., & Carver, C. S. (1983). Two sides of the self: One for you and one for me. In J. Suls & A. G. Greenwald (Eds.), *Psychological perspectives on the self* (Vol. 2). Hillsdale, NJ: Erlbaum.

Schein, E. H. (1980). *Organizational psychology* (3rd ed.). Englewood Cliffs, NJ: Prentice-Hall.

Schelling, T. (1975). *Strategy of conflict.* Cambridge, MA: Harvard University Press.

Scherer, S. E. (1974). Proxemic behavior of primary school children as a function of their socioeconomic class and subculture. *Personality and Social Psychology Bulletin, 2,* 67–70.

Scherwitz, L., Berton, K., & Leventhal, H. (1978). Type A behavior, self-involvement, and cardiovascular response. *Psychsomatic Medicine, 40,* 593–609.

Schettino, A. P., & Bordon, R. J. (1976). Group size versus group density: Where is the affect? *Personality and Social Psychology Bulletin, 2,* 67–70.

Schlenker, B. R. (1974). Social psychology and science. *Journal of Personality and Social Psychology, 29,* 1–15.

Schlenker, B. R. (1976). Social psychology and science: Another look. *Personality and Social Psychology Bulletin, 2,* 418–420.

Schmitt, R. (1957). Density, delinquency and crime in Honolulu. *Sociology and Social Research, 41,* 274–276.

Schmutte, G. T., & Taylor, S. P. (1980). Physical aggression as a function of alcohol and pain feedback. *Journal of Social Psychology, 110,* 235–244.

Schopler, J., & Stockdale, J. E. (1977). An interference analysis of crowding. *Journal of Environmental Psychology and Nonverbal Behavior, 1,* 81–88.

Schramm, W., Lyle, V., & Parker, E. B. (1961). *Television in the lives of our children.* Stanford, CA: Stanford University Press.

Schulman, J., Shaver, P., Colman, R., Emrich, B., & Christie, R. (1973). Recipe for a jury. *Psychology Today,* 6(12), 37.

Schulz, R. (1976). Effects of control and predictability on the physical and psychological well-being of the institutionalized aged. *Journal of Personality and Social Psychology, 33,* 563–573.

Schulz, R., & Hanusa, B. H. (1978). Long-term effects of control and predictability-enhancing interventions: Findings and ethical issues. *Journal of Personality and Social Psychology, 36,* 1194–1201.

Schwartz, B., Lacey, H., & Schuldenfrei, R. (1978). Operant psychology as factory psychology. *Behaviorism, 6,* 229–254.

Schwartz, G. E., Fair, P. L., Salt, P., Mandel, M. R., and Klerman, G. L. (1976). Facial muscle patterning to affective imagery in depressed and non-depressed subjects. *Science, 192,* 489–491.

Schwartz, S. H. (1970). Elicitation of moral obligation and self-sacrificing behavior: An experimental study of volunteering to be a bone marrow donor. *Journal of Personality and Social Psychology, 15,* 283–293.

Schwartz, S. H., & Clausen, G. T. (1970). Responsibility, norms and helping in an emergency. *Journal of Personality and Social Psychology, 16,* 299–310.

Schwartz, S. H., & Howard, J. A. (1982). Helping and cooperation: A self-based motivational model. In V. J. Derlega & J. Grzelak (Eds.), *Cooperation and helping behavior.* New York: Academic Press.

Schwartz, S. H., & Howard, J. A. (1984). Internalized values as motivators of altruism. In E. Staub, D. Bar-Tal, J. Karylowski, & J. Reykowski (Eds.), *The development and maintenance of pro-social behavior: International perspectives on positive development.* New York: Plenum.

Scientific American (1981, September). Science and the citizen. *Scientific American, 106.*

Scott, C. A., & Yalch, R. F. (1978). A test of the self-perception explanation of the effects of rewards on intrinsic interest. *Journal of Experimental Social Psychology, 14,* 180–192.

Scott, W. A. (1968). Attitude measurement. In G. Lindzey & E. Aronson (Eds.), *The handbook of social psychology* (2nd ed.). Reading, MA: Addison-Wesley.

Sears, D. O., Freedman, J. L., & Peplau, L. A. (1985). *Social psychology.* Englewood Cliffs, NJ: Prentice-Hall.

Sears, R. R., Whiting, J. W. M., Nowlis, V., & Sears, P. S. (1953). Some child-rearing antecedents of agression and dependency in young children. *Genetic Psychological Monographs, 47,* 135–236.

Seaver, W. B., & Patterson, A. H. (1976). Decreased fuel-oil consumption through feedback and social commendation. *Journal of Applied Behavior Analysis, 9,* 147–152.

Seavey, W. (1960). I am not my guest's keeper. *Vanderbilt Law Review, 13,* 699–702.

Secord, P. F., Backman, C. W., & Slavitt, D. R. (1976). *Understanding social life.* New York: McGraw-Hill.

Segal, M. W. (1974). Alphabet and attraction: An unobtrusive measure of the effect of propinquity in a field setting. *Journal of Personality and Social Psychology, 30,* 654–657.

Segall, M. H. (1976). *Human behavior and public policy.* New York: Pergamon.

Seidman, E. (1983). Unexamined premises of social problem solving. In E. Seidman (Ed.), *Handbook of Social Intervention.* Beverly Hills, CA: Sage.

Seligman, C. (1985). Information and energy

conservation. *Marriage and Family Review, 9,* 135–149.

Seligman, C., Becker, L. J., & Darley, J. M. (1981). Encouraging residential energy conservation through feedback. In A. Baum and J. E. Singer, *Advances in environmental psychology* (Vol. 3). Hillsdale, NJ: Erlbaum.

Seligman, C., Darley, J. M., Fazio, R. H., Becker, L. J., & Pryor, J. B. (1979). Predicting summer energy consumption from homeowners' attitudes. *Journal of Applied Social Psychology, 9,* 70–90.

Seligman, C., Fazio, R. H., & Zanna, M. P. (1980). Effects of salience of extrinsic rewards on liking and loving. *Journal of Personality and Social Psychology, 38,* 453–460.

Seligman, M. E. P. (1975). *Learned helplessness.* San Francisco: Freeman.

Sells, L. W. (1978). Mathematics—a critical filter. *The Science Teacher, 45,* 28–29.

Serbin, L. A., & O'Leary, K. D. (1975). How nursery schools teach girls to shut up. *Psychology Today, 9,* 56–58.

Shanab, M. E., & Yahya, L. A. (1977). A behavioral study of obedience in children. *Journal of Personality and Social Psychology, 35,* 530–536.

Shanteau, J., & Nagy, G. F. (1979). Probability of acceptance in dating choice. *Journal of Personality and Social Psychology, 37,* 522–533.

Shapiro, A., & Swensen, C. (1969). Patterns of self-disclosure among married couples. *Journal of Counseling Psychology, 16,* 179–180.

Shapiro, D., & Crider, A. (1968). Psychophysiological approaches in social psychology. In G. Lindzey & E. Aronson (Eds.), *The handbook of social psychology* (2nd ed). Reading, MA: Addison-Wesley.

Shave, E. J. (1928). A new type of scale for measuring attitudes. *Religious Education, 23,* 364–369.

Shaver, P., & Rubenstein, C. (1979). Living alone, loneliness and health. Paper presented at the 87th Annual Convention of the American Psychological Association, New York.

Shaw, B. F. (1985). Closing commentary: Social cognition and depression. *Social Cognition, 3,* 135–144.

Shaw, C. (1968). Juvenile delinquency: A group tradition. In J. F. Short (Ed.), *Gang delinquency and delinquent subcultures.* New York: Harper & Row.

Shaw, M. E. (1960). A note concerning homogeneity of membership and group problem solving. *Journal of Abnormal and Social Psychology, 60,* 448–450.

Shaw, M. E. (1963). Some effects of varying amounts of information exclusively possessed by a group member upon his behavior in the group. *Journal of General Psychology, 68,* 71–79.

Shaw, M. E. (1964). Communication networks. In L. Berkowitz (Ed.), *Advances in experimental social psychology* (Vol. 1). New York: Academic Press.

Shaw, M. E. (1981). *Group dynamics: The psychology of small group behavior* (3rd ed.). New York: McGraw-Hill.

Shaw, M. E., & Penrod, W. T. (1962). Does more information available to a group improve group performance? *Sociometry, 25,* 377–390.

Shepard, D. S., Foster, S. B., Stason, W. B., Solomon, H. S., McArdle, P. J., & Gallagher, G. S. (1979). Cost-effectiveness of interventions to improve compliance with anti-hypertensive therapy. Paper delivered at National Conference on High Blood Pressure Control, Washington, DC.

Sherif, C. W., Sherif, M., & Nebergall, R. E. (1965). *Attitude and attitude change: The social judgment–involvement approach.* Philadelphia: Saunders.

Sherif, M. (1936). *The psychology of social norms.* New York: Harper & Row.

Sherif, M. (1958). Superordinate goals in the reduction of intergroup conflicts. *American Journal of Sociology, 63,* 349–356.

Sherif, M. (1966). *In common predicament: Social psychology of intergroup conflict and cooperation.* Boston: Houghton Mifflin.

Sherif, M. (1970). On the relevance of social psychology. *American Psychologist, 25,* 144–156.

Sherif, M. (1979). Superordinate goals in the reduction of intergroup conflict: An experimental evaluation. In W. G. Austin & S. Worchel (Eds.), *The social psychology of intergroup relations.* Monterey, CA: Brooks/Cole.

Sherif, M., Harvey, O. J., White, B. J., Hood, W. R., & Sherif, C. W. (1961). *Intergroup conflict and cooperation: The Robbers Cave experi-*

ment. Norman, OK: University Book Exchange.

Sherif, M., & Hovland, C. I. (1961). *Social judgment: Assimilation and contrast effects in communication and attitude change.* New Haven, CT: Yale University Press.

Sherif, M., & Sherif, C. W. (1953). *Groups in harmony and tension.* New York: Harper & Row.

Sherif, M., & Sherif, C. W. (1956). *An outline of social psychology* (rev. ed.). New York: Harper & Row.

Sherif, M., & Sherif, C. W. (1967). Attitude as the individual's own categories: The social judgment–involvement approach to attitude and attitude change. In C. W. Sherif & M. Sherif (Eds.), *Attitude, ego-involvement and change.* New York: Wiley.

Sherif, M., & Sherif, C. W. (1969). *Social psychology.* New York: Harper & Row.

Sherif, M., White, B. J., & Harvey, O. J. (1955). Status in experimentally produced groups. *American Journal of Sociology, 60,* 370–379.

Sherman, S. J., & Gorkin, L. (1980). Attitude bolstering when behavior is inconsistent with central attitudes. *Journal of Personality and Social Psychology, 16,* 388–403.

Sherrod, D. R., & Cohen, S. (1979). Density, personal control and design. In J. R. Aiello & A. Baum (Eds.), *Residential crowding and design.* New York: Plenum.

Sherrod, D. R., & Downs, R. (1974). Environmental determinants of altruism: The effects of stimulus overload and perceived control on helping. *Journal of Experimental Social Psychology, 10,* 468–479.

Sherrod, D. R., Hage, J. N., Halpern, P. L., & Moore, B. S. (1977). Effects of personal causation and perceived control on responses to an aversive environment: The more control, the better. *Journal of Experimental Social Psychology, 13,* 14–27.

Sherwin, R., & Corbett, S. (1985). Campus sexual norms and dating relationships—a trend analysis. *Journal of Sex Research, 21,* 258–274.

Shotland, R. L. (1985). When bystanders just stand by. *Psychology Today, 19,* 50–55.

Shotland, R. L., & Huston, T. L. (1979). Emergencies: What are they and do they influence bystanders to intervene? *Journal of Personality and Social Psychology, 37,* 1822–1824.

Shotland, R. L., & Stebbins, C. A. (1980). Bystander response to rape: Can a victim attract help? *Journal of Applied Social Psychology, 10,* 510–527.

Shotland, R. L., & Yankowski, L. D. (1982). The R&OM response method: A valid and ethical indicator of the "truth" in reactive situations. *Personality and Social Psychology Bulletin, 8*(1), 174–179.

Shumaker, S. A., & Taylor, B. (1983). Toward a clarification of people-place relationships: A model of attachment to place. In N. Feimer & E. S. Geller (Eds.), *Environmental psychology: Directions and perspectives.* New York: Praeger.

Shure, G. H., Meeker, R. J., & Hansford, E. A. (1965). The effectiveness of pacifist strategies in bargaining games. *Journal of Conflict Resolution, 9,* 106–117.

Sieber, J. E. (Ed.) (1982a). *The ethics of social research: Surveys and experiments.* New York: Springer-Verlag.

Sieber, J. E. (Ed.) (1982b). *The ethics of social research: Fieldwork, regulation, and publication.* New York: Springer-Verlag.

Siegel, K., & Tuckel, P. (1985). The utilization of evaluation research. *Evaluation Review, 9,* 307–328.

Siegel, S., & Fouraker, L. E. (1960). *Bargaining and group decision making: Experiments in bilateral monopoly.* New York: McGraw-Hill.

Sigall, H., & Page, R. (1971). Current stereotypes: A little fading, a little faking. *Journal of Personality and Social Psychology, 18,* 247–255.

Silverman, I. (1977). Why social psychology fails. *Canadian Psychological Revue, 18,* 353–358.

Simmel, E. C., Hahn, M. E., & Walters, J. K. (Eds.) (1983). *Aggressive behavior: Genetic and neural approaches.* Hillsdale, NJ: Erlbaum.

Simmel, G. (1950). The stranger. In *The Sociology of Georg Simmel* (K. Wolff, Trans.). New York: Free Press.

Simmel, G. (1955). *Conflict and the web of group affiliations.* New York: Free Press.

Simon, J. L. (1978). *Basic research methods in*

social science (2nd ed.). New York: Random House.

Simon, J. L., & Arndt, J. (1980). The shape of the advertising response function. *Journal of Advertising Research, 20,* 11–28.

Simon, N. G. (1983). New strategies for aggression research. In E. C. Simmel, M. E. Hahn, & J. K. Walters (Eds.), *Aggressive behavior: Genetic and neural approaches.* Hillsdale, NJ: Erlbaum.

Simon, R. J. (1967). *The jury and the defense of insanity.* Boston: Little, Brown.

Simonton, D. K. (1979). Multiple discovery and invention: Zeitgeist, genius, or chance? *Journal of Personality and Social Psychology, 37,* 1603–1616.

Singer, J. D. (1964). Soviet and American foreign policy attitudes: A content analysis of elite articulations. *Journal of Conflict Resolution, 8,* 424–480.

Singer, J. E., Lundberg, V., & Frankenhaeuser, M. (1978). Stress on the train: A study of urban commuting. In A. Baum, J. Singer, & S. Valins (Eds.), *Advances in environmental psychology* (Vol. I). Hillsdale, NJ: Erlbaum.

Singer, J. L., & Singer, D. G. (1981). *Television, imagination and aggression: A study of preschoolers play.* Hillsdale, NJ: Erlbaum.

Sistrunk, F., & McDavid, J. W. (1971). Sex variable in conforming behavior. *Journal of Personality and Social Psychology, 17,* 200–207 .

Skinner, B. F. (1938). *The behavior of organisms: An experimental analysis.* New York: Appleton-Century-Crofts.

Skrypnek, B. J., & Snyder, M. (1982). On the self-perpetuating nature of stereotypes about women and men. *Journal of Experimental Social Psychology, 18,* 82–113.

Slater, P. E. (1958). Contrasting correlates of group size. *Sociometry, 21,* 129–139.

Sleet, D. A. (1969). Physique and social image. *Perceptual and Motor Skills, 28,* 295–299.

Sloan, L. R., Love, R. E., & Ostrom, T. M. (1974). Political heckling: Who really loses? *Journal of Personality and Social Psychology, 30,* 518–525.

Slovic, P., Fischhoff, B., & Lichtenstein, S. (1982). Facts versus fears: Understanding perceived risks. In D. Kahneman, P. Slovic, & A. Tversky (Eds.), *Judgment under uncertainty: Heuristics and biases.* Cambridge, England: Cambridge University Press.

Smelser, N. J. (1963). *Theory of collective behavior.* New York: Free Press.

Smetana, J., Bridgeman, D. L., & Bridgeman, B. (1978). A field study of interpersonal distance in childhood. *Personality and Social Psychology Bulletin, 4,* 309–313.

Smith, D. E., King. M. B., & Hoebel, B. G. (1970). Lateral hypothalamic control of killing: Evidence for cholinoceptive mechanism. *Science, 167,* 900–901.

Smith, F. J. (1977). Work attitudes as predictors of attendance on a specific day. *Journal of Applied Psychology, 62,* 16–19.

Smith, F. J., & Lawrence, E. S. (1978). Alone and crowded: The effects of spatial restruction on measures of affect and simulation response. *Personality and Social Psychology Bulletin, 4,* 139–142.

Smith, G. (1983). Presentation at Yale Law School course on nuclear arms control.

Smith, M. B. (1972). Is experimental social psychology advancing? *Journal of Experimental Social Psychology, 8,* 86–96.

Smith, M. B. (1973). Is psychology relevant to new priorities? *American Psychologist, 28,* 463–471.

Smith, M. B., Bruner, J. S., & White, R. W. (1956). *Opinions and personality.* New York: Wiley.

Smith, M. B., Janis, I. L., Star, S. A., & Cottrell, L. S. (1949). *The American soldier: Combat and its aftermath.* Princeton, NJ: Princeton University Press.

Smith, M. L., & Glass, G. V. (1977). Meta-analysis of psychotherapy outcome studies. *American Psychologist, 32,* 752–760.

Smithson, M., Amato, P. R., & Pearce, P. (1983). *Dimensions of helping behavior.* New York: Pergamon.

Smoke, W. H., & Zajonc, R. B. (1962). On the reliability of group judgments and decisions. In J. J. Criswell, H. Solomon, & P. Suppes (Eds.), *Mathematical methods in small groups.* Stanford, CA: Stanford University Press.

Snyder, M. (1974). The self-monitoring of expressive behavior. *Journal of Personality and Social Psychology, 30,* 526–537.

Snyder, M. (1979). Self-monitoring. In L. Berkowitz (Ed.), *Advances in experimental social psychology* (Vol. 12). New York: Academic Press.

Snyder, M., & Campbell, B. (1982). Self-monitoring: The self in action. In J. Suls (Ed.), *Psychological perspectives on the self.* Hillsdale, NJ: Erlbaum.

Snyder, M., & Cunningham, M. (1975). To comply or not to comply: Testing the self-perception explanation of the foot-in-the-door phenomenon. *Journal of Personality Social Psychology, 31,* 64–67.

Snyder, M., & Monson, T. C. (1975). Persons, situations, and the control of social behavior. *Journal of Personality and Social Psychology, 32,* 637–644.

Snyder, M., & Tanke, E. D., (1976). Behavior and attitude: Some people are more consistent than others. *Journal of Personality, 44,* 501–517.

Snyder, M., Tanke, E. D., & Berscheid, E. (1977). Social perception and interpersonal behavior: On the self-fulfilling nature of social stereotypes. *Journal of Personality and Social Psychology, 35,* 656–666.

Solomon, L. (1960). The influence of some types of power relationships and game strategies upon the development of interpersonal trust. *Journal of Abnormal and Social Psychology, 61,* 223–230.

Sommer, R. (1969). *Personal space.* Englewood Cliffs, NJ: Prentice-Hall.

Sommer, R. (1982). The District Attorney's dilemma: Experimental games and the real world of plea bargaining. *American Psychologist, 37,* 526–532.

Sommer, R., & Olsen, H. (1980). The soft classroom. *Environment and Behavior, 12,* 3–16.

Spence, J. T., Helmreich, R., & Stapp, J. (1974). The personal attributes questionnaire: A measure of sex-role stereotypes and masculinity-femininity. *JSAS Catalog of Selected Documents in Psychology, 43*(Ms. No. 617).

Spencer, J. M., & Zammit, J. P. (1976). Mediation-arbitration: A proposal for private resolution of disputes between divorced or separated parents. *Duke Law Journal,* 911–939.

Sperlich, P. (1979). Trial by jury: It may have a future. In P. Kurland & G. Casper (Eds.), *Supreme Court review 1978.* Chicago: University of Chicago Press.

Srull, T. K. (1983). Organizational and retrieval processes in person memory: An examination of processing objectives, presentation format, and the possible role of self-generated retrieval cases. *Journal of Personality and Social Psychology, 44,* 1157–1170.

Staats, A. W. (1975). *Social behaviorism.* Homewood, IL: Dorsey Press.

Stagner, R. (1976). Traits are relevant: Theoretical analysis and empirical evidence. In N. S. Endler & D. Magnusson (Eds.), *Interactional psychology and personality.* Washington, DC: Hemisphere.

Stang, D. J. (1972). Conformity, ability and self-esteem. *Representative Research in Social Psychology, 3,* 97–103.

Star, S. A., Williams, L. M., & Stouffer, S. A. (1965). Negro infantry platoons in white companies. In H. Proshansky & B. Seidenberg (Eds.), *Basic studies in social psychology.* New York: Holt, Rinehart and Winston.

Stark, R., & Bainbridge, W. S. (1980). Networks of faith: Interpersonal bonds and recruitment in cults and sects. *American Journal of Sociology, 85,* 1376–1395.

Stasser, G., Kerr, N. L., & Davis, J. H. (1980). Influence processes in decision making: A modeling approach. In P. Paulus (Ed.), *Psychology of group influence.* Hillsdale, NJ: Erlbaum.

Statistical Abstract of the United States: 1982–1983. (1983). Washington, DC: U.S. Department of Commerce, Bureau of the Census.

Staub, E. (1978). *Positive social behavior and morality: Social and personal influences* (Vol. 1). New York: Academic Press.

Staub, E. (1984). Steps toward a comprehensive theory of moral conduct: Goal orientation, social behavior, kindness and cruelty. In W. M. Kurtines & J. L. Gewirtz (Eds.), *Morality, moral development and moral behavior: Basic issues in theory and research.* New York: Wiley.

Staw, B. M. (Ed.) (1977). *Psychological foundations of organizational behavior.* Santa Monica, CA: Goodyear.

Staw, B. M., & Salancik, G. R. (1977). *New directions in organizational behavior.* Chicago: Saint Clair Press.

Steckel, S. B. (1982). *Patient contracting.* New York: Appleton-Century-Crofts.

Steele, C., & Liu, T. (1983). Dissonance processes as self-affirmation. *Journal of Personality and Social Psychology, 40,* 5–10.

Stein, A. H., & Friedrich, L. K. (1972). Television content and young children's behavior. In J. P. Murray, E. A. Rubinstein, & G. A. Comstock (Eds.), *Television and social behavior: Volume 2. Television and social learning.* Washington, DC: U.S. General Printing Office.

Steiner, I. D. (1972). *Group process and productivity.* New York: Academic Press.

Steininger, M., Newell, J. D., & Garcia, L. T. (1984). *Ethical issues in psychology.* Homewood, IL: Dorsey Press.

Stephan, W. G. (1980). The heart and mind of social psychology. In R. F. Kidd and M. J. Saks (Eds.), *Advances in applied social psychology* (Vol. 1). Hillsdale, NJ: Erlbaum.

Stephan, W. G. (1985). Meta-analysis of the educational impact of school desegregation. In M. J. Saks & L. Saxe (Eds.), *Advances in applied social psychology* (Vol. 3). Hillsdale, NJ: Erlbaum.

Stephan, W. G., & Feagin, J. R. (1980). *School desegregation.* New York: Plenum.

Stephan, W. G., & Rosenfield, D. (1978). Effects of desegregation on racial attitudes. *Journal of Personality and Social Psychology, 36,* 795–804.

Sternberg, R. J. (1986). A triangular theory of love. *Psychological Review, 93,* 119–135.

Sternberg, R. J., & Grajek, S. (1984). The nature of love. *Journal of Personality and Social Psychology, 47,* 312–329.

Stevens, S. S. (1957). On the psychophysical law. *Psychological Review, 64,* 153–181.

Stewart, A. J., & Lykes, M. B. (1985). Conceptualizing gender in personality theory and research. *Journal of Personality, 53,* 93–101.

Stewart, A. J., & Rubin, Z. (1976). The power motive in dating couples. *Journal of Personality and Social Psychology, 34,* 305–309.

Stewart, R. (1965). Effects of continuous responding on the order effect in personality impression formation. *Journal of Personality and Social Psychology, 1,* 161–165.

Stogdill, R. M. (1950). Leadership, membership, and organization. *Psychological Bulletin, 47,* 1–14.

Stogdill, R. M. (1959). *Individual behavior and group achievement.* New York: Oxford University Press.

Stokols, D. (1972). On the distinction between density and crowding: Some implications for future research. *Psychological Review, 79,* 275–278.

Stokols, D. (1976). The experience of crowding in primary and secondary environments. *Environment and Behavior, 8,* 49–86.

Stokols, D., & Novaco, R. (1981). Transportation and well-being: An ecological perspective. In I. Altman, J. Wohlwill, & P. Everett (Eds.), *Human behavior and environment: Advances in theory and research* (Vol. 5). New York: Plenum.

Stokols, D., Rall, M., Pinner, B., & Schopler, J. (1973). Physical, social and personal determinants of the perception of crowding. *Environment and Behavior, 5,* 87–117.

Stokols, D., & Shumaker, S. A. (1980). People in places: A transitional view of settings. In J. Harvey (Ed.), *Cognition, social behavior and the environment.* Hillsdale, NJ: Erlbaum.

Stone, G. (1979). Patient compliance and the role of the expert. *Journal of Social Issues, 35,* 34–59.

Stone, W. F. (1974). *The psychology of politics.* New York: Free Press.

Stoner, J. A. F. (1961). A comparison of individual and group decisions involving risk. Unpublished master's thesis, School of Industrial Management, Massachusetts Institute of Technology.

Storms, M. D. (1973). Videotape and the attribution process: Reversing actors' and observers' points of view. *Journal of Personality and Social Psychology, 27,* 165–175.

Storms, M. D., & Nisbett, R. E. (1970). Insomnia

and the attribution process. *Journal of Personality and Social Psychology, 16,* 319–328.

Stouffer, S. A., Lumsdaine, M. H., Williams, R. M., Smith, M. B., Janis, I. L., Star, S. A., & Cottrell, L. S. (1949). *The American soldier: Combat and its aftermath.* Princeton, NJ: Princeton University Press.

Stouffer, S. A., Suchman, D. E., De Vinney, L. C., Star, S. A., & Williams, R. M., Jr. (1949). *The American soldier: Adjustment during army life.* Princeton, NJ: Princeton University Press.

Straus, M. A., Gelles, R. J., & Steinmetz, S. K. (1979). *Behind closed doors: Violence in the American family.* Garden City, NY: Doubleday/Anchor.

Strauss, A. (1978). *Negotiations: Varieties, contexts, processes and social order.* San Francisco: Jossey-Bass.

Strauss, G. (1976). Organization development. In R. Dubin (Ed.), *Handbook of work, organization, and society.* Chicago: Rand McNally.

Streff, F. M., & Geller, E. S. (1986). Strategies for motivating safety belt use: The application of applied behavior analysis. *Health Education Research, 1,* 47–59.

Strickland, B. R. (1977). Internal-external control of reinforcement. In T. Blass (Ed.), *Personality variables in social behavior.* Hillsdale, NJ: Erlbaum.

Strickland, R. H., Aboud, F. E., & Gergen, K. J. (Eds.) (1976). *Social psychology in transition.* New York: Plenum.

Strodtbeck, F. (1951). Husband-wife interaction over revealed differences. *American Sociological Review, 16,* 468–473.

Strodtbeck, F. L., & Hook, L. H. (1961). The social dimensions of a twelve-man jury table. *Sociometry, 24,* 397–415.

Strodtbeck, F. L., James, R. M., & Hawkins, C. (1957). Social status in jury deliberation. *American Sociological Review, 22,* 713–719.

Stroebe, W. (1979). The level of social psychological analysis: A plea for a more social social psychology. In L. H. Strickland (Ed.), *Soviet and Western perspectives in social psychology.* New York: Pergamon.

Stroop, J. R. (1932). Is the judgment of the group better than that of the average member of the group? *Journal of Experimental Psychology, 15,* 550–562.

Strouse, J., & Fabes, R. (1985). Formal v. informal sources of sex education: Competing forces in the sexual socialization of adolescents. *Adolescence, 78,* 251–264.

Strube, M. J., Berry, J. M., & Moergen, S. (1985). Relinquishment of control and Type A behavior: The role of performance evaluation. *Journal of Personality and Social Psychology, 49,* 831–842.

Struening, E. L., & Guttentag, M. (Eds.) (1975). *Handbook of evaluation research* (Vols. 1 and 2). Beverly Hills, CA: Sage.

Strull, W. M., Lo, B., & Charles, G. (1984). Do patients want to participate in medical decision making? *Journal of the American Medical Association, 252,* 2990–2994.

Suedfeld, P., Bochner, S., & Wnek, D. (1972). Helper-sufferer similarity and a specific request for help: Bystander intervention during a peace demonstration. *Journal of Applied Social Psychology, 2,* 17–23.

Suedfeld, P., & Rank, A. D. (1976). Revolutionary leaders: Long-term success as a function of changes in conceptual complexity. *Journal of Personality and Social Psychology, 34,* 169–178.

Suedfeld, P., & Tetlock, P. (1977). Integrative complexity of communications in international crises. *Journal of Conflict Resolution, 21,* 169–184.

Suedfeld, P., Tetlock, R. E., & Ramirez, C. (1977). War, peace and integrative complexity: UN speeches on the Middle East problem, 1947–1976. *Journal of Conflict Resolution, 21,* 427–441.

Suggs, D., & Sales, B. D. (1978). The art and science of conducting the voir dire. *Professional Psychology, 9,* 367–388.

Suls, J. (Ed.) (1982). *Psychological perspective on the self* (Vol. 1). Hillsdale, NJ: Erlbaum.

Summers, G. F. (1970). *Attitude measurement.* Chicago: Rand McNally.

Sumner, W. G. (1906). *Folkways.* Boston: Ginn.

Sundstrom, E. (1975). An experimental study of crowding: Effects of room size, intrusion, and goal-blocking on nonverbal behaviors, self-disclosure, and self-reported stress. *Journal of*

Personality and Social Psychology, 32, 645–654.

Sundstrom, E., & Altman, I. (1974). Field study on dominance and territorial behavior. *Journal of Personality and Social Psychology, 30,* 115–125.

Sussman, N. M., & Rosenfeld, H. M. (1982). Influence of culture, language and sex on conversational distance. *Journal of Personality and Social Psychology, 42,* 66–74.

Swap, W. C. (1977). Interpersonal attraction and repeated exposure to rewarders and punishers. *Personality and Social Psychology Bulletin, 3,* 248–251.

Szasz, T. (1984). *The myth of mental illness: Foundations of a theory of personal conduct.* New York: Harper & Row.

Tagliocozzo, D. L., & Mauksch, H. O. (1979). The patient's view of patient's role. In E. G. Jaco (Ed.), *Patients, physicians and illness.* New York: Free Press.

Tajfel, H. (1970). Experiments in intergroup discrimination. *Scientific American, 223,* 96–102.

Tajfel, H. (1978). *Differentiation between social groups: Studies in social psychology of intergroup relations.* London: Academic Press.

Tanford, S., & Penrod, S. (1984). Social influence model: A formal integration of research on majority and minority influence processes. *Psychological Bulletin, 95,* 189–225.

Tannenbaum, P. H., & Zillmann, D. (1975). Emotional arousal in facilitation of aggression through communication. In L. Berkowitz (Ed.), *Advances in experimental social psychology* (Vol. 8). New York: Academic Press.

Tapp, J. L., & Levine, F. J. (Eds.) (1977). *Law, justice and the individual in society: Psychological and legal issues.* New York: Holt, Rinehart and Winston.

Task Force on Psychology and Public Policy (1984). Psychology and public policy. *American Psychologist, 41,* 914–921.

Tavris, C., & Jayaratne, T. (1976). How happy is your marriage? *Redbook, 147*(2), 90–92, 132, 134.

Tavris, C., & Wade, C. (1984). *The longest war: Sex differences in perspective* (2nd ed.). San Diego, CA: Harcourt Brace Jovanovich.

Taylor, F. W. (1903). Group management. *Transactions of the American Society of Mechanical Engineers, 24,* 1337–1480.

Taylor, F. W. (1911). *Principles of scientific management.* New York: Harper & Row.

Taylor, J. B., & Parker, H. A. (1964). Graphic ratings and attitude measurement: A comparison of research tactics. *Journal of Applied Psychology, 48,* 37–42.

Taylor, R. B. (1984). Toward an environmental psychology of disorder: Delinquency, crime and fear of crime. In D. Stokols and I. Altman (Eds.), *Handbook of environmental psychology.* New York: Wiley.

Taylor, R. B., & Gottfredson, S. (1986). Environmental design, crime and prevention: An examination of community dynamics. In A. J. Reiss, Jr., & M. Tonry (Eds.), *Communities and crime* (Vol. 18). Chicago: University of Chicago Press.

Taylor, R. B., Gottfredson, S. D., & Brower, S. (1984). Block crime and fear: Defensible space, local social ties, and territorial functioning. *Journal of Research in Crime and Delinquency, 21,* 301–331.

Taylor, R. B., Shumaker, S. A., & Gottfredson, S. D. (1985). Neighborhood level linkages between physical features and local sentiments. *Journal of Architectural Planning and Research, 2,* 261–275.

Taylor, S. E. (1975). On inferring one's attitudes from one's behavior: Some delimiting conditions. *Journal of Personality and Social Psychology, 31,* 126–131.

Taylor, S. E. (1979). Hospital patient behavior: Reactance, helplessness, or control? *Journal of Social Issues, 35,* 156–184.

Taylor, S. E. (1986). *Health psychology.* New York: Random House.

Taylor, S. E., & Clark, L. F. (1986). Does information improve adjustment to noxious events? In M. J. Saks & L. Saxe (Eds.), *Advances in applied social psychology* (Vol. 3). Hillsdale, NJ: Erlbaum.

Taylor, S. E., & Crocker, J. (1981). Schematic bases of social information processing. In E. T. Higgins, C. P. Herman, & M. P. Zanna (Eds.), *Social cognition: The Ontario Symposium* (Vol. 1). Hillsdale, NJ: Erlbaum.

Taylor, S. E., & Fiske, S. T. (1975). Point-of-view and perceptions of causality. *Journal of Personality and Social Psychology, 32,* 439–445.

Taylor, S. E., Lichtman, R. R., & Wood, J. V. (1984). Attributions, beliefs about control, and adjustments to breast cancer. *Journal of Personality and Social Psychology, 46,* 489–502.

Taylor, S. E., Wood, J. V., & Lichtman, R. R. (1983). It could be worse: Selective evaluation as a response to victimization. *Journal of Social Issues, 39,* 19–40.

Taylor, S. P., & Gammon, C. B. (1975). Effects of type and dose of alcohol on human physical aggression. *Journal of Personality and Social Psychology, 32,* 169–175.

Taylor, S. P., Gammon, C. B., & Capasso, D. R. (1976). Aggression as a function of the interaction of alcohol and threat. *Journal of Personality and Social Psychology, 34,* 938–941.

Taylor, S. P., & Leonard, K. E. (1983). Alcohol and human physical aggression. In R. Geen & E. Donnerstein (Eds.), *Aggression: Theoretical and empirical reviews* (Vol. 2). New York: Academic Press.

Taylor, S. P., Vardaris, R. M., Rawtich, A. B., Gammon, C. B., Cranston, J. W., & Lubetkin, A. I. (1976). The effects of alcohol and delta-9-tetrahydrocannabinol on human physical aggression. *Aggressive Behavior, 2,* 153–161.

Tedeschi, J. T., & Reiss, M. (1981). Identities, the phenomenal self and laboratory research. In J. T. Tedeschi (Ed.), *Impression management theory and social psychological research.* New York: Academic Press.

Teger, A. I. (1980). *Too much invested to quit.* New York: Pergamon.

Telch, M. J., Killen, J. D., McAlister, A. L., Perry, C. L., & Maccoby, N. (1982). Long-term follow-up of a pilot project on smoking prevention with adolescents. *Journal of Behavioral Medicine, 5,* 1–8.

Tellegen, A., Kamp, J., & Watson, D. (1982). Recognizing individual differences in predictive structure. *Psychological Review, 80,* 95–105.

Tennis, G. H., & Dabbs, J. M. (1975). Sex, setting and personal space: First grade through college. *Sociometry, 38,* 385–394.

Tetlock, P. E. (1979). Identifying victims of groupthink from public statements of decision makers. *Journal of Personality and Social Psychology, 37,* 1314–1324.

Thibaut, J. W., & Kelley, H. H. (1959). *The social psychology of groups.* New York: Wiley.

Thibaut, J. W., & Walker, L. (1975). *Procedural justice: A psychological analysis.* Hillsdale, NJ: Erlbaum.

Thomas, A., Chess, S., & Birch, H. G. (1970). The origin of personality. *Scientific American, 223,* 102–109.

Thomas, E. A. C., & Malone, T. W. (1979). On the dynamics of two-person interactions. *Psychology Review, 86,* 331–360.

Thomas, M. H., & Drabman, R. S. (1978). Effects of television violence on expectations of others' aggression. *Personality and Social Psychology Bulletin, 4,* 73–76.

Thomas, M. H., Horton, R. W., Lippincott, E. C., & Drabman, R. S. (1977). Desensitization to portrayals of real-life aggression as a function of exposure to television violence. *Journal of Personality and Social Psychology, 45,* 450–479.

Thompson, S. C. (1981). Will it hurt less if I can control it? A complex answer to a simple question. *Psychological Bulletin, 90,* 89–101.

Thompson, S. C., & Kelley, J. J. (1981). Judgments of responsibility for activities in close relationships. *Journal of Personality and Social Psychology, 41,* 469–477.

Thurow, L. C. (1982, April 1). How to rescue a drowning economy. *The New York Review of Books,* pp. 3ff.

Thurstone, L. L. (1928). Attitudes can be measured. *American Journal of Sociology, 33,* 529–544.

Thurstone, L. L. (1928). The intelligence of policemen. *Journal of Personnel Research, 1,* 64–74.

Thurstone, L. L., & Chave, E. J. (1929). *The measurement of attitude.* Chicago: University of Chicago Press.

Titmuss, R. M. (1971). *The gift relationship: From human blood to social policy.* New York: Vintage.

Tobias, S. (1982). Sexist equations. *Psychology Today, 15,* 14–18.

Toch, H. (1965). *The social psychology of social movements.* New York: Bobbs-Merrill.

Toch, H. (1980). *Violent men* (rev. ed.). Cambridge, MA: Schenkman.

Tolman, C. W. (1965). Emotional behavior and social facilitation of eating in domestic chicks. *Animal Behavior, 13,* 493–496.

Tolor, A., & Reznikoff, M. (1967). Relation between insight, repression-sensitization, internal-external control, and death anxiety. *Journal of Abnormal Psychology, 72,* 426–430.

Tornatzky, L. G., & Solomon, T. (1982). Contributions of social science to innovation and productivity. *American Psychologist, 37,* 737–746.

Tresemer, D. (1974). Fear of success: Popular but unproven. *Psychology Today, 7,* 82–85.

Triandis, H. C. (1977). *Interpersonal behavior.* Monterey, CA: Brooks/Cole.

Triandis, H. C. (1980). Values, attitudes, and interpersonal behavior. In H. Howe & M. Page (Eds.), *Nebraska symposium on motivation* (Vol. 27). Lincoln: University of Nebraska Press.

Triplett, N. (1898). The dynamogenic factors in pacemaking and competition. *American Journal of Psychology, 9,* 507–533.

Trist, E. L., Higgin, G. W., Murray, H., & Pollack, A. B. (1963). *Organizational choice.* London: Tavistock Publications.

Trites, D., Galbraith, F. D., Sturdavent, M., & Leckwart, J. F. (1970). Influence of nursing unit design on the activities and subjective feelings of nursing personnel. *Environment and Behavior, 2,* 203–234.

Trivers, R. L. (1971). The evolution of reciprocal altruism. *Quarterly Review of Biology, 46,* 35–37.

Tuchman, B. (1956). *Bible and sword: England and Palestine from the Bronze Age to Balfour.* New York: New York University Press.

Turner, A. G. (1982). What subjects of survey research believe about confidentiality. In J. E. Sieber (Ed.), *The ethics of social research: Surveys and experiments.* New York: Springer-Verlag.

Turner, C. W., Layton, J. F., & Simons, L. S. (1975). Naturalistic studies of aggressive behavior: Aggressive stimuli, victim visibility, and horn honking. *Journal of Personality and Social Psychology, 31,* 1198–1107.

Turner, J. C., & Giles, H. (Eds.) (1981). *Intergroup behavior.* Chicago: University of Chicago Press.

Turner, R. H. (1964). Collective behavior. In R. E. L. Faris (Ed.), *Handbook of modern sociology.* Chicago: Rand McNally.

Turner, R. H., & Killian, L. M. (1957). *Collective behavior.* Englewood Cliffs, NJ: Prentice-Hall.

Tversky, A., & Kahneman, D. (1973). Availability: A heuristic for judging frequency and probability. *Cognitive Psychology, 5,* 207–232.

Ulrich, R. E., Stachnik, T. J., & Stainton, N. R. (1963). Student acceptance of generalized personality interpretation. *Psychological Reports, 13,* 831–834.

Unger, R. K. (1979). Toward a redefinition of sex and gender. *American Psychologist, 34,* 1085–1094.

U. S. Bureau of the Census (1981). *Statistical abstract of the United States: 1981* (102nd ed.). Washington, DC.

Urwick, L. (1943). *The elements of administration.* New York: Harper & Row.

Valzelli, L. (1981). *The psychobiology of aggression and violence.* New York: Raven Press.

Vandenberg, S. G., & Kuse, A. R. (1979). Spatial ability: A critical review of the sex-linked major gene hypothesis. In M. A. Witlig and A. C. Peterson (Eds.), *Sex-related differences in cognitive functioning: Developmental issues.* New York: Academic Press.

Vansell, M., Brief, A. P., & Schuler, R. S. (1981). Role conflict and role ambiguity: Integration of the literature and directions for future research. *Human Relations, 34,* 43–71.

Varela, J. A. (1971). *Psychological solutions to social problems: An introduction to social technology.* New York: Academic Press.

Vernon, P. E. (1964). *Personality assessment: A critical survey.* New York: Wiley.

Vinokur, A. (1971). A review and theoretical analysis of the effects of group processes upon individual and group decisions involving risk. *Psychological Bulletin, 76,* 231–250.

Vinsel, A., Brown, B., Altman, I., & Ross, C. (1980). Privacy regulation, territorial displays, and effectiveness of individual functioning. *Journal of Personality and Social Psychology, 39,* 1104–1115.

Virinis, J. S., & Roll, S. (1970). Primary and secondary male characteristics: The hairiness and large penis stereotypes. *Psychological Reports, 26,* 123–126.

Vroom, V. H., Grant, L. D., & Cotton, T. S. (1969). The consequences of social interaction in group problem solving. *Organizational Behavior and Human Performance, 4,* 77–95.

Wack, J., & Rodin, J. (1978). Nursing homes for the aged: The human consequences of legislation-shaped environments. *Journal of Social Issues, 34,* 6–21.

Wagner, R. V. (1975). Complementary needs, role expectations, interpersonal attraction, and the stability of working relationships. *Journal of Personality and Social Psychology, 32,* 116–124.

Waitzkin, H., & Stoeckle, J. D. (1976). Information control and the micropolitics of health care: Summary of an ongoing research project. *Social Science and Medicine, 10,* 163–176.

Wales, H. W. (1985). Tilting at crime: The perils of eclecticism. *Georgetown Law Journal, 74,* 481–497.

Walker, T. G., & Main, E. C. (1973). Choice shifts in political decision making: Federal judges and civil liberties cases. *Journal of Applied Social Psychology, 3,* 39–48.

Wallace, D. H., & Wehmer, G. (1972). Evaluation of visual erotica by sexual liberals and conservatives. *Journal of Sex Research, 8,* 147–153.

Wallston, B. S., & Wallston, K. A. (1984). Social psychological models of health behavior: An examination and integration. In A. Baum, S. E. Taylor, & J. E. Singer (Eds.), *Handbook of psychology and health* (Vol. 4). Hillsdale, NJ: Erlbaum.

Wallston, K. A., & Wallston, B. S. (1983). Who is responsible for your health? The construct of health locus of control. In G. Saunders and J. Suls (Eds.), *Social psychology of health and illness.* Hillsdale, NJ: Erlbaum.

Wallston, K. A., Wallston, B. S., & DeVellis, R. (1978). Development of the multi-dimensional health locus of control (MHLC) scale. *Health Education Monographs, 6,* 161–170.

Walster, E., Aronson, E., & Abrahams, D. (1966). On increasing the persuasiveness of a low-prestige communicator. *Journal of Experimental Social Psychology, 2,* 325–342.

Walster, E., Aronson, V., Abrahams, D., & Rottman, I. (1966). Importance of physical attractiveness in dating behavior. *Journal of Personality and Social Psychology, 4,* 508–516.

Walster, E., Berscheid, E., & Walster, G. (1973). New directions in equity research. *Journal of Personality and Social Psychology, 25,* 151–176.

Walster, E., & Piliavin, J. A. (1972). Equity and the innocent bystander. *Journal of Social Issues, 28,* 165–189.

Walster, E., Traupmann, J., & Walster, G. W. (1978). Equity and extra-marital sexuality. *Archives of Sexual Behavior, 7,* 127–141.

Walster, E., & Walster, G. W. (1978). *Love.* Reading, MA: Addison-Wesley.

Walster, E., Walster, G. W., & Berscheid, E. (1978). *Equity: Theory and research.* Boston: Allyn & Bacon.

Walster, E., Walster, G. W., & Traupmann, J. (1978). Equity and premarital sex. *Journal of Personality and Social Psychology, 36,* 82–92.

Walters, R. H. (1966). Implications of laboratory studies of aggression for the control and regulation of violence. *Annals of the American Academy of Political Science, 364,* 60–72.

Wandersman, A. (1984). Citizen participation. In R. Hellin, R. Price, S. Reinharz, S. Riger, & A. Wandersman, (Eds.), *Psychology and community change* (2nd ed.). Homewood, IL: Dorsey.

Wandersman, A., Jakubs, J. F., & Giamartino, G. (1981). Participation in block organization. *Journal of Community Action, 1,* 40–48.

Wapner, S., Kaplan, B., & Cohen, S. B. (1973). An organismic developmental perspective for understanding transactions of men and environment. *Environment and Behavior, 5,* 255–289.

Warner, S. (1965). Randomized response: A survey technique for eliminating evasive answer bias. *Journal of the American Statistical Association, 60,* 63–69.

Warr, P., & Parry, G. (1982). Paid women's employment and women's psychological well-being. *Psychological Bulletin, 91,* 498–516.

Warren, R. (1974). *Community in America.* Chicago: Rand McNally.

Warshaw, P. R., & Davis, F. D. (1985). Disentangling behavioral intention and behavioral expectation. *Journal of Experimental Social Psychology, 21,* 213–228.

Washington v. *Davis,* 426 US 229 (1976).

Waters, H. F., & Malamud, P. (1975). Drop that gun, Captain Video. *Newsweek, 85,* 81–82.

Watson, J. B. (1919). *Psychology from the standpoint of a behaviorist.* Philadelphia: Lippincott.

Waxler, N. E., & Mishler, E. G. (1978). Experimental studies of families. In L. Berkowitz (Ed.), *Group processes.* New York: Academic Press.

Webb, E. J., Campbell, D. T., Schwartz, R. D., & Sechrest, L. (1981). *Unobtrusive measures: Non-reactive research in the social sciences* (2nd ed.). Chicago: Rand McNally

Weber, R., & Crocker, J. (1983). Cognitive processes in the revision of stereotypic beliefs. *Journal of Personality and Social Psychology, 45,* 961–977.

Weeks, D. G., Michela, J. L., Peplau, L. A., & Bragg, M. E. (1980). The relation between loneliness and depression: A structural equation analysis. *Journal of Personality and Social Psychology, 39,* 1238–1244.

Weick, K. E. (1979). *The social psychology of organizing* (2nd ed.). Reading, MA: Addison-Wesley.

Weigel, R. H., & Loomis, J. W. (1981). Televised models of female achievement revisited: Some progress. *Journal of Applied Social Psychology, 11,* 58–63.

Weigel, R. H., & Newman, L. S. (1976). Increasing attitude-behavior correspondence by broadening the scope of the behavioral measure. *Journal of Personality and Social Psychology, 33,* 793–802.

Weigel, R. H., Wiser, P. L., & Cook, S. W. (1975). The impact of cooperative learning experiences on cross-ethnic relations and attitudes. *Journal of Social Issues, 31,* 219–244.

Weiner, B. (1980). *Human motivation.* New York: Holt, Rinehart and Winston.

Weiner, B. (1985). An attributional theory of achievement, motivation and emotion. *Psychological Review, 92,* 548–573.

Weiner, B., Frieze, I., Kukla, A., Reed, L., Rest, S., & Rosenbaum, R. M. (1972). Perceiving the causes of success and failure. In E. E. Jones, D. E. Kanouse, H. H. Kelley, R. E. Nisbett, S. Valins, & B. Weiner (Eds.), *Attribution: Perceiving the causes of behavior.* Morristown, NJ: General Learning Press.

Weiner, F. H. (1976). Altruism, ambiance and action: The effects of rural and urban rearing on helping behavior. *Journal of Personality and Social Psychology, 34,* 112–124.

Weinstein, C. S. (1981). Classroom design as an external condition for learning. *Educational Technology, 21,* 12–19.

Weinstein, C. S. (1982). Special issue on learning environments: An introduction. *Journal of Man-Environment Relations, 1,* 1–9.

Weinstein, N. D. (1977). Noise and intellectual performance: A confirmation and extension. *Journal of Applied Psychology, 62,* 104–107.

Weiss, B. (1974). Earlier menstruation, longer adolescence. *Psychology Today, 8*(6), 59.

Weiss, C. H. (1977a). Research for policy's sake: The enlightenment function of social research. *Policy Analysis, 4,* 531–543.

Weiss, C. H. (1977b). *Using social research in public policy making.* Lexington, MA: Lexington Books.

Weiss, L., & Lowenthal, M. F. (1975). Life-course perspective on friendship. In M. F. Lowenthal, M. Thurner, & D. Chiriboga (Eds.), *Four stages of life.* San Francisco: Jossey-Bass.

Weiss, R. S. (1973). *Loneliness: The experience of emotional and social isolation.* Cambridge, MA: MIT Press.

Weitzman, L. J., & Rizzo, D. (1974). Images of males and females in elementary school textbooks. New York: NOW Legal Defense and Education Fund.

Wells, G. L., Leippe, M. R., and Ostrom, T. R. (1979). Guidelines for empirically assessing the fairness of a lineup. *Law and Human Behavior, 3,* 285–293.

Wells, G. L., & Murray, D. M. (1984). Eyewitness confidence. In G. Wells & E. Loftus (Eds.), *Eyewitness testimony: Psychological perspectives.* New York: Cambridge University Press.

Werner, C. (1978). Intrusiveness and persuasive impact of three communication media. *Journal of Applied Social Psychology, 8,* 145–162.

West, S. G., Gunn, S. P., & Chernicky, P. (1975). Ubiquitous Watergate: An attributional analysis. *Journal of Personality and Social Psychology, 32,* 55–65.

Wetzel, C. G. (1982). Self-serving biases in attribution: A Bayesian analysis. *Journal of Personality and Social Psychology, 43,* 197–209.

Wetzel, C. G., & Insko, C. A. (1982). The similarity-attraction relationship: Is there an ideal one? *Journal of Experimental Social Psychology, 18,* 253–276.

Wetzel, C. G., Schwartz, D., & Vasu, E. S. (1979). Roommate compatibility: Is there an ideal relationship? *Journal of Applied Social Psychology, 9,* 432–445.

Wheeler, L., Deci, E. L., Reis, H. T., & Zuckerman, M. (1978). *Interpersonal influence* (2nd ed.). Boston: Allyn & Bacon.

Whitaker, D. S., & Lieberman, M. A. (1964). *Psychotherapy through the group process.* New York: Atherton.

White, G. L. (1980). Physical attractiveness and courtship progress. *Journal of Personality and Social Psychology, 39,* 660–668.

White, G. L., Fishbein, S., & Rutstein, J. (1981). Passionate love and the misattribution of arousal. *Journal of Personality and Social Psychology, 41,* 56–62.

White, R. K. (1966). Misperception and the Vietnam War. *Journal of Social Issues, 22* (Whole No. 3).

White, R. K. (1968). *Nobody wanted war.* New York: Doubleday.

Whitley, B. E. (1983). Sex-role orientation and self-esteem: A critical meta-analytic review. *Journal of Personality and Social Psychology, 44,* 765–778.

Whyte, M. K. (1973). Bureaucracy and modernization in China: The Maoist critique. *American Sociological Review, 38,* 149–163.

Whyte, W. F. (1943). *Street corner society: The social structure of an Italian slum.* Chicago: University of Chicago Press.

Whyte, W. F. (1948). *Human relations in the restaurant industry.* New York: McGraw-Hill.

Wicker, A. W. (1969). Attitudes versus actions: The relationship of verbal and overt behavioral responses to attitude objects. *Journal of Social Issues, 25*(4), 41–78.

Wicker, A. W. (1971). An examination of the "other-variables" explanation of attitude-behavior inconsistency. *Journal of Personality and Social Psychology, 19,* 18–30.

Wicker, A. W. (1979). *An introduction to ecological psychology.* Monterey, CA: Brooks/Cole.

Wicklund, R. A. (1982). How society uses self-awareness. In J. Suls (Ed.), *Psychological perspectives on the self* (Vol. 1). Hillsdale, NJ: Erlbaum.

Wicklund, R. A., & Brehm, J. W. (1976). *Perspectives on cognitive dissonance.* Hillsdale, NJ: Erlbaum.

Wiggins, J. S., Wiggins, N., & Conger, J. C. (1968). Correlates of heterosexual somatic preference. *Journal of Personality and Social Psychology, 10,* 82–90.

Wilder, D. A. (1977). Perception of groups, size of opposition, and social influence. *Journal of Experimental Social Psychology, 13,* 253–268.

Will, J., Self, P., & Datan, N. (1974). Material behavior and perceived sex of infant. Paper presented at American Psychological Association convention.

Williams, E. (1975). Coalition formation over telecommunications media. *European Journal of Social Psychology, 5,* 503–507.

Williams, J. E., & Best, D. L. (1982). *Measuring sex stereotypes: A thirty-nation study.* Beverly Hills, CA: Sage.

Williams, J. G., & Solano, C. H. (1983). The social reality of feeling lonely: Friendship and reciprocation. *Personality and Social Psychology Bulletin, 9,* 237–242.

Williams v. *Florida* 399 U.S. 78 (1970).

Willie, C. V., & Greenblatt, S. L. (1981). *Community politics and educational change: Ten school systems under court order.* New York: Longman.

Willis, R. (1965). Conformity, independence and and anti-conformity. *Human Relations, 18,* 373–388.

Wills, T. A., Weiss, R. L., & Patterson, G. R. (1974). A behavioral analysis of the determinants of marital satisfaction. *Journal of Consulting and Clinical Psychology, 42,* 802–811.

Wilson, E. O. (1975). *Sociobiology and the new synthesis.* Cambridge, MA: Harvard University Press.

Wilson, J. Q., & Herrnstein, R. J. (1985). *Crime and human nature,* New York: Simon & Schuster.

Wilson, T. D., & Linville, P. W. (1982). Improving the academic performance of college freshmen: Attribution therapy revisited. *Journal of Personality and Social Psychology, 42,* 367–376.

Wilson, T. D., & Linville, P. W. (1985). Improving the performance of college freshmen with attributional techniques. *Journal of Personality and Social Psychology, 49,* 287–293.

Wilson, W. R. (1979). Feeling more than we can know: Exposure effects without learning. *Journal of Personality and Social Psychology, 37,* 811–821.

Winch, R. F. (1958). *Mate-selection: A study of complementary needs.* New York: Harper & Row.

Wineman, J. D. (1982). Office design and evaluation: An overview. *Environment and Behavior, 14,* 271–298.

Wineman, J. D. (Ed.) (1985). *Behavioral issues in office design.* New York: Van Nostrand Reinhold.

Winett, R. A., Kagel, J. H., Battalio, R. C., & Winkler, R. C. (1978). The effects of monetary rebates, feedback, and information on residential electricity conservation. *Journal of Applied Psychology, 63,* 73–80.

Winett, R. A., & Neale, M. S. (1979). Psychological framework for energy conservation in buildings: Strategies, outcomes and directions. *Energy and Buildings, 2,* 101–116.

Winter, D. G. (1973). *The power motive.* New York: Free Press.

Wirth, L. (1938). Urbanism as a way of life. *American Journal of Sociology, 44,* 1–24.

Wishner, J. (1960). Reanalysis of "Impressions of Personality." *Psychological Review, 67,* 96–112.

Wispé, L. (1978). *Altruism, sympathy and helping: Psychological and sociological principles.* New York: Academic Press.

Wispé, L. (1986). The distinction between sympathy and empathy: To call forth a concept, a word is needed. *Journal of Personality and Social Psychology, 50,* 314–321.

Witkin, H. A., Mednick, S. A., Schulsinger, F., Bakkestrom, E., Christiansen, K. O., Goodenough, D. R., Philip, J., Rubin, D. B., & Stocking, M. (1976). Criminality in XYY and XXY men. *Science, 198,* 547–555.

Wittig, M. A., & Skolnick, P. (1978). Status versus warmth as determinants of sex differences in personal space. *Sex Roles, 4,* 493–503.

Wixon, D. R., & Laird, J. D. (1976). Awareness and attitude change in the forced-compliance paradigm: The importance of when. *Journal of Personality and Social Psychology, 34,* 376–384.

Wolf, S. (1985). Manifest and latent influence of majorities and minorities. *Journal of Personality and Social Psychology, 48,* 899–908.

Wolfgang, M. E., & Strohm, R. B. (1971). The relationship between alcohol and criminal homicide. *Quarterly Journal of Statistics on Alcohol, 17,* 411–425.

Woll, S. (1986). So many to choose from: Decision strategies in videodating. *Journal of Social and Personal Relationships, 3,* 43–52.

Wolpe, J. (1973). *The practice of behavior therapy.* New York: Pergamon.

Woodside, A. G., Sheth, J. N., & Bennett, P. D. (1977). *Consumer and industrial buying behavior.* New York: Elsevier.

Woodward, J. (1965). *Industrial organization: Theory and practice.* London: Oxford University Press.

Worchel, S. (1974). The effect of three types of arbitrary thwarting on the instigation to aggression. *Journal of Personality, 42,* 301–318.

Worchel, S. (1979). Conflict and the reduction of intergroup conflict: Some determining factors. In W. G. Austin & S. Worchel (Eds.), *The social psychology of intergroup relations.* Monterey, CA: Brooks/Cole.

Worchel, S. & Teddlie, C. (1976). The experience of crowding: A two-factor theory. *Journal of Personality and Social Psychology, 34,* 30–40.

Worringham, C. J., & Messick, D. M. (1983). Social facilitation of running: An unobtrusive study. *Journal of Social Psychology, 121,* 23–29.

Worthington, M. (1974). Personal space as a

function of the stigma effect. *Environment and Behavior, 6,* 289–295.

Wortman, C. B., & Brehm, J. W. (1975). Responses to uncontrollable outcomes: An integration of reactance theory and the learned helplessness model. In L. Berkowitz (Ed.), *Advances in experimental social psychology* (Vol. 8). New York: Academic Press.

Wrightsman, L. S., & Deaux, K. (1984). *Social psychology in the 80's* (4th ed.). Monterey, CA: Brooks/Cole.

Wyer, R. S., & Carlston, D. E. (1979). *Social cognition, inference, and attribution.* Hillsdale, NJ: Erlbaum.

Wyer, R. S., Jr., & Gordon, S. E. (1982). The recall of information about persons and groups. *Journal of Experimental Social Psychology, 18,* 128–164.

Wyer, R. S., Jr., & Srull, T. K. (1980). The processing of social stimulus information: A conceptual integration. In R. Hastie, T. M. Ostrom, E. B. Ebbeson, R. S. Wyer, D. L. Hamilton, & D. E. Carlston (Eds.), *Person memory: The cognitive basis of social perception.* Hillsdale, NJ: Erlbaum.

Yakimovich, D., & Saltz, E. (1971). Helping behavior: The cry for help. *Psychonomic Science, 23,* 427–428.

Yalom, I. D. (1975). *The theory and practice of group psychotherapy* (2nd ed.). New York: Basic Books.

Yalom, I. D., & Rand, K. (1966). Compatibility and cohesiveness in therapy groups. *Archives of General Psychology, 13,* 267–276.

Yarmey, A. D., & Jones, H. P. T. (1983). Is the study of eyewitness identification a matter of common sense? In S. Lloyd-Bostock and B. Clifford (Eds.), *Evaluating witness evidence.* Chichester, England: Wiley-Interscience.

Yerkes, R. M. (1918). Psychology in relation to the war. *Psychological Review, 25,* 85–115.

Young, J. E. (1982). Loneliness, depression and cognitive therapy: Theory and application. In L. A. Peplau & D. Perlman (Eds.), *Loneliness: A sourcebook of current theory, research, and therapy.* New York: Wiley.

Younger, J. C., Walker, L., & Arrowood, A. J. (1977). Post-decision dissonance at the fair. *Personality and Social Psychology Bulletin, 3,* 284–287.

Yukl, G. (1981). *Leadership in organizations.* Englewood Cliffs, NJ: Prentice-Hall.

Zajonc, R. B. (1965). Social facilitation. *Science, 149,* 269–274.

Zajonc, R. B. (1968). Attitudinal effects of mere exposure. *Journal of Personality and Social Psychology Monograph Supplement, 9,* 2–27.

Zajonc, R. B. (1980). Compresence. In P. B. Paulus (Ed.), *Psychology of group influence.* Hillsdale, NJ: Erlbaum.

Zajonc, R. B. (1980). Feeling and thinking: Preferences need no inferences. *American Psychologist, 35,* 151–175.

Zaleznik, A., Christiansen, C. R., & Roethlisberger, F. J. (1958). *The motivation, productivity and satisfaction of workers: A production study.* Boston: Harvard University Press.

Zander, A., Cohen, A. R., & Stotland, E. (1959). Power relations among professions. In D. Cartwright (Ed.), *Studies in social power.* Ann Arbor: University of Michigan Press.

Zanna, M. P., Olson, J. M., & Fazio, R. H. (1980). Attitude-behavior consistency: An individual difference perspective. *Journal of Personality and Social Psychology, 38,* 432–440.

Zanna, M. P., Sheras, P. L., Cooper, J., & Shaw, C. (1975). Pygmalion and Galatea: The interactive effect of teacher and student expectancies. *Journal of Experimental Social Psychology, 11,* 279–287.

Zartman, I. W., & Berman, M. R. (1982). *The practical negotiator.* New Haven, CT: Yale University Press.

Zavalloni, M., & Louis-Guerin, C. (1979). Social psychology at the crossroads: Its encounters with cognitive and ecological psychology and the interactive perspective. *European Journal of Social Psychology, 9,* 307–321.

Zeisel, H. (1966). An international experiment on the effects of a Good Samaritan law. In J. Ratcliffe (Ed.), *The Good Samaritan and the law.* Garden City, NY: Doubleday (Anchor Books).

Zeisel, H. (1971). . . . And then there were none: The diminution of the federal jury. *University of Chicago Law Review, 38,* 710–724.

Zeisel, H., & Diamond, S. S. (1974). Convincing empirical evidence on the six-member jury. *University of Chicago Law Review, 41,* 281–295.

Zeisel, J. (1975). *Sociology and architectural design.* New York: Free Press.

Zeisel, J. (1981). *Inquiry by design: Tools for environment-behavior research.* Monterey, CA: Brooks/Cole.

Zellner, M. (1970). Self-esteem, reception, and influenceability. *Journal of Personality and Social Psychology, 15,* 310–320.

Zillmann, D. (1971). Excitation transfer in communication-mediated aggressive behavior. *Journal of Experimental Social Psychology, 7,* 419–434.

Zillmann, D. (1979). *Hostility and aggression.* Hillsdale, NJ: Erlbaum.

Zillmann, D. (1985). Arousal and aggression. In R. G. Geen & E. Donnerstein (Eds.), *Aggression: Theoretical and empirical reviews.* New York: Academic Press.

Zillmann, D., & Bryant, J. (1982). Pornography, sexual callousness, and the trivialization of rape. *Journal of Communication, 32,* 10–21.

Zillmann, D., Bryant, J., & Carveth, R. A. (1981). The effect of erotica featuring sadomasochism and bestiality on motivated intermale aggression. *Personality and Social Psychology Bulletin, 7,* 153–159.

Zillmann D., & Cantor, J. (1972). Directionality of transitory dominance as a communication variable affecting humor appreciation. *Journal of Personality and Social Psychology, 24,* 191–198.

Zillmann, D., & Cantor, J. R. (1976). Effect of timing of information about mitigating circumstances on emotional responses to provocation and retaliatory behavior. *Journal of Experimental Social Psychology, 12,* 38–55.

Zillmann, D., & Cantor, J. R. (1977). Affective responses to the emotions of a protagonist. *Journal of Experimental Social Psychology, 13,* 155–165.

Zimbardo, P. G. (1969). The human choice: Individuation, reason, and order versus deindividuation, impulse, and chaos. In W. J. Arnold & D. Levine (Eds.), *Nebraska Symposium on motivation.* Lincoln: University of Nebraska Press.

Zimbardo, P. G. (1977). *Shyness.* Reading, MA: Addison-Wesley.

Zimbardo, P. G., Ebbesen, E. B., & Maslach, C. (1969). *Influencing attitudes and changing behavior.* Reading, MA: Addison-Wesley.

Zimbardo, P. G., Ebbesen, E. B., & Maslach, C. (1977). *Influencing attitudes and changing behavior* (2nd ed.). Reading, MA: Addison-Wesley.

Zinder, N. D. (1983, January/February). Fraud in science. *Science, 83,* pp. 94–95.

Zlutnick, S., & Altman, I. (1972). Crowding and human behavior. In J. Wohlwill and D. Carson (Eds.), *Environment and the social sciences: Perspectives and applications.* Washington, DC: American Psychological Association.

Zuckerman, M., DePaolo, B. M., & Rosenthal, R. (1981). Verbal and non-verbal communication of deception. In L. Berkowitz (Ed.), *Advances in experimental social psychology* (Vol. 14). New York: Academic Press.

Zuckerman, M., Koestner, R., & Alton, A. O. (1984). Learning to detect deception. *Journal of Personality and Social Psychology, 46,* 519–528.

Zuckerman, M., Lazzaro, M. M., & Waldgeir, D. (1979). Undermining effects of the foot-in-the-door technique with extrinsic rewards. *Journal of Applied Social Psychology, 9,* 292–296.

PHOTO CREDITS

Page numbers appear in boldface.

Chapter 1: **xxviii–1** Clay, Jeroboam; **16** © 1980 Susan Berkowitz, Taurus; **17** Karp, Omni-Photo Communications; **18** © Frank Siteman 1983, The Picture Cube; **24** Copyright Sepp Seitz 1981, Woodfin Camp; **29** Wolinsky, Stock, Boston.

Chapter 2: **34–35** Franken, Stock, Boston; **37** © Eric Kroll 1978, Taurus; **40** © 1980 Druskis, Jeroboam; **43** Copyright © 1987, Kroll, Taurus; **45** Dr. Paul Ekman; **46** Antman, The Image Works; **58** AP/Wide World; **64** © Grecco, Stock, Boston; **76** Carey, The Image Works.

Chapter 3: **80–81** Bellerose, Stock, Boston; **84** © Ira Berger 1981, Woodfin Camp; **90** © Christopher Morrow, Stock, Boston; **96** Zeiberg, Taurus; **99** © 1985, Peter Menzel, Stock, Boston; **101** © Frank D. Smith 1981, Jeroboam; **117** Copyright Sepp Seitz 1982, Woodfin Camp.

Chapter 4: **122–123** © Billy Barnes, Southern Light; **126** © Griffiths, Omni-Photo Communications; **131** © Fredrik D. Bodin, Stock, Boston; **136** Silverman, Stock, Boston; **143** © 1984 Dave Schaefer, Monkmeyer; **159** Karp, Omni-Photo Communications.

Chapter 5: **164–165** Bellerose, Stock, Boston; **168** Franken, Stock, Boston; **172** Southwick, Stock, Boston; **180** Lea, Omni-Photo Communications; **193** © 1984, Malave, Stock, Boston.

Chapter 6: **208–209** Huffman, Monkmeyer; **211** Franken, Stock, Boston; **228** © 1978, Budnik, Woodfin Camp; **230** Burroughs, Jeroboam; **243** © 1979, Herwig, Stock, Boston.

Chapter 7: **248–249** Diakoupolis, Stock, Boston; **252** Bodin, Stock, Boston; **262** © 1978 Leonard, Woodfin Camp; **267** Culver; **276** Lejeune, Stock, Boston; **280** Griffiths, Omni-Photo Communications; **283** © 1983, Fortin, Stock, Boston.

Chapter 8: **288–289** Clay, Jeroboam; **305** Holland, Stock, Boston; **311** © Reno, Jeroboam; **322** Franken, Stock, Boston.

Chapter 9: **328–329** Franken, Stock, Boston; **339** Carey, The Image Works; **345** Berndt, Stock, Boston; **346** Moore, Taurus; **349** Schuyler, Stock, Boston; **363** © Karp, Omni-Photo Communications.

Chapter 10: **368–369** UPI/Bettmann Newsphotos; **379** © Kroll, Taurus; **387** Herwig, The Picture Cube; **390** Alphapress, Jeroboam; **395** UPI/Bettmann Newsphotos.

Chapter 11: **412–413** Smolan, Stock, Boston; **418** Brown, Stock, Boston; **434** © Timothy Eagan 1978, Woodfin Camp; **436** Carey, The Image Works; **441** Eckert, Jr., EKM-Nepenthe; **447** Morrow, Stock, Boston.

Chapter 12: **456–457** Hayman, Stock, Boston; **466** © Christopher Morrow 1982, Stock, Boston; **479** © Hrynewych, Stock, Boston; **481** © Arthur Grace, Stock, Boston; **488** AP/Wide World.

Chapter 13: **496–497** UN Photo; **502** © Steve Hansen, Stock, Boston; **505** © Sandra Johnson 1982, The Picture Cube; **511** Schuyler, Stock, Boston; **532** Karel/Sygma.

NAME INDEX

Note: Italicized page numbers indicate material in tables, figures, and Applications.

SUBJECT INDEX

Note: Italicized page numbers indicate material in tables, figures, and Applications.

About the Authors

MICHAEL J. SAKS

Michael J. Saks has taught social psychology to undergraduate and graduate students, as well as to professors of law and judges, at the University of Virginia, Georgetown University, and Boston College. He is currently on the staff of the College of Law at the University of Iowa. His research has won awards from the Society for the Psychological Study of Social Issues and the American Psychological Association, and has been cited in several decisions by the U.S. Supreme Court. He has written more than 65 articles and books, most notably *Social Psychology in Court.*

Dr. Saks earned his Ph.D. from Ohio State University and is a graduate of Yale Law School.

EDWARD KRUPAT

Edward Krupat taught social psychology at Rutgers University and Boston College before coming to the Massachusetts College of Pharmacy and Allied Health Sciences, where he is Professor of Psychology and director of an undergraduate program in health psychology. He also holds a research appointment at Boston University's Center for Applied Social Science. Dr. Krupat has done research in the areas of health psychology and environmental social psychology. He is the author of *People in Cities: The Urban Environment and Its Effects.* In 1980 he received a National Science Foundation Science Faculty Development Award which allowed him to spend a year at the Medical School of the University of California, San Francisco, working with the Graduate Group in Psychology in such areas as patient communication and satisfaction.

Dr. Krupat received his Ph.D. from the University of Michigan.